THE ECONOMICS OF PUBLIC SPENDING

The Economics of Public Spending

Edited by
DAVID MILES
GARETH MYLES
IAN PRESTON

OXFORD
UNIVERSITY PRESS

*This book has been printed digitally and produced in a standard specification
in order to ensure its continuing availability*

OXFORD
UNIVERSITY PRESS

Great Clarendon Street, Oxford OX2 6DP
Oxford University Press is a department of the University of Oxford.
It furthers the University's objective of excellence in research, scholarship,
and education by publishing worldwide in

Oxford New York

Auckland   Cape Town   Dar es Salaam   Hong Kong   Karachi
Kuala Lumpur   Madrid   Melbourne   Mexico City   Nairobi
New Delhi   Shanghai   Taipei   Toronto
With offices in
Argentina Austria Brazil Chile Czech Republic France Greece
Guatemala Hungary Italy Japan South Korea Poland Portugal
Singapore Switzerland Thailand Turkey Ukraine Vietnam

Oxford is a registered trade mark of Oxford University Press
in the UK and in certain other countries
Published in the United States
by Oxford University Press Inc., New York

ISBN 978-0-19-926033-1

Preface

This book is designed to investigate the extent of government expenditure and its success in meeting its objectives. It does this by taking each area of expenditure in turn and employing a specialist in that area to analyse the data and the theory. These chapters are supported by an introduction that provides a background on the public sector and discusses the general theory of public expenditure.

The project has come about following a series of seminars on public expenditure at the Institute for Fiscal Studies held between July 1999 and June 2001. Authors were invited to contribute and to present preliminary versions of the papers at these seminars. Formal discussants were nominated for each paper and there was also intensive informal discussion. The papers collected here are those prepared in the months immediately following those seminars.

The book is intended to be a self-contained survey of public expenditure suitable for undergraduates, practitioners and anyone else with an interest in the public sector. It could provide the foundation for a course in its own right or as a matching text for reading on government income generation. Public expenditure is an area with relatively few dedicated publications, so that we hope that this text proves a useful addition to the literature.

There are numerous people that the editors wish to thank. First, the authors of the chapters deserve special praise for committing to the project at an early stage and for delivering their manuscripts so efficiently. We also thank participants at the associated seminars and particularly the discussants, Roy Carr-Hill, Lorraine Dearden, Andrew Dilnot, Carl Emmerson, Costas Meghir, Ron Smith, Michael Spackman and John van Reenen. The Institute for Fiscal Studies provided the financial support that underpinned this project. Among the staff of the Institute for Fiscal Studies special thanks are due to Robert Markless, Jean Haddock and Chantal Crevel-Robinson for organizational support, Judith Payne for production of the manuscripts and Emma Hyman for publicity. Finally, we wish to thank the staff of Oxford University Press, particularly Andrew Schuller, for their assistance.

David Miles
Gareth Myles
Ian Preston

August 2002

Contents

1

Introduction: The Economics of Public Spending

DAVID MILES[1], GARETH MYLES[2] AND IAN PRESTON[3]

I. INTRODUCTION

The public sector affects the lives of all those who live in developed economies. Public expenditure pays to defend nations against invasion. It finances schools and universities in which people are educated. When people are ill, it provides medical care and financial support. Public expenditure provides pensions for the old and finances the police to protect people from crime. It also provides entertainment and infrastructure. Much of this is taken for granted and commonly passes unremarked. But this scale of public provision is a relatively recent phenomenon. Why and how we have reached this position?

In the UK public expenditure is around 42 per cent of gross domestic product, and in the US around 35 per cent. At the start of the twentieth century, public expenditure was 10 per cent of gross domestic product. It grew rapidly over the first half of that century until it reached its present levels by the end of the 1960s. Since then, the level of public expenditure has stabilised.

The purpose of this book is to look at the detail behind these broad figures. It is about assessing the role and extent of public expenditure across a wide range of areas of economic life and the particular related policy issues within each area. Each chapter focuses upon a specific area of public expenditure, reviews the relevant data and describes the key policy issues. The economics of public expenditure is an area of research that is often overlooked since much economic analysis focuses on how revenue should be generated and much less on how that revenue is spent. We hope that this book will help to redress that balance.

This chapter describes the economic theory that underpins much analysis of public expenditure. The ideas that it contains are frequently drawn upon in the chapters that follow. It provides a self-contained introduction that is designed to be accessible to any reader with a grasp of elementary economics. The bulk of the chapter then

We are grateful to Andrew Dilnot for comments and to Betty Gruber and others at the IMF for advice and assistance in constructing consolidated general government spending figures.

[1] Imperial College London and Institute for Fiscal Studies.
[2] University of Exeter and Institute for Fiscal Studies.
[3] University College London and Institute for Fiscal Studies.

discusses why we might need a public sector at all and the determination of the level of expenditure. It identifies what is optimal and addresses the difficulties involved in achieving this optimum. A brief review of relevant data follows.

II. PUBLIC AND PRIVATE GOODS

It is striking how great aggregate public expenditure is in developed economies and the diversity of purposes for which public expenditure is made. Why is this so? What role does the government play in the economy that justifies its size? Why is government involved in so many areas of economic activity? Why, in the US, is a *third* of expenditure undertaken by the government? And why, in several of the mixed economies in Europe, is around *half* attributable to government?

Economists find it useful to classify goods into types depending upon the way in which they are consumed. At one extreme is the *pure private* good, consumed by any one individual only if consumed by no other. These are goods, such as food or clothing, where consumption is rivalrous and consumption by one individual excludes consumption by any other. At the other extreme is the *pure public good*, collectively consumed by all. These are goods, such as national defence or fresh air, where consumption is non-rivalrous in the sense that any one individual can consume the benefits without lessening the ability of anyone else to do so; they are also non-excludable in the sense that it is infeasible to prevent any individual from enjoying the benefits if they wish to.

Pure private and pure public goods mark extreme cases between which there are many intermediate possibilities. Some goods, such as broadcasting, provide non-rivalrous benefits but exclusion is possible. Others, such as public highways, provide services which are consumed collectively but in a manner which involves partial rivalry in that, at times, one person's use adds to the congestion suffered by others. The phrase *impure public goods* is sometimes used for these intermediate cases which in practice cover most goods with any degree of publicness.

The case for public provision in the case of pure public goods is well established and is explained below. However pure public goods are rare and most public consumption is of goods which are either impurely public or arguably purely private. We need to think through the issues involved in public provision of each of these types of good.

1. The Minimal State

A good place to start is to ask how the economy would function in the absence of government. The best way to approach this is to return to the most basic economic situation. This will provide a clear motive for a minimal level of government expenditure. Further development of the argument will then give reasons for additional expenditure.

Many political philosophers since Hobbes (1651) and Locke (1690) have considered the hypothetical disadvantages of life without government. The absence of personal security and want of order would lead, in the words of Hobbes, to a 'life of man, solitary, poore, nasty, brutish and short'. The provision of the basic 'night-watchman' services of protection from violence and enforcement of legal order is usually seen as a minimal requirement of civilised society and justification for a basic role for government. Since this cannot be achieved without call on the resources necessary to sustain a judicial system, this provides a justification for at least some public spending.

These services are not purely public since different cases compete for police and court time; but the benefits of living under the rule of law are largely public. It is clearly possible to debate how these costs should be met. Both police and legal services could be sold on a private market with purchases made as and when necessary. Alternatively, they could be financed by voluntary contributions of individuals. Although possible, both of these methods have significant drawbacks, some of which will be discussed in the next section. Practice has revealed that the most common solution is to have them provided by a central body—the government—who funds them via taxes levied upon the population. Even so, private markets do exist for additional personal security.

Besides providing protection against personal violence, the minimal state also plays an important role in facilitating economic activity. Indeed, until a judicial system defines property rights, even such a basic economic act as exchange of commodities is problematic. Such property rights determine the ownership of commodities and regulate the terms under which they can be transferred from one owner to another. To quote Hobbes again, without government 'it is consequent . . . that there be no propriety, no dominion, no mine or thine distinct; but onely that to be every man's that he can get; and for so long, as he can keep it'.

Once property rights and rules of trade are defined and the government has undertaken to protect them by prohibiting and punishing theft, exchange of private commodities between individuals can occur. If undertaken voluntarily by informed individuals, then such trade must be mutually beneficial since, were it not so, one of the individuals would refuse to participate in the trade. By necessity, if trade takes place on these terms until the parties wish to trade no further, an efficient outcome will be reached with no further gains remaining to be made. In this role the government acts to make gains from trade possible; this can be seen as the most basic form of government intervention designed to improve the *efficiency* of the economy.

These arguments can be applied to the international sphere. Neighbouring societies may seek to appropriate the resources or imperil the personal safety of a society's population by use of force. Faced with this threat, the society would seek to protect itself with the government as the obvious, perhaps the only, vehicle for the organisation of its defence. This role too is typically seen as part of the function of the minimal state.

Although economists may disagree on the limit to which the public sector should intervene in the economy, few would argue in favour of reducing it below that of the minimal state. The minimal role of such a state is necessary to ensure the smooth flow of economic transactions and to protect economic gains from outside appropriation. This does no more than provide the environment in which trade can take place.

2. Pure Private Goods

Let us suppose that property rights define a secure basis for trade, a body exists to police and enforce them and a legal system to settle any disputes. What further economic role could exist for government?

Consider first the allocation of pure private goods. Suppose that there are a sufficiently large number of perfectly informed consumers so that none can individually exert any significant impact on the price at which these goods are traded. If each consumer maximises satisfaction subject to their budget constraint, then the rate at which they are prepared to sacrifice one good for the other (their marginal rate of substitution or MRS) will be equated to the rate at which the market allows them to sacrifice one for the other (the price ratio). If all face the same price ratio, the marginal rates of substitution are equalised across consumers. Each person is prepared to sacrifice one good for another at the same rate as any other person and there is therefore no further scope for mutually beneficial trade between consumers. No government intervention in the allocation of private goods can make any consumer better off without making another worse off—the equilibrium without government intervention is efficient.

Now consider production of the goods by a large number of firms. Maximisation of profit ensures that the rate at which the economy can transform one good into the other by reallocating productive resources (the marginal rate of transformation or MRT) is also equated to the common price ratio and therefore to the common MRS among consumers. There is therefore no change to production which can make any consumer better off without making someone else worse off. In summary, the result of individual consumer optimisation and competitive, price-taking behaviour by firms is the efficiency condition for any two consumers i and j and any two good x and y

$$MRS_{xy}^{i}=MRS_{xy}^{j}=MRT_{xy} \tag{1}$$

There are many allocations of resources within the economy which have this efficiency property. Any competitive equilibrium as just described will be one of them. Which particular one obtains in the absence of government intervention will depend upon the allocation of resources before trade and production as determined by the property rights which the government defines.

An economic case for government intervention in the economy needs therefore to rest upon either of two grounds. Perhaps the assumptions made about the nature of consumption or production are wrong—there may exist public goods, consumers may not be perfectly informed, there may exist firms with power to affect prices by their activities and so on. Arguments made on this basis are concerned with efficiency. Alternatively, the particular competitive equilibrium which arises from the property rights defined, although efficient, may be regarded as less desirable than an alternative which the government regards itself as justified in favouring—perhaps because it is less grossly unequal. Arguments made on this basis are arguments about distribution.

3. Pure Public Goods

The reasoning regarding public goods is very different. To see what is involved assume that quantity G of the public good is provided at price p_G per unit and consider the incentives of the consumers. They have two options. Either they can purchase the public good and pay a total price of $p_G G$ or, since a public good is non-excludable, they can consume it without any payment. The latter option is clearly preferable for self-interested people, so no rational and self-interested consumer would ever pay for the public good in these circumstances. The argument is slightly more complex if the quantity provided depends on the number of purchasers, but there is still an incentive not to pay and to consume what is funded by the contribution of others. Such an incentive is always absent with a pure private good since consumption can only take place if a purchase is made.

This incentive problem in the purchase of public goods is called the *free-rider problem*: all consumers have reason to free-ride on what others provide. Its consequence is that public goods cannot be efficiently provided by the same form of price mechanism used to direct the production and purchase of purely private goods. If this were attempted, the free-riding activity of each consumer would result in too little of the public good being purchased relative to what is efficient. It is this failure of the market which provides a potential role for the government to, do better than the market by providing the public good in appropriate quantities.

The properties of an efficient allocation with public goods can be characterised by reconsidering (1). The reasoning underlying this efficiency condition is that an extra unit of private good x can be allocated either to consumer i or to j. Efficiency requires that the marginal value i and j place on x relative to the value placed on any other good such as y (measured by the MRS) is equal. If it were not, there would be gains from reallocating x from the consumer with the lower relative valuation to the consumer with the higher valuation and reallocating y in the opposite direction. In turn, this valuation must be related to the marginal cost of producing that extra unit, which can be measured by the MRT. The situation is different for a public good. If an extra unit is produced then *all* consumers benefit. Efficiency is then achieved when the sum of marginal valuations is equal to the marginal cost. This reasoning is summarised in the *Samuelson rule* for optimal provision

$$\sum_{h=1}^{H} \text{MRS}_{Gy}^{h} = \text{MRT}_{Gy} \tag{2}$$

where H is the number of consumers who benefit from provision of the public good (see Samuelson, 1954, for the original argument). In this rule MRS_{Gy}^{h} is interpreted as the marginal benefit that h derives from an extra unit of provision of the public good. As argued above, the operation of private markets will not typically lead to satisfaction of this condition.

This single condition does not define a unique, optimum quantity of the public good to be provided—it is a property holding jointly of an allocation defined by a quantity of the public good *and* an allocation of the private good *y* among consumers. In general, different quantities will be efficient depending upon the distribution of private goods across the individuals in the population.

III. EFFICIENCY ARGUMENTS FOR PUBLIC SPENDING

The previous section outlined the difference between efficiency considerations for the polar cases of pure private and pure public goods. In this section we develop more nuanced arguments for public spending applied to intermediate cases and under less-stringent assumptions, but still focusing on questions of efficiency.

1. Externalities

In the idealised, competitive economy with purely private goods, economic agents interact only through the price system. To all intents and purposes, each agent is contained within their own private environment and is completely unaffected by the actions of others *except* to the extent to which those others collectively affect prices. When economic activities interact other than through the price system, then market failure will arise. Such interactions are called *externalities* and responses to their existence provide a justification for some government action.

Public goods provide one example of an externality: because of their non-rivalry, their provision by one consumer will benefit all. The discussion of externalities therefore generalises the discussion above. Other relevant examples of externalities can be given. One person's consumption of health services which prevents them contracting infectious diseases or hastens their recovery from them affects the likelihood of others contracting the diseases and therefore generates an externality. Acting selfishly, people would fail to take account of the benefits to others of consuming these services and the level of consumption would be less than socially optimal. A case therefore exists for government to take over provision of these health services and provide them at the optimum level.

The fact that an externality leads to market failure can easily be seen by considering a simple two-consumer economy. Suppose there are two goods, x which generates no externality and y which generates a positive externality. When one individual consumes y then it benefits not only them but also the other person. Let x_i and y_i stand for the ith person's consumption of x and y. Not only the first consumer but also the second consumer has a marginal valuation of the first consumer's consumption, y_1. When considering the *social* benefit from the first consumer's consumption one needs to take account of both of these (and the same is obviously true when considering the second person's consumption too).

Efficiency is more complex than simply equating the isolated marginal rates of substitution to a common marginal rate of transformation. Instead one should take the first individual's MRS between y_1 and x_1, add the second person's MRS between y_1 and x_1 and equate the sum to a common MRT (and *vice versa* with regard to the second person's consumption, y_2). The efficiency condition becomes

$$\text{MRS}^1_{xy_1} + \text{MRS}^2_{xy_1} = \text{MRS}^1_{xy_2} + \text{MRS}^2_{xy_2} = \text{MRT}_{xy}. \tag{3}$$

The difference between (3) and (1) is the appearance of the externality effects in the condition for social efficiency. These will, in general, result in the market equilibrium being inefficient. This conclusion follows from the difference between private and social marginal benefits. In particular, in a case like this where there is a *positive externality* then the consumption of good y will tend to be higher in an efficient equilibrium than in the market outcome. The reasoning can be extended fairly straightforwardly to negative externalities for which the converse holds.

There are several policy responses the government can make to accommodate the effects of externalities. The most direct is to take formal control of the allocation of commodities. In the health example it could assume responsibility for health care provision. This response creates a justification for public spending on items concerned.

But alternative interventions exist. Allocation could be controlled by legal stipulation, such as minimal health care obligations or compulsory vaccination. Choices can also be affected by the use of a corrective subsidy (or taxation for negative externalities). When used to combat externalities, these are termed *Pigouvian subsidies* or *taxes*. As has been noted for the case of public goods, the ability of the government to respond to a market failure such as this is limited by the information that it has available.

If the number of agents concerned is small enough for private bargaining to be feasible, then there may be no need for intervention. The agents will find it in their interests to bargain about the level of the externalities—for instance, the sufferer of a negative externality will be willing to pay to have the level of the externality reduced. If this bargaining continues until all gains are exhausted, then by definition an efficient outcome is achieved. This sort of resolution is the subject of the famous *Coase Theorem* (see Coase, 1960). The relevance of such observations is limited when large numbers are affected by the externality and no institutions exist to facilitate bargaining.

2. Information

Another feature of the economy which can cause market failure, and therefore create a case for government intervention, is imperfect information. It is important to note that limited information *per se* is not problematic. In fact, an economy in which all agents have the same limited information will reach an efficient equilibrium given the information that is available. Agents choose actions to maximise the expected benefits and no reallocation of resources taking place before the information is improved will be able to raise the level of welfare expected by any consumer without reducing that of another.

What is problematic is asymmetry of information between agents. The classic problems caused are usually divided into problems of adverse selection and moral hazard. Let us see how they might apply to an area where government spending is common—insurance against health problems or against unemployment. Take adverse selection first. Assume that the population divides into those with high and low risk of the outcome against which insurance is needed and assume that people know their type. That is to say the population divides into people who know their constitution creates a high risk of ill health and those who know themselves to be healthy (or those who know they find holding down a job difficult and those who know they can easily find work). Assume further that firms that might provide insurance against ill health or unemployment cannot observe what type individuals are. This is the asymmetry of information.

Suppose that such firms offer insurance at premiums which reflect the average risk in the population. Since these premiums will be less than fair for low-risk buyers, the low-risk consumers may choose not to buy the policies. This raises the average risk of those who do buy and hence requires premiums to rise if insurers are to remain solvent. This makes policies even less attractive to those with low risks. Eventually, low risk types may leave the market entirely; this is the classic outcome of *adverse selection* where the high risk drive out the low risk. Only the high-risk people can therefore find insurance at fair terms and this may drive everyone else out of the market.

Informational problems in the insurance market can reveal themselves both through adverse selection (policies attracting too many bad risks) and also through the *moral hazard* problem. Consider a company that offers insurance that always covers all bad outcomes, but that cannot observe the actions of the individuals it insures. Taking out insurance reduces the incentive for insured individuals to take actions that reduces the risk. If an individual is insured against unemployment, for example, then the cost of shirking within a job (and risking dismissal) is low and the incentives to search for jobs low. The risk will therefore rise above the level observed before the insurance was offered and the profits of the insurance company will be reduced, or even become losses. This changing of behaviour is the moral hazard—individuals cannot be relied upon to act in the manner the insurance company would like. The consequence is that the more cover an insurance company offers, the higher becomes the probability of the insured outcome. In extreme cases, no insurance will be offered at all. No company will offer unemployment insurance because it knows that doing so will discourage unemployed insurees from looking for work.

Government intervention can sometimes improve upon these informational inefficiencies. To do so, though, the government must either be able to take actions that the private agents cannot take or must have information that the private agents do not. For example, in the health context the government may be able to enforce compulsory take up of insurance so that it can cross-subsidise insurance premiums across different groups of the population. In the unemployment insurance context, it may be able to enforce scrutiny of job search intensity that would be considered too invasive if permitted to private firms. In each case direct government provision of insurance may improve on the market outcome.

3. Paternalism

Up to this point, the discussion has followed the standard tradition in economics of assuming that the preferences of the consumers should be respected by the government. That is, the government should see an increase in welfare as occurring when one or more of the consumers considers their personal welfare to be higher without any considering it lower. The nature of the preferences that lead to the increases, or decreases, in perceived personal utility are not questioned.

There are clearly limits to how far this position is in practice taken by governments. Concern that parents may not invest adequately in the education of their children leads to government education provision and requirements for a minimum numbers of years of schooling. Fears that myopic consumers cannot be relied on to invest adequately in pensions leads to the forced saving implicit in government pension provision.

What unites these examples is the concept of a *merit good*. This is a good which the government insists must be consumed in at least a minimal quantity by all consumers. This can be achieved through the government providing the good directly and ruling that all must consume. This may be because the government wants to overrule individual preferences which they judge, in a paternalistic way, to be 'wrong', or may be because the government, more benignly, believes that it has access to better information than consumers. In the latter case, it would arguably be better for the government to simply reveal its information, assuming it trusts consumers to absorb it.

If merit goods arise because the government overrules individual preferences a set of new and important issues arises. Now government policy is based on the presumption that individuals should possess preferences other than those they do have. Because of this, economic efficiency cannot be measured with respect to individual preferences and must be judged with respect to the preferences imposed by the government.

4. Market Power

The efficiency of the competitive economy is built on the assumption that no economic agent can unilaterally affect market prices. Facing what they perceive as fixed prices, economic agents act in ways that collectively secure the efficiency of the market allocation. But an agent with market power, for example a monopolistic firm or trade union, acts in a way that takes account of the marginal effect of their action upon the price. The resulting equilibrium will not be efficient.

The consequences of market power can be seen by considering monopoly in further detail. A monopolist restricts output to raise price above the marginal cost of production. Compared to the competitive outcome, this leads to lower output and consumption, and a transfer from consumers to the firm as more of consumers' willingness to pay is appropriated by the firm as profit. There is also a deadweight loss in that what consumers lose is less than what the firm gains—this loss is a measure of the inefficiency of the monopoly. A trades union is a monopolist in the supply of labour. It will restrict labour supply in order to raise the wages of its members. This causes a transfer from the profits of the firms using that labour to the union members and it generates deadweight loss too.

The effects of market power can be lessened through a range of policy responses. The most direct is to nationalise monopolistic firms and to run them with social efficiency rather than profit maximisation as the goal. If this happens then the firms' balance sheets are drawn into the public accounts—the cost of the firms' investment becomes a part of public spending just as its revenues contribute to public funds.

Social efficiency would require marginal cost pricing to be operated. However, doing so may raise questions of profitability. Natural monopolies arise when production requires the payment of significant fixed costs (such as the investment in a cable network) and the market can only profitably sustain a single firm. Forcing such a firm to charge marginal cost would lead to it failing to cover its fixed costs and therefore would be unsustainable in the long run. The losses could be covered by public subsidies (with a risk that further inefficiencies might be introduced through the cost of raising the subsidy). Alternatively, the firm could be directed to use optimal break-even prices (called Ramsey prices in this context) but then the outcome would be a second-best departure from marginal cost pricing.

An alternative to nationalisation is the regulation of the firms, for example, by placing limitations on pricing policy. The growth of market power can also be limited through competition policy. This can include both the prevention of mergers and takeovers and the encouragement of competition by assisting the development of competing firms and the breaking-up of dominant firms. But again, the extent to which this can be undertaken may be limited by the natural monopoly problem. Finally, intervention can take the more indirect form of corrective taxation.

IV. FINDING OUT ABOUT PREFERENCES

Having determined the criteria for optimal provision, the question of whether the government can achieve this level of provision needs to be addressed. We have already noted the possible failure of the market to provide efficiently. These observations do not imply that the government can achieve an efficient outcome, but only that it may get closer than the market does. One key reason why the government may have difficulty doing this is related to *informational constraints*. The level of public goods described by (2) can be provided only if the government has both the information to calculate the solution and the means to finance the provision without introducing other distortions, and consequent inefficiencies, into the economy. This section covers the first of these conditions and the next section addresses financing.

The particular difficulty in the calculation of (2) is that the government does not know the preferences of consumers. Such information is vital if the marginal benefits of providing specific goods or services are to be determined. This is not a problem in markets for pure private goods since consumers reveal this information via their trading activities. Since there is no similar market for public goods this information is not revealed in the same way. It may be felt that the government could ask consumers to reveal their preferences, for instance, through the use of consumer surveys. Unfortunately the answers that emerge from such surveys will depend upon the *incentives* that the consumers perceive to reveal the truth.

Consider the case in which consumers expect that the higher the preference for public goods they express the more they personally will have to pay to fund them. This situation is precisely analogous to that faced by a private firm attempting to charge for public goods. Each consumer will have an incentive to understate their valuation and attempt to free-ride on the valuations of others. Consequently, the survey would report valuations below the true levels and, if the government acted on the basis of this information, too little of the public good would be provided.

This conclusion is dependent upon the assumption of a direct link between reported valuation and required contribution. More complex mechanisms have been constructed that provide incentives for truthful valuation.

1. Demand Revelation

Consider the simple example of the provision of a public good, such as street lighting, that will benefit all the residents of a given street. Say that the cost of providing the facility is c and there are n residents to pay for it. The ith resident is willing to pay an unknown amount b_i for the benefit received from it. According to the Samuelson rule it should be provided if and only if $\Sigma_i \, b_i \geqslant c$.

First, suppose the government asks residents to state their valuation, provides the facility if the sum of stated benefits exceeds the cost and charges each resident their declared valuation. Each resident has a clear incentive to understate their valuation in the hope of free-riding on the payment of others. The efficient outcome will not be reached.

Let the government instead adopt the following naive procedure: ask the residents to state a value on the benefit they will obtain from the facility. Provide the facility if the sum of stated benefits exceeds the cost and charge each resident an equal share of the cost. With this charging scheme, what matters for each consumer is whether their benefit exceeds or falls short of what they are asked to pay. If the benefit is in excess of the charge, then they will be in favour of the facility being provided, otherwise they will not.

Now consider the incentives at work. Let the benefit less the charge for each resident, $b_i - c/n$, be termed their net valuation of the facility. First, take a resident whose net valuation is positive. As described, if the facility is provided, there is no connection between reported valuation and charge. Hence, a resident in this position has an incentive to overstate their valuation in an attempt to ensure that the facility is provided–they can do this without incurring any additional charge. Second, take a resident whose net valuation is negative. They will have to pay the charge if it is provided but only receive a benefit that is less than this. Their incentive is then to understate the valuation in an effort to ensure that the facility is not provided. Consequently, all of the residents (except those where the net valuation is exactly zero) have an incentive to make a false statement of valuation. There can be no expectation then that the process of asking for valuations will lead to an economically efficient decision.

The theory of *mechanism design* explores how the process can be modified to provide incentives for a statement of correct valuation. It is clear that this must involve changing the relationship between statement of valuation and the payment that is made. In neither of the naive examples did this relation provide the right incentives.

One simple mechanism which does work is the following [based on ideas introduced by Groves (1973) and Clarke (1971)]. Provide the facility if the sum of stated benefits exceeds the cost and charge each resident the net stated cost to everyone else of providing the facility. In other words, modify the mechanism to charge the ith resident $\sum_{j\neq i}((c/n)-b_j)$ if the facility is provided and nothing otherwise. If their true net valuation plus the reported net valuations of other consumers is negative, they will have an incentive to report truthfully and not have the facility go ahead. Conversely, if their true net valuation plus the sum of others' reports is positive they should reveal the true value. Overstating the benefit could only lead to the facility being provided at a cost they do not wish to pay and understating can only lead to the facility not being provided when they were willing to bear the cost. The mechanism therefore leads to truthful revelation and to satisfaction of the Samuelson rule.

Although it elicits truthful valuations, there remain difficulties with this form of mechanism. Recall that each resident pays an amount equal to minus the sum of net valuations of the other residents. These payments will generally not sum to zero across residents. If they are negative on aggregate then the mechanism is costly to implement. This is not surprising since it is extracting information and this can only be done at a price. The cost must then be financed by government expenditures. In this case, the benefits of obtaining correct valuations have to be offset against the cost of raising the necessary finance, typically through distortionary taxes. The practical implementation is also difficult if large numbers of consumers are involved. It might work when there are only a few but in most cases applying this scheme is not a practical proposition.

2. Voting

Given these problems, how are preferences elicited in practice? One answer to this question is to interpret voting in elections as a way of revealing information about preferences for public goods. In some votes, such as referenda in US states or in Swiss cantons, the vote may be over a single precise issue. More generally, elections bundle together a whole host of issues of which public spending is only a part. It is immediately clear that in the latter case the vote will provide only imperfect information on preferences for public goods. For instance, in an election an issue such as immigration or penal reform might be the major concern to voters. A party can then get elected because of its stance on these issues even though its public good proposals are seen by the majority of voters as less satisfactory than its opponents.

Even when the vote is directly about the level of provision of a public good (for instance, a referendum on the level of defence spending), voting mechanisms are still not perfect. The most commonly used method is simple majority voting where each voter has a single vote and the chosen alternative is that which receives the most votes. Under certain conditions it is possible to be precise about the outcome. Suppose preferences over the level of public spending (given the proposed system of financing) are *single peaked* for all individuals, which is to say that for any level of spending if a voter would prefer spending to be higher they would never also prefer spending to be lower. The *median voter theorem* predicts that, under such conditions, the level of spending that will prevail with majority voting is the median preferred spending level. To see why, imagine lining the voters up in an order reflecting how much public spending they wish to have. Then the median voter is the person in the middle of this line and the level of public spending chosen by voting will be the quantity that they wish to have. When this quantity is compared with that satisfying efficiency criteria, such as the Samuelson rule, it may be higher, lower or the same. Consequently voting cannot be relied upon to achieve an efficient outcome. Voting provides only limited information. It reveals the number in favour of each alternative but says nothing about the strength of preference. In welfare terms the latter is important if decisions about competing objectives are to be made.

The median voter model assumes that all voters would exercise their right to vote. In practice this is not so with turnout for most elections well below 100 per cent. This is not surprising since voting is costly—it takes time and effort to travel to the polling booth and cast the vote—and the probability of personally affecting the voting will be low when the number of voters is high. Of course, some voters may find fulfilment in political participation and some may care not only about who wins but also about the balance of votes, but it remains easy to see why many voters may regard the effort of voting as wasted. Some economists regard the voluntary casting of votes as so clearly irrational that they consider the fact that so many people do vote to be a paradox (see for instance, Mueller, 1989). If some people do not participate, then voting will reveal only the preferences of those who choose to vote and these need not be a representative sample of the population. The relationship between the choice that emerges from this procedure with the efficient outcome cannot easily be predicted.

For pure public goods single peakedness of preferences seems like a plausible assumption to make so that the median voter theorem may have some applicability.

However, it has already been noted that much of public spending is actually on public provision of private or impure public goods. In these cases individuals are often allowed to supplement or substitute public provision with additional or alternative purchases in the private sector. Public health care, for example, may exist alongside a private market for certain elective medical treatments. Public education may coexist with a private schooling system. In these circumstances, single peakedness is unlikely. At low levels of spending public provision would have low quality and a typical voter might choose to opt into the private sector. Assuming they would still pay taxes to finance the public spending, moderate increases in spending would make them worse off since their tax bills would rise and they would not consume the publicly provided service. At some high enough level of public spending, however, they would choose to switch into the public sector and might begin preferring public spending to increase if their taste for the good in question is strong enough. The potential violation of single peakedness, with moderate public spending judged worse than either high or low spending, is noted by Stiglitz (1974).

More complex arguments are therefore needed to establish voting equilibrium for public spending on private goods. A series of papers by Epple and Romano (1996a,b) show how majority voting can sustain public spending on purely private goods in the presence of private alternatives. Their models assume that those consuming private alternatives continue to pay the taxes that finance public spending for others as typically happens. In the long run, the possibility of opting-out of public provision may create political pressure to allow opting-out also of tax payments.

The conditions under which one can use the median voter theorem to construct and estimate an empirical model of public spending decisions were explored by Bergstrom and Goodman (1973) and have formed the basis for many attempts to estimate preferences for local public spending in the US. The literature is reviewed by Bergstrom et al. (1982) and points to income inelastic demand for local public services.

3. Public Opinion Surveys and Other Methods

Given the impracticality of truthful demand revelation mechanisms and the problems of inferring preferences from voting, we are thrown back on other methods of getting information about preferences over public spending.

Survey data is often collected where voters are asked direct questions about their willingness to pay for increases in specific items of public spending. If respondents expect survey results to feed directly into policy then the incentive considerations raised above are relevant in interpreting answers, but if they do not then these may provide illuminating information on preferences.

Where the spending concerned is locally specific then local variation in costs of provision and levels of spending produce useful auxiliary information with which to identify preferences. Bergstrom et al. (1982) apply such methods to US data on public education spending, reaching very similar conclusions about income elasticities to the median-voter-based aggregate studies discussed above but also identifying a number of important demographic influences. Preston and Ridge (1993) apply similar methods to local public spending in the UK, concluding similarly that demand is income inelastic and most goods and services provided are impurely public.

Where spending is national no such spatial variation in costs or spending levels exist. Such survey data often suffers also from a very imprecise specification of the implied tax costs of spending changes. Brook et al. (1998) and Hall and Preston (2000) investigate demands for a wide range of national public spending items using UK data in which tax costs have been very precisely specified. Their results give very imprecisely determined economic influences from incomes and prices but clear evidence of strong and plausible influence from demographic characteristics and education. Older respondents are more favourable to defence and police spending. Respondents with children support education spending most strongly as do those with high education themselves. The highly educated also favour spending on culture and the environment more strongly than others. Consumption of private substitutes does appear to depress support for public spending.

Another method is to infer valuations indirectly by looking at the prices of related goods. For example, the value of a good school can be determined through looking at the premium placed on houses located in relevant catchment areas. Studies in the US have attempted to estimate demand for local public spending using variation in house prices across districts (see the survey in Rubinfeld, 1987).

V. PUBLIC FINANCE

Having discussed the difficulties involved with the government determining the optimal level of provision, we turn to the issue of *financing*. Efficient finance requires that the government is able to provide the funding for public goods without introducing any distortions into the economy. It can achieve this in two circumstances. First, in a command economy where the government has complete control over resource allocation. Second, when the government has access to *lump-sum taxes*. Lump-sum taxes are special in that they do not introduce distortions into the economy. Of these two cases, only the latter will be discussed. Although the command economy is analytically interesting as a special case, it has little practical relevance.

To understand the role of lump-sum taxes, it is important to be clear about what is meant by a tax being distortionary. A tax is not distortionary in the sense of undermining efficiency simply because it causes a change in behaviour. For instance, levying a tax of £1 on each person in the UK would cause all to change their behaviour simply because they are £1 less rich but it is not distortionary, assuming, of course, that all can afford to pay and none choose to leave the country because of the tax or take action to evade it. What actually makes a tax distortionary is its altering the marginal trade-off between two goods or activities. Consider placing a commodity tax on a good. This keeps the price constant between any two different purchasers of the good, but it alters the trade-off that buyers and sellers face between the taxed good and a commodity taxed at a different rate.

The arguments of the previous paragraph seem to imply that the required revenue could be raised without distortion if all goods were taxed at the same rate. Unfortunately, this is not so because in their economic activity consumers supply some commodities (such as labour) while demanding others (typically final consumption goods). When a consumer satisfies their budget constraint, the total value of demand is equal to the total value of supply. Thus, a tax system which raises the price of all goods in the same proportion raises income and expenditure equally and hence, since government revenue is the difference between the two, must raise zero revenue. Any system of commodity taxation that raises revenue cannot tax all goods at the same rate and must therefore distort choices. The same conclusion holds for income taxes and, in fact, for any taxes that are levied upon economic choices.

This returns us to lump-sum taxes. By definition, the special nature of these is that the tax liability cannot be affected by any change in behaviour. In contrast, with commodity taxation, for example, a consumer always has the option of substituting to goods with lower taxes or refraining from consuming taxed goods at all. For lump-sum taxes, the fact that tax liability cannot be affected means that choices are not distorted by the taxes. (To repeat the earlier point, this is not to say that choices are not changed; they almost certainly will be but only through the income effect of the taxes; there is no substitution effect.) Since they cannot be levied on economic choices completely non-distortionary taxes must be levied on some unalterable underlying characteristic.

This last fact is both the strength and the weakness of lump-sum taxes. It is a strength because it is what leads to the avoidance of distortion. It is a weakness because the characteristic must be an economically relevant basis for the tax and must be publicly observable and verifiable. For instance, preferences may be thought of as an unalterable characteristic. They are also economically relevant. But they are not publicly observable—choices following from preferences may be observed but these can always be changed if a tax advantage follows. In contrast, eye colour is publicly observable and unchangeable (without great cost) but there is no evidence that it is economically relevant. Hence, it is possible to tax people on the basis of the colour of their eyes, and the resulting taxes would be lump-sum, but there is no economic justification for so doing.

It might yet be argued that the difficulties raised so far are caused entirely by an attempt to differentiate the lump-sum taxes across different individuals. Put another way, are not uniform lump-sum taxes always possible? Two points can be made in response to this. First, the distribution of the tax burden across individuals is often as important as efficiency in raising revenue; more will be said about the equity aspects of taxation in the following section. Uniform lump-sum taxes perform very badly in this respect. Second, experience has shown that even uniform lump-sum taxes are very difficult to administer. The UK government attempted to finance local government through such a tax which was more or less uniform within districts in the late 1990s (apart from partial or total exemptions for groups such as students, members of religious orders and convicts). The requirement on each local government to keep a record of its population proved difficult with mobile taxpayers reluctant to register. The tax was essentially levied on existence, which seems at first sight to be an unalterable characteristic. However it proved easily alterable, at least in an administrative sense. In addition, many people just refused to pay (poll tax non-payment rates were 30 per cent even for those registered) and the authorities lacked the administrative capacity to chase them for payment. The tax was eventually scrapped both because of its administrative costs and its perceived inequity.

The conclusion that these arguments lead to is that although lump-sum taxes can in theory raise revenue without creating distortions, informational constraints render them of little practical value. Consequently, governments are forced to use distortionary tax systems in order to raise revenue. The distortions that are created then prevent efficiency criteria such as the Samuelson rule from being implemented. Instead, the government has to trade off the gains from providing public goods and other benefits of public spending against the costs of the distortions caused by their financing. An optimal trade off is achieved when the marginal gain is just equal to the marginal cost.

How the level of provision so achieved compares to that required by efficiency considerations depends on what is assumed about government information. If, for example, the government were to know preferences for public goods but used distortionary taxation, then the level of provision would typically be less than that suggested by the Samuelson rule. Though of analytical interest, this particular situation is not of great practical relevance. The practically relevant case is that of a government that does not know preferences and must also use distortionary taxation. In this case the public good supply of the government is only as successful as the method (e.g. voting) used to elicit preferences and the potential inefficiency is compounded by the distortionary financing.

The optimal level of public spending that emerges will be that which best trades off the costs and the benefits using the imperfect information. One thing about this is certain: it will not achieve full efficiency. Consequently, whether the resulting equilibrium is better or worse than that achieved by private provision is a question that needs to be addressed on a case-by-case basis.

VI. DISTRIBUTIONAL ARGUMENTS FOR PUBLIC SPENDING

The concept of economic efficiency used so far has been carefully constructed to sidestep issues of distribution. Recall that an allocation has been regarded as efficient if no alternative can be found which improves the welfare of at least one consumer without reducing that of any other. There is no reference to the relative levels of welfare of different consumers in this definition, only a focus on the direction of changes. In addition, such an efficiency criterion is unable to judge between situations in which some consumers gain and some lose. This has the advantage that it requires no contentious interpersonal comparisons to be made but has the disadvantage that it enables no comment in most practical policy situations.

In contrast, governments do generally care about the distribution of welfare both in relative levels across consumers and in the winners and losers from policy. Such concern for distribution often arises from considerations of *equity* and views about the comparability of welfare that go well beyond what is necessary for the theory of efficiency. These views can reflect either the voting behaviour of the population or the fundamental beliefs of the policymakers. They are reflected in their most direct form in the use of policies that cause redistribution of income between consumers. The income tax and social security systems transfer resources from those earning higher incomes to those who are unemployed, on low incomes or retired. There are also indirect transfers built into other government spending policies. For example, both free education and healthcare involve implicit transfers.

At its purest, the theory of redistribution is quite simple. To see this return to the economy of pure private goods discussed earlier. What differentiates consumers in this economy are their preferences and the endowment of goods that they have to exchange. Redistribution then consists of reallocating the endowments between consumers. For each allocation of endowments, there exists a different equilibrium of trade with resulting utility levels for the consumers. Therefore, by redistributing endowments, the government can choose between alternative allocations of utility across consumers. Confronting its views about equity with these allocations of utility, the government can choose its most preferred outcome. This is the equilibrium that most closely meets the equity considerations.

This direct reallocation of endowments between consumers does not raise any efficiency considerations. Effectively the theory assumes that there is a fixed initial stock of commodities that is not diminished as the government conducts its transfers. Therefore the equity objective can be met without any efficiency cost.

The limitations of this argument have already been explored in the discussion of optimal lump-sum taxation. Both the preferences of the consumers and their endowments will be private information. The government cannot therefore determine the correct degree of redistribution without inducing the consumers to reveal this information. If the incentives are not in their favour, the consumers will not do so. Consequently, the government must fall back on means of redistribution that are distortionary and have efficiency consequences. For instance, a progressive income tax with a marginal rate of tax that increases with income plus an income subsidy for those on low income is redistributive but will distort the choice of labour supply. In this case, the government has to trade-off the degree of redistribution with the disincentives that high income taxes cause for labour supply.

Governments with distributional objectives will want to disburse public funds in such a way that they go disproportionately to the most needy. Simply dispensing transfers to anyone claiming to be in need will not ensure equity objectives are met if the government has no means of checking the genuineness of the individual claims. Where possible governments will impose conditions on welfare receipt which may, for instance, involve participation in programmes, such as workfare, which would be unattractive to those not in genuine need. Alternatively, the form of the transfers may achieve a similar objective. Besley and Coate (1991) show how public provision of private goods can achieve redistributive objectives. Blackorby and Donaldson (1988) have shown how provision of transfers in kind rather than in cash can successfully induce the genuinely needy to distinguish themselves if they are the only types of people to whom the goods in question are attractive.

VII. DELIVERY OF PUBLIC SERVICES

Discussion in previous sections has pointed to arguments for governments to determine the level and pattern of spending for particular goods. This does not mean that government need actually deliver production of the services concerned itself. Provision can be through private sector firms under contract to public authorities. At the heart of debate about these issues are questions about the relative efficiency of the government in providing public goods compared to the private sector. A common argument is that the private sector can provide many public goods at lower cost than the public sector. This is one of the factors behind privatisation and contracting-out of public services (other arguments reflect the belief that the government should simply not be involved in some areas).

This raises the question of why the private sector might be more efficient. Major reasons usually cited include the potential discipline of competition for contracts and competition for corporate control both of which affect the private sector but not the public. An inefficient private firm will be unable to offer to undertake public contracts at lower cost than more efficient rivals. Even private monopolies should not endure problems of productive inefficiency if doing so exposes them to threat of corporate takeover. For these reasons, long-run cost inefficiencies should not survive in the private sector. In contrast, the public sector may continue to operate with no competitive threats to its existence and the consequent perpetuation of inefficiency.

These arguments have important implications. They suggest immediately that if the private sector is allowed the task of providing a public good it has to be subject to some form of competition or regulation. These will ensure that the pressure of the marketplace is brought to bear on its operations. Competition can be introduced either at the stage of bidding for contracts or during the operational phase. In the former case, a competitive bidding process will ensure that the terms of the contract are as attractive as possible. In the latter, the threat of lost market share should provide the necessary incentive.

These policies are not without their difficulties. The process of tendering for contracts is one that is open for abuse through the collusion of bidders. For instance, two bidders may choose to collude over higher tenders with each preferring to win one contract at a high price rather than two at a low price. There can also be collusion between the organisers of the tendering process and the bidders to secure potential rents. Moving to the other extreme, if the process becomes too competitive, a tender may be made at a price at which the contract cannot be effectively delivered. This will result in either the provision of the contract at an inferior level of quality or to the failure of the contractor.

These are not the only issues involved. A further issue of great significance is the provision of finance to support long-term investment projects. The point at stake is again whether the public or private sectors are able to provide this at least cost. Proponents of the public sector argue that since it is seen as low risk (e.g. neither the UK nor US governments have any history of defaulting on loans), the public sector is able to borrow at preferential rates. In contrast, the advantage of the private sector is that it is better able to spread risk across the market. Such spreading reduces the exposure of any single individual to risk and allows risk-reducing exploitation of covariances between returns on different projects.

The determination of who should provide is therefore an open question that has to be addressed on a case-by-case basis. In providing an answer in any particular circumstance a number of issues must be taken into account. In every case the intention is to obtain a chosen quality of provision at least cost. This may involve provision by the public sector with suitably designed incentives to prevent inefficiencies. Or it may involve private sector provision with safeguards to prevent the exploitation of monopoly power. What is clear is that there can be no presumption about the dominance of either form of provision.

VIII. PUBLIC CHOICE

Thus far we have, at least implicitly, assumed that the government is benevolent. It may be limited in its information and hence in the policy tools it can employ, but given this it does attempt to achieve the best it can for society. In terms of an economist's modelling of government, this leads to a perspective in which the government is little more than a calculating machine for optimal policies. As such, it remains a 'black-box' whose inner workings never need to be considered.

This is not a situation that all economists are comfortable with. The view of the *public choice school* (as discussed in Mueller, 1989) is that the government is not simply a benevolent welfare maximiser. Instead, they argue that its motivation and policies can only be understood by looking at the individuals and processes that comprise government. This implies that the government cannot be understood outside of the political environment in which it operates nor independently of the personal objectives of its members.

These observations lead to the conclusion that policy should be analysed not through the analysis of efficiency subject to constraint, but through study of the process of decision-making. This has to take into account the political environment in which decisions are made and the motivation of agents acting within that environment. Only when this is done can the actions of the government be understood. We shall now discuss some major themes of the public choice approach and trace their implications for public good provision.

1. Rent Seeking

The public choice school is very broad but one of the themes that unifies many of its areas is that of *rent seeking* (see, for instance, Tullock, 1967; Krueger, 1974; and other papers in Buchanan et al., 1980). Rents are defined as the surpluses that are created by economic activity over and above fair reward for factors of production. Rent seeking is the act of agents attempting to secure those surpluses. For example, monopoly profit is an example of a rent and the owners of a monopolistic firm organise its production to secure that rent. In this case, rent seeking would result in the restriction of output below the competitive level. This example illustrates the first consequence of rent seeking: it leads to economic inefficiency, in this case due to the monopoly output level being too low. To see the second major consequence of rent seeking, assume that the monopolist has to erect barriers to entry in order to secure its position. Such barriers could include expenditure on advertising and investment in excess capacity. What is common to both is that they are costly to undertake and represent wasted resources from a social perspective (even though they may be privately optimal for the monopolist). Hence rent seeking may result in resources being wasted on economically worthless activity, thus introducing a second source of inefficiency.

The application of these ideas to public goods, and political choices in general, is straightforward. The government is in a uniquely advantageous position to create rents. For example, it can create monopolies through regulation, licensing and patent policy. It can create rents for firms and individuals by its choice of tax concessions. The award of contracts to supply goods and services creates potential rents for the winners. In fact, whenever the government intervenes in the economy it is potentially creating rents.

One implication of this is that when rents are created through policy, agents in the economy will engage in rent seeking to secure them. Moreover, agents will expend resources to lobby the government to create rents. For instance, a restriction on imported goods (be it through tariffs, quotas or quality standards) will benefit home producers who will actively spend resources to secure the restriction. This is inefficient both because of the use of distortions created by the policy and because of the resources expended on rent seeking. There is a still further disturbing aspect of rent seeking: the politicians who are making the decisions are the beneficiaries of the rent seeking activity (through a range of benefits from corporate hospitality to direct bribes) and hence have an incentive to create the rents. In an extreme version of this viewpoint, the activity of the government can be explained as the creation of rents so as to auction them to the highest bidder.

Interpreted in terms of public spending, these arguments imply that there may be little link between what the government should be doing and what it actually does. The former is determined by efficiency criteria such as the Samuelson rule whereas the latter is the outcome of the interplay of forces in the creation and capture of rents. A purely rent seeking perspective of government therefore has little to say about optimum public good provision. Instead, its value comes from potentially providing a means to understand the observed outcome. That is, given an observed level and structure of public provision, applying the rent-seeking perspective may well reveal both the forces that have lead to that outcome and the issues that would need to be resolved to improve upon it.

2. Bureaucracy

The public choice school provides additional reasons to be doubtful of the capacity of the government to provide an efficient level of public goods. Moving within the structure of government, it can be observed that many planning decisions are made by bureaucrats (see Niskanen, 1968, 1971). It has already been noted that bureaucrats can distort the policy process by creating rents to be auctioned. Even if this were not possible (for instance if there were very strict governance of their activity to prevent acceptance of bribes, etc.), alternative means of generating personal gain remain. For example, it is often argued that if monetary gains are not achievable they will be substituted by non-monetary gains. In the case of a bureaucrat such non-monetary gain may be derived from the size of the department they manage or the extent of the budget that they control. If this is so, incentives exist for the bureaucrat to direct their efforts to maximising these variables.

To see the consequences of this behaviour, assume that all of the non-monetary variables can be related to the size of the departmental budget. Then the choices of the bureaucrats will always be focused on maximising this budget. This will result in the level of public spending being determined by an equilibrium between the bureaucrats' wish to increase spending and whatever constraints there may be upon spending. Such constraints could, for example, take the form of a reluctance by politicians to raise taxes beyond a given level. If the overall government budget were fixed, then the spending allocation across government departments would be determined by a game between the bureaucrats heading each department.

Regardless of the details of the processes that may occur, some general comments can be made on the end result if spending is driven by the private objectives of bureaucrats. First, it is clear that both the level and the allocation of spending will only partially, if at all, reflect the needs and preferences of the electorate. Instead spending will reflect preferences of bureaucrats and their relative political strengths. Second, it can be expected that the level of expenditure will be excessively high due to the incentives for the bureaucrats to raise expenditure.

This brief review of the public choice approach has highlighted a number of important issues. Essentially, these revolve around the limitations of governments, once elected, to implement good policies. These conclusions follow from the application of economic rationality to the processes and actors within the political sphere. If this rationality is justified outside this sphere, then there can be no argument for not applying it within so that these damaging critiques of government failure cannot be easily dismissed. The central empirical issue raised by the public choice approach concerns what the motives and preferences of politicians and bureaucrats are.

IX. EMPIRICAL OVERVIEW

1. Total Size

Figure 1 (based on data from Tanzi and Schuknecht, 2000) shows how public spending has grown over the last century in five developed economies. Only selected years are plotted—not including, for example, the years of the Second World War—with intermediate years interpolated but the figure gives a good impression of the overall trend. There is a persistent difference between the three historically higher spending European and the two lower spending non-European countries. Nonetheless all economies show a clear long run upward path in public spending relative to overall output. Starting from levels of public spending at less than 15 per cent of GDP in the late nineteenth century, the share increased sharply at around the time of the First World War but then continued to rise. It now exceeds a third of GDP in all cases and in some large economies exceeds 50 per cent.

Many explanations have been offered for this long-run increase (see, e.g. Lybeck and Henderson, 1990). For example, the changing characteristics of populations over time, particularly their increasing incomes and longevity, may have changed the demand for public services. Growing average prosperity and changes in income distribution which raise the income of the median voter will have increased demand for publicly provided goods which are income elastic, though it is far from clear which publicly provided goods these might be. Aging of the population may have raised the demand for publicly provided goods consumed by the elderly such as health care.

At the same time, ongoing processes of industrialisation and urbanisation have changed work patterns and ways of living, shifting responsibility for child care, education and care of the elderly away from the family and on to the state.

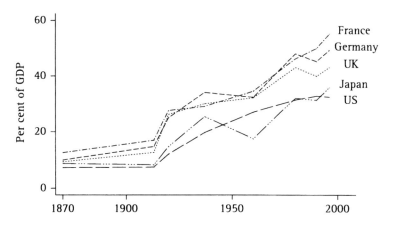

Figure 1. *Growth of total spending*

Source: Tanzi and Schuknecht (2000).

Sociological explanations of this sort can be traced back as far as the nineteenth century work of Wagner (1958).

Changes in political institutions will also affect the determination of public spending levels. Public choice arguments of the sort discussed above tend to focus on the growth of bureaucracies and organised interest groups.

Another sort of explanation focuses less on changing characteristics of voters or the political process and more on the nature of supply. Baumol (1967) argues that publicly provided goods tend to be labour intensive and subject to low technological productivity growth. Their relative price therefore tends to grow and if demand is price-inelastic then so will be the share of public spending in GDP.

2. Division of Expenditure into Categories

Figure 2 shows the growth in selected subcategories of public spending since the late nineteenth century (data are from Tanzi and Schuknecht, 2000). This is helpful in understanding the origin of the long-run increase.

The path of defence spending, which constituted one of the largest items of public spending in the late nineteenth century, has been somewhat erratic and has clearly been driven in large part by the course of international relations. Military spending in the two former Axis powers peaks at around the time of the Second World War but then falls away dramatically. Spending in the three Allied powers continued at a higher level after the war than before, reaching its height in the 1960s before also falling back. Only in the US among those nations represented does defence now constitute more than 10 per cent of spending.

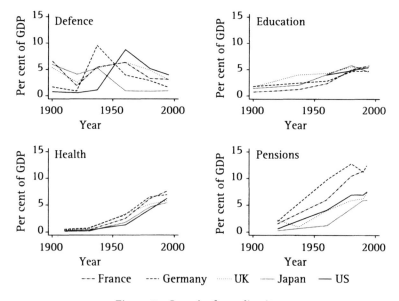

Figure 2. *Growth of spending items*

Source: Tanzi and Schuknecht (2000).

The most marked rises have come from social spending on items like health, education and pensions. Publicly provided education can be seen to have been rising gradually as a share of GDP in all five countries since the nineteenth century but particularly so since the war (and perhaps slightly earlier in the UK). Health and pensions spending have both grown considerably since the war. If we consider subsidies and transfers in total then these have risen on average fourfold between 1937 and 1995 (from about 2.1 per cent of GDP to 13.1 per cent in the US, from 10.3 per cent to 23.6 per cent in the UK, from 7.0 per cent to 19.4 per cent in Germany, from 7.2 per cent to 29.9 per cent in France and from 1.4 per cent to 13.5 per cent in Japan).

Figure 3 gives a more detailed breakdown of current public spending for three of these countries, based on IMF statistics and a classification of government functions developed by OECD and the UN (see IMF, 2001b). The percentages here are percentages of government spending. The numbers recorded below the figures are averages across the three countries and give each country equal weight. These are figures for consolidated general spending, which is to say the combined expenditure of all levels of government (as recorded in IMF, 2001a). In order to avoid double counting it is important to subtract intergovernmental transfers and we have done this using unpublished figures provided to us by the IMF statistics department.

The diversity of goods provided through the public sector is apparent. Note that spending on the goods associated with the 'minimal state'—defence and public order—appear relatively minor, making up only a tenth of spending on average. Costs of an administrative and governmental nature are recorded under the heading "general public services" and add no more than another 6 per cent on average.

Health and education, despite providing benefits of an arguably largely private nature, are substantial in all countries. Spending on housing and community amenities, on recreation and culture, and on transport and communications

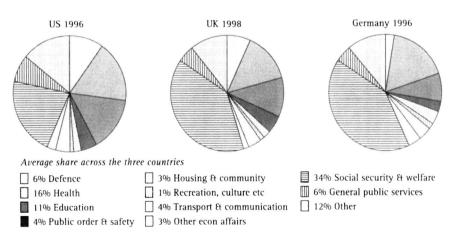

Figure 3. *Composition of consolidated general spending by country*
Source: IMF (2001a,b).

sectors are comparatively small. Subsidies to agriculture, energy, mining, manufacturing and construction sectors are brought together here under the heading of 'other economic affairs' and also appear relatively minor on average.

Social security and welfare spending is the largest single item in all countries, under this classification. This is so even in the US where it is noticeably smaller than in the three European countries. On average it constitutes over a third of spending.

3. Division Between Different Levels of Government

Figures 4–6 show how spending responsibilities are allocated between different tiers of government in these countries. This provides an interesting contrast since Germany and the US are federal countries whereas the UK is not. Nonetheless some common observations can be made. Certain items such as defence are always allocated by the centre. Redistributive functions also tend to be concentrated centrally for the good reason that redistribution between poor and rich regions is only possible that way and also that attempts at redistribution at lower levels are vulnerable to frustration through migration of richer individuals away from localities with internally redistributive programmes.

Education on the other hand seems in all these countries to be largely devolved to lower levels—either to the states or to local government. Public order is also typically dealt with at lower levels. Health spending, on the other hand, is always substantial at the central level but can also be important at lower tiers, for example in Germany.

The fact that spending is made at lower levels need not mean that it is financed from taxes levied locally. In most multiple tier systems central government partly finances lower tier functions by means of grants. These have many purposes,

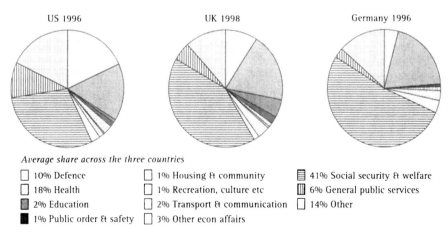

Figure 4. *Composition of central spending by country*

Source: IMF (2001a,b).

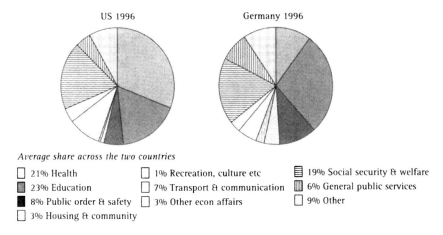

Figure 5. *Composition of state spending by country*

Source: IMF (2001a,b).

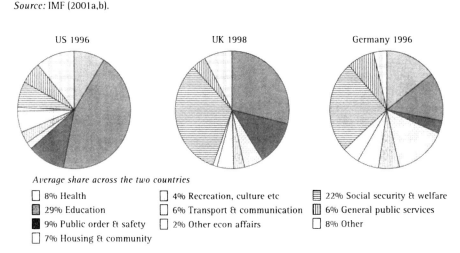

Figure 6. *Composition of local spending by country*

Source: IMF (2001a,b).

including correcting for imbalances of resources between localities and between tiers given the chosen allocation of tax instruments. Sometimes grants are lump sum and sometimes they depend on the spending activities of the lower tiers. In the latter case, the incentives of lower tiers to spend can be changed by the design of the grant formula and central government can use this as a way to encourage recognition of externalities between localities.

Figure 7 contrasts the division of spending between tiers with the division of revenue raising. Because spending here is not classified by function we are able to provide data for slightly later years and also add France to the countries covered.

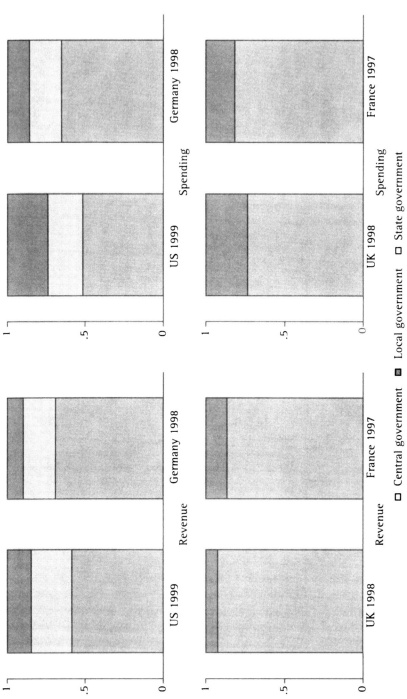

Figure 7. *Revenue and spending shares at tiers by country*

☐ Central government ■ Local government ☐ State government

Source: IMF (2001a,b).

Note that in all four countries central government raises a greater share of revenue than its share of spending. This is particularly marked for the UK, for example, where local government's share of spending is well over three times its share of revenue raised. This may be expected to generate considerable political pressure for central government intervention in local spending decisions.

X. CONCLUSION

This chapter has provided a brief background to the major themes in the economic analysis of public expenditure. We have presented some basic descriptive statistics that provide an overview of the public sector (more detailed statistics are contained in the chapters that follow). The justification for having a public sector and the issues involved in determining the optimal quantity of public goods have been reviewed. We have also noted many of the difficulties involved in turning these theoretical recommendations into practical policy applications.

The purpose of the following chapters is to explore these ideas in detail for particular areas of public expenditure. Each form of expenditure can be justified by the arguments we have considered. What makes a study of these areas so interesting are the differing degrees of difficulty encountered in implementing optimal policies and the variety of solutions that these give rise to.

REFERENCES

Baumol, W. J. (1967), 'The macroeconomics of unbalanced growth: the anatomy of the urban crisis', *American Economic Review*, vol. 57, pp. 415–26.

Bergstrom, T. C. and Goodman, R. P. (1973), 'Private demands for public goods', *American Economic Review*, vol. 63, pp. 280–96.

—, Rubinfeld, D. L. and Shapiro, P. (1982), 'Micro-based estimates of the demand function for local school public expenditures', *Econometrica*, vol. 50, pp. 1183–205.

Besley, T. and Coate, S. (1991), 'Public provision of private goods and the redistribution of income', *American Economic Review*, vol. 81, pp. 979–84.

Blackorby, C. and Donaldson, D. (1988), 'Cash versus kind, self-selection and efficient transfers', *American Economic Review*, vol. 78, pp. 691–700.

Brook, L., Hall, J. D. and Preston, I. P. (1998), 'What drives support for higher public spending?', in P. F. Taylor-Gooby (ed.), *Choice and Public Policy*, London: Macmillan.

Buchanan, J. M., Tollison, R. D. and Tullock, G. (1980), *Towards a Theory of the Rent Seeking Society*, College Station, TX: A&M Press.

Clarke, E. H. (1971), 'Multi-part pricing of public goods', *Public Choice*, vol. 11, pp. 17–33.

Coase, R. H. (1960), 'The problem of social cost', *Journal of Law and Economics*, vol. 3, pp. 1–44.

Epple, D. and Romano, R. E. (1996a), 'Public provision of private goods', *Journal of Political Economy*, vol. 104, pp. 57–84.

Epple, D. and Romano, R. E. (1996b), 'Ends against the middle: Determining public service provision when there are private alternatives', *Journal of Public Economics*, vol. 62, pp. 297–325.

Flora , P. et al. (1983), *State, Economy and Society in Western Europe 1815–1975*, vol. I, Chicago: St James Press.

Groves, T. (1973), 'Incentives in teams', *Econometrica*, vol. 41, pp. 617–31.

Hall, J. D. and Preston, I. P. (2000), 'Tax price effects on attitudes to hypothecated tax increases', *Journal of Public Economics*, vol. 75, pp. 417–38.

Hobbes, T. (1651), *Leviathan*, London, Reprinted in 1968, C. B. MacPherson (ed.), Harmondsworth: Penguin Books.

International Monetary Fund (2001a), *Government Finance Statistics Yearbook*, Washington, DC.

—— (2001b), *Government Finance Statistics Manual*, Washington, DC.

Krueger, A. (1974), 'The political economy of the rent seeking society', *American Economic Review*, vol. 64, pp. 291–303.

Locke, J. (1690), *Two Treatises of Government*, London, Reprinted in 1960, P. Laslett (ed.), Cambridge: Cambridge University Press.

Lybeck, J. A. and Henderson, M. (1988), *Explaining the Growth of Government*, Amsterdam: North-Holland.

Mueller, D. C. (1989), *Public Choice II*, Cambridge: Cambridge University Press.

Niskanen, W. A. (1968), 'The peculiar economics of bureaucracy', *American Economic Review Papers and Proceedings*, vol. 57, pp. 293–321.

—— (1971), *Bureaucracy and Representative Government*, Chicago: Aldine-Atherton.

Preston, I. P. and Ridge, M. (1995), 'Demand for local public spending: evidence from the British Social Attitudes Survey', *Economic Journal*, vol. 105, pp. 644–60.

Rubinfeld, D. L. (1987), 'The economics of the local public sector', in A. J. Auerbach and M. Feldstein (eds) *Handbook of Public Economics*, vol. II, Amsterdam: Elsevier Science.

Samuelson, P. (1954), 'The pure theory of public expenditure', *Review of Economics and Statistics*, vol. 36, pp. 387–9.

Stiglitz, J. E. (1974), 'The demand for education in public and private school systems', *Journal of Public Economics*, vol. 3, pp. 349–85.

Tanzi, V. and Schuknecht, L. (2000), *Public Spending in the 20th Century: A Global Perspective*, Cambridge: Cambridge University Press.

Tullock, G. (1967), 'The welfare cost of tariffs, monopoly and theft', *Western Economic Journal*, vol. 5, pp. 224–32.

Wagner, A. (1958), 'Three extracts on public finance', in R. A. Musgrave and A. T. Peacock (eds), *Classics in the Theory of Public Finance*, London: Macmillan.

2

Public and Private Pension Spending: Principles, Practice and the Need for Reform

JAMES BANKS AND CARL EMMERSON[1]

I. INTRODUCTION

Pensions are one of the most important single items of spending in almost all developed countries. In most countries, spending is set to rise substantially as populations age and the number of retired members of the population increases. Pensions, or more broadly social security, reform is therefore at the top of almost every government's policy agenda.[2] Indeed, a number of countries are already embarking on substantial reform processes which have meant that there are now a variety of different approaches to the problem of how to deliver retirement income to the elderly. What distinguishes Britain from most other countries is that the future costs of public pension provision are not projected to increase markedly, since past reforms have already reduced the generosity of future benefits for today's workers. A further side of these reforms—the offering of private pensions—has meant that there is already a substantial mix of private and public pension

This study forms part of the research programme of the ESRC Centre for the Microeconomic Analysis of Fiscal Policy at IFS. The authors are also grateful to the Leverhulme Trust for co-funding as part of the research programme 'The changing distribution of consumption, economic resources and the welfare of households', reference number F/368/J. Material from the Family Expenditure Survey and the Family Resources Survey, made available by the Office for National Statistics (ONS) through the ESRC Data Archive, has been used by permission of the Controller of HMSO. Neither the ONS nor the ESRC Data Archive bears any responsibility for the analysis or interpretation of the data reported here. The authors are grateful to Andrew Dilnot, Richard Disney, Emla Fitzsimons, Paul Johnson and David Miles for useful discussions and comments. The views expressed, and any errors remaining, are attributable to the authors alone.

[1] Institute for Fiscal Studies. Banks is also at University College London.
[2] Throughout this survey, we use the term social security loosely interchangeably with public pensions, as does much of the international literature, that is, to broadly refer to government provision of income to the elderly. Many of the issues of the design of public pension systems carry over into other social security benefits, and it is certainly true that the system should be considered as a whole rather than piece by piece. In the UK, pensions spending makes up around half (49%) of social security spending, with the rest being sickness and disability benefits (26%), unemployment insurance (6%) and benefits to the family (18%).

provision in the British system. Hence it is a natural country in which to survey the arguments for and against various types of pension provision.

This paper aims to survey the arguments relating to the public and private provision of retirement income, to illustrate some of the main features and approaches of current systems (both in the UK and elsewhere) and to outline the arguments relating to the need for, and the potential direction of, reform. Inevitably, however, such a survey can only be incomplete and many issues will have to be omitted or dealt with only briefly. Fortunately, however, unlike many other items of public spending, there is a huge literature on pension provision—both public and private—to which we are able to refer the interested reader. The debate does not, however, have a balanced international focus. In particular, there are a wealth of papers and volumes outlining and debating options for the US system and it is difficult to provide a survey of the literature without focusing on the issues particularly important in the US situation.[3] Such issues tend to relate to the impact of reform on national and individual saving and wealth accumulation. In contrast, the European debate tends to be more focused on the costs of existing systems, the redistribution they achieve and the impact of reform on both these factors. To some extent, a survey such as this cannot help but reflect this imbalance in the literature.

We begin our introduction by giving a brief discussion of the reasons that pension spending is projected to increase in the future, and hence why the subject of pension reform has become such a major policy issue. We also focus briefly on the implications of such trends for the measurement of the fiscal position and liabilities of the government budget. Although these two issues are not directly the subject of this survey, they provide a vital context within which to interpret the issues we discuss later.

In Section II, we consider the economics of pensions and the particular contexts in which reform is discussed. Potential market failures in the private market for

---

[3] A number of the more recent volumes on US reform options draw on international comparative evidence in the form of descriptive papers outlining particular countries' experiences with the system they have in place. Such international comparative studies have become particularly important in the case of pensions policy, probably because of the peculiar difficulties raised in the evaluation of policy options using domestic data alone. Such evaluations would either need a structural model to predict pension saving and labour supply behaviour, or need to draw on experimental evaluation evidence and pilot studies, to predict the effects of reform. There are problems with both of these methods. In the first case, there is a debate about the relevance and performance of the models of intertemporal spending and saving decisions that would lie at the heart of this approach to pension policy evaluation or selection, and the models themselves do not often deliver strong enough predictions to provide a firm basis for a particular policy intervention. In the second case, evaluation of policy experiments is made difficult by the long time-lags involved, since pension policies will have their effects over the entire lifetimes of individuals. Short-run experimental evidence can be obtained, and we describe some below, but extrapolating the conclusions of these studies either to the long run, or to the economy as a whole when the general equilibrium effects are probably substantial, is, once again, controversial. Hence considering the experiences of other countries, where policies have already been introduced and real data are being collected on their effects, has become an important tool in informing the pension policy debate. A good recent example of this approach is Gruber and Wise (1999), who exploit detailed international microeconomic evidence to generate variation that is used to evaluate the incentive effects of public pensions on retirement choices.

pension saving are highlighted, along with both paternalistic and redistributive motives for having a public pension system. We go on to consider options for the design of such systems. These can broadly vary in three dimensions—the way contributions accrue into future benefits, the conditions and form in which benefits can be received, and the agency that administers the scheme. A number of distinctions—public versus private, funded versus unfunded and defined benefit versus defined contribution—that crop up repeatedly in the menu of policies for analysis are examined. We look at what various analyses have shown to be the impact of different designs, focusing on three properties of the pension system—redistribution, insurance and risk pooling, and incentives. Finally, we examine broad classes of options for reform and assess any similarities between their approaches.

In Section III, we look specifically at how the UK system operates and consider some of the historical context in which the pension system has evolved. We look at the generosity of the UK state pension system and how the general direction of reforms over the last 20 years compares with that seen elsewhere. We also look at the way in which current public pension spending is distributed across the population, documenting the resulting incomes of today's pensioners. In particular, we focus on the mix of public and private provision, in terms of the system parameters, system structure and the resulting incomes among those who have already retired. As part of this analysis, we look at annuity income, which will become increasingly important as more individuals retire with mandatory annuitised pensions. We also look at the implied future liabilities of the UK pension system compared with those seen elsewhere and discuss possible future reforms. Section IV concludes.

1. Public Pension Systems: Rising Costs and a Need for Reform?

The reason public spending on pensions or social security is set to become more important over time is now well known. Put simply, the number of workers relative to the number of retired is projected to decline, and hence, given the current structure of most countries' public pension systems (where today's workers pay the pensions of today's retired), cost projections rapidly increase over the next 40–60 years.

The first reason behind these projected cost increases is the pure demographic trends facing developed countries. The fact that birth rates have declined and life expectancies have risen means that populations will have much higher dependency ratios (the ratio of retired individuals or households to those of working age) in the future. Figures 1–3 show how these trends have interacted for the UK over the last 60 years, and how the dependency ratio is projected to change over the next 60 years. The baby boom of the mid-1960s is clearly visible in Figure 1, with the birth rate rising from 15/1,000 to 19/1,000 over a period of 10 years, before falling back to current levels of around 12/1,000 by the mid-1970s. Coupled with the steadily increasing life expectancies for both men and women shown in Figure 2, this has meant current projections show that, by the year 2040, if retirement ages

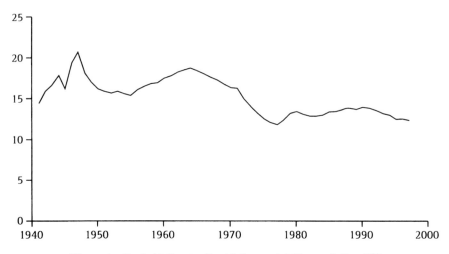

Figure 1. *Crude birth rate: live births per 1,000 population, UK*

Source: Population trends.

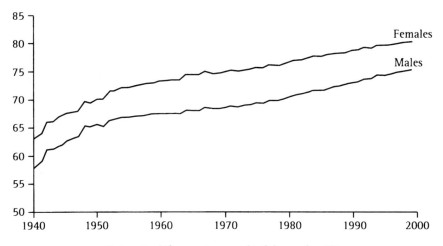

Figure 2. *Life expectancy at birth by gender, UK*

Source: Social trends dataset, Office for National Statistics website.

remain the same, the dependency ratio will have risen to above 0.4, that is, two out of every five adults will be retired (see Figure 3).

Table 1 shows long-term trends in dependency ratios across a number of countries. What is immediately clear is that all populations are ageing, and that projected increases between 1990 and 2030 will dwarf the increases experienced over the period 1960–90.

Also clear from Table 1, however, is that the UK projection—an increase of just over 60 per cent—is relatively small compared with some countries, which

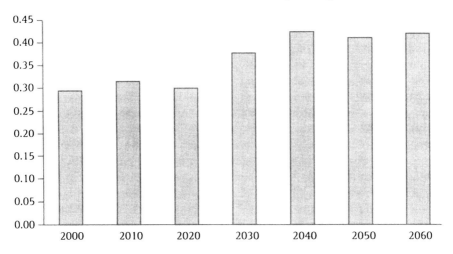

Figure 3. *Projected dependency ratio: number of retired as a proportion of number of working-age adults, Great Britain*

Note: State retirement age taken as 65 for men and 60 for women for 2000 and 2010; 65 for both thereafter.

Source: Government Actuary's Department, 1999.

Table 1. *International trends in dependency ratios*

	Dependency ratios		
	1960	1990	2030
Canada	13.0	16.7	39.1
France	18.8	20.8	39.1
Germany	16.0	21.7	49.2
Italy	13.3	21.6	48.3
Japan	9.5	17.1	44.5
Sweden	17.8	27.6	39.4
UK	17.9	24.0	38.7
US	15.4	19.1	36.8

Note: In this table, dependency ratios are the ratio of the population aged over 65 to the working-age population.

Source: Bos et al. 1994.

experience increases of between 90 per cent (France and US) and 160 per cent (Japan) over the 40-year horizon. These particular comparisons are obviously sensitive to the precise choice of year, given that baby booms and life expectancies do not move in an international synchronised way. For a more detailed analysis on a wider set of countries, see World Bank (1994). The general conclusion remains, no matter what comparison points are used. First, all developed countries are ageing and facing marked increases in dependency ratios. Second, the increase in the UK is at the lower end of the international scale.[4]

However, the increases in projected public pension costs as a result of the pure ageing of the population could be amplified if there are non-demographic factors that reduce further the ratio of workers to non-workers, for example, potential labour market trends. Increasing prosperity will change labour market economic outcomes: as societies become richer, they most likely choose to consume more leisure. On the other hand, life expectancies are simultaneously increasing, with the result that resources have to be spread over more periods, an effect that will offset the increasing wealth of individuals from economic growth and increases in real living standards. In addition, migration patterns, the increasing participation of women in the paid labour force and the extent to which increased life expectancies are positively associated with the extension of healthy (and hence potentially productive working) lives will all change the ratio of workers to retired, and hence, given the design of most current systems, change the projected future costs of public pension provision.

Since, short of natural disasters or other major population shocks, the ageing of the population is inevitable, the two sets of factors that will affect estimates of the future costs of pension provision, and hence current liabilities of social security schemes, are the potential labour market trends outlined above and the design of the scheme itself. The policy debate predominantly concerns the latter and we will focus on it in what follows, but the above discussion makes it clear that the future liabilities of public systems, even given their current design, are far from certain, and that the options and the need for reform should always be seen within the context of the changing labour market.

To some extent, the 'worries' about increasing dependency ratios relate to more general issues than just pension systems. The trends, if taken at face value, suggest that, in the future, a smaller share of the population will potentially be engaged in productive activity. The particular 'problems' of financing public pension schemes in this scenario are just one manifestation, albeit a very visible one, of the more general trend. Seen as such, however, it also becomes clear that sufficient economic growth could make the productivity of the working population increase sufficiently to offset the falling proportions of productive members. Table 1 shows,

---

[4] The ageing of a population has implications for public spending items other than just pensions. Health spending and spending on other parts of the social security system (such as disability or invalidity benefits) will presumably also increase as the proportion of the elderly rises, with the key issue being the degree to which the ageing of the population is 'active' or 'healthy', as opposed to 'unhealthy' (when the stress placed on retirement and health systems would be much greater). In what follows, we do not discuss these issues at much length, but rather focus almost entirely on the pension system. On the one hand, the issues raised by the study of pension finance with ageing populations carry over fairly straightforwardly to other parts of the welfare state. On the other, however, it must be remembered, particularly, that receipt of healthcare and invalidity, sickness and disability benefits can, to the extent that they are correlated with retirements, exacerbate any incentive problems within the system.

however, that such effects of economic growth and changing labour force participation would have to be particularly strong in the future, given the acceleration in population ageing predicted over the next 40 years or so.

The spiralling projections for future costs of pensions mean that, as far as measuring public spending goes, the analysis of social security or pensions policy immediately highlights the deficiencies of looking at the current account surplus or deficit as a way of understanding the financial liabilities of the government. As pointed out by Auerbach and Kotlikoff (1987), an accurate evaluation of the government's fiscal position ought to reflect committed future liabilities, and, in the case of some pension systems, these liabilities will be substantial as the population ages. To address this, Auerbach et al. (1991) proposed that fiscal positions should be analysed using 'generational accounts', which take into consideration projected future tax receipts and spending commitments. The relative merits of the calculations and assumptions needed to create such a set of accounts have been debated elsewhere (see Auerbach et al., 1991, 1994; Kotlikoff, 1992; but also Haveman, 1994; Congressional Budget Office, 1995; or, for an applied UK perspective; see, Cardarelli et al., 2000; Banks et al., 1999). There seems no doubt that it is the right way to think about the aggregate implications of government pension policy and the potential effects of reforms.[5] One way to analyse options for pension policy would therefore be to use such a generational accounts framework explicitly. Since accounts are being computed for an increasing number of countries, both in Europe and elsewhere (see Kotlikoff and Liebfritz, 1998), this is becoming an increasingly viable approach for certain types of policy analysis. In this chapter, however, we take a different approach, since we are interested not in the effects of a specific reform in a specific scenario but instead in more general issues. Therefore the next section sets out the economic issues in pension provision and discusses the broad policy raised.

II. THE ECONOMICS OF SOCIAL SECURITY

In this section, we look at the arguments that have been put forward relating to the economic issues surrounding the provision of economic resources to the elderly, and at the aims that such a system could or should attempt to meet. These issues are now well known within the literature, but we include them for completeness and to provide a context within which to interpret the applied policy analysis in Section III. As a result, our exposition draws from a number of classic studies of the economics of social security without necessarily referencing them on a point-by-point basis.

---

[5] The full generational accounts analysis includes projected spending on all items. For pensions, the framework is particularly appropriate since the future commitments of the government are made explicit in the pension policy of the time. This is not necessarily the case for future spending on items such as health or education, where commitments discounted for up to 50 years are less meaningful. As well as this issue, much of the debate on the generational accounts themselves has focused on the disaggregate question of the extent to which it is possible to decompose the future liabilities into the net benefits or liabilities faced by individual generations.

Readers interested in more detail on these design issues would be well advised to look at the original work of Samuelson (1958, 1975), Aaron (1966, 1982), Feldstein (1974), Diamond (1977), Diamond and Mirrlees (1986) and, for an applied UK perspective, Dilnot et al. (1984). Other more general texts with useful summaries and discussions of the issues raised here are Barr (1998, ch. 9), Myles (1995, ch. 14), Stiglitz (1988) and Rosen (1995). More recently, a number of edited volumes, in particular Sass and Triest (1997), Arnold et al. (1998) and Feldstein (1998), provide a modern debate on the options for social security reform as well as good international comparative evidence.

1. Aims

A pension system essentially ensures the delivery of income to elderly households in their retirement. To ask why there are reasons for government to intervene in this activity is to ask why the outcomes of individual or household decisions are currently suboptimal, either for individual agents or for society as a whole. This in turn leads to three possible rationales for a social security system:[6] (a) market failure is leading to individuals not having the opportunity to (efficiently) provide retirement income for themselves; (b) there is a paternalistic concern that individuals are not choosing to save enough, even though they have the appropriate opportunities; or (c) society as a whole would be better off if there were some redistribution of resources towards those not rich enough to provide adequate retirement income themselves.

It is fair to say that there is consensus that these three rationales, taken together, provide a genuine basis for government intervention in pensions and social security policy. Where there is perhaps less consensus is in the relative importance of each of the three reasons for intervention. Since each will affect the way in which the efficiency and design of a pension system should be evaluated, we discuss each, briefly, in turn.

(a) Market Failure
Potential market failures could take a number of forms. Diamond (1977), writing from the US, points to three potential candidates—the lack of safe investment opportunities offering a reasonable return, the absence of real annuities and the problems of insuring risks associated with varying length of working life— although points out that the reason for the lack of indexed investment opportunities is somewhat puzzling. The existence of both indexed government bonds and real annuities in the UK goes some way towards diminishing the first two of these three potential market failures, and indeed removes the puzzle regarding the existence of opportunities for indexed investments. There is some evidence, however, that, despite the possibility of real annuitisation, only a minority of annuities in

---

[6] A fourth more practical rationale could simply be that the state can administer retirement insurance more cheaply than the private sector, and we discuss this further below.

payment are of this form (see Finkelstein and Poterba, 1999), although this is less puzzling now, when inflation is expected to be low, than in the past.

Diamond (1977) also points out, however, that the third market failure—the inability to insure against changes in the length of working life—is both large and not necessarily very easily handled by institutions other than the public sector. Unexpected early retirements, possibly as a result of ill health, disability or redundancy, have big repercussions, since the period of time over which contributions are made is reduced and the period over which benefits are required is lengthened. Trying to insure privately generates the usual moral hazard and adverse selection problems (see Arrow, 1963; Akerlof, 1970; Rothschild and Stiglitz, 1976), given the difficulties and costs in monitoring both health status and attempts or ability to obtain suitable employment. A social security system offers one way of providing insurance against declines in earnings associated with unexpectedly early retirements, although the precise details of system design will be important in determining the degree to which the system is effective in this dimension (see Diamond and Mirrlees, 1986). Mandatory retirement insurance can solve the adverse selection problem, but on the other hand, social security could worsen the moral hazard problem associated with early retirements, depending on the way in which benefits are affected.

(b) Paternalism

At the heart of the paternalism argument is the debate over whether individuals would provide enough for their own retirement in the absence of a social security system, that is, does the government need to intervene to encourage or force individuals to undertake retirement saving? The main private mechanism for provision of resources in retirement is saving during working life, although transfers from other family members could provide additional resources. The question of how much of this would be done in the absence of a pension system is extremely difficult to answer on either a theoretical or an empirical basis.

From a theory point of view, how individuals allocate resources over their life cycle could be thought to depend on their expectations of their future economic circumstances, the way that they discount the future when taking decisions and their degree of risk aversion. The conventional neo-classical economic model for setting out these household or individual consumption and saving choices is the well-known life-cycle model, developed in the work of Duesenberry (1949) and Friedman (1957) and formalised as an empirical model of choice under uncertainty in Hall (1978). In essence, the model predicts that individuals wish to smooth the discounted expected marginal benefit of consumption across different periods of their lifetime. Saving and borrowing choices are the mechanism by which they can achieve this, given expectations about the amount of resources available to distribute.

Development and estimation of the life-cycle model spawned an enormous literature, with a number of developments being added or debated to make the model more flexible. For a full survey of the model and its implications for spending and saving behaviour, see Deaton (1992) or Browning and Lusardi (1996). In particular, developments have focused on the role of uncertainty and the precautionary motive for saving, as well as on the importance of demographic variables such as household size and the number and ages of children, in determining the life-cycle allocation of spending. The empirical literature in this area is both large and inconclusive. There is still controversy about the extent to which the model can explain the consumption and saving choices we see in data, and hence predictions relating to the 'adequacy' of saving (either observed in data or at the level that would be required given the prevailing economic conditions) made from estimated parameters of the model are always controversial.

Possibly as a result, recent studies in saving behaviour have instead focused in detail on the way in which individuals make the relatively complex planning decisions required by the life-cycle model and on the factors that will affect the formation of those plans. Two areas receiving particular attention that are relevant for determining the rationality of such choices are (a) the possible use of rule-of-thumb approximations for complex intertemporal planning decisions, and (b) self-control and the way individuals discount the future.

Bernheim (1991, 1993) argues that the optimal saving plans derived from intertemporal consumption models are too complex for many people to compute. Even in the simplest models, they require someone to make an assessment of their expected income over their entire lifetime and to form expectations of future rates of return. In addition, individuals will have to take into account expected future labour supply and household composition, as well as the level of current and future benefits provided by the government. The counter-argument to this is that one might expect individuals to develop rules of thumb that provide approximations to the optimal plan, and there are some (limited) circumstances in which such approximations have been shown to be very accurate (see Deaton, 1992). However, when circumstances are changing, rules of thumb can become unreliable and out of date. The delivery of state retirement income and other benefits, the age structure of the population, household composition and formation, life expectancies and work patterns have all changed so much that such rules, if inherited from previous generations, would provide a very poor guide for younger generations.

In practice, there may be some middle ground, with approximate rules for behaviour being developed as a result of a number of influences, including family and peers but also including some reflection and 'planning'. It is likely that such plans would not be fully rational in the sense of the models described above, but they may perform reasonably well, given a realistic specification of the economic environment. This is an important but difficult topic for future research, and one that models of bounded rationality are beginning to address. What seems fairly clear, however, is that an understanding of the way in which individuals or households form their consumption and saving plans, and the information that is used as inputs in those plans, are increasingly important inputs into pension policy design and analysis. This is confirmed by a series of interesting experiments in the US in which Bernheim and co-authors have shown that employees attending a series of financial education seminars choose to save more in various forms—in particular, in their tax-favoured employer pension (401k plan)—than those without access to the information.[7]

A second area of recent research on intertemporal rationality is the issue of self-control in intertemporal decisions. Thaler (1990) and Laibson (1994), for example, have argued that individuals have self-control problems that invalidate the standard life-cycle models since individuals are unable to postpone consumption from today to tomorrow. As such, it may be 'optimal' for them to engage in mechanisms that commit them to saving, and a required participation in some form of social security could be thought of as one of these mechanisms. Indeed, it is clear that such mechanisms, even outside pensions, although typically only partial commitment devices, do exist and are relatively widely used.

Related to these planning issues are those of how individuals discount the future when making their consumption and saving choices. Laibson (1997) and Laibson et al. (1998), for example, explore the implications of individual choices where the future is discounted differently according to how far away it is. For example, today I may prefer £60 in 15 years' time to £50 in 14 years' time, but 14 years from now I may have reversed my preferences over these two, that is, I may actually prefer £50 immediately to £60 in one year's time. The implication of this is that, although today I might think it optimal for me to start saving tomorrow, when tomorrow comes I will actually place a greater value on consumption rather than saving, so saving keeps being deferred.[8] Again, a possible solution is for people to be encouraged to engage in commitment mechanisms.

With regard to empirical research into the degree to which households save enough, a number of papers have looked at the issues involved. Diamond (1977) and Kotlikoff et al. (1982) argued empirically that consumers had insufficient savings to cover their retirement. Since then, this issue has become a controversial one, with no consensus emerging. To add to this, the measurement of individual saving itself is made more complicated when (average) capital gains are particularly high, as was the case with the returns on the US stock markets in the 1990s (see, e.g. Gale and Sabelhaus, 1999). Hence it is quite possible that simulation of economic behaviour under different models provides greater insights. Using such techniques, Hubbard et al. (1995) have shown that the structure of social insurance (and particularly asset tests) can have a strong effect on precautionary saving motives, and hence low saving may be the rational response to the current economic environment.

In the UK, Banks et al. (1998) address the question of whether households save enough for their retirement by looking at what happens to consumption around retirement. Microeconomic data suggest that consumption growth, and indeed

---

[7] See Bayer et al. (1996), Bernheim and Garrett (1996) or Bernheim et al. (1997).

[8] Of course, the reverse could be true, as pointed out by Akerlof (1998), although this is not a case often dealt with in the literature. In this case, individuals may be thought to continually put off the point where they consume their wealth, and the argument would be for them to engage in spending, as opposed to saving, commitments.

consumption, fall markedly around the time of retirement in a way that is not consistent with smoothing around this time. Banks et al. (1998) show that two-thirds of this fall in consumption growth can be explained within the life-cycle model in terms of anticipated changes in household demographics and labour market status, but that an important proportion remains unexplained. This evidence suggests either that households have not saved enough or that there are unanticipated shocks occurring around the time of retirement.

One explanation may be found in the increasing body of evidence that individuals overestimate their future pension entitlements. Dilnot et al. (1994), for example, provide evidence from the UK Retirement Survey that, for 40 per cent of individuals, retirement income was less than they had expected, and Ghilarducci (1992) gives similar evidence from the US. But there may also be other informational shocks occurring at the time of retirement. Expectations of the implications of illness or bad health might change following retirement as an individual's peer group changes.

The results of many studies (including, e.g. the Banks et al. (1998) paper) are based on a cohort of households that have already retired. But, as argued in Attanasio and Banks (1998), the economic environment has changed sufficiently in recent years that the behaviour of older generations is probably a very poor guide to the behaviour, or indeed needs, of younger generations. The empirical issue of current generations' adequacy of saving for retirement is therefore far from resolved. Even if this were not the case, inferring conclusions from the above studies about the counterfactual case, in which there were no social security at all, is another matter entirely. Since there is no developed country without some form of social security system or safety net, consumption and saving data do not exist with which to evaluate such an extreme counterfactual. In general, simulation approaches such as that taken by Hubbard et al. (1995) may, in the future, provide a way of learning about the implications of 'rational' behaviour in the presence of different institutional structures. This in turn could shed light on the degree to which observed behaviour is compatible with rational models of intertemporal choice.

To sum up this debate, there is little broad agreement in the literature relating to the adequacy of household saving or even over what the empirical concept of 'adequacy' really means. Even to the limited extent that there may be some consensus that households in the US are not saving 'enough', there is little consensus on why this may be the case—whether as a result of incorrect expectations or of behaviour that is 'irrational' in a strictly neo-classical economic sense. If one considers Germany or Italy (where pensions are generous and saving is also high), one's conclusions could be altered dramatically.

Further arguments that fit (indirectly) into the paternalistic motivations for public involvement in pension provision relate to the costs of individual decisions. That is, even if decision-making is rational, it could be that the costs of obtaining quality information on which to base choices outweigh the discounted benefits, and hence private outcomes are suboptimal when compared with the perfect information case. Alternatively, the costs of regulating private long-term saving scheme providers and ensuring that accurate information is available may be substantial. Thus, if these decision costs exist in life-cycle choices and are substantial enough, it may be the case that the centralising of these decisions may result in overall gains (as long as the government's decisions are ultimately at least as effective). The relative importance of these arguments, however, remains a matter for debate.

Ultimately, then, the relevance of paternalistic-type arguments for social security remains a matter for debate amongst economists and policymakers alike. It would be possible to argue, for example, that (a) we do not currently know how important such arguments are, (b) we will never know how important such arguments are, or (c) there may be no single answer anyway, given that the practical importance of the paternalistic motivation for pension provision depends on the degree to which we care about any resulting oversaving for those individuals who would have saved anyway. In general, if one believes consumption, saving and retirement choices are made rationally, then one is forced to rely predominantly on market failure or redistribution as a rationale for government intervention. If, on the other hand, one believes that individuals are myopic or time inconsistent, or that decisions are complex and information is costly to acquire, the paternalistic motivation for intervention can become a strong one.

Having said this, it is important to be clear that there is a difference between wanting to encourage saving and wanting to encourage saving in the form of pensions. Many of the above arguments apply to saving in general, and the paternalistic rationale for intervention could equally be construed as suggesting the need for broader investment in education and information provision, or the encouragement to hold precautionary balances, as well, or even instead.[9] This is particularly relevant when large groups of the population are holding little or no liquid wealth, as is the case in the UK (see Banks and Tanner, 1999a) and the US (see Bertaud and Starr-McCluer, 1999). The analysis of wealth inequality, and related topics such as financial exclusion, is becoming increasingly important for government policy and ought to be integrated with the analysis of pensions and retirement saving.

(c) Redistribution

One of the most important roles social security or pensions systems can play is in redistributing resources from one group of individuals or households to another, either across or within generations. Whilst this is discussed in more detail in Section II.3, with respect to the effects of different designs and possible reforms, it is worth noting that redistribution on its own is often put forward as a reason for the existence of social security policy. Indeed, if one believes that individual or household intertemporal choices are taken rationally, it is probably the strongest reason for public intervention in pension provision. Diamond (1977) points out, however, that redistribution motives, whilst legitimate, do not stand alone in

---

[9] Although, to the extent that longer horizons lead to greater 'problems' with individual choices, the argument for paternalistic intervention in retirement saving may be more important.

justifying the social security systems that exist in most countries today, which can be very varied and generate very different types of redistribution, that is, not just from rich to poor (see Creedy et al. 1993). The UK and Australian systems, for example, are almost all redistribution, whereas the continental European systems contain very little, as will be seen below. And redistribution, after all, can be undertaken in other forms of government activity; there is not necessarily a reason, from a life-cycle perspective, to tax all workers (rich and poor) in order to give benefits to the retired (both rich and poor) as would be the case in a simple pay-as-you-go system (see below).[10]

2. Design of Pension Systems

Traditional views of pension systems are, in essence, very simple, being composed of only two elements. In the first instance, contributions are made out of earned income, and in the second, a stream of benefits are received at some point in the future. Within these two elements, however, there are many possible structures for schemes, all of which have been debated at length in the literature about the design, and subsequently the reform, of social security policy. Although we discuss them separately in what follows, each issue can be thought of as affecting one of four basic properties of pension schemes: the way in which contributions accrue entitlements to future benefits, restrictions on the conditions under which one can begin to receive benefits, the form in which benefits have to be taken or the particular agencies that may administer the schemes.[11]

(a) Funding

Probably the most important, and certainly the most lengthy, discussions in the current policy debate relate to the degree of funding of a social security system.[12] In an entirely funded system, the contributions of an individual or generation (cohort) go towards a fund that is invested, accumulates and will ultimately finance the benefits received by that individual or generation when they retire.[13] In contrast, an unfunded system, commonly called pay-as-you-go (PAYG), is characterised by the contributions of current working generations paying directly for the benefits of those currently in retirement; that is, the system as a whole is financed on a year-by-year basis. A combination of approaches—partial funding—is also a possibility.

---

[10] Indeed, pension schemes may introduce redistribution that is undesirable and unintentional due to the complexity of the interactions between incomes, retirement, wealth and life expectancy.

[11] This is certainly the way that the literature has progressed since the study of Diamond (1977). Increasingly in the UK, and elsewhere (e.g. Australia), with the movement to income provision for the elderly being provided by regular means-tested benefits, this model becomes harder to apply. Essentially, the concept of a 'state pension' is becoming more blurred. We stick to this approach, however, as it provides the most convenient way to discuss the majority of the literature.

[12] In this section, we abstract from issues of how much pension should be provided, that is, what the appropriate levels of contributions and benefits should be. Such issues are important but tend to apply regardless of the particular design of the social security system.

[13] Plus, to some extent, the benefits of others if there is any risk pooling.

The US system, for example, is a predominantly PAYG system where the excess of contributions received over benefits paid is accumulated into a fund that will help finance the system in future years. But this fund is small: although it has been growing since 1983, the fund currently represents only around 5 per cent of the liabilities of the system, and 90 per cent of payroll tax receipts are still paid out immediately (Feldstein, 1998).

There are two focuses of the debate about the degree to which a public pension system should be funded. First, the applied public finance literature points out that the amount of funding will affect the future fiscal position of the government finances (see, e.g. Auerbach and Kotlikoff, 1987). With ageing populations and current structures of PAYG (or at least only partially funded) social security, the implied fiscal liabilities for government budgets can be enormous. Such changes, *ceteris paribus*, coupled with the government's intertemporal budget constraint, mean that, if left unchecked, social security systems will be leading future governments inevitably towards increases in taxes or reductions in benefits. For international evidence on the potential magnitude of these issues, see Section III or the more detailed analyses contained in studies carried out by the major international economic organisations, that is, World Bank (1994), IMF (Chand and Jaeger, 1996) and OECD (1996).

The second aspect of the funding debate is a substantial, and related, discussion about the macroeconomic implications of funding, that is the possibility that a movement towards more funding can raise the growth of the capital stock and hence that there are long-run welfare gains to be made.[14] Aaron (1966) and Samuelson (1958) showed that the potential long-run returns on contributions within a PAYG system are given by the surplus of wage growth over population growth (i.e. the increase in the tax base) plus the rate of growth of the tax rate. That is, although the scheme pays out its benefits with the contributions of current workers, any individual will receive more from the scheme, relative to the contributions they made while working, as a result of economic growth. In contrast, the return the same individual would receive in a funded scheme would be given by the average net rate of return on their fund. Thus one argument for funding is that one might expect portfolio returns to be greater than wage or GDP growth and hence funded schemes offer a greater return. Miles (1998), amongst others, shows that this has certainly been the case *ex post* for a number of countries in recent years, but goes on to point out that the *ex-ante* risk properties of the portfolio investment would have been very different, and also that the difference in returns obviously depends on the particular portfolio selected in the funded scheme.

Although funding may well provide welfare gains in the long run, it is clear that there may well be substantial transition costs involved in getting the new system to maturity. These costs could outweigh the benefits of transition (depending on the discount rates and the degree of intergenerational altruism) in any realistic

---

[14] At heart, this is not a discussion specific to pensions but an argument about welfare provision in general.

horizon because the transition itself will create a number of losers (see, e.g. Flemming, 1977; Diamond, 1998). Auerbach et al. (1994) use the Auerbach and Kotlikoff (1987) overlapping generations general equilibrium model to look at the transition paths in a suggested US reform. They argue convincingly that such a tool should be used by policymakers so that, at the least, gainers and losers can be identified when reforms are being considered. Auerbach et al. also show how different ways of financing transitions can have differing effects on economic welfare, finding an expenditure-tax-financed transition to minimise the welfare losses across their set of simulated reforms. Miles (1998) uses a similar framework to model different transition paths for European economies and shows that transition costs are potentially important in a European context—not surprisingly, since the nature of the funding problem is an order of magnitude greater in many European countries than in the US, let alone the UK (see below).

Of course, the establishment of an unfunded public pension system benefits an initial generation of retired people. By considering transition to a funded system from the point where the unfunded system has already been established, these gains are effectively ignored. This makes clear, however, that what is occurring is an intergenerational transfer, and the transition costs are essentially the inevitable 'flip side' of the initial welfare gains made at the introduction of the system.

(b) Public or Private Provision?
Related to the above arguments, but not equivalent, is the debate about whether there are advantages to social security systems being publicly or privately provided. There is a tendency for some of the literature to associate 'privatisation' with funding, but, at least in principle, it is possible to have both public funded and private unfunded schemes. The arguments for privatisation should therefore not be confused with those outlined above for or against funding.

Instead, the arguments for privatisation rest predominantly on two issues: first, the ability of a private funded system to deliver investment returns more effectively than a public sector funded scheme; and second, the susceptibility of each system to political risk. We deal with the latter in Section II.3. The former (i.e. the efficiency of a privately run system compared with a public system) depends on three factors: administrative costs, the cost of regulation and the relative (risk-adjusted) performance of investment funds across private and public sectors. Whilst one would expect the administrative costs of a public scheme to be lower than those of a private system through economies of scale, the magnitudes of all three factors are uncertain. The charge ratios in the UK private pension system, for example, could be falling as the system becomes more established. But the cost of regulation, particularly in a complex system such as the UK, could be substantial. To the extent that these costs manifest themselves as fixed costs, they will introduce unwanted redistribution into the system, in the sense that they will affect the net rates of return of poorer households by more than those of richer households.

Even if such factors worked in favour of a public system, their effect may be offset by potential differences in expected investment returns between publicly and privately managed funds. These differences could be a result of the government failing to achieve portfolio returns on the risk–return frontier. Alternatively, however, the returns could differ as a result of the public scheme choosing a different point on the frontier. The importance of this obviously depends on the correspondence of preferences for risk between government and individuals.[15] Empirical evidence in this area is scarce and would greatly inform the private versus public debate. Comparative evidence by the World Bank (1994) suggests that the rate of return on publicly administered funded schemes has historically been low.

As a final thought in this area, there may be political economy issues relating to whether such direct government intervention in corporate activity is desirable. A public funded scheme would, after all, be a major shareholder in the private sector. In particular, this could be a big issue in countries with less developed capital markets, where firms may have problems raising domestic investment finance elsewhere. To the extent that publicly funded schemes are a genuine reform possibility, this is obviously an issue for further research.

In practice, the arguments for funding and the arguments for privatisation are often taken together–that is, many authors implicitly rule out the public funded option, possibly as a result of the potentially high political risks involved in governments managing funds on behalf of individuals (see the discussion of political risk, and particularly hypothecation, below).

(c) Defined Benefit versus Defined Contribution

There are two ways in which contributions in a funded scheme can earn rights to benefits in the future. In the first type of scheme, referred to as defined benefit (DB), the benefit formula links future benefits to the history of earnings covered by the plan. In the second type–defined contribution (DC) schemes–contributions are channelled into individual accounts which accrue capital gains and interest based on portfolio returns, and the final value of the account is converted to a stream of benefits of some form on retirement.

The economic differences between the two ways of funding a pension system could be thought to be minimal since, in most respects, a DB scheme can be set up to mimic the outcomes of a DC scheme (although a DC scheme contains a degree of benefit commitment that is hard to generate in a DB scheme). The most commonly discussed difference between these structures is that, by default, a DB scheme will spread risks over generations in a way that a DC scheme will not unless it is specifically set up to do so.[16] We deal with this issue in Section II.3. Apart from this, Diamond (1999) argues that the differences are essentially in the perception

---

[15] Of course, if one believes that individual preferences are irrational with respect to risk (e.g. exhibiting loss aversion or being affected by 'framing'–the way in which the risk is described to the consumer, see Kahneman and Tversky, 1979, 1986), there may be a paternalistic reason for the government to intervene *specifically* to choose a different point on the risk–return frontier.

[16] To some extent, this is not a valid comparison. More valid may be a comparison of 'best' design as opposed to 'default' design, in which case the equivalence of the two types of provision is much closer.

of the plan in the consumer's eyes. More particularly, a DC scheme makes the financing of benefits explicit but at the cost of the outcomes or benefits being fairly unclear. The reverse is true for DB schemes—the individual benefits are visible whereas the financing of benefits is typically opaque. Once again, we return to this issue later, since it is potentially important when considering the ease with which governments can alter contributions or benefits.

A further dimension in which the two methods of delivery differ is in the way in which they respond to the need for change as a result of demographic trends. In the case of an increase in life expectancies, for example, a DB scheme would require actuarial adjustments to the rates and rules of the plan whereas a DC scheme would typically adjust automatically.

(d) The Form of Benefits

One factor that has not received quite so much attention in the literature is the design of the benefits side of pension policy and, in particular, restrictions on the way in which resources can be withdrawn in a DC scheme. The exception here is the case of state benefits in a PAYG scheme, where the issue of the structure and indexation of the state retirement pension has received much attention from policy-makers in the UK and elsewhere. Benefits from a funded scheme could, in principle, be given in the form of a lump sum, an income draw-down facility with the remaining fund continuing to accrue returns, an annuity or (as in the UK) some combination of all three. If the benefits are to be taken in the form of an annuity, there are a number of ways in which this could be provided.

Once again, the issue arises as to whether individuals would take rational choices themselves in the absence of rules over the form in which benefits can be taken. A further question is how annuity decisions will affect the surviving member of a couple on the death of the other member (Diamond, 1998). We discuss issues relating to annuity income receipt in the UK system in Section III, but the fact that, in current private annuity markets, most individuals choose nominal, as opposed to real, policies is taken by Diamond as evidence that annuity choices may not be rational. Likewise, he argues that the fact that, left on their own, people purchase single, as opposed to joint-life, annuities is further evidence to this effect. Whilst such outcomes (i.e. indexed joint-life benefit streams) could be, and are, achieved by appropriate design of a DB scheme, when pension provision is through a DC system the issues have to be either resolved by regulation or else left to individuals themselves.

Other arguments relate to the pros and cons of annuitisation. Put briefly, mandatory annuitisation is presumably better for those pure life-cycle savers who would have annuitised anyway (since, presumably, market rates will be better as a result of the removal of adverse selection issues). It is also presumably better for those who would not have annuitised but for whom annuitisation would be the best option—the by now familiar paternalistic argument. From a macroeconomic perspective, Kotlikoff and Spivak (1981) show that annuitisation lowers bequests. This could be thought to lower the level of capital stock in the economy if one believed bequests were optimal originally.[17] Annuitisation may also have effects on incentives and exposure to risk, which we will deal with below.

Finally, the absence of mandatory annuitisation can lead to moral hazard problems in the presence of other means-tested benefits. The experience of Australia has been a cautionary tale here. The existence of a compulsory private scheme without an annuitisation requirement, coupled with means-tested benefits starting five years after the age at which one can qualify for accrued private pension entitlements, has led to many households or individuals consuming their private pension wealth rapidly (particularly in the form of housing, which is exempt from the means test) and then subsequently qualifying for means-tested support (see Bateman and Piggott, 1997).

(e) Other Design Issues

There are a host of other design options and reform issues discussed in the literature which, for reasons of brevity, we do not go into in detail here. One important such example is the debate over the extent to which changes in the retirement age (i.e. the age at which one is entitled to receive benefits, as opposed to the age at which one actually retires) can offer a way out of problems associated with PAYG schemes and ageing populations, a debate popular in continental Europe (see, e.g. Chand and Jaeger, 1996; or Disney, 2000 for a critique). We deal with this briefly below. A similar set of arguments relate to the possible effects of immigrant workers on future system liabilities, essentially increasing the ratio of workers to retired, partially offsetting the pure ageing of the population.

Another set of issues concern whether households should be 'compelled' or simply 'encouraged' to participate in pension schemes. This is particularly pertinent when there are multiple tiers of pension coverage, as in the UK, often associated with a co-existence of both public and private schemes. We talk more below about the UK's 'carrot-and-stick' approach to this problem, where benefits in the state system have been eroded and tax advantages have been given to private schemes. However, if provision is voluntary, the same issues about rational choice as led to paternalism arguments will arise again. It is worth noting that the empirical studies that show households are not saving enough for their retirement show this within the context of current systems, that is, including pension wealth, not in the absence of it.

The experimental evidence from Bernheim's and his co-authors' experiments provides some of the few pieces of *ex-post* evaluation relevant to the pensions debate.[18] The studies discuss changes in saving behaviour and attitudes, particularly relating to private pensions, within a sample population, some of whom were randomly chosen to receive various forms of financial education. While the studies show that consumer education can have an effect, they also imply that

---

[17] Of course, if one believed that bequests were excessive for some reason, such a dead-weight loss could be seen as a dead-weight gain.

[18] Bayer et al. (1996), Bernheim and Garrett (1996) and Bernheim et al. (1997).

extensive, and presumably costly, programmes of consumer education and information provision may be required to raise consumers' saving in a voluntary system, if a raising of saving rates is necessary. The work also suggests that the employer may be a natural channel for such programmes, although the arguments are less strong when one considers all but the biggest firms, since the cost per employee of such educational programmes would presumably rise markedly for smaller firms.

Hence there may be problems with a voluntary approach to privatisation, particularly in redistributive terms if the decision to opt out is correlated with education, income or wealth. This is not to say that compulsion is necessarily the way forward, however, since such an approach generates its own issues, notably in determining a universal level at which to compel contributions, particularly in the presence of substantial heterogeneity (either observed or unobserved). Such an approach may also run the risk of increasing dead-weight losses in the system, since there is a danger of associated changes in incentives of the type described below.

These design issues, or for that matter those mentioned in earlier sections, will not reduce the increasing burden of pensions caused by ageing populations. Instead, what will change across different systems, or when systems are reformed, are which generations will pay the costs of population ageing and the way in which the costs will be borne. The discussion of social security reform, and particularly transition, in recent literature makes this clear. What is also clear, though, is that there are still valid and ongoing arguments regarding the relative merits of various policy options, especially funding versus PAYG and defined benefit versus defined contribution, although we would also argue that, to some extent, such distinctions are only a convenient shorthand. The real issues relate to the economic effects of various systems, and the literature has shown how similar effects and consequences can be achieved as a result of a variety of system designs. Finally, the transition costs debate makes it clear that what is 'optimal' depends on one's starting-point, and in particular the relative well-being of cohorts and the pattern of transfers between cohorts already in place.

Diamond (1996, 1997, 1998), amongst others, has emphasised that the issues are as much political as economic, since choices are essentially over who should gain and who should lose. It is certainly true that the political dimension of pensions policy should not be understated. Voters choose governments, and pension systems are ultimately chosen as part of the electoral process, so the degree to which various reform options benefit different groups of society, and the way in which these groups are changing in size and political voice, may prove a strong factor in driving reform, although it is not clear which way the effects would go. Having said this, however, the economic design of pension systems does have a role to play in affecting behaviour and incentives and hence the dead-weight loss inherent in a system. Next, we deal with these issues briefly, before moving on to talk about some of the more common reform templates that have been suggested as ways of combating the problems caused by population ageing.

3. Impacts of Pension System Design

The way in which pension and, more generally, social security systems are designed is likely to have big effects on economic behaviour and individual and social welfare. At the heart of design choices is the need to balance the gains from the redistribution and insurance offered by social security against any efficiency reductions or dead-weight losses that they may entail.

(a) Risk

Pension schemes, whilst presumably designed to offer as predictable an economic outcome as possible, provide differing degrees of insurance against different kinds of risks—in particular, demographic risks, economic risks such as those associated with future earnings, capital markets and annuitisation, and political risk. Thompson (1998) provides a comprehensive summary of these in turn, although the issues are partially confused by his focus on the differences in two specific dimensions, that is, the comparison of an unfunded DB scheme and a funded DC design. Many, but not all, differences relate to the funded/unfunded, as opposed to the DB/DC, nature of provision.

Demographic risks arise from changes in the population structure, as a result of changes in birth or mortality rates. Under a PAYG model, the bearing of these risks is determined by the adjustments of tax rates and benefit rates, which in turn are determined by the outcome of the political process. Such potential risks can be large, as can be seen by the projections for European PAYG systems, given current population projections, presented in Section III. It is worth noting that a DC scheme is not necessarily immune from such demographic risks. Whilst the value of the fund on retirement is unaffected, the stream of real benefits that the fund will be able to purchase will be affected by prevailing asset prices, annuity rates and tax rates, all of which will presumably be affected by the demographic conditions that underpin the aggregate demand and supply of assets. The potential magnitudes of such effects is another area in which research is still at an early stage (see, e.g. Schieber and Shoven, 1997).

Economic risks typically result from unanticipated changes in wages, earnings or investment returns during working life. Risky investment returns are not insured within a DC plan for obvious reasons, although a portfolio that moves towards safer assets as it gets closer to retirement date clearly reduces such risks. Whilst future wage and earnings risks are not insured within a DC scheme, since contributions to the scheme will presumably fall or lapse as a result, past earnings and wages are captured in the fund in an irreversible way.

Within most PAYG systems, on the other hand, contribution and benefit rates are not typically affected—if entitlements are linked to aggregate earnings growth, then, while real wage growth increases future liabilities, it also provides a bigger tax base with which to pay them. Investment returns are typically not important since the scheme has very few assets to invest. Funded DB schemes are potentially more complicated, with the degree of insurance depending on the design.

Well-designed benefits could, at least theoretically, offer fairly complete insurance. Poorly designed schemes could leave much of the risk borne by individuals. In particular, short averaging periods over which benefits are computed or high penalties for early withdrawal from the scheme (as a result of unemployment or job transitions) could mean that individuals' exposure to economic risk is substantial (see Brugiavini and Disney (1995) for a comparison of the DB and DC cases in the UK system).

Finally, understanding the degree to which different schemes can offer insurance against political risk is more complicated still. Thompson (1998) lists six types of political risk. The first three affect PAYG systems and are probably the most intuitive. The first relates to excessive promises—the idea that governments may be tempted to promise high returns (either as an electoral strategy or through a genuine misprojection of the population structure) which will not be delivered. Such risks are precisely those that the dynamic approach to fiscal policy suggested by Auerbach et al. (1991) is designed to highlight. The second risk arises out of possible political stalemate meaning that adjustments to contributions or benefit rates cannot be made when required. Third, in the absence of political stalemate, the government may be tempted to adjust the net benefits of the scheme for reasons other than those to do with pension saving. At the heart of this final point is a hypothecation argument. There is a real sense in which individual items of a government's budget are fungible, and the degree to which tax rises in a pension system can be identified or earmarked as paying for current benefits is limited.[19]

Thompson (1998) argues that a private DC design is not immune from political-type risk, although it may be thought that the risks are smaller. In the first instance, potential risks arise from transition costs (discussed earlier), although such risks are not present in equilibrium. Second, if there is a failure to ensure that financial assets are preserved sufficiently, individuals may be able to dissipate assets prior to retirement or draw-down assets too quickly after retirement. Finally, ineffective administration or regulation may lead to returns being less than expected. But, while these three issues are certainly problems that need to be addressed with DC scheme design, they might not necessarily be thought of as political risks *per se*. More important, perhaps, is the fact that government policy needs to be considered as a whole, not just the pension system in isolation. It then becomes immediately clear that there are political risks in any intertemporal decisions, since the government could undo any private retirement saving by adjustments elsewhere in the tax and benefit system. To argue that there is less political risk in a funded DC (or DB) system is to argue that the benefits paid (or contributions received) by such systems are in some sense more untouchable by government in a way that those in an unfunded scheme are not. The direct visibility of such changes, coupled with other practical problems in reforming private systems administered by third parties, presumably makes political risk smaller in a funded scheme. This is not to

---

[19] The US system has, however, been particularly successful at maintaining stability over contribution rates and building up a surplus in the trust fund independently of other budgetary pressures.

say that it is non-existent, as is made clear by the recent abolition of the dividend tax credit previously granted to pension funds in the UK.

(b) Redistribution

The second major issue when looking at the impacts of pension spending and pension systems is the effect, whether desired or otherwise, on redistribution. In one dimension, all pension schemes do is redistribute resources—over the lifetime of an individual from times in which they are high to times in which they are (expected to be) low. The more interesting dimensions, however, are across and within cohorts or generations of households. Many of the points relating to redistribution will relate closely to those on risk mentioned above, since the characteristics of schemes in each of these dimensions are linked. Once again, however, although such issues are important to bear in mind when thinking about possible policy reforms, it is also important to remember that further redistribution can be achieved, or redistribution can be undone, by other government policies. Hence it is ultimately always important to look at the redistribution properties of the tax and benefit system as a whole. This is not to say that it is not important to understand the way in which individual parts of government activity contribute to this whole.

Within PAYG systems, some redistribution from (contemporaneously) rich to poor is often a result of the particular benefits accrual formula. This redistribution could occur on the benefits side by offering guaranteed minimum pensions, offering supplementary flat benefits for everyone or using progressive benefit formulas, or on the contributions side if earnings only accrue benefits within particular ranges of earnings. In general, then, public unfunded schemes inherently redistribute in many dimensions: from the short-lived to the long-lived (i.e. from men to women, from poor to rich) as well as from the rich to the poor. Such redistributions and their interactions can be complex to understand. In the UK, for example, the rules for the State Earnings-Related Pension Scheme, and subsequent changes to these rules, have had large effects on the redistribution within the system that were certainly misunderstood and possibly unintended (see Dilnot et al., 1994).

An equally important issue, perhaps, is the intergenerational redistribution that is inherent in moving from an unfunded to a funded system. More precisely, such a move redistributes resources substantially away from the transition generations who have to 'pay twice'. Ultimately, however, as pointed out above, society's attitude to these transitional redistributions will depend on (a) the size of the transition costs and the generations on which they are incident, (b) the degree of intergenerational altruism, and (c) the degree to which future generations' utility, or welfare, is discounted by current generations.

Once in place, funded schemes also redistribute resources, but in different ways according to their design. A DB scheme redistributes across generations and, in most cases, from those with short tenure in the scheme to those with long tenure. On the other hand, unless mandated explicitly, a DC scheme with compulsory annuitisation redistributes from poor to rich and, in some circumstances, from men to women depending on the form of the annuitisation requirements. These latter results arise because mandatory annuitisation (with single-rate annuities) means that those living disproportionately long will gain most benefits (which have to be 'priced' at an average rate) by enjoying them for the longest time. Whilst it is clear from Figure 2 that women are expected to live longer than men, a number of studies have also shown that there is a correlation between wealth and life expectancy (see Attanasio and Hoynes, 1995; Disney et al., 1998; Attanasio and Emmerson, 1999).

(c) Incentives
The final issue relating to the design of social security systems is that of the incentives created by the schemes. In particular, the literature has focused on two areas—first, working-age labour supply and saving, and second, retirement. In the first case, labour supply and saving decisions will inevitably be distorted by pension schemes, since they alter the return to work and substitute for other forms of long-run saving. The size of the distortion, however, will depend on individual discount rates and on scheme design. If discount rates are high, contributions will be perceived essentially as a tax, since the future benefits will be discounted away, and there will be income and substitution effects on labour supply as in the standard framework. On the other hand, if future benefits are well understood, then one might expect some adjustment of saving behaviour. In an early empirical study, Feldstein (1974) used time-series data on pension wealth, consumption and saving to estimate that, on balance, social security reduced saving, a result that was hotly debated. Subsequent estimation has failed to establish a strong consensus over the magnitude of possible effects. In a more recent study, Attanasio and Brugiavini (1999), using a quasi-experimental framework on cross-sectional data from an Italian reform, find estimates of the offset that vary by age and lie between 30 and 80 per cent. This would suggest substantial substitutability between pension saving and other forms of saving.

The other dimension in which incentives generated by pension schemes may matter is in retirement decisions. The international comparative project of Gruber and Wise (1999) provides good evidence on these effects for state systems. Across countries, they show a striking correlation between the age at which benefits become available and departure from the labour force. They also show that the structure of a number of systems generates significant financial disincentives to work beyond early retirement ages (the age at which one is *first* entitled to receive benefits) and that such disincentives are also correlated with retirement behaviour. With regard to private schemes, the importance of occupational pension 'windows' in the UK provides anecdotal evidence that the incentive effects may be equally powerful in determining retirement behaviour.

Even if social security does distort decisions and incentives—which it presumably does, the question being more 'by how much?'—such distortions may not be a bad thing. After all, redistribution and insurance can only be achieved if one is willing to pay in terms of efficiency. What the social security debate has pointed out, however, are the potential magnitudes of the trade-offs and the importance of particular designs in minimising distortions whilst providing the equivalent redistributive and insurance outcomes.

4. Recipes for Reform

We end this analysis of economic issues by providing a brief summary of how the above factors have been put together to generate structures for proposed reform. Invariably, there are a number of different approaches to the question of how we should reform unfunded social security systems, and indeed on the degree to which such reforms are needed and over what time-scale. Broadly speaking, though, Disney (2000), following Chand and Jaeger (1996), has categorised proposals for reform into four broad groups.

The first model is to restructure the benefit and/or contribution rates, possibly coupled with changes to the retirement age. Noting that the tax rate needed to finance the scheme is a function of wages (w), benefit levels (b), the number of contributing workers (L) and the number of eligible pensioners (P), one can write

$$t = \frac{b}{w} \frac{P}{L},$$

and hence changes in any of these four variables will affect the costs of the scheme to the taxpayer. Such proposals have been called 'parametric' since they keep the nature and structure of the system unchanged and alter only particular parameters within that structure. For an example of the simulated effects of this approach in a number of countries, see Chand and Jaeger (1996). The advantage of such an approach is that it is not too drastic, and indeed its proponents typically argue that the demographic projections are such that a funding crisis can be avoided with only small parametric adjustments as long as they are made sufficiently early (see, e.g. Munnell, 1998). Whilst this argument was made for the US, it is not clear that it is so relevant where the demographic situation is more acute (e.g. in Italy or Japan).

Parametric reforms may often be used in conjunction with other more structural changes, as is the case with the UK reforms described below. The first disadvantage of pure parametric reform, however, is that the precise adjustment needed will be extremely sensitive to assumptions on the future of the system, and by the time such assumptions can be assessed against likely outcomes, any compensating interventions needed will be much greater. In addition, the arguments for parametric reform are presumably more relevant where the demographic conditions are relatively less unfavourable (e.g. in the US) as opposed to other countries (such as Italy or Germany) where they are severe. Finally, there may be a sense in which specific parameters of the system may be less effective than others. It is far from clear that movements in the retirement age,[20] for example, will be effective.

---

[20] With parametric reform, one has to be very precise about which parameter one is discussing. In this case, it could be the age at which one is first entitled to receive benefits at a reduced rate, or the age at which one is entitled to receive full benefits, or the age at which one actually retires.

On the contributions side, given that an increasingly large proportion of the work-force are retiring earlier than the statutory retirement age, any increase in the state retirement age will not necessarily generate increased contributions. Also, the degree to which less benefits will need to be paid will be determined by the degree to which early retirers are retiring on to other (possibly means-tested) benefits or are covered by other forms of income. Hence parametric reform can be a technic-ally complicated option, and the desirability of one option over another may well depend on particular assumptions or projections.

The second broad approach to reform delineated by Disney (2000) is the 'actuarially fair' approach (which underpins recent reforms in Sweden, Poland and Latvia as well as Italy), although we would argue that this can be seen as, in some sense, a particular case of structural adjustment, the only difference being in the one-off nature typically proposed in the context of the latter. By 'actuarially fair' reform is meant an explicit linking of the benefits in the scheme to the contribu-tions, while retaining the unfunded nature of the system. 'Notional accounts' are set up to mimic DC plans (i.e. with individualised retirement benefits that are con-ditional on contributions) but with the scheme remaining unfunded. The approach is to calculate implicitly the implied rate of return (given wage and population growth projections) and then set the accrual rate of pensions to achieve this. Post-retirement benefit indexations are linked explicitly to demographics. Disney (1999) points out a number of problems with this approach. Namely, there is still no guarantee that the 'Aaron–Samuelson' condition for equilibrium of the unfunded scheme on which the rate of return adjustments are based—that the rate of return on contributions is equal to the surplus of wage growth over population growth—will continue to hold in the future. Presumably, such calculations will be very sensitive to the projections used, and there may be a need for repeated adjust-ments over time. Second, Disney (1999) argues that there may be some downward rigidity in adjustments for political reasons, pointing out that when the growth of wages falls below inflation, it is unlikely that pensions will be set to grow by less than the cost of living. Finally, and more structurally, he argues that such reforms, by making the benefit–contribution link transparent, take away the rationale for public (unfunded) schemes in the first place, and may become politically unsustainable, given that the implicit returns will be observed directly and then compared with possibly high market returns available on private retirement saving alternatives.

The third model for reform, favoured by some US authors (e.g. Kotlikoff, 1996a,b; Feldstein, 1998), is a wholesale privatisation and a switch to DC plans, that is, some form of 'individual accounts'. Examples of reforms on these lines are the Chilean reform of 1980 (followed in a number of other Latin American coun-tries) and, to some extent, the Australian reform of 1992. Whilst such a move to funding will probably increase returns and may have other benefits, as described above, the main issue in such a reform is the management of the transition costs, an issue that has generated substantial debate (see, e.g. Auerbach and Kotlikoff, 1991). The other concern is over redistribution, since within-cohort redistribution will be all but eliminated in such a move (apart from that implicit in mandatory annuitisation). Thus other redistributive mechanisms may need to be introduced simultaneously and their costs would need to be added to the costs of the reform.

The final reform package, favoured by the World Bank, and increasingly being introduced, particularly in developing countries, is a partial privatisation and a movement towards a 'mixed-pillar' or 'multi-tier' system. Such an approach is close to the wholesale privatisation option, but with a retention of some part of the state system for some individuals, thus, presumably, ensuring some redistributive role for pensions and reducing the need for offsetting changes elsewhere. Such an approach, coupled with some parametric reforms to the unfunded part of the system, would be a good description of the route taken by the UK in the series of reforms since the late 1980s, which has been referred to as a voluntary or 'back-door' privatisation (Disney and Johnson, 1998). In this case, the advantages over and above the clean-break privatisation are that the transition costs can be spread more widely and that some redistribution can remain. However, the transition still has to be managed carefully, and, if individuals' decisions to opt out are correlated with wealth, there can be standard adverse selection issues and the opportunity for within-cohort redistributions can be reduced. Finally, the degree to which individuals may understand the options on offer, and their relative pros and cons, may be an important factor to consider, as was clearly the case in the UK's introduction of personal pensions and the subsequent mis-selling scandals.

Although each of the four reform strategies has its advocates (in all cases, very eminent experts), it seems to us that there is no genuine agreement on which route is preferable, and indeed on the extent to which the routes truly differ in altering the underlying economic conditions. In a practical sense, the actuarially fair route is very similar in spirit to the parametric approach (particularly since parametric reforms will presumably happen repeatedly as opposed to only once). The final 'mixed' approach is precisely a combination of the parametric and structural approaches, with the degree of each being a crucial but unspecified factor.

The absence of an 'optimal' route for reform is what one would expect in so far as the route required will presumably depend upon each country's particular circumstances, with regard to its demographic situation, economic projections, and the aims and structure of the system that is already in place. It seems sensible to suggest that the preferred reform option should differ in differing situations and that reform should be approached on a country-by-country basis. In the international debate on reform, agreement now exists about the potential effects that need to be considered in designing reform. In this sense, we would argue that the structural options for reform are now well understood, and the main strategies adopted from now on will depend upon two sets of practical issues. The first relate to the political economy of pension reform, since these issues will determine the precise nature and direction of the reform process. The second set of issues relate to the economic evaluation of the magnitude of the potential transition costs incurred by a switch to a funded system, which in turn will depend on a wide variety of financial and labour market factors that are currently not known with very much certainty. Examples include the magnitude, nature and importance of income uncertainty, the magnitude, variance and persistence of shocks to asset returns, the size of the risk premium, the degree of mean reversion in stock prices and the degree of risk aversion of individuals.

In the European policy debate, there is still little articulation of, let alone agreement over, the practical benefits of each reform approach. Indeed, it is not clear to us that the complete set of options has been spelled out explicitly. Recent papers (Miles and Timmerman, 1999; Boldrin et al. 1999) have used simulation analysis of possible transitions to a fully funded model to suggest that a movement towards funded schemes in a clean-break privatisation is not likely to be the solution to the problems Europe faces as a result of its ageing populations. This is essentially because the demographic problems are so severe that the transition costs are likely to be enormous. However, detailed debates of the implications of parametric reforms, partial privatisations or actuarially fair adjustments have only, to our knowledge, been looked at in a minority of country-specific analyses.

III. SOCIAL SECURITY SYSTEMS IN PRACTICE: THE UK EXPERIENCE

This section describes how the UK pension system has evolved in practice, with reference to the theoretical framework outlined above. The pension system is clearly an extremely important area of government spending–in 1998–99, the UK government spent over £100 billion (around 30 per cent of total public spending) on social security and welfare benefits, of which half went to elderly people. Moreover, this public spending interacts with individuals' decisions to make their own provision for retirement income. Flows into funded private pension schemes amounted to some £15 billion (Office for National Statistics, 1996).

A description of the UK pension system will generally suffer from an inevitable degree of simplification as a result of the various complexities of the system. Again, we would refer interested readers to other works on the subject. For a balanced view, we would suggest, in particular, Budd and Campbell (1998), Dilnot et al. (1994), Disney and Johnson (1998), Disney (1996) or Blundell and Johnson (1999), who all provide descriptions of the UK system in comparative volumes.

It should also be remembered that one of the key features of the UK state pension system is that it is almost continuously undergoing 'radical' reforms, as is the case at the moment. Hence discussions of likely future reforms tend to become dated very quickly. Indeed, this is one reason why relating the UK system, in particular, to the principles of pension provision defined earlier is difficult. Such principles often refer to systems in maturity, so they are effectively redundant in practice, since the UK system has not yet been in equilibrium and does not look like being so for some time. This in turn is a reminder that pension reform occurs as a result of political changes which, at least in the UK, tend to occur frequently. As late as 1992, for example, the Labour Party was proposing an increase in generosity of state involvement in pensions and, conversely, in 1997, the Conservatives proposed funding the basic state pension. Neither of these reforms seems particularly likely to occur in the UK in the foreseeable future. Since the UK pension system is, however, a product of numerous reforms introduced by different governments over the last 50 years, it is perhaps not surprising that it contains a degree of incoherence and complexity. This in turn makes it difficult to understand the genuine impacts of the system with respect to the issues outlined above, that is, redistribution, risk and incentives. Of course, the obvious implication of this is that perhaps the best reforms that could be made are ones aimed at simplifying the current system rather than adding additional complexity, unless strong arguments can be made to justify this complexity.

This section looks at the UK's approach to public and private pension provision and contrasts it with those of other countries. This highlights the vast diversity of pension schemes around the globe and also the corresponding levels of income that they deliver.

1. The Current Social Security Framework

State pension provision in the UK is split into two tiers. The first consists of the *basic state pension*, which is a flat-rate contributory pension, financed on a PAYG basis. In addition, many elderly adults receive a significant amount of income-related benefits—namely, the minimum income guarantee, housing benefit and council tax benefit. The second tier consists of the *State Earnings-Related Pension Scheme*, more commonly known by its acronym SERPS, which is also financed on a PAYG basis. However, this earnings-related element to the state pension system was only introduced in the UK in 1978, which is much later than happened in many European countries, such as Germany and Italy. Since funded schemes were already in existence by this time, provisions have always been included to allow individuals to 'opt out' of SERPS into funded private pension schemes.

Private savings vehicles are an extremely important part of the UK pension system. The current generation of UK pensioners receive 40 per cent of their income from private sources, and government policy is to aim for this to increase to 60 per cent by 2050 (Department of Social Security, 1998a). This private retirement income comes mainly in the form of *occupational pensions*, which typically operate on a DB basis. In future, *personal pensions*, which operate on a DC basis, will form a significant proportion of retirement income as they have become increasingly popular since they were first available as an alternative to SERPS in 1988. Around one-half of those earning above the lower earnings limit (LEL)[21] are currently members of a DB scheme and one-quarter are members of a personal pension. The remainder are still accruing SERPS entitlements. In what follows, we discuss each part of the UK pension system in more detail.

---

[21] This is the point at which individuals start to accrue rights to contributory benefits, which in 1999–2000 is set at £66 per week.

(a) The First Tier of Coverage: Basic State Pension

The UK first introduced a state pension as early as 1906. This was a means-tested benefit payable to those aged over 70 with 'good character'. The basic state pension, which still exists today, was introduced in 1948 as part of Beveridge's social insurance scheme. It paid a flat rate of £1.30 a week, equivalent to about 14 per cent of average earnings, financed by flat-rate employee contributions (Beveridge, 1942). This was in contrast to the earnings replacement 'Bismarckian' systems that developed in Germany, France and Italy (see Johnson, 1999). These provide a genuine level of social insurance so that individuals with higher levels of earnings during their working lives, and hence higher levels of social security contributions, will receive a more generous pension from the state.

In the UK, individuals with sufficient National Insurance contributions[22] receive the basic state pension when they reach the state retirement age, which was set in 1948 at 65 for men and 60 for women, its current ages.[23] Between 1948 and 1975, the basic state pension was indexed on an *ad hoc* basis, and increases over the period meant that its value was preserved relative to average earnings. The 1975 Social Security Act committed future governments to increasing the basic state pension by the greater of price or earnings growth, and its generosity reached around 20 per cent of average earnings in the early 1980s. Since 1981, indexation of the basic state pension has been to increases in the retail price index. As the UK has experienced real earnings growth over the last two decades, the basic state pension is now worth just 15 per cent of average earnings, as shown in Figure 4. Should price indexation continue each year, then by 2050 the basic state pension will only be worth 7 per cent of average earnings.[24]

Individuals need to have made National Insurance contributions for 90 per cent of their working lives in order to qualify for a full basic state pension. However, since credits are available for periods of unemployment, illness or disability, around 86 per cent of men and 49 per cent of women qualify for the full amount (Department of Social Security, 1998a). These figures are expected to continue to rise in future, due to reforms such as the introduction of home responsibilities protection (HRP)[25] and the abolition of the right for married women to 'opt out' of the basic state pension, and also because of increased labour market participation by women.[26]

---

[22] These comprise employee payments as a percentage of earnings between lower and upper earnings limits, and employer contributions on earnings above the LEL. The structure of these contributions has been repeatedly reformed (see Chennells et al., 1999).

[23] Legislation already in place will increase the retirement age for women by six months every year from 2010 until 2020, when equalisation at 65 will be achieved for everyone born after 1955.

[24] Assuming real earnings growth of $1\frac{1}{2}$ per cent a year. Implications of price indexation of the basic state pension, the LEL and the upper earnings limit are discussed in Disney and Whitehouse (1991).

[25] This gives credits for years in which individuals bring up children or care for other dependants.

[26] See Dilnot et al. (1984) and Disney (1996) for a discussion of the contributory principle. Johnson and Stears (1996) discuss implications of current and future levels of entitlement to the basic state pension.

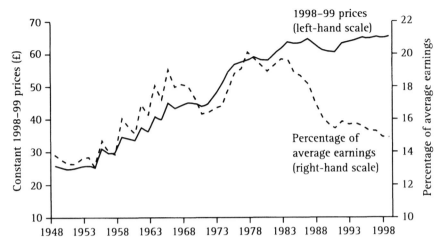

Figure 4. *Value of the basic state pension in 1998–99 prices and as a percentage of average earnings*

Sources: HM Treasury, 1996; Office for National Statistics website.

There is no possibility of early retirement benefits, but individuals are able to defer receipt of the basic state pension for up to five years, in return for which they receive an increase in their pension entitlement of 3.6 per cent. This is in contrast to the US and German systems, which provide allowances for individuals to claim state pension benefits before they reach the retirement age, albeit at a reduced rate. In the UK, the number of deferrals has fallen, with just 9 per cent of pensioners in the 70- to 74-year-old age-group receiving increments on their pensions, compared with 19 per cent of those aged over 80 (Department of Social Security, 1999b). This appears to be largely a result of the abolition of the earnings rule in 1989, which means that individuals can now continue to receive earnings after the retirement age without having their pension entitlement reduced (Whitehouse, 1990; Blundell and Johnson, 1999). As we mentioned earlier, this corresponds to evidence suggesting that the design of these systems does influence retirement behaviour (Tanner, 1998; Gruber and Wise 1999).

(b) The First Tier of Coverage: Means-Tested Benefits

The current system design means that, in principle, no individual is actually left in retirement with just the basic state pension, since it is now worth less than the level of support given to pensioners through means-tested benefits. The main means-tested benefit for the elderly—the minimum income guarantee (the benefit formerly known as income support)—is currently worth £75 per week, some £8.25 more than the basic state pension. In practice, however, some are left with incomes below this level since only 68–79 per cent of eligible pensioners actually claimed income support.[27] This is likely to be as a result of both stigma and the fact that many individuals becoming eligible for means-tested benefits in retirement have never previously received state benefits. The government has stated that 'over the longer term . . . [its] aim is that [the minimum income guarantee] should rise in line with earnings'. This is unlike the basic state pension, which is to remain indexed to prices. This policy of focusing additional state spending on those in greatest need contrasts starkly with the German, French and Italian pension approach of providing genuine social insurance and hence higher pensions to individuals with higher lifetime earnings.

Pensioners are also eligible to claim two other income-related benefits–housing benefit, which, as its name suggests, provides help with housing costs, and council tax benefit, which relieves the burden of local taxation on low-income households. Currently, some 40 per cent of pensioners receive some form of income-related benefit (Department of Social Security, 1999b). By international standards, this high level of income-related support to pensioners is an outlier with the exception of Australia, which operates an almost entirely means-tested pension system. Such high levels of means testing in retirement have led to concerns among policy-makers about the number of people facing a disincentive to work and save for retirement, and qualitative studies suggest that such concerns are certainly evident in the population at large (see Banks and Tanner, 1999b).

By making assumptions about the level of earnings growth and annuity rates in the future, it is possible to calculate how much an individual needs to have saved in order to purchase a stream of income equivalent to the level of means-tested benefits. For example, it is quite possible that an individual retiring in 2050 would need some £130,000 in 1999 prices to purchase an annuity equal to the minimum income guarantee (MIG).[28] Of course, this overstates the degree of disincentives provided by the MIG, since any employee earning above the LEL will be eligible for a state pension. However, the maximum possible state pension for someone retiring in 2050 is equivalent to a fund worth £110,000, even if the individual has a full 49-year contribution record, which is still £20,000 short of the value of the means-tested floor. This is due to the fact that, once in retirement, the level of state pension is indexed to prices while the MIG increases in line with earnings.

(c) The Second Tier of Coverage: SERPS and Occupational Schemes

Since the basic state pension was flat-rate and at a level likely to be unacceptably low for many workers, it is not surprising that supplementary pension coverage grew substantially over the 1950s and 1960s, particularly given the growth in real incomes over the period. Membership of occupational pension schemes, which on the whole operate on a DB basis, increased from 28 per cent of employees in 1953 to 53 per cent in 1967 (Pension Law Review Committee, 1993).

---

[27] Estimates from Department of Social Security (1998b), revised in DSS Press Release 98/300.

[28] Assuming real earnings growth of $1\frac{1}{2}$ per cent a year, annuity rates of 4 per cent and no real growth in rents or council tax bills. Should rents and council tax bills also increase by $1\frac{1}{2}$ per cent, then this figure rises to nearly £165,000.

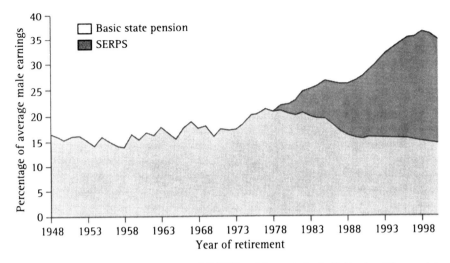

Figure 5. *Total basic state pension and SERPS entitlements for individuals with complete contribution histories, by year of retirement*

Notes: Assumes a full contribution record–44 years for men and 39 years for women. Figures for basic state pension as a share of average earnings differ slightly from those in Figure 4 since a slightly different earnings index has been used. However, the broad pattern is the same regardless of the choice of index.

Source: Government Actuary's Department, 1999.

The reforms introduced in the 1975 Social Security Act were, in part, a response to the fact that those individuals who were unable to join an occupational pension scheme were left reliant on the state for their pension. Hence the level of compulsory saving was increased: from 1978, all employees had to contribute to the SERPS unless they were a member of a DB occupational pension scheme that was guaranteed to be at least as generous as SERPS,[29] in which case they were allowed to opt out of the state scheme. In opting out of SERPS, individuals and their employers paid a reduced rate of National Insurance contributions, and individuals relinquished SERPS entitlements but would continue to qualify for the basic state pension. Figure 5 shows the degree of first- and second-tier state pension coverage in the UK for an individual who earned the male average in each year of his or her working life.

An indication of how relatively ungenerous the UK pension system is compared with other OECD countries is given by Table 2, taken from Johnson (1999). The table shows quite clearly that there is a large degree of variation in the generosity of state schemes across the countries listed, from 25 to 50 per cent of average male earnings for someone on half average male earnings and from 38 to 192 per cent

---

[29] This was known as the guaranteed minimum pension, which has since been abolished. For a more complete discussion of the 1975 reforms, see, for example, Disney and Johnson (1998).

Table 2. *International comparison of replacement rates for individuals with different levels of male earnings*

	Individuals earning		
	Half average male earnings	Average male earnings	Twice average male earnings
Canada	50	51	51
France	48	95	165
Germany	34	72	150
Italy	32	82	192
Netherlands	41	41	41
New Zealand	38	38	38
UK	25	34	48
US	32	55	64

Note: Net replacement rates are taken as a percentage of the earnings of those approaching retirement, except for Germany and the US where they are taken as a percentage of overall average earnings.

Source: Johnson, 1999.

of this level for someone earning twice average male earnings. Countries such as Germany, France and Italy offer earnings replacement schemes and, as a result, individuals with higher lifetime earnings receive higher state pensions. By contrast, the Netherlands and New Zealand offer the same flat-rate pension regardless of the level of earnings (and hence contributions made). The UK, Canada and the US have schemes where the pension does vary with earnings, albeit to lesser degrees. An important aspect to bear in mind when looking at these types of replacement rates is that they tend to understate the replacement rate for any single individual. This is because, with real earnings growth, the level of income amongst the working population will be higher than that experienced by the retired when they worked, and replacement rates such as those in Table 2 are computed cross-sectionally without taking such effects into account. This will, of course, not change the dispersion, or relativities, between countries, as long as wage growth across cohorts is broadly comparable.

(d) The Second Tier of Coverage: Personal Pensions
The right to 'opt out' of SERPS was expanded to DC pension schemes in the 1986 Social Security Act, taking effect from 1988. These funds, known as approved personal pensions (APPs) or simply personal pensions (PPs), received a portion of an individual's National Insurance contributions paid into the account on the individual's behalf.[30] This payment was set at such a level that, under reasonable

---

[30] This is known as the contracting-out rebate (COR). Budd and Campbell (1998) provide a discussion of the 1985 Green Paper and the subsequent 1986 Social Security Act which also introduced the possibility of individuals contracting out into occupational DC schemes.

rates of return, individuals would receive a pension at least as generous as the SERPS entitlement that they were forgoing.

Since 1988, DC personal pension schemes have become extremely popular. This is perhaps not surprising, given the fact that personal pensions were and continue to be one of the most tax-privileged forms of saving. Contributions are made from income free of income tax, returns accumulated in the fund are also untaxed and a quarter of the fund can be taken tax-free on retirement.[31] In addition to this, initially the COR did not vary with age and the government also paid a bonus 2 per cent contribution into individuals' funds as an extra incentive to contract out in this way. This meant that the young in particular were likely to benefit from contracting out of SERPS and into a personal pension.[32] By 1995–96, there were some five-and-a-half million people contributing to personal pension schemes in the UK (Department of Social Security, 1999b), with membership being particularly high among 25- to 34-year-olds (Whitehouse, 1998).

While DC personal pension schemes have become more popular, take-up of DB occupational pension schemes among full-time men has fallen since the early 1980s. This is similar to the trend observed in the US, where the introduction of 401k plans (occupational DC plans) resulted in a lower take-up of occupational DB schemes. In addition to the introduction of personal pensions, other changes have contributed to the reduction in coverage of DB pension schemes, such as the increase in importance of small and medium-sized firms, the increase in the number of self-employed and the increase in labour market mobility. Membership of DB schemes among women has continued to grow; however, this is at least partly due to legislation that has made such schemes more accessible to part-time workers in particular (Disney and Stears, 1996; Barrientos, 1998).

(e) Annuities

As discussed in Section II, an important part of the design of a social security system is how payments are made in retirement. State pensions and DB private pensions in the UK are equivalent to annuitised wealth, although they may have different degrees of indexation. Those with DC private pensions are forced to annuitise the majority of their private pension savings. The element of the fund that comes from the COR has to be used to purchase a protected rights annuity, which pays the same for men and women, that is, insurance firms are not allowed to offer better terms to men despite their lower life expectancy. This must be done between the ages of 60 and 75. The remainder of an individual's pension fund consists of voluntary pension saving (i.e. saving over and above the compulsory

---

[31] See Dilnot and Johnson (1993), Emmerson and Tanner (2000) or Banks and Tanner (1999a) for more details on the taxation of private pensions in the UK. Some international comparisons are contained in Whitehouse (1999).

[32] This was due to a combination of the impact of compound interest and the fact that cuts to SERPS had reduced its generosity to younger cohorts. See Disney and Whitehouse (1992) or Dilnot et al. (1994) for more details of the incentives to 'opt out' of SERPS.

second tier), of which one-quarter can be taken as a tax-free lump sum while the rest has to be annuitised between the ages of 50 and 75.[33]

Individuals are, however, given a range of options for how to annuitise their savings, for example, whether they are fixed in nominal terms, indexed to prices or linked to some investment. Annuities can also be on either a single- or a joint-life basis.[34] Those choosing to defer annuitisation make income withdrawals from their fund, subject to certain minimum and maximum amounts.[35] If the individual dies before they have annuitised the fund, then it can be converted into cash, subject to a tax of 35 per cent.[36] This is likely to be very important for those with a bequest motive (Khorasanee, 1996), since, while individuals could purchase a joint-life annuity, the value of a fund with a draw-down facility is clearly greater, conditional on the comparison between draw-down rules and annuity rates.

Individuals can also choose to convert part of the lump sum, or for that matter any other savings, into an annuity if they wish. However, there is evidence that those purchasing an annuity voluntarily receive a lower rate than those making a compulsory purchase. This suggests the presence of adverse selection, namely, that it is those individuals who expect to live longer than average who are choosing to purchase voluntary annuities (Finkelstein and Poterba, 1999).

(f) Future Reforms

Despite the fact that the UK pension system has been under almost continuous reform for almost a quarter of a century, the current government has proposed more changes. Many of the proposals are a continuation of the direction of reform since 1981. The government is to continue focusing additional support on the poorest pensioners by increasing the level of means-tested benefits rather than increasing the generosity of the basic state pension.[37] SERPS is to be abolished and replaced by the State Second Pension (SSP), which will eventually become a flat-rate top-up to the basic state pension. This makes SSP more generous to lower earners than its predecessor, SERPS, and will help to alleviate some disincentives by increasing the returns to work and saving among lower earners. However, since benefits in retirement will be indexed to prices, while the MIG will continue to be linked to earnings, many individuals will still find themselves on means-tested benefits at some point in their retirement (Agulnik et al. 1999; Disney et al. 1999).

In addition, further growth of private sector coverage is also planned with the introduction of *stakeholder pensions*, which are essentially bench-marked

---

[33] Prior to the 1995 Finance Act, annuitisation had to be done at the time of retirement. Murthi et al. (1999) examine protected rights and compulsory annuities in the UK.

[34] McDonald (1999) provides a description of compulsory annuity options.

[35] These are currently set at 35 and 100 per cent of the annual amount that an annuity purchased with the fund would provide. *Source*: Tolley's (1999, Section 65.5 (ii)).

[36] Tolley's, 1999, Sections 65.2 and 65.5 (viii).

[37] As pointed out earlier, such means-tested benefits do not necessarily fit into the framework for 'pensions' outlined above. However, whether such a switch is seen as a contraction of public spending on pensions or not is essentially a semantic debate.

Table 3. *Use of 'voluntary' incentives and greater compulsion in pension reforms with transitions to greater levels of funding*

	Year of reform	Switching for new entrants	Switching for current work-force
Argentina	1994	Voluntary	Voluntary
Bolivia	1997	Mandatory	Mandatory
Chile	1981	Mandatory	Voluntary
Colombia	1994	Voluntary	Voluntary
Croatia	2000	Mandatory	Mandatory, aged < 40 Voluntary, aged 40–50
El Salvador	1998	Mandatory	Mandatory, aged < 35 Voluntary, aged 35–55
Hungary	1997	Mandatory	Voluntary
Kazakhstan	1997	Mandatory	Mandatory
Mexico	1997	Mandatory	Mandatory
Peru	1993	Voluntary	Voluntary
Poland	1999	Mandatory	Mandatory, aged < 30 Voluntary, aged 30–50
UK	1988	Voluntary	Voluntary
Uruguay	1996	Mandatory	Mandatory, aged < 40 and higher income

Source: Disney et al., 1999.

personal pension schemes that may be more appropriate for lower earners.[38] One potentially important aspect of the reforms is the fact that employers will be compelled to designate a stakeholder scheme for their employees and make payroll deductions on their behalf. With regard to the paternalistic arguments outlined earlier, this employer involvement may help increase pension saving by enabling individuals to get in the habit of making regular contributions to a stakeholder pension direct from their pay-packets. In essence, however, the introduction of stakeholder pensions is a continuation of the partial privatisation of the UK pension system that has been occurring since 1986.

Some other countries, such as Argentina, have also opted for this voluntary, 'sticks-and-carrots' approach to reform. However, other countries have followed different routes.[39] Some have moved towards increased funding through compulsion. This can be done either by making such schemes compulsory for just new entrants to the labour market or just younger individuals, or, at the other extreme, by making schemes compulsory for all workers (Disney et al., 1999). The routes taken by various countries are shown in Table 3.

[38] See Disney et al. (1999), Emmerson and Tanner (1999) and Agulnik et al. (1999) for a further discussion of the government's proposals.

[39] For a discussion of such transitions, see, for example, World Bank (1994).

Table 4. *Financing of UK pension rights, 1995*

Type of pension	Value of accrued rights (£ billion)
Basic state pension	605
SERPS	150
Unfunded public sector schemes	195
Total unfunded schemes	950
Funded occupational schemes	585
Personal pensions	165
Total funded schemes	750
Total UK pension rights	1,700

Source: Pension Provision Group, 1998.

While the UK has adopted a voluntary approach towards private social security provision, the combination of ungenerous state benefits and financial incentives to 'opt out' into private pensions has led to the private sector playing an important and growing role. Table 4 shows precisely how important the private funded pension system is in the UK in comparison with the accrued rights in the state-run PAYG pension systems. State liabilities in 1995 were worth some £950 billion (around 130 per cent of GDP). Reporting to the government in 1998, the Pension Provision Group commented that '[unfunded] public sector schemes might be more suitable candidates than SERPS if a further move towards pre-funding were considered to be desirable' (Pension Provision Group, 1998). The recommendation was ignored, however, in the subsequent move to the introduction of stakeholder pensions. Table 4 also shows that the remaining liabilities in state earnings-related pensions are small compared with assets in the private sector totalling £750 billion.

Box 1 shows how the UK pension system looked in 1980 when SERPS had just been introduced, and how it may look in 2010 given the proposals for what the government has described as a 'radical reform of the whole pension system' (Department of Social Security, 1998a). By 1980, the UK system consisted of a first tier involving the basic state pension and social assistance, which was the principal means-tested benefit for those on low incomes. The second tier of coverage consisted of private occupational pension schemes and SERPS. Above that was a third tier of voluntary saving for retirement. By 2010, the pension system could look far more complicated, due to the introduction in 1988 of the right for individuals to opt out of SERPS (and, more problematically, their employer's pension scheme) into a defined contribution private pension. In addition, individuals with defined benefit pensions are now able to make additional contributions into private schemes through additional voluntary contributions (AVCs) and free-standing additional voluntary contributions (FSAVCs). The current government has also initiated the introduction of stakeholder pensions from April 2001.

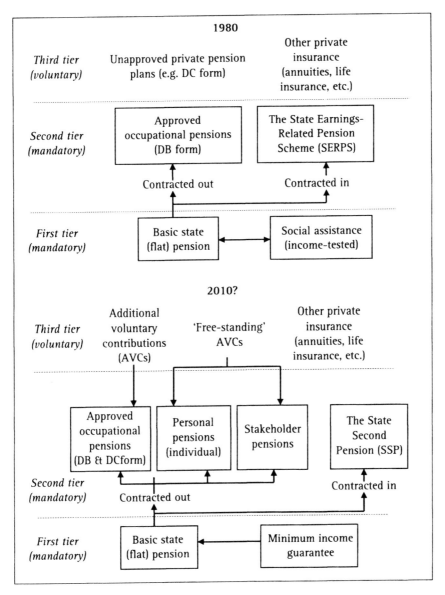

Box 1. *Two snapshots of the UK pension system*

Source: Disney et al., 1999.

These reforms since 1980 have clearly increased individual choice, but at the cost of making the pension system far more complicated.

2. The Current Cost of the UK Social Security System

The most expensive single item of government expenditure in the UK is the basic state pension, which costs some £32 billion per year (3.8 per cent of GDP), which is just under a third of the entire social security budget. In addition to this, pensioners receive state spending in the form of SERPS and also significant amounts of means-tested benefits. Figure 6 shows UK state pension spending as a share of GDP from 1957–58 to 1998–99. It indicates that, between 1957 and 1982, spending doubled from 2.5 per cent to just over 5 per cent of GDP. Since then, spending has fallen slightly, despite the introduction of SERPS and an increasing proportion of individuals aged over the retirement age. This is predominantly because entitlements were initially low as the scheme was immature, and since then, indexation changes, and indexation itself, have kept the costs down when expressed as a proportion of GDP. Public spending on pensions also rose as a share of total government expenditure between 1958 and 1982, despite the fact that total government spending was also rising as a share of GDP over this period. Since 1982, pensions spending has remained broadly constant as a share of general government expenditure (GGE), as there has been a slight decline in overall spending as a share of GDP.

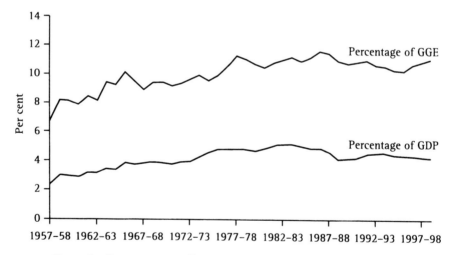

Figure 6. *Government spending on pensions, as a percentage of GDP and as a percentage of GGE*

Note: Includes spending from the National Insurance Fund on the retirement pension and lump-sum payments to pensioners.

Source: Spending from ONS *Annual Abstract of Statistics* (various years). GDP from Office for National Statistics website. GGE from HM Treasury (1999b).

The top half of Table 5 shows the breakdown of public pension spending items in the UK in 1998–99. Total direct state spending totals just over 5 per cent of GDP. In addition, elderly people receive other spending in the form of disability and industrial injury benefits, the cost of which is estimated at around £5 billion (Pension Provision Group, 1998). They also receive a disproportionate amount of spending on health, for example, a large proportion of NHS spending goes towards Hospital and Community Health Services (HCHS), 41 per cent of which goes on the over-65s despite their population share of 16 per cent (Department of Health, 1999).

These figures for government spending do not represent the true cost to the state since they ignore the cost of tax expenditures on the elderly (Atkinson, 1987). Government estimates of these costs are also provided, in the lower half of Table 5, showing the cost to the government of these tax expenditures to be £20.5 billion, some 2.4 per cent of GDP. However, unlike the direct spending items, the

Table 5. *State resources spent on the provision of retirement income, 1998–99*

	Billions of pounds	Percentage of GDP
Direct spending items		
Contributory benefits		
Basic state pension[a]	32.0	3.8
SERPS	3.7	0.4
Non-contributory benefits		
Basic state pension[a]	0.0	0.0
Income support (minimum income guarantee)	3.6	0.4
Housing benefit	3.8	0.5
Council tax benefit	1.1	0.1
Total	44.4	5.2
'Expenditure' on tax concessions		
Income tax allowances		
Age-related allowances	1.1	0.1
Income tax relief on:		
Occupational pension schemes	8.9	1.1
Contributions to personal pensions[b]	2.5	0.3
National Insurance contributions[c]		
Occupational schemes (DB)	6.0	0.7
Occupational schemes (DC)	0.1	0.0
Personal pensions	2.0	0.2
Total	20.5	2.4
Total 'expenditure' on state support	64.9	7.6

[a] Includes Christmas bonus.
[b] Includes retirement annuity premiums and FSAVCs.
[c] Relates to the cost of the COR only, not the cost of exempting employer National Insurance contributions.
Sources: Department of Social Security (1999a,b), Inland Revenue (1999) and HM Treasury (1999a,b).

costings of the tax expenditures come with substantial health warnings. First, the costs of income tax relief on occupational and personal pension schemes are the cost of the government not taxing either the contributions into the scheme or the pension when drawn, in comparison with taxing both. Clearly, if pensions were taxed in this way, it would be unlikely that anyone would hold retirement savings in this form, and hence the figures for income tax relief probably overstate the tax expenditures. A more appropriate figure would be the cost of the tax relief on the lump sum.

In contrast, the tax expenditure for National Insurance contributions could well be an understatement of the exchequer costs. On the one hand, the cost of the reduced rate of National Insurance for those contracted out of SERPS should be zero, since an actuarially fair rebate would imply the schemes were worth the same. Work commissioned by the National Audit Office in 1990 found that, up to April 1993, the overall cost of reduced National Insurance from incentives paid to individuals' personal pension funds, after netting off the reduced entitlements to SERPS, was some £5.9 billion in 1988 prices over the five-year period (Budd and Campbell, 1998). There is also a further subsidy to saving in a private pension. Employers' contributions to private schemes are exempted from both employer and employee National Insurance contributions. This exemption makes private pensions heavily tax-favoured assets when compared with others available in the UK. Moreover, there seems to be no justification for this differential tax treatment of employers' and employees' pension contributions (for more on this issue, see Emmerson and Tanner, 2000). The net cost of these subsidies could be substantially higher than the £8 billion provided by the official government estimates, depending on the generosity of the COR compared with the SERPS entitlement forgone and the proportion of private contributions that are made by the employer.

Comparing the purely direct state expenditures internationally shows that the UK is a relatively low spender. Figure 7 shows OECD figures for public pension spending as a share of GDP. With the exception of Australia, which only provides a means-tested state pension system, the UK is currently one of the lowest spenders, alongside the US, Canada, New Zealand, and the Netherlands. Those countries that opted for full social-insurance-style systems (France, Germany, and Italy) have substantially higher levels of state spending. The issue of the future projected costs of the UK system will be discussed further in Section III.4. First, however, we look at the level and distribution of pensioner income that arise from the relatively low levels of state spending in the UK.

3. Current UK Pensioner Incomes

Perhaps the best description of a pension system is given by the level and distribution of income that it provides to individuals in retirement. The composition of pensioner incomes will also show the relative importance of state and private savings in the provision of retirement income. However, the incomes received by today's generation of pensioners clearly do not reflect the current pension system

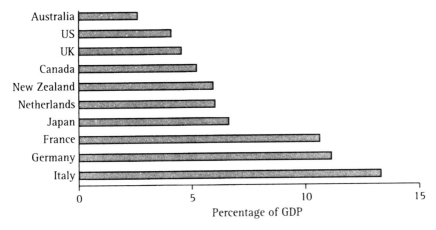

Figure 7. *Public spending on pensions in 10 OECD countries, 1995*

Source: Roseveare et al. 1996.

but instead are the product of the various reforms to the UK system over the last 40–60 years. For example, individuals retiring between 1998 and 2000 could have 20 years of contributions to the original SERPS which, as a result of subsequent cuts, is far more generous than the expected entitlements of younger individuals. As Table 2 has already shown, the UK state pension system provides relatively low levels of income which vary only slightly with an individual's working-life income.

This tells only half the story, however, since a significant and growing proportion of pensioner income comes from private sources. This has implications not only for the level of income received by the retired but also for how that income is distributed. Interestingly, despite the large degree of diversity between different countries' pension systems, Johnson (1999) found that the relative resources of elderly people were comparable. More precisely, out of eight OECD countries, only in Australia were average pensioner incomes not in the range 81–105 per cent of the average incomes of the working population. For example, in Italy, which operates an extensive (and expensive) earnings-related pension scheme, pensioner incomes were at the same level relative to the working population as found in the UK, the US, Canada, and the Netherlands, all of which have substantially smaller public sector involvement.

Table 6 shows that, on average, pensioner couples now receive nearly £250 a week, while single pensioners receive almost £130. These figures represent real growth in pensioner incomes of some 60 per cent over the period 1979 to 1996–97 for both single pensioners and pensioner couples. This is substantially higher than the real growth in incomes for the entire population, which, over the same period, was just over 40 per cent. Looking across the income distribution, this real growth in pensioner incomes has occurred disproportionately among richer pensioners,

Table 6. *Income and real growth in income of pensioners,*
1979 to 1996–97 (net income before housing costs)

	Quintile of the pensioner income distribution					
	All	1	2	3	4	5
Pensioner couples						
1979	155	94	109	127	162	243
1996–97	248	126	158	199	266	436
Real growth	60%	34%	45%	57%	65%	80%
Single pensioners						
1979	81	54	63	72	81	117
1996–97	129	68	93	110	138	205
Real growth	61%	22%	28%	47%	77%	85%

Note: Pounds per week, July 1996 prices.

Source: Department of Social Security, 1999*b*.

with pensioner couples in the top 20 per cent of the pensioner income distribution now receiving an average of £436 per week. This contrasts to the periods from 1961–62 to 1971–72 and from 1971–72 to 1981–82 when pensioner income growth was highest in lower quintiles (Retirement Income Inquiry, 1996; Johnson and Stears, 1995).

Table 7 provides a breakdown of the relative importance of each source of income, by age and pensioner type, and highlights how the mix of public and private pensions varies across the elderly population. Not surprisingly, younger pensioners have, on average, a higher share of their income from earnings, with the exception of 60- to 64-year-old men, who receive a considerable proportion of income from means-tested and other state benefits such as disability benefits. State pension income, which consists of both the basic state pension and SERPS, is a more important source of income for older individuals and single pensioners, mainly as a consequence of these types of pensioners being poorer on average. Finally, couples receive more income, on average, from private pensions.

Figure 8 shows how important each of these sources of income is for each quintile of the pensioner income distribution. Perhaps the most striking feature of the figure is that there is very little difference in income across the first four quintiles, while income in the richest quintile is substantially higher. Also clear from the picture is the flat-rate nature of the basic state pension since receipt is approximately the same in each quintile (small differences arise as a result of different average household sizes across quintiles having effects through the equivalence scale). Receipt of means-tested state benefits is highest in the third quintile, due to higher levels of housing benefit payments pushing pensioners who are on low incomes and living in rented accommodation into higher quintiles. This would no longer be the case if a measure of income after housing cost deductions were used. The fourth quintile receives higher levels of income from private pensions than those

Table 7. *Composition of pensioner income, by status and age-group (per cent)*

	Age-group				
	60–64	65–69	70–74	Over 75	All over 60
Couples					
State pension	4.6	40.6	55.4	57.8	42.2
Means-tested benefits	12.8	3.5	3.3	5.4	5.7
Other benefits	28.8	12.6	5.4	5.7	12.0
Private pension	34.1	26.8	25.0	22.3	26.5
Investment	7.0	7.2	6.6	6.7	6.9
Earnings	12.7	9.4	4.3	2.1	6.8
Single men					
State pension	–	43.4	57.0	56.2	45.7
Means-tested benefits	36.2	10.8	11.5	12.7	15.3
Other benefits	29.9	12.3	4.4	5.2	10.1
Private pension	25.6	21.8	18.9	18.0	20.1
Investment	6.8	6.1	6.0	6.6	6.4
Earnings	1.1	5.5	2.1	1.2	2.4
Single women					
State pension	42.8	55.8	57.6	58.8	56.2
Means-tested benefits	17.0	14.6	15.6	17.7	16.7
Other benefits	11.5	4.6	4.5	5.6	5.9
Private pension	16.3	16.9	15.5	12.2	14.1
Investment	5.1	5.3	6.3	5.3	5.3
Earnings	7.3	2.8	0.6	0.3	1.5

Notes: Percentages may not sum to 100 due to rounding. 'Means-tested benefits' includes income from all means-tested benefits (income support, council tax benefit, and housing benefit). 'Other benefits' includes all non-means-tested benefits, such as invalidity or incapacity benefit.

Source: Emmerson and Johnson (1998) using data from the 1995–96 Family Resources Survey.

lower down the income distribution, while the richest quintile receives higher levels of income from investment and earnings as well as higher levels of private pension income.

(a) Annuity Income
As discussed in Section II, annuitised forms of income are an extremely important part of the design of the UK social security system. In addition to income from state pensions and defined benefit private pensions, individuals also receive significant amounts of income from the annuitisation of savings from defined contribution private pensions. Prior to the introduction of APPs in 1988, the only individuals who could 'opt out' of SERPS into a DC scheme were the self-employed and those employees whose employer did not offer a DB scheme. These schemes were known as Section 226 plans. Among the current generation of pensioners with annuities, most are likely to have saved in a Section 226 plan rather than a personal pension

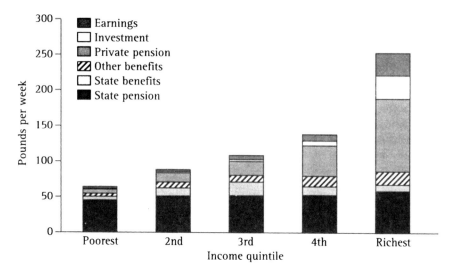

Figure 8. *Equivalised net income of pensioners by income quintile*

Notes: 'State benefits' includes income support, council tax benefit and housing benefit. 'Other benefits' includes other, non-means-tested benefits such as invalidity or incapacity benefit.

Source: Emmerson and Johnson (1998) using data from the 1995–96 Family Resources Survey.

scheme. However, in future, as younger generations reach retirement, annuity income from APPs will become relatively more important.

Table 8 shows how important annuity income is for the current UK population. Only a small proportion of individuals have income from annuitised wealth, although couples are more likely to have income in this form than single people. The increase in annuity receipt among younger age-groups is likely to reflect the increase in self-employment (and hence Section 226 pensions) over the last 20 years rather than the introduction of personal pensions in 1988, since most of the current generation of pensioners would have been better off in SERPS than in a personal pension. Among those who do have annuity income, it tends to be a relatively important source of income, providing on average £47 per week to single males, £36 per week to single females and £51 per week to couples.

Comparison of those with annuity income and those without shows that those with tend to have higher levels of education and are more likely to own their own homes. They also tend to have higher levels of income and higher levels of savings, for example, looking at 70- to 80-year-olds, 59 per cent of those with an annuity have savings of more than £20,000 compared with 24 per cent of those without annuity income (Banks and Emmerson, 1999). The average level of income among older groups will be affected by two forms of differential mortality. First, the group of single women will contain more women who are widowed as opposed to never married, with widowed women being more likely to have some annuity income since they may have inherited their deceased partner's entitlement. Second, those

Table 8. *Importance of private annuity income in the UK*

	Percentage with annuity	Number with annuity	Annuity income (£ p.w.)[a]	Proportion of total income from annuity[a]
Single men				
Under 60	0.2%	12,531	–	–
60–69	5.1%	24,987	54.10	0.222
70–79	3.9%	17,149	(38.57)	(0.171)
Over 80	3.7%	9,655	–	–
All	0.9%	64,322	47.34	0.176
Single women				
Under 60	0.2%	12,654	–	–
60–69	2.7%	24,341	42.69	0.165
70–79	2.1%	28,392	30.02	0.204
Over 80	2.4%	24,049	40.18	0.218
All	0.8%	89,436	36.07	0.189
Couples				
Under 60	0.3%	78,641	39.30	0.095
60–69	5.8%	245,783	53.36	0.172
70–79	5.3%	122,625	53.55	0.185
Over 80	3.3%	18,282	(41.29)	(0.168)
All	1.2%	465,331	50.56	0.162

[a] Annuity income is the average among all those with some annuity income.

Note: Parentheses denote sample sizes of less than 50. Sample sizes of less than 25 are not reported.

Source: Family Resources Survey, 1996–97 and 1997–98.

individuals with lower levels of lifetime income will be less likely to survive to older ages. Attanasio and Emmerson (1999) provide quantitative evidence on the size of this effect in the UK, showing that differential mortality effects are larger within the bottom part of the wealth distribution.

4. The Sustainability of the UK Pension System

Perhaps the most striking feature of the UK pension system with that of its European neighbours is that the state pension system is entirely 'sustainable', at least in terms of its future costs. This is a direct result of the low level of generosity of the UK public pension system, highlighted in Section III.2, in combination with the fact that the ageing problem is far less stark in the UK than in some European countries (see Table 1). Several reforms introduced since 1980 have had the effect of substantially reducing future state expenditures. In the terminology of Section II, these reforms have been a combination of 'parametric' reforms, which have substantially reduced future state liabilities (and hence the generosity of future state pensions), and 'carrot-and-stick' reforms aimed towards greater

Table 9. *Future costs of SERPS after various reforms*

	1994–95	2000–01	2010–11	2020–21	2030–31
Original regime	1.8	4.2	12.0	25.0	41.0
After 1986 Social Security Act	1.8	4.2	9.2	14.5	18.7
After 1995 Pensions Act	1.8	4.2	8.4	10.9	12.0

Note: Billions of pounds, 1994–95 prices.

Sources: Government Actuary, 1994 and 1995; Retirement Income Inquiry, 1996.

levels of voluntary private provision. The two most important of the parametric reforms were the indexing of the basic state pension to prices from 1981 and the rise in the retirement age for women from 60 to 65 by 2030 (see footnote 22).

In addition to increasing the retirement age, two other parametric reforms to SERPS are worth highlighting. Both have reduced future expenditures (and hence generosity) to less than one-quarter of what they would otherwise have been. The first was a reduction in the amount that a widow can inherit from her deceased partner's pension from 100 to 50 per cent from April 2000. A second and more subtle (yet very substantial) change was made to the way in which SERPS entitlements accrue through changes to the indexation of net contributions within the scheme in the reform of 1995. For more details, see Retirement Income Inquiry (1996).

One of the main reasons why these cuts were initiated is that, when SERPS was first introduced, projections for future costs were only calculated up to 2008–09, well before its maturity date. Table 9 shows the cost of SERPS at various stages and the degree to which its generosity has been reduced. If anything, these figures are underestimates, since it should be remembered that, due to continuous underestimates of longevity, the earlier forecasts were underestimates of what the true future costs would have been.[40]

Such reforms illustrate the main difference between the historical approaches of the UK and of the US in running their unfunded public schemes. In the UK, the policy has been to adjust contribution rates and future benefits continually in order to keep the system in balance, conditional on actuarial projections of future costs. In the US, on the other hand, the stance has been to hold contributions and benefits fixed and allow the scheme to accumulate a surplus or deficit over time—hence the partially funded nature of the US system.

Table 10 shows the latest Government Actuary forecasts for expenditure on state pensions. The support ratio, which is the ratio of contributors to pension recipients, is forecast to fall slightly between 2000 and 2010 and then rise as the retirement age for women is increased. It is then forecast to fall sharply beyond 2020. Expenditures on both the basic state pension and SERPS are forecast to rise in real

---

[40] Hemming and Kay (1982) produced forecasts that highlighted the extent of the future liabilities. Disney (1998) highlights the fact that official government forecasts for the future number of pensioners have consistently been revised upwards due to underestimates of longevity.

Table 10. *Long-term projections for the national insurance fund (July 1999)*

	2000–01	2010–11	2020–21	2030–31	2050–51
Demographic forecasts					
Contributors (millions)	20.2	21.6	22.2	21.5	21.3
Pensioners (millions)	11.0	12.3	12.6	15.2	15.8
Support ratio	1.8	1.7	1.8	1.4	1.4
State expenditure *(£ billion, 1999–2000 prices)*					
Basic state pension	34.4	38.0	41.3	49.4	51.2
SERPS	5.2	9.9	12.6	14.9	15.8
Total expenditure[a]	48.6	57.7	65.9	76.2	79.0
Total expenditure as a share of GDP (%)	5.4	5.6	5.5	5.5	4.2
Joint employee and employer contribution rates (%)[b]	19.9	18.9	18.1	18.6	15.2
GDP per pensioner spending (1999–2000 = 100)	99.5	93.0	87.8	75.4	56.2

[a] Includes incapacity benefit, jobseeker's allowance and some other more minor benefits and expenses.
[b] Contribution rates exclude the 1.95 per cent currently payable to the National Health Service and are based on the rate structure introduced in the Social Security Act 1998.

Source: Government Actuary's Department, 1999.

terms due to higher levels of coverage. However, expenditure as a share of GDP—the measure of 'sustainability' more often used in the literature—is forecast to stay relatively constant. An important consideration in whether the system will follow current trends, however, will be whether these increasingly low levels of expenditures are politically sustainable, given increasing numbers of pensioners in the population receiving *relatively* less public pension. After all, the amount of GDP spent by the government per pensioner is forecast to fall to 75 per cent of what it is today by 2030. Under the current system, this is projected to fall even further, to around half of the levels in 2000–01, by 2050. While the proposed SSP will be more generous than SERPS to lower earners, the actual impact on government spending will depend on how many individuals take out stakeholder pensions. In any case, the overall cost of the reforms will depend on whether the government achieves its aims of indexing the minimum income guarantee in line with average earnings, and the Government Actuary's forecasts do not include spending on means-tested benefits for the elderly.

An international context for the projected trends in UK public pension spending is provided by Table 11. The final column of the table is taken from Chand and Jaeger (1996) and shows the sum of projected future deficits (each expressed as a percentage of projected future GDP) over the 55-year horizon of their study. These vary hugely across countries. The future liabilities in the UK system are by far the smallest and are actually projected to fall after 2030 once the ageing of the

Table 11. *Projected future state spending on pensions as a percentage of GDP*

	2000	2010	2020	2030	2040	2050	Net liability, 1995–2050[a]
Canada	5.0	5.3	6.9	9.0	9.1	8.7	67.8
France	9.8	9.7	11.6	13.5	14.3	14.4	113.6
Germany	11.5	11.8	12.3	16.5	18.4	17.5	110.7
Italy	12.6	13.2	15.3	20.3	21.4	20.3	75.5
Japan	7.5	9.6	12.4	13.4	14.9	16.5	106.8
New Zealand	4.8	5.2	6.7	8.3	9.4	9.8	20.4
UK	4.5	5.2	5.1	5.5	4.0	4.1	4.6
US	4.2	4.5	5.2	6.6	7.1	7.0	25.7

[a] The sum of projected future deficits, each expressed as a percentage of projected future GDP.

Sources: Roseveare et al. (1996); Chand and Jaeger (1996) for net pension liabilities.

population begins to slow down. In contrast, France, Germany, Italy, and Japan, all of which already have relatively expensive public pension systems, face costs increasing by 50 per cent or more over the same horizon.

It is clear, then, that the issues with future public spending on pensions are not the same in the UK as in some of the other European countries. Whereas other public pension systems may face increasing costs in the medium to long term, these will, if current policy persists, not occur in the UK. In contrast, therefore, the issue for the UK will be whether the particular mix of public and private, funded and unfunded, provision that has arisen as a result of two decades of continual reform will be able to deliver the redistribution required.

IV. CONCLUSIONS

Given that there is a vast literature on all aspects of pensions and pension spending, any attempt to summarise it is fated to be at least partially inadequate. It is fair to say that economists have learnt a lot in the last 20 years about the issues involved. But there is also a sense in which diminishing returns to scale may have begun to set in. Certainly, in the international academic debate, the need, and options, for reform are relatively well understood, although there may be less understanding and agreement on this in a country-(or continent-)specific policy sense, where more applied research is needed in many cases. In particular, more needs to be known about financial markets and the relative returns (and riskiness of returns) on risky assets in comparison with safe assets and in comparison with labour income, since such calculations underpin our estimates of how large any transition costs from pension reform may be. Ultimately, however, conditional on policymakers' knowledge of pension issues being at the 'frontier', many developed countries are at the point where value judgements need to be made in order to set the direction for policy on future public and private pensions.

The message we take from the 'sustainability' debate is that, if current trends continue, there is no easy way out. Funding is not necessarily the whole answer, since asset prices may adjust adversely. Movements towards funding may not be a feasible option in some scenarios as a result of substantial transition costs and political issues. But something has to give, because the ageing of the population is inevitable. Not counting large-scale population shocks, however, there are still a number of margins on which systems could adjust. Two of these are the relative generosity and structure of pension systems. But others are departures of trends in labour market behaviour, social preferences or economic growth from those experienced in recent years. The future of unfunded pension systems is still, in every sense, uncertain.

The UK system combines a particular mix of public and private pension provision that makes it an interesting but complex system to study. In 1984, Dilnot et al. argued that British social security was like a 'patchwork quilt falling apart at the seams'. Since then, the pension component, at least, has become substantially *more* complicated. We have shown how public and private pension spending now combine to deliver a mix of income sources to elderly households, and that the particular mix varies widely across population groups.

One striking feature of the evolution of the UK system over the last 20 years (i.e. since the introduction of SERPS) is the number of reforms that have been introduced with little or no prior debate. All genuine economic analysis has been conducted after the reforms were implemented. This is in stark contrast to the US approach of having a long and detailed debate with, as yet, no reform at all. Successive reforms to the UK system have left it complicated and, to some extent, unwieldy. In our overview, we have had to discuss, or at least mention, nine distinct pension vehicles (basic state pension, SERPS, occupational pension schemes, PPs, AVCs, FSAVCs, and the imminent stakeholder pensions, MIG, and SSP). It could be argued that the only saving grace of such a complicated system is that no one understands it, thus making it (politically) easy to reform. But the heterogeneity in pension histories created by the evolution of the UK system, which has never been in equilibrium and will not be for some time, will inevitably result in difficulties in designing future reforms that meet well-defined economic and social goals without such reforms either becoming expensive or creating groups of losers.

To the extent that there are distortions in pension systems, their degree is determined by individuals' perceptions of the economic environment. With imperfect or costly information, individual choices are more likely to be suboptimal as the complexity of the system increases, as was clearly demonstrated in the mis-selling scandal surrounding the introduction of PPs. Policies relating to financial information and education (i.e. aiming to improve public understanding of the pension system rather than to reform the system itself further) may therefore be becoming increasingly important in the UK, and are certainly, in our opinion, a candidate for interesting future research.

In our overview, we have also shown that the international situation is diverse, in terms of both the structure of systems and the way in which their costs are projected to change, given current trends. In the US, the funding problem is not as severe as in some other countries, but there is still a perceived need for reform, and potential reforms are extremely well debated. In Europe, this is not the case. Applied studies examining the options using rigorous macroeconomic and micro-economic analysis, in the way that has been done in the US, are only just begin-ning to emerge. This may be partly because situations within Europe are very diverse. Some projected liabilities are massive, others less so. But such differences mean that expectations of potential further integration of economic and financial systems must surely play a role in informing policy analysis, given the length of horizons over which pension reforms need to be analysed. Our view of the applied European literature is that there is still a lot to be learnt before the options are clear.

Consideration of European differences is particularly interesting in another dimension. We have shown that the future liabilities of several countries are potentially large, but it is important to remember that, to some extent, this may be because those countries have chosen, through the political process, to have gener-ous pension arrangements. While it is clear that many countries may eventually reduce the generosity of their pension schemes, this will only occur as a result of the political process in those countries. Some countries may choose to retain relat-ively generous systems and simply increase the contribution rates of future gener-ations. While this may be less popular with younger workers, who will be making higher payroll contributions as a result, the political voice of the retired should not be ignored. This may be particularly important, given that they will make up a larger proportion of the voting population and may also tend to focus their votes more on certain issues.

Given the advanced and voluminous debate on economic issues, it seems to us that many of the most important research issues for the future of public pensions now relate to either political economy or financial markets, not necessarily the economic design of pension policy *per se*. This is particularly the case if one considers likely routes through transition to funding, since such routes depend heavily on discounted intergenerational altruism, the size of various groups of the population and the way in which the political system transmits these groups' pref-erences to government policy. Such topics are beginning to come to the fore, and the surveys of social security by Mulligan and Sala-i-Martin (1999a, b, c) point to possible directions in this area.

Finally, we would point out that one of the distinguishing characteristics of pensions is that they are long-term investments, often with fixed costs, so indi-viduals can get locked in (either explicitly or implicitly). In this scenario, there are clear arguments for stability and simplicity of economic systems, whether public or private. What is required is an intertemporal economic environment that allows individuals to plan their consumption, labour supply, and saving choices. At the very least, social security reforms, major or minor, should not be made to aid the management of short-run or even medium-run fluctuations in government finances. Nor should they be made on ideological grounds alone, for example as a result of some belief in the inherent value of private provision. Whilst the dynamic issues mean that early reform can minimise the scale of the intervention needed, having to introduce subsequent reforms as a result of inappropriate initial changes can cause further problems.

REFERENCES

Aaron, H. (1966), 'The social insurance paradox', *Canadian Journal of Economics*, vol. 32, pp. 371–4.
— (1982), *Economic Effects of Social Security*, Washington, DC: Brookings Institution.
Agulnik, P., Barr, N., Falkingham, J. and Rake, J. (1999), *Partnership in Pensions? Responses to the Pensions Green Paper*, CASE paper no. 24, London: Centre for Analysis of Social Exclusion, London School of Economics.
Akerlof, G. A. (1970), 'The market for lemons: quality uncertainty and the market mechanism', *Quarterly Journal of Economics*, vol. 84, pp. 488–500.
— (1998), 'Discussion of "Self-control and saving for retirement"', *Brookings Papers on Economic Activity*, 1: 98, pp. 185–9.
Arnold, R. D., Graetz, M. J. and Munnell, A. H. (eds) (1998), *Framing the Social Security Debate: Values, Politics and Economics*, Washington, DC: Brookings Institution Press.
Arrow, K. J. (1963), 'Uncertainty and medical care', *American Economic Review*, vol. 53, pp. 941–73.
Atkinson, A. (1987), 'Income maintenance and social insurance', in A. J. Auerbach and M. Feldstein (eds), *Handbook of Public Economics*, vol. 2, Amsterdam: Elsevier.
Attanasio, O. P. and Banks, J. W. (1998), 'Household saving: analysing the saving behaviour of different generations', *Economic Policy*, vol. 27, pp. 549–83.
— and Brugiavini, A. (1999), 'Social security and household saving', University College London, mimeo.
— and Emmerson, C. (1999), 'Differential mortality in the UK', Institute for Fiscal Studies, mimeo.
— and Hoynes, H. (1995), 'Wealth accumulation and differential mortality', National Bureau of Economic Research, Working Paper 5126; *Journal of Human Resources*, forthcoming.
Auerbach, A., Gokhale, J. and Kotlikoff, L. J. (1991), 'Generational accounts: a meaningful alternative to deficit accounting', in D. Bradford (ed.), *Tax Policy and the Economy*, vol. 5, Cambridge, MA: MIT Press.
—, — and — (1994), 'Generational accounts: a meaningful way to evaluate fiscal policy', *Journal of Economic Perspectives*, vol. 8, pp. 73–94.
— and Kotlikoff, L. (1987), *Dynamic Fiscal Policy*, Cambridge: Cambridge University Press.
— and – (1991), 'Demographics, fiscal policy and US saving in the 1980s and beyond', in L. H. Summers (ed.), *Tax Policy and the Economy*, Cambridge, MA: MIT Press.
Banks, J., Blundell, R. W. and Tanner, S. (1998), 'Is there a retirement-savings puzzle?', *American Economic Review*, vol. 88, pp. 769–88.
—, Disney, R. and Smith, Z. (1999), 'What can we learn about pension reform from generational accounts for the UK?', Institute for Fiscal Studies, Working Paper no. 99/16.
— and Emmerson, C. (1999), *The Characteristics of UK Annuitants*, Briefing Note no. 4/99, London: Institute for Fiscal Studies.

Banks, J. and Tanner, S. (1999a), *Household Saving in the UK*, London: Institute for Fiscal Studies.

— and — (1999b), 'Perceptions of saving: an economic analysis of focus group evidence', Institute for Fiscal Studies, mimeo.

Barr, N. (1998), *The Economics of the Welfare State*, Oxford: Oxford University Press.

Barrientos, A. (1998), 'Supplementary pension coverage in Britain', *Fiscal Studies*, vol. 19, pp. 429–46.

Bateman, H. and Piggott, J. (1997), *Private Pensions in OECD Countries: Australia*, Labour Market and Social Policy Occasional Paper no. 23, Paris: Organisation for Economic Co-operation and Development.

Bayer, P. J., Bernheim, B. D. and Scholz, J. K. (1996), 'The effects of financial education in the workplace: evidence from a survey of employers', Stanford University, Working Paper no. 96-011.

Bernheim, B. D. (1991), *The Vanishing Nest Egg: Reflections on Saving in America*, New York: Priority Press.

— (1993), *Is the Baby Boom Generation Preparing Adequately for Retirement?*, Summary Report, New York: Merrill Lynch.

— and Garrett, D. M. (1996), 'The determinants and consequences of financial education in the workplace: evidence from a survey of employees', Stanford University, Working Paper no. 96-007.

—, — and Maki, D. M. (1997), 'Education and saving: the long term effects of high school financial curriculum mandates', Stanford University, Working Paper no. 97-012.

Bertaud, C. and Starr-McCluer, M. (1999), 'Household portfolios in the United States', paper prepared for the European University Institute's Conference on Household Portfolios, Florence, Italy, 17–18 December.

Beveridge, W. (1942), *Social Insurance and Allied Services*, Cmd 5404, London: HMSO.

Blundell, R. W. and Johnson, P. (1999), 'Pensions and retirement in the United Kingdom', in J. Gruber and D. Wise (eds), *Social Security and Retirement around the World*, Chicago: Chicago University Press.

Boldrin, M., Dolado, J., Jimeno, J. and Peracchi, F. (1999), 'The future of pensions in Europe', *Economic Policy*, vol. 14, pp. 287–320.

Bos, E., Vu, M. T., Massiah, E. and Bulatao, R. A. (1994), *World Population Projections, 1994–95 Edition: Estimates and Projections with Related Demographic Statistics*, Washington, DC: World Bank/Baltimore, MD: Johns Hopkins University Press.

Browning, M. and Lusardi, A. (1996), 'Household saving: micro theories and micro facts', *Journal of Economic Literature*, vol. 34, pp. 1797–855.

Brugiavini, A. and Disney, R. (1995), 'The choice of private pension plans under uncertainty', Institute for Fiscal Studies, Working Paper no. 95/5.

Budd, A. and Campbell, N. (1998), 'The roles of the public and private sectors in the UK pension system', in M. Feldstein (ed.), *Privatizing Social Security*, National Bureau of Economic Research; Chicago: Chicago University Press.

Cardarelli, R., Sefton, J. and Kotlikoff, L. J. (2000), 'Generational accounting in the UK', *Economic Journal*, forthcoming.

Chand, S. and Jaeger, A. (1996), *Ageing Populations and Public Pension Scheme*, Occasional Paper no. 147, Washington, DC: International Monetary Fund.

Chennells, L., Dilnot, A. and Roback, N. (1999), 'A survey of the UK tax system', Institute for Fiscal Studies, mimeo [http://www.ifs.org.uk/taxsystem/final1.pdf].

Congressional Budget Office (1995), *Who Pays and When? An Assessment of Generational Accounting*, Washington, DC: Congress of the United States, Congressional Budget Office.

Creedy, J., Disney, R. and Whitehouse, E. (1993), 'The earnings related state pension, indexation and life-time redistribution in the UK', *Review of Income and Wealth*, vol. 40, pp. 257–78.

Deaton, A. S. (1992), *Understanding Consumption*, Oxford: Clarendon Press.

Department of Health (1999), *Department of Health Annual Report: The Government's Expenditure Plans 1999/00*, Cm. 4203, London: DoH.

Department of Social Security (1998a), *A New Contract for Welfare: Partnership in Pensions*, Cm. 4179, London: DSS.

—— (1998b), *Income Related Benefits: Estimates of Take-Up in 1996–97*, London: DSS.

—— (1999a), *Social Security Departmental Report: The Government's Expenditure Plans 1999/00*, Cm. 4214, London: DSS.

—— (1999b), *Social Security Statistics 1999*, London: Government Statistical Service.

Diamond, P. A. (1977), 'A framework for the analysis of social security', *Journal of Public Economics*, vol. 8, pp. 275–98.

—— (1996), 'Proposals to restructure social security', *Journal of Economic Perspectives*, vol. 10, pp. 67–88.

—— (1997), 'Political aspects of social security reform', in S. A. Sass and R. K. Triest (eds), *Social Security Reform: Conference Proceedings*, Boston: Federal Reserve Bank of Boston.

—— (1998), 'The economics of social security reform', in R. D. Arnold, M. J. Graetz and A. H. Munnell (eds), *Framing the Social Security Debate: Values, Politics and Economics*, Washington, DC: Brookings Institution Press.

—— (1999), 'Social security reform–Lecture 1: Social security policy; Lecture 2: Social security and the labour market; Lecture 3: Social security and the capital market', The 1999 Lindahl Lectures, 19–21 October (sponsored by Nordbanken).

—— and Mirrlees, J. (1986), 'Payroll-tax financed social insurance with variable retirement', *Scandinavian Journal of Economics*, vol. 88, pp. 25–50.

Dilnot, A., Disney, R., Johnson, P. and Whitehouse, E. (1994), *Pensions Policy in the UK: An Economic Analysis*, London: Institute for Fiscal Studies.

—— and Johnson, P. (1993), *The Taxation of Private Pensions*, London: Institute for Fiscal Studies.

——, Kay, J. and Morris, N. (1984), *The Reform of Social Security*, Oxford: Clarendon Press.

Disney, R. (1996), *Can We Afford to Grow Older? A Perspective on the Economics of Ageing*, Cambridge, MA: MIT Press.

—— (1998), 'Social security reform in the UK: a voluntary privatisation', paper presented to 'Social Security Reform: International Comparisons' conference, Rome, 16–17 March.

—— (1999), 'Notional account pension reform strategy: an evaluation', World Bank, Pension Primer Series on Notional Accounts.

—— (2000), 'Crises in public pension programmes in OECD: what are the reform options?', *Economic Journal Features*, vol. 110, pp. 1–23.

——, Emmerson, C. and Tanner, S. (1999), *Partnership in Pensions: An Assessment*, Commentary no. 78, London: Institute for Fiscal Studies.

—— and Johnson, P. (1998), 'The United Kingdom: a working system of minimum pensions?', in H. Siebert (ed.), *Redesigning Social Security*, Institut für Weltwirtschaft an der Universität Kiel; Tübingen: Mohr Siebeck.

——, —— and Stears, G. (1998), 'Asset wealth and asset decumulation among households in the Retirement Survey', *Fiscal Studies*, vol. 19, pp. 153–74.

——, Palacios, R. and Whitehouse, E. (1999), 'Individual choice of pension arrangement as a pension reform strategy', Institute for Fiscal Studies, Working Paper no. 99/18; *Scandinavian Journal of Economics*, forthcoming.

Disney, R., and Stears, G. (1996), 'Why is there a decline in defined benefit plan membership?', Institute for Fiscal Studies, Working Paper no. 96/4.

— and Whitehouse, E. (1991), 'How should the basic state pension be indexed?', *Fiscal Studies*, vol. 12, no. 3, pp. 47–61.

— and — (1992), *The Personal Pensions Stampede*, London: Institute for Fiscal Studies.

Duesenberry, J. S. (1949), *Income, Saving, and the Theory of Consumer Behaviour*, Cambridge, MA: Harvard University Press.

Emmerson, C. and Johnson, P. (1998), 'Pension provision in the United Kingdom', Institute for Fiscal Studies, mimeo.

— and Tanner, S. (1999), *The Government's Proposals for Stakeholder Pensions*, Briefing Note no. 1/99, London: Institute for Fiscal Studies.

— and — (2000), 'A note on the tax treatment of private pensions and Individual Savings Accounts', *Fiscal Studies*, this issue.

Feldstein, M. (1974), 'Social security, induced retirement, and aggregate capital accumulation', *Journal of Political Economy*, vol. 82, pp. 905–26.

— (ed.) (1998), *Privatizing Social Security*, National Bureau of Economic Research; Chicago: Chicago University Press.

Finkelstein, A. and Poterba, J. (1999), 'Selection effects in the market for individual annuities: new evidence from the United Kingdom', National Bureau of Economic Research, Working Paper no. 7168.

Flemming, J. S. (1977), 'Optimal payroll taxes and social security funding', *Journal of Public Economics*, vol. 7, pp. 329–49.

Friedman, M. (1957), *A Theory of the Consumption Function*, Princeton, NJ: Princeton University Press.

Gale, W. and Sabelhaus, J. (1999), 'Perspectives on the household saving rate', *Brookings Papers on Economic Activity*, pp. 181–224.

Ghilarducci, T. (1992), *Labor's Capital: The Economics and Politics of Private Pensions*, Cambridge, MA: MIT Press.

Government Actuary (1994), *Pensions Bill (1994): Report by the Government Actuary on the Financial Provisions of the Bill on the National Insurance Fund*, London: HMSO.

— (1995), *National Insurance Fund Long Term Financial Estimates*, London: HMSO.

Government Actuary's Department (1999), *National Insurance Fund Long Term Financial Estimates*, London: The Stationery Office.

Gruber, J. and Wise, D. (eds) (1999), *Social Security and Retirement around the World*, Chicago: Chicago University Press.

Hall, R. E. (1978), 'Stochastic implications of the permanent income hypothesis: theory and evidence', *Journal of Political Economy*, vol. 96, pp. 229–57.

Haveman, R. (1994), 'Should generational accounts replace public budgets and deficits?', *Journal of Economic Perspectives*, vol. 8, pp. 95–111.

Hemming, R. and Kay, J. A. (1982), 'The costs of the State Earnings-Related Pension Scheme', *Economic Journal*, vol. 92, pp. 300–19.

HM Treasury (1996), *Tax Benefit Reference Manual*, 1995–96 edition, London: HM Treasury.

— (1999a), *Financial Statement and Budget Report*, March 1999, London: The Stationery Office.

— (1999b), *Pre-Budget Report*, November 1999, London: The Stationery Office.

Hubbard, G., Skinner, J. and Zeldes, S. (1995), 'Precautionary saving and social insurance', *Journal of Political Economy*, vol. 103, pp. 360–99.

Inland Revenue (1999), *Inland Revenue Statistics 1999*, London: The Stationery Office.

Johnson, P. (1999), *Older Getting Wiser*, Sydney: Institute of Chartered Accountants in Australia.

— and Stears, G. (1995), 'Pensioner income inequality', *Fiscal Studies*, vol. 16, no. 4, pp. 69–93.

— and — (1996), 'Should the basic state pension be a contributory benefit?', *Fiscal Studies*, vol. 17, no. 1, pp. 105–12.

Kahneman, D. and Tversky, A. (1979), 'Prospect theory: an analysis of decisions under risk', *Econometrica*, vol. 47, pp. 263–91.

— and — (1986), 'Rational choice and the framing of decisions', *Journal of Business*, vol. 59, pp. s251–s278.

Khorasanee, M. Z. (1996), 'Annuity choices for pensioners', *Journal of Actuarial Practice*, vol. 4, pp. 229–55.

Kotlikoff, L. J. (1992), *Generational Accounting*, New York: Free Press.

— (1996a), 'Privatising social security at home and abroad', *American Economic Review*, vol. 86, pp. 368–72.

— (1996b), 'Privatization of social security: how it works and why it matters', National Bureau of Economic Research, Working Paper no. 5330.

— and Leibfritz, W. (1998), 'An international comparison of generational accounts', National Bureau of Economic Research, Working Paper no. 6447.

— and Spivak, A. (1981), 'The family as an incomplete annuities market', *Journal of Political Economy*, vol. 89, pp. 372–91.

—, — and Summers, L. H. (1982), 'The adequacy of savings', *American Economic Review*, vol. 72, pp. 1056–69.

Laibson, D. (1994), 'Self control and saving', Ph.D. thesis, Massachusetts Institute of Technology.

— (1997), 'Golden eggs and hyperbolic discounting', *Quarterly Journal of Economics*, vol. 112, pp. 443–77.

—, Repetto, A. and Tobacman, J. (1998), 'Self-control and saving for retirement', *Brookings Papers on Economic Activity*, 1: 98, pp. 91–196.

McDonald, O. (1999), *Investment in Retirement: Are Annuities the Answer?*, London: Association of Unit Trusts and Investment Funds.

Miles, D. (1998), 'The implications of switching from unfunded to funded pensions systems', *National Institute Economic Review*, no. 163.

— and Timmerman, A. (1999), 'Risk sharing and transition costs in the reform of pension systems in Europe', *Economic Policy*, vol. 30, pp. 253–86.

Mulligan, C. B. and Sala-i-Martin, X. (1999a), 'Gerontocracy, retirement and social security', National Bureau of Economic Research, Working Paper no. 7117.

— and — (1999b), 'Social security reform in theory and practice (I): facts and political theories', National Bureau of Economic Research, Working Paper no. 7118.

— and — (1999c), 'Social security reform in theory and practice (II): efficiency theories, narrative theories and implications for reform', National Bureau of Economic Research, Working Paper no. 7119.

Munnell, A. H. (1998), 'Introduction', in R. D. Arnold, M. J. Graetz and A. H. Munnell (eds), *Framing the Social Security Debate: Values, Politics and Economics*, Washington, DC: Brookings Institution Press.

Murthi, M., Orszag, J. M. and Orszag, P. (1999), 'The value for money of annuitants in the UK: theory, experience and policy', University of London, Birkbeck College, Centre for Pensions and Social Insurance, Working Paper no. 9-99.

Myles, G. D. (1995), *Public Economics*, Cambridge: Cambridge University Press.

OECD (1996), *Ageing in OECD Countries: A Critical Policy Challenge*, Social Policy Study no. 20, Paris: Organisation for Economic Co-operation and Development.

Office for National Statistics (1996), *The United Kingdom National Accounts: The Blue Book 1996*, London: The Stationery Office.

Pension Law Review Committee (1993), *Consultation Document on the Law and Regulation of Occupational Pension Schemes*, London: Pension Law Review Committee.

Pension Provision Group (1998), *We All Need Pensions: The Prospects for Pension Provision*, London: The Stationery Office.

Retirement Income Inquiry (1996), *Pensions 2000 and Beyond: Analysis of Trends and Options*, vol. 2, London: Retirement Income Inquiry.

Rosen, H. S. (1995), *Public Finance*, 4th edition, Chicago: Irwin.

Roseveare, D., Leibfritz, W., Fore, D. and Wurzel, E. (1996), 'Ageing populations, pension system and government budgets: simulations for 20 OECD countries', Organisation for Economic Co-operation and Development, Working Paper no 168.

Rothschild, M. and Stiglitz, J. (1976), 'Equilibrium in competitive insurance markets: an essay on the economics of imperfect information', *Quarterly Journal of Economics*, vol. 90, pp. 629–49.

Samuelson, P. A. (1958), 'An exact consumption-loan model of interest with or without the social contrivance of money', *Journal of Political Economy*, vol. 66, pp. 467–82.

—— (1975), 'Optimal social security in a life-cycle growth model', *International Economic Review*, vol. 16, pp. 539–44.

Sass, S. A. and Triest, R. K. (eds) (1997), *Social Security Reform: Conference Proceedings*, Boston: Federal Reserve Bank of Boston.

Schieber, S. J. and Shoven, J. B. (1997), 'The consequences of population ageing for private pension fund savings and asset markets', in M. D. Hurd and N. Yashiro (eds), *The Economic Effects of Aging in the United States and Japan*, Chicago: Chicago University Press.

Stiglitz, J. (1988), *Economics of the Public Sector*, 2nd edition, New York: Norton.

Tanner, S. (1998), 'The dynamics of male retirement behaviour', *Fiscal Studies*, vol. 19, pp. 175–96.

Thaler, R. H. (1990), 'Anomalies, saving, fungibility and mental accounts', *Journal of Economic Perspectives*, vol. 4, pp. 193–205.

Thompson, L. H. (1998), 'Individual uncertainty in retirement income planning under different public pension regimes', in R. D. Arnold, M. J. Graetz and A. H. Munnell (eds), *Framing the Social Security Debate: Values, Politics and Economics*, Washington, DC: Brookings Institution Press.

Tolley's (1999), *Income Tax 1999–00*, Croydon: Tolley Publishing Company Limited.

Whitehouse, E. (1990), 'The abolition of the pensions earnings rule', *Fiscal Studies*, vol. 11, no. 3, pp. 55–70.

—— (1998), 'Pension reform in Britain', World Bank, Social Protection Discussion Paper no. 9810.

—— (1999), 'The tax treatment of funded pensions', World Bank, Social Protection Discussion Paper no. 9910.

World Bank (1994), *Averting the Old Age Crisis: Policies to Protect the Old and Promote Growth*, New York: Oxford University Press.

3

Expenditure on Healthcare in the UK: A Review of the Issues

CAROL PROPPER[1]

I. INTRODUCTION

Public expenditure on healthcare in the UK is large. In 2000, just under £50 billion was spent by the state on healthcare, a sum that accounted for around 6 per cent of GDP. On top of these large public expenditures, individuals buy healthcare and pharmaceuticals directly, and private expenditure on healthcare in the UK totalled about £9 billion in 2000. Nor is high public and private expenditure on healthcare just a British phenomenon. Governments and private individuals throughout the OECD contribute large sums for healthcare expenditure. In fact, within the OECD and the G7 group of countries, UK expenditure per capita is low. The UK spends around 7 per cent of GDP per capita on healthcare, while the G7 average is 9 per cent and the OECD average is 8 per cent. However, in comparison with both the OECD and G7 countries, the share of expenditure accounted for by the public sector is high. The UK share is around 85 per cent, while the average for the G7 group is 70 per cent and for the OECD is 75 per cent.

The large scale of public intervention is justified on both efficiency and equity grounds,[2] but while it is common for governments to intervene in the market for healthcare, it is also clear that the form and extent of this intervention vary considerably across countries. This raises questions of whether the UK spends sufficient sums of either public or private finance on healthcare, whether the balance between public and private finance is optimal and whether the way in which those sums are spent achieves either the efficiency or equity goals of the population. To answer such questions is beyond the scope of a single review. Instead, this review focuses on a set of topics that are relevant to current debates about the financing of UK healthcare and also shed light on these broader questions.

The author would like to thank Olwen Renowlden for data assistance and Simon Burgess for his very helpful advice. Funding from the Leverhulme Trust is gratefully acknowledged. Any errors are the author's.

[1] Department of Economics and CMPO University of Bristol, CASE London School of Economics and CEPR.

[2] See Barr (1998) and Emmerson et al. (2000) for a review of both efficiency and equity arguments for government intervention in healthcare markets.

The first topic reflects the debate that other forms of health service organisation may be an improvement on that currently in operation in the UK. I examine the relationship between the organisation of the system and three sets of outputs that are measures of: first, the efficiency of the system; second, the equity of the system; and third, the outcomes of the system. These are expenditure per capita, the distribution of payments for, and receipt of, healthcare resources and measures of health (health outcomes). This examination is based on comparison of performance across comparable countries, which has its strengths and weaknesses, which are explored below. The second topic examines the lessons from the internal market reforms that were implemented in the UK in the early 1990s. These reforms are part of a general move in healthcare organisation towards increased competition, and the review examines the implications for efficiency. The third topic examines the role for private finance in the funding of UK healthcare. I examine the extent of private finance in the UK healthcare system and the interrelationships between public and private finance, with the aim of deriving the implications for the evolution of public healthcare finance in the UK system.

The organisation of the chapter is as follows. Sections II and III examine the performance of the current system. Section II presents the trends in healthcare expenditure in the UK and compares the UK, in terms of financing and organisation of the healthcare system, with other OECD countries. Section III presents the performance of the UK system in terms of the distribution of resources. Section IV presents evidence from recent international comparative studies to examine the relationship between organisational design and the performance of the healthcare system in terms of per capita expenditure. Section V examines the relationship between system design and equity in the payment for, and in the receipt of, resources. Section VI examines the relationship between system design and health outcomes and the distribution of these outcomes. Section VII examines the internal market reforms and Section VIII examines the role of private finance and issues in the dynamics of UK healthcare expenditure. The final section draws out the lessons for the finance of UK healthcare expenditure and for future research.

II. THE UK LEVEL OF EXPENDITURE ON HEALTHCARE

1. Trends in UK Healthcare Expenditure

Healthcare expenditure in the UK can be broadly divided into public expenditure, which is mainly spent on the National Health Service (NHS), and private expenditure, which is defined as expenditure by the household and corporate sector on healthcare (including dentistry and over-the-counter medicines). Estimates of public expenditure are somewhat more reliable than estimates of private expenditure, but whichever estimates are used, the bulk of expenditure in the UK (around 85 per cent in 2000) is public.

Figure 1 presents real spending on the NHS as a proportion of GDP from 1960 to 1999. The graph shows that the share of the NHS in national income has grown

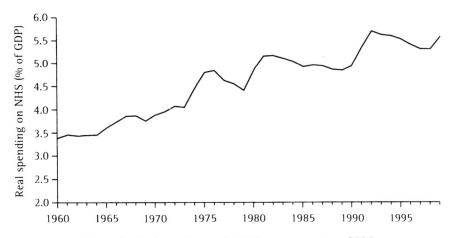

Figure 1. *Real spending on the NHS as a percentage of GDP*

Source: Emmerson et al., 2000.

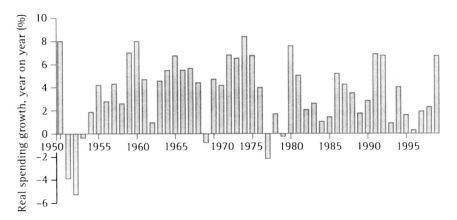

Figure 2. *Real year-on-year growth in spending on the NHS*

Source: Emmerson et al., 2000.

from under 3.5 per cent to just under 6 per cent in 40 years. But it is also clear that this increase has not been constant and that there have been years in which the share has fallen, to be then followed by years in which expenditure has increased faster than the long-run trend. Figure 2 presents the percentage year-on-year increase in real NHS expenditure. This shows considerable variation around the average of 3.4 per cent annual growth for the period. There were periods of negative growth during the mid-1950s and the early and late 1970s, and there have been periodic large increases of a size comparable to, or even slightly larger than, the settlements made by the Labour administration for 2000 and 2001 and forecast to 2004.

Propper

Figure 3 presents private expenditure as a share of GDP. The scale indicates the smaller share of private expenditure and the graph also shows that private spending remained small, and indeed even fell, up to the late 1970s. Figure 4 presents the percentage year-on-year growth in private expenditure in real terms. The large falls first in the mid-1960s and then again in the mid-1970s are apparent. The 1980s show a pattern of strong growth, but this tailed off during the early 1990s, and there has been considerable volatility in growth rates in the second half of the 1990s.

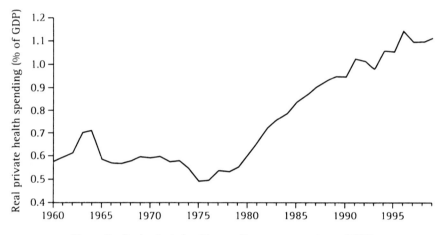

Figure 3. *Real private health spending as a percentage of GDP*

Note: 'Private' = Total − Public.

Source: OECD Health database 2000.

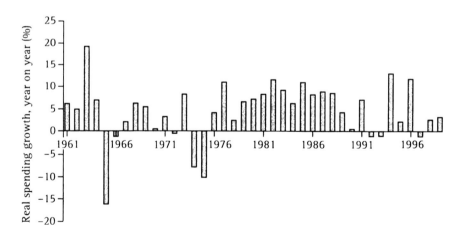

Figure 4. *Real year-on-year growth in private expenditure*

Note: 'Private' = Total − Public.

Source: OECD Health database 2000.

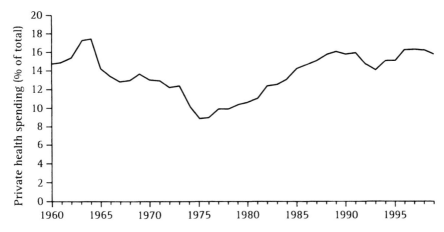

Figure 5. *Private health spending as a percentage of total health spending*
Source: OECD Health database 2000.

Figure 5 presents private expenditure as a percentage of total expenditure on healthcare from 1960 to 1999. This shows that the share that was private rose in the early 1960s, fell from a peak in 1964 to a low in 1975, rose again up to 1991, then fell as NHS expenditure increased rapidly with the advent of the internal market in 1991, then rose from 1993 to 1997 and fell again in the late 1990s.

In summary, the picture that emerges is one of long-run growth in both public and private expenditure but, around this long-run trend, of considerable year-on-year volatility in both public and private annual growth rates and also in the share that is private.

2. The UK Compared

Tables 1 and 2 present the UK's position, in terms of total expenditure and the share that is public, in comparison with two groups of countries—the OECD and the G7 countries. The tables indicate substantial differences in the level of healthcare expenditure across countries, even within the relatively homogeneous industrialised countries of the OECD. Table 1 illustrates health expenditure per capita as measured in purchasing power parities (PPPs) in the OECD. In 1998, these ranged from less than $1,000 (e.g. Hungary and Korea) to more than $2,500 (Switzerland $2,794 and the US $4,178).[3] Within these countries, the position of the UK is towards the bottom end. There is also a range in the share that health expenditure accounts for in GDP. The highest share is in the US, the lowest in Korea. Again, the position of the UK is near the bottom of the OECD group.

---

[3] In comparison, in low-income countries, these amounts are much smaller—$10 per capita in many African countries, and less than $100 per capita in most of Asia and Latin America. The share in GDP is also smaller.

Table 1 also shows the proportion of healthcare that is publicly financed. The unweighted average across all OECD countries is 75 per cent, and only in the US and Korea is the proportion less than 50 per cent. In some countries (e.g. the UK, the Nordic countries and the Czech Republic), almost all healthcare expenditure is paid for by the public purse.

Table 2 presents these data for the more homogeneous group of G7 countries. Again, the UK is somewhat of an outlier, with the lowest average expenditure per capita on healthcare and the highest public share.

The crude share of public finance hides important differences in the finance and delivery of healthcare. Finance for public healthcare is raised by a mixture of

Table 1. *Total expenditure on healthcare and share that is public: OECD countries, 1998*

	Total healthcare expenditure per capita (US$ PPP)	Total healthcare expenditure as a share of GDP (%)	Public finance as a share of total (%)
Australia	2,043	8.5	69.3
Austria	1,968	8.2	70.5
Belgium	2,081	8.8	89.7
Canada	2,312	9.5	69.6
Czech Republic	930	7.2	91.9
Denmark	2,133	8.3	81.9
Finland	1,502	6.9	76.3
France	2,077	9.6	76.4
Germany	2,424	10.6	74.6
Greece	1,167	8.3	56.8
Hungary	705	6.8	76.5
Iceland	2,103	8.3	84.3
Ireland	1,436	6.4	75.8
Italy	1,783	8.4	68.0
Japan	1,822	7.6	78.3
Korea	730	5.0	45.8
Luxemburg	2,215	5.9	92.3
Netherlands	2,070	8.6	70.4
New Zealand	1,424	8.1	77.1
Norway	2,425	8.9	82.8
Poland	496	6.4	73.3
Portugal	1,237	7.8	66.9
Spain	1,218	7.1	76.9
Sweden	1,746	8.4	83.8
Switzerland	2,794	10.4	73.4
UK	1,461	6.7	83.7
US	4,178	13.6	44.7

Source: OECD Health database 2000.

Table 2. *Total expenditure on healthcare and share that is public:*
G7 countries, 1998

	Total healthcare expenditure per capita (US$ PPP)	Total healthcare expenditure as a share of GDP (%)	Public finance as a share of total (%)
Canada	2,312	9.5	69.6
France	2,077	9.6	76.4
Germany	2,424	10.6	74.6
Italy	1,783	8.4	68.0
Japan	1,822	7.6	78.3
UK	1,461	6.7	83.7
US	4,178	13.6	44.7

Source: OECD Health database 2000.

general taxation, social insurance (payroll tax) contributions and local taxation. Examples of systems in which general taxation dominates are the UK and Denmark. An example of a country that uses earmarked social insurance contributions is the Netherlands. Private finance is usually raised by insurance premiums and/or out-of-pocket payments. Private insurance can be used to provide supplementary cover to public cover where those covered are offered no tax breaks (e.g. the UK) or to provide cover for those without comprehensive public cover (e.g. the Netherlands) or to provide cover against public sector co-payments levied on prescription medicines, dental care etc. (e.g. France and Denmark). Out-of-pocket payments can be predominantly co-payments, with the third party usually paying the major share of the bill (e.g. the UK, the Netherlands, the US and Denmark) or can amount to substantial use of the private sector on a fee-paying basis (e.g. Italy, Spain and Portugal).

While the public sector plays a key role in finance, the provision (i.e. supply) of healthcare varies widely in terms of public/private mix. In the OECD, delivery spans from being nearly 100 per cent in the public sector (e.g. Sweden) to being substantially the role of the private sector (e.g. Switzerland and the US). Even where finance is predominantly social-insurance- or tax-based, countries may use mainly private providers. Canada, for example, has predominantly public finance but private providers. Table 3 illustrates the mixture of public and private finance and provision in the OECD.

Given the importance of healthcare expenditure as a share of GDP and of public expenditure, and the differences in institutional arrangements for financing and delivering healthcare, an obvious question is the extent to which differences in expenditure and outcomes are associated with the organisation of the healthcare system. This is examined in Section IV.

Table 3. *Classification of countries by public/private mix of provision and finance in healthcare*

Public/private mix	Country		
Mainly public provision, public finance	Denmark Finland Greece Iceland	Ireland Italy Norway Portugal	Spain Sweden UK
Mixed provision, public finance	Australia Austria Belgium	France Germany Japan	Luxemburg New Zealand
Mainly private provision, public finance	Canada		
Mixed provision, mixed finance	Netherlands		
Mainly private provision, private finance	Switzerland	US	

Source: OECD, 1994.

III. THE UK ALLOCATION OF PUBLIC HEALTHCARE EXPENDITURE

It is clear that successive UK governments have had a strong commitment to equity in healthcare finance and delivery. In this section, I examine the extent to which this commitment has been realised and whether it has translated into an equitable distribution of health outcomes.

1. The Allocation of Resources

Since 1974, an explicit goal in the allocation of public funds for healthcare has been that these funds should be allocated according to need. Throughout the 1960s, it had become increasingly obvious that the distribution of resources within the NHS bore little resemblance to the principles of equal allocation for equal need and more to the historic distribution of hospitals. In 1976, the Department of Health decided to allocate funds to the 14 regions of the NHS on the basis of need, as measured by standardised mortality ratios (SMRs), themselves a measure of morbidity and a proxy for need. A region's need, and therefore its allocation, would be calculated on the difference between national and regional SMRs. The resource allocation (RAWP) formula covered about three-quarters of the NHS current expenditure budget but did not cover either capital expenditure or payments to general practitioners (family doctors–GPs) or dentists. At its inception, the scheme meant monies were allocated according to the RAWP formula to regions, but, within regions, allocations to areas, and below them districts, were decided by each region.

Over time, there was both greater devolvement of monies according to RAWP-type principles down to district level[4] and criticism of the use of SMRs as a measure

---

[4] A district covers around 100,000 people.

Table 4. *Meeting of RAWP targets*

1985–86	1987–88	1990–91	1992–93	1993–94
Coefficient of variation between regions				
0.103	0.097	0.093	0.091	0.140
1993–94	*1994–95*	*1995–96*	*1996–97*	*1997–98*
Range of distance from target: districts				
36.80	25.70	27.60	20.96	14.39

Source: Glennerster et al., 2000.

of need. However, despite this criticism, the basic approach was not modified till the mid-1990s. In part, this was because there was general agreement over the principle, and, in part, it was because movements to target allocations (those generated by the RAWP formula) were gradual and dictated by politicians. Movement to target was achieved by allocation of 'new' healthcare resources. Regions kept the same real budget as last year and, if above target, received no new funds. Extra real resources, if made available at Treasury level, went to below-target regions. During the 1990s, the formula was adjusted to incorporate better measures of need and to deal with the fact that changes in the way the NHS delivers care meant the primary units of allocation were units of around 100,000 people.

Le Grand et al. (1990) and Le Grand and Vizard (1998) provide an assessment of the extent to which movements to target reduced inequalities in allocations across regions. The average distance from target fell from the inception of the scheme to the late 1980s. Table 4 shows that variation in average healthcare spending per person at regional level fell from the mid-1980s to 1992–93, though it rose in 1993–94 (the last year reported by the authors) and that variation in the difference from targets at district level fell during the 1990s.

Recent evidence on the allocation of expenditure at below regional level is provided by a study of the distribution of health expenditure at ward level within three urban local authorities in England for 1995–96. Bramley et al. (1998) seek to allocate all sources of healthcare funding in three relatively deprived cities to wards.[5] In practice, exact allocation of healthcare expenditure to individuals within small geographical areas is not possible from the administrative sources used in this study, and for some of the expenditure allocated, allocation is on the basis of location of the provider (family doctor or hospital) rather than of the individual user of service. In addition, for hospital services, detailed costs of services are not known and instead the researchers have to allocate the average to all users. Given these caveats, Bramley et al. conclude that the distribution of healthcare expenditure by ward within the three cities was generally less dispersed than other forms of

[5] Wards are small geographical areas with populations of around 5,000 people.

public expenditure, and was pro-sick and hence generally higher in more deprived wards. When allowance is made for the population age structure of the wards, the spending becomes more pro-deprived.

Broadly, it appears that the allocation of healthcare spending at region, district and possibly also ward level has been such that variations in allocations have fallen and spending is close to being allocated according to the measures of need used in the allocation formulae.

2. The Receipt of Healthcare

Equity in the geographical distribution of resources does not necessarily imply equity in the distribution of healthcare across individuals with different incomes. In a series of studies, Propper and her co-authors examine equity in the delivery of healthcare standardised for medical need. These studies estimate the extent to which violations of the principle 'equal treatment for equal need' are systematically related to income in the UK. The studies use individual-level data from household surveys that contain data on individuals' access to resources, their use of healthcare services and their self-reported health status. Answers to the self-assessed health questions used in these surveys have been found to be good predictors of subsequent mortality in a variety of industrialised countries (van Doorslaer et al., 1997). Individuals' incomes are defined as their equivalised household incomes. Medical need is defined as self-assessed health, and various measures of this are used. Several forms of care (GP care, out-patient care and in-hospital care) are examined. The approach of using data on users and non-users contrasts with many other studies of equity in the allocation of healthcare, which look only at users of healthcare (Propper (1998) reviews these).

O'Donnell and Propper (1991) examine whether there are departures from 'equal treatment for equal need' that are systematically related to income using data from the mid-1980s and conclude that the distribution of NHS care is weakly pro-poor. Propper and Upward (1992) examine the distribution of healthcare utilisation standardised for need by income group for the UK for the years 1974, 1982, 1985 and 1987. These results are presented in Table 5. The columns present the share of

Table 5. *Percentage shares of NHS expenditure standardised for need*

	1974	1982	1985	1987
Income quintile				
Bottom	24.6	22.5	22.7	22.7
2nd	21.6	20.3	22.7	21.2
3rd	19.3	21.1	19.7	19.9
4th	17.9	21.7	18.9	19.8
Top	16.6	14.5	16.1	16.3
Concentration index	−0.083	−0.092	−0.070	−0.062

Source: Propper and Upward, 1992.

NHS expenditure received by each income quintile after standardising for self-reported morbidity. In 1974, the lowest income quintile received nearly 25 per cent of total NHS standardised expenditure. The comparable figure in 1987 was just under 23 per cent. The last line in each column presents the concentration index. This is a measure of the departure of the cell averages from proportionality and thus is a measure of the departure from equal treatment for equal need. The value of the index ranges from -1 to $+1$, where a negative (positive) number indicates pro-poor (pro-rich) inequity.[6] The results indicate a mildly pro-poor distribution in all four years. Propper (1998) finds a similar distribution for 1991 and 1994.

3. Inequalities in Outcomes

However, whilst the mechanisms for allocation become ever more complex, evidence on the distribution of health has raised fundamental issues about the effectiveness of the allocation formula in achieving equitable health outcomes. While RAWP allocations have reduced regional disparities in funding, there is a growing body of research that suggests that inequalities in health across geographical areas have not fallen since the 1970s and may indeed be rising.

The Acheson Report (Department of Health, 1998) concluded that, in many respects, inequalities in health had not improved since the 1970s when RAWP began, and in some cases had worsened. For example, health status within London had improved in the better-off (in terms of income) local areas whilst it had fallen in the poorer areas. Shaw et al. (1999) found that standardised mortality ratios for the under-65-year-olds were 2.6 times higher in those local constituencies[7] with the worst health outcomes than in the constituencies with the best health.[8] Infant mortality patterns were similar—infant mortality in the poorest-health constituencies was 2.0 times the level in the best-health constituencies.

There is also evidence of increasing health inequality from studies of variation across individuals. Using data from repeated (cross-sectional) household surveys, Propper and Upward (1992) calculate the concentration index of self-reported health status for individuals ranked by their equivalised household income. They find the rich to have better health and that income-related inequalities increased between 1974 and 1985, but then fell in 1987, to below the levels of 1982.

Many of those who study inequalities in health in the UK (e.g. Shaw et al., 1999) argue that the solution lies not in improving healthcare but in changing individuals' access to resources. From their detailed review of resource allocation in the NHS, Glennerster et al. (2000) conclude that allocating resources according to need will be inherently limited to the extent to which it can overcome differences in health status. Part of the reason is a technical one: making equal allocations for

---

[6] For details of the methodology, see van Doorslaer and Wagstaff (1992) and van Doorslaer et al. (2000).

[7] A constituency is the small area used for elections to the national parliament.

[8] Health outcome of the constituency defined in terms of SMRs for the under-65s.

equal need assumes equal efficiency of productive units. But they see the more important reason as being that equalising resources at an area level will not eliminate the differences in individual behaviour that lead to differences in actual expenditure across individuals. The problem is compounded by the well-known fact that variations in health seem to be largely determined by factors outside of the healthcare system, some well known and others less so.[9]

IV. DOES THE ORGANISATION OF THE HEALTHCARE SYSTEM DETERMINE EXPENDITURE?

International comparisons have been used to attempt to answer questions such as 'does the overall organisation of the healthcare system have any impact on health expenditure?', 'does the use of a gatekeeper to the hospital sector result in lower expenditure?', does the method of remunerating doctors affect expenditure?' and 'do increases in the supply of doctors result in increases in health expenditure?'. Such international comparisons have also examined the impact of income and of demographic factors on total expenditure.

These international comparisons tend to be beset by several problems (Gerdtham and Jonsson, 2000). The first is the weak theoretical base for the determinants of aggregate health expenditure. There is no clearly accepted model for the macroeconomic analysis of health expenditure. Few of the estimated models make clear the causal relationships between aggregate expenditure and the organisation of the healthcare sector. The importance of the physician as the agent for the patient and the key supplier of healthcare, the fact that health services are often provided on the basis of 'need' rather than willingness to pay and the use of non-price rationing (e.g. waiting-lists) make the usual separation of demand from supply difficult. Second, the data may vary in their reliability. It can be difficult to capture the precise institutional details of a healthcare system. It can be difficult, for example, to determine which expenditures to include in healthcare when the same care may be covered in different countries by the social security system, the health sector or the social services sector (an obvious example being care for the elderly). The specifics of the healthcare sector within countries mean that classification of financing and delivery systems can often be somewhat arbitrary. For example, variables representing the public fraction of healthcare expenditure, the use of high-cost procedures and the type of reimbursement system are often only approximations to the underlying influences of interest. The distinctions between institutional arrangements of different countries are usually captured by the use of dummy variables, but this means they often cannot be distinguished from country effects. Third, many of the extant studies rely on fairly small samples, and increasing the sample size increases the heterogeneity of the sample. Fourth, many of the estimates have not

---

[9] In one of the few studies of variation in expenditure across a reasonably homogeneous population, Cremieux et al. (1999) find a positive association between expenditure on healthcare and better life expectancy and lower infant mortality across Canadian provinces.

incorporated dynamics, even though observed differences in health expenditure are likely to be the result of both permanent and transitory differences.[10]

Given these problems, it is perhaps not surprising that relatively few robust results emerge from cross-country comparisons of the determinants of healthcare expenditure. A recent survey (Gerdtham and Jonsson, 2000) concludes that results must be treated with caution, but identifies the following results. With respect to the non-institutional variables (those factors that are not features of the healthcare financing and delivery system), a common and extremely robust finding is that the effect of per capita income on expenditure is positive and often close to unity. On the other hand, the effect of population age structure is generally insignificant. Institutional features appear to have the following impact on expenditure. The use of primary-care gatekeepers (the UK's General Practice system whereby individuals must be referred for treatment and diagnosis in the hospital sector by their family doctor), the use of direct patient payment for care followed by reimbursement from a public or private insurer, the use of capitation payments for physicians in the ambulatory sector and the public provision of health services (proxied by the ratio of public beds to total beds) are all associated with lower health expenditures. Use of in-patient expenditure is associated with higher healthcare expenditures. Evidence on other features of the healthcare system, for example, the use of budget ceilings on in-patient care and whether doctors are salaried or paid on a fee-for-service basis, is less clear-cut.

These results indicate that both income and institutional factors determine healthcare expenditure, suggesting that, as countries grow, so will their healthcare expenditure, but the extent of growth will be determined by the precise nature of the healthcare system. Looked at another way, these studies point to the importance of micro-incentives—incentives at the level of the supplier and the demander of healthcare. These issues are discussed in more detail below for the UK.

While these studies give some indication of the features of a healthcare system that may matter, two further caveats need to be borne in mind. The first is that cross-country studies to date have examined expenditure and not efficiency. Whilst governments may be concerned with expenditure and expenditure growth, the real issue that is important for the design of healthcare systems is efficiency. However, without a way of adjusting expenditure for quality, efficiency cannot be measured. It is argued that this focus on expenditure distorts international comparisons. For example, it is argued that looking only at expenditure ignores the costs imposed by waiting-lists, which tend to be used in countries that have lower expenditure per capita, and so erroneously equates higher expenditure with inefficiency.[11] More generally, the position of the US as an outlier with both high expenditure and higher (unmeasured) quality means that results are often not robust to leaving the US out of the analysis.

---

[10] One commentator on early studies in this area concludes: 'We have had crude data, misspecified equations, contentious theory and cavalier history' (Culyer, quoted in Gerdtham and Jonsson, 2000).

[11] For an example of this argument, see Danzon (1992).

Second, none of these studies has fully addressed the issue that the organisational form and financing of healthcare expenditure are endogenous. For example, centralised control of, or influence on, health budgets is itself a response to low income, budget deficits and a desire to control costs. Such endogeneity will bias the estimates of the coefficients on the institutional design factors in the estimates. Finally, even income may not be exogenous in the long run, as the level of healthcare affects productivity.

1. Age and Expenditure

Perhaps one surprising result from the studies is the lack of an impact of age or of other measures of need (e.g. unemployment) on healthcare expenditures. The impact of ageing on government expenditure has been a major concern for both governments and academic writers (e.g. Bos and von Weisacker, 1989). Severe consequences were expected for the healthcare sector when population ageing was argued to be the cause of rises in government expenditure up to the mid-1980s (OECD, 1988).[12]

However, recent analyses of cross-country expenditure data conclude that the age effect is correlated with income (richer countries in the sample have older populations) and show that, holding income constant, age *per se* has little effect. Recent analysis of country-specific micro-data on healthcare expenditure indicates that expenditures on healthcare are concentrated in the last few months of life. An analysis of micro-data for a sample of Swiss individuals in the last eight quarters of life during the period 1983–92 (Zweifel et al., 1999) indicates that the amount of healthcare expenditure depends on remaining lifetime but not on calendar age, at least for those over 65. From this, Zweifel et al. infer that the positive relationship between age and healthcare expenditure that can be observed in cross-sectional data may be caused by the fact that, at age 80, for example, there are many more individuals living in their last two years than there are at age 65. The impact of ageing will thus be to push the high levels of healthcare expenditure to later in individuals' lives rather than to increase per capita expenditure.

Cutler and co-authors (Cutler and Meara, 1998, 1999; Cutler and Sheiner, 1999) carry out detailed analysis of the relationship between ageing and health using data on healthcare expenditures in the US under the Medicare programme for elderly persons. Cutler and Meara (1999) analyse the increase in Medicare spending during the 1980s and 1990s. During these decades, Medicare spending doubled in real terms despite the fact that the health of Medicare beneficiaries improved over the period. In attempting to reconcile these two facts, the authors show that most of the growth has been amongst the oldest old. Between 1985 and 1995, spending among those aged 65–69 rose by 2 per cent annually. In contrast, spending for those over 85 rose by 4 per cent. However, the source of this increase is not increased use of acute care (for which the growth rate amongst the young elderly

---

[12] Emmerson et al. (2000) provide projections of the impact of ageing on expenditure for the UK.

is in fact higher than that amongst the old elderly) but increased use of post-acute services.

Cutler and Meara (1999) speculate that this increase in use might reflect three factors. The first is 'gaming' in response to the reimbursement mechanisms used in Medicare. In-patient care is reimbursed prospectively, so hospitals receive the same payment regardless of whether they provide rehabilitative care or not. However, post-acute care is reimbursed on a cost basis when services are used. So, if hospitals unbundle the post-acute care from the in-patient setting, they collect additional revenues at no extra cost. The second factor is that some of the additional services might reflect real extra services, perhaps substituting for care previously provided by a family member. Getting reimbursement for such care was made easier in the late 1980s. Finally, Cutler and Meara argue that some of the increase in expenditure might be fraud. The nature of their data means that they are unable to establish the relative strength of these factors.

This analysis illustrates the importance of the interaction of demography, health status and the institutional arrangements for reimbursement and delivery of care. Ageing *per se* does not necessarily mean that individuals are more in need of healthcare; in fact, in the US data at least, older groups are healthier than in the past. However, even though healthier, they use more resources. This is in part due to changes in family choice (due to changes in taste and in income) and the availability of better rehabilitative care, but also due to the particular nature of the reimbursement arrangements for publicly funded care in the US. In other words, again the literature points to the importance of micro-incentives and the responses of agents to these incentives in determining the level and composition of expenditure.

It is also possible that the impact of age will be affected by endogenous government budgetary responses. Getzen (1992) finds no empirical relationship between ageing and expenditure and argues (as an *ad hoc* justification of his findings) that, during the 1980s, the existence of budget deficits meant that governments acted to damp down the increased demand that arose from an ageing population. He concludes therefore that ageing *per se* does not automatically mean greater healthcare expenditure: the effect will depend on the overall fiscal position of the government. This contention remains to be tested.

V. DOES THE ORGANISATION OF THE HEALTHCARE SYSTEM DETERMINE EQUITY?

There is considerable evidence that policymakers within OECD countries are concerned about equity in healthcare. As shown in Table 1, the share of the state in healthcare expenditure is high, and many countries have achieved close to universal coverage of their population for the majority of healthcare services (OECD, 1993).

The simple share of public finance in total healthcare expenditure hides the fact that OECD countries finance their healthcare through a mixture of taxes, social insurance contributions, private insurance premiums and direct payments at point of use (known as out-of-pocket payments). These various payment sources have very different implications for both vertical and horizontal equity in the payment for healthcare, and may also have an impact on equity in the receipt of healthcare.

1. Equity in the Finance of Healthcare

Wagstaff et al. (1999) examine the progressivity of the healthcare financing system in 13 OECD countries. Progressivity is measured using the Kakwani index, which is equal to the difference between the concentration index for payments and the Gini coefficient for gross (i.e. pre-healthcare-payment) income. This index measures departures from proportionality. A zero value of the index indicates proportionality in payments (i.e. all individuals pay the same proportion of their income for healthcare), and a negative (positive) value indicates a regressive (progressive) structure. Indices are calculated for the five sources of payment for healthcare: direct taxes, indirect taxes, social insurance, private insurance and direct payments. Indices for total taxes (direct and indirect), total public (taxes plus social insurance), total private and total expenditures are computed as weighted averages of the relevant separate indices.

The results indicate that direct taxes used to finance healthcare are progressive. This is particularly true in the UK, Ireland and Germany, but less true in Sweden and Finland, where a relatively high share of direct taxation for healthcare finance comes from local income taxes, which are less progressive than national taxation. Indirect taxes are regressive in all of the countries in the study. Social insurance is generally progressive, apart from in the Netherlands and Germany, where higher income groups are excluded from the social insurance schemes used to finance healthcare. The progressivity of private insurance depends upon what private insurance buys. In countries where private insurance buys cover against public sector co-payments (e.g. Denmark and France), progressivity is lower where co-payments are higher (because poorer individuals spend a higher proportion of their income on insurance against co-payments). In countries where private insurance is taken out as (often 'double' cover) supplementary to cover provided by the state (e.g. Italy, the UK, Portugal and Spain), insurance is generally progressive. This is because those who pay for cover twice are richer individuals. Where insurance is the sole form of cover for the majority of the population (the US and Switzerland), it is highly regressive. Where it is the sole form of cover for richer individuals (Germany and the Netherlands), it is progressive. Finally, out-of-pocket payments are generally a highly regressive means of raising revenue, though their regressivity varies across countries, reflecting the differences across countries in exemptions from out-of-pocket payments.

The net effect of these different payment mechanisms on the progressivity of healthcare finance across 12 of the 13 countries is given in Table 6. The countries are ranked in terms of progressivity of healthcare finance, with the most regressive at the top. The position in the ranking depends on the weight of the different payment mechanisms in the total healthcare financing package. Broadly, it can be

Table 6. *Progressivity of healthcare financing*

	Year of analysis	Progressivity of all payments for healthcare
Switzerland	1992	−0.1402
US	1987	−0.1303
Netherlands	1992	−0.0703
Germany	1989	−0.0452
Portugal	1990	−0.0445
Sweden	1990	−0.0158
Denmark	1987	−0.0047
Spain	1990	0.0004
France	1989	0.0012
Finland	1996	0.0181
Italy	1991	0.0413
UK	1993	0.0510

Note: Progressivity measured as Kakwani index, so a negative (positive) value indicates a regressive (progressive) structure.

Source: Wagstaff et al., 1999.

seen that countries that rely most heavily on private insurance have the least progressive healthcare financing system. Tax-financed systems are proportional or progressive. Countries that rely heavily on social insurance have less regressive systems than those that rely most on private insurance, but have less progressive systems than those that use tax finance (the exception being France, where over 70 per cent of revenues are raised by social insurance).[13]

2. Equity in the Delivery of Healthcare

The principle of equity in the delivery of healthcare is widely adopted in OECD country policy documents (van Doorslaer and Wagstaff, 1992). But differences in the mix of public and private financing, and in the delivery systems, across these countries may mean that these equity goals are not met in practice. van Doorslaer et al. (2000) estimate the extent to which violations of the principle 'equal treatment for equal need' are systematically related to income in 13 OECD countries. The study uses individual-level data from household surveys. This contrasts with many other studies of equity in the allocation of healthcare, which have looked only at users of healthcare. Individuals' incomes are their equivalised household

---

[13] van Doorslaer et al. (1999) examine the impact of healthcare payment sources on vertical and horizontal equity and redistribution. They find that the vertical effect (unequal treatment of unequals) is far more important than horizontal inequity (unequal treatment of equals). Public finance systems tend to have small positive redistributive effects and less differential treatment of equals, while private financing sources generally have (larger) negative redistributive effects that are, to a substantial degree, caused by differential treatment.

Table 7. *Extent of progressivity in delivery of all medical care*

	Year of analysis	Progressivity of delivery of all medical care[a]
Switzerland	1992	0.040
US	1987	0.009
Netherlands	1992	−0.038
Sweden	1990	−0.014
Denmark	1994	−0.060
Finland	1996	−0.029
UK	1989	−0.016

[a] A negative (positive) value indicates a progressive (regressive) system.

Note: Countries are ranked in order of increasing progressivity in finance (from Wagstaff et al., 1999).

Source: van Doorslaer et al., 2000.

incomes, and various forms of care are examined. Departures from proportionality (equal treatment for equal need) are measured by an index that ranges in value from −1 to +1, where a negative (positive) number indicates pro-poor (pro-rich) inequity.[14]

In all the countries studied, individuals in lower income groups are more intensive users of the healthcare system. The poor use more services of the general practitioner, the medical specialist and the hospital. But after standardising for the level of need for care, there is little or no evidence of significant inequality in the delivery of healthcare overall. Interpreted literally, these results indicate that, in the late 1980s and early 1990s, the healthcare systems of these countries appeared to perform reasonably well on the horizontal equity criterion of equal treatment for equal need.

Furthermore, there is no evidence of a link between the healthcare financing system and equity in *delivery* of care. Table 7 shows the extent of departures from equal treatment for equal need across countries, where the countries are ranked in terms of their progressivity in finance (from Wagstaff et al., 1999). As can be seen, countries that are the most progressive in terms of finance are not those that have the most pro-poor distribution of healthcare. For example, the UK has the most progressive financing system of the group in the table, but equity in delivery is more pro-poor in Finland, Denmark and the Netherlands.

While this study finds no evidence of significant inequity in the delivery of healthcare overall, it does find that significant pro-rich inequality arises for physician contacts. This seems to be due mainly to a higher use of medical specialist services by higher income groups and a higher use of GP care amongst lower income groups. This finding appears to be fairly general and emerges in different countries with very diverse characteristics regarding access to specialists and provider incentives. It occurs in countries with universal coverage (Scandinavia)

---

[14] For details of the methodology, see van Doorslaer et al. (2000).

Table 8. *Percentage saying government should definitely be responsible for healthcare for the sick*

	West Germany	Britain	Italy	Sweden
1985	54	85	87	n.a.
1990	57	85	88	n.a.
1996	51	82	n.a.	71

Source: Taylor-Gooby, 1999.

as well as those without (US), in countries with (Denmark and the Netherlands) and without (Belgium) a GP gatekeeper role and in countries with (Belgium) and without (Denmark) substantial cost sharing by patients. On the other hand, this finding does not emerge in two other countries that have few features in common (the UK and Switzerland).

The lesson that may be drawn from the studies to date of equity in the finance and delivery of healthcare is that changes to the finance side would appear to have more impact on equity than changes to the delivery side. However, such conclusions may be premature. The analysis on the delivery side was not able to adjust for differences in quality of care across individuals and relies upon analysis of data drawn from a variety of country-specific surveys. Second, the results on the finance side are not incompatible with a position in which countries whose citizens care about fairness in healthcare finance adopt more progressive finance (i.e. use taxation rather than social insurance or private insurance and use less co-payment). In other words, the financing system might be endogenous to the beliefs about fairness.

A study of attitudes towards the role of the state in financing healthcare, carried out by Taylor-Gooby in 1999, shows that there is a considerable difference in the level of support for government responsibility for the sick. Table 8 presents the answers to a question asked in four countries over time, and shows considerable variation in the level of support for the principle. In addition, the ranking of these countries in terms of support for the statement is similar to their ranking in terms of progressivity of healthcare financing. Again, further research using comparable datasets is needed to ascertain the link between equity beliefs and financing arrangements.

VI. DOES THE ORGANISATION OF THE HEALTHCARE SYSTEM DETERMINE HEALTH OUTCOMES?

1. The Level of Health

The above analyses have been concerned with expenditure on the healthcare system and the level and distribution of healthcare. Health expenditure is, however, an input; arguably, what individuals care about is the output of the healthcare sector—in other words, health. Obviously, there are many factors other than healthcare that determine an individual's health status, but one measure of performance of healthcare systems is the extent of health of the population. Tables 9 and 10 present two commonly used measures of outcomes—life expectancy and infant mortality—for the G7 countries. These tables make it clear that the UK performs relatively badly on these summary statistics, though not as badly as the US, which is the biggest healthcare spender. When countries are ranked in terms of their expenditure, the performance of the UK is perhaps a little better, in that it is the lowest spender but has outcomes better than the lowest (though the comparison is less favourable to the UK if the US is excluded).

Table 9. *Life expectancy in G7 countries, 1996*

| | Life expectancy at birth (years) | | Ranking | | |
| | | | Life expectancy | | Spending[a] |
	Females	Males	Females	Males	
Japan	83.6	77.0	1	1	6
France	82.0	74.2	2	5	3
Canada	81.4	75.7	3	2	4
Italy	81.3	74.9	4	3	5
Germany	79.9	73.6	5	6	2
UK	79.5	74.3	6	4	7
US	79.4	72.7	7	7	1

[a] Spending is ranked according to share of health spending in GDP.

Source: Emmerson et al., 2000 (from OECD Health database 1999).

Table 10. *Infant mortality in G7 countries, 1996*

| | Infant mortality[a] | Ranking | |
		Infant mortality[a]	Spending[b]
Japan	4.3	1	6
France	4.9	2	3
Canada	5.3	3	4
Italy	6.0	4=	5
Germany	6.0	4=	2
UK	6.2	6	7
US	8.0	7	1

[a] Infant mortality is defined as the number of deaths at age under 1 year per 1,000 live births.
[b] Spending is ranked according to share of health spending in GDP.

Source: Emmerson et al., 2000 (from OECD Health database, 1999).

Examination of outcomes for specific illnesses and conditions tends to show that the UK performs badly compared with the rest of the G7 group (Coleman, 1999; Emmerson et al., 2000). The UK has high death rates from ischaemic heart disease and relatively poor survival rates for some common cancers (lung, heart, breast and prostate; Sikora, 1999). It is argued that these poor survival rates are indicators of failures in the medical system, although these failures may be due to lack of money or poor organisation of services (e.g. lack of concentration of cancer services) or both.

While Tables 9 and 10 suggest that the UK is not performing that well, more detailed cross-country analyses of the relationships between expenditure and mortality tend to find little relationship between expenditure and mortality. In early research, Leu (1986) finds no relationship between medical care expenditures and lower mortality after controlling for per capita income. Hitiris and Posnett (1992), using OECD data, find limited evidence of a relationship between health-care expenditures and mortality rates, despite using a large pooled time series of countries and allowing for heteroscedasticity and autocorrelation.

Interestingly, the relative position of the UK on the measures has worsened during the 1990s: prior to this date, the UK position was generally above average for the G7 group. More formal cross-country analyses indicate some convergence within EU countries over time in healthcare spending and outcomes (Nixon, 2000). Those countries that had lower-than-average healthcare expenditure and lower-than-average outcomes in the 1960s appear to have caught up with higher spenders and those with better outcomes. Conversely, those countries with good relative positions in the 1960s and 1970s appear to have had a fall in their relative position. So countries with worsening trends in infant mortality over the period 1960–95 include Belgium, Denmark, France, Finland, Greece, Ireland, the Netherlands, Sweden and the UK. Belgium, Germany (females only), Denmark, Spain (males only), the Netherlands, Sweden and the UK experienced worsening trends in terms of life expectancy. Viewed this way, the relatively poor current position of the UK might simply reflect regression towards the mean.

2. Inequality in the Distribution of Outcomes across Countries

van Doorslaer et al. (1997) examine income-related inequalities in health across nine European countries. Using data from household surveys, they calculate the concentration index of the distribution of self-reported health status.[15] Individuals were ranked by equivalent household income. Ill health was measured by the responses to questions in which respondents were asked to rate their health. Answers to these questions have been found to be good predictors of subsequent mortality in a variety of industrialised countries. In all countries, income-related health inequality is found to be significant. The authors explore the statistical

---

[15] For details of the calculation of the concentration index, see van Doorslaer et al. (1997).

association between these inequalities and two measures of healthcare expenditure and the level and distribution of income for the nine countries. They find that there is little association between health inequalities and GDP per capita, health spending and the percentage of healthcare spending that is public. On the other hand, they find evidence of a positive association between health inequalities and income inequality, as measured by the Gini coefficient for after-tax income.

VII. LESSONS FROM THE INTERNAL MARKET REFORMS

The UK, along with several other OECD countries, implemented a major reform of its healthcare system in the 1990s. In 1991, the internal market reforms were introduced. These separated the functions of provision and of purchase of hospital-based healthcare, creating one set of agents responsible for provision and another responsible for purchase. NHS hospitals were to be given greater autonomy from central and local control, and purchasers were created from area-based authorities that had previously administered hospitals and from a self-selected group of primary-care physicians (Culyer et al., 1990). The intention of the reforms was to create competition on the supply side of the market. Purchasers were free to buy hospital-based healthcare from any provider, including the small private sector. Providers would compete for contracts to supply care, which, it was argued, would encourage efficiency (Maynard, 1991).

These reforms are part of a more general healthcare reform process intended to increase competition in healthcare markets.[16] It is generally agreed that such reforms have brought about less change than their architects hoped.[17] However, within a UK context, the reforms have highlighted the importance of incentives for providers and purchasers of healthcare. An assessment of the reforms concludes that 'the incentives were too weak and the constraints too strong' (Le Grand et al., 1998). The constraints come, in part, from the controls imposed by central government (Propper, 1995).

One area over which there was less central control was the behaviour of General Practice Fundholders. In the internal market, two main classes of buyer were created: a self-selected group of family physicians (general practitioners, or GPs), called General Practice Fundholders (GPFHs), and health authorities. The reforms gave GPs choice, and GPFHs the ability to pay for this choice, for a subset of treatments.

[16] Culyer et al. (1990) and Maynard (1991) provide an overview of the NHS reforms. Propper (1995) provides an assessment of the limits to reform. Glied (2000) provides a review of the US literature on managed care. Chalkley and Malcomson (2000) review issues in government contracting for healthcare services. Le Grand and Bartlett (1993) provide a review of the wider set of 'quasi-market' reforms enacted in the UK.

[17] Le Grand, Mays and Mulligan (1998) provide an assessment of the UK reforms. Saltman and Figueras (1998) review the experience of managed competition. A more sociological assessment of several reforms is provided in *Social Science and Medicine*, vol. 52 (2001).

The fundholding scheme ran from 1991 to 1999. The scheme was voluntary, and practices joined in different years over the scheme's life. By its end, nationally about half of all general practices were fundholders. GPFHs held a budget from which they were expected to pay for only particular, specified types of care, including a specified subset of all procedures that an elective hospital patient might have. These included common elective procedures and accounted for about 70 per cent of all elective admissions. GPFHs placed contracts for these procedures with hospitals. These contracts commonly included information about price and some dimensions of quality, including, in some instances, waiting times (Glennerster et al., 1994). The contracts were likely to link payment to activity, with GPFHs basically paying hospitals for each case treated.

Any surplus from the fund could be retained by fundholders to use in their practices. As GPFHs were self-employed contractors subject to relatively little financial monitoring, exactly how these funds were spent was not subject to detailed scrutiny, and, at the very least, practice improvements translate into higher income when the GP exits from the practice. Research on the behaviour of GPFHs shows that GPs were generally active in making changes in the internal market (Glennerster et al., 1994), and detailed analyses of the financial incentives embodied in the scheme suggest that GPFHs responded to financial, as well as nonfinancial, incentives. The implementation of the reforms was undertaken in such a way that GPFHs had budgets based on their referrals in the year immediately prior to entry into the scheme. This gave them incentives to increase their use of hospital services prior to entering the scheme in order to inflate their budgets (which they could then hold at this level for the life of the scheme). Croxson et al. (2001) show that fundholders did respond to these financial incentives by increasing their referrals to hospital prior to entry into the scheme, so inflating their budgets upwards for the duration of the fundholding scheme. Gravelle et al. (2001) show that fundholding practices responded to positive prices by admitting fewer patients than non-fundholding practices. They also responded to changes in waiting times and patient characteristics in a way that was consistent with the positive financial costs of making referrals.

Evidence on the prices charged by NHS hospitals to GPFHs and the District Health Authority buyers indicates that external incentives—competition—also influenced behaviour. The Department of Health set regulations such that price was meant to equal average cost. However, this rule was not (and probably could not be) monitored. A limited number of studies of the impact of supply-side competition on prices were undertaken. These show that higher levels of competition were associated with lower prices, particularly for services that had lower costs (Propper, 1996; Propper et al., 1998). These studies also suggest that NHS hospitals gave greater discounts to those buyers who were more able to move their contracts between sellers.

So, while, in general, the regulatory activities of central government might have limited the responses of agents in the internal market, it does appear that, even with such regulation, agents did respond to financial incentives.

VIII. THE ROLE OF PRIVATE FINANCE AND THE DYNAMICS OF HEALTHCARE EXPENDITURE

While the size of the private sector relative to the public is small, private finance accounts for around 15 per cent of healthcare expenditure in the UK. This private expenditure includes co-payments for pharmaceuticals, direct payment for care provided outside the NHS and payments for health insurance. Setting aside co-payments for pharmaceuticals (which are free for the elderly, the young and those in receipt of social security), private payments are made by individuals who are richer. Besley et al. (1999) find the privately insured to be more likely to be wealthier, more likely to live in prosperous areas of the UK, more likely to be more educated, more likely to be in work and more likely to be supporters of the Conservative Party. Propper et al. (2001) also find evidence of a cohort effect in purchase: younger individuals are currently more likely to purchase than their older counterparts. Not surprisingly, adding in the expenditure on private care to NHS expenditure makes the UK distribution of health expenditure less progressive (O'Donnell et al., 1993).

There are a number of essentially static arguments in favour of a private sector that operates alongside a public sector system. First, there are a limited number of economic models that show that systems in which there is private provision alongside public are welfare-increasing. Besley and Coate (1991) argue that systems in which there is *de jure* universal provision, but in which richer individuals are *de facto* allowed to 'opt out', can be redistributive, even when public provision is financed by a non-redistributive mechanism such as a head tax. Gouveia (1997) argues that allowing the rich to 'opt out' maintains the existence of a public system by keeping tax payments down to levels supported by a coalition of the rich and the poor. The second, often-advanced, argument is that the private sector allows individuals choice. The third is that, for a given budget, individuals who use the private sector may actually benefit those who remain in the public sector: if richer individuals use private care but pay taxes for public care, then this will reduce demand in the public sector, so increasing the resources available per capita in the public sector. For example, in the UK, it is argued that those who use the private sector for treatment reduce waiting times for those who remain in the public sector.

But the dynamics of the process may be somewhat different. If the wealthier receive less of their healthcare through the public system, their commitment to contribute taxes to the system may decrease. In addition, without the 'sharp elbows' of the middle classes to keep up quality, the quality of the public sector may fall. A fall may lead to lobbying for lower taxes for the public scheme and a reduction in budgets. If opting-out does depend on the quality of the public sector, reductions in the budget will lead to less use of the system by richer individuals. This will, in turn, lead to further calls for reductions in the budget. So attempts to cut public expenditure may lead to the public sector becoming a 'poor service for the poor'.

The relationship between private financing and the evolution of the public system turns on the relationship between the quality of the public sector, use of the public and private sectors and political support for the public sector. The argument that private finance will lead to a downward spiral towards a 'poor service for the poor' depends upon the premises that support for public sector financing is negatively associated with private demand and that the demand for a privately financed alternative is affected by the quality of the public sector.

In practice, there are several possible relationships between support for public finance and use of private healthcare. Users of private healthcare services may be less supportive of public services on ideological grounds or because they simply see little personal return from public services they do not use. Alternatively, users of private services may be frustrated with the level of service available from the public sector, although ideologically they may prefer higher state spending to achieve higher service levels and quality for all. Use of the public or private sector may affect attitudes. Users dissatisfied with the level of service in the public sector may switch to the private sector. Users of the private sector may like the quality of service they receive and no longer see themselves as potential beneficiaries of the public service, and in turn lessen their support for state provision.

At an EU level, Mossialis (1997) finds a positive relationship between expenditure per capita and satisfaction with the healthcare services, though there are two outliers (Denmark and Italy). In addition, he finds a north–south divide in citizens' satisfaction with healthcare systems, with those in the north being more satisfied, those in the south being less so and the UK (and Ireland) lying between the two. In an examination of the dynamics of expenditure across countries (using OECD data), Globerman and Vining (1998) find no relationship between the current share of public expenditure in a country and past shares of public expenditure on healthcare in that country. In other words, low current levels of public expenditure do not necessarily imply low levels of expenditure in the future.

At a national level, evidence from the UK suggests that those who use the private sector are, in general, less supportive of public financing of healthcare. Users of private healthcare services and, more particularly, users of private medical insurance are less supportive of increases in expenditure on the NHS or the equity goals of the NHS (Burchardt et al., 1999; Hall and Preston, 1998). There is also evidence from the UK that the *quality* of the NHS is associated with use of the private sector: longer waiting-lists have been found to be linked with higher levels of demand for private medical insurance (Besley et al., 1999), though not with *use* of the private sector (Burchardt et al., 1999). Besley et al. and Calnan, et al. (1993) also find evidence of a link between dissatisfaction with the quality of the NHS and private insurance purchase in the UK. However, both studies stress that it is dissatisfaction with the quality of service, rather than the concept of public provision, that drives people into the private sector.

But there is considerably less evidence that private use leads to *change* in attitudes. Burchardt and Propper (1999) find that use of private healthcare in the UK in the early 1990s did not lead to clear-cut changes in attitudes towards the NHS over the following five years. Furthermore, over this five-year period, the attitudes of both private sector and NHS users changed, and the changes in attitudes of both sets of users were very close. It appears that, in the UK at present, it is *use of a service* that leads to attitude change and not whether that individual uses a public or a private service.

These studies point to an interaction between NHS utilisation, private utilisation and attitudes, which suggests that the state of the NHS might have an impact upon the utilisation of the private sector alternative by the individual. The evidence is less clear as to whether this will translate into lower support for the NHS and for taxes for the NHS. Judge et al. (1998) find that levels of dissatisfaction with healthcare fluctuated between 1983 and 1996 but rose towards the end of the period to be higher than during the previous 13 years. A strong association exists (at national level) between actual levels of expenditure on the NHS, spending priorities and dissatisfaction with the NHS. Public support for higher spending and levels of dissatisfaction with the NHS rose in the second half of the 1980s when funding increases were relatively small, fell back again in the early 1990s when spending rose, then rose again as spending slowed down in the mid-1990s. However, the same study finds little support for major changes in the traditional method of tax finance for the NHS during this period. In a study of attitudes to public sector funding, Brook et al. (1997) find that the use of private sector alternatives for healthcare is an important determinant of what individuals think is a funding priority for themselves, but is a less important determinant of what they perceive to be in the national interest.

Given this evidence, it appears that a decrease in expenditure on the NHS may lead to increased use of the private sector, but this will not lead to a large shift in support away from the NHS. Increasing NHS expenditure may therefore paradoxically put greater pressure on the NHS as more individuals use the higher-quality public service. Conversely, the findings also suggest that there may be scope for more private finance at the margin without threatening the tax base of the NHS.

In considering extensions to private finance, it is necessary to take into account possible supply-side responses. Under the current performance monitoring arrangements within the NHS, in which hospitals are set waiting-list or waiting-time targets, Martin and Smith (1999) find that an increase in waiting-lists results in larger increases in supply than reductions in demand. They attribute this to the fact that hospital managers are strongly monitored in terms of waiting-time/waiting-list targets. In addition, physicians who work in the private sector generally also work in the public sector and are not strongly monitored in terms of hours of work supplied to the NHS. So any exogenous increase in demand for private services (say a tax break for private purchase) or a change in quality of the NHS will affect both sectors.

Measures to stimulate private finance could lead to a worsening of service in the NHS as staff moved into the private sector to meet the increased private demand. If the fall in demand for NHS care were sufficiently large, NHS waiting-lists would then fall. This might stimulate some NHS demand, but it might also reduce the pressure on managers to exert effort, and, if the Martin and Smith estimates are taken at face value, would result in less NHS activity. So, in the short run, giving tax breaks could harm NHS users. The benefit to private users would depend on whether prices in the private sector rose and on the difference in the benefits of treatment—including the difference in waiting times—in the two sectors.

IX. CONCLUSIONS

This review has examined the financing of the UK healthcare sector using evidence from both international comparisons and within the UK. The international comparisons suggest the following. The lower expenditure per capita of the UK can, in part, be attributed to organisation of the healthcare system. Features of the UK system, such as the use of primary-care gatekeepers (the UK's General Practice system whereby individuals must be referred for treatment and diagnosis in the hospital sector by their family doctor) and of budgets set at a system-wide level, appear to keep expenditure below what would be expected, given national income. The evidence on equity in finance and delivery indicates that, on the finance side, the UK has one of the most progressive systems. On the delivery side, the NHS is not worse, and indeed somewhat better, in terms of equity in the use of healthcare resources, than several other OECD countries that spend considerably more per capita on their healthcare.

On the other hand, the international evidence on expenditure cannot be taken as evidence of efficiency, as no adjustment is made for quality. Further, the evidence also indicates that these positive properties of the UK system may not translate into health outcomes. The UK has, on some measures, poorer health outcomes than similar countries and a poorer distribution of health. While these outcomes might be better than expected, given the level of funding, the fact that little relationship between funding and mortality has been found at cross-country level makes such an inference something of a leap of faith. The distribution of outcomes appears to be more related to the distribution of income than to any measures of healthcare spending.

What international comparisons also hint at is the importance of incentives at the level of the supplier and the demander. Funding analyses show that the UK use of gatekeepers and payment of doctors by salary rather than fee-for-service mean expenditure per capita is lower than it would be with other design features. However, cross-country analyses are generally at a level at which it is hard to isolate the impact of such incentives: to understand these micro-incentives, it is necessary to examine data in which the incentive structures can be more clearly identified.

Examination of responses to the financial incentives embodied in the UK internal market reforms indicates that physicians and healthcare providers do appear to respond to financial incentives in a tax-financed, predominantly publicly provided healthcare system. Referral patterns of GPs reflected financial (and other) rewards. Where competition was stronger, prices appeared to be lower. However, it is also clear that responses of agents were limited by the structures established, and the actions taken, by central government to 'manage the market'.

In terms of the type of finance, the review suggests that there are no clear equity grounds for moving away from tax finance. The present tax-financed system is more equitable than either social insurance or private insurance. On the other hand, there are growing pressures on the NHS, which are reflected in public attitudes. The evidence suggests that a marginal extension of private finance will not necessarily erode public support for the NHS.

Finally, the review highlights the importance of moving on from a focus on what are basically inputs—expenditure and its distribution—to an examination of outcomes and the links between inputs and outputs. The UK appears to meet its equity goals well in terms of how it spends public finance, but this is not mirrored by an increase in equity in health outputs. The existence of health inequalities raises the issue that the focus by governments on inputs and amounts of money spent is somewhat skewed. As important is a focus on what is being achieved for this money. To assess the extent to which health outcomes have much to do with expenditure on healthcare, greater research effort needs to be directed to looking at the impact of expenditure on health. In other words, economists need to direct effort to the study of the efficiency of production. This, in turn, suggests a greater focus on the responses of suppliers and demanders to incentives.

REFERENCES

Barr, N. (1998), *The Economics of the Welfare State*, 3rd edn, Oxford: Oxford University Press.

Besley, T. and Coate, S. (1991), 'Public provision of private goods and the redistribution of income', *American Economic Review*, vol. 81, pp. 979–84.

—, Hall, J. and Preston, I. (1999), 'The demand for private health insurance: do waiting lists matter?', *Journal of Public Economics*, vol. 72, pp. 155–81.

Bos, D. and von Weisacker, R. K. (1989), 'Economic consequences of an ageing population', *European Economic Review*, vol. 33, pp. 345–54.

Bramley, G. et al. (1998), *Where Does Public Spending Go? Pilot Study to Analyse the Flows of Public Expenditure into Local Areas*, DETR Regeneration Research Report, London: Department of the Environment, Transport and the Regions.

Brook, L., Hall, J. and Preston, I. (1997), 'What drives support for higher public spending?', Institute for Fiscal Studies, Working Paper no. W97/16.

Burchardt, T., Hills, J. and Propper, C. (1999), *Private Welfare and Public Policy*, York: Joseph Rowntree Foundation.

— and Propper, C. (1999), 'Does the UK have a private welfare class?', *Journal of Social Policy*, vol. 28, pp. 643–65.

Calnan, M., Cant, S. and Gabe, J. (1993), *Going Private: Why People Pay for their Health Care*, Oxford: Oxford University Press.

Chalkley, M. and Malcomson, J. (2000), 'Government purchasing of health care services', in A. J. Culyer and J. Newhouse (eds), *The Handbook of Health Economics*, vol. 1A, Amsterdam: North-Holland.

Coleman, M. P. (1999), *Cancer Survival Trends in England and Wales 1971–1995: Deprivation and NHS Region*, Series SMPS no. 61, London: The Stationery Office.

Cremieux, P.-Y., Ouellette, P. and Pilon, C. (1999), 'Health care spending as determinants of health outcomes', *Health Economics*, vol. 8, pp. 627–39.

Croxson, B., Propper, C. and Perkins, P. (2001), 'Do doctors respond to financial incentives: UK family doctors and the GP Fundholder scheme', *Journal of Public Economics*, vol. 79, pp. 375–98.

Culyer, A., Maynard, A. and Posnett, J. (eds) (1990), *Competition in Health Care: Reforming the NHS*, Basingstoke: Macmillan.

Cutler, D. and Meara, E. (1998), 'The medical costs of the young and the old: a forty year perspective', in D. Wise (ed.), *Frontiers in Aging*, Chicago: University of Chicago Press.

— and — (1999), 'The concentration of medical spending: an update', National Bureau of Economic Research, Working Paper no. W7279.

— and Sheiner, L. (1999), 'Demographics and medical care spending: standard and non-standard effects', in A. Auerbach and R. Lee (eds), *Demographics and Fiscal Policy*, Cambridge: Cambridge University Press.

Danzon, P. M. (1992), 'Hidden overhead costs: is Canada's system really less expensive?', *Health Affairs*, Spring, pp. 21–43.

Department of Health (1998), *Independent Inquiry into Inequalities in Health Report*, Acheson Report, London: The Stationery Office.

Emmerson, C., Frayne, C. and Goodman, A. (2000), *Pressures in UK Healthcare: Challenges for the NHS*, Commentary no. 81, London: Institute for Fiscal Studies.

Gerdtham, U. G. and Jonsson, B. (2000), 'Cross-country studies of health care expenditure', in A. J. Culyer and J. Newhouse (eds), *The Handbook of Health Economics*, vol. 1A, Amsterdam: North-Holland.

Getzen, T. E. (1992), 'Population ageing and the growth of health care expenditures', *Journal of Gerontology: Social Sciences*, vol. 47, pp. S98–104.

Glennerster, H., Hills, J. and Travers, T. (2000), *Paying for Health Care, Housing and Education*, Oxford: Oxford University Press.

—, Matsaganis, M. and Owens, P. (1994), *Implementing GP Fundholding: Wild Card or Winning Hand?*, Buckingham: Open University Press.

Glied, S. (2000), 'Managed care', in A. J. Culyer and J. Newhouse (eds), *The Handbook of Health Economics*, vol. 1B, Amsterdam: North-Holland.

Globerman, S. and Vining, A. (1998), 'A policy perspective on "mixed" health care financial systems of business and economics', *Journal of Risk and Insurance*, vol. 65, pp. 57–80.

Gouveia, M. (1997), 'Majority rule and the public provision of a private good', *Public Choice*, vol. 93, pp. 221–44.

Gravelle, H., Duskeiko, M. and Sutton, M. (2001), 'The demand for elective surgery: time and money prices in the UK National Health Service', University of York, Centre for Health Economics, mimeo.

Hall, J. and Preston, I. (1998), 'Public and private choice in UK health insurance', Institute for Fiscal Studies, Working Paper no. W98/19.

Hitiris, T. and Posnett, J. (1992), 'The determinants and the effects of health expenditure in developed countries', *Journal of Health Economics*, vol. 11, pp. 173–81.

Judge, K., Mulligan, J.-A. and New, B. (1998), 'The NHS: new prescription needed?', in R. Jowell, J. Curtis, A. Park, L. Brook, K. Thomson and C. Bryson (eds), *British Social Attitudes: The 14th Report*, London: Ashgate/SCPR.

Le Grand, J. and Bartlett, W. (eds) (1993), *Quasi-Markets and Social Policy*, Houndmills: Macmillan.

Le Grand, J., Mays, N. and Mulligan, J. (eds) (1998), *Learning from the NHS Internal Market*, London: King's Fund.

— and Vizard, P. (1998), 'The National Health Service: crisis, change or continuity?', in H. Glennerster and J. Hills (eds), *The State of Welfare: The Economics of Social Spending*, Oxford: Oxford University Press.

—, Winter, D. and Woolley, F. (1990), 'The National Health Service: safe in whose hands?', in J. Hills (ed.), *The State of Welfare: The Welfare State in Britain since 1974*, Oxford: Oxford University Press.

Leu, R. (1986), 'The public–private mix and international health care costs', in A. J. Culyer and B. Jonsson (eds), *Public and Private Health Services*, Oxford: Basil Blackwell.

Martin, S. and Smith, P. (1999), 'Rationing by waiting lists: an empirical investigation', *Journal of Public Economics*, vol. 71, pp. 141–64.

Maynard, A. (1991), 'Developing a health care market', *Economic Journal*, vol. 101, pp. 1277–86.

Mossialis, E. (1997), 'Citizens' views on the healthcare system in the 15 member states of the European Union', *Health Economics*, vol. 6, pp. 109–16.

Nixon, J. (2000), 'Convergence of health care spending and health outcomes in the European Union 1960–95', University of York, Centre for Health Economics, Discussion Paper no. 183.

O'Donnell, O. and Propper, C. (1991), 'Equity and the distribution of NHS resources', *Journal of Health Economics*, vol. 10, pp. 1–20.

—, — and Upward, R. (1993), 'Equity in the finance and delivery of health care in Britain', in E. van Doorslaer, A. Wagstaff and F. Rutten (eds), *Equity in the Finance and Delivery of Health Care: An International Perspective*, Oxford: Oxford University Press.

OECD (1988), *Ageing Population: The Social Policy Implications*, Paris: Organisation for Economic Co-operation and Development.

— (1993), *Health Care Systems: Facts and Trends 1960–1991*, Health Policy Study no. 3, Paris: Organisation for Economic Co-operation and Development.

— (1994), *The Reform of Health Care Systems: A Review of Seventeen OECD Countries*, Health Policy Study no. 5, Paris: Organisation for Economic Co-operation and Development.

Propper, C. (1995), 'Agency and incentives in the NHS internal market', *Social Science and Medicine*, vol. 40, pp. 1683–90.

— (1996), 'Market structure and prices: the responses of hospitals in the UK National Health Service to competition', *Journal of Public Economics*, vol. 61, pp. 307–35.

— (1998), *Who Pays for and Who Gets Health Care? Equity in the Finance and Delivery of Health Care in the United Kingdom*, Nuffield Occasional Papers, Health Economics Series, Paper no. 5, London: Nuffield Trust.

—, Rees, H. and Green, K. (2001), 'The demand for private insurance in the UK: a cohort analysis', *Economic Journal*, vol. 111, pp. C180–C200.

— and Upward, R. (1992), 'Need, equity and the NHS: the distribution of health care expenditure 1974–87', *Fiscal Studies*, vol. 13, no. 2, pp. 1–21.

—, Wilson, D. and Soderlund, N. (1998), 'The effects of regulation and competition in the NHS internal market: the case of GP Fund-Holder prices', *Journal of Health Economics*, vol. 17, pp. 645–74.

Saltman, R. B. and Figueras, J. (1998), 'Analysing the evidence on European health care reforms', *Health Affairs*, vol. 17, no. 2, pp. 85–108.

Shaw, M., Dorling, D., Gordon, D. and Davey-Smith, G. (1999), *The Widening Gap: Health Inequalities and Policy in Britain*, Bristol: Policy Press.

Sikora, K. (1999), 'Cancer survival in Britain', *British Medical Journal*, vol. 19, pp. 461–2.

Taylor-Gooby, P. (1999), 'Commitment to the welfare state', in R. Jowell, J. Curtis, A. Park, L. Brook, K. Thomson and C. Bryson (eds), *British Social Attitudes: The 15th Report*, Aldershot: Gower.

van Doorslaer, E. and Wagstaff, A. (1992), 'Equity in the delivery of health care: some international comparisons', *Journal of Health Economics*, vol. 11, pp. 389–411.

—, — et al. (1997), 'Socioeconomic inequalities in health: some international comparisons', *Journal of Health Economics*, vol. 16, pp. 93–112.

—, — et al. (1999), 'The redistributive effect of health care finance in twelve OECD countries', *Journal of Health Economics*, vol. 18, pp. 291–313.

—, — et al. (2000), 'Equity in the delivery of health care in Europe and the US', *Journal of Health Economics*, vol. 19, pp. 553–83.

Wagstaff, A., van Doorslaer, E. et al. (1999), 'Equity in the finance of health care: some further international comparisons', *Journal of Health Economics*, vol. 18, pp. 263–90.

Zweifel, P., Felder, S. and Meier, M. (1999), 'Ageing of population and health care expenditure: a red herring?', *Health Economics*, vol. 8, pp. 485–96.

4

Education and Public Policy

JAYASRI DUTTA, JAMES SEFTON AND MARTIN WEALE[1]

I. INTRODUCTION

In this survey, we aim to discuss the economic aspects of education and to evaluate the relevant facts, in the UK and across comparable industrial countries.

Economists usually concentrate on the productive aspect of education; it is the most important way by which societies can, and do, invest in human capital.[2] The fact that education increases the skill levels of individuals and contributes to the rise and spread of technological progress is beyond dispute. One may ask, nevertheless, how large these effects are, who pays the costs and who obtains the benefits. It is a type of investment where public financing is substantial, even in countries where the level of state participation in economic activity is otherwise low. The proportion of education financed by central, state or local governments is at least 75 per cent in the major industrial countries and is often in the region of 95 per cent. There are several good economic reasons for this to be the case. In this survey, we evaluate the quantitative importance of these reasons and their implications for public policy, both actual and potential.

Education generates higher incomes for private individuals; it is generally believed that the whole is more than the sum of its parts and that the social returns to education exceed private returns. Better-educated workers are likely to be more productive at their own jobs; they may, at the same time, raise the productivity of their colleagues, by demonstration, discussion or dissemination. The importance of peer-group effects of this kind are self-evident in our everyday tasks of teaching and research. Their importance has valuable implications for the role of public financing as well as for the organisation of education. Economic reasoning says that private individuals are likely to underinvest in activities that generate *positive*

The authors are grateful to many people for helpful discussions. In particular, Mike Biggs, Jacques Dreze, George Kapetanios, Sig Prais, Rebecca Riley, Richard Smith, Mario Tirelli and Dirk te Velde have been extremely helpful with various aspects of preparing this paper. Financial support from the Economic and Social Research Council under grants R022 251064 and L138 251022 is gratefully acknowledged.

[1] Jayasri Dutta is in the Faculty of Economics and Politics, University of Cambridge. James Sefton and Martin Weale are at the National Institute of Economic and Social Research.

[2] For a sociological critique of this, see Fevre et al. (1999).

externalities. The importance of peer effects, and other externalities, is critical in determining location, districting and access rules for the state school system, as well as the choice of target schools or universities for preferential funding.[3] An argument with similar economic flavour relies on the fact that the provision of education may display economies of scale—the education of, say, the 51st pupil in a class imposes negligible costs. This sort of argument is of particular importance in policy debates on class sizes. In Sections III and IV, we review the available evidence on the private and social returns to education; we have little to say, as yet, about returns to scale in its provision.

A second justification comes from the facts that the returns to education are risky and that private individuals may underinvest because of their inability to diversify the resulting *income risk.* The argument is typically made for higher education (see, e.g. Kodde, 1986). The likely increase in skills and productivity depends on inherent ability as well as chance. The possibility of the former implies that the latter cannot be insured and that the income risks must be borne by the worker. Anticipating this, a school-leaver may choose not to go to university, which is a high-return investment with high risk. Public subsidies to higher education lower the cost of the investment; the taxes used to finance these subsidies may succeed in lowering the associated risk. We evaluate this argument in Section V.

The arguments so far speak to the relative efficiency of public education. The third reason calls upon *equity* and is of special relevance to school education: public financing is important if school-age children cannot borrow against future incomes to finance their own education. Otherwise, the quantity and quality of education will be entirely dependent on their parents' ability to pay. Loury (1981) makes a persuasive argument that, in the long run, the inequitable is, in fact, inefficient, because purely private financing lowers the average skill level far below its potential. In Sections VI and VII, we review the issue of distributional effects of public expenditures on education and the evidence about its implications for inter-generational mobility, both economic and social.

Data for about a dozen OECD countries allow us to make comparisons. By virtually any criterion, the UK does not do well in these comparisons. The proportion of national income spent on education is much lower than in other English-speaking countries or in Northern Europe. A relatively small proportion of this is spent on higher education: the UK has the lowest expenditure rate in our sample. Arguably, the returns to educational spending are likely to be high at earlier stages; which is not the same as saying that higher education should be starved of funding. In Section III, we present the costs and benefits of university education and, for five countries, quote figures for the rate of return.

The OECD data measure aggregates. In the presence of selective higher education, these estimates may overstate the return to an expansion of higher education,

---

[3] Benabou (1996) evalutes the effects of such rules on the distribution of earnings in the presence of peer externalities.

because of selection biases on ability as well socio-economic backgrounds. In Section VIII, we report a more careful analysis of the British experience. The rates of return are indeed lower—but, for most subjects, compete well with an assumed return on physical capital of 7–9 per cent p.a.

There remains the crucial question 'Who should pay for this?' As we argued before, the case for substantial public funding is relevant to primary and secondary education. There is less of a case for higher education, on equity as much as efficiency grounds. The gains from higher education are appropriated by the graduates; and, even now, there remains a participation bias in higher education, with more students from better, and higher-income, backgrounds.[4] Should the median taxpayer subsidise the future earnings of the relatively privileged?

The alternative is higher fees: an increase of fees raises real concerns about the possibility of tilting the scales even further against children from poorer backgrounds. The experience of the US—which has substantially higher intergenerational mobility than the UK, despite a large fee-based university system—may reassure us on this count.[5] Certainly, a student loan system is financially feasible. There may be good arguments for public administration of such a system, where the fee is paid back as a graduate tax. Taxation, unlike loans, can be equitable and impose fewer risks on individuals. Indeed, it is reasonable to imagine a rationalisation of the structure of fees, by which medicine or engineering degrees are charged differently from humanities degrees. We evaluate the suggestion in Section VIII. For the moment, we aim to establish whether this is a desirable direction of change; we have not attempted a full fiscal analysis of the alternative policy packages.

II. EDUCATION EXPENDITURES

Just how much do countries spend on education? Tables 1–4 summarise the very broad facts about educational expenditures and their financing. These and other cross-country aggregates are from OECD (1998).

The Scandinavian countries have the highest levels of spending on education as a proportion of GDP although not per pupil in absolute terms; most education is financed by the state, irrespective of the level. The US has a relatively low level of public participation; while this is no surprise, the total expenditure (public and private) is one of the highest. For purposes of comparison, expenditure rates in the UK are among the lowest in the sample, and particularly so for university education: indeed, it is an outlier in an otherwise clear picture of Anglo-Saxon bias towards higher education. These facts are of particular importance in evaluating rates of return, as we do next. The fact that overall expenditure rates in the UK are typically unavailable is unfortunate and due to the absence of systematic accounting of private school expenditures.

---

[4] Tables 9 and 10 emphasise this. Around 40 per cent of university graduates have parents with professional qualifications.

[5] See, for example, Dearden et al. (1997).

Table 1. *Spending on education as a percentage of GDP: all levels*

	1990		1995	
	Total (%)	Public (%)	Total (%)	Public (%)
Australia	4.9	4.3	5.6	4.5
Austria	–	5.2	–	5.3
Belgium	–	4.8	–	5.0
Canada	5.7	5.4	7.0	5.8
Denmark	6.4	6.2	7.1	6.5
Finland	6.4	6.4	6.6	6.6
France	5.6	5.1	6.3	5.8
Germany	–	–	5.8	4.5
Ireland	5.2	4.7	5.3	4.7
Italy	–	5.8	4.7	4.5
Japan	4.7	3.6	4.7	3.6
Netherlands	–	–	4.9	4.6
New Zealand	–	5.5	–	5.3
Norway	–	6.2	–	6.8
Spain	4.9	4.2	5.7	4.8
Sweden	–	–	6.7	6.6
Switzerland	–	5.0	–	5.5
UK	–	4.6	–	4.3
US	–	–	6.7	5.0
OECD	–	–	5.9	4.7

Source: OECD (1998).

Table 2. *Levels of education: spending as a percentage of GDP, 1995*

	Primary (%)	Secondary (%)	University (%)	Other tertiary (%)
Australia	1.6	2.1	1.5	0.3
Austria	1.2	2.7	0.9	0.1
Canada	2.1	2.2	1.5	0.9
Denmark	1.3	2.6	1.1	0.2
Finland	1.8	2.4	1.3	0.3
France	1.2	3.2	1.1	–
Germany	1.8	2.1	1.0	0.1
Ireland	1.3	2.1	1.3	–
Italy	1.1	2.1	0.8	–
Japan	1.3	1.7	0.9	0.1
Netherlands	1.2	2.0	1.3	–
Spain	1.8	2.3	1.0	–
Sweden	2.0	2.5	1.7	–
UK	–	–	0.7	–
US	1.8	2.0	2.0	0.4
OECD	1.6	2.1	1.5	0.3

Note: Data missing for Belgium, New Zealand, Norway and Switzerland.

Source: OECD (1998).

Table 3. *Public funding as a percentage of expenditures, 1995*

	School[a]	Tertiary[b]	All
Australia	87	65	79
Austria	98	–	97
Belgium	100	–	–
Canada	94	61	82
Denmark	98	99	98
France	93	84	91
Germany	76	92	78
Ireland	96	70	90
Italy	100	84	97
Japan	92	43	75
Netherlands	94	88	93
Spain	87	76	84
Sweden	100	94	98
UK	–	72	–
US	90	48	75
OECD	91	75	86

[a] Includes primary and secondary.
[b] Includes university.

Notes: Data missing for Finland, New Zealand, Norway and Switzerland. Based on final funds after transfers.

Source: OECD (1998).

Table 4. *Expenditure per student, 1995 (in US dollars)*

	Primary	Secondary	University
Australia	3,121	4,899	11,572
Austria	5,572	7,118	7,687
Belgium	3,270	5,770	6,043
Canada	–	–	12,217
Denmark	5,713	6,247	7,656
Finland	4,253	4,946	7,412
France	3,379	6,182	6,569
Germany	3,505	6,543	8,101
Ireland	2,144	3,395	7,249
Italy	4,673	5,348	4,932
Japan	4,065	4,465	9,337
Netherlands	3,191	4,351	9,026
New Zealand	2,638	4,120	8,380
Spain	2,628	3,455	4,966
Sweden	5,189	5,643	13,168
Switzerland	5,893	7,601	18,365
UK	3,328	4,246	7,225
US	5,371	6,812	19,965
OECD	3,595	4,971	12,018

Notes: Data missing for Norway. Conversion to US dollars at purchasing power parity.

Source: OECD (1998).

We note that 28 per cent of education expenditure at the secondary level in the UK is accounted for by private schools, which are attended by about 10 per cent of all secondary pupils (see, e.g. Biggs and Dutta, 1999); the per capita expenditure on a private education is thus more than three times that in state schools. This is relevant to our discussion on distributional effects (Section VI); it may also be a partial indicator of the nature of scale economies in education provision.

III. THE RETURN TO EDUCATION

The most basic economic analysis of education is conducted in terms of the returns to education. Spending on education is an investment which can be looked at in the same way as any other. One can work out either the increase in income per year of stage of schooling completed or the return to particular types of education, comparing the earning power of graduates with that of those who leave education with A levels. Estimation of these differentials is notoriously difficult, and actual estimates cover a very wide range. Psacharopoulos (1993) quotes figures for the private return to higher education ranging from 0.7 per cent p.a. in Canada for humanities degrees (estimated in 1985) to 48 per cent p.a. for social science degrees in the UK in 1971.

The calculated figures are, however, typically based on the cross-section data of a survey of earnings in a particular year. The returns are calculated on the assumption that the income differences observed in that particular year persist throughout the remaining life of someone choosing whether to pursue a particular course of study or not. This in turn means that there may be substantial fluctuations in returns from one year to the next, so that claims about the temporal behaviour of earnings differentials must be treated with caution. For example, Mincer (1994) quotes figures for the rate of return to college education in the US that show the return falling to below 4 per cent p.a. in 1979 and then recovering to over 10 per cent p.a. by 1986. As there are no confidence intervals provided, we have little to go on to determine the extent to which this is mere sampling variation. Since the return falls gradually from its level of around 9 per cent p.a. in the mid-1960s and recovers steadily from its low point, it does seem that there is a real fall and then rise in the premium. On the other hand, Willis (1986) quotes rates of return to higher education in the US for the same period; these do not show the decline in the late 1970s that Mincer explains.

In any calculation of this type, there is real concern as to how much the observed differences in earnings or employment reflect innate differences in ability rather than schooling. Three of the 11 post-war Prime Ministers (Sir Winston Churchill, Lord Callaghan and Mr Major) had not been to university. If they had, any calculation of the effects of university education would have included their and similar successes in it. There are a number of other biases that can creep into the calculations. Some argue that earning power depends on social background; but so does the likelihood of going to university. The effect of social factors may well inflate the measured return to education. As universities ration places by performance, graduates are unlikely to represent a random draw from the population of A-level students. Three As at A level are probably a very good predictor of future performance; relatively few students with three As choose not to go to university.

A number of corrections have been made for these biases. For example, Harmon and Walker (1995) look at the return to secondary education in the UK by comparing those who stayed at school into the fourth form both before and after the 1947 and 1973 raisings of the school-leaving age. This method plainly cannot be applied very generally. Other studies have looked at the differences between twins (see, e.g. Ashenfelter and Krueger, 1994). There are questions over estimation methods used. Blackburn and Neumark (1995) argue that, provided early indicators of ability are introduced, ordinary least squares estimation offers a satisfactory result. Blundell et al. (1997) use a 'matching' approach, with ability test scores at age seven among the regressors, along with other background and demographic variables designed to control for the other factors affecting the education decision; their careful study of the cohort represented in the National Child Development Survey means that their methods cannot be used for snapshot calculations from less detailed data sources.

1. Evaluating Costs and Benefits

University education takes time during which teaching costs are incurred and wages are not earned. After taking a degree at university, a graduate decides whether or not to take a job, and finds one with some probability. In fact, a university education raises the rate of labour force participation, as well as the probability of finding a job. It is certainly associated with increased earning on the job, once found. All of these contribute to a greater expected income for a graduate; this higher income is earned for the many working years remaining.

In Table 5, we show the costs and benefits of university education. First of all, we present the cost of education per annum, with local prices converted to US dollars at purchasing power parities, and the average duration of university education. We also report differences in labour force participation and unemployment rates. We indicate the overall income differential per year associated with a university education, for a selection of countries for which the raw data are available. This is calculated from published earnings differentials (also shown in the table, averaged over all age-groups), adjusted for the different participation and unemployment rates experienced by those with university education relative to those with only upper secondary education. Finally, we present, for the small number of countries for which they are available, the estimates of the private and social rates of return to university education calculated by the OECD. The private rate of return is the discount rate that equates the private cost of education—measured as any fees that students have to pay, plus the loss of post-tax earnings due to university attendance but less any maintenance grants paid—to the benefits of education, measured by the increase in earnings, again after tax and other deductions and after adjusting for differential participation and unemployment. The social rate of return compares

Table 5. *Costs and benefits of a university education*

	Annual cost (US$)[a]	Average duration (years)	Labour force participation rates (%)		Unemployment rates (%)		Earnings differentia (%)
			(S)	(U)	(S)	(U)	(U)
Australia	11,572	3.1	90	93	6	4	61
Canada	12,217	4.8	89	92	9	5	52
Denmark	8,157	3.6	89	94	6	4	55
France	6,569	6.2	90	92	8	6	85
Germany	9,001	5.3	85	93	8	5	52
Ireland	7,249	3.5	92	94	6	3	71
Italy	4,932	4.4	80	92	6	5	73
Netherlands	9,026	3.4	87	90	3	3	35
New Zealand	8,380	3.3	93	93	3	2	71
Spain	4,966	5.0	91	91	12	9	45
Switzerland	18,365	7.9	94	95	3	5	46
UK	7,225	4.2	89	94	8	4	61
US	19,965	4.2	88	93	6	2	83

[a]Annual expenditure per full-time-equivalent student converted to US dollars at purchasing power parity.

Note: All figures are for men aged 25–64 in 1996.
(S) refers to those with secondary education only.
(U) refers to those with university education.

Source: OECD (1998).

the social costs and the social benefits. The former include the cost of providing university education, whether it is borne by the student or not, and the value of earnings lost before any deductions. The social benefits are measured by the increase in gross earnings, adjusted for participation and unemployment effects, but do not allow for any external benefits of education.

The rate-of-return figures are not available very widely. In Section VIII, we add our own estimates of the position in the UK in 1995. However, the data shown here do suggest that the social return to higher education, at around 10 per cent p.a., is comparable to or slightly above the social return to physical capital. This may be a reason for countries to expand their higher education provision somewhat. The private rates of return suggest that, for any suitable individual, investment in higher education is a very good deal. Private returns are higher than social returns because governments bear some of the costs of higher education. In view of these data, one might ask, at least for the countries for which data are available, whether this is reasonable.

IV. EDUCATION AND ECONOMIC GROWTH

We deduced, in the previous section, that higher education is a good investment. Here, we ask a slightly different question, motivated by the fact that Microsoft and other similar high-tech and high-growth firms are partly the *consequence* of high-quality education. What is the measured effect of education on technological progress and economic growth? We review the evidence in the light of growth accounting methods, which follow Solow (1957), and in the context of growth regressions, popularised by Baumol et al. (1989) and Barro and Sala-i-Martin (1995).

Growth in output, or GDP, is due in part to growth inputs and in part to technological progress which allows societies to produce more from the same resources. Solow (1957) provides an elegant decomposition. Suppose g_y is the rate of growth of aggregate output and g_L and g_K are the rates of growth of aggregate inputs of labour and capital. We can measure the rate of total input growth as a weighted average of g_L and g_K, the weights being the expenditure shares of each factor.[6] Call this $g_I = \lambda g_L + (1 - \lambda)g_K$, with λ being the share of wages in national income. g_I measures input growth; the remaining growth in output is attributable to technological progress. This remainder is often called the (Solow) residual, and growth effects of phenomena *other* than labour and capital are quantified by their relation to this residual. Education, to the extent that it enhances productivity of individual workers, should appear in an appropriate measure of g_L, the growth of labour input; its external effects, on technology growth, should then appear a second time, in the residual. At this point, regression analysis is valuable in measuring the overall impact. Roughly, a relation between individual education and individual

---

[6] The method is fully justified if production displays constant returns to scale and each factor is paid its marginal product. Even otherwise, it provides a reasonable accounting device to measure technical progress.

productivity represented by earning power measures 'level effects'—more education raises the level of income—while a cross-country link between residual growth
and education measures potential 'growth effects', as the level of education may
affect the rate of technological progress and output growth.

1. Growth Accounting

Education affects human capital; how should we account for this in growth
accounting?

A first answer suggests that the effective quantity of labour used in production
should be measured in efficiency units, rather than in, say, man-hours. If g_L is the
rate of growth of the effective labour force, it must depend on the rate of growth
in hours worked, say g_n, and the rate of growth of labour quality due to education,
say g_e. The real question here is how the latter should be measured. If an average
graduate is paid twice as much as a school-leaver with O levels, and if it is assumed
that rates of pay reflect marginal productivity, it would be sensible to give graduates twice as much weight as workers with O levels. An approximate means of
making this calculation is offered by the next equation, from Mincer (1974); here,
s is years of schooling, x is years of work and y is income:

$$\log y = 6.20 + 0.107s + 0.081x - 0.0012x^2. \tag{1}$$

Equation (1) suggests that earnings increase by 10 per cent for every year of
schooling, providing ready-made weights for consolidating a labour force built up
from people with varying levels of education. It also draws attention to the fact
that separate corrections must be made for changes to the age structure of the
labour force.[7]

The calculation described above suggests that one type of labour is a perfect substitute for another type of labour: one graduate can always replace two school-leavers
with O levels. This assumption is, to say the least, open to criticism. A slightly different approach, suggested by Mankiw et al. (1992), is as follows. Suppose that skilled
labour, with higher education, and unskilled labour are separate factors, both necessary for production. It is a simple task to extend the growth accounting method to a
three-factor production function, and thus measure growth in labour input as the
weighted sum of growth in these two components. Input growth is now defined to be
$g_I = \lambda_s g_s + \lambda_u g_u + (1 - \lambda_s - \lambda_u)g_K$: the subscripts 's' and 'u' refer to skilled and
unskilled labour respectively and λ are their factor shares. Human capital is then just
another factor in the aggregate production function. Mankiw et al. estimate λ_u and λ_s
to be about one-third each, which provides a useful mnemonic and reconciles the
usual stylisation that λ_L is two-thirds. Importantly, the calculation assumes constant
returns to scale. If factors are paid their marginal product, the social return on human
capital formation is simply the sum of private returns.

---

[7] The estimates presented by Ashenfelter and Krueger (1994) suggest a higher return, of the order of
12–16 per cent per year of schooling, but the difference is not statistically significant.

There have been a number of studies of this sort which have identified the contribution of education to economic growth. Matthews et al. (1982, p. 113) suggest that, between 1873 and 1924, the UK's effective labour force was increasing at 0.5 per cent p.a. due to the spread of education, after a rate of 0.3 per cent p.a. between 1856 and 1873. The rate increased to 0.6 per cent p.a. between 1937 and 1964 and fell back to 0.5 per cent p.a. between 1964 and 1973. Over the whole period from 1856 to 1973, the actual growth in man-hours worked was 0.2 per cent p.a., with a larger population offset by a shorter working week. But the effective labour input increased by 1.2 per cent p.a., with changes in the age, nationality and sex mix contributing 0.2 of a percentage point p.a. and changes in the intensity of work adding another 0.3 of a percentage point p.a. in addition to the effects identified above. Thus, improved education accounted for almost half of the identified growth in the labour input in the UK between 1856 and 1973.

Denison (1967) compares levels of education and their variation in the US with those in eight European countries (Belgium, Denmark, France, Germany, Italy, the Netherlands, Norway and the UK) with a view to understanding why growth rates differed. He concludes educational differences tended to hinder the European countries relative to the US, despite the fact that per capita growth was faster in Europe. Thus output per person employed grew 2.08 percentage points p.a. faster in Germany than in the US, but -0.41 of a percentage point was accounted for by education. The quality of the US labour force improved much faster than that of Germany's.

These observations illustrate that, while education can have an important effect on economic growth, it is not necessarily the most important influence: in Germany, non-residential capital formation accounted for $+0.62$ percentage points p.a. of the difference, and it can easily have an impact in the opposite direction from the overall difference in economic growth. From a public policy perspective, the observation that increased education leads to higher output is no more useful than the observation that investment in manufacturing leads to more manufacturing output. The key policy question is whether investment in education offers a good return to society at large. Growth accounting methods assume that all returns can be privately captured; the social rates of return in Section III measure the accounting rate of return in this situation. For evidence on external effects, we turn to the now considerable body of regression evidence.

2. Regression Methods

In the last 10 years or so, the careful growth accounting method for estimating the effects of education on economic growth has lost favour and been replaced by a much broader-brush regression method. Suppose we observe growth in output and in labour and capital inputs for a range of countries. In regression format, the Solow equation writes as

$$g_{yi} = \lambda_L g_{Li} + \lambda_K g_{Ki} + \gamma_i + u_i, \tag{2}$$

where the subscript *i* refers to a typical country in the sample. This equation can be estimated, and the quantities $\gamma_i + u_i$ yield the productivity growth residual. Clearly, estimation is meaningful only if the residual is uncorrelated with input growth. Many difficulties arise with the measurement of capital and its depreciation. Nevertheless, the approach is useful if we aim to quantify the growth effects of some relevant variables, or policy decisions, by positing that γ_i depends on these. If, for example, it is suspected that education levels have growth effects, the natural hypothesis is $\gamma_i = \alpha + \beta e_i$, with e_i the level of educational attainment.

Quite a large number of such regressions are estimated by, and reported in, Barro and Sala-i-Martin (1995). They conclude that education—and especially publicly funded education—does have significant growth effects. These effects can be attributed to secondary and to higher education levels. An increase in education expenditures by 1 per cent of GDP increases growth rates by 0.15 of a percentage point; in later work, Barro (1998) suggests a yet higher estimate. An extra year of secondary or higher education, which represents (say) a 10 per cent increase in expenditures, will raise growth rates by 1 percentage point per year. It may be useful to compare this with Table 2. A single percentage point of GDP on secondary and higher education is the difference between Italy and the US, and this makes sense from what we imagine about their rates of technological progress; but it is also less than the difference between the UK and Ireland, with Ireland having the higher expenditure rate, which would recommend caution in interpretation. Quantitative reliability apart, these results suggest that the social rate of return may be much larger than the returns we quote.[8]

Benhabib and Spiegel (1994) conduct a careful analysis, measuring the incremental effect of the *level* of education on the rate of technological progress, correcting for the effects of other variables likely to be correlated with it. Their results suggest that the effect of education is indirect: it is associated with greater levels of research and development expenditures, higher rates of innovation and higher rates of new technology adoption. Once these factors are included, the growth effects of education are no longer significant. A quantitative analysis requires measurement of these intermediate inputs, which we have not attempted in this study. The important issue here is that these indirect effects can be priced and need not be pure externalities.

Clearly, the quantitative importance of education externalities is not yet established beyond doubt. They do, probably, exist; the available data present serious difficulties with measurement. Data on years of schooling are typically unavailable and equations were often estimated using the proportion of adults who had attained a particular level as a 'proxy'. Second, in many such regressions, the initial level of educational attainment, rather than its change, is used as an explanatory variable. The meaning of this can only be imagined. Consider a growth regression being carried out for a panel that includes a large number of developing countries, most of which

---

[8] Regression analysis suggests that growth effects are of constant elasticity form, that is, $g = e^\gamma$. This form displays decreasing returns, and hence higher returns at lower levels of investment.

had very little education in 1940. If the proportion attaining a particular level in 1960 is used in place of growth in attainment, the coefficient is very difficult to interpret. Even if enrolment rates stay constant at the 1960 level, the proportion of the working-age population with school education will rise steadily between, say, 1960 and 2000, as uneducated people leave the labour force and are replaced by educated people. Thus, depending on the education policy and the demographic structure, any level of education at the start of the period may be closely correlated with the increase in the education attainment of the labour force during the period of concern. Barro and Sala-i-Martin (1992) do provide information on number of years of education. They show, for example, that, over the period 1960–85, the average number of years of schooling per worker in the OECD rose from 6.5 to 8.6. Using Mincer's value of a 10 per cent increase in output for each extra year of education, this implies that the effective labour force rose by 0.8 per cent p.a. on average as a consequence of improved educational standards, with UK experience slightly below the OECD average, as indeed it is for most educational spending indicators.

Judson (1998) provides further empirical support for the link between education and economic performance and growth, with more detailed analysis. She suggests that the effect of education spending on economic growth depends on how that spending is allocated between primary, secondary and higher education. An efficient allocation equates the returns to the marginal pupil in each of the three types and she is able to calculate the extent to which countries depart from an efficient allocation. Countries that allocate their education spending efficiently find that education supports economic growth; those that are very inefficient find that it does not.

There is never a last word on a topic of this sort; Temple (1999) accurately reflects the unease with empirical analysis of education and growth with the phrase 'there is much work still to be done on the role of human capital'. It is difficult to disagree. Certainly it would be verging on the foolhardy to make policy on the strength of the estimates so far available.

V. RISK AND HIGHER EDUCATION

It is often believed that higher education, or skill acquisition, is risky. The risks cannot be fully diversified. As a result, individuals may underinvest in training. This is an argument partly for providing subsidies to private individuals, which most European governments routinely practise by paying for higher education from the government budget. Partly, it is an argument for a careful design of income taxation, to reduce the associated risks.

The economic argument is a relatively straightforward application of the economics of uncertainty and asymmetric information. Suppose individuals differ in innate ability, which here captures all characteristics relevant to being a more productive skilled worker. Typically, individuals know their own ability better than others do.[9]

---

[9] This may well be disputed, given the battery of tests and examinations that the average person takes until the age of 18 and the volumes of data produced in psychometrics.

Suppose that productivity, employment and incomes depend on this innate ability as well as on pure chance. It is the latter that is risky and potentially diversifiable. Outsiders–including insurance firms, or banks handing out student loans–cannot observe the former *ex ante* and so are unable to distinguish pure bad luck from bad judgement of the person's prospects, *ex post*. Indeed, cheaper loans or insurance may be likely to attract pools of low-ability workers. In response, income insurance is not offered or is offered at prohibitive premiums. Skilled workers must thus bear income risks. If skill premiums are risky, individuals may choose to invest less often, or lower amounts, in human capital than in the presence of income insurance.[10]

There are three steps in the argument, each in need of quantification. Are skill premiums risky and by how much? To what extent are they non-diversifiable? What is the extent of underinvestment?

There are relatively few answers as yet available. First, the question of risk. We know that labour incomes are uncertain; for the argument to hold water, it should be the case that the incomes of skilled workers are *more* uncertain than those of unskilled workers. From our own earlier work, on the British Household Panel Survey, we know that this claim is simply not true. In Dutta et al. (1999), we evaluate a model of income dynamics fitted separately to individuals with and without higher education. It turns out that the variance of incomes for those with higher education is lower than that for the rest, a finding echoed in our study of the General Household Survey described in Section VIII. As skill premiums are positive (about 17 per cent), higher education yields higher return with lower risks, and its coefficient of variation is 0.83, compared with 0.68 for the secondary-school-leavers. These estimates, being based on panel data, partially correct for individual-specific ability effects.[11]

This would suggest that there is not much to worry about. The second question is particularly difficult to answer, as it asks about the extent to which individuals can, and do, insure against income uncertainty; in other words, how large is the benefit from full income insurance, and is this larger for skilled workers? Consumption studies routinely report failures of the permanent income hypothesis (see, e.g. Campbell and Mankiw, 1991). Theoretical or simulation work suggests that the welfare cost of these failures may be quite small, especially with higher income groups, as saving provides a significant method of self-insurance (see, e.g. Sefton et al., 1998). We can thus conjecture that the costs of bearing risk actually fall, rather than rise, with higher education, because average incomes are that much higher.

Finally, does the prospect of risk discourage prospective students from attending university? This may seem an odd question, given our findings that a university

---

[10] This argument adapts the framework of Rothschild and Stiglitz (1976). Spence (1976) suggests that higher education performs an important role in signalling the ability of students, which function is hampered if education is subsidised.

[11] These numbers are for steady-state distributions associated with the estimated non-linear dynamics. Skill premiums are more risky for individuals at the very top of the ability distribution, whose earnings are also much higher.

education may lower the burden of risk. Kodde (1986) estimates the direct impact of perceived risks on the education decisions of Dutch school-leavers. Students were asked to report their likely income prospects if they took a university degree; these were then correlated with the participation decision after correcting for observable characteristics. Notice that risk perceptions are subjective, rather than deduced from observed income variations for different sorts of degrees. Nevertheless, his findings are counter-intuitive: perceived risks do not reduce the decision to participate in higher education. Indeed, coefficient estimates are often positive rather than merely insignificant.[12]

1. Insuring Human Capital

The line of argument pursued above has clear implications for how to pay for higher education. We have seen earlier that the return to higher education accrues privately to the skilled. Certainly these returns are high enough, on average, for higher education, and its expansion, to be fiscally sustainable. In the following, we summarise an argument made by Kodde (1986).

Consider two distinct ways of paying for university education. In the first, a student is asked to pay a fixed charge, which may depend on the nature of the degree taken, is payable out of future income, but does not depend on actual income or labour force participation.[13] This mimics the structure of a pure student loan with each degree separately priced. In the second, individuals pay a graduate tax; the *tax rate* may be degree-specific (e.g. 10 per cent for a medical, law or engineering degree but 2 per cent for Ancient History); the actual amount paid depends on income earned, so that an engineering graduate who works as an (unsuccessful) musician pays relatively little by way of tax, though more than he or she would have paid for a degree in music. The latter method provides income insurance which the former does not. Indeed, efficient tax rates can be set in order to offset fully the extent of underinvestment. The structure now adopted in the UK is a hybrid. Graduates have a fixed amount to repay after graduating and they contribute 9 per cent of their income above £10,000 in each year to repaying their debts. It follows that very low earners and those who do not participate in the labour market do not face any repayments.

VI. EDUCATION AND INEQUALITY

One of the important *political* arguments for state intervention in the provision of education—especially school education—is equity, within and across generations. If education is expensive, only the rich can afford it. The poor remain poor because they do not have access to the quality (and quantity) of education available to the rich.

---

[12] An increase in riskiness may actually increase, rather than decrease, investment; this is true if risk aversion increases with income. Most studies of attitudes towards risk suggest that this is not the case.

[13] Indeed, the poll tax introduced in the late 17th century did have charging rates that depended on qualifications. It proved no more durable than either its predecessor or its successor.

This argument hinges on imperfections in capital markets. If the main cost of education is income forgone, and if extra education raises subsequent earning power by a constant proportion independently of each individual's potential, then the financial return to education will be the same for most individuals. If individuals—parents or their children—are able to borrow, considerations of equity become irrelevant. In light of our earlier results, virtually every parent could deduce that a good education provides a better investment than most physical or financial assets, and certainly pays for bank loans at the usual interest rates they face.

The source of imperfections in the capital market are not difficult to deduce. Children cannot inherit debts; nor can parents underwrite a debt obligation for under-age children. Clearly, this particular difficulty is important for school, rather than university, education. Galor and Zeira (1993) suggest a plausible story of why higher education may be subject to similar borrowing constraints. Typically, banks charge a premium on lending over borrowing rates, partly to account for costs due to non-payment and its prevention. Individuals who face different borrowing and lending rates borrow less often, and the incidence falls on the education of the poor.

Loury (1981) considers an efficiency argument for state intervention in the presence of imperfect capital markets. Imagine that the effect of education on labour productivity and earnings has decreasing marginal productivity. If so, the return on education expenditures is likely to be exceptionally high for the poor, who have little to spend and cannot borrow. To illustrate the point, suppose every parent is willing to spend 5 per cent of his or her income on his or her children's education. Aggregate productivity is higher if 5 per cent of national income is spent uniformly on the education of all children, relative to a situation where every child gets an education costing 5 per cent of their parents' income and no more. A society with fully state-funded schools will have higher growth than one with fully private education. Persson and Tabellini (1994), in yet another growth regression, find empirical support for this hypothesis: state education reduces inequality, and inequality is harmful for growth.

Chiu (1998), following Meade (1937), suggests a different mechanism whereby the cost of education is higher for students from poor than from rich backgrounds. He assumes that the capital market is imperfect, so that individuals cannot smooth out their consumption over their lifetimes. This raises the utility cost of education to a poor student and implies, once more, that underinvestment is more likely for poorer students. Hence, inequality is harmful for growth. It also follows that policies such as student loans will lead to an increased demand for post-compulsory education. Eeckhout (1999) provides a microeconomic model that yields similar conclusions. It is unclear whether the fear raised by Meade—that people will dislike loans because of the resulting loss of control of their lives—has been removed by the expansion of home-ownership and consumer credit.

These analyses of education and inequality have looked at education as though it is a single indivisible commodity. The reality is that quality varies considerably. It is often believed that richer people have better access to education for their children, either by living in areas with better schools or by educating their children privately.

Biggs and Dutta (1999) show that the degree of participation in the private sector is likely to be fairly sensitive to the amount of public spending. If private education is better than state education, the ability to afford it is an important factor leading to a high correlation between parents' incomes and children's incomes. The authors suggest that, with plausible parameters, raising the proportion of GDP spent on education by the state from 5.5 to 6 per cent will reduce the correlation between parents' incomes and children's incomes from 0.6 to 0.2, and produce a much more equal distribution of incomes, reducing standard measures of inequality by almost a half. At the same time, they suggest that there is a U-shaped link between public spending on education and national income. With a high level of public spending, everyone uses the state system and the level of human capital is high. Lower levels of spending reduce the educational quality of those in the public sector but drive more children into the private sector. Initially, the first effect dominates while, for further reductions, the second effect is stronger again and national income begins to rise.

There is, of course, a related issue over the quality of schooling provision and what makes good schools. Do the poor have access to poor education because state education is badly run? We do not give this topic the space that it deserves but limit ourselves to one account (Prais, 1996a). The London Borough of Barking and Dagenham for many years had schools that delivered poor results. In 1990, it decided to improve its schools and joined forces with the National Institute of Economic and Social Research to study school teaching in Zürich. There, as in Barking, there are problem schools teaching children from poor backgrounds in a language that is not their mother tongue. But levels of attainment seemed much higher. Inspectors and teachers from Barking visited Swiss schools to study how the Swiss taught and to develop, from this, new methods of teaching Maths to primary school children. Over the last four years, the attainment levels of Barking children in Maths at age 11 have risen from 10 points below the national average to the national average. This average has also risen sharply over the period. Generalising from one experiment is, of course, dangerous, but teaching teachers how to teach may be cheap compared with some of the other suggested ways of improving school quality.[14]

VII. SOCIAL MOBILITY AND INCOMES

There is a considerable body of evidence suggesting that there is a strong link between the earnings of parents and those of their children and also that the link is greater in the UK than in the US. A certain amount of caution is needed because the range of estimates is fairly wide. But in the UK, the evidence from the National Child Development Survey suggests that 33-year-olds in 1991 inherited about half of the relative earning power of their fathers in 1974 (Dearden et al., 1997).

---

[14] The most notorious of these is reducing class size. Politicians often argue that classes need to be smaller. They do not explain how they know this; the evidence does not support it (Prais, 1996b).

This might be taken as evidence to support the view that inequality persists across generations. In this and the following section, we look at the interaction of this with social mobility and educational attainment (Table 6).

Table 7 shows the Markov matrix for social mobility in Britain. Each entry represents the probability of a male child in full- or part-time work being in a particular socio-economic group as a function of the socio-economic group of his father. The data are taken from the 1991 General Household Survey, the last to record this. The table shows the mean of the log of the income of the people in each socio-economic group, μ_j, and also its standard deviation, σ_j. An interesting comparison can be made with the similar data for 1949 presented by Prais (1955). His figures, reproduced in Table 8, show that (a) there is a much greater chance that the sons of male manual workers will also be manual workers and (b) a much larger proportion of the steady-state population are manual workers. The proportion of sons of male professional

Table 6. *Key to occupations in Tables 7–11*

P	Professional
E	Employer/Manager
NM1	Non-manual, intermediate
NM2	Non-manual, junior
M1	Skilled manual
M2	Semi-skilled manual
M3	Unskilled manual

Table 7. *The social transition matrix in Great Britain, 1991*

Son's occupation	Father's occupation							
	P	E	NM1	NM2	M1	M2	M3	Steady state
P	0.27	0.12	0.11	0.14	0.06	0.05	0.02	0.11
E	0.27	0.33	0.21	0.23	0.17	0.17	0.15	0.23
NM1	0.17	0.17	0.26	0.16	0.11	0.09	0.09	0.15
NM2	0.07	0.12	0.11	0.15	0.07	0.05	0.10	0.09
M1	0.15	0.19	0.19	0.19	0.39	0.39	0.43	0.27
M2	0.06	0.07	0.12	0.12	0.16	0.22	0.15	0.13
M3	0.02	0.01	0.01	0.02	0.05	0.03	0.06	0.02
Mean log income	9.86	9.83	9.59	9.31	9.38	9.08	8.89	
Standard deviation (log income)	0.49	0.54	0.45	0.65	0.48	0.61	0.78	

Note: Key to occupations is given in Table 6.

Source: 1991 General Household Survey.

Table 8. *The social transition matrix in England, 1949*

Son's occupation	Father's occupation							
	P	E	NM1	NM2	M1	M2	M3	Steady state
P	0.39	0.11	0.04	0.02	0.01	0.00	0.00	0.02
E	0.15	0.27	0.10	0.04	0.02	0.01	0.01	0.04
NM1	0.20	0.23	0.19	0.11	0.08	0.04	0.04	0.09
NM2	0.06	0.12	0.19	0.21	0.12	0.09	0.08	0.13
M1	0.14	0.21	0.36	0.43	0.47	0.39	0.36	0.41
M2	0.05	0.05	0.07	0.12	0.17	0.31	0.24	0.18
M3	0.02	0.02	0.06	0.06	0.13	0.16	0.27	0.13

Note: Key to occupations is given in Table 6.

Source: Prais, 1955.

and managerial workers who become manual workers has not changed much. Thus *embourgeoisement* has disproportionately benefited the sons of male manual workers.

The table allows us to estimate how much of the persistence in incomes is a class phenomenon. We assume that the son of a man in socio-economic group i is randomly allocated a socio-economic group, with P_{ij}–the probability of being in group j given a father in group i–being shown in Table 7. Second, we assume that the log income of each person in j is drawn randomly from a normal distribution with mean μ_j and standard deviation σ_j. We set up a panel of 5,000 dynasties, each indexed by the subscript n, and simulate it for 10 generations. By the end of the 10 generations, the social distribution has converged to its steady state and we can link the incomes of those in the 10th generation to the incomes of those in the 9th generation using the regression

$$y_{n,10} = \alpha y_{n,9} + \beta + \varepsilon_n. \tag{3}$$

If the link between father's and son's socio-economic group were the main factor explaining the link between father's and son's income, we would expect to see a value of α approaching that found from the National Child Development Survey. In fact, with the parameters set out above, we find $\alpha = 0.16$. In other words, the link between fathers' and sons' incomes is very much stronger than can be explained simply by the persistence of socio-economic groups. It has the implication that the sons of male managers are better managers, or at least better-paid managers, than the sons of male manual workers. Social class effects summarise about a third of the link between fathers' and sons' earnings.

1. Education and Social Mobility

But, for the component associated with social class, we can examine whether education plays a positive role, using the framework described by Boudon (1973, ch. 4).

Table 9. *Probability of educational attainment by father's socio-economic group*
(male child currently in full-time work)

Son's educational attainment	Father's occupation						
	P	E	NM1	NM2	M1	M2	M3
Degree	0.42	0.22	0.27	0.18	0.07	0.05	0.05
HE < degree	0.15	0.16	0.20	0.18	0.13	0.09	0.05
A levels	0.18	0.17	0.15	0.15	0.13	0.10	0.07
GCSE A–C	0.15	0.21	0.20	0.21	0.19	0.19	0.15
GCSE D–G	0.02	0.07	0.04	0.06	0.11	0.11	0.11
None	0.07	0.18	0.14	0.20	0.38	0.45	0.56

Notes: Key to occupations is given in Table 6. HE = higher education.

Table 10. *Probability of socio-economic group classed by education*

Father's occupation	Son's educational attainment					
	Degree	HE < degree	A levels	GCSE	GCSE A–C	None D–G1
P	0.40	0.14	0.07	0.03	0.01	0.01
E	0.30	0.32	0.29	0.25	0.17	0.14
NM1	0.24	0.19	0.14	0.10	0.04	0.04
NM2	0.02	0.05	0.08	0.10	0.04	0.04
M1	0.03	0.26	0.36	0.40	0.56	0.48
M2	0.00	0.03	0.06	0.11	0.15	0.21
M3	0.00	0.00	0.01	0.02	0.03	0.08

Notes: Key to occupations is given in Table 6. HE = higher education.

In Table 9, we show the probability that a male child currently in full-time work reached a particular level of education. The table shows clearly the well-known fact that the sons of male professionals and managers are much more likely to go to university than the sons of male unskilled workers. We denote by V_{ij} the probability that someone from socio-economic group i reached education level j. Table 10 shows the probability that someone with education level j is in socio-economic group k. We denote this by W_{jk}. If it is the case that males with fathers from socio-economic group i are randomly allocated across educational attainment with probabilities given by V_{ij}, and that people with particular educational attainment are randomly allocated across their own socio-economic group with probability W_{jk}, then it follows that the elements of the Markov matrix linking fathers' and sons' socio-economic groups are given by

$$Q_{ik} = \sum_j V_{ij} W_{jk}. \tag{4}$$

Table 11. *A Synthetic matrix of socio-economic mobility probabilities*

Son's occupation	Father's occupation						
	P	E	NM1	NM2	M1	M2	M3
P	0.21	0.13	0.15	0.12	0.07	0.05	0.04
E	0.28	0.25	0.27	0.25	0.22	0.20	0.19
NM1	0.18	0.14	0.15	0.13	0.10	0.09	0.07
NM2	0.05	0.06	0.05	0.06	0.06	0.05	0.05
M1	0.22	0.32	0.28	0.33	0.40	0.42	0.43
M2	0.05	0.09	0.07	0.09	0.13	0.14	0.16
M3	0.01	0.02	0.02	0.02	0.04	0.04	0.05

Note: Key to occupations is given in Table 6.

The resulting transition matrix is shown in Table 11. A comparison of this with Table 7 indicates the extent to which the link between class and education explains social transition. Plainly, the tables are reasonably similar, but without a clear alternative hypothesis it is difficult to say how good the model is. This comparison of Q_{ik} with the actual transition matrix, P_{ij}, indicates that a model that attributes lack of social mixing to education does a reasonable job in explaining the observed social transition matrix.

It would be too soon to conclude from these results that equal access to the education system would provide equal employment opportunities for all. But the similarity between the synthetic and actual transition matrices does suggest that, if the sons of men in the different social classes had similar educational chances, then the inheritance of social class would be much reduced. There is plainly a great deal to do in this respect, and one might regret the tendency to blame the élite institutions rather than the educational system and cultural environment in general for this. If many state schools leave children with the belief that they will not fit into Oxford or Cambridge Universities, one could reasonably ask 'What is wrong with the school system?' rather than, as the question is usually put, 'What is wrong with the ancient universities?'.

Even though the social transition matrix allows us to identify less than half of the persistence between fathers' and sons' incomes, it does appear that this component of the persistence at least is partly due to the lower take-up of A-level and higher education by the sons of male manual workers. Unless one believes that this reflects hereditary characteristics, it represents a waste of resources that public policy should offset. The rates of return identified in our analysis of OECD data suggest that public action is likely to prove a good investment.

VIII. HIGHER EDUCATION IN THE UK

In fact, considerable progress has been made in expanding the scope of higher education over the last 15 years. In this section, we examine whether, despite this, it still offers a good investment for an individual.

Table 12. *Men's qualifications and earnings*

Age	Degree				A level			
	20–29	30–39	40–49	50–69	20–29	30–39	40–49	50–69
Percentage of male cohort qualified to level shown								
1981	8.2	11.3	6.7	5.8	18.5	10.8	6.2	4.1
1986	12.5	15.2	11.9	9.2	19.6	13.9	6.9[a]	
1991	10.3	13.5	15.7	10.2	20.8	16.1	11.1	7.3
1996	15.3	18.3	21.1	11.6	25.3	17.2	15.3	10.6
Median earnings (median of whole population = 100)								
1981	103	161	218	249	93	123	135	119
1986	103	164	176	183	90	111	120[a]	
1991	116	164	189	183	85	121	122	115
1996	107	167	165	160	81	119	119	116

[a] All men aged 40–69.

Source: General Household Survey.

In 1995, 26.6 per cent of 19- and 20-year-olds were undertaking full-time higher education (with 21.8 per cent at universities). In 1987, the comparable figures were 12.4 per cent of the population with 10.3 per cent in universities and polytechnics.[15] Thus the proportion of the cohort at university has approximately doubled over the period. Table 12 shows how the proportion of working men with the relevant qualifications has changed since 1981. This obviously lags the expansion of the throughput of the higher education system. But, at the same time, we can see a visible tendency for older men to improve their qualifications. The proportion of men aged 40–49 with degrees in 1996 is markedly higher than the proportion of 30- to 39-year-olds 10 years earlier.

While this has happened, expenditure per student has fallen sharply; the increase in student numbers has been achieved with little real increase in overall expenditure. Teaching expenditure per student in 1985–86 was £8,470 per student in the then universities. In polytechnics and other local authority colleges, it was £4,250. In 1990, the figure for universities was £7,680 and in the polytechnics (excluding other local authority colleges) it was £4,810. In 1996–97, the expenditure per student was £4,790. All these figures are in 1998 prices. The shift from student grants to loans yields an additional saving. Expenditure on all maintenance grants reached £840 million in 1985–86 (in current prices) and rose only to £1,250 million in 1996–97 despite the increase in student numbers. With the almost complete abolition of higher education maintenance grants from Autumn 1999, this is set to fall to around £300 million. Loans to students are still treated as expenditure in the public accounts, so these data are misleading as to the true extent of student support.

---

[15] The polytechnics and universities were merged in 1992.

Table 13. *Classification of subject groups*

Group A	Group B	Group C
Subjects allied to medicine	Engineering	Biological sciences
Agriculture	Architecture etc.	Humanities
Physical sciences	Mass communication	
Maths and computing	Education	
Social studies		
Business studies		
Design		
General courses		

Table 12 also shows median earnings of men in each age-group relative to median male earnings in the economy as a whole. The data are shown for both graduates and A-level non-graduates with no other higher education qualification. These figures do not give the impression that graduate salaries have been depressed by the expansion of graduate numbers for younger workers, although they have fallen for men over 40. The data for A-level workers may indicate that their position has worsened relative to the median, raising the prospect that over-supply of A-level non-graduates has damaged the market.

A fuller perspective can be obtained by looking at the rates of return to university degrees. We estimate the return to graduates in 1995, as compared with those with two or more A levels who leave the full-time education system at that point. The basic equation we estimate relates earnings to educational attainment. We look at whether the person has any GCSE grades A–C or equivalent, and take account of the number. We also identify people who have two or more A levels, but no degree, who have below degree-level higher education and we distinguish those who gained their degrees by attending universities or polytechnics. The equation is estimated only for people in full-time work, and therefore indicates the benefit of a degree for someone who works full-time. A preliminary run suggested that we could consolidate non-medical degree subjects into the three groups shown in Table 13, with medicine as a fourth subject. Each of the dummy variables enters in two forms, as a level effect and multiplied by the age of the individual,[16] but in the regression we present, we have suppressed insignificant variables; this also meant that the distinction between universities and polytechnics was not maintained. We explored a role for dummies multiplied by age squared but did not find any. Apart from the fact that qualification dummies are used instead of years of study, the equation has the form suggested by Willis (1986). We also tested whether men under 30 earned significantly less than the model predicted, as a means of examining whether the expansion in graduate output since 1985 had

---

[16] The use of both level and age-interactive dummies means that it does not matter a great deal whether the equation is in terms of age or work experience.

depressed wages. There was no evidence of this: a dummy was positive but insignificant. The equation is estimated by ordinary least squares. Data limitations mean that it is not possible to allow either for sample selection issues or for endogeneity of education choices.

While the equation presented in Table 14 gives 'plausible' results, there is one aspect in which it is very peculiar. It does not show the heteroscedasticity that one would expect. If earnings of individuals followed something close to a random walk, then the variance of the residuals should be a function of age. If the effect of a degree on the earnings of individuals is uncertain, then the variance of the earnings of graduates should be higher than that of those of non-graduates, unless there is an adequate negative correlation between the effect of A levels on earnings and the effect of a degree. The effect of uncertainty on investment in higher education is as important as on any other aspect of investment. But without a satisfactory identification of the effects of uncertainty, our assessment of its importance below has to be conjectural.

Table 14. *The determinants of men's earnings in 1995*

	Coefficient	Standard error	t statistic
Age	0.1030	0.0051	20.3
Age^2	-0.0012	0.0001	-19.3
ZGCSE × Age	-0.0022	0.0007	-3.1
NGCSE	-0.0156	0.0086	-1.8
NGCSE × Age	0.0009	0.0003	3.5
ALev × Age	0.0038	0.0009	4.4
OHE × Age	0.0039	0.0006	6.7
DegA	0.1043	0.0393	2.7
DegC	-0.2044	0.0752	-2.7
Med × Age	0.0166	0.0031	5.3
Deg × Age	0.0054	0.0010	5.2
Univ	0.1146	0.0384	3.0
Constant	7.4887	0.1007	74.4

$R^2 = 0.35$
Standard error $= 0.45$

Dependent variable: log of annual equivalent earnings.
3,191 observations, General Household Survey 1995–96.

Key:
ZGCSE $= 1$ if no GCSE grade A–C exams or equivalent,
NGCSE $=$ number of GCSE grade A–C exams or equivalent,
ALev $= 1$ if two or more A levels,
OHE $= 1$ if two or more A levels and higher education below degree level,
DegA $= 1$ if a degree from Group A (Table 13),
DegC $= 1$ if a degree from Group C (Table 13),
Med $= 1$ if a medical degree,
Deg $= 1$ if any degree,
Univ $= 1$ if last place of full-time education was university or polytechnic.

There is a further aspect of the regression that we should mention. Earlier studies (Weale, 1992) suggested that polytechnic[17] graduates were at a substantial income disadvantage relative to university graduates, and this was borne out by the estimation of a similar regression for 1985 (available from the authors on request). That showed a difference of 11 per cent in the average earnings of the two groups. By 1995, that difference had fallen to a statistically insignificant 3 per cent, and we restricted that to zero in the equation presented. Thus, as compared with 1985, it looks as though the income disadvantage of having been to a polytechnic has more or less disappeared.

Finally, we should draw attention to a matter the regression cannot examine. As mentioned above, the General Household Survey stopped asking people about their father's social class in 1992. We have therefore been unable to identify effects of background on earning power. However, we note that Bennett et al. (1992) find, from data for the mid-1980s, that the return to higher education is bigger for children from disadvantaged backgrounds. This is consistent with a view that, without the benefits of university education, children are handicapped by their background, but that university goes some way towards levelling the playing field. The fact that Weale (1992) found, looking at 1980 graduates six years after graduation, that attendance at grammar and public schools gave an income advantage of 5 and 15 per cent respectively over attendance at comprehensive schools suggests that universities did not level the field completely. It would be interesting to know whether this is still true. In the mean time, there is a risk that the regression suffers from an omitted 'background' variable.

1. Private Rates of Return

From the equation in Table 14, we can calculate private and then social rates of return for higher education. These are, of course, subject to some of the reservations expressed in Section III. But we calculate the earnings profiles for average male graduates and A-level non-graduates, both with five grade A–C GCSEs, assuming that the non-graduates start work at age 18 and the graduates at age 21. In both cases, we assume the 1995 tax and National Insurance structure and calculate the figures for a single man. If we denote by $y_t(A)$ the expected income of a non-graduate with A levels at age t and by $y_t(D)$ the comparable figure for a graduate (with loans treated as income and fees and repayments treated as expenditure), then the rate of return is the value of r that equates the present values of the streams of earnings, satisfying

$$\sum_{t=18,64} \frac{y_t(A)-y_t(D)}{(1+r)^{t-18}} = 0. \tag{5}$$

---

[17] Polytechnics became 'new universities' in 1992.

This can usually be found by iteration. However, we have to make some assumption about the method of student support available. We assume that each student receives a government loan of £3,635 p.a. while a student. Of this, £1,000 is used to pay fees and £2,635 provides 'income'. There is no real interest on the loan and it is repaid out of salary after graduation. The graduate pays 9 per cent of gross salary over £10,000 until the loan is repaid. These figures are 1999 values. We assume that, had the current system been in operation in 1995, the amounts would have been adjusted by the movement in average earnings (taken from the New Earnings Survey) in 1995 relative to 1998. Thus the parameters of the loan and fee structure are multiplied by 336.3/384.5.

However, we also assume that students have both to work while studying and to borrow in order to support themselves. We assume commercial borrowing of £2,000 p.a. combined with earnings of £1,000 p.a. in 1995 values. It is assumed that the commercial borrowing is funded at a real rate of interest of 7 per cent p.a. and that the graduate is expected to repay it over five years after graduating. This is assumed to be an outcome imposed by a lender rather than the consequence of optimal saving by the graduate. This has the effect of raising the return to the degree provided it is above the commercial rate and depressing it if it is already below the commercial rate. Rates of return calculated assuming that the model parameters are correct are shown in the first row of Table 15.

The calculation needs to take account of the effects of uncertainty. There are two aspects to this. The first is that the coefficients from the regression equation are uncertain. Since the rate of return is a non-linear function of the regression coefficients, the expected value of the rate of return cannot be calculated simply by setting

Table 15. *Private rates of return to a degree gained through full-time study*

| | Degree[a] | | |
	Group A	Group B	Group C
Rate of return estimated from model (% p.a.)	16.2	9.9	−11.7
Welfare gain	36.3%	19.8%	−26.7%
Rate of return with parameter uncertainty (% p.a.)	16.3	9.7	−3.0[b]
Standard error	2.5	2.8	8.5
Welfare gain	36.0%	19.3%	−27.3%
Number of failed cases	−	−	467
Rate of return with parameter & individual uncertainty (% p.a.)	17.1	10.4	0[b]
Standard error	7.6	7.1	10.0
Welfare gain	35.3%	18.3%	−28.2%
Number of failed cases	4	36	442
Years to repay loan	6.1	6.9	8.3

[a] For composition of groups, see Table 13.
[b] These figures should be interpreted in the light of the comments in the text.

the regression coefficients to their expected values. In any case, it is desirable to give some indication of the precision with which the rate of return is estimated.

We denote the vector of regression coefficients by $\mathbf{b}$. The vector $\mathbf{c}^D(t)$ is the value of the exogenous variables used to calculate the forecast income of a graduate; $\mathbf{c}^A(t)$ is the analogous vector for an A-level worker. In other words,

$$y_t^D - y_t^A = \exp(\{\mathbf{c}^D(t)' - \mathbf{c}^A(t)'\}\mathbf{b}).\tag{6}$$

We consider a panel of 1,000 individuals, indexed by the subscript k. Each individual faces a set of parameters $\mathbf{b}_k$, where $\mathbf{b}_k = \mathbf{b} + \varepsilon_k$ with $\varepsilon_k \sim N(0, V(\mathbf{b}))$, so that, for each individual,

$$y_{kt}^D - y_{kt}^A = \exp(\{\mathbf{c}^D(t)' - \mathbf{c}^A(t)'\}\mathbf{b}_k).\tag{7}$$

These are earnings gross of taxation and we have to adjust to after-tax figures in order to calculate the net return as well as taking account of the various loans needed for study. The rate of return for the kth individual is calculated from the individual-specific earnings differentials. The expected rate of return and its standard deviation are calculated as the mean and standard deviation of r_k. These figures do not take any account of any postgraduate training received. This is unlikely to be an important bias because the return to the typical postgraduate course has historically been very low (Weale, 1992). Nor do the figures take account of the effect of education level on employment rates and on labour market participation. This may be important, particularly when negative rates of return are found, if graduates are less likely to take early retirement than A-level workers.

The second question concerns the uncertainty that affects the individual student arising from the difference between average log income and actual log income. Here, as noted above, we have been unable to identify the incremental uncertainty associated with a degree. The overall standard deviation of log income in the regression in 1995 was 0.45 but we were unable to identify any extra uncertainty associated with a degree. We also present results assuming that a degree course adds a random term with a standard deviation of 0.1 in addition to the parametric effects and that this persists through the individual's working life. Thus, in this case, for the kth individual,

$$y_{kt}^D - y_{kt}^A = \exp(\{\mathbf{c}^D(t)' - \mathbf{c}^A(t)'\}\mathbf{b}_k + \eta_k),\tag{8}$$

where $\eta_k \sim N(0, 0.1)$.

Table 15 quotes figures for different types of degree calculated (a) using the estimated parameters of the model, (b) after taking account of the parametric uncertainty, and (c) after compounding the effects of parametric uncertainty with those of individual uncertainty. We do not present figures for the return to medical degrees; these obviously need to take account of postgraduate training as well as degree courses. The figures for the first two groups are reasonably robust to the precise choice of variables included in the regression.

However, the rate of return is calculated iteratively and, typically, if the return to a degree is very poor, the solution method can fail to converge. We have reported the failure rate in our sample of 1,000 synthetic graduates in each subject group, and it can be seen that it is high for the Group C degrees. This in turn means that figures for Group C with uncertainty are calculated from only the more successful cases. The figures for Groups A and B suggest that the biases arising in the calculation of the rates of return from the model parameters alone are not very great, but the indication of the uncertainty surrounding them is very important.

We complement this analysis of uncertainty with one in terms of utility, which therefore takes account of risk aversion. We make the simplifying assumption that utility is a function of income and not of expenditure. This fails to take account of the benefits of consumption smoothing, but the scope to which the latter is possible depends in part on access to credit markets. We assume that $U(z_{tk}) = - z_{tk}^{-2}$, where z_{tk} is the disposable resources of the individual in each period after taxation and fees and after any loan repayments. Loans drawn down are included in z_{tk} at the appropriate point. The lifetime utility, V_k, of the kth individual is calculated by summing using a discount rate of 5 per cent p.a. $V_k = \sum_{t=18}^{64} U(z_{tk}) \times 1.05^{t-18}$. We can calculate this both for someone who has only A levels and for a graduate to show the welfare gain from a degree. It can be seen that the welfare gain figures in Table 15, which reflect expected utility, suggest that this is affected only slightly by uncertainty, perhaps explaining why Kodde (1986) is unable to find negative effects. This in turn leads us to speculate that, if larger loans were available to students in Groups A and B, the gearing effect on raising welfare would more than offset the extra uncertainty. Expected welfare would be increased and more students would be drawn to higher education.

2. Social Rates of Return

In Table 16, we show estimates of the social rates of return to the three types of degree. These are calculated by comparing A-level and graduate salaries gross of tax. The cost of producing a graduate is assumed to be £4,790 p.a., which we adjusted to 1995 price levels, plus earnings forgone during study. These are the earnings of an A-level worker less the £1,000 p.a. the student is assumed to earn

Table 16. *Social rates of return to a degree gained through full-time study*

	Degree[a]		
	Group A	Group B	Group C
Parameter uncertainty	11.4	7.5	−3.5[b]
Standard error	1.3	2.1	9.1
Number of failed cases	−	−	436

[a] For composition of groups, see Table 13.
[b] This figure should be interpreted in the light of the comments on estimating the rate of return.

while studying. Social rates of return are lower than private rates but, except for Group C graduates, they are very respectable.

Why, indeed, does the rate of return seem to remain good despite the increase in the graduate population? Mason (1996 and 1998) finds, from detailed case studies, that there is some evidence of graduate underemployment and that there are also quality concerns about students from less-good departments in both old and new universities. But Machin (1998) argues that the pattern of demand has, overall, shifted in favour of skilled workers, allowing overall differentials to be maintained, and Riley and Young (1999) support this conclusion. This may explain why reasonable rates of return have been maintained. Perhaps, following Arrow and Capron (1959), we can conclude that employers' attitudes to graduates are a bit like the old complaints about the shortage of domestic servants: they would like to pay less than they have to for the labour that they do hire and they blame an inability to recruit on a shortage instead of on an unwillingness to pay market rates. On the other hand, the anecdotal evidence could be an indicator that, with the most recent graduates, oversupply is starting to appear and we may be in the early stages of a period in which high returns lead to an eventual oversupply followed by a period of poor returns.

IX. PROSPECTS

There are two important questions raised by this analysis. First of all, is there a case for raising university participation further? Second, might one expect it to rise even if charges on students are increased? The answer to both these questions is probably yes. The current private rates of return are such as to make higher education an attractive investment. However, further work is probably needed to assess the benefits of higher education for more marginal students, and this probably requires another survey of graduates comparable with the 1986 survey of 1980 graduates. Alternatively, it may be possible to put together a sample of reasonable size by merging a number of General Household Surveys in order to establish whether we are in the early stages of the price–quantity fluctuations that can result from oversupply.

But, subject to this qualification, raising the tuition fee to £2,000 p.a. would reduce rates of return to higher education by less than 1 percentage point p.a. In view of this, it does seem difficult to justify the continuing subsidy to the private sector implicit in the difference between the cost of a student and the fee charged.

The theoretical work identifies a real concern that charging for education can deter children from poor backgrounds and thus perpetuate inequality. The student loan scheme is intended to address this inequality, but there must be a question about whether it does so adequately while it is inadequate to support a student and provide fees. On the other hand, the evidence of very high returns to students from disadvantaged backgrounds provides an incentive to study that is absent from the models showing that inequality can be perpetuated. But it would be difficult to rely on this alone, since we do not know whether there is an additional element of pre-selection involved here. It may be that only the most determined children of manual workers go to university and that, even without a university education, they might be able to do reasonably well in the labour market. Our rate-of-return calculations do not identify this, but they do suggest that, in subjects with good rates of return, the effect of uncertainty on the expected welfare gain is not likely to be very large.

There is a separate question concerning the functioning of the universities. While this survey article has not really addressed the question of how universities should be funded, there is nevertheless an important comparison that should be made. In the UK, student participation has increased despite higher charges. This is indicative of a combination of an easing of rationing and an increased demand for graduates. But there is stiff opposition to the notion that universities should be able to set their own fee levels. At the same time, at least in economics, it is clear that universities are having trouble in attracting at least British teaching staff. In the US over the last 10 years or so, the first-division universities have increased their charges as the costs of maintaining good research faculties have risen. But they have also increased the availability of scholarships to students from modest backgrounds. Demand for places with them has increased, despite the increase in fees; the perceived higher returns to university education have meant that the process has allowed the universities to increase their revenues without feeling a loss of quality of the student body (Clotfelter, 1996).

Given this example, the question must arise of whether British universities should be allowed to come to their own judgement about the appropriate balance between teaching and research and how best to deliver this. For example, instead of an effective prohibition on universities from charging top-up fees, the Minister might require the universities to follow the US example and offer a suitable range of scholarships as a condition for receipt of public funds. The US experience suggests that this would allow the best universities to maintain or enhance their international reputations for research while at the same time retaining a vibrant undergraduate community.

REFERENCES

Arrow, K. and Capron, W. (1959), 'Dynamic shortages and price rises: the engineer-scientist case', *Quarterly Journal of Economics*, vol. 73, pp. 292–308.

Ashenfelter, O. and Krueger, A. (1994), 'Estimates of the returns to schooling from a new sample of twins', *American Economic Review*, vol. 84, pp. 1157–73.

Barro, R. (1998), *The Determinants of Economic Growth*, Cambridge, MA: MIT Press.

—— and Sala-i-Martin, X. (1992), 'Convergence', *Journal of Political Economy*, vol. 100, pp. 223–51.

—— and —— (1995), *Economic Growth*, Cambridge, MA: Harvard University Press.

Baumol, W., Blackman, S. B. and Wolff, E. (1989), *Productivity and American Leadership: The Long View*, Cambridge, MA: MIT Press.

Benabou, R. (1996), 'Equity and efficiency in human capital investment: the local connection', *Review of Economic Studies*, vol. 63, pp. 237–64.

Benhabib, J. and Spiegel, M. (1994), 'The role of human capital in economic development: evidence from aggregate cross-country data', *Journal of Monetary Economics*, vol. 34, pp. 143–73.

Bennett, R., Glennester, H. and Nevison, D. (1992), 'Investing in skill: to stay or not to stay on', *Oxford Review of Economic Policy*, vol. 8, no. 2, pp. 130–45.

Biggs, M. and Dutta, J. (1999), 'The distributional effects of education expenditures', *National Institute Economic Review*, no. 169, pp. 68–77.

Blackburn, M. and Neumark, D. (1995), 'Are OLS estimates of return to schooling biased downward?', *Review of Economics and Statistics*, vol. 77, pp. 217–29.

Blundell, R., Dearden, L., Goodman, A. and Reed, H. (1997), *Higher Education, Employment and Earnings in Britain*, London: Institute for Fiscal Studies.

Boudon, R. (1973), *Mathematical Structures of Social Mobility*, Amsterdam: Elsevier.

Campbell, J. Y. and Mankiw, N. G. (1991), 'The response of consumption to income: a cross-country investigation', *European Economic Review*, vol. 35, pp. 723–56.

Chiu, W. H. (1998), 'Income inequality, human capital accumulation, and economic perform-ance', *Economic Journal*, vol. 108, pp. 44–59.

Clotfelter, C. (1996), *Buying the Best: Cost Escalation in Elite Higher Education*, Princeton: Princeton University Press.

Dearden, L., Machin, S. and Reed, H. (1997), 'Intergenerational mobility in Britain', *Economic Journal*, vol. 107, pp. 47–66.

Denison, E. (1967), *Why Growth Rates Differ*, Washington, DC: Brookings Institution.

Dutta, J., Sefton, J. and Weale, M. (1999), 'Income dynamics in the United Kingdom', National Institute of Economic and Social Research, Discussion Paper no. 116.

Eeckhout, J. (1999), 'Educational mobility: the effect on efficiency and distribution', *Economica*, vol. 66, pp. 317–34.

Fevre, R., Rees, G. and Gorard, S. (1999), 'Some sociological alternatives to human capital theory and their implications for research on post-compulsory education and training', *Journal of Education and Work*, vol. 12, pp. 117–40.

Galor, O. and Zeira, J. (1993), 'Income distribution and macroeconomics', *Review of Economic Studies*, vol. 60, pp. 35–52.

Harmon, C. and Walker, I. (1995), 'Estimates of the economic return to schooling in the UK', *American Economic Review*, vol. 84, pp. 1278–86.

Judson, R. (1998), 'Economic growth and investment in education: how allocation matters', *Journal of Economic Growth*, vol. 3, pp. 337–59.

Kodde, D. (1986), 'Uncertainty and the demand for education', *Review of Economics and Statistics*, vol. 68, pp. 460–7.

Loury, G. C. (1981), 'Intergenerational transfers and the distribution of earnings', *Econometrica*, vol. 49, pp. 843–67.

Machin, S. (1998), 'Recent shifts in wage inequality and the wage returns to education in Britain', *National Institute Economic Review*, no. 166, pp. 87–96.

Mankiw, G., Romer, D. and Weil, D. (1992), 'A contribution to the empirics of economic growth', *Quarterly Journal of Economics*, vol. 107, pp. 407–37.

Mason, G. (1996), 'Graduate utilisation in British industry: the initial impact of mass higher education', *National Institute Economic Review*, no. 156, pp. 93–103.

— (1998), *Change and Diversity: The Challenge Facing Chemistry Higher Education*, London: Royal Society for Chemistry.

Matthews, R. C. O., Feinstein, C. H. and Odling-Smee, J. (1982), *British Economic Growth: 1856–1973*, Oxford: Clarendon Press.

Meade, J. (1937), *Economic Analysis and Policy*, Oxford: Oxford University Press.

Mincer, J. (1974), *Schooling, Experience, and Earnings*, New York: National Bureau of Economic Research.

Mincer, J. (1994), 'Investment in US education and training', National Bureau of Economic Research, Discussion Paper no. 4844.

OECD (1998), *Education at a Glance*, Paris: Organisation for Economic Co-operation and Development.

Persson, T. and Tabellini, G. (1994), 'Is inequality harmful for growth?', *American Economic Review*, vol. 84, pp. 600–21.

Prais, S. (1955), 'Measuring social mobility', *Journal of the Royal Statistical Society*, Series A, vol. 118, pp. 56–66.

—— (1996a), 'Class-size and learning: the Tennessee experiment', *Oxford Review of Education*, vol. 22, pp. 399–414.

—— (1996b), 'Reform of mathematical education in primary schools: the experiment in Barking and Dagenham', *National Institute Economic Review*, no. 157, pp. 3–8.

Psacharopoulos, G. (1993), 'Returns to education: a global update', World Bank, Policy Research Paper no. 1067.

Riley, R. and Young, G. (1999), 'The skill bias of technological change in the UK', National Institute of Economic and Social Research, mimeo.

Rothschild, M. and Stiglitz, J. (1976), 'Equilibrium in competitive insurance markets: an essay in the economics of imperfect information', *Quarterly Journal of Economics*, vol. 90, pp. 630–49.

Sefton, J., Dutta, J. and Weale, M. (1998), 'Pension finance in a calibrated model of savings and income distribution', *National Institute Economic Review*, no. 166, pp. 97–107.

Solow, R. M. (1957), 'Technical change and the aggregate production function', *Review of Economics and Statistics*, vol. 39, pp. 312–20.

Spence, M. (1976), *Market Signalling*, Cambridge, MA: MIT Press.

Temple, J. (1999), 'The new growth evidence', *Journal of Economic Literature*, vol. 37, pp. 112–56.

Weale, M. (1992), 'The benefits of higher education: a comparison of universities and polytechnics', *Oxford Review of Economic Policy*, vol. 8, no. 2, pp. 35–47.

Willis, R. (1986), 'Wage determinants: a survey and re-interpretation of human capital earnings functions', in O. Ashenfelter and R. Layard (eds), *Handbook of Labour Economics*, vol. I, Amsterdam: North-Holland.

5

Unemployment and Workers' Compensation Programmes: Rationale, Design, Labour Supply and Income Support

I. INTRODUCTION

Social insurance programmes are costly, making up the largest single component of government expenditures in many countries. These programmes are also not without controversy. Different sets of commentators view them as encouraging sloth, on the one hand, or necessary to prevent severe deprivation, on the other hand. Both sets of commentators are partly right. In this paper, I will focus on unemployment insurance (UI) programmes which provide compensation for the unemployed and workers' compensation (WC) insurance for those injured or made ill by their employment.

I focus on UI and WC programmes because the other main components of social insurance—retirement and health benefits—have been covered in earlier chapters in this book.[2] UI and WC are also of interest in their own right for several reasons. Since the programmes are for able-bodied individuals or those who are generally expected to return to work, the trade-offs between insurance and moral hazard are potentially more pronounced than in the case of other programmes. While the costs of UI and WC are lower than those for retirement or health programmes, they are still very large. As is discussed below, UI and WC expenditures are typically several per cent of GDP.

UI and WC share many attributes. Both programmes are primarily for workers who are temporarily unable to work. Both programmes condition benefits on

The author would like to thank Alan Auerbach, Bertil Holmlund, Alan Krueger, Costas Meghir and seminar participants at the Institute for Fiscal Studies and University of California, Berkeley for their comments and Bradley Heim for outstanding research assistance.

[1] Department of Economics and Institute for Policy Research, Northwestern University and NBER.
[2] See papers in this volume by Banks and Emmerson on public and private pensions and Propper on health spending in the UK.

past earnings and generally discontinue benefits once a worker returns to work. Because of these basic similarities, the dimensions on which the programmes differ are informative in several ways for both policy-makers and researchers. For policy-makers, these differences often reveal the differing objectives and constraints of the two programmes. In other cases, the differences provide alternative models for policy-makers to follow, since the current programme structures have partly come about through historical accident. For researchers, the differences in how the programmes have been studied often suggest new approaches and topics, as researchers have often acted opportunistically given handy data and have not analysed key issues.

I begin by discussing the economic rationales for government involvement in these areas. The natural beginning point is the market imperfections that justify government involvement, and these are explored in Section II. I then describe, in Sections III and IV, the design of the US programmes in detail and provide some more limited information on the programmes in other countries.

I also discuss the main distortion generated by the programmes—namely, the effect of the programmes on labour supply.[3] One may ask, 'Why can't the labour supply parameters estimated in the voluminous labour economics literature just be plugged into the social insurance formulae?'. In my view, a separate consideration of the labour supply effects of UI and WC is justified for at least three reasons. First, the labour supply parameters estimated in the public finance and labour economics literatures may not apply to social insurance programmes because people are imperfectly informed as to the rules of the programmes, or because the preferences of those who are eligible for social insurance programmes may be different from those of the population at large. For example, a severe disability may change the way an individual trades off labour for leisure. More generally, the people who are on the margin of going on a social insurance programme are likely to have different preferences from the wider population.

Second, the labour supply elasticities estimated in the labour economics literature span a huge range. Literature surveys such as Pencavel (1986) and Killingsworth (1983) find wide dispersion in estimates of income and substitution effects. Fuchs et al. (1998) also find that there is little agreement among economists on the magnitude of labour supply elasticities. A major shortcoming in the broader labour supply literature is that it is difficult to identify exogenous changes in wages or incomes that can be used to estimate labour supply responses. The variation in social insurance programmes may provide natural experiments with which to estimate labour supply parameters and test the relevance of labour supply models.

Third, the design of social insurance programmes raises theoretical labour supply issues that are not often dealt with in the labour economics literature. For example, most of the labour supply literature deals with how workers adjust their number of hours worked per week, whereas the incentives of social insurance

---

[3] There are other distortions that should be mentioned, such as the effect of UI on precautionary saving. See, for example, Engen and Gruber (2001).

programmes often affect the decision of whether to participate at all in the labour force.[4] In addition, programmes such as UI influence job search intensity, which does not figure in standard labour supply models. I will discuss the theoretical effects of UI and WC on labour supply as well as the empirical literature. While the literature is most extensive for the US evidence, I will bring in empirical evidence from several other countries.

In Section V, I discuss the main positive effect of UI and WC. The classic rationale for the programmes is the short-run support they provide for those who are temporarily without the ability to work. This income support may prevent the consumption of recipients from dropping sharply as their incomes fall. There are also potential long-term consequences of this short-term assistance, as discussed in Section VI. Support during unemployment may allow the unemployed to find better jobs and, in the case of WC, may allow the injured to recover more fully from their injuries.

I should emphasise that this is not the first survey of UI and WC. There are excellent prior surveys of the effects of unemployment insurance[5] and the effects of workers' compensation.[6]

II. ECONOMIC RATIONALE FOR THE PROGRAMMES

1. Unemployment Insurance

The main rationale for UI is that it provides insurance for workers who may lose their jobs, which may cause a substantial loss in earnings for these individuals.[7] This rationale is appropriate for workers whose unemployment is unexpected, but not for individuals with frequent and predictable spells of unemployment, say in seasonal jobs. If UI is a desirable benefit, this argument does not explain why government-provided or mandated benefits are necessary. A possible explanation is that adverse selection may lead firms not to offer insurance, since it would attract people likely to leave their jobs. This reason is probably not central in a UI system like the USA's, under which only job losers are eligible for benefits, not those who quit or are fired.

---

[4] A reason for the disproportionate effect of social insurance programmes on the work/non-work decision is that the programmes typically do not proportionally change the return to work. Rather, they often provide a large benefit at zero hours of work and high implicit tax rates over a range of low, but positive, hours. For UI and WC, the tax rate is often near or even above 100 per cent.

[5] See Hamermesh (1977), Welch (1977), Danziger et al. (1981), Gustman (1982), Atkinson (1987), Atkinson and Micklewright (1990), Devine and Kiefer (1991), Anderson and Meyer (1993) and Holmlund (1998) for surveys of the UI literature.

[6] See Ehrenberg (1988), Krueger (1990a), Moore and Viscusi (1990) and Kniesner and Leeth (1995) for surveys of the WC literature.

[7] For a good analysis of UI as insurance for workers, see Baily (1977). Brown and Kaufold (1988) have argued that this insurance will increase human capital investment by workers. An empirical investigation of the insurance value of UI is in Neill (1989).

Probably a more important explanation for government UI provision is adverse selection at the firm level. If private insurance companies sold UI to firms, the insurance companies would also suffer from the adverse selection problem, as those firms most prone to unemployment would be the most likely to buy the insurance. This difficulty does not prevent private companies from offering medical insurance and workers' compensation insurance. However, the size of UI losses due to the lay-off of a large fraction of a firm's workforce may greatly exceed the size of losses from medical insurance or workers' compensation.

Perhaps the most compelling reason for publicly provided UI is that unemployment risks are not easily diversifiable for private insurance companies. Unlike workplace injuries, claims for UI tend to be concentrated in recessions. A severe recession could involve claims of tens of billions of dollars over a few years, which would financially strain and potentially bankrupt private insurance companies.

Another argument for government-mandated UI that is more difficult to evaluate is that subsidising job search by the unemployed may increase societal welfare. UI may increase search activity, and search activity may increase the probability of a good job match. This argument must rest on a reason for the value of the job match to society being different from that to the individual searching for a job and the firm seeking employees.

The other common rationale for UI is that it provides an automatic stabiliser in downturns, by maintaining the purchasing power of the unemployed. This argument requires that the timing of the benefit payments and tax charges be counter-cyclical. Hamermesh (1977) describes several studies of this effect and suggests that it is a crucial role of UI. However, the importance of this argument depends crucially on the true character of business cycles. If cycles are due to 'shocks' to technology, as suggested by real business cycle theorists, then UI will reduce welfare by decreasing efficiency.[8] If cycles are due partly to insufficient aggregate demand, then the increases in demand during downturns provided by UI may increase welfare.

A final reason for UI might be income redistribution. If this goal is to be attained, it requires that the actual programme be implemented in a way that distributes more benefits net of taxes to lower income groups.[9]

2. Workers' Compensation

To understand the rationale for WC, it is useful to think first about information, wages and compensating differentials in an abstract economy. Consider a simplified world where labour markets are competitive, workers have perfect information about job risks and there are no mobility barriers. Then there would be fully compensating wage differentials for job risks, and firms would offer the optimal wage

---

[8] See Christiano (1984) for a discussion of such effects.
[9] This issue is briefly discussed in Section V.

rates and levels of injury reduction such that the marginal cost of injury reduction would equal the marginal benefit from injury reduction.

Abstracting from worker responses, if WC is introduced with no administrative costs and at a price equal to firm benefit payouts (and benefits at an amount needed to compensate workers for injuries), then we would see no change in firm injury prevention and a fall in wages equal to the value of the insurance to the worker.

The main argument for WC is probably that workers do not have perfect information about job risks. The most glaring example is occupational diseases such as asbestosis, where the dangers have only recently become known. This lack of knowledge is not surprising in such a case, given the long exposure period and the lengthy latency period before the onset of the disease. Nevertheless, this example illustrates the difficulty workers have in being fully knowledgeable regarding job risks. A second argument for a government-mandated WC system is that by making injury compensation routine (and limiting firms' liabilities), such a system reduces worker uncertainty and also reduces administrative and dispute costs relative to an ad hoc system of legal remedies.

III. UNEMPLOYMENT INSURANCE: PROGRAMME FEATURES AND LABOUR SUPPLY EFFECTS

Unemployment insurance is one of the most extensively studied government programmes in the USA and elsewhere. As mentioned earlier, there are several excellent prior surveys of UI.

1. Main Features of US Unemployment Insurance Programmes

UI programmes differ sharply across states in the USA due to the provisions of the Social Security Act of 1935, which created the current system and gave states great latitude in designing their programmes. State UI programmes differ in the earnings required for eligibility, the level of benefits (the replacement rate, the minimum and maximum benefit), the potential duration of benefits and other parameters. Table 1 reports key features of 12 state programmes in 2000. It is apparent from this table that there are large differences in programme parameters across states. These cross-state differences and their frequent changes over time have been a fundamental source of the identifying variation used to estimate the effects of these programmes.

Approximately 97 per cent of all wage and salary workers are in jobs that are covered by UI. The main categories of workers not covered are the self-employed, employees of small farms and household employees whose earnings are below the threshold amount. Despite this near universal coverage, less than 40 per cent of the unemployed received UI in many recent years.[10] The cause of this low rate of

---

[10] See Blank and Card (1991) and Anderson and Meyer (1997b) for studies of the reasons for the low rate of UI receipt.

Table 1. *Main characteristics of state unemployment insurance programmes in the USA*

State	Base period earnings required ($)	Replacement rate[a] (%)	Minimum weekly benefit ($)	Maximum weekly benefit ($)	Quarters of work required for 26 weeks of benefits
California	1,125	39–57	40	230	1.56–2.28
Florida	3,400	50	32	275	4
Illinois	1,600	49.5[b]	51	296–392	1.38
Massachusetts	2,400	50–61.9[b]	24–36	431–646	2.77–3.44
Michigan	3,090	67[c]	88	300	2.67
Mississippi	1,200	50	30	190	3
Missouri	1,500	52	40	220	3.12
Nebraska	1,600	52–65	36	214	3–3.9
New Jersey	2,060	60[b]	61	429	2.67
New York	2,400	50	40	365	1.5
Texas	1,776	52	48	294	3.85
Median state	1,576	52	39	292	3.12

[a]Where a range is given, a benefit schedule is used in which the replacement rate is higher for lower-paid workers.
[b]Illinois, Massachusetts and New Jersey have dependants' allowances.
[c]Of average after-tax weekly wage.

Source: National Foundation for Unemployment Compensation & Workers' Compensation, 2000.

receipt is largely that individuals who are new entrants or re-entrants to the labour force, individuals who have irregular work histories and individuals who quit or are fired from their last job are typically not eligible for benefits. Such individuals are frequently excluded by minimum earnings requirements for eligibility ranging from $130 in Hawaii to $3,400 in Florida, with a typical state requiring previous earnings just over $1,500.[11]

UI benefits are paid on a weekly basis and, except for minimum and maximum benefit amounts, are usually between 50 and 60 per cent of previous earnings.[12] All states have a maximum weekly benefit amount, which varies from a low of $190 in Mississippi to over $600 in Massachusetts if dependants' allowances are included. The median state had a maximum benefit of about $292 in 2000. About 35 per cent of claimants receive the maximum benefit. For these individuals, the fraction of their previous earnings replaced by UI can be much lower than 50 per cent. The minimum weekly benefit is typically very low; the median state has a minimum of about $39.

In almost all states, benefits last up to 26 weeks. However, in all but eight states, total benefits paid are restricted to some fraction of previous earnings or weeks worked. Table 1 indicates that a typical state requires just over three quarters (39 weeks) of work for a claimant to be eligible for 26 weeks of benefits. This provision causes the potential duration of benefits to be less than 26 weeks for approximately half of all recipients.[13] In all but 11 states, there is a waiting period of one week after the beginning of unemployment until one can receive benefits.

In 1970, a permanent federal–state extended benefits programme was established to provide additional weeks of benefits to individuals who exhaust their regular state benefits in periods of high unemployment. When a state's insured unemployment rate is sufficiently high, weeks of benefits are extended 50 per cent beyond that which an individual would be entitled to under state law, with the extension not to exceed 13 weeks. In addition, in times of high unemployment, Congress has typically passed *ad hoc* laws temporarily extending benefits further. Because the unemployment rate has been low in recent years, benefits have only rarely been extended, despite a change that relaxed the threshold for benefit extensions in 1993.

Prior to 1979, UI benefits were not subject to federal income taxation, but in 1979 they became taxable for high-income individuals. In 1982 taxation of UI

---

[11] More precisely, earnings during the first four of the five full calendar quarters prior to the quarter an individual files for benefits. Five states now use alternative time frames that differ from this rule.

[12] A typical benefit schedule would compute the weekly benefit amount as high-quarter earnings divided by 23. High-quarter earnings are typically the highest calendar quarter of earnings during the first four of the five full calendar quarters prior to the quarter an individual files for benefits.

[13] A typical state calculates potential weeks of benefits as the minimum of 26 and base period earnings divided by three times the weekly benefit amount. Base period earnings are usually calculated as earnings during the first four of the five calendar quarters prior to the quarter an individual files for benefits.

was extended to most individuals, and in 1987 benefits became taxable for all recipients.[14] UI benefits are not, however, subject to OASDHI (social security and Medicare) payroll taxes.

A convenient indicator of the work disincentive of UI is the fraction of previous after-tax earnings replaced by after-tax benefits—the after-tax replacement rate. This replacement rate has fallen dramatically in recent years, particularly due to the taxation of benefits, and is now typically under a half. As recently as 1986, some people had replacement rates near one (often those lifted by the minimum benefit), implying that they would receive from UI nearly what they would earn if they returned to work.[15] This situation is much less common today. Strong disincentives to work part-time remain, though, as benefits are typically reduced dollar for dollar for earnings greater than a fairly small amount (the earnings disregard).

2. Unemployment Insurance Financing

UI financing in the USA is unique in that a firm's tax rate depends on its lay-off history. In other countries, benefits are funded through general revenues or payroll taxes that are not determined by a firm's lay-offs. The dependence of a firm's tax rate on previous UI use is called experience rating. Federal law levies a 6.2 per cent tax on the first $7,000 in wages a year paid to an employee. The law provides for a credit of 5.4 per cent to employers that pay state taxes under an approved UI system, so that all employers pay at least 0.8 per cent.

State experience rating systems take many forms, but the two most common are reserve ratio (30 states and District of Columbia) and benefit ratio (17 states) experience rating.[16] In reserve ratio systems, a firm's tax rate depends on the difference between taxes paid and benefits accrued divided by average covered payroll. Taxes paid and benefits accrued are typically summed over all past years and are not discounted, whereas average payroll is typically the average over the last three years. In benefit ratio systems, a firm's tax rate depends on the ratio of benefits paid to taxable wages, both generally averaged over the last three years.

In reserve ratio states, a firm's tax rate increases in steps as its reserve ratio decreases (in benefit ratio states, tax rates rise as the benefit ratio rises). However, for most firms in almost all states, the tax rates do not adjust sufficiently when the ratios change to cause firms to pay the full marginal UI costs of laying off a worker. In addition, there are large ranges at the top and bottom over which a firm's lay-off history has no effect on its tax payments. This provides an incentive to

---

[14] In 1979, UI benefits became taxable for married taxpayers filing jointly with income over $25,000 and for single filers with income over $20,000. In 1982, the cut-offs changed to $18,000 and $12,000 respectively.

[15] See Feldstein (1974) for an earlier discussion and evidence on high replacement rates.

[16] See National Foundation for Unemployment Compensation & Workers' Compensation (2000). Michigan and Pennsylvania are counted as benefit ratio states even though they have hybrids of reserve ratio and benefit ratio systems.

lay off workers temporarily and subsidises industries with seasonal variation in employment. Forty states have a tax base that is higher than the federal base of $7,000. Alaska has the highest, at $22,600. Overall, in 1998, UI taxes were a highly regressive 1.9 per cent of taxable wages and 0.6 per cent of total wages.[17]

3. Unemployment Insurance Programmes Outside the USA

We should emphasise that there are often very different institutions in other countries to insure the unemployed. Moreover, programmes for the unemployed are often combined with other programmes, and those eligible for one type of benefit are often eligible for another in certain circumstances. These features often make cross-country comparisons problematic. Subject to these caveats, in Table 2 we report UI expenditures as a share of GDP and in absolute terms for seven countries.[18] Analogous expenditures on compensation for work injuries are reported for comparison. There are pronounced differences across countries. Among the countries shown, the UK has the lowest share of GDP devoted to UI expenditures, at 0.25 per cent, while four other countries have shares at least 10 times as big. Part of the explanation for the low GDP share in the UK is that UI expenditures provide a benefit that does not vary with previous earnings and is set at a fairly low level. For example, a single individual over age 25 was entitled to a weekly benefit of £52.20 ($77) in 2000. This amount is about a quarter of the typical maximum benefit in the USA.

Table 2. *International comparisons of expenditures on unemployment insurance and workers' compensation*

	Unemployment insurance		Employment injuries (workers' compensation)	
	% of GDP	$US million	% of GDP	$US million
Canada	2.52	13,776	0.85	4,624
Denmark	4.54	6,113	0.24	325
Germany	3.40	65,049	0.60	11,427
Japan	0.46	19,788	0.25	10,744
Sweden	2.95	5,460	0.81	1,502
UK	0.25	2,445	–	–
USA	0.50	28,334	0.74	41,654

Notes: Expenditures include cash and in-kind benefits, and administrative and other expenditures. All figures are in nominal US dollars and pertain to 1993 (1991 for the USA).

Source: International Labour Organisation, 2001.

[17] See Anderson and Meyer (2001) for an analysis of the distributional effects of UI taxes and benefits.
[18] For summary measures of the replacement rate and benefit duration in OECD countries, Nickell (1998) provides a nice overview.

One of the countries with a GDP share over 2.5 per cent is Canada. The Canadian UI programme provides an interesting comparison, as Canada is a close neighbour of the USA and has similar per capita income and industry base. Surprisingly, Canadian expenditures are almost half those in the USA, despite Canada having a population less than 11 per cent as large. While Canadian weekly benefits are slightly higher and last slightly longer on average than US benefits, the major difference between the countries is in the ratio of the number of UI recipients to the number of unemployed. An unemployed individual is approximately three-and-a-half times more likely to receive benefits in Canada than in the USA. This difference is hard to explain on the basis of the composition of unemployment in the two countries or current statutory qualification rules, though Canadian benefits were certainly more generous in the 1970s and 1980s than those in the USA. The amount of earnings in the past needed to qualify for benefits is only slightly higher in Canada. Those who have left their previous job are usually not eligible in the USA but are often eligible in Canada. It is also true that without experience rating, Canadian employers have less incentive to enforce eligibility rules. However, these features appear to explain only a small part of the difference. Furthermore, the timing of when UI became more generous in Canada than in the USA does not fit particularly well with when the two countries' unemployment rates diverged.[19]

4. Theoretical Responses of Labour Supply to Unemployment Insurance

UI affects at least five dimensions of labour supply. First, it can increase the probability of unemployment by affecting worker and firm actions to avoid job loss. Second, programme characteristics affect the likelihood that a worker will file a claim for benefits once he or she has been laid off. Once a claim has been made, we expect that labour supply will be affected by the adverse incentives of the UI programme. Third, once on the programme, UI can extend the time a person is out of work. Most research on the labour supply effects of UI has focused on this issue. Fourth, the availability of compensation for unemployment can shift labour supply by changing the value of work to a potential employee. Finally, there are additional effects, such as the work responses of spouses of unemployed workers. We discuss these five effects in turn.[20]

First, we discuss the effects of UI on the incidence of unemployment. UI can induce eligible workers to search less hard for a different job or work less hard on the current job, both of which can lead to a lay-off. There has been some modelling of this issue; for example, Mortensen (1990) examines the effect of

---

[19] See Card and Riddell (1993, 1997), Riddell and Sharpe (1998) and Riddell (1999) for detailed comparisons of the US and Canadian UI systems and discussions of the role of UI in explaining unemployment rate differences between the two countries.

[20] This classification of the labour supply effects of UI leaves out some effects that can be considered labour supply effects, such as possible improvements in the matching of workers to jobs.

UI on job search while employed. However, these effects have not been extensively studied. There is a substantial theoretical literature on how the availability of UI may make lay-offs more common when firms face variable demand for their product. The presence of UI, particularly UI that is not fully experience rated, may make firms more likely to lay off workers and may make employees more willing to work in firms that are prone to lay-offs (see Baily, 1977; Feldstein, 1976). While this response to UI is partly a labour demand effect, it is also partly a labour supply response as workers are induced to take jobs with higher lay-off risk because of UI.[21]

Second, the generosity of UI benefits may affect the probability that a person claims benefits conditional on a lay-off. As the generosity of benefits rises, it is more likely that the stigma and transaction costs of applying for UI will be outweighed by the benefits. Furthermore, whether someone initially receives UI is partly related to how long they are out of work. In nearly all states, a UI claimant must be out of work for over a week to be eligible for benefits.[22] It is more likely that a person will remain out of work for the waiting week if benefits are high. In addition to affecting programme costs, the increased claim rate in turn affects the number of weeks worked, because once a person is on the UI rolls, he or she becomes subject to the implicit taxes on work and the consequent work disincentives.

Third, conditional on beginning an unemployment spell, the duration of time out of work is affected by UI. This issue has received the most attention in the UI literature. Both labour supply and search models suggest that higher and longer-duration UI benefits will cause unemployed workers who receive UI to take longer to find a new job. An elegant, yet fairly realistic, search model is provided by Mortensen (1977), though there are many search models incorporating UI.[23] Mortensen models workers as choosing a search intensity and a reservation wage while facing a stationary known wage offer distribution and a constant arrival rate of job offers (for a given search intensity). If the worker is offered a job at a wage that exceeds the reservation wage, he or she accepts it. Mortensen incorporates two key features of the UI system in the USA into the model: benefits are assumed to be paid only for a specified duration rather than in every period of an unemployment spell, and new entrants or workers who quit jobs do not qualify for benefits.[24]

In this framework, the main labour supply effect of UI is to lengthen unemployment spells. This effect can be seen in the model, as increases in either the level or potential duration of benefits raise the value of being unemployed, reducing search intensity and increasing the reservation wage. Thus, the exit rate from unemployment, $\lambda(s)[1-F(w)]$, falls as both s and $1-F(w)$ fall, where $\lambda(\cdot)$ converts search effort s into job offers, w is the reservation wage and F is the cumulative distribution function of wage offers.

---

[21] This effect of UI occurs through an outward shift in the labour supply curve to high lay-off jobs, so it partly falls under the fourth effect of UI below.

[22] This waiting week can be thought of as the deductible (the excess) in the UI insurance policy.

[23] See, for example, Mortensen (1986).

[24] See Burdett (1979) for an analysis of a similar model.

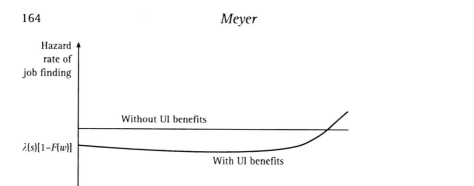

Figure 1. *The job finding rate and unemployment insurance benefits*

   Mortensen's model also implies our fourth labour supply effect of UI, known as
the 'entitlement' effect. This effect of UI raises the escape rate from unemployment
for workers who currently do not qualify for benefits and for qualified workers
close to when benefits are exhausted. That is, because the potential for receiving
benefits on a future job makes work more attractive, workers who are ineligible for
UI search harder to find a job. Higher benefits reduce the escape rate for recipients
when time until exhaustion is high and increase the escape rate around the time
of exhaustion. This pattern of UI effects on the hazard of leaving unemployment
is illustrated in Figure 1. Since the entitlement effect is likely to be small relative
to the standard search subsidy effect in many countries, the average duration
of unemployment is likely to rise with increases in both the level and potential
duration of benefits.
   The effect of UI on unemployment durations has also been modelled using the
standard static labour supply model. In a version of this model, Moffitt and
Nicholson (1982) assume people have preferences over two goods–income and
leisure. Unemployment in this model raises utility because of its leisure value.
The wage on a new job is fixed and a job can be found at any time. At the time of
job loss, an individual chooses income and weeks of unemployment subject to
a budget constraint that can be seen in Figure 2. The budget constraint becomes
flatter as the level of UI benefits increases, and it is extended outward as the potential duration of benefits increases. Both effects make unemployment more attractive, thus making it more likely that an individual will choose to be unemployed
longer.
   The two models make very different assumptions but have similar predictions.
In the Mortensen model, one is uncertain when a job will be found and what the
wage will be. One remains unemployed until a sufficiently high-paying job is
found. In the Moffitt and Nicholson model, one can find a job at any time at a fixed
wage. Their model emphasises the leisure value that a period of unemployment

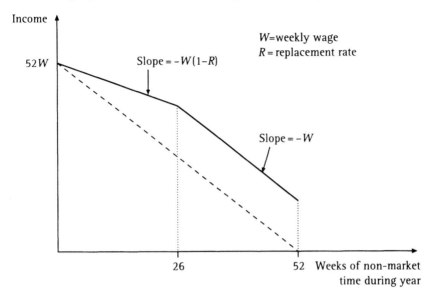

Figure 2. *How unemployment insurance alters the budget constraint*

may have if one optimises over a long period of time such as a year. This explanation has its greatest plausibility when there is a significant demand for home production or when it is difficult to take a vacation once a new job has begun.[25]

We should note that UI affects the labour supply of employed and unemployed workers in other ways. We have already mentioned the Mortensen entitlement effect where unemployed workers who are currently not eligible for benefits search harder because a job with UI is more valuable. In a standard labour supply framework, a similar mechanism would shift out the labour supply curve of the unemployed. This type of effect should also apply to the employed. Because UI makes employment more attractive if individuals realise that they may be laid off at some time in the future, the labour supply curve shifts outward (ignoring financing). Anderson and Meyer (1997a), following Summers (1989) and Gruber and Krueger (1991), describe how labour supply may shift in this way in response to the provision of benefits.

UI may also reduce work by spouses and limit part-time work. One of the responses to unemployment in the absence of UI may be an increase in hours worked by the spouse of an unemployed worker. This spousal labour supply is likely to be 'crowded out' at least in part by unemployment benefits that reduce the loss in family income when one spouse is unemployed.

As for part-time work, the incentives mentioned earlier discourage part-time work. In particular, we would expect that when there is a decrease in the allowable

---

[25] Implicit in this discussion is the assumption that the search requirement for UI receipt can be satisfied at low cost.

earnings before an individual's benefits are reduced (the disregard), there will be a decrease in part-time work and a smaller increase in full-time work (McCall, 1996). In addition, those seeking part-time work are ineligible for benefits in most states. These workers' earnings are taxed to finance the programme, yet they are disqualified from receiving benefits. This issue has aroused controversy in recent years.

Finally, we should emphasise that the above results are based on partial equilibrium analyses, that is, they do not include the effect of the behaviour of UI recipients on those who do not receive UI. This issue is discussed briefly below.

5. Empirical Evidence on Unemployment Insurance Labour Supply Effects

There are excellent surveys, as mentioned earlier, that include summaries of the labour supply effects of UI. Atkinson (1987), in particular, provides concise summaries of the literature up to the mid-1980s. In this survey, we will not replough that ground, but rather focus on mostly newer studies, though we will discuss the results in relation to some of the earlier summaries of the literature.

(a) Identification of Unemployment Insurance and Workers' Compensation Effects

Before discussing estimates of UI programme effects, it is useful to make some general comments that apply to both the UI and WC literatures. While good evidence on UI and WC effects from outside the English-speaking countries is becoming more common (especially for UI), there are reasons to believe that the best evidence on the effects of UI and WC—especially for programmes with features similar to those in the states—is likely to come from the USA. With 50 states and the District of Columbia having essentially the same systems but with often sharply different benefit levels and other characteristics, one has transparent variation in incentives that is arguably exogenous and can be used to estimate the effects of UI and WC. Moreover, there are often differing incentives across groups within a state, and sharp changes in programme characteristics for one group but not another, providing additional levers to identify the effects of the programmes.

That states differ in many respects, and that their policies are often driven by these differences, does not invalidate many of the approaches that can be taken with US data. There certainly is work showing that state UI and WC benefits are affected by underlying state attributes.[26] Nevertheless, the best work using data from the states relies on sharp changes in policies (and uses comparison groups), while the underlying determinants of policies tend to move slowly. For example, studies using data immediately before and after benefits have been increased sharply are likely to be immune from a political economy critique, especially when the forces that lead to these policy changes are understood. Other sensible

---

[26] For example, see Adams (1986) for UI and Besley and Case (1994) for WC.

approaches include, for example, the examination of policies that affect one group but not another or have sharply different effects on different groups. For example, US benefit schedules generally do not provide high benefits for all those in a particular state. Rather, they provide very different benefit replacement rates depending on one's earnings, and these schedules differ sharply across states and over time.

This is not to say that US evidence is applicable to all countries or that non-US studies cannot be convincing. Only a narrow range of policies can be directly evaluated using US data because state differences in UI programmes are all within the confines of the parameters of a federal system and because state WC programmes are similar (due in part to influential commissions, the efforts of national insurance organisations, unions and multi-state employers). Furthermore, the economic, cultural and institutional background in other countries may render the US experience not directly transferable. Nevertheless, in the vast majority of non-US studies (and many US studies), it is difficult to see the identifying variation in UI or WC programme characteristics across units that allows researchers to estimate programme effects. Atkinson and Micklewright (1985), in their review of UI research, argue that micro-data studies that do not describe their sample and other basic facts are 'likely to be meaningless' (p. 241). We would stress that the same is true of studies that do not make clear the source of differences in programme incentives across individuals and why those sources are likely to be exogenous. Other problems arise in cross-country studies that have difficulty holding constant the many country-specific features that affect unemployment.

Before describing the central tendencies of the empirical work on UI and WC labour supply effects, we describe an empirical approach that has been used successfully in a number of recent studies. Specifically, a number of recent studies have examined changes in state laws that affected some individuals but not others, or reforms that provided plausible comparison groups through another means (see Meyer, 1995a, for a review of these methods).

A useful place to start is the numerous papers that examine the effects of UI on the length of unemployment spells. In a typical study that does not use exogenous variation from policy changes, the length of unemployment is regressed on the benefit level or the replacement rate, the past wage or earnings, and demographic characteristics. Welch (1977) criticises this conventional methodology by pointing out that within a given state at a point in time, the weekly UI (or WC) benefit is a constant fraction of previous earnings except when an individual receives the minimum or maximum weekly benefit. Thus, regressions of spell length on weekly benefits and previous earnings consequently cannot distinguish between the effect of UI or WC and the highly correlated influence of previous earnings. This result is especially true if we are uncertain about exactly how previous earnings affect spell length. This identification problem, which is created by the dependence of programme generosity on an individual's previous earnings, is common to many social insurance programmes besides UI and WC, including social security and disability insurance. Other sources of differences in benefits, such as family composition and earnings, are also likely to have independent effects on spell length, making their use in identification suspect. In many studies of UI outside the USA, eligibility for UI or benefit generosity is often taken as exogenous even though it depends on an individual's work history and place of employment. This problem also arises when other outcomes are examined, such as saving.

Several papers exploit potentially exogenous variation in UI benefit levels from increases in state maximum weekly benefit amounts. These natural experiments are used to estimate the effects of UI on the length of unemployment, re-employment earnings and the incidence of UI claims. Early work in the spirit of this approach can be found in Classen (1979) and more closely Solon (1985). Classen examines benefit changes, but relies mostly on departures from a linear effect of earnings on outcomes as a measure of benefit effects. Solon examines the length of UI receipt in Georgia just before and after the introduction of federal income taxation of UI for high-income individuals in 1979. In the typical study of spell lengths, the variation in UI benefits comes from some combination of different replacement rates in different states, different minima and maxima, and maybe some variation in these parameters over time. Many of the natural-experiment-type papers are able to isolate one component of this variation which can be used separately to identify the effects of UI.

The main idea for one of the natural experiment papers that we use as a prototype can be seen by examining Figure 3, which displays a typical state schedule relating the weekly UI (or WC) benefit amount to previous earnings. The solid line is the schedule prior to a change in a state law that raises the minimum and maximum weekly benefit amount (WBA). The dashed line is the schedule after the benefit increase. Between the minimum and the maximum, the weekly benefit amount is a constant fraction of previous earnings (in the case of UI in most states,

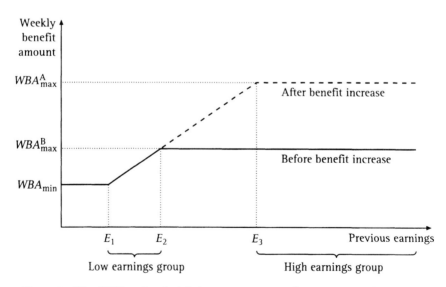

Figure 3. *UI or WC benefit schedule in a common natural experiment study approach*

the highest quarter of earnings during the first four of the last five calendar quarters prior to the quarter of filing for benefits).

For people with previous earnings of at least E_3 (the high earnings group), one can compare the mean weeks of UI received and re-employment earnings of people who filed for UI benefits just prior to and just after the change in the benefit schedule.[27] Those who file before the increase receive WBA^B_{max}, while those filing afterwards receive WBA^A_{max}. An individual's filing date generally determines his or her UI benefit amount for his or her entire benefit year (the one-year period following the date of claim). Thus, two individuals with quarterly earnings greater than E_3 will receive different weekly benefits for their entire period of receipt if one filed a few days before and the other a few days after the effective date of the benefit increase. This is the main idea of this approach. Most of the remaining methodological issues in the approach involve correcting for possible differences between the individuals filing just before and just after the benefit increase. One may also need to account for the dependence between observations from a given earnings group for a given year. In this example, one can use as a comparison group those with earnings between E_1 and E_2 (the low-earnings group) who file just before and just after the benefit increase. The benefits these individuals receive are unaffected by the increase in the maximum benefit amount. The so-called difference-in-differences estimator would then be used. In studies of this type, an additional comparison group may come from states that did not experience a benefit increase.

One should not construe this argument as saying that all studies that use this type of approach are convincing and that studies that do not are not convincing. Rather, this example shows that one can make clear the sources of variation that allow the estimation of programme effects, and that one can then make a case for their exogeneity (or lack thereof).

(b) Unemployment Insurance and Unemployment or Claim Incidence

There is a substantial literature that finds a large effect of UI on the incidence of unemployment or the incidence of UI claims. Table 3 summarises some of these studies. They are mostly concerned with labour demand, but we include them for completeness. Feldstein (1978) examines the effect of benefits on lay-offs, finding a large effect. The subsequent studies focus on how incomplete experience rating interacts with benefit generosity to affect lay-offs. In these studies, a key variable is the marginal tax cost of a lay-off, denoted by e, which is the fraction of the UI cost of an additional lay-off (in present value) that a firm can expect to pay in future taxes. The extent to which e is below one, then, is a measure of the degree to which experience rating is incomplete. The three studies—Topel (1983), Card and Levine (1994) and Anderson and Meyer (1994)—all find large effects of incomplete experience rating on lay-offs. The first two studies find substantially larger effects

---

[27] In principle, one could also examine the effects of increases in the minimum weekly benefit amount. However, in many cases few people receive the minimum benefit and it is raised infrequently.

Table 3. *Studies of unemployment insurance and the incidence of lay-offs*

Empirical specification	Data and identification	Findings
Feldstein (1978). Linear regression of temporary lay-off probability on the after-tax UI replacement rate, controlling for age, union status, race, marital status, gender, a linear effect of the wage, and industry and occupation (in some specifications).	US March 1971 Current Population Survey (CPS) data for experienced labour force members who were not labour force re-entrants and not self-employed. Identified by differences in benefits across states and individuals within state.	Elasticity of temporary lay-off unemployment rate with respect to the replacement rate ranging from 0.74 to 0.91. 'The average UI benefit replacement rate implied by the current law can account for about half of temporary layoff unemployment.'
Topel (1983). Estimation of time-constant lay-off and re-employment hazard rate using cross-section data on labour force status and unemployment. Key UI variable is subsidy rate $b[1/(1-t) -e]$, where b is the benefit, t is the income tax rate and e is the fraction of the cost of a marginal lay-off that the firm pays through experience rating.	US March 1975 CPS data on full-time, full-year labour force participants. Identified by differences in benefit and experience rating schedules across states interacted with industry unemployment rates.	'. . . the layoff unemployment rate would have been about 30 per cent lower if the subsidy to unemployment caused by the current UI system had been eliminated.' Argues that most of the effect is through incomplete experience rating increasing lay-offs.
Card and Levine (1994). Estimation of annual and seasonal temporary lay-off, permanent lay-off and other unemployment rates. Linear models for the probability of unemployment with e (see above for definition) as the main regressor are used, with state, state $\times$ year and industry $\times$ year controls in some specifications.	US CPS outgoing-rotation-group data for five industries in 36 states from 1978 to 1985. Identified by differences in experience rating schedules across states interacted with industry unemployment rates.	We estimate that a move to complete experience-rating would reduce the temporary layoff unemployment rate by about 1.0 percentage point (or roughly 50 per cent) in the trough of a recession, and by about the same amount in the lowest demand months of the year.
Anderson and Meyer (1994). Linear probability models of temporary job separations and all job separations with firm-specific measure of e (see above for definition) and controls for past firm lay-offs. Some specifications difference the data to remove firm and individual fixed effects.	US Continuous Wage and Benefit History (CWBH) administrative data on both workers and firms from six states during 1978–84. Identified by the differential effects of changes in state tax schedules on different firms.	Our preferred estimates imply that incomplete experience rating is responsible for over twenty per cent of temporary lay-offs.

using state-by-industry proxies for the tax cost than is found by the third study, which employs firm-level tax costs. A recent study—Anderson and Meyer (2000)—finds substantial effects of experience rating in a study of the reintroduction of experience rating in Washington State in the 1980s. It is hard to translate these results into effects of the level of benefits, but it should be clear that incomplete experience rating could not have an effect on lay-offs unless there were substantial UI benefits. In a paper that is explicitly about labour demand, Anderson (1993) finds that UI-induced adjustment costs have a substantial effect on the seasonality of employment.

A second group of studies, summarised in Table 4, examine how UI benefits and other variables affect the frequency of claims for UI conditional on unemployment or a job separation. Corson and Nicholson (1988) and Blank and Card (1991) both examine aggregate data and Panel Study of Income Dynamics (PSID) micro data. They both find substantial effects of the level of benefits in aggregate data, but they come to conflicting results using the micro data. Anderson and Meyer (1997b) find substantial effects in administrative micro data. Overall, an elasticity of unemployment or claims with respect to benefits in the neighbourhood of 0.5 is a reasonable summary of these studies.

(c) Unemployment Insurance and Unemployment Durations
The results of many of the more recent studies of unemployment durations, as well as of some older studies that rely on changes in benefits for identification, are reported in Table 5 for the USA. Several of the studies, including Classen (1979), Solon (1985) and Meyer (1990, 1992a), find elasticities of duration with respect to the level of benefits in excess of 0.5. The elasticity estimates with respect to the potential duration (length) of benefits tend to be much lower.

The non-US results reported in Table 6 are more varied. Very large effects of potential duration in Canada but no benefit level effect are found by Ham and Rea (1987), while Hunt (1995) finds very large effects of the level and potential duration of benefits in Germany. The studies of Sweden (Carling et al., 1996) and Norway (Roed and Zhang, 2000) find much smaller effects, though the sources of identification in the former study are far from clearly exogenous. A very thoughtful recent study by Carling, Holmlund and Vejsiu (2001) examines data before and after a benefit cut in Sweden and finds an elasticity over 1.0. The authors discuss earlier research analysing a previous cut which also found large effects. Other work, by Abbring, van den Berg and van Ours (2000), suggests large effects of benefit cuts on unemployment duration in the Netherlands, but it is difficult to separate out benefit cuts from other policies in their work. An elasticity of unemployment duration with respect to benefits of 0.5 is not an unreasonable rough summary, though there are a wide range of estimates in the literature. Such an elasticity is not very different from the central tendency of the duration elasticities reported in the Atkinson (1987) survey.

One should note that the elasticity of unemployment with respect to benefits is the sum of the lay-off/claim elasticity and the duration elasticity. To see this result,

Table 4. *Studies of unemployment insurance and benefit take-up*

Empirical specification	Data and identification	Findings
Corson and Nicholson (1988). Aggregate claims ratio regressed on replacement rate (= average weekly benefit of recipients divided by average weekly wage of employed).	US state-by-year aggregate data on the fraction of unemployed that receive UI.	Elasticity over 0.5.
Micro claims data regressed on variable for income taxation of UI, but replacement rate not used.	PSID individual data on UI claims.	Large effect of benefit taxation variable.
Blank and Card (1991). Aggregate claims ratio adjusted for estimated eligibility regressed on replacement rate (= average weekly benefit of recipients divided by average weekly wage of employed).	US state-by-year aggregate data on the fraction of unemployed that receive UI.	Replacement rate elasticities of 0.32–0.58.
Micro claims data regressed on state average replacement rate. No variable for income taxation of UI included.	PSID individual data on UI claims.	Insignificant effect of replacement rate. Coefficient usually of 'wrong' sign.
Meyer (1992b). Difference-in-differences analysis of claim incidence by earnings group, industry and region.	New York administrative data on UI claims from 1988 and 1989. Identification comes from a 36 per cent increase in the maximum benefit.	'The numbers are consistent with large effects of the higher benefits on the relative incidence of claims.'
Anderson and Meyer (1997b). Linear and logit models of UI receipt conditional on separation. Explanatory variables include logarithms of: weekly benefit, 1–tax on benefits, 1–tax on earnings, and potential duration of benefits. Some specifications with flexible controls for past earnings, state and state × time.	US Continuous Wage and Benefit History (CWBH) administrative data on both workers and firms from six states during 1978–84. Identified by differences in benefit schedules across states, changes in these schedules and changes in income taxation of benefits.	Elasticity of benefit take-up with respect to benefits of 0.33 to 0.60. Slightly smaller elasticities with respect to 1–tax on benefits. Elasticities of take-up with respect to potential duration about half as large as those with respect to the benefit level.

Table 5. *Studies of unemployment insurance and duration of unemployment in the USA*

Empirical specification	Data and identification	Findings
Classen (1979). Linear and log-linear regression of unemployment duration on benefits using deviations of relationship from linearity at benefit maximum as an estimate of benefit effects. Tobit models were also estimated.	US CWBH administrative data from Arizona from the year before and year after a 1968 benefit increase.	Benefit elasticity of 0.6 in levels and 1.0 in logarithms.
Solon (1985). Hazard model for exit from unemployment with key variable $b(1 - \rho t)$ to capture taxation of benefits, where b is the weekly benefit, t is the income tax rate and ρ reflects incomplete perception of taxes.	US CWBH data for Georgia before and after the introduction of income taxation of UI benefits for high-income families.	After-tax benefit elasticity of duration equal to 1.0.
Moffitt (1985). Flexible discrete hazard model of exit from unemployment with explanatory variables for benefit level, potential duration of benefits at start of spell, past wages and state unemployment rate.	US CWBH data for 13 states, 1978–83. Identification from differences in benefit schedules across states and changes in benefits and potential duration of benefits over time.	The results indicate that a 10-percent increase in the UI benefit increases spells by about half a week and that a 1-week increase in potential duration increases spells by about 0.15 weeks. These numbers suggest a benefit elasticity of about 0.4 and a potential duration elasticity of 0.34.
Meyer (1990) and Katz and Meyer (1990). Hazard model for exit from unemployment with non-parametric baseline hazard and variables for benefit level, and measures of time until benefits run out. Includes controls for state unemployment and past wages, and state indicator variables.	Subset of Moffitt (1985) data with some recoding. Identification same as for Moffitt, but the inclusion of state indicators weights it toward changes in schedules and differential treatment across states of those with different levels of earnings.	Elasticity of duration with respect to weekly benefit of 0.8 and with respect to potential duration of benefits of 0.5.

Table 5. *Contd.*

Empirical specification	Data and identification	Findings
Meyer (1992a). Comparisons of durations of those filing three months before and after 17 benefit increases. Most of increases due to automatic cost-of-living adjustments. Estimates with and without controls for demographics.	US CWBH data for six states. Identification of benefit effects comes from changes in benefits due to cost-of-living adjustments in period of high inflation.	A range of estimates, but central tendency of elasticity of duration with respect to the benefit amount of 0.6.
Meyer (1992b). Difference-in-differences analysis of claim duration with extensive controls.	See Table 4.	Duration elasticities of 0.24–0.42, though several estimates are smaller.
Card and Levine (2000). Hazard models of exit from unemployment receipt.	US administrative data for New Jersey. Examines programme that offered 13 weeks of 'extended benefits' for six months in 1996. The programme was part of a political compromise over funding care for indigent hospital patients.	Elasticity of duration with respect to potential duration of benefits of 0.1.

Table 6. *Studies of unemployment insurance and the duration of unemployment outside the USA*

Empirical specification	Data and identification	Findings
Ham and Rea (1987). Models the hazard from unemployment as a function of a polynomial of the duration of unemployment, initial entitlement and its square, weekly benefits and wages, and the provincial and industrial unemployment rates. Estimation is by maximum likelihood.	Canadian Employment and Immigration Longitudinal Labour Force Files with weekly data on men aged 18–64, for 1975–80. Identification comes from legislative changes in the benefit rate, individuals with weekly wages above the maximum earnings and changes in weeks of entitlement.	Benefit effect of wrong sign or insignificant. The potential duration coefficients were both significant in all specifications. An increase in the initial potential benefit duration of one week was estimated to increase expected duration of unemployment by 0.26–0.33 weeks (an elasticity of 1.02–1.33).
Hunt (1995). Models exit from unemployment in a competing risks hazard framework combined with a difference-in-differences approach. Control variables are an individual's age group, the time period, the interaction of time and age (treatment groups), and various demographic variables.	German Socioeconomic Panel public use file, for the years 1983–88. 2,236 individuals under age 57. One policy change reduced benefits to the childless unemployed, and three policy changes extended the duration of benefits to unemployed individuals of a certain age (49+ for the first policy, 44+ for the second and 42+ for the third). The control group consisted of unemployed individuals aged 41 or less. Identification comes from the differential effect of the policy changes on the treatment and control groups.	The extension of benefits lowered by 46% the hazard from unemployment for those aged 44–48, but the other benefit extensions had insignificant effects. For those aged 44–48, the implied elasticity of mean duration with respect to the maximum duration of UI was 2.27. In several cases, the extensions cut escapes to employment and out of the labour force. The cut in benefits for the childless significantly increased employment. The author notes that many of the effects are implausibly large.
Carling et al. (1996). The hazard of leaving unemployment (to any alternative) is modelled using an unrestricted baseline hazard and is estimated semi-parametrically.	Sweden. Non-disabled unemployed workers under 55 registered at public employment agencies in three months of 1991.	Elasticity of exit to employment with respect to the benefit level is estimated at −0.06.

Table 6. *Contd.*

Empirical specification	Data and identification	Findings
Explanatory variables include indicators for receiving UI benefits or KAS (cash assistance that gives smaller benefits for a shorter period of time), age, education, training, gender, citizenship and the regional unemployment rate.	Identification from variation in claimant status across individuals. UI recipients were members of a UI fund for at least 12 months, and had worked for a certain number of days in the past 12 months. KAS provided compensation for those not covered by UI and who met work or school requirements, and included labour force entrants.	
Roed and Zhang (2000). Flexible hazard rate model.	Norway. Register data on all unemployment spells between August 1990 and December 1999. Benefit variation due to changes in indexation over the year is used for identification.	Elasticity of hazard with respect to benefit of −0.35 for men and −0.15 for women.
Carling et al. (2001). Flexible hazard rate model of exits to employment and competing risks model of exits to employment, labour market programmes and non-participation.	Sweden. Register-based longitudinal data from 1994 to 1996. Data from before and after cut in replacement rate from 80 to 75%.	'Our implied elasticity of the hazard rate with respect to benefits is about 1.6 . . .'

let weeks unemployed, W, be the product of incidence, I, and duration, D. Then, letting the UI benefit be B, we have

$$W = ID \tag{1}$$

and

$$\frac{dW}{dB}\frac{B}{W} = \frac{B}{W}\left(D\frac{dI}{dB} + I\frac{dD}{dB}\right) = \frac{B}{I}\frac{dI}{dB} + \frac{B}{D}\frac{dD}{dB}. \tag{2}$$

Overall, the combined effect of benefits on unemployment through incidence and duration is suggested to be near one by these studies. This result is consistent with the aggregate analysis of 20 OECD countries by Nickell (1998), who finds an elasticity of unemployment with respect to the replacement rate of close to one.

Besides cross-sectional regression analyses of benefit effects on duration, we also have evidence from a recent series of randomised social experiments in the USA that are surveyed in Meyer (1995b). Four cash bonus experiments made payments to UI recipients who found jobs quickly and kept them for a specified period of time. Six job search experiments evaluated combinations of services, including additional information on job openings, more job placements and more extensive checks of UI eligibility. The bonus experiments show that economic incentives do affect the speed with which people leave the UI rolls. As a result, UI is not a completely benign transfer, but rather it affects claimants' behaviour, as shown by the declines in weeks of UI receipt found for all of the bonus treatments. The job search experiments found that various combinations of services to improve job search and increase enforcement of work search rules reduce UI receipt. It is hard to extrapolate from these experimental results to elasticities, since the treatments were very different from benefit changes, but the estimates probably suggest moderate effects of UI. Individuals were clearly able to change the speed with which they went back to work when faced with financial incentives to do so, but the effects were not particularly large. The experiments also indicated that job search assistance and reporting requirements have a substantial effect on unemployment duration.

(d) Unemployment Insurance Spillovers

An important issue on which more evidence is needed is the degree of spillover effects from UI recipients to other unemployed individuals. Might the spells of non-recipients become shorter, if UI recipients cut back on search activities and thus competed less strenuously for available jobs? The possibility of such spillovers has been emphasised by Atkinson and Micklewright (1985) and others. Levine (1993) examines this question empirically using the CPS and the National Longitudinal Survey of Youth. He finds that increases in the generosity of UI benefits appear to decrease the unemployment of those who do not receive UI. This is important work that suggests that previous work on UI and unemployment durations may have overestimated the overall effects of UI on unemployment rates. There is little other direct evidence on the question of whether general equilibrium effects of UI are much smaller than partial equilibrium effects. We should note that it is also possible that the adverse unemployment effects of UI will be magnified in general equilibrium. Carling et al. (2001) argue that UI will raise wage pressure in economies where wage bargaining is pervasive, thus reinforcing its adverse incentive effects on job search.

(e) Other Labour Supply Effects of Unemployment Insurance

Table 7 summarises two studies of other aspects of labour supply that are affected by UI. Cullen and Gruber (2000) find that higher unemployment benefits are associated with less work by the wives of unemployed men. The authors find that there is substantial crowd-out of this form of family 'self-insurance'. Their estimates suggest that for every dollar of UI received by the husband, wife's earnings fall by between 36 and 73 cents. McCall (1996) examines the effects of UI on part-time work. He finds that the level of the disregard (the amount of earnings allowed before benefits are reduced) has a significant effect on the probability of part-time employment during the first three months of joblessness. There is also some work on the extent to which the presence of UI shifts out the labour supply of those who are employed (Anderson and Meyer, 1997a) and of those whose benefits are about to run out (Katz and Meyer, 1990). The first paper finds some support for potential workers valuing the benefits (and labour supply thus shifting out), but the estimates are imprecise. The second paper finds little support for the hypothesis that higher UI benefits raise job-finding just prior to benefit exhaustion.

IV. WORKERS' COMPENSATION: PROGRAMME FEATURES AND LABOUR SUPPLY EFFECTS

1. Main Features of US Workers' Compensation Programmes

States have complete discretion in designing their workers' compensation programmes. Nevertheless, state programmes have many standard features. Coverage under WC in the USA is about as universal as that under UI. Approximately 97 per cent of the non-federal UI-covered workforce is covered, plus all federal employees. Unlike UI, a worker is eligible for WC benefits immediately on starting work, even without a previous earnings history.

State WC programmes cover the medical costs of a work-related injury or illness as well as four main types of cash benefits (also called indemnity benefits). First, 'temporary total' benefits are paid to workers who are totally unable to work for a finite period of time. All WC claims are initially classified as temporary total cases and temporary total benefits are paid; if the disability persists beyond the date of maximum medical improvement, the case is reclassified as a permanent

Table 7. *Studies of other unemployment insurance effects on labour supply*

Empirical specification	Data and identification	Findings
McCall (1996). The exit from unemployment to full-time or part-time work is modelled using a competing risks hazard model. Explanatory variables include an indicator for UI receipt, the replacement rate, the disregard (amount that can be earned without reducing benefits) and interactions of these variables.	US CPS Displaced Worker Supplements from 1986, 1988, 1990 and 1992. Identification from cross-state differences in disregard and changes in disregards (state fixed effects specifications).	Significant effect of disregard on probability of part-time employment during the first three months of joblessness.
Cullen and Gruber (2000). The labour supply of wives modelled as a linear function of potential UI benefits, demographic variables, the unemployment rate, the average wage of women similar to the wife and lagged husband's job characteristics. Dependent variables are the share of months employed and average hours worked per month. OLS, Tobit and 2SLS estimates with benefits received instrumented for using potential benefits.	US Survey of Income and Program Participation (SIPP) data from the 1984–88 and 1990–92 waves. Married couples where both husband and wife are between 25 and 54. 2,560 spells of unemployment.	Estimates of the implied income elasticity of labour supply for wives range from −0.49 using OLS to −1.07 using 2SLS. In a specification check, potential UI benefits also had a significant negative effect on the labour supply of women with employed husbands, suggesting that these estimates may overstate the true effect of UI benefits.

disability.[28] About 70 per cent of all claims are for temporary total disabilities. Second, if a worker remains totally disabled after reaching maximum medical improvement, he or she is eligible for 'permanent total' benefits. In most states, permanent total and temporary total benefits provide the same weekly payment, but in some states there is a limit on cumulative permanent total benefits. Benefits equal a fraction (typically two-thirds) of the worker's pre-disability average weekly wage, subject to a minimum and maximum payment. Figure 3, described earlier, displays a typical state benefit schedule. The maximum allowable benefit varies substantially across states, and is often linked to the number of the worker's dependants. Approximately half of workers earned a wage high enough that if they incurred a temporary total disability, their benefit would be limited by the maximum level in their state. Third, workers who suffer a disability that is partially disabling but is expected to last indefinitely qualify for 'permanent partial' benefits. An employee who loses the use of a limb, for example, would receive permanent partial benefits. These benefits are typically determined on the basis of a schedule that links benefits to specific impairments. For example, an employee who lost the use of an arm in a work-related accident in Illinois in 2000 was entitled to a maximum benefit of $269,943. Finally, dependants of workers who are killed on the job are paid survivors' benefits.

Each state law requires a waiting period ranging from 3 to 7 days before indemnity benefit payments begin. However, workers are compensated retroactively for the waiting period if their disability persists beyond a specified time period. Table 8 illustrates the interstate variation in WC benefit minima, maxima, replacement rates, waiting periods and retroactive periods for 12 states. Comparing this table with Table 1, we notice that WC has much higher replacement rates and maximum benefits than UI. A typical state has a WC replacement rate of two-thirds but a UI replacement rate of just over a half. The typical state has a maximum WC benefit nearly twice its maximum UI benefit. Furthermore, WC benefits are not subject to income or payroll taxes.

The high replacement rates combined with the exclusion of WC from income taxation often lead to after-tax replacement rates near or above one. A couple of representative examples illustrate this point. Suppose an individual's taxable family income was under $43,850 in 2000 and she was subject to a 5 per cent state income tax. Then, the combination of state income, federal income and OASDHI payroll taxes implied a 27.65 per cent total marginal tax rate. For someone whose benefit was not limited by the maximum benefit and who had a pre-tax replacement rate of two-thirds, the after-tax replacement rate was 92 per cent. If income was over $43,850, the family was in a higher federal income tax bracket with a total marginal tax rate of 40.65 per cent; the implied after-tax replacement rate was 112 per cent. When a worker has higher take-home pay not working than working, there is a strong disincentive to work.

---

[28] The date of maximum medical improvement is the time at which a doctor determines that an injured worker will not recover further from an injury.

Table 8. *Main characteristics of state workers' compensation programmes in the USA*

State	Minimum weekly benefit ($)	Maximum weekly benefit ($)	Replacement rate	Waiting period (days)	Retroactive period (weeks)
California	126.00[a]	490.00	66%	3	2
Florida	20.00	541.00	66%	7	2
Illinois	100.90–124.30[a,b]	899.81	66%	3	2
Massachusetts	149.93	749.69	60	5	3
Michigan	170.00	611.00	80[c]	7	2
Mississippi	25.00[d]	303.35	66%	5	2
Missouri	40.00	578.48	66%	3	2
Nebraska	49.00[a]	487.00	66%	7	6
New Jersey	151.00	568.00	70	7	8 days
New York	40.00[a]	400.00	66%	7	2
Texas	80.00	531.00	70[e]	7	4
Median state	100.00	529.00	66%	3	2

[a] In California, Illinois, Nebraska and New York, the minimum is actual earnings if less than the amount listed.

[b] In Illinois, minimum benefit increases if additional dependants are present.

[c] In Michigan, the replacement rate is a percentage of after-tax earnings.

[d] In Mississippi, the minimum does not apply in cases of partial disability.

[e] In Texas, the replacement rate is 75% if earnings are less than $8.50 per hour.

Source: US Chamber of Commerce, 2000.

These sharp work disincentives also apply to those who were working full-time but are considering part-time or temporary work after their injury, probably causing a fifth type of benefits, for those who work even though they earn much less than previously–'temporary partial benefits'–to be uncommon. A WC recipient with low earnings upon re-employment typically loses $2 in benefits for every $3 earned. Given that WC is not subject to income or payroll taxes, the return to working part-time or at a much lower wage than previously earned is negligible or even negative.

2. Workers' Compensation Financing

WC is mostly financed through insurance premiums paid by firms. WC experience rating is much tighter than UI experience rating, with large firms almost perfectly experience rated. The premium rates as a fraction of payroll range from 0.1 per cent in banking to over 20 per cent in construction and trucking in some states. To determine its premium, a firm is placed in one or more of 600 classifications that are a mixture of industry and occupation codes. These classifications determine manual rates, which, when multiplied by payroll, give the premium for a small firm. A large firm's rate is a weighted average of the manual rate and the firm's incurred loss rate, typically over a three-year period in the past. The weight put on the firm's incurred loss rate increases with firm size, with the weight equalling one for very large firms.

3. Comparisons of UI and WC Programme Costs in the USA

Some striking patterns are evident in Table 9, which reports aggregate benefits and revenues for UI and WC during the past 20 years. The cyclicality of UI benefit payments is pronounced, with benefit payments high in 1982–83 and 1992–93 in response to the downturns near the beginning of those periods. Any cyclicality is less apparent for WC, but a secular rise in WC benefit payments and costs followed by a decline after 1993 is evident. Why WC costs rose so quickly and then fell is only partly understood. The rise was likely associated with benefit increases and associated behavioural responses, as well as the rise in medical costs, while the recent fall is partly due to a decline in injury rates.

4. Workers' Compensation Outside the USA

We should emphasise that there are often very different institutions in other countries to compensate those injured on the job. Moreover, programmes for the injured are often combined with other programmes, and those eligible for one type of benefit are often eligible for another in certain circumstances. In particular, there is often no easy translation from the US WC programme to an equivalent in another country, since the USA lacks national health insurance and WC provides medical benefits.

Table 9. *Financial characteristics of workers' compensation and unemployment insurance programmes (millions of US dollars)*

	Workers' compensation		Unemployment insurance	
	Benefit payments	Costs	Benefit payments	Tax collections
1980	13,618	22,256	14,070	15,010
1981	15,054	23,014	15,580	15,630
1982	16,407	22,764	21,240	15,950
1983	17,575	23,048	28,850	18,010
1984	19,685	25,122	16,340	24,060
1985	22,470	29,320	14,360	24,450
1986	24,647	33,964	15,700	22,880
1987	27,317	38,095	15,080	24,180
1988	30,703	43,284	13,280	23,820
1989	34,316	47,955	13,500	21,750
1990	38,237	53,123	16,860	21,360
1991	42,170	55,216	24,420	20,630
1992	45,668	57,394	36,770	23,010
1993	45,330	60,820	35,070	25,230
1994	44,586	60,475	26,220	27,960
1995	43,373	57,054	20,990	28,900
1996	42,065	55,057	22,000	28,550
1997	40,586	52,040	20,300	28,200
1998	41,693	52,108	19,410	27,370
1999	–	–	20,720	26,480

Note: All amounts are in nominal dollars.

Sources: Nelson (1988a, 1988b, 1991); Mont et al. (2000); US House of Representatives, Committee on Ways and Means (1990, 1998, 2000).

In Canada, WC is fairly similar to that in the USA, with substantial variation in programmes across provinces. Replacement rates are typically 90 per cent of earnings net of income taxes, pension contributions and UI contributions. The waiting period and retroactive period are typically just one day, and firms in most cases must purchase insurance through a provincial fund.

In the UK, those who suffer an industrial accident or contract an industrial disease are generally eligible for the industrial injuries disablement benefit (IIDB), and about half of recipients also receive an additional allowance for reduced earnings. The level of benefit varies with the degree of disablement but does not vary with previous earnings. It is capped at a low level: IIDB in 2000 was a maximum of £109.30 ($161) per week. As a result, this benefit provides little insurance to middle- and upper-income workers in the UK. The programme appears to be more of a backstop akin to US welfare programmes, and expenditures are fairly modest.

5. Theoretical Responses of Labour Supply to Workers' Compensation

WC affects at least four dimensions of labour supply. First, it can affect the likelihood of an on-the-job injury. Much research on the labour supply effects of WC has focused on this issue. Second, programme characteristics affect the likelihood that workers will make a claim, given an injury. Once a claim has been made, we expect that labour supply will be affected by the adverse incentives of WC. Third, once on the programme, WC can extend the time a person is out of work. Finally, the availability of compensation for on-the-job injuries can shift labour supply by changing the value to a worker of various jobs. We discuss these four effects in turn.

There is an extensive literature on how the provision of benefits can possibly make the occurrence of an injury more likely. This research is motivated by the idea that workers (and firms) will take fewer actions to prevent an injury when the injury becomes less costly due to the availability of benefits that compensate workers. Krueger (1990a) provides a simple model of this situation. Let expected utility of the job be written as

$$E[U] = \{1 - p(e)\} U(W) + p(e)V(B) - e, \tag{3}$$

where $p(e)$ is the probability of an injury, e is the worker's effort devoted to injury prevention (care taken, use of earplugs, etc.), $U(W)$ is the utility when working at wage W and $V(B)$ is the utility of the WC benefit B when injured. The first-order condition for the choice of e that maximises utility, assuming an interior solution, is

$$p'(e)\{V(B) - U(W)\} - 1 = 0. \tag{4}$$

By differentiating (4) and using the second-order condition, one can show that

$$\frac{\partial e}{\partial B} = \frac{p'V'}{p''(U-V)} < 0, \quad \text{assuming} \quad p' < 0,\, p'' > 0 \text{ and } U - V > 0. \tag{5}$$

Thus, the provision of WC benefits may reduce effort at injury reduction (a dimension of labour supply) and increases the probability of an injury. On the other hand, we should note that more generous WC benefits could decrease injuries through their effect on firm incentives, as discussed by Ruser (1985) and Ehrenberg (1988).

Second, the generosity of WC benefits may affect the probability that a person claims benefits conditional on having an injury. As the generosity of benefits rises, it is more likely that the benefits of receiving WC will outweigh the costs, which consist of lost earnings plus the transaction costs of establishing eligibility and possibly the stigma of WC receipt. As a result of higher benefits, there may also be more claims in marginal cases where it is unclear whether the injury is work related and more cases involving outright fraud.[29] Furthermore, whether someone initially receives WC is partly related to how long they are out of work. A WC claimant cannot receive benefits until after a waiting period of typically three days. It is more likely that an injured worker will be out of work longer than this waiting period when benefits are high. Once a person is then on the WC rolls,

---

[29] For anecdotal evidence that higher benefits may also lead to fraud and overstated claims, see the *New York Times*, 29 December 1991, p. 1.

he or she becomes subject to the implicit taxes on work and the consequent work disincentives. Therefore, additional claims will lead to a labour supply response as well as to higher costs.

Third, the duration of time out of work is affected by WC. As with UI, this issue is one on which a substantial part of WC research has focused. The duration of time out of work while receiving WC can be thought of as determined by a sequence of decisions. In each period following an injury, an individual compares the benefits received from WC (and the leisure time when not working) with the earnings received when working. A worker's decision would also reflect the disutility of working with an injury (which would tend to fall as an individual recovers) and the increase in productivity with recovery. An additional factor in a person's decision is that a longer stay out of work might facilitate a full recovery, reducing future pain and increasing future productivity. In this setting, higher WC benefits would tend to delay a return to work but make a full recovery more likely, just as higher UI could lead to a better job match.

One should note that permanent benefits under WC have an income effect but no substitution effect. Permanent partial benefits, which are frequently paid as a lump-sum settlement, also do not affect the marginal incentives to return to work; they only reduce work by increasing income.

One additional labour supply response is the extent to which labour supply shifts out in response to WC benefits because they make employment more attractive. This issue is examined theoretically and empirically in Gruber and Krueger (1991).[30]

6. Empirical Evidence on Workers' Compensation Labour Supply Effects

There are excellent surveys that include summaries of the labour supply effects of WC, such as Ehrenberg (1988), Krueger (1990a), Moore and Viscusi (1990) and Kniesner and Leeth (1995). The empirical research on the labour supply effects of WC, while extensive, is probably less developed than the research on UI. Furthermore, while European researchers have recently produced many convincing studies of UI, research on WC outside the USA has lagged.

(a) The Incidence of Injuries and Workers' Compensation Claims
Table 10 summarises a large number of studies that examine the effect of WC programme parameters on the incidence of injuries or the incidence of WC claims. Most of these studies, especially the early ones, examine aggregate data at the state-by-year level or the industry-by-state-by-year level. These studies tend to find that more generous WC is associated with higher injury rates, but the effect is usually small. This may be an accurate estimate or a result of the use of aggregate variables and proxies that are required when researchers use state or state-by-industry data. The studies also tend to find higher claims elasticities than injury

---

[30] Also see Holmlund (1983).

Table 10. *Studies of workers' compensation and the incidence of injuries or claims*

Study	Unit of observation and sample	Dependent variable	Benefit elasticity
Chelius (1982)	US state by two-digit SIC manufacturing industry; 36 states from 1972 to 1975.	Injuries per 100 full-time workers.	0.14
Ruser (1985)	US state by three-digit SIC manufacturing industry; unbalanced panel of 41 states from 1972 to 1979.	Injuries per 100 full-time workers. Injuries with lost workdays per 100 full-time workers.	0.062 0.116
Butler (1983)	US manufacturing industries by year; 15 industries over 32 years in South Carolina.	Closed WC cases reported in the fiscal year per worker.	0.290
Butler and Worrall (1983)	US state by year; 35 states from 1972 to 1978.	Temporary total claims of non-self-insured firms per worker.	0.344
Krueger (1990a)	US individuals in 47 states in 1984 and 1985.	WC claims.	0.45
Krueger and Burton (1990)	US state-level data for 29 states in 1972, 1975, 1978 and 1983.	Premiums per employee or manual rate.	Not significantly different from zero
Butler and Worrall (1991)	US state-level data for 1954–81.	WC claim costs.	0.68
Butler et al. (1997)	US individuals at a large nationwide firm during 1990–93.	Frequency of disability claims. Indemnity cost per worker.	−0.45 to 1.24 (with median of 0.78) 0.06–2.90 (with median of 1.27)

elasticities, a result that is expected given the additional effect of higher benefits on claims conditional on an injury. The estimated benefit elasticities cluster around 0.2 or 0.3, though the only studies that use individual micro data–Krueger (1990a) and Butler et al. (1997)–find appreciably larger elasticities of the claims rate with respect to benefits. There is also a short literature examining whether claims for hard-to-diagnose injuries and injuries for which treatment can be delayed are more common when benefits are higher and on days when the injury is more likely a non-work injury (such as Mondays). The evidence on these issues is quite mixed.[31]

(b) The Duration of Time Out of Work After an Injury
Most work on the incentive effects of WC has focused on the programme's effect on injury rates or the number of claims rather than on the duration of claims. However, there has been a great deal of recent research on the effects of WC on the duration of time out of work which we summarise in Table 11. Early work by Butler and Worrall (1985) examined low-back injuries in Illinois. They found elasticities between 0.2 and 0.4, depending on the statistical technique used. When Worrall et al. (1988) examined data pooled from 13 states, however, they did not find a consistent relationship between the level of benefits and the length of spells.

   Meyer et al. (1995) examined data from a natural experiment provided by two very large increases in benefit levels in Kentucky and Michigan. This natural experiment enabled them to compare the behaviour of people who are injured before the benefit increases with that of those injured after the increases. By using the approach outlined in Section III(5a), the paper provides a test of the effect of benefit changes on the duration of claims where the sources of identification are readily apparent. The authors find that a 60 per cent increase in the benefit level is associated with an increase in spell duration of approximately 20 per cent. The elasticities range from 0.27 to 0.62, with most clustering between 0.3 and 0.4. Overall, the elasticity estimates are very similar in the two states. These results suggest substantial labour supply effects of WC benefits. Subsequent papers that have followed this natural experiment approach and examined the effects of benefit increases have found large effects. Krueger (1990b), Gardner (1991) and the Curington (1994) results for severe impairments all imply duration elasticities over 0.7. On the other hand, the minor impairment results in Curington (1994) and the recent work of Neuhauser and Raphael (2001) suggest smaller effects, though the latter paper argues that the elasticities are understated due to claim composition changes.

   Again, note that the elasticity of lost work time with respect to benefits is the sum of the injury or claims elasticity and the duration elasticity, as we indicated in Section III(5c). Combining the injury or claims elasticity estimates with the duration elasticity estimates suggests an elasticity of lost work time with respect to

---

[31] See Smith (1990), Card and McCall (1996) and Ruser (1998).

Table 11. *Studies of workers' compensation and the duration of claims*

Study	Unit of observation and sample	Dependent variable	Benefit elasticity
Butler and Worrall (1985)	Low-back injuries in Illinois.	Length of claim using hazard models.	0.2–0.4
Worrall et al. (1988)	Low-back injuries in 13 states.	Length of claim using hazard models.	0.0
Meyer et al. (1995)	All injuries in Kentucky (1979–81) and Michigan (1981–82).	Length of claims; comparisons of means and log(duration).	0.3–0.4
Krueger (1990b)	All injuries in Minnesota, 1986.	Length of claims; comparisons of means and log(duration).	>1.5
Gardner (1991)	All injuries in Connecticut, 1985–90.	Mean length of claims.	0.9
Curington (1994)	All injuries in New York, 1964–83.	Severe impairment durations.	0.7–1.3
		Minor impairment durations.	0.1–0.2
Aiuppa and Trieschmann (1998)	France. Administrative region-level data from Caisse Nationale for years 1973–91.	Indemnity costs per injured employee.	0.78
Neuhauser and Raphael (2001)	California Workers' Compensation Institute administrative data from two years before and after 1994 and 1995 benefit increases.	Duration of temporary disability claims.	0.25–0.35, but much larger with selection correction

WC benefits of between 0.5 and 1.0. This elasticity is probably slightly smaller than the UI elasticity, but it implies large effects on work time.

(c) Other Labour Supply Effects of Workers' Compensation

Gruber and Krueger (1991) examine the extent to which WC makes employment more attractive for those currently not receiving benefits, leading labour supply to shift out. They find a substantial shift in their study, concluding that workers value a dollar of WC benefits at about a dollar. This increase in labour supply may dampen the labour supply reductions of WC, particularly for high-injury jobs that would otherwise be less desirable.

V. INCOME SUPPORT AND CONSUMPTION SMOOTHING

The insurance provided by UI and WC and their distributional effects are probably their most important benefits. Nevertheless, the US literature on income support and poverty reduction due to UI is quite slim. Work on the insurance value of UI is even less common. Unfortunately, like other benefits of social insurance, the insurance value of UI and WC is difficult to analyse. It is much easier to analyse the disincentive effects of UI and WC than it is to quantify the beneficial effects of the programmes. The disincentive effects can often be analysed with programme data, but the benefits typically require more in-depth information, such as long histories of earnings, income and consumption.

Danziger and Gottschalk (1990) examine how UI fits into the safety net for the unemployed in the USA. They emphasise that since a large fraction of those with the lowest earnings are ineligible, the role of UI is quite limited. However, while UI is received by a minority of the unemployed, it does play a significant role in poverty reduction. Older studies found that UI benefits are fairly progressive.[32] Examining both benefits and taxes, Anderson and Meyer (2001) show that despite being financed through a regressive tax, the net benefits of UI are disproportionately received by those in low-income deciles.

Gruber (1997) examines the consumption smoothing benefits of UI. Since unemployment is a risky event, risk-averse people would want to purchase insurance against it (at a fair price). One can save to self-insure, but pooling risks for a given person over time is not as efficient as pooling risks across people at a point in time. Such self-insurance would be incomplete, as an optimising individual would not save enough to cover the losses of unemployment because that would leave too few resources for consumption most of the time.

Using US PSID data for 1968–87, Gruber (1997) examines whether consumption falls less upon unemployment when UI is more generous. He finds a large consumption smoothing role for UI, concluding that a 10 percentage point rise in the

---

[32] See Hutchens (1981) and Feldstein (1977) which corrects and updates Feldstein (1974).

replacement rate reduces the fall in food consumption upon unemployment by 2.65 per cent.

In other papers, Gruber has examined the extent to which families self-insure against unemployment and how these efforts are crowded out by government-provided UI. Engen and Gruber (2001) find that more generous UI leads to lower savings, though the magnitudes are small. Given the consumption loss in self-insuring through precautionary saving, a small response might not be too surprising. On the other hand, the work of Cullen and Gruber (2000), which was discussed earlier, suggests substantial ability to self-insure by those with a spouse and substantial crowding-out of this behaviour as UI becomes more generous. The authors find that each dollar of UI receipt reduces spousal earnings by 36–73 cents. This last result suggests that further research should explore whether the effects of UI on consumption and savings are sharply different for the unmarried. Further work should try to reconcile the large spousal labour supply crowd-out effect with the large remaining effect of UI on consumption.

These results for the USA are very different from recent work on Canada by Browning and Crossley (2001), who find much smaller effects of UI on consumption smoothing. They argue that their most important finding is that the benefit effect is very heterogeneous. Most households are insensitive to the level of benefits, while those without liquid assets or with a spouse who is not employed are very sensitive to the level of benefits. This last result also partially disagrees with the interaction effects implied by the results of Gruber and co-authors. While Browning and Crossley try to reconcile their results with those of Gruber, they are not able to offer much to explain the differences.

A recent paper by Bentolila and Ichino (2001) provides evidence on unemployment and consumption smoothing from a broader group of countries. The authors examine the USA and the UK, as well as Germany, Italy and Spain. They find that consumption falls less with unemployment in Italy and Spain. This result is not attributed to UI, as it is argued that UI is less generous in Italy and Spain; rather, it is attributed to more extensive transfers from family members.

In other work related to the insurance value of UI, Dynarski and Gruber (1997) examine the extent to which families are able to smooth variation in labour earnings. They find that the most important smoothing mechanisms are the government tax and transfer system and self-insurance through saving. Sullivan (2001) examines the ability of the unemployed to smooth their consumption using unsecured debt. He finds evidence that unsecured debt plays a substantial role for most people, but that those with low initial assets or low income are unwilling or unable to borrow. We should also note that Meyer and Rosenbaum (1996) find that the same people tend to receive UI year after year, but the number of weeks received each year varies greatly over time even for these regular users. This result gives a somewhat mixed picture about the degree of predictability of unemployment and the need for insurance, but overall suggests substantial uncertainty.

Research on the distributional and insurance value of WC in the USA is even less common than similar work on UI. There are many studies that examine the fraction of lost income replaced by WC (see Boden and Galizzi, 1998, for a nice survey). In the case of temporary injuries, the statutory rules imply that, in most cases, 80–100 per cent of prior after-tax earnings are replaced in the short run, though the percentage is often lower or higher. However, so-called temporary claims often have long-term effects. Galizzi et al. (1998) examine a sample of people with back injuries in Wisconsin. Their results suggest that a substantial share of those who receive only temporary total benefits have earnings losses that persist long after full recovery supposedly occurred and benefit payments ended.

In the case of injuries classified as permanent, the earnings losses are often very large. Using data from California, Reville and Schoeni (2001) estimate that 4–5 years after an injury, earnings are about 25 per cent lower than they otherwise would have been. Galizzi et al. (1998) also find evidence that those with permanent injuries are more likely than comparison groups to have a car or home repossessed or to suffer other financial difficulties. This evidence strongly suggests that injured workers often suffer large adverse shocks to their financial well-being, as well as the pain and loss of functioning due to an injury. However, there is currently no research that examines the well-being of injured workers and the extent to which the WC system in combination with other programmes insures them against being injured. In other words, studies have yet to combine information on the pattern of WC payments after an injury (which are often front-loaded) with earnings information and information on transfers from other programmes such as the Supplemental Security Income (SSI) programme and the Social Security Disability Insurance (SSDI) programme. This information has also not been combined with information on consumption or other measures of well-being, as has been done in the UI literature. In addition, the distributional aspects of WC programmes have not been extensively examined.

VI. JOB SEARCH AND INJURY RECOVERY

The research on the effect of UI on the level of earnings upon re-employment is not very developed, and what has been written is not very definitive. UI should allow a worker to raise his or her reservation wage and be more selective in the job taken. There is some suggestion from Classen (1979) and Meyer (1992a) that policy changes that encourage longer unemployment spells do not lead to higher wages, and some evidence from the US UI experiments (Meyer, 1995b) that encouraging shorter unemployment spells through various incentives does not significantly reduce wages.

The work on injury recovery effects of WC is also not well developed. Higher WC benefits should allow a worker to spend more time out of work and recover more fully from an injury. There is some research on worker conditions several years after injuries, such as Galizzi et al. (1998), but the relationship between benefit parameters and recovery is not explored. This issue is briefly examined in Reville and Schoeni (2001), who compare long-term earnings losses before and after temporary total benefits were raised 21 per cent in California. They find small and insignificant effects of the benefit change on later earnings, but suggest that their test has little statistical power.

VII. CONCLUSIONS

The empirical work on unemployment insurance and workers' compensation insurance reviewed in this chapter finds that the programmes tend to increase the length of time employees spend out of work. Most of the estimates of the elasticities of lost work time that incorporate both the incidence and duration of claims are close to 1.0 for UI and between 0.5 and 1.0 for WC. These elasticities are substantially larger than the labour supply elasticities typically found for men in studies of the effects of wages or taxes on hours of work; such estimates are centred close to zero (see, e.g. Killingsworth, 1983; Pencavel, 1986). They are also larger than the consensus range of estimates of the labour supply elasticity for women, which is highly dispersed but centred near 0.4. These seemingly disparate results may, in part, be reconciled by the likelihood that elasticities are larger when a response can easily occur through participation or weeks worked rather than through an adjustment of the number of hours worked per week. Labour supply responses to WC and UI benefits occur mainly through decisions about weeks worked, and labour supply responses of women mainly concern participation and weeks worked. Male labour supply elasticities, by contrast, are primarily determined by an adjustment of the number of hours worked per week, a margin on which employees may have relatively little flexibility. These observations suggest that it would be misleading to apply a universal set of labour supply elasticities to diverse problems and populations.

Temporary total WC insurance benefits and UI benefits may also generate relatively large labour supply responses because they lead to only a short-run change in the returns to working. For example, receipt of benefits under UI is not for an indefinite period. Thus, workers may intertemporally substitute their labour supply while benefits are available, generating larger work responses than predicted by long-run labour supply elasticities.

In addition, UI and temporary total WC benefits make the net wage (after-tax wage minus after-tax benefits) very low, often close to zero in the case of WC benefits. This situation is different from a typical cut in wages for two reasons. First, the income effect does not counterbalance the substitution effect to the usual extent since benefits are provided and income often does not fall appreciably. In the case of a replacement rate of 0.8, the net wage falls by 80 per cent but current income only falls by 20 per cent. In the usual case of wage variation, a drop in the wage dramatically lowers income, and thus the income effect tends to mitigate the substitution effect. Second, the level of the net wage may be so low that it is out of the range of typical variation in cross-section wages or wage variation due to taxes. Thus, estimates based on other sources of wage variation may be less applicable to UI and WC.

Despite labour supply responses to social insurance programmes, it should be clear that the desirability of social insurance depends on the *intended* as well as unintended effects (or, more appropriately put, undesired side effects) of the programmes. Thus, a finding of labour supply responses to incentives is not necessarily cause for abandoning a programme. The undesired side effects must be balanced against the improved welfare from providing income maintenance to those in need. These two effects have been explicitly balanced in some research, such as Gruber (1997).

There is some evidence that UI substantially smooths consumption of the unemployed. These estimates suggest a substantial insurance value to UI. The evidence also shows that the UI programme is fairly redistributive. Nevertheless, the benefits of the UI programme are not as firmly established as the labour supply distortions, and they merit extensive further study. These issues are even more apparent for WC. There is substantial evidence of material hardship on the part of those suffering workplace injuries even after the effects of the current WC system and other transfers. However, a clear and comprehensive picture of the benefits of the WC programme cannot be extracted from the pieces of information that we currently have.

A final point worth highlighting is that less research has been conducted on WC than on UI, despite its much larger size (at least in the USA). In my view, WC is under-researched relative to its importance to the economy and merits further study. WC programmes exhibit substantial variability over time or across states, and large data-sets are available that can be analysed, so there is potential for many valuable research projects. Also, while the UI literature for Europe is rapidly catching up to the US literature, relatively little work has been done on WC-like programmes outside the USA.

REFERENCES

Abbring, J. H., van den Berg, G. J. and van Ours, J. C. (2000), 'The effect of unemployment insurance sanction on the transition rate from unemployment to employment', Free University, Amsterdam, Working Paper.

Adams, J. (1986), 'Equilibrium taxation and experience rating in a federal system of unemployment insurance', *Journal of Public Economics*, vol. 29, pp. 51–77.

Aiuppa, T. and Trieschmann, J. (1998), 'Moral hazard in the French workers' compensation system', *Journal of Risk and Insurance*, vol. 65, pp. 125–33.

Anderson, P. M. (1993), 'Linear adjustment costs and seasonal labor demand: evidence from retail trade firms', *Quarterly Journal of Economics*, vol. 108, pp. 1015–42.

— and Meyer, B. D. (1993), 'Unemployment insurance in the United States: layoff incentives and cross-subsidies', *Journal of Labor Economics*, vol. 11, pp. S70–95.

— and — (1994), 'The effect of unemployment insurance taxes and benefits on layoffs using firm and individual data', National Bureau of Economic Research, Working Paper no. 4960.

— and — (1997a), 'The effects of firm specific taxes and government mandates with an application to the U.S. unemployment insurance program', *Journal of Public Economics*, vol. 65, pp. 119–44.

— and — (1997b), 'Unemployment insurance takeup rates and the after-tax value of benefits', *Quarterly Journal of Economics*, vol. 112, pp. 913–38.

Anderson, P. M. and Meyer, B. D. (2000), 'The effects of the unemployment insurance payroll tax on wages, employment, claims and denials', *Journal of Public Economics*, vol. 78, pp. 81–106.

—— and —— (2001), 'The distributional consequences of unemployment benefits and taxes', Northwestern University, mimeo.

Atkinson, A. B. (1987), 'Income maintenance and social insurance', in A. Auerbach and M. Feldstein (eds), *Handbook of Public Economics*, Amsterdam: North-Holland.

—— and Micklewright, J. (1985), *Unemployment Benefits and Unemployment Duration*, London: Suntory-Toyota International Centre for Economics and Related Disciplines, London School of Economics and Political Science.

—— and —— (1990), 'Unemployment compensation and labor market transitions: a critical review', *Journal of Economic Literature*, vol. 29, pp. 1679–727.

Baily, M. N. (1977), 'On the theory of layoffs and unemployment', *Econometrica*, vol. 45, pp. 1043–64.

Bentolila, S. and Ichino, A. (2001), 'Unemployment and consumption: are job losses less painful near the Mediterranean?', CEMFI, mimeo.

Besley, T. and Case, A. (1994), 'Unnatural experiments? Estimating the incidence of endogenous policies', National Bureau of Economic Research, Working Paper no. 4956.

Blank, R. M. and Card, D. E. (1991), 'Recent trends in insured and uninsured unemployment: is there an explanation?', *Quarterly Journal of Economics*, vol. 106, pp. 1157–90.

Boden, L. I. and Galizzi, M. (1998), *Measuring Income Losses of Injured Workers: A Study of the Wisconsin System*, Cambridge, MA: Workers Compensation Research Institute.

Brown, E. and Kaufold, H. (1988), 'Human capital accumulation and the optimal level of unemployment insurance provision', *Journal of Labor Economics*, vol. 6, pp. 493–514.

Browning, M. and Crossley, T. F. (2001), 'Unemployment insurance benefit levels and consumption changes', *Journal of Public Economics*, vol. 80, pp. 1–24.

Burdett, K. (1979), 'Unemployment insurance payments as a search subsidy: a theoretical analysis', *Economic Inquiry*, vol. 17, pp. 333–42.

Butler, R. J. (1983), 'Wage and injury response to shifting levels of workers' compensation', in J. Worrall (ed.), *Safety and the Workforce*, Ithaca, NY: Cornell University Press.

——, Gardner, B. D. and Gardner, H. H. (1997), 'Workers' compensation costs when maximum benefits change', *Journal of Risk and Uncertainty*, vol. 15, pp. 259–69.

—— and Worrall, J. D. (1983), 'Workers' compensation: benefit and injury claim rates in the seventies', *Review of Economics and Statistics*, vol. 50, pp. 580–9.

—— and —— (1985), 'Work injury compensation and the duration of nonwork spells', *Economic Journal*, vol. 95, pp. 714–24.

—— and —— (1991), 'Claims reporting and risk bearing moral hazard in workers' compensation', *Journal of Risk and Insurance*, vol. 49, pp. 191–204.

Card, D. and Levine, P. B. (1994), 'Unemployment insurance taxes and the cyclical and seasonal properties of unemployment', *Journal of Public Economics*, vol. 53, pp. 1–29.

—— and —— (2000), 'Extended benefits and the duration of UI spells: evidence from the New Jersey extended benefit program', *Journal of Public Economics*, vol. 78, pp. 107–38.

—— and McCall, B. P. (1996), 'Is workers' compensation covering uninsured medical costs? Evidence from the "Monday effect"', *Industrial and Labor Relations Review*, vol. 49, pp. 690–706.

—— and Riddell, W. C. (1993), 'A comparative analysis of unemployment in Canada and the United States', in D. Card and R. B. Freeman (eds), *Small Differences That Matter: Labor*

Markets and Income Maintenance in Canada and the United States, Chicago, IL: University of Chicago Press and National Bureau of Economic Research.

— and — (1997), 'Unemployment in Canada and the United States: a further analysis', in B. C. Eaton and R. G. Harris (eds), *Trade, Technology and Economics: Essays in Honour of Richard Lipsey*, Cheltenham: Edward Elgar.

Carling, K., Edin, P., Harkman, A. and Holmlund, B. (1996), 'Unemployment duration, unemployment benefits, and labor market programs in Sweden', *Journal of Public Economics*, vol. 59, pp. 313–34.

—, Holmlund, B. and Vejsiu, A. (2001), 'Do benefit cuts boost job finding? Swedish evidence from the 1990s', *Economic Journal*, vol. 111, pp. 766–90.

Chelius, J. (1982), 'The influence of workers' compensation on safety incentives', *Industrial and Labor Relations Review*, vol. 35, pp. 235–42.

Christiano, L. J. (1984), 'A reexamination of the theory of automatic stabilizers', *Carnegie-Rochester Conference Series on Public Policy*, vol. 20, pp. 147–206.

Classen, K. P. (1979), 'Unemployment insurance and job search', in S. A. Lippman and J. J. McCall (eds), *Studies in the Economics of Search*, Amsterdam: North-Holland.

Corson, W. and Nicholson, W. (1988), *An Examination of Declining UI Claims during the 1980's*, Unemployment Insurance Occasional Paper no. 88-3, Washington, DC: US Department of Labour, Employment and Training Administration.

Cullen, J. and Gruber, J. (2000), 'Does unemployment insurance crowd out spousal labor supply?', *Journal of Labor Economics*, vol. 18, pp. 546–72.

Curington, W. P. (1994), 'Compensation for permanent impairment and the duration of work absence: evidence from four natural experiments', *Journal of Human Resources*, vol. 29, pp. 888–910.

Danziger, S. and Gottschalk, P. (1990), 'Unemployment insurance and the safety net for the unemployed', in W. L. Hansen and J. F. Byers (eds), *Unemployment Insurance*, Madison, WI: University of Wisconsin Press.

—, Haveman, R. and Plotnick, R. (1981), 'How income transfer affects work, savings, and the income distribution: a critical review', *Journal of Economic Literature*, vol. 19, pp. 975–1028.

Devine, T. J. and Kiefer, N. M. (1991), *Empirical Labor Economics: The Search Approach*, New York, NY: Oxford University Press.

Dynarski, S. and Gruber, J. (1997), 'Can families smooth variable earnings?', *Brookings Papers on Economic Activity*, pp. 229–84.

Ehrenberg, R. G. (1988), 'Workers' compensation, wages, and the risk of injury', in J. F. Burton, Jr. (ed.), *New Perspectives in Workers' Compensation*, Ithaca, NY: ILR Press.

Emmerson, C. and Leicester, A. (2001), *A Survey of the UK Benefit System*, Briefing Note no. 13, London: Institute for Fiscal Studies (www.ifs.org.uk/taxsystem/benefitsurvey.pdf).

Engen, E. M. and Gruber, J. (2001), 'Unemployment insurance and precautionary saving', *Journal of Monetary Economics*, vol. 47, pp. 545–79.

Feldstein, M. S. (1974), 'Unemployment compensation: adverse incentives and distributional anomalies', *National Tax Journal*, vol. 27, pp. 231–44.

— (1976), 'Temporary layoffs in the theory of unemployment', *Journal of Political Economy*, vol. 84, pp. 837–57.

— (1977), 'New evidence on the distribution of unemployment insurance benefits', *National Tax Journal*, vol. 30, pp. 219–21.

— (1978), 'The effect of unemployment insurance on temporary layoff unemployment', *American Economic Review*, vol. 68, pp. 834–46.

Fuchs, V. R., Krueger, A. B. and Poterba, J. M. (1998), 'Economists' views about parameters, values, and policies: survey results in labor and public economics', *Journal of Economic Literature*, vol. 36, pp. 1387–425.

Galizzi, M., Boden, L. I. and Liu, T. (1998), *The Workers' Story: Results of a Survey of Workers Injured in Wisconsin*, Cambridge, MA: Workers Compensation Research Institute.

Gardner, J. A. (1991), *Benefit Increases and System Utilization: The Connecticut Experience*, Cambridge, MA: Workers Compensation Research Institute.

Gruber, J. (1997), 'The consumption smoothing benefits of unemployment insurance', *American Economic Review*, vol. 87, pp. 192–205.

— and Krueger, A. (1991), 'The incidence of mandate employer-provided insurance: lessons from workers' compensation insurance', in D. Bradford (ed.), *Tax Policy and the Economy 5*, Cambridge, MA: National Bureau of Economic Research.

Gustman, A. L. (1982), 'Analyzing the relation of unemployment insurance to unemployment', in R. Ehrenberg (ed.), *Research in Labor Economics*, 5, Greenwich, CT: JAI Press.

Ham, J. C. and Rea, S., Jr. (1987), 'Unemployment insurance and male unemployment duration in Canada', *Journal of Labor Economics*, vol. 5, pp. 325–53.

Hamermesh, D. S. (1977), *Jobless Pay and the Economy*, Baltimore, MD: Johns Hopkins University Press.

Holmlund, B. (1983), 'Payroll taxes and wage inflation: the Swedish experience', *Scandinavian Journal of Economics*, vol. 85, pp. 1–15.

— (1998), 'Unemployment insurance in theory and practice', *Scandinavian Journal of Economics*, vol. 100, pp. 113–41.

Hunt, J. (1995), 'The effect of unemployment compensation on unemployment duration in Germany', *Journal of Labor Economics*, vol. 13, pp. 88–120.

Hutchens, R. (1981), 'Distributional equity in the unemployment insurance system', *Industrial and Labor Relations Review*, vol. 34, pp. 377–85.

International Labour Organisation (2001), *Cost of Social Security 1990–96*, Geneva. Available from www.ilo.org/public/english/protection/socsec/publ/css/cssindex.htm

Katz, L. F. and Meyer, B. D. (1990), 'The impact of the potential duration of unemployment benefits on the duration of unemployment', *Journal of Public Economics*, vol. 41, pp. 45–72.

Killingsworth, M. R. (1983), *Labor Supply*, New York, NY: Cambridge University Press.

Kniesner, T. J. and Leeth, J. D. (1995), *Simulating Workplace Safety Policy*, Boston, MA: Kluwer Academic Publishers.

Krueger, A. B. (1990a), 'Incentive effects of workers' compensation insurance', *Journal of Public Economics*, vol. 41, pp. 73–99.

— (1990b), 'Workers' compensation insurance and the duration of workplace injuries', National Bureau of Economic Research, Working Paper no. 3253.

— and Burton, J. F., Jr. (1990), 'The employers' cost of workers' compensation insurance: magnitudes, determinants, and public policy', *Review of Economics and Statistics*, vol. 72, pp. 228–40.

Levine, P. B. (1993), 'Spillover effects between the insured and uninsured unemployed', *Industrial and Labor Relations Review*, vol. 47, pp. 73–86.

McCall, B. (1996), 'Unemployment insurance rules, joblessness, and part-time work', *Econometrica*, vol. 64, pp. 647–82.

Meyer, B. D. (1990), 'Unemployment insurance and unemployment spells', *Econometrica*, vol. 58, pp. 757–82.

— (1992a), 'Using natural experiments to measure the effects of unemployment insurance', Northwestern University, mimeo.

— (1992b), 'Quasi-experimental evidence on the effects of unemployment insurance from New York State', Northwestern University, mimeo.

— (1995a), 'Natural and quasi-experiments in economics', *Journal of Business and Economic Statistics*, vol. 13, pp. 151–62.

— (1995b), 'Lessons from the U.S. unemployment insurance experiments', *Journal of Economic Literature*, vol. 33, pp. 91–131.

— and Rosenbaum, D. T. (1996), 'Repeat use of unemployment insurance', National Bureau of Economic Research, Working Paper no. 5423.

—, Viscusi, W. K. and Durbin, D. (1995), 'Workers' compensation and injury duration: evidence from a natural experiment', *American Economic Review*, vol. 85, pp. 322–40.

Moffitt, R. (1985), 'Unemployment insurance and the distribution of unemployment spells', *Journal of Econometrics*, vol. 28, pp. 85–101.

— and Nicholson, W. (1982), 'The effect of unemployment insurance on unemployment: the case of federal supplemental benefits', *Review of Economics and Statistics*, vol. 64, pp. 1–11.

Mont, D., Burton, J. F., Jr. and Reno, V. (2000), *Workers' Compensation: Benefits, Coverage, and Costs, 1997–98, New Estimates*, Washington, DC: National Academy of Social Insurance.

Moore, M. J. and Viscusi, W. K. (1990), *Compensation Mechanisms for Job Risks: Wages, Workers' Compensation, and Product Liability*, Princeton, NJ: Princeton University Press.

Mortensen, D. T. (1977), 'Unemployment insurance and job search decisions', *Industrial and Labor Relations Review*, vol. 30, pp. 505–17.

— (1986), 'Job search and labor market analysis', in O. Ashenfelter and R. Layard (eds), *Handbook of Labor Economics*, vol. 2, Amsterdam: North-Holland.

— (1990), 'A structural model of UI benefit effects on the incidence and duration of unemployment', in Y. Weiss and G. Fishelson (eds), *Advances in the Theory and Measurement of Unemployment*, New York, NY: St. Martin's Press.

National Foundation for Unemployment Compensation & Workers' Compensation (2000), *Highlights of State Unemployment Compensation Laws*, Washington, DC: NFUCWC.

Neill, J. R. (1989), 'A welfare-theoretic evaluation of unemployment insurance', *Public Finance Quarterly*, vol. 17, pp. 429–44.

Nelson, W. J., Jr. (1988a), 'Workers' compensation: coverage, benefits and costs, 1985', *Social Security Bulletin*, vol. 51, no. 1, pp. 4–9.

— (1988b), 'Workers' compensation: 1980–84 benchmark revisions', *Social Security Bulletin*, vol. 51, no. 7, pp. 4–21.

— (1991), 'Workers' compensation: coverage, benefits and costs, 1988', *Social Security Bulletin*, vol. 54, no. 3, pp. 12–20.

Neuhauser, F. and Raphael, S. (2001), 'The effect of an increase in workers' compensation benefits on the duration and frequency of benefit receipt', University of California, Berkeley, mimeo.

Nickell, S. (1998), 'Unemployment: questions and some answers', *Economic Journal*, vol. 108, pp. 802–16.

Pencavel, J. H. (1986), 'Labor supply of men: a survey', in O. Ashenfelter and R. Layard (eds), *Handbook of Labor Economics*, vol. 1, Amsterdam: North-Holland.

Reville, R. T. and Schoeni, R. F. (2001), 'Disability from injuries at work: the effects on earnings and employment', RAND Labor and Population Programme Working Paper Series no. 01-08.

Riddell, W. C. (1999), 'Canadian labour market performance in international perspective', *Canadian Journal of Economics*, vol. 32, pp. 1097–134.

— and Sharpe, A. (1998), 'The Canada–US unemployment rate gap: an introduction and overview', *Canadian Public Policy*, vol. 24, pp. 1–37.

Roed, K. and Zhang, T. (2000), 'Does unemployment compensation affect unemployment duration?', Frisch Centre for Economic Research, Oslo, mimeo.

Ruser, J. W. (1985), 'Workers' compensation insurance, experience-rating, and occupational injuries', *RAND Journal of Economics*, vol. 16, pp. 487–503.

— (1998), 'Does workers' compensation encourage hard to diagnose injuries?', *Journal of Risk and Insurance*, vol. 65, pp. 101–24.

Smith, R. S. (1990), 'Mostly on Monday: is workers' compensation covering off-the-job injuries?', in P. S. Borba and D. Appel (eds), *Benefits, Costs, and Cycles in Workers' Compensation*, Boston, MA: Kluwer.

Solon, G. (1985), 'Work incentive effects of taxing unemployment benefits', *Econometrica*, vol. 53, pp. 295–306.

Sullivan, J. X. (2001), 'Borrowing during unemployment: unsecured debt as a safety net', Northwestern University, mimeo.

Summers, L. H. (1989), 'Some simple economics of mandated benefits', *American Economic Review: Papers and Proceedings*, vol. 79, pp. 177–83.

Topel, R. H. (1983), 'On layoffs and unemployment insurance', *American Economic Review*, vol. 73, pp. 541–59.

US Chamber of Commerce (2000), *Analysis of Workers' Compensation Laws, 2000*, Washington, DC: US Chamber of Commerce.

US House of Representatives, Committee on Ways and Means (various years), *Green Book*, background material and data on programmes within the jurisdiction of the Committee on Ways and Means, Washington, DC: US Government Printing Office.

Welch, F. (1977), 'What have we learned from empirical studies of unemployment insurance?', *Industrial and Labor Relations Review*, vol. 30, pp. 451–61.

Worrall, J. D., Butler, R. J., Borba, P. and Durbin, D. (1988), 'Estimating the exit rate from workers' compensation: new hazard rate estimates', Rutgers University, mimeo.

6

What We Spend and What We Get: Public and Private Provision of Crime Prevention and Criminal Justice

ANN DRYDEN WITTE AND ROBERT WITT[1]

I. INTRODUCTION

Communities that cannot provide an acceptable level of security for persons and property will not survive long. Economists have long pointed out that, even if such communities were to survive, they would not prosper. Communities where the strong are allowed to victimise the weak freely will be small, and surviving members will have to spend most of their resources on defence.

When property can be freely taken by theft and deception, no one has the incentive to invest. Protection of property from taking is the most basic of all property rights. Without this protection, the problem of the commons is pervasive.

Adam Smith believed that the protection of person and property was the most important duty of government after national defence. Yet, somewhat surprisingly, economists interested in public economics have rarely analysed the nature of the government's role in providing domestic security for citizens. A search of both general and advanced textbooks on public economics revealed no text that considered government expenditures and the government role in crime prevention and criminal justice.

In this chapter, we seek to use the perspective and tools of public economics to examine crime control and criminal justice. We begin by presenting both general and specific measures of the level and nature of crime for a variety of countries. Not surprisingly, crime is pervasive. However, the level of crime varies substantially across countries. In Section III, we outline the arguments for at least some public provision of crime prevention, enforcement, prosecution, defence and adjudication. We briefly consider sentencing. In Section IV, we describe the

The authors are grateful to Roy Carr-Hill and seminar participants at the Institute for Fiscal Studies for useful discussions and comments. The views expressed, and any errors remaining, are attributable to the authors alone.

[1] Witte is at Wellesley College and the National Bureau of Economic Research (NBER). Witt is at the University of Surrey.

Fiscal Studies (2001) vol. 22, no. 1, pp. 1–40. © Institute for Fiscal Studies, 2001

relative roles of the private and public sectors in the provision of crime control and criminal justice. In the penultimate section, we summarise some research on the effectiveness of public expenditures on crime control and criminal justice. We conclude by suggesting some potentially productive research directions.

II. WHAT IS THE PROBLEM?

Crime is everywhere. Even though countries define crime differently in their criminal codes, no country is without crime. Some things are crimes almost everywhere. These have come to be called the core or traditional crimes—murder, robbery, rape, theft, burglary, fraud and assault. Even for these crimes, measuring the extent of the activity is, to say the least, difficult. Perpetrators have strong incentives to keep their activities secret, and discovery by public or private enforcement agencies is limited both by resources and by evidence.

Crime is, of course, not limited to the traditional crimes. Trafficking in illegal or stolen property is widespread and increasingly transnational. Financial and environmental crimes, sometimes carried out by large multinational enterprises, can and often do cause mass human suffering and financial losses. One need only think of the Bhopal disaster or the BCCI scandal.

Obtaining an overall measure of the extent of crime that is comparable across countries is a daunting task. Fortunately, researchers at the World Bank have carefully compiled, analysed and aggregated indicators for the 'rule of law', graft and political instability and violence from 13 different sources for over 150 countries. See Kaufmann et al. (1999a,b) for a list of sources and methodology used. They provide an aggregate measure for each indicator that ranges from −2.5 to 2.5. Countries with higher numbers are deemed to be more law-abiding. Kaufmann et al. provide standard errors as well as point estimates for each country.

Kaufmann et al.'s rule of law provides, as far as we are aware, the broadest (in terms of both types of crime and geography) indicator of crime that is available. To obtain a measure for the rule of law, Kaufmann et al. aggregate a number of indicators that measure the extent to which agents have confidence in and abide by the rules of society. The indicators include perceptions of the incidence of both violent and non-violent crime, the effectiveness and predictability of the judiciary and the enforceability of contracts. Kaufmann et al. indicate that, together, these indicators measure the success of a society in developing an environment in which fair and predictable rules form the basis for economic and social interaction.

Figure 1 displays Kaufmann et al.'s measures for the rule of law for selected countries. The diamond in the centre of the country name is the point estimate. The lines emanating from the point estimates provide the 90 per cent confidence interval for each estimate.

From these data, it is clear that some countries (e.g. Switzerland and Singapore) have much stronger rules of law than other countries (e.g. the Congo and Iraq). It is also clear that reasonable estimates for the middle-range countries (e.g. Brazil,

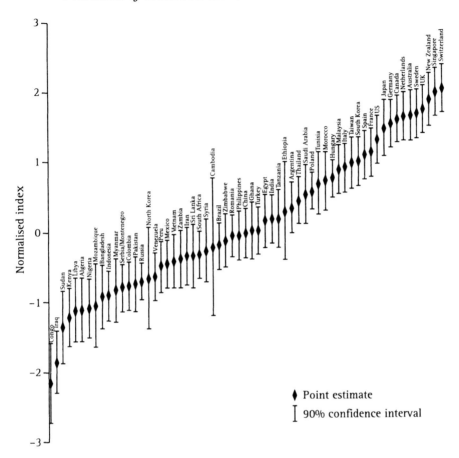

Figure 1. *Rule of law, 1997–98*

Source: Kaufmann et al. (2000).

India and Turkey) do not differ significantly. Still, these estimates provide a useful broad assessment of the extent of the crime problem across countries.

Kaufmann et al.'s indicator for graft is designed to measure perceptions of corruption, an important aspect of crime (see Figure 2). Kaufmann et al. describe this measure as indicating the degree to which public power is used for private gain. This measure of crime is narrower than the rule of law considered previously, but it still provides a valuable measure of the extent of an important and often overlooked aspect of crime. Rankings are generally similar, but not identical, to those for the rule of law. For example, Italy is quite like Spain in terms of the rule of law but has a much lower rating than Spain for graft. Tunisia is quite like Brazil in terms of graft but has a higher measure for the rule of law than does Brazil.

While graft measures public property offences, Kaufmann et al.'s political instability and violence indicator might be considered as a measure of the likelihood of

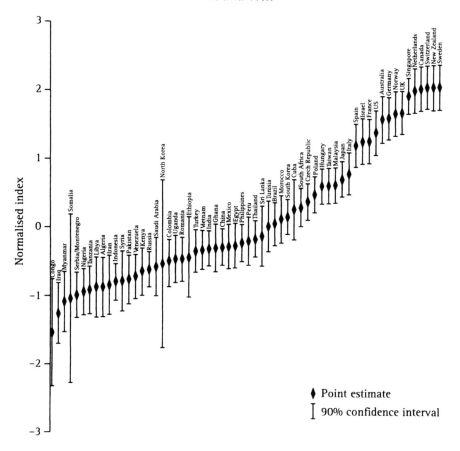

Figure 2. *Graft, 1997–98*

Source: Kaufmann et al. (2000).

violent crime related to government. Figure 3 presents a measure of public perceptions regarding the likelihood that the government in power will be destabilised or overthrown by unconstitutional or violent means. On this indicator, Italy ranks above Spain, and Algeria joins the Congo and Iraq at the bottom of the scale.

Turning from general measures of lawfulness to measures for the core crimes, one finds less information both in terms of the number of countries for which comparable data are available and in terms of the crimes for which the extent is measured. Before proceeding, it is important to note that reports of crime to the police—the most broadly cited statistics in many countries—are generally more a measure of the functioning of the criminal justice system than of crime (Newman, 1999).

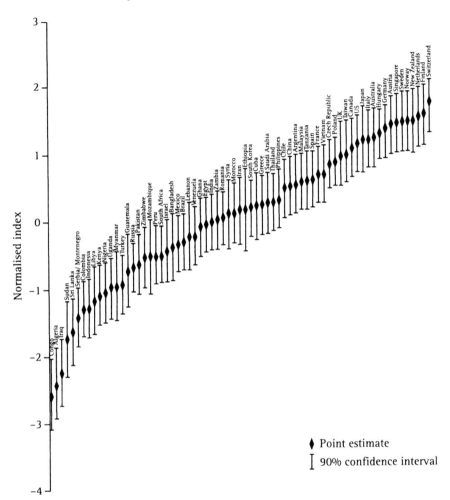

Figure 3. *Political instability and violence, 1997–98*

Source: Kaufmann et al. (2000).

That being said, some crimes are more difficult to hide than others. For example, murder is generally known because a dead body rarely remains successfully hidden for long. In stable countries, the number of murders (homicides) is generally quite well recorded by the police.[2] Further vital statistics provide a check on the number of homicides in countries with well-functioning public health departments.

The United Nations Crime and Justice Survey (UNCJS), the International Police Organisation (INTERPOL) and the World Health Organisation (WHO) provide independent estimates of the extent of homicide for a variety of countries.

---

[2] Newman (1999, p. 11).

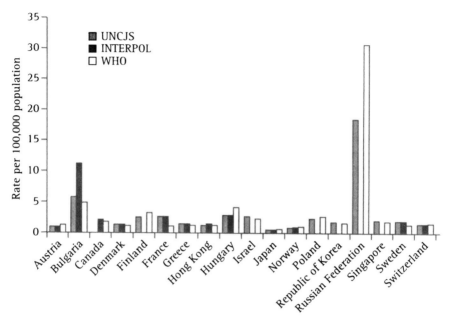

Figure 4. *Homicide rates per 100,000 population, 1993*
Source: Notes to Box 0.7 of Newman (1999).

WHO reports only on successful, completed acts of homicide from vital statistics. The UNCJS and INTERPOL rely either directly or indirectly on the reports of national criminal justice systems.[3]

As can be seen in Figure 4, the three sources of data generally agree rather closely on the homicide rate for most countries. However, there are notable exceptions. For example, the different sources provide quite different estimates for Bulgaria and the Russian Federation. While the sources of data indicate quite different magnitudes for these countries, all sources indicate that they have higher murder rates than other countries for which data were available. For other countries, homicide rates range from under one per 100,000 (i.e. Japan and Norway) to over two per 100,000 (e.g. Finland and Israel).

For crimes other than murder, measurement is more difficult. Surveys of victims provide reasonably accurate measures of offences for which there is an identifiable victim who knows that he has been victimised and is willing to report it in a survey setting. For international comparisons, the International Crime Victim Surveys (ICVSs) that were carried out in 1989, 1992–94 and 1996 provide results for a number of industrialised, transition and developing countries.[4] These surveys

---

[3] Raw data on homicide from the UNCJS and INTERPOL include attempts as well as completed murders. We use figures given in the notes to Box 0.7 of Newman (1999).

[4] For a description of methodologies and countries included, see Note 3 to Box 0.9 of Newman (1999).

use consistent definitions of offences, while official statistics depend on the definition of offences in the criminal law, which can vary widely from country to country. The surveys asked about the following offences: (1) contact crimes (robbery, sexual offences, threats and assaults), (2) burglary (including attempts), (3) car crimes (car theft, theft from car and car damage) and (4) other thefts (motorcycle theft, bicycle theft and other personal theft).

These surveys reveal that more than half of urban residents report having been a victim of one or more of the covered offences during the last five years. Being the victim of a crime is a common occurrence in all urban areas. Rates of victimisation are highest in Africa and Latin America, where almost three-quarters of urban residents report having been victimised during the last five years. Rates are lowest in Asia, where 45 per cent of urban residents report victimisation in a five-year period. Victimisation rates in the US, England and Wales, and West Germany are quite similar, with between 60 and 65 per cent of urban residents reporting victimisation during a five-year period.

The ICVS asked respondents about their perception of the relative seriousness of various types of crimes. Western European and North American countries tended to rank violent crimes (e.g. robbery with a weapon) most seriously, while African, Asian, Central and Eastern European, and Latin American countries ranked car theft as the most serious of the offences considered.

Urban residents have over a 50 per cent chance of being the victim of a contact crime during a five-year period in Colombia and less than a 10 per cent chance of being the victim of a contact crime in Switzerland. In Western Europe, the Netherlands reports the highest level of victimisation for contact crimes (22 per cent of urban residents report victimisation). This reported rate of victimisation is approximately the same as Russia's. In the US, approximately 20 per cent of urban residents report that they have been victims of contact crimes during a five-year period.

Car theft is most frequently reported in New Zealand (just under 50 per cent of urban residents report car thefts during a five-year period) and least frequently reported in China (less than 2 per cent of the Chinese report car thefts during a five-year period). These numbers point up the importance of opportunity. For most property crimes, victimisation rates are higher in wealthier countries where there is more of value to steal. Theft is significantly correlated with holdings of durable goods.

It is more difficult to gauge the extent of crimes other than murder and those covered by the ICVS. Official records of crime, such as the US Federal Bureau of Investigation (FBI)'s Uniform Crime Reports (UCRs), reflect many things in addition to the underlying crime rate (for example, the willingness of residents to report crimes to the police and the reporting practices of police agencies). We discuss a few attempts (mainly cross-national) to study other types of offending here.

The ICVS, like most victimisation surveys, is concerned with offences where individuals or households are the victims. A few victimisation surveys have also sought to discern the extent to which businesses are victimised. For example, a 1993 survey of commercial establishments in England and Wales reports that eight out of 10 retailers and two out of three manufacturers experience one or more crimes covered by the survey in 1993. Commercial victimisation appears to be highly concentrated, with 3 per cent of retailers experiencing 59 per cent of the crime reported in the survey. The reported risk of victimisation and the amount of the loss were higher for retailers and manufacturers than for households (Mirrlees-Black and Ross, 1995a,b).

As is well known, the core crimes with the exception of fraud are, like basketball, primarily a young man's game. In a very interesting study, Jurgen-Tas et al. (1994) report the results of surveys of young people (aged 14–21) in 12 countries that were carried out in 1992. As can be seen in Figure 5, rates of self-reported offending vary substantially across the areas studied. For example, young people in Athens report the highest rates of violent crime, with more than half of the respondents reporting that they had committed an offence during the last year. Young people in Helsinki report the highest rates of property crime (just under 40 per cent) and young people in England and Wales the highest rate of drug-offending (26 per cent).

Regardless of whether one considers general measures of law-abidingness, victimisation reports or self-reports of crime by the young, the message is the same—there is a lot of crime. That being the case, we turn to the next issue. What, if anything, should the public sector do about it?

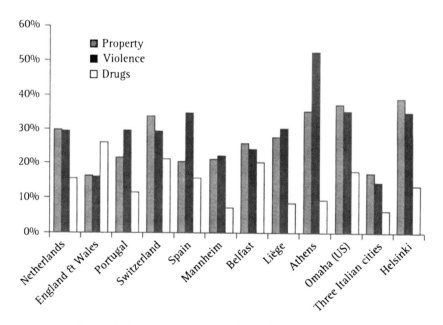

Figure 5. *Percentage reporting offences during the last 12 months*
Source: Box 0.10 of Newman (1999).

III. WHAT PUBLIC ROLE?

As Hart (1994, p. 91) has noted, communities must have restrictions on the free use of violence, theft and deception if they are to survive and prosper. To put it somewhat differently, societies will place restrictions on the core or traditional crimes—murder, rape, robbery, theft, burglary, fraud and assault.

The question is how these restrictions will be imposed. In what Hart calls primitive societies, they may be imposed by custom and informal means of social control. However, as communities grow, develop and become more heterogeneous, restrictions against committing the core crimes tend to become a matter of religious or governmental rules or a mixture of both.

Today, the legal systems that outlaw the core crimes can be classified broadly into three types: (1) civil law, (2) common law and (3) Islamic law (Newman, 1999). Only in Islamic law do we find a mixture of religious and governmental restrictions against the core crimes. Islamic law tends to encourage non-governmental response to the core crimes, including murder (Groves et al., 1987). Islamic law tempers retaliation by encouraging forgiveness. Under Islamic law, a victim or a victim's family may waive retaliation and receive instead a money payment from the perpetrator of the crime. In such a situation, the government will not become involved with either the offender or the offence. Only if the perpetrator and victim cannot agree does the government become involved.

In both the common law and civil law traditions, it is the government that forbids the core crimes. The civil law tradition originated as a combination of Roman law and papal statements of the Roman Catholic church. However, most countries that follow the civil law tradition today (e.g. France, Germany, Brazil, Russia and Indonesia) rely on secular legislation as the source of restrictions against the core crimes. Under a civil law system, there is a sharp separation of powers. Legislatures make the law and judges apply it.[5]

By way of contrast, the common law tradition relies on the customs of the people as its original source. Much of common law became codified over time. For example, restrictions against the core crimes are now generally legislated. However, judges may and do interpret the legislated law in particular cases. The judge has the ability to make laws in the common law tradition but not in the civil law tradition. Countries that use the common law tradition include England, India and the US.

Why do most developed countries empower one or more arms of government to determine what is criminal? The rise of the power of government to determine what is a crime coincides with the rise of the nation state, industrialisation and urbanisation. The rulers of the new nation states sought to monopolise control over the use of force in the hands of their servants for quite obvious reasons. Industrialisation and urbanisation weakened the force of traditional or customary law. The rise of

---

[5] In developed countries, the civil law and common law traditions have become more similar since the Second World War.

secular society weakened religious restrictions against the core crimes, although religious restriction can still be very important in preventing crime.

Standardisation and codification of criminal laws lowered the transaction costs required for both interpersonal interaction and property transfers. Reliable and standardised rules allowed for greater economies of scale by lowering the costs of trade and travel over larger areas. As noted earlier, protection of property from taking by theft or fraud is the most basic of all property rights and is necessary to prevent the problem of the commons. The newly emergent nation state was in a unique position to undertake the codification and had the incentive to do so to solidify its power.

Many believe that crime is very distinct from other types of illegal acts because crimes are believed not only to harm the victim but also to harm other members of society. Crimes, particularly the core crimes, are believed to be offences against society, not merely offences against the individual (Kaplan et al., 1991; Cooter and Ulen, 2000). In economic terms, crime produces negative externalities and will be too high if there is no public intervention.

An additional distinguishing feature of crimes as opposed to most civil offences, such as torts, is that conviction of a crime requires a finding of *mens rea* (a guilty mind). If enforcement costs were zero, we might want to eliminate the core crimes. By way of contrast, we only wish to encourage an efficient level of prevention expenditures in the case of torts. The intent to do physical harm or to transfer property by force or deception requires stronger deterrence than does accidental occurrence and may even justify putting the offender in a position where he can no longer offend (i.e. incapacitating the offender).

Some have argued that many crimes should be handled like torts, with the victim bringing a case for compensation (e.g. Friedman, 2000). Others argue that crimes are very different from torts. For some crimes (e.g. rape and robbery), some argue that no amount of compensation can make the victim whole (Cooter and Ulen, 2000). Others argue that the intent required for a crime requires punishment or retaliation (*United States v. Bergman*, 1976).

Regardless of the position one takes in these arguments, even the most ardent proponents of treating many things that are currently crimes as torts find a need to criminalise in some circumstances. For example, Friedman (2000) suggests that criminalisation is necessary for acts in which the victims are anonymous (e.g. highway robbery) or defendants are 'judgment-proof' (too poor to pay compensation to victims). The matter in dispute is what acts should be criminal.

1. Police

The police do many things, but we are concerned only with their crime-control functions. These functions include crime prevention and the apprehension of offenders.

(a) Preventing Crime
What is the proper role of government in preventing crime? As we will show later, crime prevention is now generally split between the private and public sectors,

with the private sector generally spending more on prevention than the public sector.

Much crime prevention does not involve the use of force, and hence the argument for public provision is greatly weakened. When crime prevention does require the use of force, the case for public provision is stronger (Hart et al., 1997). Public monopoly of and control over the legitimate use of force are central to the provision of standard levels of security for persons and property. Further, to be effective, the police require the sympathy and co-operation of the public. Public police may be better able to nurture these needed characteristics.

Public police forces are relatively new and emerged along with large, heterogeneous urban areas. They arose in response to a public outcry for more order. The first public police force was established in London in 1829 to provide a full-time day and night patrol to prevent crime. Sir Robert Peel, who was mainly responsible for establishing the force under the Metropolitan Police Act, insisted that political patronage be excluded from appointments and promotions (Miller, 1977, as excerpted in Kaplan et al., 1991). Boston established a public police force in 1837 to prevent violence between Protestants and Catholics. New York City's Municipal Police Act established a semi-military day and night patrol force in 1845. The New York force was not insulated from political patronage (Kaplan et al., 1991, pp. 141–5).

(b) Apprehending Offenders

The police are asked not only to prevent crime but also to apprehend offenders when crime does occur. Apprehension often requires the use of force, and hence a reasonably good case can be made for public provision (Hart et al., 1997). Also, in contrast with many civil offences such as automobile accidents, the identity of the perpetrator may be unknown to the victim (Polinsky and Shavell, 1999). Even if the perpetrator's identity is known, the victim may well not be willing to press a case.

As noted earlier, crime can produce very high negative externalities (e.g. fear of going out when someone has recently been murdered in the neighbourhood) and so both prevention of crime and apprehension of criminals will be inadequately supplied by the private sector. Prevention and apprehension are also likely to be much higher in wealthier than in poorer neighbourhoods if these activities are financed by the private sector.

To summarise, both efficiency and equity arguments call for public financing of at least a minimal level of police services in larger communities. The wealthy will often choose to purchase additional prevention to protect both their person and their property.

The fact that the police's crime-fighting activities can involve the use of force in a wide array of situations suggests that public provision rather than contracting with the private sector will likely be best for these activities (Hart et al., 1997). Other police functions (e.g. record-keeping) may well be better contracted out than provided by the public sector.

2. Prosecution

The role of the state in prosecuting crime clearly depends upon whether crime is seen mainly as an offence against the state or as an offence against the victim. Countries as diverse as China, France and the US see crime mainly as an offence against the state or the community as a whole, and public officials generally prosecute criminal cases. However, the powers and type of officials empowered to prosecute crimes vary substantially across countries. In continental Europe, the prosecutor is an appointed career civil servant of the central government with a close relationship to the court. Most prosecutors in the US are locally elected officials with substantial autonomy from both the judicial and the executive branches of government (Kaplan et al., 1991, pp. 289–91).

In China, private citizens (generally the victim or the victim's relatives) prosecute less serious crimes, while the state prosecutes more serious offences (Newman, 1999, p. 40). From an economic point of view, this split can be justified because of the larger negative externalities arising from more serious crimes.

Traditional English common law sees crime as an offence against the victim, not as an offence against some broader community. It was not until 1879 that England created an Office of Public Prosecutions. The Director of this Office is a career civil servant. The actual trial of cases is assigned to barristers in private practice designated as Crown Counsel. For a discussion, see Newman (1999, p. 132) or Kaplan et al. (1991, pp. 287–306).

One can easily argue for public expenditures to secure prosecution of crimes that cause large negative externalities, since private parties would be expected to bring too few suits. Arguments for public provision of prosecution generally rest on the need to maintain a high level of standards in the prosecution of serious criminal cases. As Kaplan et al. (1991, p. 311) express it, 'the prosecutor is also a representative of the government upon whom the courts, and society, impose a standard of ethics which may transcend any particular rule'. Contracts for prosecutors would tend to be quite incomplete. Privately contracted prosecutors would have strong incentives to lower standards in order to lower costs (Hart et al., 1997).

3. Defence

Most developed countries, whether following a civil or a common law legal tradition, provide public funding to allow indigent defendants to hire legal counsel in serious criminal cases. The need for representation is probably stronger under the adversarial common law tradition, where the judge can only consider the evidence brought before him, than under the inquisitional civil tradition, where the judge can actively search for information.

Economic arguments for the provision of defence counsel for the indigent rest mainly on equity grounds, although it would be possible to argue that it is inefficient to imprison the innocent poor. Horizontal equity dictates that the equally situated should be treated equally. In terms of the core crimes, equal situation might well be defined as being equally innocent or equally guilty. Defendants without legal counsel will clearly not be in a situation that is equivalent to the situation of those who are able to purchase competent legal counsel.

The US has a large, complicated and much criticised 'system' for providing defence counsel for the indigent. The sixth amendment to the US Constitution establishes the right to counsel in federal criminal prosecutions. However, most of the core crimes are prosecuted at the local level, not at the federal level. During the 1960s and 1970s, a series of US Supreme Court cases (e.g. *Gideon v. Wainwright* (1963) and *Argersinger v. Hamilin* (1972)) established indigents' right to counsel for all criminal prosecutions that carry a sentence of imprisonment.

The Supreme Court did not indicate how state and local government were to provide indigent defence counsel or what source of funds would be used to pay for indigent defence. Currently, local governments (e.g. the counties) are primarily responsible for providing defence counsel for the indigent. The majority of funding for indigent defence comes from local government, although the state share of funding has grown over the years (Smith and DeFrances, 1996).

The system for providing indigent defence in the US varies markedly from place to place. However, three basic methods are used:

- *Assigned counsel programmes* appoint indigent counsel on a case-by-case basis. The counsellor is chosen from members of the local, private bar.
- Under *contract attorney programmes*, the local or state government contracts with individual private attorneys, private law firms or local bar associations to provide indigent defence.
- Under *public defender programmes*, salaried staff of full-time or part-time attorneys provide indigent defence. The public defenders may be employed by state or local government or by non-profit corporations contracted to provide indigent defence (Kaplan et al., 1991, p. 351).

About three-quarters of inmates in state prisons and about half of those in federal prisons in the US received publicly provided legal counsel for the offence for which they were serving time (Smith and DeFrances, 1996). The quality of publicly provided legal counsel varies widely both across the US states and, in many states, across local jurisdictions. In 1986, the cost per case of providing defence counsel ranged from a low of $63 in Arkansas to a high of $540 in New Jersey (Kaplan et al., 1991, p. 353).

Horizontal equity is not achieved by the current US system for indigent defence. Further, as noted by Judge Richard Posner, criminal defendants have less access to the private market for lawyers than do defendants in civil cases where damage awards are possible (*Merritt v. Faulkner*, 1983).

4. Adjudication

The need for impartial adjudication of guilt in criminal cases is widely accepted. In traditional societies, this adjudication was often by a body of chiefs or elders.

In the course of economic development and urbanisation, criminal law and criminal procedure became increasingly complex and a widely respected, informal body to adjudicate became more difficult to construct and use. The increasing complexity and impersonality of adjudication has led to the increasing use of trained personnel to referee the trial or inquisition (e.g. to enforce criminal procedure) and establish matters of law. Still, adjudication is, in many countries, a task that is carried out jointly by lay citizens and trained personnel.

For example, in the US, a jury of peers (selected from voter registration lists or other compilations of residents) determines the facts and the guilt or innocence of the accused. The judge referees the proceedings (e.g. enforces proper procedure and the admission of evidence), instructs the jury, determines matters of law and decides on the sentence a convicted defendant will receive after being found guilty.[6] In the US, judges may be elected or appointed and the judiciary is separated from the executive or legislative branch of governments.

In Germany, lay judges often sit with professional judges in criminal trials (Aronowitz, 2000). By way of contrast, in Japan, the jury system has, by and large, been suspended and judges chosen on the basis of national-level examinations adjudicate in criminal trials (Moriyama, 2000).

As noted by Judge Richard Posner, impartial adjudication is central to a well-functioning judicial system. As Posner (1992, p. 534) puts it, 'the rules of the judicial process have been designed both to prevent the judge from receiving a monetary payoff from deciding a case in a particular way and to minimise the influence of politically effective interest groups on his decisions'. Posner's first requirement suggests that for-profit provision of adjudication is a non-starter. His second requirement suggests that some insulation from electoral politics may be desirable.

But why do so many adjudication systems involve the lay public? One possible justification for lay involvement in adjudication may be to obtain both public support for and tempering of legal outcomes in the criminal arena. For example, it is well known that juries will often not convict when the potential penalty is not in accord with community feelings regarding what is appropriate.

5. Punishment

Punishments for criminal offence range widely: death (capital punishment); deprivation of liberty (up to imprisonment for life); corporal punishment; control in freedom (e.g. probation and parole); fines; warnings or admonitions; and community service orders. According to the fifth UNCJS, which obtained information on crime and criminal justice for 1993–94 for a wide variety of countries, deprivation of liberty (i.e. imprisonment) was the most common form of criminal punishment, with 35 per cent of cases resulting in this type of sentence. Fines were

---

[6] When criminal sentences were largely indeterminate (e.g. 5 years to life), judges and parole boards had substantial discretion. The move to determinate sentencing (e.g. sentencing guidelines) decreased the amount of sentencing discretion available to judges.

the next most common sentence and were used in 33 per cent of the cases (Newman, 1999, pp. 89–90).

The relative use of fines and imprisonment varies widely across countries. For example, according to the UNCJS, adjudicated criminal cases in Colombia always result in imprisonment, 96 per cent of criminal cases resulted in imprisonment in Greece, 92 per cent in Mexico and 60 per cent in Italy. By way of contrast, 95 per cent of adjudicated cases in Japan resulted in a fine, 82 per cent in Myanmar, 79 per cent in England and Wales and 70 per cent in Egypt and in Germany.

After carrying out a quantitative examination of sentencing practices, Shinkai and Zvekic conclude that the level of development of the country, economic situation or region could not explain variations in sentencing practices. They conclude that cross-national variations in sentencing patterns are best explained by the 'availability and acceptability of the sentencing options' (Newman, 1999, p. 91).

Economists have been interested in optimal sentencing since the work of Becker (1968) and Stigler (1970). Economists generally conclude that fines should be preferred whenever they can be imposed. See, for example, Posner (1992, p. 227). The argument for fines rests on their production of revenue for the state, the victim or both and the high costs of imprisonment. The major economic arguments for the use of imprisonment for the core crimes rest on the fact that many who commit crimes are too poor to pay a fine that would provide optimal deterrence. For a discussion, see Kaplow and Shavell (1999). This is so both because of their penury and because many of the core crimes have low probabilities of the offender being penalised and, hence, would require very high fines if optimal deterrence were to be achieved. For example, in New South Wales (Sydney and surrounding communities), crime statistics for 1996 indicate that, as a whole, those who break and enter buildings, steal cars, rob or assault others have only a 4 per cent chance of being convicted and less than a 1 per cent chance of going to prison. The reason for the low probability of apprehension and punishment for these crimes is mainly victims' failures to report the offences to the police (54 per cent of offences are reported), the police's failures to record reported offences (40 per cent of crimes are recorded by the police) and the police's failures to find the perpetrator (7 per cent of crimes are cleared by the police) (Newman, 1999, p. 75).

Another economic argument for imprisonment rather than fines is that imprisonment quite successfully incapacitates offenders and fines do not. The social benefit of this incapacitation depends upon the extent to which offenders will continue to offend and on the elasticity of supply of offenders. This suggests that imprisonment of consistently violent offenders will have higher social benefits than will imprisonment of those who commit a 'crime of passion'. Certainly, it argues against the tendency in the US to use scarce prison resources for drug dealers. As my son, who lives on the lower east side of New York, says, 'Mom, they are like cockroaches—as soon as one leaves, there is another to replace him'. Society achieves little decrease in drug dealing by incarcerating drug dealers.

The arguments presented up to this point suggest that wealthy offenders with little likelihood of offending again should be fined, not imprisoned. While this is largely the case, it is not always so. Why? Before turning to possible economic arguments for imprisoning such offenders, we will consider the reasons judges provide.

In *United States v. Bergman* (1976), a 64-year-old rabbi with an excellent reputation for community service was convicted of fraudulently charging the government for services rendered by nursing homes that he owned. In sentencing Bergman to a short term of imprisonment, Judge Marvin Frankel carefully enunciated his reasoning. He concluded that both general deterrence and equal justice required a prison sentence in this case.

It is also interesting to consider Judge Kimba Wood's reasoning when sentencing the US junk bond inventor, Michael Milken, to prison. She found that a prison term was necessary in the Milken case to achieve general deterrence (i.e. the need to prevent others from violating the law). Her reasoning is interesting. She found that prison sentences are viewed as one of the most powerful deterrents to the financial community. She also reasoned that crimes such as securities fraud, which are hard to detect, require greater punishment in order to deter others from committing them (Kaplan et al., 1991, pp. 571–5).

In some ways, the arguments of Judge Frankel and Judge Wood are like those of economists, but in other ways they are quite different. Both Bergman and Milken were capable of paying large fines (indeed, Milken paid very large fines). Being barred for life from working in the securities industry effectively incapacitated Milken, and Judge Frankel found it unlikely that Bergman would ever offend again. This leaves only the economic argument of optimal deterrence. Would it have been possible to achieve optimal general deterrence by only fining Bergman and Milken? The judges ruled not, but I suspect that many economists would argue that, given the wealth of these two criminals, a large enough fine would have effectively deterred others.

This leaves Judge Frankel's second argument, equal justice. Economists are not accustomed to thinking about equal justice but are accustomed to thinking about horizontal equity. As we argued earlier, in the criminal justice setting, horizontal equity might be seen as treating equally guilty parties equally. Sending the judgment-proof poor to prison and allowing the equally guilty rich to pay a fine might strike some economists as horizontally inequitable.

IV. PUBLIC AND PRIVATE PROVISION OF PREVENTION AND CRIMINAL JUSTICE

The previous section gave reasons why we might have public expenditures on crime prevention and criminal justice. In this section, we will focus on (1) how much overall spending there should be on crime prevention and criminal justice, (2) public expenditures on crime prevention and criminal justice, (3) individual crime prevention activities and (4) the partial privatisation of criminal justice activities.

1. Optimal Level of Expenditures on Crime Prevention and Criminal Justice

In many industrialised countries, an increasing amount of public and private resources is devoted to crime prevention. What counts as prevention? Examples include specific crime prevention programmes (e.g. juvenile delinquency, school, ex-offender job training, rehabilitation and counselling programmes), employment of security guards, installation of locks, burglar alarms, CCTV systems and many other innovations in crime preventive technology, and policing. The socially or individually optimal level of crime prevention is where the marginal benefit of reduction in crime equals the marginal cost of extra prevention. However, as Freeman (1999) has noted, to estimate the marginal dollar value of the reduction in crime due to any crime prevention policy is hard because of the difficulties associated with measuring reductions in monetary and non-monetary costs (e.g. reduced non-monetary loss from being victimised).

To calculate the trade-off of the marginal value of the reduction in crime due to the criminal justice system is even trickier than for prevention. The criminal justice system is diverse and multifaceted. There are a host of agencies involved and, at the margins, these agencies engage in much work having little to do with criminal justice. Thus, when the youth services of an English town asked the simple question 'did our interventions against offending come to a profit or loss last year?', the answer required a considerable research effort. A criminal justice 'audit' was set in train to estimate the costs of operating the criminal justice system. For a discussion of such an audit, see Shapland (2000), who notes that such work helps us to understand the respects in which criminal justice is indeed a 'system'. Efforts to gauge precisely the unit cost of each stage of criminal justice (e.g. average costs to provide support to victims during the reporting and investigation stage) have a wider significance. Only by comparing the use of resources with such data can one see the effective priorities of the system—that is, upon what it spends its money. Informed comparison of, say, spending on victim–offender mediation compared with spending on refuges for rape victims can then be made.

Interest in rigorous evaluations of crime prevention programmes has increased in recent years. Sherman et al. (1997), for example, introduce a scientific methods scale to assess the methodological quality of evaluation studies in the US, and Goldblatt and Lewis (1998) report similar research from the UK. Partially in response to this trend, the UK government established a three-year Crime Reduction Programme (1999–2002), which included an assessment of the effectiveness and cost-effectiveness as a foundation for setting priorities and allocating resources. Cost-effectiveness and cost–benefit analyses of criminal justice agencies and programmes require estimates of both the costs of crime and the cost of the agency or programme. As noted earlier, estimating the cost of crime is difficult. However, estimates are becoming more common. For example, Brand and Price (2000) provide estimates of the cost of crime for the UK, which include monetary and non-monetary costs to victims. Cost–benefit analyses of crime prevention programmes have also been carried out in other industrialised countries (see references cited in Brand and Price).

There appears to be a broad consensus in the international community on the process required to ensure cost-effectiveness in reducing crime: increased collaboration between institutions (see Walker and Sansfacon, 2000). These institutions include communities, families, schools, businesses and government agencies, such as law enforcement, education, health, labour, social services, housing and urban planning departments. For France, Walker and Sansfacon provide confirmation of the importance of co-ordination of crime prevention programmes between government agencies in reducing crime. The authors describe 'Local Prevention Contracts' in which mayors, chief prosecutors, police chiefs and the national official for education sign contracts to support local crime prevention projects covering most urban areas in France. Also, a community might end up with a group of young workers who share the experience of work with the police as safety and security assistants or as social mediation agents.

In addition to increases in partnerships with other organisations, there has been some interesting work on police tactics. On the one hand, the Kansas City preventive patrol experiment (Kansas City, MO, Missouri Police Department, 1977) concluded that reduced police response time does not reduce crime. On the other hand, community policing with a clear focus (e.g. directed police patrol in crime hot spots) has shown substantial evidence of crime reduction in the US (Sherman et al., 1997). Despite the fact that there is evidence that many different crime prevention programmes can effectively prevent crime (see Section V), the police and prisons remain the two most fiscally important areas of criminal justice expenditure in almost all developed countries.

2. Public Expenditures

In analysing expenditures on criminal justice, it should be borne in mind that, in most countries, the police, courts and prisons are administered by many different agencies or departments of government. Consequently, within countries, it is difficult to identify expenditures since financing is often conducted in separate government departments which may be unrelated to criminal justice itself (see Newman, 1999, pp. 137–8). It should also be noted that, while information problems concerning annual expenditures on criminal justice exist within countries over time, comparisons at cross-national level are sometimes even more problematic. Difficulties arise, in the main, from the way different countries define crime, justice and other relevant concepts (see Howard, Newman and Pridemore, 2000, for a survey of comparative criminology issues).[7]

---

[7] Clearly, differences in accounting practices may seriously affect capital and labour expenditure estimates reported by countries to agencies such as the UNCJS.

According to the Bureau of Justice Statistics, the total amount spent on criminal justice by all levels of government in the US in 1996 was $120 billion. Lindgren and Gifford (2000) report that $53 billion was for police protection, $41 billion for corrections (e.g. prisons and jails) and $26 billion for judicial and legal costs. In the US, government spending on crime as a percentage of GDP was roughly $1\frac{1}{2}$ per cent in 1996. Tables 1 and 2 summarise the estimates of criminal justice expenditures for a number of major industrialised countries. These cross-country aggregates are from van Dijk and de Waard (2000) and relate mainly to 1997 and 1998.

The US and England and Wales have the highest levels of spending on crime as a proportion of GDP, with Denmark and France recording the lowest expenditure rates. A striking feature of Table 1 is the relatively low level of police expenditure

Table 1. *Expenditures per Mille of GDP (1998 prices)*

	Judiciary	Prosecution	Police	Prison	Total
Australia	*1.12*	*0.28*	7.37	1.76	10.53
Austria	*2.49*	*0.17*	8.79	1.15	12.60
Canada	1.20	0.34	7.23	2.48	11.25
Denmark	1.22	0.21	4.86	1.35	7.64
England and Wales	1.24	0.46	10.82	2.55	15.07
France	*1.05*	*0.26*	6.10	0.85	8.26
Germany	*2.72*	*0.79*	5.86	1.06	10.43
Netherlands	1.12	0.56	7.30	2.59	11.57
Sweden	1.67	0.42	6.07	2.18	10.34
US	2.91	0.47	6.75	5.51	15.64

Note: Estimates are italicised.

Source: van Dijk and de Waard (2000, p. 49).

Table 2. *Expenditures per capita (in Euros, 1998 prices)*

	Judiciary	Prosecution	Police	Prison	Total
Australia	*25*	*6*	160	38	229
Austria	*57*	*4*	203	26	290
Canada	28	8	169	58	263
Denmark	30	5	117	32	184
England and Wales	23	9	205	49	286
France	*23*	*6*	132	19	180
Germany	64	*19*	137	25	245
Netherlands	23	11	151	54	239
Sweden	33	8	119	43	203
US	81	13	188	154	436

Notes: Estimates are italicised. Fixed exchange rates for Euro-zone countries; purchasing power parity 1998 for other countries.

Source: van Dijk and de Waard (2000, p. 50).

for the US compared with the high level in England and Wales. This difference may reflect the high ratio of private to public police in the US relative to England and Wales but may also reflect differential salary levels within and across these countries.

It is no surprise that the expenditure on prisons is much higher in the US than in other countries, given the substantial increases in the US incarceration rate over the last three decades. For purposes of comparison, expenditure rates on prisons in France are the lowest in the sample.

From Table 2, we note that the US is the biggest per capita spender, with expenditures of 436 euros per head, followed by Austria and England and Wales. The lowest per capita spenders are France and Denmark, with 180 and 184 euros respectively.

During the past two decades, the number of police per head of population for both industrialised and developing countries has increased, although the greatest increases have been seen in industrialised countries. As Newman (1999) points out, there exists a strong positive correlation between expenditure on criminal justice and economic wealth (as measured by GDP per capita). Table 3 focuses on police expenditure per capita and GDP per capita. In general, we see that richer countries spend more per head on policing. However, Japan is one clear exception, with a very high GDP but low police expenditure. Rough calculations suggest that developing countries (e.g. Colombia, Cyprus, Jordan, Saint Vincent and Grenadines, and Slovenia) spend more on police as a percentage of GDP relative to industrialised countries.[8]

Rapidly growing prison populations in many countries have led to an upsurge of interest in discerning the impact of this costly increase on crime rates. For example, recent work in the US, using either state-level panel data on crime rates from the FBI's Uniform Crime Reports (e.g. Levitt, 1996) or time-series data (e.g. Witt and Witte, 2000), finds increased imprisonment to be associated with significant declines in the reported crime rate. It is important to note that this work considers the effect of increased imprisonment on crimes reported to the police. As noted earlier, reported crime can change even when actual crime does not. For example, victims can decide to report more or less crime to the police and the police can decide to record more or less of the crime that they uncover.

As of mid-1999, the US had incarcerated 1,860,520 individuals in its prisons and jails. This represents an incarceration rate of one in every 147 US residents. Estimates of the annual cost of locking up an inmate in the US can be found in Donohue and Siegelman (1998). For example, they estimate (p. 5) that the annual cost of incarcerating an additional inmate is approximately $36,000 (in 1993 dollars). Although this estimate includes the costs of building, occupying a prison cell and lost legitimate wages, it ignores a number of social benefits (e.g. the benefit from seeing an individual punished) and social costs (e.g. the effects of imprisonment on future legitimate work experience).

---

[8] In some countries, the military assumes some police functions. For example, in the US, the military was used to help fight the 'war on drugs'.

Table 3. *Police expenditure and GDP per capita, 1994*

	GDP per capita (US$)	Expenditure on police per capita (US$)	Expenditure on police as a percentage of GDP (%)
Colombia	1,847	18.72	1.01
Costa Rica	2,463	7.42	0.30
Croatia	3,867	20.57	0.53
Cyprus	9,754	136.59	1.40
Denmark	28,245	145.28	0.51
Finland	19,048	112.23	0.59
France	24,608	148.90	0.61
Greece	7,465	60.01	0.80
Hong Kong	22,590	185.65	0.82
Hungary	4,072	6.09	0.15
India	309	0.20	0.06
Japan	36,782	18.40	0.05
Jordan	1,095	15.42	1.41
Madagascar	208	0.05	0.02
Malta	7,394	77.09	1.04
Netherlands	21,536	204.09	0.95
Romania	1,274	4.13	0.32
St Vincent and Grenadines	2,248	41.45	1.84
Singapore	23,556	100.94	0.43
Slovenia	7,206	98.13	1.36
Spain	12,201	27.73	0.23
Sweden	22,499	157.29	0.70
Switzerland	36,096	299.53	0.83
Turkey	2,227	9.66	0.43

Source: Adapted from Newman (1999, p. 302).

As well as differences in expenditure on police and courts between developed and developing countries, richer countries also tend to spend more on prisons, although Japan again, with its high GDP, spends relatively little on prisons (Newman, 1999). Table 4 shows UNCJS figures for annual public expenditures per convicted prisoner. These data are derived by multiplying the expenditure (salaries and fixed assets) on corrections (penal and correctional institutions) reported by each country in local currency by an exchange rate and then dividing by the number of convicted adult prisoners reported in 1994. With the exception of Northern Ireland, which has its own unique characteristics, Switzerland is currently one of the highest spenders, alongside Sweden, the US, Denmark and England and Wales. Interestingly, these are countries identified in Figure 1 as having stronger rules of law.

An examination of expenditures per convicted prisoner indicates some interesting facts. Japan has relatively low levels of spending on prisons per head of the population, while at the same time it spends a high amount per prisoner. Another

Table 4. *Annual expenditure per convicted prisoner, 1994*

	Expenditure per convicted prisoner (US$ p.a.)
Northern Ireland	158,197
Switzerland	112,145
Sweden[a]	90,806
US[a]	73,205
Denmark	64,932
England and Wales	61,721
Bermuda	56,510
Japan	47,873
Scotland	46,235
Luxemburg	43,885
Cyprus	39,284
Slovenia	31,786
Hong Kong	28,341
Portugal	22,442
Finland	18,908
Austria	17,980
Belgium	15,767
Uruguay	10,949
Republic of Korea	10,122
Hungary	9,788
Singapore	9,593
Czech Republic	8,903
Brunei Darussalam[a]	4,253
Colombia	4,028
Turkey	3,384
Slovakia	2,962
Panama	2,871
Costa Rica	1,923
Croatia	1,231
Guyana	542
Madagascar	70

[a]1990 data.

Source: Newman (1999, p. 142).

fact that stands out is that developing countries have lower levels of prison expenditure per prisoner than industrialised countries. These particular comparisons are obviously sensitive to the precise choice of day of year, given that the number of admissions to prison is not taken into account (see Newman, 1999, p. 337).

3. Individual Efforts to Prevent Crime

In general, an individual will purchase crime prevention goods and services when the cost of prevention is less than the expected benefits from prevention.

One aspect of the debate over the modes of crime prevention is the separation between private and public expenditures. There are a number of explanations as to why certain individuals may only be concerned about private expenditures. The failure of government programmes to stem the growth in crime may provide one example, but an alternative explanation may lie in terms of how individual objectives are determined. The median-voter model, originally developed in the political sciences, may be applied to shed light on the level of private prevention expenditures. In democracies, things such as police services will be set at the level desired by the median voter (generally considered to be the voter with median income). Individuals and firms with above-median income may quite rationally choose to increase their level of protection by buying in the private market. Under such circumstances, it could be argued that richer individuals and firms purchase relatively more protection, because they personally stand to gain more from this than from the alternative low-protection strategy.

Expenditures by individuals and private organisations on crime prevention are more difficult to estimate than public expenditures. In 1992, the latest year in the US for which we have a bench-mark input–output table, private household purchases of detective and protective services amounted to $944 million and purchases of security systems services amounted to $1,301 million. Clearly, these are not the only private purchases related to crime prevention and criminal justice. Purchases of legal services by private households cost about $44 billion in 1992, but we have no information on what part of this cost was related to criminal cases. There are also expenditures on modifications to existing structures (e.g. bars on windows), car alarms and other anti-theft devices that do not show up explicitly in the estimates. The above private expenditures do not include expenditures by businesses and other organisations, which have substantial crime prevention and apprehension expenditures, as is clear from a trip to any major company or university in the US. Unfortunately, such estimates are not readily available in the UK due to the absence of systematic accounting of private crime prevention expenditures.

Cooter and Ulen (2000, p. 458) quote figures for US private expenditures on crime prevention in 1993 of $65 billion. Sources cited in Anderson (1999) estimate that expenditures on private protection in 1993 were $69 billion. Philipson and Posner (1996) cite a yet higher estimate of $300 billion (including expenditures by businesses and other enterprises on security guards and other measures of self-protection). Laband and Sophocleus (1992) provide a similar estimate.

Anderson (1999) concludes that the aggregate burden of crime, taking into account the value of lost property, transfers and losses to victims of crime (e.g. worth of assets from victims, lost productivity, medical expenses and diminished quality of life), is $1,705 billion. This estimate seems excessive, given that it is approximately one-fifth of the US GDP reported in 1999.[9]

---

[9] We have been unable to find estimates of private expenditure on crime prevention goods and services for other countries.

It would appear that private and public anti-crime initiatives can be either substitutes or complements. Philipson and Posner (1996), for example, show that the proportion of homes with burglar alarms in a state falls with improved public sector crime protection schemes. Ayres and Levitt (1998) find that the introduction of a Lojack system for recovering stolen cars (hidden radio transmitter that enables the police to locate the stolen vehicle) reduces overall car crime.

Measures of the cost of crime and of private expenditures on crime prevention and criminal justice are sparse, and yet such numbers are central to being able to talk intelligently about either the public/private trade-off or the optimal level of overall expenditures on crime prevention and criminal justice. This is an area ripe for detailed and careful empirical work.

4. Partial Privatisation of Criminal Justice Activities

What role does the private sector play in the criminal justice system? The American example is, perhaps, the most dramatic in the variety of private sector activities that characterise its criminal justice system. Benson (1998) provides a comprehensive account of the public sector contracting out to the private sector. Examples of this partial privatisation include police services, drug treatment facilities, airport security, prisons and correctional facilities.

It is now commonplace for private firms to provide a whole range of services previously supplied by governments. Corrections Corporation of America and Wackenhut Corrections Corporation, for example, provide correctional, security and other related services to government agencies around the world. Wackenhut contracts include security at the US Embassy in El Salvador, supplying the entire police force for a nuclear power plant in Illinois and providing correctional facilities in New Zealand.

Benson (1998) provides evidence to show that private security and community policing initiatives have been extremely successful in reducing crime. Examples include private residential streets, private patrols and neighbourhood watch, the deterrent effect of gun ownership[10] and technology (Lojack example mentioned above). In addition to these private sector efforts, he argues that the criminal justice system should employ more resources in giving reparation for loss or injury inflicted to the victims of crime. Benson notes that private sanctions imposed by firms (e.g. firing an employee who steals from the firm) are now being substituted for public sector criminal prosecution.

The contracting-out by governments around the world of prison management services to private companies has grown rapidly over the last decade. As Figure 6 documents, the total number of prisoners held in private facilities rose sharply from 15,300 in 1990 to 145,160 in 1999. For example, the number of private

---

[10] The deterrent effect of private gun ownership is very controversial. See Cook and Ludwig (2000). As a whole, Benson's book has been the subject of considerable controversy. It would be very useful to have scholars with different perspectives consider the benefits and costs of privatisation of crime prevention and criminal justice.

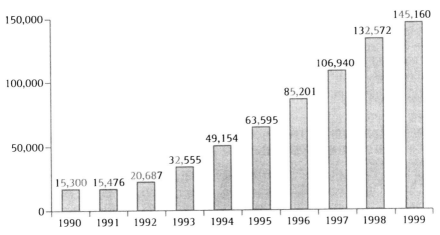

Figure 6. *Rated growth capacity of private secure adult correctional facilities*
Source: Thomas (2000), http://web.crim.ufl.edu/pcp/census/1999/Figure1.html.

prisoners in the US has grown from about 1,200 in 1985 to 122,871 at the end of 1999, which represents 6.6 per cent of the total prison population. Estimates of the number of private prisoners in other countries, at the end of 1999, are Australia (7,459), England and Wales (7,161), the Netherlands (737), New Zealand (384), Scotland (500) and South Africa (6,048). With the exception of Australia, these totals are very small relative to the total number of prisoners.

The US, Australia and the UK have been the main countries to experiment with private prisons. At the end of 1999, the numbers of privately managed secure adult facilities in the US, Australia and the UK were 158, 15 and 10, respectively. Corrections Corporation of America and Wackenhut Corrections Corporation have the largest global market share of contracts to run private prisons.

Perhaps because of increased privatisation of governmental functions and the claim that private prisons are cheaper per prisoner than public prisons, the issue of privatisation of prisons has become highly contentious (see, e.g. Shaw, 1994; Biles, 1997; Hart et al., 1997; Benson, 1998). Arguments for governments to manage prisons generally rest on the need to maintain a high level of standards in the quality of prison services and in the behaviour of prison employees. Contracts for private prison operators would tend to be quite incomplete: privately contracted firms would have strong incentives to lower standards in order to minimise costs (Hart et al., 1997). There are a number of recent examples where this has actually happened. A prison in Louisiana was recently taken away from the private sector because of unacceptable conditions. Others argue that it is not necessarily the contractual incompleteness that has an adverse effect on quality, but rather the inability or unwillingness of the client to enforce contract terms (Domberger and Jensen, 1998).

There has been a substantial growth in private policing in many countries. As Newman (1999, p. 126) observes, 'while private policing has a long history in industrial countries, it is also becoming a major growth industry in emerging market economies'. Sources cited in Newman estimate that the number of security guards in Singapore (with a population of 2.6 million) is approximately 15,000 to 20,000, which is at least twice the police strength. A high ratio of private to public police is also found in other developed economies. For example, the US has a security guard (or officer)/police ratio of three to one (see Newman, 1999, p. 127).

V. WHAT WE KNOW ABOUT THE RELATIVE EFFECTIVENESS OF CRIME PREVENTION AND CRIMINAL JUSTICE

Just how effective are specific crime prevention programmes? What are the major benefits of incarceration? In this section, we do two things. First, we survey briefly a range of crime prevention strategies that seem to work in the US. Second, we look at the arguments that have been put forward relating to the economic issues surrounding the benefits of incarceration. Standard texts on law and economics (e.g. Cooter and Ulen, 2000) discuss four types of social benefits derived from imprisonment—namely, retribution, rehabilitation, deterrence and incapacitation. Given the difficulty of measuring the first two, we shall concentrate on deterrence and incapacitation. It should be noted, however, that much of the empirical literature does not distinguish between deterrence and incapacitation effects. In the case of imprisonment, separating incapacitation from general deterrent effects is difficult since the two are jointly produced.

1. Specific Crime Prevention Programmes

Potential effective crime prevention programmes could take a number of forms. Sherman et al. (1997), writing from a US perspective, point to a number of successful programmes. These include community-based mentoring and after-school recreation programmes, intensive work with at-risk families with young children, intensive residential training programmes for at-risk youth, extra police patrols in high-crime hot spots and a number of situational crime prevention schemes, such as neighbourhood watch and building and community redesign programmes.

The recently completed evaluation of the Children at Risk (CAR) programme found that youths in the treatment group had participated in more social and educational activities, exhibited less anti-social behaviour, committed fewer violent crimes and used and sold fewer drugs than did youths in the control group (see Harrell et al., 1999). CAR was a drug and delinquency prevention programme for high-risk adolescents between the ages of 11 and 13 who lived in five cities (Austin, Bridgeport, Memphis, Savannah and Seattle). The programme consisted of eight components considered key to comprehensive delinquency prevention: case management, family services, educational services, after-school and summer activities, mentoring, incentives, community policing and enhanced enforcement, and criminal-juvenile justice intervention. One interesting result was that positive effects of the programme on drug use, crime and risk factors were not generally observed at the end of the programme. This may indicate that CAR was simply a secondary prevention programme when youths got into trouble.

The Job Corps programme in the US has long been a central part of federal government efforts to provide training for disadvantaged youths. Recent evidence suggests that participation in the programme significantly reduced arrest and conviction rates, as well as time spent in jail (see Schochet et al., 2000). The arrest rate was reduced by about 6 percentage points and the impacts on arrest rates were very similar across male and female sub-groups.

Evaluation of the effectiveness of private crime prevention activities is much more difficult to find. However, given the recent epidemic of households and firms buying locks, alarms or other forms of protection in response to the threat of crime, researchers have started considering how these activities can have negative or positive spillover effects for the neighbourhood community. For example, Ayres and Levitt (1998) conclude that the Lojack system for recovering stolen cars, mentioned in Section IV, provides an example of a positive externality due to a general deterrent effect.

Related to the above initiatives are those of how communities organise themselves when allocating resources to crime prevention programmes. Hawkins (1999), for example, explores the implications of a 'Communities That Care' system, where prevention science is used to guide the type of prevention policies suitable according to profiles of risk and protection.

2. Deterrence

There is a reasonably large theoretical and empirical literature in economics that considers both the deterrent (specific and general) and incapacitative effects of imprisonment. For example, economists and others have sought to discern whether increased imprisonment lowers the crime rate. How does the deterrent effect of formal sanctions arise?

Following the theoretical work of Becker (1968), much empirical work by economists has focused on the role of the criminal justice system in determining criminal activity. In short, economists have argued, using both theory and empirical work, that if the cost of crime is raised, by increasing the probability of apprehension or imposing more or longer sentences, less of it will occur.[11] Deterrence refers to the effect of possible punishment on individuals contemplating criminal acts.[12] Deterrence may flow both from criminal justice system actions and from social actions (i.e. the negative response of friends and associates to criminal behaviour). To date, attempts by economists to measure deterrent effects have concentrated on the effects of the criminal justice system, while work by sociologists has concentrated on 'social sanctions'. See Nagin (1998) for a survey of this literature.

---

[11] Actually, the deterrence hypothesis was widely explored both empirically and theoretically prior to economists' re-entry to the study of crime in the late 1960s.

[12] Marginal deterrence refers to a situation where individuals commit less harmful rather than more harmful acts if expected sanctions rise with harm (see Polinsky and Shavell, 1999).

The potential criminal's perceptions regarding social sanctions are difficult to measure, although work on peer-group (e.g. Evans et al., 1992) and community effects (e.g. Sampson and Groves, 1989) may be able to capture some aspects of perceived social sanctions. In terms of the effects of education, a consistent finding is that students who attend schools with strong ethical values (e.g. parochial schools) offend less than students attending modern urban high schools (see, e.g. Tauchen et al., 1994). This effect may stem from higher levels of social sanctions against crime in schools with strong ethical standards or from the better family and community settings of at least some students.

In an interesting paper, Williams and Sickles (1999) provide an extension of Ehrlich (1973) by including an individual's social capital stock into his utility and earnings functions. Social capital, including things such as reputation and social networks, is used as a proxy to account for the effect of social norms on an individual's decision to participate in crime. This assumes that the stigma associated with arrest depreciates an individual's social capital stock. Williams and Sickles clarify this point further by arguing that employment and marriage create a form of state dependence, which reduces the likelihood of criminal involvement. In other words, an individual with a family, job or good reputation has more to lose if caught committing crimes than those without such attachments. Dynamics arise from current decisions affecting future outcomes through the social capital stock accumulation process. The paper's main result is that criminals behave rationally in the sense that they account for future consequences of current-period decisions.[13]

Glaeser et al. (1996, p. 543) make a similar point in the context of family structures, claiming that 'the average social interactions among criminals are higher when there are not intact family units. The presence of strong families interferes with the transmission of criminal choices across individuals'. The importance of family structure (along with other variables such as deterrence and returns to crime) in explaining urban crime is also the key point of Glaeser and Sacerdote (1999).

In the literature, deterrence is broken into two components. The first component, called specific deterrence, encompasses the effect of punishment on the individual punished. The second component, called general deterrence, encompasses the effect of punishment on the general public. Specific deterrence is generally reflected by including measures that reflect the individual's past experience with the criminal justice system (e.g. Witte, 1980 or Trumbull, 1989). The implicit assumption is that offenders form their perceptions regarding possible punishment based on their own experience with the criminal justice system.[14] For example, the

---

[13] Many of these insights into the dynamics of crime were originally discussed in Williams (1996).

[14] We know little about how individuals form their perceptions of likely sanctions if they offend, although Paternoster and his colleagues (see, e.g. Nagin and Paternoster, 1991) have done interesting empirical work and Sah (1991) has developed a model for the perceived probability of punishment. In a study of institutionalised young adults (college students and prison inmates), Lattimore et al. (1992) find that individuals transform probabilities when making risky choices. Risk-seeking is common over long-shot odds, and subjects are less sensitive to changes in mid-range probabilities than is assumed by expected utility models.

offender's perceived probability of arrest might be proxied by the ratio of his past self-reported offences to arrests and his perceived punishment by some sort of average of the punishments he has received in the past. There is an important potential difficulty in using this type of specific deterrence measure. If there is autocorrelation in criminal behaviour, these measures of specific deterrence will be correlated with the error term in the crime equation. One might instrument these variables by using community-level or peer-group measures.

It has proven much more difficult to obtain reasonable measures of general deterrent effects. As an example, consider the probability of arrest. In a standard model of criminal choice, an individual's probability of arrest depends upon his level of criminal activity, his ability to avoid arrest and exogenous factors related to the criminal justice system. When contemplating a crime, the individual is faced with a schedule of probabilities that relates the nature and extent of his criminal activity to the probability of arrest. See Cook (1979) or Tauchen et al. (1994) for a discussion. An analogy would be to a taxpayer who, when making labour supply and tax-reporting decisions, is faced with a schedule that relates taxable income to the schedule of tax rates.

Just as there is no single tax rate, there is no single probability of arrest. There is a different probability of arrest for each and every possible set of criminal choices. For example, we would expect that, for a given individual, the probability of arrest would be much higher for robbery than for petty theft.

Changes in criminal justice policy or in the level of criminal justice resources alter the probability schedule facing a potential criminal. For example, an increase in criminal justice resources such as that contained in the 1994 US Crime Bill might raise the probability of being arrested for each criminal act—that is, it might cause the schedule relating the probability of arrest to criminal activity to shift up. The 'war on drugs' caused certain sections of the probability schedule (the sections associated with drug offences) to shift up and other sections to shift down (the sections associated with violence offences). It is these types of exogenous changes in the criminal justice system that should be used to reflect deterrent effects, not a community-level probability of arrest. This approach to representing deterrence has been used by Block et al. (1981) and Tauchen et al. (1994).

There are a number of practical problems that arise in testing for deterrent effects. In particular, we consider three estimation issues: measurement error, endogeneity and non-stationarity.

Models of criminal behaviour are usually estimated using official reported crime statistics. Such recorded offences are influenced both by victims' willingness to report crime and by police recording practices and procedures. At the level of the individual police department, both administrative and political changes can lead to abnormalities in reported data or to failures to report any data. For example, the measurement error in crime rates may arise because hiring more police leads to more crimes reported. Consequently, estimates derived from regressing crime rates on the number of police (or on arrest rates) may be severely distorted by the impact of measurement error. Until quite recently, measurement error was not widely considered in the economics literature. However, the importance of the issue and potential solutions were considered very early by Carr-Hill and Carr-Hill (1972) and Carr-Hill and Stern (1973).

More recently, Corman and Mocan (2000) report that complaints to the police about murder, robbery, burglary and motor vehicle theft 'decline in response to increases in arrests'. They use detailed information from the New York Police Department and modern time-series estimation techniques. By using data for a single police department, they avoid some of the measurement error inherent in studies that use cross-department statistics. However, changes in victim reporting behaviour are not considered.

Murder is the one crime for which police reports are quite good. Corman and Mocan (2000) report that the elasticity of murders reported to the police with respect to the arrest rate is approximately −0.3, indicating that a 10 per cent increase in the growth rate of arrests reduces the growth rate of murders by 3 per cent. A number of authors have noted recently that much of the decline in murder rates in developed countries has stemmed from a decrease in domestic assaults. Corman and Mocan do not include measures to reflect the change in public and police attitudes regarding domestic violence in their equations. In general, economists' work on crime is only beginning to incorporate family and community effects.

Not very surprisingly, economists have concentrated their attention on the possibility that crime and sanctions are jointly determined. The main point is that increases in sanctions may cause decreases in crime, but increases in sanctions may also be a response to higher crime rates. Since the 1970s, there has been a considerable effort to find instruments (i.e. exogenous factors) to identify the effects of sanctions on the supply of crime. For example, Levitt (1996) uses instrumental variables to estimate the effect of prison population on crime rates. Prison-overcrowding litigation in a state is used as an instrument for changes in the prison population.

In order to identify the effect of police on crime, Marvell and Moody (1996) and Levitt (1997) propose different procedures. Marvell and Moody are concerned with the timing sequence between hiring police and crime. Using lags between police levels and crime rates to avoid simultaneity, they test for causality in the spirit of Granger (1969). Although they find Granger causation in both directions, the impact of police on crime is much stronger than the impact of crime on police. In a recent paper, Levitt (1997) uses the timing of elections (when cities hire more police) as an instrumental variable to identify a causal effect of police on crime. He finds that increases in police, instrumented by elections, reduce violent crime but have a smaller impact on property crime. Levitt does not consider the impact of elections on either victim or police reporting behaviour.

A substantial problem that has been ignored in the vast majority of empirical studies is non-stationarity of crime rates. A time series is said to be non-stationary if (1) the mean and/or variance does not remain constant over time or (2) the covariance between observations depends on the time at which they occur. In the

US, the UCR crime index appears strongly non-stationary (see, e.g. Witt and Witte, 2000). Here, the authors have attempted to estimate and test a model using time-series cointegration techniques. The empirical results suggest a long-run equilibrium relationship between crime, prison population, female labour supply and durable consumption.

3. Incapacitation

Incapacitation refers to an offender behind bars being unable to commit new crimes against members of society outside prison.[15] Therefore, unless there is an infinitely elastic supply of criminals, incapacitation will reduce crime to below what it would otherwise have been. However, as argued in Section III with respect to drug dealers, if the supply of offenders is reasonably elastic, the incapacitation effect may be very small (see Freeman, 1996). In addition, for some individuals, incarceration may only affect the timing rather than the total number of crimes they commit.

These uncertainties of the effects of prison on crime are illustrated in a recent report by the Justice Policy Institute (2000) on incarceration and crime trends in Texas. As of the end of 1999, there were 706,600 Texans in prison, on jail parole or on probation, the largest population of people under the jurisdiction of a state's prison system in the US. However, there is little evidence that Texas's severe correctional system is responsible for the fall in crime: Texas crime rates have not experienced the declines witnessed in other parts of the US, where prison population growth has been much slower.

The basic intuition of the optimal sanction is that individuals should be put in prison and kept there as long as the expected net harm exceeds the costs of imprisonment. Polinsky and Shavell (1999) argue that prison should only be used to incapacitate individuals whose net harm is relatively high. In addition, these authors highlight two points about incapacitation. First, since expected harm caused by individuals usually declines with their age, it may be worth having fewer older people in prison. Second, past behaviour is the best predictor of future behaviour. Thus the criminal justice system should impose a prison sentence on someone who has committed a harmful act rather than incapacitating someone who has the potential to commit a crime. In practice, you have to commit a crime to go to prison.

While the theory of optimal incapacitation policy is well established (see Shavell, 1987), the empirical work faces some difficulties. The central difficulty is how to separate the deterrent and incapacitation effects associated with imprisonment. One approach, discussed at length in Ehrlich (1981), is to compare regression estimates of the actual effect of imprisonment on crime with theoretical estimates of maximum incapacitation effects. Some authors, such as Levitt (1998), seek to identify some observable substitution effects of the probability of arrest for one

---

[15] As discussed in Polinsky and Shavell (1999), incapacitation can take forms other than imprisonment—for example, loss of a driver's licence prevents an individual from doing harm while driving.

crime on the incidence of a substitute crime. Other authors, such as Kessler and Levitt (1999), have used California's adoption of 'three strikes and you're out' sentencing rules to separate the deterrence and incapacitation effects of punishment.

Recently, some researchers have focused their attention on whether sanctions depend on offence history. Glaeser and Sacerdote (2000) provide evidence to show that repeat offenders are more likely to receive longer sentences. Offenders with a high expected probability of recidivism are more likely to commit crimes in the future and thus more likely to be worth incapacitating by imprisonment. Glaeser and Sacerdote use a variety of data sources to examine the sentences given to murderers in the US. They find that sentences are longer when there is a greater value to incapacitation or greater deterrence elasticity. However, contrary to the predictions of the economic model of optimal punishment, they find victim characteristics are important in explaining sentencing among vehicular homicides (e.g. drivers who kill women get 56 per cent longer sentences, whereas drivers who kill blacks get 53 per cent shorter sentences).

VI. CONCLUSIONS AND SOME SUGGESTIONS FOR RESEARCH

Crime is pervasive. However, the extent of crime is hard to measure. Cross-nationally, we have the best measures for murder. However, even for murder, estimates from different sources can vary widely. Given differences in criminal laws, defendant protections and statistical systems, broad measures of law-abidingness (e.g. those developed by the World Bank) and cross-national victimisation and self-report surveys offer the best hope of comparing the level of other types of offences across countries. Crime statistics coming from the criminal justice system (e.g. offences reported to the police) provide valuable information but do not generally provide reliable estimates of crime either across countries or across time.

To date, much work by economists on crime has used criminal justice statistics and interpreted these statistics as measures of the underlying level of crime. This first-generation work has been valuable, but it is now time to move forward. Two directions appear particularly promising. First, in order to interpret criminal justice data, we need to know more about the behaviour of both crime victims and the criminal justice system. For example, in order to interpret properly results that use police reports as a measure of crime, we need to understand both victim reporting behaviour and police recording practices. Second, work seeking to estimate the deterrent effects of the criminal justice system could benefit from using sources of data on crime other than data from the criminal justice system (e.g. victimisation surveys). Studies that use a number of indicators of crime (e.g. multi-indicator models) are likely to provide more meaningful results than studies that use any single indicator.

So far, studies by economists of crime have focused on relatively few issues (e.g. the deterrent effect of police resources and imprisonment). There have been relatively few studies of the way in which such important criminal justice system entities as prosecutors' offices and public defenders operate.[16]

Most, if not all, criminal justice systems operate with budgets that are not adequate to process all cases fully. To deal with this 'overcrowding', one or more agencies are given discretion in how they handle cases. Different criminal justice systems grant differing amounts of discretion to different agencies at different points in time. For example, in the US during the 1960s, judges and parole boards had substantial discretion. The determinate sentencing movement limited the discretion of judges and parole boards. Discretion was not eliminated; it was simply shifted to prosecutors from judges and parole boards. How much discretion in criminal justice systems is optimal? Where should the discretion be lodged?

Public finance economists have provided valuable work on optimal taxation. As far as we are aware, there has been little work on optimal criminal law or optimal criminal justice funding. What acts should we criminalise? What is the optimal level of funding for the police, prosecutors, courts and corrections? What should the split between private and public spending be? While private prisons have received some attention, private policing has received less.

Much criminal justice research has focused on preventing crime through the punitive actions of the criminal justice system (e.g. deterrence and incapacitation). Another line of research has focused on preventing crime by working with high-risk youth. The two lines of research are not well integrated. Yet an optimal portfolio of crime prevention strategies requires a combination of punitive and supportive efforts.

REFERENCES

Anderson, D. A. (1999), 'The aggregate burden of crime', *Journal of Law and Economics*, vol. 42, pp. 611–42.

Argersinger v. Hamilin, 407 U.S. 25 (1972).

Aronowitz, A. (2000), 'Germany', *World Factbook of Criminal Justice Systems*, http://www.ojp.usdoj.gov/bjs/pub/ascii/wfbcjger.txt, accessed 7 July 2000.

Ayres, I. and Levitt, S. D. (1998), 'Measuring positive externalities from unobservable victim precaution: an empirical analysis of Lojack', *Quarterly Journal of Economics*, vol. 113, pp. 43–77.

Becker, G. (1968), 'Crime and punishment: an economic approach', *Journal of Political Economy*, vol. 76, pp. 169–217.

Benson, B. L. (1998), *To Serve and Protect*, New York: New York University Press.

Biles, D. (1997), 'Private prisons: welcome or not?', *Australian Journal of Forensic Sciences*, vol. 29, pp. 3–8.

Block, M., Nold, F. and Sidak, J. (1981), 'The deterrent effect of antitrust enforcement', *Journal of Political Economy*, vol. 89, pp. 429–45.

Brand, S. and Price, R. (2000), *The Economic and Social Costs of Crime*, Home Office Research Study no. 217, London: Home Office.

---

[16] There has been some work by economists in the US on plea bargaining (see Reinganum, 1988).

Carr-Hill, G. and Carr-Hill, R. (1972), 'Reconviction as a process', *British Journal of Criminology*, vol. 12, pp. 35–43.

Carr-Hill, R. A. and Stern, N. H. (1973), 'An econometric model of the supply and control of recorded offences in England and Wales', *Journal of Public Economics*, vol. 2, pp. 289–318.

Cook, P. J. (1979), 'The clearance rate as a measure of criminal justice effectiveness', *Journal of Public Economics*, vol. 11, pp. 135–42.

——, and Ludwig, J. (2000), *Gun Violence: The Real Costs*, New York: Oxford University Press.

Cooter, R. and Ulen, T. (2000), *Law and Economics*, 3rd edn, Reading, MA: Addison-Wesley.

Corman, H. and Mocan, H. N. (2000), 'A time-series analysis of crime and drug use in New York City', *American Economic Review*, vol. 90, pp. 584–604.

Domberger, S. and Jensen, P. (1998), 'Contracting out by the public sector: theory, evidence, prospects', *Oxford Review of Economic Policy*, vol. 13, pp. 67–78.

Donohue, J. J. and Siegelman, P. (1998), 'Allocating resources among prisons and social programs in the battle against crime', *Journal of Legal Studies*, vol. 27, pp. 1–43.

Ehrlich, I. (1973), 'Participation in illegitimate activities: a theoretical and empirical investigation', *Journal of Political Economy*, vol. 81, pp. 521–65.

—— (1981), 'On the usefulness of controlling individuals: an economic analysis of rehabilitation, incapacitation and deterrence', *American Economic Review*, vol. 71, pp. 307–22.

Evans, W., Oates, W. and Schwab, R. (1992), 'Measuring peer group effects: a study of teenage behavior', *Journal of Political Economy*, vol. 100, pp. 966–91.

Freeman, R. (1996), 'Why do so many young American men commit crimes and what might we do about it?', *Journal of Economic Perspectives*, vol. 10, pp. 25–42.

—— (1999), 'The economics of crime', in O. Ashenfelter and D. Card (eds), *Handbook of Labor Economics*, vol. 3c, Amsterdam, New York and Oxford: Elsevier Science, North-Holland.

Friedman, D. (2000), *Law's Order*, Princeton, NJ: Princeton University Press.

Gideon v. Wainwright, 372 U.S. 335 (1963).

Glaeser, E. L. and Sacerdote, B. (1999), 'Why is there more crime in cities?', *Journal of Political Economy*, vol. 107, pp. S225–58.

—— and —— (2000), 'The determinants of punishment: deterrence, incapacitation and vengeance', National Bureau of Economic Research, Working Paper no. 7676.

——, —— and Scheinkman, J. (1996), 'Crime and social interactions', *Quarterly Journal of Economics*, vol. 111, pp. 507–48.

Goldblatt, P. and Lewis, C. (eds) (1998), *Reducing Offending: An Assessment of Research Evidence on Ways of Dealing with Offending Behaviour*, Home Office Research Study no. 187, London: Home Office.

Granger, C. (1969), 'Investigating causal relations by econometric models and cross-spectral methods', *Econometrica*, vol. 37, pp. 424–38.

Groves, W., Newman, G. and Corrado, C. (1987), 'Islam, modernization and crime: a test of the religious ecology thesis', *Journal of Criminal Justice*, vol. 13, pp. 23–9.

Harrell, A., Cavanagh, S. and Sridharar, S. (1999), *Evaluation of the Children at Risk Program: Results 1 Year after the End of the Program*, Washington, DC: US Department of Justice, Office of Justice Programs.

Hart, H. L. A. (1994), *The Concept of Law*, Oxford: Oxford University Press.

Hart, O., Shleifer, A. and Vishny, R. (1997), 'The proper scope of government: theory and an application to prisons', *Quarterly Journal of Economics*, vol. 112, pp. 1163–202.

Hawkins, J. D. (1999), 'Preventing crime and violence through communities that care', *European Journal on Criminal Policy and Research*, vol. 7, pp. 443–58.

Howard, G. J., Newman, G. and Pridemore, W. A. (2000), 'Theory, method, and data in comparative criminology', in D. Duffee (ed.), *Criminal Justice 2000, Measurement and Analysis of Crime and Justice*, vol. 4, Washington, DC: National Institute of Justice.

Justice Policy Institute (2000), *Texas Tough? An Analysis of Incarceration and Crime Trends in the Lone Star State*, http://www.cjcj.org.

Jurgen-Tas, J., Terlouw, G. and Klein, M. (eds) (1994), *Delinquent Behavior of Young People in the Western World*, Amsterdam: Kugler Publications.

Kansas City, Mo., Missouri Police Department (1977), *Response Time Analysis*, Kansas City, MO.

Kaplan, J., Skolnick, J. and Feeley, M. (1991), *Criminal Justice*, 5th edn, Westbury, NY: Foundation Press.

Kaplow, L. and Shavell, S. (1999), 'Economic analysis of law', National Bureau of Economic Research, Working Paper no. 6960.

Kaufman, D., Kraay, A. and Zoido-Lobaton (1999a), 'Aggregating governance indicators', World Bank, Working Paper no. 2196.

—, — and — (1999b), 'Governance matters', World Bank, Working Paper no. 2195.

—, — and — (2000), *Aggregate Governance Indicators Data and Charts*, http://www.worldbank.org/wbi/governance/gov_matrs_new.htm, accessed 28 June 2000.

Kessler, D. and Levitt, S. (1999), 'Using sentence enhancements to distinguish between deterrence and incapacitation', *Journal of Law and Economics*, vol. 42, pp. 343–63.

Laband, D. N. and Sophocleus, J. P. (1992), 'An estimate of resource expenditures on transfer activity in the United States', *Quarterly Journal of Economics*, vol. 107, pp. 959–83.

Lattimore, P. J., Baker, J. and Witte, A. D. (1992), 'The influence of probability on risky choice: a parametric examination', *Journal of Economic Behavior and Organisation*, vol. 17, pp. 377–400.

Levitt, S. (1996), 'The effect of prison population size on crime rates: evidence from prison overcrowding litigation', *Quarterly Journal of Economics*, vol. 111, pp. 319–51.

— (1997), 'Using electoral cycles in police hiring to estimate the effect of police on crime', *American Economic Review*, vol. 87, pp. 270–90.

— (1998), 'Why do increased arrest rates appear to reduce crime: deterrence, incapacitation, or measurement error?', *Economic Inquiry*, vol. 36, pp. 353–72.

Lindgren, S. A. and Gifford, L. S. (2000), *Criminal Justice Expenditure and Employment Extracts Program*, National Criminal Justice 178273, Washington, DC: US Department of Justice, Bureau of Justice Statistics.

Marvell, T. and Moody, C. (1996), 'Specification problems, police levels, and crime rates', *Criminology*, vol. 34, pp. 609–46.

Merritt v. Faulkner, United States Court of Appeals, Seventh Circuit, 1983. 697 F.2d 761.

Miller, W. (1977), *Cops and Bobbies: Police Authority in New York and London, 1830–1870*, Chicago: University of Chicago Press.

Mirrlees-Black, C. and Ross, A. (1995a), *Crime against Retail Premises in 1993*, Research Findings no. 26, London: Home Office.

— and — (1995b), *Crime against Manufacturing Premises in 1993*, Research Findings no. 27, London: Home Office.

Moriyama, T. (2000), 'Japan', *World Factbook of Criminal Justice Systems*, www.ojp.usdoj.gov/bjs/pub/ascii/wfbcjjap.txt, accessed 8 July 2000.

Nagin, D. (1998), 'Criminal deterrence research: a review of the evidence and a research agenda for the outset of the 21st century', in M. Tonry (ed.), *Crime and Justice: An Annual Review of Research*, vol. 23, Chicago: University of Chicago Press.

Nagin, D. and Paternoster, R. (1991), 'The preventive effect of the perceived risk of arrest', *Criminology*, vol. 29, pp. 561–73.

Newman, G. (ed.) (1999), *Global Report on Crime and Justice*, New York: Oxford University Press.

Philipson, T. J. and Posner, R. A. (1996), 'The economic epidemiology of crime', *Journal of Law and Economics*, vol. 39, pp. 405–33.

Polinsky, A. M. and Shavell, S. (1999), 'The economic theory of public enforcement of law', National Bureau of Economic Research, Working Paper no. 6993.

Posner, R. (1992), *Economic Analysis of Law*, 4th edn, Boston: Little Brown and Company.

Reinganum, J. (1988), 'Plea bargaining and prosecutorial discretion', *American Economic Review*, vol. 78, pp. 713–25.

Sah, R. (1991), 'Social osmosis and patterns of crime', *Journal of Political Economy*, vol. 99, pp. 1272–95.

Sampson, R. and Groves, W. (1989), 'Community structure and crime: testing social-disorganisation theory', *American Journal of Sociology*, vol. 94, pp. 774–802.

Schochet, P. Z., Burghardt, J. and Glazerman, S. (2000), *National Job Corps Study: The Short-Term Impacts of Job Corps on Participants' Employment and Related Outcomes*, Princeton, NJ: Mathematica Policy Research, Inc.

Shapland, J. (2000), 'Auditing criminal justice', in N. G. Fielding, A. Clarke and R. Witt (eds), *The Economic Dimensions of Crime*, London and New York: MacMillan Press and St Martin's Press.

Shavell, S. (1987), 'The model of optimal incapacitation', *American Economic Review: Papers and Proceedings*, vol. 77, pp. 107–10.

Shaw, S. (ed.) (1994), *Privatisation and Market Testing in the Prison Service*, London: Prison Reform Trust.

Sherman, L. W., Gottfredson, D., Mackenzie, D., Eck, J., Reuter, P. and Bushway, S. (1997), *Preventing Crime: What Works, What Doesn't, What's Promising*, Washington, DC: US Department of Justice, Office of Justice Programs.

Smith, S. and DeFrances, C. (1996), *Indigent Defense*, National Criminal Justice 158909, Washington, DC: US Department of Justice, Bureau of Justice Statistics.

Stigler, G. (1970), 'The optimum enforcement of laws', *Journal of Political Economy*, vol. 78, pp. 526–36.

Tauchen, H., Witte, A. D. and Griesinger, H. (1994), 'Criminal deterrence: revisiting the issues with a birth cohort', *Review of Economics and Statistics*, vol. 76, pp. 399–412.

Thomas, C. W. (2000), Home Page, http://web.crim.ufl/pcp/, accessed 6 August 2000.

Trumbull, W. (1989), 'Estimation of the economic model of crime using aggregate and individual data', *Southern Economic Journal*, vol. 94, pp. 423–39.

United States v. Bergman, United States District Court, Southern District of New York, 1976, 416 F.Supp.496.

van Dijk, F. and de Waard, J. (2000), *Legal Infrastructure of the Netherlands in International Perspective*, Amsterdam: Ministry of Justice, http://www.minjust.nl:8080/c_actual/rapport/index.htm.

Walker, I. and Sansfacon, D. (2000), *Investing Wisely in Crime Prevention: International Experiences*, Washington, DC: US Department of Justice, Office of Justice Programs.

Williams, J. (1996), 'On the dynamic decision to participate in crime', Ph.D. thesis, Rice University.

— and Sickles, R. (1999), 'Turning from crime: a dynamic perspective', mimeo, University of Adelaide.

Witt, R. and Witte, A. D. (2000), 'Crime, prison and female labor supply', *Journal of Quantitative Criminology*, vol. 16, pp. 69–85.

Witte, A. D. (1980), 'Estimating the economic model of crime with individual data', *Quarterly Journal of Economics*, vol. 94, pp. 59–87.

7

On Sharing NATO Defence Burdens in the 1990s and Beyond

TODD SANDLER AND JAMES C. MURDOCH[1]

I. INTRODUCTION

In little more than four months, the Communist regimes in Europe, which had posed the greatest threat to European security for 40 years, unravelled as the Berlin Wall tumbled on 9-10 November 1989, a democratic coalition government formed in Czechoslovakia on 7 December 1989, Ceausecu's regime collapsed on 22 December 1989 and the first free elections in a generation took place in East Germany on 18 March 1990.[2] These events were followed by a unified Germany joining NATO (3 October 1990), the official disbandment of the Warsaw Pact (1 July 1991) and the demise of the Soviet Union (20 December 1991). But these developments, which marked the end to the cold war, were not the only factors behind the momentous change in the nature of European defence. Iraq's invasion of Kuwait on 1 August 1990 underscored that security threats to NATO's resource supplies and interests could come from 'rogue states' that operate outside international conventions and norms.[3] This war also highlighted the recent revolution in military technologies, which would be greatly perfected before their next large-scale deployment against Serbia in 1999. Changes in European defence also derived from NATO's adoption of a new strategic doctrine in 1994 that calls for crisis management and peace enforcement in places even outside of Europe whenever NATO's vital interests are at risk.[4] Still other influential developments included NATO's expansion to

The authors greatly appreciate data assistance given by Aaron Birkland. They have also profited from comments provided by Ron Smith. Sandler's research was supported, in part, by a NATO Fellowship. The views expressed are solely those of the authors.

[1] Sandler is the Robert R. and Katheryn A. Dockson Chair in International Relations and Economics, University of Southern California; Murdoch is the Director of the Bruton Center at the University of Texas-Dallas.

[2] Dates in this paragraph come from NATO Office of Information and Press (1995, pp. 295-351) and Sandler and Hartley (1999, pp. 52-7).

[3] On rogue states and the threats that they pose, see Klare (1995) and Sandler and Hartley (1999, pp. 182-92).

[4] This new doctrine and its genesis were discussed in Gompert and Larrabee (1997), Jordan (1995), Sandler and Hartley (1999) and Thomson (1997).

encompass some ex-Warsaw-Pact members and the significant downsizing of defence budgets among most NATO allies with the exception of Greece and Turkey.

These changes came so suddenly as to catch NATO policymakers unprepared: almost overnight, threats to NATO security were no longer necessarily from the east, nor were they necessarily even within Europe. As such, allied forces now required the ability to be rapidly projected to theatres outside of Europe. The next generation of weapons had to be more suited to these new concerns and less geared to those of the cold war era of nuclear deterrence. Security challenges also stemmed from transnational terrorism as grievances in other regions of the world (e.g. the Middle East) erupted in European terrorist acts designed to capture world attention.[5] The potential collapse of the transition economies and their potential return to Communism presented yet another danger, which can be largely addressed through foreign assistance intended to keep these emerging-market economies buoyant.

Throughout its 50 years, NATO burden sharing has been a divisive issue. All too frequently, the US has alleged that it has carried an 'unfair' and disproportionately large amount of the alliance burden (US Committee on Armed Services, 1988). In recent years, the US Department of Defense (DOD) must annually submit to Congress a report assessing allied contributions to the common defence (see, e.g. US DOD, 1996, 1999). The European allies have countered these charges of under-contributions by pointing out that much of US defence spending is on non-European concerns and by devising alternative burden-sharing measures that put their contributions in a better light. Moreover, some European allies emphasised that they assumed disproportionate burdens for UN peacekeeping and for other activities (e.g. NATO infrastructure). Any assessment of burden sharing faces at least two problems: (1) how to measure relative burdens and (2) what activities to include in this burden-sharing accounting.

To analyse the distribution of burdens among NATO allies, researchers have followed the seminal study of Olson and Zeckhauser (1966) and applied the theory of pure public goods.[6] Subsequent studies have hypothesised that defence expenditures yield multiple outputs that vary in their degree of publicness (van Ypersele de Strihou, 1967; Sandler, 1977). By changing the mix of public and private benefits associated with defence activities, recent changes to NATO's strategic doctrine, weapon technologies, perceived threat and membership composition can alter burden-sharing behaviour.

A primary purpose of this chapter is to investigate burden sharing in NATO in the 1990s in light of recent changes. We apply theoretical insights from a joint

---

[5] For a current assessment of the threat of transnational terrorism, consult Enders and Sandler (1999, 2000) and US Department of State (1999).

[6] This extensive literature has been surveyed recently by Murdoch (1995) and Sandler and Hartley (1999). Key articles include McGuire (1990), Murdoch and Sandler (1982 and 1984), Olson and Zeckhauser (1966), Oneal (1990), Oneal and Elrod (1989), Palmer (1990a,b, 1991), Russett (1970), Sandler (1975, 1987, 1993), Sandler and Cauley (1975), Smith (1989) and van Ypersele de Strihou (1967).

product model representation of alliances (Section II) to suggest empirical tests of burden-sharing behaviour so as to assess the impact of recent alterations in NATO's strategic environment on allied support of the alliance (Section III). Empirical tests of burden sharing in the 1990s are based on two alternative public finance principles: an ability-to-pay measure (Section IV) and a benefits-received measure (Section V). Another purpose is to hypothesise how burden sharing will change during the coming decade (Section VI). We are particularly interested in this change under alternative expansion scenarios. A third purpose is to devise a security burden-sharing measure that broadens security-promoting activities to go beyond defence spending (Section VII). Concluding remarks round out the study in Section VIII.

The empirical tests indicate that there is no evidence of disproportionate burden sharing for 1990–99, so that the large allies are not shouldering the defence burdens for the small allies. In the latter 1990s, there is, however, a tiny drift upward in the positive (but insignificant) correlation between defence burdens and the allies' national income, which suggests a gradual return to disproportionate burden sharing, consistent with our theoretical prediction. This return is anticipated to be more pronounced in the years to come as changes in NATO's strategic environment have time to influence actions. When derived benefits are compared with actual defence burdens carried, the match between the two is still significant, indicating that the joint product model with its private inducement to support defence is still relevant. If alliance-wide public benefits increase in the ensuing decade as predicted, then this match may eventually become insignificant. When alternative expansion scenarios are examined, the extent of disproportionality of burden sharing increases if the alliance continues to grow.

II. ALTERNATIVE PUBLIC GOOD MODELS

1. A Pure Public Good Model of Alliances

If defence is purely public for the allies, then the benefits associated with defence must be non-rival and non-excludable. Defence benefits are non-rival among allies when one ally's consumption of the unit of defence does not detract, in the slightest, from the consumption opportunities still available to other allies *from that same unit*. Deterrence, as provided by strategic nuclear weapons (e.g. Trident submarines or B-2 stealth bombers), is non-rival among allies because, once deployed, these weapons' ability to deter enemy aggression is independent of the number of allies (or citizens) on whose behalf the retaliatory threat is made, provided that the promised retaliation is automatic and believable. If the allies underwriting deterrence have a 'first-strike' advantage so that they can destroy enough of the enemy's nuclear arsenal in a pre-emptive attack, then any return fire would be minimal and the retaliatory pledge attains greater credibility. When, moreover, the strategic arsenal is sufficiently large to absorb an attack and still possess enough surviving missiles to deliver an unacceptable punishment to a would-be aggressor, the threatened retaliation is credible and can be made on behalf of 15, 18 or more allies.

The benefits of a defence activity are non-excludable if they cannot be withheld at an affordable cost by the provider. For strategic nuclear forces, benefits are non-excludable whenever the defence provider(s) cannot fail to deliver the pledged retaliatory response against an invader of another ally. If an attack on one ally causes unacceptable collateral damage to the allies underwriting the retaliatory response, then the promised retribution is likely to ensue. This automatic response can also be triggered when the deterrence-providing allies have sufficient investment interests, military troops, citizens or other assets in a targeted ally to suffer greatly from any attack. During the cold war, the large numbers of US troops and their dependants stationed in West Germany, the UK and Italy served as a tripwire to a US response if these host allies were attacked. Thus it is understandable that, at first, the Europeans were opposed to the announced US troop withdrawals from Europe after the cold war, despite their complaints of negative externalities stemming from hosting US troops. Given the proximity of France and the UK to other NATO allies in Europe, these two nuclear allies would have great difficulty in excluding their European allies and neighbours from any promised retaliation owing to collateral damage.

Alliances that rely on deterrence to forestall an attack share a purely public defence good, for which some essential implications follow. First, defence burdens are anticipated to be shared unevenly with the largest allies, which have the most to lose from an attack, assuming a disproportionately large burden in relation to their gross domestic product (GDP).[7] The prediction that the large, wealthy allies will shoulder the defence burdens for smaller, poorer allies is the 'exploitation hypothesis'. If, for example, the large ally spends $250 billion on defence and a small ally desires to spend just $5 billion, then the small ally is likely to spend very little, relying instead on the protection that spills over from its large formidable ally. This conclusion rests on the purely public assumption where the defence efforts of one ally are perfectly substitutable for those of another. If, however, this substitutability is limited, then this disproportionality is curtailed. Second, defence spending will be allocated in a suboptimal fashion, which follows because each ally considers only its own marginal benefits and the associated marginal costs when deciding defence provision. Optimality for a pure public defence good requires that the alliance-wide sum of marginal benefits be equated to marginal costs.[8] Third, the absence of rivalry in consumption implies that all friendly nations can be included in the alliance, in so far as only benefits arise from the expansion of an alliance. Fourth, co-operation needs to be fostered to address suboptimal defence levels and can take the form of 'tight' alliance linkages, whereby allies sacrifice some of their autonomy over their defence decision to the collective

---

[7] This was first formulated by Olson (1965) and Olson and Zeckhauser (1966).

[8] This was established in Samuelson (1954, 1955). Sandler and Hartley (1999, ch. 2) has a much more in-depth analysis of these implications.

or a central authority (Sandler and Forbes, 1980). Fifth, the match between benefits received from defence and the actual defence burden is anticipated for many allies to be weak owing to free riding, which shows up as a negative relationship between an ally's real defence outlays and those of its allies.

2. Joint Product Representation of Alliances

Researchers noticed that after the mid-1960s (see Section IV) many of the implications of the pure public good model of alliances did not hold (e.g. Russett, 1970) and, in response, offered a generalisation in the form of a joint product model in which defence yields multiple outputs whose publicness varies. In particular, defence activities can produce deterrence (a pure public benefit), damage limitation or protection for times of conflict (an impure public benefit) and ally-specific outputs (private benefits).[9] Defence outputs are impurely public among allies when the associated benefits are either partially or wholly excludable by the provider, or else partially rival among the allies. Consider conventional forces, deployed along an alliance's perimeter to keep an opposing side from penetrating its front. Because the actual deployment decision can exclude one or more allies, conventional armaments and troops display partially excludable benefits. Such forces are subject to a spatial rivalry in the form of 'force thinning' as a given army is spread over a longer exposed border. Coalescing troops in one place along an alliance's border leads to vulnerabilities elsewhere, and it is these resulting vulnerabilities that imply rivalry in consumption.

Ally-specific benefits occur when a defence activity helps only the providing ally and yields no benefit spillovers to others. In large part, the UK efforts to thwart terrorism in Northern Ireland only benefited the UK. The same can be said of the British forces stationed 12,000 km away in the Falklands, or British efforts to expel Argentine troops from the Falklands between 2 April and 14 June 1982. The recent build-up of Greek and Turkish forces to protect their respective partitions of Cyprus yield largely ally-specific benefits. Unlike public defence outputs, private ally-specific benefits motivate an ally to provide defence, since these benefits cannot be derived from another ally's defence efforts. Similarly, excludable impurely public defence benefits—say, derived from conventional forces assigned to the ally's borders—also provide incentives for an ally to contribute.

Consider the differences in the mix of outputs and the publicness of benefits derived from strategic and conventional weapons. By their nature, strategic weapons do not readily lend themselves to producing ally-specific benefits. Such weapons cannot be used to threaten an insurgency into submission, nor can they be assigned to thwart terrorism or provide disaster relief. If, moreover, these forces have sufficient range, they can be deployed almost anywhere with little or no thinning of strength, so that strategic nuclear forces yield primarily alliance-wide

---

[9] Ally-specific benefits are private among allies but public within an ally.

purely public benefits. Some ally-specific benefits follow from the provider's control of the launch button, whose possession can allow it to extract some hegemonic concessions (Morrow, 1991). In contrast, conventional forces possess a large share of ally-specific benefits and impurely public benefits. While it is true that formidable conventional forces deter an enemy, they can also further many ally-specific interests. Their deployment during a conflict is impurely public owing to force thinning. In essence, the extent of publicness is reflected in the ratio of excludable benefits (i.e. ally-specific and damage-limiting benefits) to total benefits received from a defence activity's outputs. This ratio depends on the reigning strategic doctrine, weapon technology, perceived threats and alliance composition. For example, curbing the threat posed by the proliferation of nuclear forces, which is part of NATO's new crisis-management doctrine, yields purely public benefits to NATO allies and any nation in harm's way from such weapons.

The implications of the joint product model are at variance with those of the purely public deterrence representation of an alliance. First, a high ratio of excludable benefits implies that an ally must support its own defence, regardless of its economic size, if it is going to be protected. As this ratio increases, the exploitation hypothesis is anticipated to lose its relevancy, so that any disproportionality between an ally's size and its defence burden is predicted to decline. Second, the presence of excludable benefits allows markets and club arrangements to promote preference revelation, thereby achieving a closer equality between marginal benefits and marginal costs. As the ratio of excludable benefits approaches one, this equality of margins becomes closer to being satisfied, thus implying greater optimality. Free riding can be curtailed with a sizeable helping of excludable benefits. Third, alliance size restrictions hinge on the thinning of forces; allies with large exposed borders cause more thinning and must contribute more conventional forces to offset this thinning externality (Sandler, 1977). Because ally-specific benefits are not shared and deterrence can be shared at zero costs, neither of these types of benefits determines membership size. Fourth, alliance links can be kept loose and unintegrated when the ratio of excludable benefits is large, in so far as inefficiencies are small, calling for little co-operative correction. Fifth, the larger is this ratio, the better is the match between benefits received and defence burdens, because a payment must be made to acquire the excludable benefits.

The location and geographical properties of a prospective ally make a difference for both the desirability of including this ally and the extent of its bargaining strength if included. A conventional alliance can save costs owing to the sequestration of interior borders that no longer require protection (Gardner, 1995, pp. 401–6; Sandler, 1999). Consider an alliance of three contiguous square countries of equal sizes lined up in a row.[10] Suppose that each country's sides are

---

[10] The formation and expansion of NATO was analysed in Sandler (1999) based on cost savings from interior borders.

of unit length costing 1 to protect. If each country provides its own defence, then each expends 4 in protecting its perimeter from an attack in all directions. If, instead, the countries form an alliance, then only 8 sides need protecting, leading to a cost saving of 4. The middle country possesses a bargaining advantage, because without its participation there would be no cost savings. Countries with long exposed borders are less desirable entrants and, if admitted, are at a bargaining disadvantage when cost savings from sequestered borders are distributed. Potential non-contiguous allies, such as the Baltic states (Latvia, Estonia and Lithuania), in which just Lithuania has a common 91-kilometre border with Poland, have little to offer NATO and are unlikely entrants.

III. NATO DOCTRINES AND BURDEN SHARING

1. Mutual Assured Destruction: 1949-66

NATO was initially confronted with a daunting challenge: a Soviet Union bent on a westward expansion as it acquired satellite states. Unlike the NATO allies, which had converted a large share of their defence industries to peacetime uses by 1949, the Soviet Union had continued to run its defence industries at the same wartime pace. As a consequence, the Soviet Union had acquired a conventional weapon advantage, which meant that NATO had to rely on US superiority in strategic nuclear weapons to counter any Soviet aggression. Thus the alliance adopted a strategic doctrine of mutual assured destruction (MAD), whereby any Soviet territorial expansion involving NATO allies would trigger a devastating nuclear attack. Directive MC 48, approved in 1954 by the North Atlantic Council, allowed NATO to use strategic weapons to counter such aggression (Rearden, 1995, p. 73). Any such US retaliatory response had credibility owing to a US first-strike advantage, by which Soviet nuclear assets could be neutralised by a pre-emptive strike. Thus the pledged US response could be exercised with impunity. This reliance on strategic weapons meant that NATO's security rested on purely public deterrence.

2. Flexible Response Eras: 1967-80 and 1981-90

The embarrassment experienced by the Soviet Union when it had to back down during the Cuban missile crisis, owing to the US pre-emptive advantage, set in motion a Soviet build-up of its strategic forces. As the US lost some of its strategic advantage, NATO needed a new defence doctrine that would not result in an immediate nuclear exchange during an exigency. In 1967, NATO adopted directive MC 14/3, which embodied the doctrine of flexible response, whereby NATO would respond in a measured way to Warsaw Pact challenges. The doctrine envisioned a commensurate response to acts of aggression and allowed for an escalation if necessary. As a result of this doctrine, strategic, tactical and conventional forces became complementary as they had to be used together, so that the extent of substitutability between allied forces and the incentives to free ride diminished (Murdoch and Sandler, 1984). NATO allies that failed to maintain their conventional forces became the weak link that might draw an attack.

By relying on all three kinds of weapons, this 1967 doctrine meant that defence activities within NATO yielded joint products with varying degrees of publicness. In Table 1, we list the defining events and doctrines for MAD and three subsequent strategic eras. On the right-hand side of the table, the implications of the appropriate underlying model are tabulated. By 1981, a host of events, as given on the left-hand side of Table 1, increased the share of non-excludable, purely public benefits and, in so doing, are predicted to have the influences indicated on the right. For example, the nuclear allies' build-up and modernisation of their strategic arsenals increased the share of jointly produced non-excludable public outputs. The deterrence derived from French and British enhanced strategic forces provided non-excludable and non-rival benefits to the other European allies.

When NATO adopted the forward-defence strategy or 'deep strike' in 1984, this flexible-response upgrade shifted the focus away from NATO's eastern perimeter by relying on precision-guided munitions to target and destroy the Warsaw Pact's rear-echelon forces. The new strategy reduced thinning and the impurity of conventional forces, since their deployment along the front loses some of its importance; nevertheless, this upgraded doctrine's reliance on conventional forces still meant that excludable joint products are important. In Table 1, we hypothesise that the net influence of these strategic, procurement and technological events was to augment the share of non-excludable benefits derived from defence. In other words, these events increased the publicness of the defence activity and enhanced the concerns over disproportionate burdens and suboptimality, which the first era of flexible response greatly corrected.

3. Crisis-Management Doctrine: 1991–2000

With the fall of the Berlin Wall in November 1989 and the subsequent dissolution of the Warsaw Pact, the flexible-response strategy to an eastern attack lost much of its relevance. The immediate impact was defence downsizing to take advantage of a peace dividend. As the large allies downsized to a greater extent relative to the smaller allies, defence burdens should at first shift to the latter—a tendency enhanced by Greek and Turkish military build-ups. The Gulf War of 1991 underscored that threats to NATO's interests can come from so-called rogue nations. As Communist regimes in Europe collapsed, ethnic conflicts, once held in check by powerful governments, erupted and threatened stability in Europe.

These developments and the need to reshape NATO to the post-cold-war era resulted in a new strategic doctrine (see Table 1), which first emerged at a Rome summit on 7–8 November 1991 when the Ministers acknowledged that NATO must assume responsibility for ensuring Europe's security from challenges both within and beyond NATO's boundaries (Asmus, 1997, p. 37). During an Oslo summit in

Table 1. *NATO doctrines, defining events and underlying model*

Doctrines and defining events	Model	Implications
Mutual assured destruction 1949–66		
• Reliance on US strategic forces • MC 48: NATO use of nuclear weapons • NATO conventional inferiority • Soviet nuclear force vulnerability	Deterrence as a pure public good	• Disproportionate burdens • Suboptimality and free riding • Inclusive alliance (do not limit size) • Need for co-operation and tight links • Poor match between benefits received and defence burdens
Doctrine of flexible response 1967–80		
• Reliance on conventional and strategic forces • Thinning of conventional forces • MC 14/3 in 1967: flexible response doctrine • Complementarity between strategic and conventional forces • US troops and investments in Europe	Joint products	• Reduced disproportionality of burdens • Less suboptimality • Exclusive alliances (limit size) • Looser alliance linkages • Better match between benefits received and defence burdens
Doctrine of flexible response 1981–90		
• France and UK strategic build-up • Reagan procurement and strategic build-up • Precision-guided munitions • 'Deep strike' or forward-defence strategy	Joint products with more purely public benefits	• Some increase in disproportionality • More suboptimality • Less exclusive alliance • Need for tighter alliance links • Reduced match between benefits received and defence burdens
Crisis management 1991–2000		
• Fall of Berlin Wall (9–10 November 1989) • Dissolution of Warsaw Pact and Soviet Union • Downsizing of defence spending • Desert Shield and Desert Storm • Rome Summit (7–8 November 1991) • Oslo Declaration (June 1992) • Brussels Summit (10–11 January 1994) • Bosnia IFOR and SFOR • NATO expansion (April 1999) • Kosovo and KFOR	Joint products with still more purely public benefits likely in the future	• Some increase in disproportionality • More suboptimality and free riding • Less exclusive alliance • Need for tighter alliance links • Reduced match between benefits received and defence burdens • These predictions will take some time to show up as downsizing initially placed more burdens on the small allies

1992, NATO included peacekeeping as part of its new strategic crisis-management doctrine, which required the development of multilateral rapid-deployment forces with air, land and maritime components, known as Combined Joint Task Forces (CJTFs). At the Brussels Summit on 10–11 January 1994, NATO allies agreed officially to develop these CJTFs and to broaden the strategic doctrine to include policing the non-proliferation of nuclear and other weapons of mass destruction. NATO peacekeeping troops were deployed in Bosnia in December 1995 as an Implementation Force (IFOR) for the Dayton peace agreement. A year later, this force became the Stabilisation Force (SFOR), which is still in Bosnia in 2000. In June 1999, another contingent of NATO peacekeeping troops were dispatched as part of the Kosovo Peacekeeping Force (KFOR), following the NATO springtime bombing campaign against Serbia.

There are a number of factors that promote a hypothesised increase in publicness. First, peacekeeping and crisis-management activities, if successful, provide an increased measure of world stability and security that benefits all nations—contributors and non-contributors—so that benefits are non-excludable and non-rival.[11] Second, allies that acquire sufficient capacity to project forces to trouble spots are likely to provide a free ride in times of crises for allies that have not invested in this capability. During the Gulf War, the US transported much of the coalition's equipment from Europe (Klare, 1995). Only the four largest allies—the US, the UK, France and Germany—are currently making sizeable investments in their power-projecting capacity (Sandler and Hartley, 1999). Third, R&D breakthroughs associated with the revolution in military technologies can yield non-rival, though excludable, benefits. The US, the UK and France spend the most on weapon R&D (Hartley, 1997, p. 31). The experience in Kosovo is instructive: most of the bombing missions were flown by the US military because of the sophisticated ordnance involved and the adverse weather conditions. As the technology gap in weapons expands between the large and small allies, this disproportionality of burdens should increase. This follows because only the few largest NATO allies can afford the huge fixed costs associated with the new generations of weapons. In fact, only the US has the means to make the necessary investments, so that the technology gap, so prevalent during Kosovo, is apt to open wider.

This increased share of purely public joint products will eventually increase free riding and thus place a greater burden on the richest allies once the effects of downsizing are finished. In addition, there is eventually expected to be a reduced match between defence benefits received and burdens carried, so that greater co-operation will someday be needed if allied efforts are to be efficiently allocated. The search for these relationships in Sections IV and V requires some caveats. The crisis-management shares of the allies' defence budget are still small for 1990–99, so that this movement to increased publicness may not yet be evident. Similarly,

---

[11] On the publicness of peacekeeping, see Khanna et al. (1998, 1999).

the build-up of rich allies' transport capacity is occurring in 1998–2005 and, except for 1998–99, will not be reflected in the data.[12]

IV. ABILITY TO PAY AND BURDEN SHARING

The standard burden-sharing measure for defence, used to reflect the ability to pay, is the share of GDP devoted to military expenditures (i.e. ME/GDP). Division by GDP normalises the burden based on the allies' capacity to pay. Other burden-sharing measures (e.g. military expenditures per capita and military manpower per capita) have been applied, but are less useful because they either include only a portion of the military activity or else do not really account for an ally's true ability to underwrite its defence spending.[13] Since the Olson and Zeckhauser (1966) study, disproportionality of defence burdens is typically tested non-parametrically by checking the correlation between the allies' defence burdens ranks and their GDP ranks. If a significant positive correlation exists, then this indicates that the rich allies carried a disproportionately large burden of defence spending. The standard test statistics are the Spearman rank correlation coefficient (ρ) and the Kendall rank correlation coefficient or the Kendall tau (τ).

The alternative (H_a) and null (H_0) hypotheses for a rank correlation test are

H_a: Within NATO, there is a positive association between the allies' GDP and their share of GDP devoted to military expenditure.

H_0: There is no association between these variables.

Table 2 indicates the past findings of these tests for various periods from 1950 to 1992. Previous studies have *all* found a significant positive rank correlation for 1950–66, thus rejecting the null hypothesis in favour of the alternative hypothesis. These results are consistent with the pure public deterrence model's prediction that the rich allies carried the defence burden of the small allies during the MAD era. At the start of flexible response, the positive correlations were insignificant except for 1973 during the Vietnam War. This finding suggests that considerations other than size directed burden sharing during the beginning of flexible response when ally-specific and excludable joint products provided allies with greater interests to contribute to defence. Thus this empirical result is consistent with the joint product model's prediction that economic size becomes less of a determinant of defence burden sharing. During the second half of flexible response in the early 1980s, there was some increase in this correlation, which remained insignificant.

We now update these earlier burden-sharing studies using data from 1988–99. The null hypothesis is tested with the non-parametric Spearman rank correlation coefficient (Mendenhall and Beaver, 1991). Spearman's ρ statistic is calculated in

---

[12] For example, the US plans to spend over $20 billion on strategic mobility over the next five years (US Congressional Budget Office, 1997, Table 3).

[13] Hartley and Sandler (1999) provide a discussion of alternative burden-sharing measures and why ME/GDP is the most appropriate ability-to-pay measure.

Table 2. *Past studies of defence burdens and ability to pay*

Study	Test	Year(s)	Conclusion
Olson and Zeckhauser, 1966	Spearman rank correlation	1964	Significant positive rank correlation between ME/GNP and GNP.
van Ypersele de Strihou, 1968	Regression	1955, 1963	Significant coefficient on GNP when ME/GNP is regressed against the log of GNP.
Russett, 1970	Kendall τ	1950–67	Significant rank correlation between ME/GNP and GNP for all sample years, with a marked decline in correlation starting in 1961.
Sandler and Forbes, 1980	Kendall τ	1960–75	Significant rank correlation between ME/GDP and GDP for 1960–66. Thereafter, the relationship is insignificant except for 1973.
Oneal and Elrod, 1989	Percentage of variance explained	1953–84[a]	Significant percentage of variance of ME/GDP is explained by GDP during 1953–68. After 1968, only an insignificant percentage of this variance is explained.
Khanna and Sandler, 1996	Kendall τ	1960–92	Many significant rank correlations between ME/GDP and GDP during 1960–66. No significant rank correlations are found after 1966. During the late 1970s and early 1980s, these correlations are elevated but not significant.

[a]For selected years.

the same fashion as the familiar Pearson correlation coefficient except that the *ranks* of the data replace the actual measurements, making the statistic robust to outliers and minor measurement errors that do not alter the rankings. Moreover, this statistic makes no parametric demands on the distributions of the GDP and defence burden data. This is ideal for our situation in so far as some relatively large allies (e.g. the US) are grouped with some small ones (e.g. Luxemburg), making it unlikely that the GDP observations are generated from the same distribution. The tests of the relationship between defence burden and GDP are apt to suffer from confounding influences. For instance, a longer exposed border generally necessitates greater defensive expenditures. To the extent that larger nations tend to have greater GDP, the strength of the defence burden and GDP relationship appears greater owing to this confounding variable. To assess the role of potential confounding influences, we also test the hypotheses using Spearman's partial correlation coefficients. Intuitively, a partial coefficient measures the correlation of the residuals of two regressions: the first set comes from a regression of defence burden ranks on (say) exposed borders, while the second comes from a regression on GDP and exposed borders. With the partial correlation coefficient, we thus remove any explanatory power of the confounding variable before computing the statistic.[14]

The dataset for the updated burden-sharing tests in Sections IV and V includes observations on military expenditures, GDP, exchange rates, population (POP), imports (IMP), exports (EXP) and exposed borders. For the 15 NATO allies (minus Iceland), we have data for 1988–99. The data on ME for 1988–98 were obtained from Stockholm International Peace Research Institute (1999), while ME estimates for 1999 of the NATO allies were taken from NATO (1999). In the case of exposed borders (length in kilometres of borders with non-NATO nations plus coastlines), data were obtained from the US Central Intelligence Agency (1999). With some minor exceptions, data on the remaining variables were taken from International Monetary Fund (1999a,b).[15] Each ally's openness measure equals its sum of exports and imports as a share of the country's GDP. Currency-based data for ME, GDP, IMP and EXP were expressed in nominal US dollars using the current average exchange rate for each year of data with the exception of the EU countries in 1999. For these observations, data were expressed in US dollars using the 1 January 1999 exchange rates adjusted by the value of the Euro on 1 July 1999.

In Table 3, the Spearman rank correlations between defence burdens and GDP are given annually for the 1988–99 period. Numbers in parentheses beneath the various Spearman ρ coefficients indicate the prob-values or the probability of a type I error when testing for no association. Prob-values of 0.05 or less would reflect statistically significant coefficients. In the second column, the simple rank correlation coefficients, ρ_{12}, are displayed, all of which are insignificant. The positive and insignificant rank correlations for 1988–96 decline in value during the post-cold-war period, indicating less correlation between economic size and defence burdens. This finding is consistent with the smaller allies cutting back on defence spending during this period by less than the large allies. Additionally, the absence of correlation between economic size and defence burdens suggests the continued applicability of the joint product model during the post-cold-war era. In 1997–99, there is a small increase in this rank correlation, which might forebode

---

[14] While several non-parametric statistics are available to test for association, two in particular—Kendall's τ and Spearman's ρ—readily extend to partial measures. We employed the Spearman ρ because the sampling distribution for Kendall's partial t is unknown. To obtain prob-values for this t, we would have to resort to some sort of simulation (e.g. Hoflund, 1963). Although not presented here, we also estimated the alternative Kendall's τs and found that the patterns of the correlations are essentially identical to those reported with Spearman's ρ below.

[15] The exceptions are as follows. The GDPs for Portugal in 1997–1999 were inferred from the ratio of ME to GDP as reported in US Department of Defense (1999). For countries with incomplete series on imports and exports, our measure of openness in Section V was estimated as the previous year's value. In cases where population is missing, we used the previous year's value to complete the series.

Sandler and Murdoch

Table 3. *Spearman rank correlations between defence burdens (ME/GDP) and GDP*

	ρ_{12}[a]	$\rho_{12,3}$[b]	$\rho_{12,34}$[c]
1988	0.31	0.35	0.32
	(0.27)	(0.22)	(0.29)
1989	0.27	0.33	0.33
	(0.33)	(0.24)	(0.27)
1990	0.31	0.35	0.31
	(0.27)	(0.22)	(0.30)
1991	0.18	0.22	0.22
	(0.53)	(0.44)	(0.58)
1992	0.21	0.25	0.20
	(0.44)	(0.39)	(0.52)
1993	0.20	0.23	0.17
	(0.48)	(0.43)	(0.59)
1994	0.11	0.16	0.07
	(0.68)	(0.59)	(0.83)
1995	0.06	0.12	0.04
	(0.82)	(0.69)	(0.89)
1996	0.05	0.09	0.03
	(0.87)	(0.75)	(0.92)
1997	0.09	0.12	0.05
	(0.75)	(0.69)	(0.87)
1998	0.08	0.11	0.04
	(0.79)	(0.71)	(0.89)
1999[d]	0.12	0.23	0.07
	(0.64)	(0.37)	(0.79)

Note: Numbers in parentheses are prob-values, indicating the probability of a type I error when testing the null hypothesis of no association between ME/GDP and GDP versus the alternative hypothesis of a positive association.

Variables: 1 = ME/GDP; 2 = GDP; 3 = GDP/POP; 4 = exposed borders.

[a]Simple rank correlation coefficient.
[b]Partial rank correlation coefficient with GDP/POP held constant.
[c]Partial rank correlation coefficient with GDP/POP and exposed borders held constant.
[d]The number of allies is 18 for 1999, since Iceland is excluded.

that the crisis-management doctrine and other developments are beginning to have their anticipated impact on burden sharing. It is, however, apt to take more years of crisis-management activities and the build-up of mobile forces before the predicted disproportionality shows up. The last two columns of Table 3 contain partial rank correlation coefficients with GDP per capita held constant and with GDP per capita and exposed borders held constant, respectively. Both partial rank correlation coefficients show an identical pattern to that of the simple rank correlation. When GDP per capita is held constant, the positive correlations are slightly elevated from the simple rank correlations. A similar result applies for 1988–91 but not for 1992–99 when both GDP per capita and exposed borders are held constant. After 1992, this partial rank correlation displays the same trend as the simple rank correlation but is smaller.[16] These findings imply no exploitation of the large by the small during the post-cold-war period.

V. BENEFIT MEASURES AND BURDEN SHARING

Benefits from defence spending arise from what is protected by both conventional and strategic arsenals: the ally's industrial base, its population and its exposed borders. To calculate an overall measure for these defence benefits, we followed the methodology of Sandler and Forbes (1980) and computed each ally's share of NATO's GDP (i.e. ally's GDP/NATO GDP), its share of NATO's population and its share of NATO's exposed borders. Myriad weighting schemes can be devised to aggregate these three benefit measures to derive some aggregate benefit share for each ally. In essence, the appropriate weights depend on an ally's preferences, which are neither known nor easily observed. As a reasonable proxy in light of our ignorance, we weighted these shares equally by adding them up and dividing by three for an 'average benefit share'.

If the average benefit share is a good predictor of an ally's actual defence burden share within NATO (ME/NATO ME), then the distributions of the two measures should be similar, that is, there should be no systematic difference between them. This new burden-sharing measure represents *between-ally* sharing in contrast to the earlier ME/GDP measure which denotes *within-ally* sharing based on country-specific variables. To determine the correspondence between defence burdens and its benefits, we used a Wilcoxon signed-rank test which is a non-parametric alternative to the familiar paired difference test (Mendenhall and Beaver, 1991).[17] The alternative hypothesis (H_{2a}) and null hypothesis (H_{20}) are

H_{2a}: The distributions of defence burdens and average benefit shares for the NATO allies are different.

H_{20}: The distributions of defence burdens and average benefit shares for the NATO allies are the same.

In our case of $N = 15$ for 1990–98, the critical value for the Wilcoxon R statistic is 25 at the 5 per cent level of significance for a two-tailed test. The null hypothesis is rejected when R is less than or equal to 25. For 1999, $N = 18$ and the critical Wilcoxon R statistic is then 40.

---

[16] Other partial rank correlations, not displayed, (e.g. holding exposed borders constant) indicate the same results: all coefficients are insignificant and the coefficient pattern over time is the same as those in Table 3.

[17] The Wilcoxon test involves (i) assigning ranks based on the absolute value of the differences between the two measures and (ii) computing the sum of the ranks with positive differences and the sum with negative differences. The smaller of these two rank sums is the R statistic of interest, and its critical values are available in most introductory statistics books.

Before presenting the results for the 1990s, we review three studies that compared defence burdens and average benefit shares for earlier periods. Sandler and Forbes (1980) uncovered a much closer match between defence burdens and their benefit proxies in 1975 than in 1960 during MAD, where the underlying distributions were different. Khanna and Sandler (1996, 1997) were unable to reject the null hypothesis H_{20} at intervals for 1965, 1970, 1975, 1980 and 1990, thus leading to the conclusion that during much of the flexible-response era there was a statistically significant match between defence burdens and their benefits. This finding supports the joint product model over the purely public deterrent model as the underlying paradigm. For 1985, however, at the height of the Reagan defence build-up, the null hypothesis is rejected in favour of the alternative hypothesis. Thus the Reagan administration's concentration on procurement and the build-up of strategic, tactical and other armaments appeared to increase the extent of publicness in the defence activity and, in so doing, induced more free riding, thus breaking the match between defence burdens and defence benefits.

Our update for the 1990s is indicated in Tables 4 and 5, where defence burdens and average benefit shares are displayed annually for 1990–94 and 1995–99, respectively. Data sources were the same as those described in Section IV for the Spearman test. As in this previous test, current-year nominal data were converted to nominal US dollars using that year's exchange rates. For each country, its share of NATO's GDP, population and exposed borders were computed and then averaged. In each table, the left column beneath each year is the actual defence burden, while the right column is the average benefit share. For example, in 1990, France assumed 8.45 per cent of NATO total defence spending, while it received a benefit share of 6.39 per cent, thus implying an overpayment. In that same year, the Netherlands covered 1.47 per cent of NATO's aggregate defence spending, which is almost a perfect match for its average benefit share of 1.54 per cent. Other figures are interpreted similarly.

The Wilcoxon R statistics for these years are: 39 in 1990; 39 in 1991; 37 in 1992; 33 in 1993; 35 in 1994; 37 in 1995; 40 in 1996; 38 in 1997; 41 in 1998; and 45 in 1999. Because none of the R statistics is less than 25 (or 40 for 1999), we cannot reject the null hypothesis; hence there is evidence of a match between defence burdens and our proxy measure of defence benefits for each year of the 1990s.[18] Based on this comparison, the joint product model still describes behaviour in the post-cold-war years, but the match is less significant for 1999, consistent with the increasing share of public benefits. As long as the associated distributions for defence burdens and benefits are the same, there is support for NATO's current loosely integrated alliance, because suboptimality is limited by this concordance.

Figure 1 splices together a key finding of the Khanna and Sandler (1996) study with that of this study. The three time series displayed show the difference between

---

[18] We also computed the defence burdens and benefits for 1988 and 1989, and found R statistics of 35 and 29, respectively. In neither case did we reject the null hypothesis at the 5 per cent level for a two-tailed test.

Table 4. *Defence burdens and average benefit shares in NATO using population, GDP and exposed borders as proxies for benefits: 1990–94*

	1990		1991		1992		1993		1994	
	Defence burden	Average benefit share	Defence burden	Average benefit share	Defence burden	Average benefit share	Defence burden	Average benefit share	Defence burden	Average benefit share
Belgium	0.92	1.03	0.96	1.00	0.81	1.02	0.78	1.01	0.84	1.01
Denmark	0.52	1.30	0.56	1.28	0.56	1.28	0.56	1.27	0.58	1.28
France	8.45	6.39	8.90	6.20	8.86	6.27	8.86	6.16	9.45	6.19
Germany	8.39	7.58	8.23	8.67	8.25	8.97	7.74	8.92	7.73	8.99
Greece	0.77	2.11	0.79	2.10	0.86	2.11	0.85	2.10	0.92	2.10
Italy	4.64	5.93	5.07	5.81	4.91	5.76	4.28	5.24	4.34	5.19
Luxemburg	0.02	0.04	0.02	0.05	0.02	0.05	0.02	0.05	0.03	0.05
Netherlands	1.47	1.54	1.51	1.51	1.55	1.53	1.47	1.53	1.52	1.54
Norway	0.67	2.81	0.69	2.80	0.75	2.80	0.66	2.78	0.72	2.78
Portugal	0.37	0.98	0.44	0.98	0.50	1.00	0.46	0.98	0.46	0.97
Spain	1.80	3.73	1.90	3.71	1.78	3.72	1.72	3.50	1.58	3.44
Turkey	1.05	4.12	1.18	4.08	1.21	4.11	1.47	4.21	1.13	4.10
UK	7.89	6.69	8.99	6.59	7.92	6.50	7.09	6.27	7.33	6.33
Canada	2.29	25.82	2.33	25.77	2.13	25.63	2.14	25.62	2.03	25.55
US	60.74	29.93	58.42	29.45	59.90	29.24	61.91	30.35	61.33	30.47
NATO–Europe	36.97	44.26	39.25	44.78	37.97	45.13	35.95	44.03	36.64	43.98
NATO–North-America	63.03	55.74	60.75	55.22	62.03	54.87	64.05	55.97	63.36	56.02

Notes: Figures represent percentage shares of NATO's total for each variable. For example, defence burden indicates the ally's defence spending divided by total NATO defence spending. Average benefit share denotes the sum of each ally's shares of NATO's population, NATO's GDP and NATO's exposed borders, divided by three. The totals for NATO–Europe and NATO–North-America may not add up due to rounding.

Table 5. Defence burdens and average benefit shares in NATO using population, GDP and exposed borders as proxies for benefits: 1995–99

	1995		1996		1997		1998		1999	
	Defence burden	Average benefit share	Defence burden	Average benefit share	Defence burden	Average benefit share	Defence burden	Average benefit share	Defence burden	Average benefit share
Belgium	0.94	1.06	0.91	1.02	0.83	0.97	0.82	0.96	0.75	0.90
Czech Republic									0.25	0.59
Denmark	0.66	1.31	0.66	1.31	0.62	1.28	0.63	1.27	0.59	1.21
France	10.12	6.34	9.95	6.23	9.17	5.93	9.01	5.90	8.28	5.53
Germany	8.72	9.34	8.36	9.03	7.38	8.51	7.33	8.77	6.80	7.69
Greece	1.07	2.12	1.20	2.12	1.22	2.11	1.29	2.10	1.27	2.02
Hungary									0.16	0.70
Italy	4.10	5.12	5.03	5.28	4.82	5.13	5.12	5.06	4.82	5.43
Luxemburg	0.03	0.06	0.03	0.05	0.03	0.05	0.03	0.05	0.03	0.05
Netherlands	1.70	1.60	1.68	1.56	1.52	1.50	1.50	1.50	1.38	1.41
Norway	0.72	2.81	0.79	2.82	0.74	2.81	0.71	2.78	0.68	2.69
Poland									0.70	2.14
Portugal	0.57	0.99	0.56	0.98	0.56	0.97	0.53	0.95	0.50	0.91
Spain	1.83	3.50	1.85	3.49	1.66	3.38	1.65	3.36	1.59	3.18
Turkey	1.40	4.18	1.61	4.20	1.60	4.26	1.84	4.22	2.20	3.94
UK	7.17	6.29	7.40	6.30	7.89	6.52	8.17	6.56	7.54	6.25
Canada	1.92	25.50	1.81	25.52	1.71	25.57	1.50	25.47	1.60	24.67
US	59.06	29.80	58.18	30.07	60.25	31.01	59.85	31.06	60.87	30.66
NATO–Europe	39.02	44.69	40.01	44.41	38.04	43.43	38.65	43.47	37.54	44.66
NATO–North-America	60.98	55.31	59.99	55.59	61.96	56.57	61.35	56.53	62.46	55.34

Notes: See Table 4.

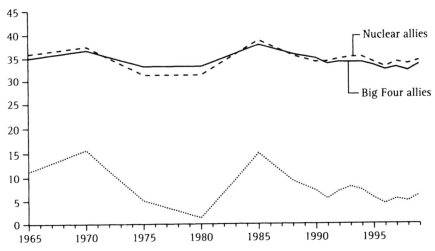

Figure 1. *Difference between actual and predicted defence burdens:*
NATO–North-America, big four and nuclear allies

actual defence burdens and those predicted by the average benefit share for the two North American allies, the three nuclear allies and the four largest allies (i.e. the three nuclear allies plus Germany). In so far as each time series shows the same pattern, we focus on the time series for North America, where this difference declined between 1970 and 1980 as flexible response shifted more defence burdens to Europe. The Reagan build-up reversed this shift. Since 1985, the overall trend for this difference is downward, except for 1999 where a small rise is noted. The pattern for exploitation, reflected by these time series for various aggregates of the large allies, is closely in keeping with our theoretical predictions.

Next, we broadened the proxy for average benefit shares to include a fourth benefit measure of openness. In a secure environment, an ally also gains from international trade. To devise a measure for the relative benefit that an ally derives from its openness ({exports+imports}/GDP), we calculated an ally's share of NATO's aggregate openness, which equals an ally's openness divided by the sum of these openness measures for the alliance. Average benefit shares were then computed by summing each ally's four benefit shares and dividing by four. In Table 6, we depict defence burdens and the new average benefit shares for five selected years in the 1990s. Other years display very similar values. The Wilcoxon signed-rank test statistic equals: 37 in 1991; 29 in 1992; 28 in 1993; 30 in 1994; 32 in 1995; 32 in 1996; 31 in 1997; and 33 in 1998.[19] For these new R statistics, we cannot reject the null hypothesis at the 5 per cent level of significance. Thus we again conclude that there is evidence of a match between defence burdens paid

---

[19] Because openness data were not available for 1999, this year was not examined with the four-proxy benefit measure.

Table 6. *Defence burdens and average benefit shares in NATO using openness, population, GDP and exposed borders as proxies for benefits: selected years*

	1991		1993		1995		1997		1998	
	Defence burden	Average benefit share	Defence burden	Average benefit share	Defence burden	Average benefit share	Defence burden	Average benefit share	Defence burden	Average benefit share
Belgium	0.96	4.07	0.78	3.93	0.94	3.97	0.83	4.05	0.82	4.04
Denmark	0.56	2.70	0.56	2.63	0.66	2.61	0.62	2.59	0.63	2.59
France	8.90	5.79	8.86	5.72	10.12	5.84	9.17	5.63	9.01	5.60
Germany	8.23	7.80	7.74	7.85	8.72	8.10	7.38	7.57	7.33	7.76
Greece	0.79	2.67	0.85	2.67	1.07	2.56	1.22	2.50	1.29	2.49
Italy	5.07	5.25	4.28	4.96	4.10	4.99	4.82	4.95	5.12	4.89
Luxemburg	0.02	4.77	0.02	4.57	0.03	4.25	0.03	4.10	0.03	4.10
Netherlands	1.51	3.75	1.47	3.67	1.70	3.64	1.52	3.60	1.50	3.60
Norway	0.69	3.94	0.66	3.94	0.72	3.82	0.74	3.90	0.71	3.88
Portugal	0.44	2.34	0.46	2.21	0.57	2.28	0.56	2.24	0.53	2.23
Spain	1.90	3.73	1.72	3.67	1.83	3.79	1.66	3.84	1.65	3.83
Turkey	1.18	3.83	1.47	4.00	1.40	4.19	1.60	3.88	1.84	3.84
UK	8.99	6.16	7.09	6.08	7.17	6.12	7.89	6.25	8.17	6.29
Canada	2.33	20.59	2.14	20.78	1.92	20.90	1.71	21.05	1.50	20.97
US	58.42	22.61	61.91	23.32	59.06	22.93	60.25	23.85	59.85	23.89
NATO–Europe	39.25	56.80	35.95	55.90	39.02	56.17	38.04	55.10	38.65	55.14
NATO–North-America	60.75	43.20	64.05	44.10	60.98	43.83	61.96	44.90	61.35	44.86

Notes: Figures represent percentage shares of NATO's total for each variable. For example, defence burden indicates the ally's defence spending divided by total NATO defence spending. Average benefit share denotes the sum of each ally's shares of NATO's population, NATO's GDP, NATO's exposed borders and NATO's openness, divided by four. The totals for NATO–Europe and NATO–North-America may not add up due to rounding.

and defence benefits received. This inclusion of another benefit measure indicates that the results are not so sensitive to the benefit proxies chosen.

VI. ALTERNATIVE NATO EXPANSION SCENARIOS

With the inclusion of the Czech Republic, Hungary and Poland in NATO in March 1999, NATO confronts new concerns about burden sharing. As the alliance expands, a greater heterogeneity of tastes is introduced at a time when the theory of alliances predicts more disproportionate burden sharing in the future with large allies assuming increased burdens in terms of the proportion of GDP devoted to defence. The Partnership for Peace (PFP) programme, started in 1994, is geared to preparing other nations for NATO membership and fostering co-operation between NATO and the countries of eastern and central Europe (Gompert and Larrabee, 1997; Sandler and Hartley, 1999, p. 19).

To investigate what might be the impact of alternative expansion scenarios, we conducted a thought experiment which allows for nine possible alliance-composition scenarios:

- Scenario 1 is NATO 15 (excluding Iceland and the three entrants);
- Scenario 2 is NATO 18 (excluding Iceland);
- Scenario 3 is NATO 18, Slovenia and Slovakia;
- Scenario 4 is NATO 18, Slovenia, Slovakia and Romania;
- Scenario 5 is NATO 18, Slovenia, Slovakia, Romania and the three Baltic states (Estonia, Latvia and Lithuania);
- Scenario 6 consists of Scenario 2 allies plus the neutrals (Austria, Finland, Ireland, Sweden and Switzerland);
- Scenario 7 consists of Scenario 3 allies plus the neutrals;
- Scenario 8 consists of Scenario 4 allies plus the neutrals;
- Scenario 9 consists of Scenario 5 allies plus the neutrals.

Scenario 1 is, of course, NATO prior to March 1999, while Scenario 2 is NATO today. The remaining scenarios are numbered from 3 to 5 or from 6 to 9, according to their likelihood of being realised, where smaller numbers are associated with more likely cases. These scenarios and their likelihood are based on locational and spatial considerations (i.e. exposed borders and geographical position) as well as political considerations as analysed in Sandler (1999). For example, Slovenia and Slovakia are the most likely entrants, because each has relatively little exposed border so that their admittance saves on cost by sequestering interior borders of existing allies. Moreover, these two countries do not face insurgencies or border disputes. In contrast, the inclusion of the Baltic states does little, except for a small contiguous border with Poland, to sequester borders. Moreover, their inclusion is rigorously opposed by Russia, thus implying political costs.

Our thought experiment first consisted of computing the Spearman rank correlations between defence burdens and GDP for various scenarios in 1998 to ascertain how burdens would be shared. This experiment implies that new allies do not alter their share of GDP for defence, which, if the behaviour of the three recent entrants is any indication, is a reasonable assumption. As in the case of the NATO 15, the data for these three NATO entrants, the other prospective entrants and the neutral nations are obtained as follows: ME from Stockholm International Peace Research Institute (1999); exposed borders from US Central Intelligence Agency (1999); and POP from International Monetary Fund (1999a,b).

In Table 7, we display various Spearman rank correlation coefficients and their prob-values. The scenarios are indicated in the first column, while the number of

Table 7. *Spearman rank correlations between ME/GDP and GDP for various membership scenarios: 1998*

Scenario[a]	No. of observations	ρ_{12}[b]	$\rho_{12,3}$[c]	$\rho_{12,4}$[d]	$\rho_{12,34}$[e]
1	15	0.08	0.11	0.01	0.04
		(0.79)	(0.71)	(0.98)	(0.89)
2	18	0.10	0.19	−0.05	0.04
		(0.68)	(0.47)	(0.86)	(0.88)
3	20	0.14	0.25	−0.07	0.04
		(0.55)	(0.30)	(0.76)	(0.87)
4	21	0.16	0.27	−0.07	0.06
		(0.49)	(0.25)	(0.78)	(0.82)
5	24	0.37	0.40	0.24	0.29
		(0.07)	(0.06)	(0.28)	(0.19)
6	23	0.15	0.25	−0.01	0.09
		(0.49)	(0.25)	(0.96)	(0.69)
7	25	0.14	0.28	−0.04	0.11
		(0.50)	(0.19)	(0.87)	(0.61)
8	26	0.14	0.29	−0.04	0.12
		(0.50)	(0.16)	(0.85)	(0.57)
9	29	0.30	0.40	0.20	0.30
		(0.11)	(0.04)	(0.30)	(0.13)

Note: Numbers in parentheses are prob-values, indicating the probability of a type I error when testing the null hypothesis of no association between ME/GDP and GDP versus the alternative hypothesis of a positive association.
Variables: 1 = ME/GDP; 2 = GDP; 3 = GDP/POP; 4 = exposed borders.
[a]Scenario 1 is NATO 15 excluding Iceland.
 Scenario 2 is NATO 15 plus three new entrants (Czech Republic, Hungary and Poland).
 Scenario 3 is NATO 18, Slovenia and Slovakia.
 Scenario 4 is NATO 18, Slovenia, Slovakia and Romania.
 Scenario 5 consists of Scenario 4 plus three Baltic countries (Estonia, Latvia and Lithuania).
 Scenario 6 is NATO 18 plus five neutrals (Austria, Finland, Ireland, Sweden and Switzerland).
 Scenario 7 is NATO 18, five neutrals, Slovenia and Slovakia.
 Scenario 8 consists of Scenario 7 plus Romania.
 Scenario 9 consists of Scenario 8 plus three Baltic countries.
[b]Simple rank correlation coefficient.
[c]Partial rank correlation coefficient with GDP/POP held constant.
[d]Partial rank correlation coefficient with exposed borders held constant.
[e]Partial rank correlation coefficient with GDP/POP and exposed borders held constant.

observations is given in the second column. In the third column, the simple rank correlations increase in value as the number of allies increases for the five scenarios without the neutrals. This result suggests that, as the alliance expands, the extent of disproportionate burden sharing increases. This outcome is in complete agreement with the general principles of collective action where free riding increases with group size (Olson, 1965; Sandler, 1992). For the scenarios involving the neutrals, this increasing disproportionality only arises with the addition of the Baltic states. Interestingly, the neutrals share burdens today not too dissimilarly from other small allies in regards to the proportion of GDP devoted to defence. When Scenarios 2 and 6 are compared for the simple rank correlation, there is increased disproportionality, but it is rather limited for the addition of so many nations. Scenarios 5 and 9 suggest that the inclusion of the Baltic states is apt to have an important negative impact on burden sharing. Nearly identical patterns arise for the partial Spearman rank correlations in the fourth and sixth columns. When, however, the partial rank correlation holds only exposed borders constant, no clear pattern emerges in the fifth column except that the addition of the Baltic states leads to an augmented disproportionality in burden sharing.

As a second thought experiment, we computed the average benefit shares and defence burdens for Scenarios 2–9, where the former were based on each ally's shares of POP, GDP and exposed borders. In Table 8, we display these defence burdens and benefit shares for only five of eight scenarios to conserve space.[20] The Wilcoxon R statistic, along with the critical values below which the null hypothesis is rejected at the 5 per cent level, is displayed in the last row. The null hypothesis is rejected in favour of the alternative hypothesis of different underlying distributions for Scenarios 5 and 9, but not for Scenarios 2, 4 and 6. For the scenarios not depicted in Table 8, the Wilcoxon R and its critical value (in parentheses) are: 61 (52) for Scenario 3; 87 (90) for Scenario 7; and 91 (98) for Scenario 8. Thus defence burdens and defence benefits do not match for the inclusion of the Baltic states and three of the four scenarios involving the neutral countries. These findings suggest that expanding the NATO alliance much beyond the inclusion of Slovenia, Slovakia and Romania will create greater inefficiency in resource allocation as benefits and burdens of defence are poorly matched.

VII. SECURITY BURDEN SHARING

Until now, there has been no convincing or successful effort in the literature to define a broader security burden-sharing measure that includes allies' defence efforts, peacekeeping support and foreign-aid activities. Surely peacekeeping bolsters overall security, while foreign assistance does the same by creating more robust and stable economies in developing countries. It is instructive to see how the US DOD addresses this security burden-sharing issue in its annual *Report on Allied Contributions to Common Defense* to the US Congress (see, e.g. US DOD,

---

[20] The values for the other scenarios are available from the authors upon request.

Table 8. *Defence burdens and average benefit shares for various enlargement scenarios using population, GDP and exposed borders as proxies for benefits: 1998*

	Scenario 2 (N = 18)		Scenario 4 (N = 21)		Scenario 5 (N = 24)		Scenario 6 (N = 23)		Scenario 9 (N = 29)	
	DB	ABS	DB	ABS	DB	ABS	DB	ABS	DB	ABS
Austria	NA	NA	NA	NA	NA	NA	0.38	0.75	0.38	0.70
Belgium	0.81	0.92	0.81	0.90	0.81	0.89	0.79	0.88	0.79	0.85
Czech Republic	0.25	0.60	0.25	0.56	0.25	0.56	0.24	0.54	0.24	0.50
Denmark	0.63	1.24	0.62	1.22	0.62	1.21	0.61	1.21	0.61	1.19
Estonia	NA	NA	NA	NA	0.01	0.44	NA	NA	0.01	0.44
Finland	NA	NA	NA	NA	NA	NA	0.40	0.67	0.40	0.65
France	8.91	5.65	8.88	5.54	8.88	5.51	8.67	5.35	8.64	5.22
Germany	7.25	8.31	7.23	8.15	7.22	8.11	7.06	7.84	7.03	7.67
Greece	1.28	2.04	1.28	2.02	1.28	2.00	1.25	2.01	1.24	1.97
Hungary	0.13	0.69	0.13	0.57	0.12	0.57	0.12	0.63	0.12	0.52
Ireland	NA	NA	NA	NA	NA	NA	0.15	0.40	0.15	0.39
Italy	5.07	4.82	5.05	4.70	5.05	4.67	4.93	4.50	4.91	4.36
Latvia	NA	NA	NA	NA	0.01	0.19	NA	NA	0.01	0.19
Lithuania	NA	NA	NA	NA	0.03	0.25	NA	NA	0.03	0.24
Luxemburg	0.03	0.05	0.03	0.05	0.03	0.05	0.03	0.05	0.03	0.05
Netherlands	1.49	1.43	1.48	1.40	1.48	1.39	1.45	1.37	1.44	1.34

Norway	0.70	2.74	0.70	2.72	0.70	2.68	0.68	2.49	0.68	2.45
Poland	0.73	2.17	0.73	2.07	0.73	2.04	0.71	2.10	0.71	1.96
Portugal	0.52	0.91	0.52	0.89	0.52	0.88	0.51	0.88	0.51	0.86
Romania	NA	NA	0.16	1.21	0.16	1.20	NA	NA	0.15	1.16
Slovakia	NA	NA	0.09	0.28	0.09	0.28	NA	NA	0.09	0.26
Slovenia	NA	NA	0.07	0.22	0.07	0.21	NA	NA	0.07	0.18
Spain	1.63	3.20	1.62	3.14	1.62	3.11	1.58	3.08	1.58	2.99
Sweden	NA	NA	NA	NA	NA	NA	1.04	1.07	1.03	1.05
Switzerland	NA	NA	NA	NA	NA	NA	0.68	0.77	0.68	0.75
Turkey	1.82	3.98	1.82	3.87	1.82	3.83	1.77	3.85	1.77	3.71
UK	8.08	6.31	8.06	6.20	8.05	6.15	7.87	6.04	7.84	5.90
Canada	1.49	25.11	1.48	24.95	1.48	24.59	1.45	24.93	1.44	24.47
US	59.19	29.85	59.00	29.34	58.97	29.18	57.62	28.60	57.41	27.98
Wilcoxon R[a]	53 (40)		65 (59)		78 (81)		77 (73)		103 (127)	

Abbreviations and notes: NA = not applicable.

DB = defence burden.

ABS = average benefit share.

Notes: Figures represent percentage shares of NATO's total for each variable. For example, DB indicates the ally's defence spending divided by total NATO defence spending. ABS denotes the sum of each ally's shares of NATO's population, NATO's GDP and NATO's exposed borders, divided by three.

[a]Values in parentheses indicate the critical value below which the null hypothesis is rejected at the 5% level.

1996, 1999). In essence, this report merely presents a rank for each security-enhancing activity and allows readers to draw their own conclusions. Suppose that Norway is highly ranked in peacekeeping and foreign assistance but is lowly ranked in its defence burden as a share of GDP. Are we then to conclude that Norway assumes a respectable burden? This is a hasty conclusion because the expenditure levels on peacekeeping and foreign aid are typically dwarfed by that on defence, so that doing more than one's share on the first two does not necessarily offset a small defence burden. Taking an average of these ranks, as done by Hartley and Sandler (1999), is also ill advised because this procedure implicitly assumes that the amounts spent are of similar magnitudes.

The security burden index proposed here adjusts for differential spending on alternative security-promoting activities. If security derives from defence, peacekeeping and foreign aid, then the proposed measure sums the expenditures on each and then divides this sum by GDP. Ranks are assigned for these security burdens and then compared with each ally's GDP ranks. We performed these computations for 1994–97 in the base case of 15 NATO allies, using data on defence spending, peacekeeping expenditure and foreign aid from US DOD (1999). Because this report presents the data in real 1998 US dollars, current-year nominal values for other variables (e.g. GDP) had to be converted into real 1998 US dollars. These real figures were obtained by first 'deflating' the own-country values to 1998 with their respective GDP price deflator before converting to dollars with the 1998 average exchange rate. Deflation of the own-country values is accomplished by multiplying by the ratio of the 1998 price deflator to the annual price deflator. The price deflators are from International Monetary Fund (1999a and 1999b).[21]

In Table 9, we present the various Spearman rank correlation coefficients between our security burden measure and GDP. The most interesting finding is that the results in Table 9 are closely related to those in Table 3, where only defence burdens are correlated with GDP for comparable years. In fact, the broader measure shows a slightly elevated, but highly insignificant, positive correlation. The elevated values suggest not only that the defence burdens overwhelm the peacekeeping and foreign assistance burdens for these years, but also that the smaller countries are not, on average, carrying more of the latter two combined burdens. If peacekeeping continues to grow in importance and if, moreover, these burdens are shouldered by the large allies, as projected here, then the rank correlation between the security burdens and GDP will increase and may culminate in disproportionate burden sharing as in the MAD era. Clearly, the argument that a broader security measure would reverse findings based solely on defence burdens is not supported here. The technique put forward for computing a security burden can be extended to include additional security-promoting activities.

---

[21] For countries with incomplete GDP price deflator series, we applied the rate of change in the consumer price index (also available from International Monetary Fund, 1999a) to the available GDP price deflators to complete the series.

Table 9. *Spearman rank correlations between security burdens and GDP (N = 15)*

	ρ_{12} [a]	$\rho_{12,3}$ [b]	$\rho_{12,34}$ [c]
1994	0.19	0.21	0.13
	(0.49)	(0.46)	(0.68)
1995	0.14	0.16	0.07
	(0.61)	(0.58)	(0.82)
1996	0.11	0.13	0.04
	(0.69)	(0.66)	(0.89)
1997	0.11	0.13	0.04
	(0.69)	(0.66)	(0.89)

Note: Numbers in parentheses are prob-values, indicating the probability of a type I error when testing the null hypothesis of no association between the security burden and GDP versus the alternative hypothesis of a positive association.
Variables: 1 = ME/GDP; 2 = GDP; 3 = GDP/POP; 4 = exposed borders.
[a]Simple rank correlation coefficient.
[b]Partial rank correlation coefficient with GDP/POP held constant.
[c]Partial rank correlation coefficient with GDP/POP and exposed borders held constant.

VIII. CONCLUDING REMARKS

Although the threat of nuclear Armageddon has subsided greatly since the conclusion of the cold war, Europe and its North American allies still confront myriad common security challenges from crisis management, ethnic unrests, weapons of mass destruction proliferation, rogue nations, transnational terrorism and a Russia at war with some of its ex-republics. As the nature of the threats changes, NATO must respond with new weapons, technology, logistical doctrines and strategies. By changing the publicness character of the shared defence activities, these developments can have profound influences on resource allocation within NATO. The NATO alliance provides a means for collective security at a bargain price, but poses collective action problems from free riding, inefficient resource allocations and disproportionate burden sharing.

This chapter has applied the theoretical and empirical tools from the economic study of alliances to take stock of free riding, burden sharing and related issues in the past. More important, we have provided an up-to-date analysis of these resource-allocation concerns for NATO in the 1990s. In the process, we have shown that the joint product model still applies during the current crisis-management era. There continues to be a concordance between benefits received and defence burdens borne by the allies. Moreover, there is no evidence yet of disproportionate burdens being shouldered by the large allies. At this point in time, NATO's loosely integrated institutional structure therefore remains appropriate.

Nevertheless, theoretical arguments are put forward that hypothesise that defence burden sharing will become more disproportionately carried by the large allies in the future as spending on crisis management, force mobility, weapons non-proliferation and high-technology weapons increases as a proportion of the defence budget. If this prediction is realised, then NATO's institutional structure may need to be tightened and, in so doing, allies' discretion will be reduced.

We have also presented alternative NATO expansion scenarios that may result in an increased exploitation of the large by the small if the alliance continues to expand. It would be useful to re-examine NATO's burdens in another five years to evaluate if the predicted trend to disproportionate burden sharing and a greater share of purely public output is realised.

REFERENCES

Asmus, R. D. (1997), 'Double enlargement: redefining the Atlantic partnership after the Cold War', in D. C. Gompert and F. S. Larrabee (eds), *America and Europe: A Partnership for a New Era*, Cambridge: Cambridge University Press.

Enders, W. and Sandler, T. (1999), 'Transnational terrorism in the post-Cold War era', *International Studies Quarterly*, vol. 43, pp. 145–67.

— and — (2000), 'Is transnational terrorism becoming more threatening? A time series investigation', *Journal of Conflict Resolution*, vol. 44, pp. 307–32.

Gardner, R. (1995), *Games for Business and Economics*, New York: John Wiley & Sons.

Gompert, D. C. and Larrabee, F. S. (eds) (1997), *America and Europe: A Partnership for a New Era*, Cambridge: Cambridge University Press.

Hartley, K. (1997), 'The Cold War, great-power traditions and military posture: determinants of British defence expenditure after 1945', *Defence and Peace Economics*, vol. 8, pp. 17–35.

— and Sandler, T. (1999), 'NATO burden sharing: past and future', *Journal of Peace Research*, vol. 36, pp. 665–80.

Hoflund, O. (1963), 'Simulated distributions for small n of Kendall's partial rank coefficient', *Biometrika*, vol. 50, pp. 520–2.

International Monetary Fund (1999a), *International Financial Statistics Yearbook: 1998*, Washington, DC: IMF.

— (1999b), *International Financial Statistics, September 1999*, Washington, DC: IMF.

Jordan, R. S. (1995), 'NATO's structural changes in the 1990s', in S. V. Papacosma and M. A. Heiss (eds), *NATO in the Post-Cold War Era: Does It Have a Future?*, New York: St Martin's Press.

Khanna, J. and Sandler, T. (1996), 'NATO burden sharing: 1960–1992', *Defence and Peace Economics*, vol. 7, pp. 115–33.

— and — (1997), 'Conscription, peacekeeping, and foreign assistance: NATO burden sharing in the post-Cold War era', *Defence and Peace Economics*, vol. 8, pp. 101–21.

—, — and Shimizu, H. (1998), 'Sharing the financial burden for UN and NATO peacekeeping: 1976–1996', *Journal of Conflict Resolution*, vol. 42, pp. 176–95.

—, — and – (1999), 'The demand for UN peacekeeping, 1975–1996', *KYKLOS*, vol. 52, pp. 345–68.

Klare, M. (1995), *Rogue States and Nuclear Outlaws: America's Search for a New Foreign Policy*, New York: Hill and Wang.

McGuire, M. C. (1990), 'Mixed public–private benefit and public-good supply with applications to the NATO alliance', *Defence Economics*, vol. 1, pp. 17–35.

Mendenhall, W. and Beaver, R. J. (1991), *Introduction to Probability and Statistics*, 8th edn, Boston: PWS-Kent Publishing.

Morrow, J. D. (1991), 'Alliances and asymmetry: an alternative to the capability aggregation model of alliances', *American Journal of Political Science*, vol. 35, pp. 904–13.

Murdoch, J. C. (1995), 'Military alliances: theory and empirics', in K. Hartley and T. Sandler (eds), *Handbook of Defense Economics, Vol. 1*, Amsterdam: North-Holland.

—— and Sandler, T. (1982), 'A theoretical and empirical analysis of NATO', *Journal of Conflict Resolution*, vol. 26, pp. 237–63.

—— and —— (1984), 'Complementarity, free riding, and the military expenditures of NATO allies', *Journal of Public Economics*, vol. 25, pp. 83–101.

NATO (1999), 'Financial and economic data relating to NATO defence: 1975–1999', NATO Press Release M-DPC-2(1999)152, 2 December, Brussels: NATO.

NATO Office of Information and Press (1995), *NATO Handbook*, Brussels: NATO.

Olson, M. (1965), *The Logic of Collective Action*, Cambridge, MA: Harvard University Press.

—— and Zeckhauser, R. (1966), 'An economic theory of alliances', *Review of Economics and Statistics*, vol. 48, pp. 266–79.

Oneal, J. R. (1990), 'The theory of collective action and burden sharing in NATO', *International Organization*, vol. 44, pp. 379–402.

—— and Elrod, M. A. (1989), 'NATO burden sharing and the forces of change', *International Studies Quarterly*, vol. 33, pp. 435–56.

Palmer, G. (1990a), 'Alliance politics and issue areas: determinants of defense spending', *American Journal of Political Science*, vol. 34, pp. 190–211.

—— (1990b), 'Corralling the free rider: deterrence and the western alliance', *International Studies Quarterly*, vol. 34, pp. 147–64.

—— (1991), 'Deterrence, defense spending, and elasticity: alliance contributions to the public good', *International Interactions*, vol. 7, pp. 157–69.

Rearden, S. L. (1995), 'NATO strategy: past, present, and future', in S. V. Papacosma and M. A. Heiss (eds), *NATO in the Post-Cold War Era: Does It Have a Future?*, New York: St Martin's Press.

Russett, B. M. (1970), *What Price Vigilance?*, New Haven, CT: Yale University Press.

Samuelson, P. A. (1954), 'The pure theory of public expenditure', *Review of Economics and Statistics*, vol. 36, pp. 387–9.

—— (1955), 'A diagrammatic exposition of a theory of public expenditure', *Review of Economics and Statistics*, vol. 37, pp. 350–6.

Sandler, T. (1975), 'The economic theory of alliances: realigned', in C. Liske, W. Loehr and J. McCamant (eds), *Comparative Public Policy: Issues, Theories, and Methods*, New York: John Wiley & Sons.

—— (1977), 'Impurity of defense: an application to the economics of alliances', *KYKLOS*, vol. 30, pp. 443–60.

—— (1987), 'NATO burden sharing: rules or reality?', in C. Schmidt and F. Blackaby (eds), *Peace, Defense and Economic Analysis*, Houndmills: Macmillan Press.

—— (1992), *Collective Action: Theory and Applications*, Ann Arbor, MI: University of Michigan Press.

Sandler, T. (1993), 'The economic theory of alliances: a survey', *Journal of Conflict Resolution*, vol. 37, pp. 446–83.

—— (1999), 'Alliance formation, expansion, and the core', *Journal of Conflict Resolution*, vol. 43, pp. 727–47.

—— and Cauley, J. (1975), 'On the economic theory of alliances', *Journal of Conflict Resolution*, vol. 19, pp. 330–48.

—— and Forbes, J. F. (1980), 'Burden sharing, strategy, and the design of NATO'; *Economic Inquiry*, vol. 18, pp. 425–44.

—— and Hartley, K. (1999), *The Political Economy of NATO: Past, Present, and into the 21st Century*, Cambridge: Cambridge University Press.

Smith, R. (1989), 'Models of military expenditures', *Journal of Applied Econometrics*, vol. 4, pp. 345–59.

Stockholm International Peace Research Institute (1999), *World Armaments and Disarmaments: SIPRI Yearbook*, Oxford: Oxford University Press.

Thomson, J. A. (1997), 'A new partnership, new NATO military structures', in D. C. Gompert and F. S. Larrabee (eds), *America and Europe: A Partnership for a New Era*, Cambridge: Cambridge University Press.

US Central Intelligence Agency (1999), *The World Factbook, 1999*, Washington, DC: US General Printing Office.

US Committee on Armed Services (1988), *Interim Report of the Defense Burden Sharing Panel*, US House of Representatives, 100th Congress, Second Session, Committee Report no. 23, Washington, DC: US Government Printing Office.

US Congressional Budget Office (1997), *Moving US Forces: Options for Strategic Mobility*, Washington, DC: US Government Printing Office.

US Department of Defense (1996), *Report on Allied Contributions to the Common Defense: A Report to the United Congress by the Secretary of Defense*, Washington, DC: US DOD.

—— (1999), *Report on Allied Contributions to the Common Defense: A Report to the United States Congress by the Secretary of Defense*, Washington, DC: US DOD.

US Department of State (1999), *Patterns of Global Terrorism 1998*, Washington, DC: US Department of State.

van Ypersele de Strihou, J. (1967), 'Sharing the defence burden among western allies', *Review of Economics and Statistics*, vol. 49, pp. 527–36.

—— (1968), 'Sharing the defense burden among western allies', *Yale Economic Essays*, vol. 8, pp. 261–320.

8

Public and Private Spending
for Environmental Protection:
A Cross-Country Policy Analysis

DAVID PEARCE AND CHARLES PALMER[1]

I. INTRODUCTION: THE GROWTH OF PUBLIC SPENDING

The increase in public spending in advanced economies has been well documented (Peacock and Wiseman, 1961; Maddison, 1984, 1991, 1995; Tanzi and Schuknecht, 2000). Traditionally, interest in public spending has been driven by the debate about the relative merits of the role of the state in the modern economy. Crudely put, those who favour less intervention call for less public spending, and those who favour more intervention call for more spending. In turn, the degree of intervention is thought to be linked to the driving forces of economic growth and, by implication, the prospects for increasing per capita human well-being. Few now argue,[2] as they might have done in the latter part of the nineteenth century, that the bigger the share of GNP absorbed by government spending, the better the prospects for growth or, if not growth, the better the prospect for social well-being.

Public expenditure growth has, of course, been dominated by the major components of state provision: pensions, social security, education and health. In this paper, we focus on a neglected element of expenditure, environmental protection. Environmental protection appears to be a classic case of a public good: expenditure generates improvements that benefit large numbers of people simultaneously (joint consumption) and there are few prospects for exclusion.[3] The jurisdiction of the publicness also varies: measures to control local air pollution, for example, will have local public good characteristics. Measures to control transboundary air

---

[1] Department of Economics and Centre for Social and Economic Research on the Global Environment (CSERGE), University College London.

[2] For an exception, see Ng (2001), who argues that economists' efforts to estimate the marginal social cost of public spending are flawed. Attention has been focused on the 'true' cost of taxation, deadweight losses adding considerably to the cost of raising revenue, but little attention has been paid to any offsetting gains on the spending side. Once the focus shifts to what makes people *happy*, as opposed to income- or consumption-based surrogates for utility, public spending may secure net gains in happiness.

[3] The exceptions generally relate to land- or water-based assets, for example, nature reserves.

Fiscal Studies (2001) vol. 22, no. 4, pp. 403–456. © Institute for Fiscal Studies, 2001

pollution (usually, acidifying and eutrophying emissions such as sulphur and nitrogen) will have regional jurisdictions. Measures to control global pollutants such as carbon dioxide have global jurisdictions. Traditional public finance theory suggests that public goods will be underprovided in a market-oriented economy. Hence there is a clear role for the state in providing those goods. Tanzi and Schuknecht (2000) note some of the more recent reactions to this popular economic notion of state provision. Few believe any longer that governments are altruistic social welfare maximisers. Forms of government control are often found to be inefficient as public good providers. Public expenditure cannot be reversed as easily as it can be expanded, and the instruments ostensibly under the control of government are not in fact in their full control, nor is there full understanding of the effects of policy choices. The move away from the presumption that state provision is best suggests that there should be more private provision of public goods. In terms of environmental expenditures, we would expect to see some shift away from the public provision of environmental goods to their private provision.

The first issue to be investigated, then, is the public/private mix of environmental protection expenditure. Environmental policy has always been characterised by substantial private expenditures, simply because of the nature of regulations, such as standard-setting, which put the burden on the private sector. But there has been an attempt to shift the burdens of protection further away from the public purse to the private sector, usually by experimenting with new forms of regulation that involve self-regulation by corporations. Additionally, trends towards privatisation of utilities such as water and energy should result in significant reclassification of public expenditures as private expenditures. Unfortunately, as we shall see, this is not a trend that can be discerned from the published data. In general, the quality of the recorded data on environmental expenditures is extremely bad and this permits only limited policy analysis to be carried out.

A second policy issue that has been much debated in the environmental economics literature is the extent to which environmental policy has been a 'drag' on economic growth and competitiveness. The focus here has generally not been on the public spending aspect of environmental control—which could conceivably affect competitiveness through the crowding-out of private investment—so much as on the burdens borne by the private sector through environmental standard-setting. We therefore review the extent to which the evidence supports the regulatory burden hypothesis.

Third, we investigate the hypothesis of an 'environmental Kuznets curve' (EKC) for environmental protection expenditures. The EKC hypothesis suggests that economies at an early stage of economic transition tend to deteriorate their environments. After some point, however, environmental quality increases. Part of this change is due to structural transformations within the economy (e.g. from heavy industry to light industry or from dirty to clean fuels—both of which have an effect in terms of reducing environmental expenditures compared with the counterfactual situation in which these transformations do not occur). But, in most explanations of the EKC, part of the downward turn is also thought to be due to the demand for environmental quality growing as per capita income rises. The literature has extensively investigated the relationship between per capita income and various pollutants, but there has been a general neglect of environmental protection expenditures and their relationship to income. On the other hand, there is a modest political economy literature that asks why environmental concerns are apparently stronger in some countries than in others. Hence we can ask what the links are between environmental expenditures and potential determining factors.

Overall, then, the chapter sets out to investigate three issues:

- the relationship between public and private protective expenditures;
- the evidence for or against 'regulatory drag' due to environmental expenditures;
- the EKC hypothesis and the determinants of environmental demand.

Before turning to these issues, it is important to set out what we know about environmental expenditures.

II. PUBLIC EXPENDITURE GROWTH

Table 1 provides a brief overview of the level of overall public expenditure, expressed as a percentage of GDP, in selected countries. One immediate observation is that the estimates for some years vary according to source. Those where the disparity is more than five percentage points are shown in bold. Second, the picture is one of continuous growth of the public sector, but there is a suggestion that this has levelled off in Italy and the US, and possibly in the UK.

Table 1. *Government expenditure as a percentage of GDP*

	1880	1913	1938	1950	1973	1990–92	1996
France–M	11.2	8.9	**23.2**	27.6	38.8	51.0	–
France–T	12.6	17.0	29.0	–	–	49.8	55.0
Germany–M	10.0	17.7	42.4	30.4	42.0	46.1	–
Germany–T	10.0	14.8	34.1	–	–	45.1	49.1
Italy–T	13.7	17.1	31.1	–	–	53.4	52.7
Sweden–T	5.7	10.4	16.5	–	–	59.1	64.2
Switzerland–T	16.5	14.0	24.1	–	–	33.5	39.4
UK–M	9.9	13.3	28.8	34.2	41.5	**51.2**	–
UK–T	9.4	12.7	30.0	–	–	39.9	43.0
Japan–M	9.0	14.2	30.3	19.8	22.9	33.5	–
Japan–T	8.8	8.3	25.4	–	–	31.3	35.9
US–M	–	8.0	19.8	–	–	**38.5**	–
US–T	7.3	7.5	19.7	–	–	32.8	32.4

Note: Figures shown in bold are those where the disparity between sources is more than 5-percentage points.

Source: M = Maddison (1995); T = Tanzi and Schuknecht (2000).

III. THE GROWTH IN ENVIRONMENTAL EXPENDITURE

Little is known about environmental expenditures before 1970. Expenditures may be made by government (central and local) and by regulated agents, mainly corporations. The private component tends to reflect the expenditures that arise because of regulations, especially regulations that establish environmental standards. Depending on the country, standards may be set on the basis of allowable emissions, ambient concentrations of pollutants in the receiving environment or permitted technology. Technology-based standards are very common and usually centre on the notion of 'best available technology' (BAT) or some variant of this (Pearce, 2000). 'Best' here refers to technology that is regarded as suitable in terms of its environmental performance. Clearly, determining what expenditure borne by the private sector is due to the standard is complex. Strictly, it would be the difference in cost between the BAT and the technology that otherwise would have been adopted. Such cost differences are hard to estimate without knowledge of the counterfactual technology. Added complications are that there will be differential running costs and potential effects on output. In practice, very crude estimates of technology costs are used to estimate actual expenditures.

One main source of broadly comparable expenditures is the OECD, which has collected 'pollution abatement and control expenditures' (PAC) data since the 1980s.[4] PAC expenditures are defined as 'the flow of investment and current expenditure that is directly aimed at pollution abatement and control, and which is incurred by the public sector, the business sector and private households' (OECD, 1993). Coverage is mainly related to water pollution control, air pollution control and waste management. Waste and water dominate the expenditure statistics. Excluded from PAC data are any expenditures on, for example, national parks, nature reserves, exploitation of natural resources and workplace protection. The OECD makes an attempt to determine which expenditures are 'directly aimed' at PAC, rather than counting all expenditures that may have some environmental benefit (e.g. energy efficiency expenditures that yield positive rates of return to the household or corporation). Of necessity, making this kind of distinction gives rise to further uncertainties in the database. The OECD also makes an effort to avoid double counting, for example, some abatement may be subsidised and it is important to determine whether this subsidy appears as a central government expenditure or as a private sector expenditure on the subsidised equipment.

Appendix A sets out the available OECD data. Figures 1a–1c summarise the data in graphical form for absolute levels of expenditure in constant prices. Figures 2a–2c summarise the data expressed in per capita terms—an attempt to normalise the data. It has to be stressed that the data are uncertain and even the OECD's own estimates change over time. We have taken the latest available summary data (OECD, 1999), which are expressed in terms of percentage of GDP. To arrive at

---

[4] PAC monographs were published in 1990, 1993 and 1996 (OECD, 1990, 1993, 1996) but data appear to have been collected before 1990 and after 1996.

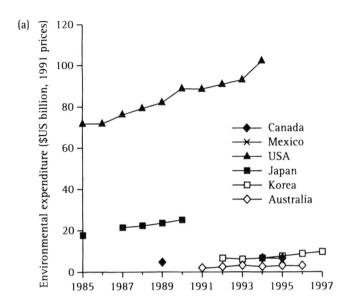

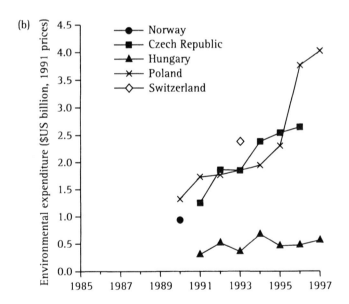

Figure 1. *Environmental expenditure (private + public): (a) non-European OECD countries; (b) non-EU15 European OECD countries; (c) EU15 OECD countries*

Note: See footnote 4.

Source: OECD (1999).

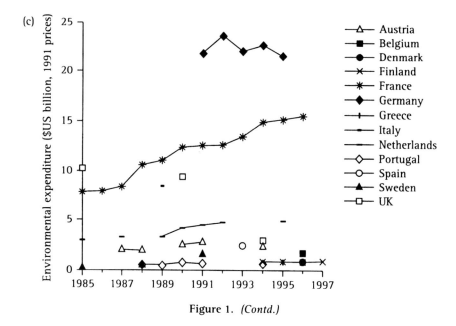

(c)

Figure 1. *(Contd.)*

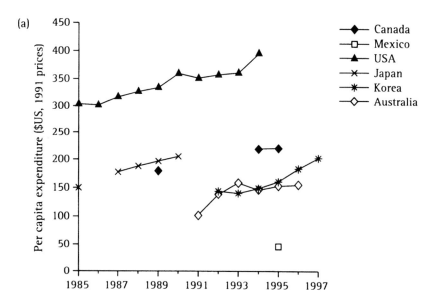

(a)

Figure 2. *Per capita environmental expenditure (private + public): (a) non-European OECD countries; (b) non-EU15 European OECD countries; (c) EU15 OECD countries*

Note: See footnote 4.

Source: OECD (1999).

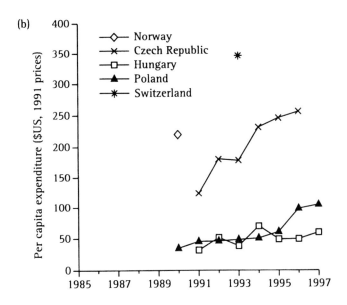

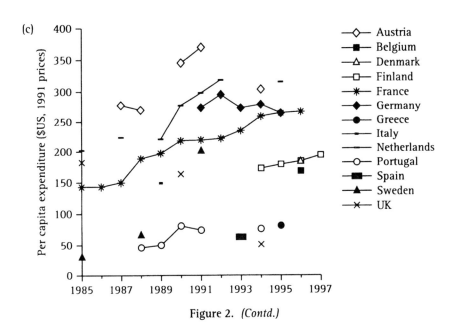

Figure 2. *(Contd.)*

per capita absolute expenditures in real terms, we have multiplied the percentage of GDP data by the OECD's own estimates of GDP and divided by the OECD estimates of country populations. Per capita data and absolute estimates are presented: the former make some allowance for the fact that some expenditures will be population-related, the latter acknowledge the public good element of environmental expenditures. The issue of the reliability of the data is addressed below.

The OECD data are largely confined to water pollution control, air pollution control and waste management.[5] Table 2 gives approximate orders of magnitude for the sectoral breakdown of expenditures for selected OECD countries. Some patterns are discernible. First, the household sector typically bears a small cost burden relative to the corporate and government sectors, ignoring, of course, the role of household taxation in financing government expenditure. The US household sector bears a much higher burden than that in the European countries shown, due to the US procedure of allocating vehicle emission abatement to vehicle purchasers, i.e. including households. Otherwise, household burdens appear fairly consistent across the different countries.

Second, corporate expenditures are higher in the US and the UK, but lower in the Netherlands and France. The OECD offers no clues as to why this is the case.

Third, the US expenditures total around $400 per capita, the Netherlands totals around $300 per capita, and France and the UK total around $200 per capita each. Arguably, this pattern reflects popular perceptions of the relative strengths of environmental concern in the different countries, an issue to which we return.

Fourth, there are some environmental sectoral rankings. Water pollution is ranked first in terms of public expenditure in three of the four countries, and again (just) for three of the four countries in terms of corporate expenditure. Waste tends to be the next most important category, with the exception of the Dutch corporate burden.

European Union data are assembled by EUROSTAT[6] for the period 1988–96. Prior to 1988, some estimates are available in ERECO (1993). Appendix B summarises the relevant information. Unfortunately, the quality of the EUROSTAT data is very poor, and the database has not been used in what follows.[7] We have also investigated UK data, and Appendix C summarises what is known about that information. UK estimates of environmental expenditure exist for only a few years and are biased towards expenditure by the corporate sector. Only one attempt appears to have been made to collect estimates for overall levels of expenditure beyond pollution abatement and embracing all sectors (UK Department of the Environment, 1992). Again, therefore, we make use of these data only to the extent that they help illuminate issues arising as we proceed.[8]

---

[5] The figures for the UK (Figures 1c and 2c) show a marked downturn in environmental expenditure in the 1990s. We consider this to be the result of a misprint in the original OECD documents: 0.3 per cent of GDP should read 1.3 per cent. We have not changed the figure here.

[6] At www.europa.eu.int/comm/eurostat

[7] Not only are the data poor, but the *presentation* of the data is poor: columns in tables are mislabelled, no indication is given as to whether estimates are in current or constant prices, and terminology is not explained. EUROSTAT's website simply adds to the confusion.

[8] Data on environmental expenditure in developing countries are sparse, see Appendix D.

Table 2a. *Breakdown of environmental expenditures:*
selected OECD countries (US dollars, circa 1990)

Country: sector	Expenditure per capita		
	Public	Corporations	Households
US			
Water	97	51	n.a.
Waste	51	88	n.a.
Air	4	69	31
Total	152	208	31+
UK			
Water	11	81	n.a.
Waste	33	38	11
Air	13	30	1
Total	57	149	12+
France			
Water	86	24	11
Waste	63	22	4
Air	n.a.	20	3
Total	149+	66	18
Netherlands			
Water	92	48	n.a.
Waste	77	18	n.a.
Air	3	45	18
Total	172	111	18+

Source: OECD (1996).

Table 2b. *Percentage breakdown of distributional*
burden of environmental expenditures

Country: sector	Expenditure per capita		
	Public	Corporations	Households
US	39	53	8
UK	26	68	6
France	64	28	8
Netherlands	57	37	6

Source: Table 2a.

IV. HOW RELIABLE ARE ENVIRONMENTAL EXPENDITURE DATA?

One reason for the comparative absence of econometric exercises involving environmental expenditures could be that analysts have judged the data to be unreliable. There appear to be no exercises testing for data reliability outside of the USA. The US studies are enabled by the collection of reasonably consistent and regular data using the PACE system (pollution abatement and control expenditures) by the US Census Bureau. The US studies relate only to private, corporate expenditures and produce ambiguous answers. Joshi et al. (2000) suggest that environmental expenditures in the US steel industry are grossly *underestimated* by a factor of around 10. On the other hand, Morgenstern et al. (1997, 2000) suggest that, for a wide range of manufacturing industries, reported costs are *overestimates* of true costs.

The obvious starting point for an analysis is to compare the 'correct' notion of cost with what is reported in the statistics. What get reported tend to be expenditures that industry regards as being due to environmental legislation. But these can obviously differ from true economic costs for various reasons. Economic cost would be measured by the change in the combined sum of producers' and consumers' surplus. Any lost consumer surplus element is obviously omitted by industrial reporting. Changes in producers' surplus may also be problematic. If the expenditure takes the form of capital equipment, there may be some negative effect on other capital investments. Public capital expenditure could crowd out private investment generally, and private environmental expenditure could compete for limited capital funds at the corporate level. Hence some analysts regard the true cost of environmental expenditure as involving forgone long-run profitability and economic growth due to these crowding-out effects. There may also be 'new source bias' whereby mandated standards relate to new plant but perversely exempt old plant, discouraging investment in new, more efficient technology. Conventional operational costs may also rise due to the impact of the abatement measure on operating efficiency (e.g. sulphur emission controls may lower energy conversion efficiency). Clearly, there are a fair number of ways in which environmental expenditures may have *negative* impacts on cost structures. This has been the presumption in the literature that tries to assess 'true' control costs, and has also been instrumental in the literature on the relationship between environmental policy and economic growth and productivity.

There are reasons for supposing that there may be offsetting factors that lower rather than raise costs. First, mandated expenditures may raise awareness within the corporation about ways of saving costs on energy and materials. This is more likely to be the case when regulations permit process changes rather than add-on abatement equipment (Morgenstern et al., 1997, 2000). Potentially more significant, and emphasised in the literature on corporate environmental management, is the complementarity between profit and environmental expenditure in contexts where firms are not operating on the production possibility frontier. The most famous example of this view is attributed to Porter (1990, 1991) and Porter and van der Linde (1995a,b). The 'Porter hypothesis' is not clear-cut, but is generally taken to imply that firms are not operating at full efficiency and that some form of regulation acts as a catalyst that makes firms realise more productive potential through resource efficiency. This is the familiar 'win–win' argument in the corporate environmental literature. The corporate environmental accounting literature has tended to suggest some balance of effects, that is, a proper reporting of the wider costs and the offsetting gains that may accrue (Schaltegger and Burritt, 2000).

Morgenstern et al. (1997, 2000) estimate translog cost functions (Heathfield and Wibe, 1987) for selected US manufacturing industries based on 800 separate plants.

Inputs include capital, labour, energy, materials and environmental abatement effort. Abatement effort is assumed to be fixed in the sense that expenditures are determined exogenously by regulation, and output is also assumed to be fixed, that is, varying output in response to environmental regulation is not an option. The full effects of regulation should then show up in raised costs. Morgenstern et al. stress the need to allow for differences in productivity between plants–differences that, in their view, are unlikely to be caused by environmental regulations (inter-plant variation is affected by factors such as location). Hence they opt for models that involve *not* pooling the data but separately estimating within-plant effects. They find that pooled effects produce *larger* estimates of regulatory impacts on costs, whereas the expectation should be that the longer-run effects would be smaller. The authors focus on the marginal cost of regulation rather than the overall cost impact, that is, on

$$\frac{\partial C}{\partial R} = \frac{C}{R} [\alpha + \beta X],$$

where C is cost, R is regulatory expenditure, X is a vector of log output, regulatory expenditure and input prices, and α and β are the parameters to be estimated.

Based on Morgenstern et al.'s fixed-effects model (i.e. the non-pooled data), the results suggest that the industry average effect of a dollar of regulatory expenditure is to raise costs by just $0.13, that is, there are $0.87 of offsetting gains. For steel, there is a net increase in costs of $1.16, but this is far lower than the effect found in other studies, for example, Joshi et al. (2000). For plastics, there are net reductions in costs–a $4 saving–that is, something like the Porter hypothesis is at work on this industry. For petroleum, environmental expenditures are fairly neutral, that is, each dollar of regulatory expenditure is associated with an offsetting dollar of savings. Finally, for pulp and paper, the additional cost is $0.82. Note, however, that Morgenstern et al.'s random-effects model (pooled data) produces estimates more in line with the 'pessimistic' view of regulatory controls. Table 3 reports the overall results and also shows the results from some of the other literature.

Table 3. *Marginal industrial costs of environmental expenditures (USA):*
effect on cost of $1 of extra expenditure

Study	Paper	Plastics	Oil	Steel	Average
Morgenstern et al. (1997)					
Fixed effects	0.8	−4.2	−0.1	1.2	0.1
Random effects	1.2	0.2	5.1	3.4	3.7
Gray and Shadbegian, 1995					
Fixed effects	0.6	n.a.	1.0	2.8	
Random effects	1.7	n.a.	1.3	3.3	
Joshi et al. (2000)					
Random effects	n.a.	n.a.	n.a.	9.2–10.7	

Notes: Figures are rounded. Morgenstern et al. and Joshi et al. adopt the translog cost function approach. Gray and Shadbegian use a growth accounting approach.

To some extent, the issue reflects the judgemental issue of whether it is better to adopt the fixed-effects, within-plant model or the pooled, random-effects model. There is an additional choice between the growth accounting approach (in which output is allowed to vary) and the cost function approach. The cost function and growth accounting approaches produce different results, the latter being on the more pessimistic side than the former. But the cost function approach applied to one sector, steel, produces very different results on the basis of the random-effects model alone. If Morgenstern et al. (1997, 2000) are right, there is a powerful defence for the view that regulation is 'good' for costs rather than bad, although the precise mechanisms whereby regulation gets translated into cost reductions are not investigated.

In terms of the analyses reported in this paper, we have no basis for judging whether the bias in estimation is systematic over time or over countries. Hence we have no option but to work with the data that are available. The necessary caveats are therefore in order. But there are other problems with the data. First, capital and recurrent expenditures are summed in the OECD database. Capital expenditures appear to be recorded in the year of their occurrence and are not annualised. This raises the potential for some years to show large expenditures which are not repeated in following years, depending on the nature of the relevant legislation. Second, what is recorded is pollution abatement expenditure, whereas environmental expenditure is larger in scope. It would, for example, cover nature protection. Table C.4 in Appendix C suggests that, for the UK, pollution control expenditures constitute around 60 per cent of the total of environmental expenditures. Third, the focus in the OECD data is on government and corporations and it is unclear how far household expenditures are adequately covered. Appendix C looks at this issue in the context of UK data.

V. IS THERE A SHIFT TO PRIVATE CONTROL EXPENDITURE?

The first question we raised was the extent to which environmental public goods originally provided by the public sector were now provided by the private sector, albeit on an 'involuntary' basis through regulation. We hypothesised that this shift would occur because of the concerns in recent decades to reduce the size of public expenditure generally and to shift regulation towards 'voluntary and negotiated agreements' and because of privatisation. However, the OECD data do not readily support the idea that there has been a significant shift away from the public provision of environmental goods to their private provision. Table 4 summarises the public/private mix of environmental protection expenditure between 1985 and 1997 for those OECD countries with data covering two or more years. Japan and Portugal have by far the lowest levels of private environmental expenditure as a proportion of total environmental expenditure. Perhaps surprisingly, the former communist countries of Eastern Europe, such as Poland and the Czech Republic, have the highest relative levels of private environmental expenditure. From the

Table 4. *Private environmental expenditure as a percentage of total environmental expenditure: selected OECD countries*

	1985	1986	1987	1988	1989	1990	1991	1992	1993	1994	1995	1996	1997
Australia							33.3	50.0	44.4	37.5	37.5	37.5	
Austria			44.4	41.2		45.0	42.9			41.2			
Canada					33.3					36.4	45.5		
Czech Republic									73.7	66.7	66.7	66.7	
Finland										45.5	54.5	45.5	45.5
France	33.3		33.3	27.3	27.3	41.7	33.3	33.3	30.8	35.7	28.6	28.6	
Germany							43.8	41.2	43.8	43.8	46.7		
West Germany	53.3	50.0	50.0	50.0	50.0	50.0	43.8	43.8	40.0	46.7	42.9		
Hungary								71.4	40.0	33.3	33.3	50.0	
Japan	10.0		9.1	9.1	9.1	18.2							
Korea									46.7	46.7	46.7	50.0	41.2
Netherlands	28.6		40.0		35.7	47.1	38.9	36.8			27.8		
Poland						71.4	80.0	60.0	60.0	70.0	72.7	64.7	64.7
Portugal				20.0	20.0	12.5	14.3			14.3			
UK	46.2					60.0							
USA	64.3	57.1	57.1	57.1	57.1	60.0	53.3	53.3	60.0	56.3			

Source: OECD, 1999.

mid-1980s to the mid-1990s, France, Germany,[9] the Netherlands and the US all experienced declines in private environmental expenditure as a proportion of total environmental spending. Hence, during this period, public environmental expenditure increased at a faster rate than private expenditure, which suggests that the burden of environmental protection is not shifting away from the public to the private sector as expected. Equally, we are unable to say if this is a genuine trend, because of the poor quality of the data.

VI. ARE ENVIRONMENTAL EXPENDITURES A DRAG ON ECONOMIC GROWTH?

A common argument that may help to mobilise lobbies against environmental expenditures is that they act as a 'drag' on industrial competitiveness and hence economic growth. The argument is potentially most powerful in the context of legislation that imposes costs on the private sector, but there is also a weaker link in terms of public expenditures as a means of 'crowding out' private investment and hence productivity.

While it is not always clear what is meant by competitiveness, it has at least two components: 'macro'-competitiveness (i.e. the competitiveness generally of any nation *vis-à-vis* other countries and trading blocs) and sectoral competitiveness (i.e. competition between sectors within a nation). Macro-competitiveness is frequently invoked in discussions about environmental policy. However, it is not clear how this form of competitiveness can be damaged by environmental regulation so long as the relevant competition is between countries with flexible exchange rates. The effect of any cost changes in one country, even assuming they were significant, would feed through changes in exchange rates, not through loss of market share.

There are several comprehensive surveys of the effects of environmental regulation generally on macro-competitiveness. Various tests of the proposition that environmental expenditures affect competitiveness negatively have been considered:

- the extent to which net exports of environmentally regulated goods change with regulations; or
- the extent to which net exports of environmentally regulated goods perform less well than those of less regulated goods;
- the extent to which firms facing heavy regulation locate outside the regulating country (the 'pollution haven hypothesis');
- the extent to which investment occurs away from strictly regulating countries; and
- the extent to which productivity is affected by regulation.

Net exports have not been found to be significantly affected by regulations (Jaffe et al., 1995; Sorsa, 1994). Corporations' location decisions are generally

---

[9] West Germany until 1991, and then Germany including the former East Germany.

unaffected by environmental costs, primarily because they tend to be a small fraction of total costs (Jaffe et al., 1995; Eskeland and Harrison, 1997). There is no evidence that firms invest more abroad in pollution-intensive industries to compensate for higher environmental costs at home (Eskeland and Harrison, 1997; World Bank, 1999).

1. The 'Porter Hypothesis'

The idea that regulation may *improve* competitiveness is associated with Porter and the 'Porter hypothesis' (Porter, 1990a,b, 1991; Porter and van der Linde, 1995a,b). There is some doubt as to what the Porter hypothesis is meant to be. For example, it seems fairly clear that Porter does not think that *any* form of environmental regulation will induce cost reductions and competitiveness gains. Seemingly, only regulations that focus on prevention rather than amelioration or end-of-pipe technology will have this effect. Also there is the suggestion that the regulations should be market-based rather than in the traditional command-and-control mode. If so, then the hypothesis may not differ much from the traditional advocacy of most environmental economists in favour of market-based instruments such as taxes and tradable quotas.

What are the mechanisms through which the Porter hypothesis is supposed to operate? The general context is clearly intended to be bounded rationality: firms simply do not operate like neo-classical optimisers with perfect information. Accordingly, somehow illuminating an area where the 'mental account' of resource efficiency is located should induce some sort of 'win–win' solution whereby costs are reduced and environmental quality improved. Jaffe, Newell and Stavins (2000) suggest that Porter has five mechanisms in mind: (a) regulation forces attention to be paid to wastefulness; (b) regulation requires information to be generated and information has public good characteristics that mean it is likely to be undersupplied; (c) regulation reduces uncertainty about the returns that can be secured from innovations in environmental technology; (d) there is a first mover advantage in having high standards and responding to them, since other countries are likely to develop such standards later on; and (e) most generally, regulation creates a climate of thinking about innovation. As Jaffe et al. (2000) note, none of these mechanisms is uncontroversial. For example, regulation may create information but it is unclear if governments have better claims to know about the missing information than firms. (Indeed, most modern approaches resting on asymmetric information assume the opposite.) More to the point, adopting cost-reducing technologies does not necessarily mean that the adoption process has passed a cost–benefit test from the firm's point of view. Finally, a point not made in the literature but that seems worth stating is that 'win–win' theorems are undeniably popular and are not confined to this aspect of corporate behaviour. Win–win solutions may be illusory but politically attractive because they hold out the prospect of facing real and potentially painful trade-offs.

One can imagine other mechanisms being at work that could provide indirect support for the Porter view. More regulation benefits firms manufacturing environmental compliance equipment. This is important because markets for pollution control technology and services are projected to rise well into the hundreds of billions of dollars in the next decade. Or it may be that firms finding it easy to comply with regulations squeeze out those that find it less easy to comply, increasing the market share of the lower-cost firms. Those who anticipate market changes, for example, to smaller more-fuel-efficient vehicles, might gain. There may be other benefits—as environmental concerns become 'globalised', so the green image of corporations is becoming internationally important. This raises the possibility that market share can be increased through environmental credentials, a benefit likely to accrue to first movers only, as Porter surmises. Similarly, environmental standards in the so-called 'lax environmental standard' countries are in fact rising rapidly, which is one of the reasons why the pollution haven hypothesis is not fulfilled. Again, those making first moves in strict environmental compliance could secure export market share because they are already locked into clean technology suitable for the expanding markets in comparison with their competitors.

Overall, however, most economists have been very sceptical of the Porter hypothesis. If it were true, it would imply that corporations are very ignorant of the potential for cost reductions and that they require the stimulus of regulation to recognise such opportunities. This seems fairly unlikely (Jaffe et al., 1995; Oates et al., 1994). Sorsa (1994) finds no evidence to suggest that rising standards improve competitiveness. Whereas Porter and van der Linde (1995a) cite case studies to support their propositions, Oates et al. survey the same corporations, and others, and find that they generally regarded the adopted clean technology as imposing a net cost on them, not a net benefit.[10]

2. Productivity Effects

Most studies find that US productivity has been negatively affected by environmental regulation. The rate of growth of total factor productivity (i.e. output per unit of all inputs) has been lower in the USA than in other major countries such as Japan and Europe. Considerable efforts have therefore gone into trying to explain this comparatively poor performance. The comparatively strict environmental legislative regime in the USA has often been cited as a major, and sometimes the major, factor in explaining this difference. The issue can be addressed in three phases:

- *Stage 1:* Assess the evidence that conventionally measured output per unit input is adversely affected by environmental regulation as historically practised.

---

[10] Albrecht (1999) does find some support for the Porter hypothesis in the context of the chlorofluorocarbon industry (CFCs). CFCs have been severely regulated via national implementation of the Montreal Protocol. Du Pont was an early mover in switching out of CFCs into substitutes and gained market share.

- *Stage 2:* Assess what the effect would have been had the environmental regulation taken a different form, especially through more widespread adoption of market-based approaches. The US has made extensive use of strict command-and-control regulations combined with an excessively bureaucratic and litigious liability system (Stewart, 1993). The US experience of negative productivity effects may not therefore be generalisable.

- *Stage 3:* Assess whether the measure of productivity used in the literature is in fact the right measure. In particular, what happens when the negative economic impacts of environmental degradation are taken into account?

As Repetto et al. (1996) note, the effect of environmental regulation on productivity must be negative, almost by definition. Most environmental regulation in advanced economies has been based on technological standards such as 'best available technology'. Hence any regulation forces firms to purchase abatement technology, which is not productive in the sense of contributing to the firm's output. Hence output must be less than it otherwise would have been if the resources used for abatement were allocated to productive uses. Costs rise and there is no off-setting increase in output. This conclusion need not follow if the measures used to reduce pollution themselves contribute to productivity, an issue addressed earlier in the context of the reliability of environmental expenditure data.

Table 5 lists the more recent studies on the links between regulation and productivity (the literature goes back to the 1970s). Notably, most of the studies again relate to the US. Most also use a specific dataset on pollution control expenditures. As noted earlier, one study, by Morgenstern et al. (1997, 2000), produces markedly different results from the other studies. It suggests that each dollar of environmental expenditure raises production costs by only 13 cents. This may be compared with up to $12 in previous studies. Indeed, the Morgenstern et al. (1997) study has a lower limit of $-$1, that is, each dollar of expenditure *saves* $1 of cost. Morgenstern et al. suggest their result arises because the other studies assume that plants are homogeneous, i.e. that the effects on productivity will be the same regardless of plant age, location and management. Once heterogeneity is assumed, the negative productivity effects fall dramatically.

As far as the Stage 1 question goes, then, the literature seems overwhelmingly to support the view that conventional productivity measures are negatively affected by environmental expenditures. But this result could be peculiar to the USA and could arise from a highly restrictive assumption about the nature of the factors affecting productivity at the plant level.

The next stage asks whether a different configuration of environmental policy would have the same negative effects on productivity as might be suggested by the conventional literature. In particular, if policy had been driven by market-based approaches, would the effects have been the same? Surprisingly, little analysis seems to have been carried out on this question. This raises the possibility that, if there are negative productivity effects, they arise because policy has simply been inefficient. The reasons for supposing that market-based instruments (MBIs)

Table 5. *Studies of the effects of environmental regulation on (conventionally measured) productivity*

Study	Country	Effect of environment regulation
Barbera and McConnell (1990)	US	10–30 per cent of reduced productivity growth 1970–80 compared with 1960–70 due to environmental regulation
Jorgensen and Wilcoxen (1990)	US	GNP growth lower than would have been 1973–85, bDFy 0.07 of a percentage point due to mandated environmental investments and by 0.3 of a percentage point due to environmental operating costs
Conrad and Morrison (1989)	Canada, Germany	Negative effects
Nestor and Pasurka (1994)	Japan, Germany	Negative effects
Joshi, Krishnan and Lave (2000)	US steel-making	For 1995, each $1 of environmental expenditures raises (marginal) cost of production by $7–12
Gray and Shadbegian (1993, 1995)	US pulp/paper, oil refineries, steel	Each $1 of environmental expenditures raises (marginal) cost of production by $3–4; less effect found in the later paper
Robinson (1995)	US manufacturing	'Significant negative effect'
Morgenstern, Pizer and Shih (1997, 2000)	US	Each $1 of environmental expenditure raises (marginal) cost of production by $0.13 (note the contrast with previous studies); range is *minus* $1 to plus $1.25
Bruvoll, Glomsrod and Vennemo (1995)	Norway	Negligible impact on economic growth rates (less than 0.1 of a percentage point)

would produce markedly lower impacts on productivity are now well known. First, the flexibility introduced by MBIs means that firms can adopt cost-minimising strategies to comply with regulations. Tietenberg (2000) suggests that traditional policies range from being 2 to 22 times more expensive than MBI-based policies. Even a modest 'multiplier' of 2 would have a dramatic effect on the analysis of productivity effects. Second, MBIs probably have a dynamic effect on abatement technology, markedly reducing its cost due to the incentive to avoid taxes or buy tradable permits. Thus abatement technology itself would be cheaper under an MBI system.

A further feature of prevailing policy is that it might not pass a cost–benefit test, that is, it might be inefficient anyway. Hahn (1996) finds that only 18 per cent of 92 US regulations pass a cost–benefit test. Only 19 per cent of the US Environmental Protection Agency's regulations pass such a test. Unfortunately, there is no comparable information for other countries. But it can be conjectured that the result may not be very different. If so, any negative productivity effects of environmental regulation may reflect the inefficiency of the way policy is implemented, rather than policy per se.

Even if negative productivity effects are an issue, the final concern is whether productivity is being correctly measured. Repetto et al. (1996) measure the damages of the environmental impacts arising from economic activity and then deduct them from the output measure. Viewed from another standpoint, regulation will have environmental benefits which should be added to the conventional productivity measure. Undertaking studies of the US electricity industry, pulp and paper industry and farming, Repetto et al. find that conventional measures of the change in productivity for the period from 1970 to the early 1990s were -0.35 per cent, $+0.16$ per cent and $+2.3$ per cent respectively. But the revised productivity measures allowing for the benefits of environmental improvement are $+0.68$ per cent, $+0.44$ per cent and $+2.41$ per cent. For electricity and paper, then, the proper measurement of productivity makes a stark difference. There is a general lesson here for the current concern to focus on 'resource productivity' (i.e. increases in the ratio of output to resource inputs). An unduly narrow focus on, say, GDP as the output measure tends to miss the central point that the main importance of resource productivity lies in its bilateral environmental effects—reducing the rate of use of resources and the corresponding reduction in emissions from producing the output.[11] It is these effects, valued at the relevant shadow environmental prices, that are likely to justify the focus on resource productivity policies.

VII. IS THERE EVIDENCE OF AN EKC FOR ENVIRONMENTAL EXPENDITURE?

The EKC hypothesis suggests that there is an inverted U-shaped curve for environmental quality when measured against income per capita. In economies at the beginning of an economic development process, one might expect the resources allocated to environmental conservation to be limited. Essentially, environment is sacrificed in the name of economic growth or, put another way, natural capital is depleted and substituted by other factors of production, especially man-made capital. After a point, however, the demand for environmental quality grows and this eventually results in the pollution–income curve peaking and then turning down; further increases in per capita income are associated with reductions in pollution.

---

[11] Indeed, the contribution of resource productivity to overall productivity is likely to be small. Growth accounting approaches based on generalised production functions would make the contribution dependent on (a) the rate of change in resource productivity and (b) the share of natural resources in GDP. For other than resource-rich countries, the latter will tend to be small.

There is an extensive literature testing for the presence of EKCs. Early analyses suggested strong relationships between income and pollution (e.g. Grossman and Krueger, 1995) but more recent work (e.g. Harbaugh et al., 2000) has questioned the early findings. EKCs appear to be less obviously present once attention focuses away from 'conventional' pollutants towards various natural resources and more 'modern' pollutants such as carbon dioxide.

Explanations for the shape of the EKC abound. Generally, the following features of the growth process might be expected:

(a) Rising per capita income will 'drag through' more materials and energy consumption and hence more waste—environmental quality will, without policy action, decline as income grows.

(b) A change in the *structure* of output will, after a point at least, reduce impacts per unit GNP. Additionally, pollution-intensive processes may be exported from rich to poor countries (Suri and Chapman, 1998)—pollution could effectively be 'exported'.

(c) A change in the *demand* for the environment will, if the environment is income-elastic, translate into *policy measures*. Such policy measures require advanced institutions and, in turn, these institutions tend to evolve only in richer countries.

(d) A change in *technology* will occur as growth induces capital replacement that embodies technologies with lower environmental impact.

On this analysis, the question is how far (c) and (d) and the benign aspects of (b) offset the effects of (a) and the damaging effects of (b). The EKC literature does not, in fact, resolve this issue, since most of it contents itself with a straightforward link between income and environmental degradation. Only limited efforts have been made to 'decompose' the relationship in terms of factors (a)–(d) above. What is tested tends to have the general form

$$\frac{E_{it}}{POP_{it}} = a + b\frac{Y_{it}}{POP_{it}} + c\left(\frac{Y_{it}}{POP_{it}}\right)^2 + \varepsilon$$

or

$$E_{it} = a + b\frac{Y_{it}}{POP_{it}} + c\left(\frac{Y_{it}}{POP_{it}}\right)^2 + \varepsilon,$$

where E is the environmental change variable (emissions, change in land cover of forests etc.), Y is GNP, POP is population, t is time, i is location, a, b and c are parameters to be estimated and ε is an error term. The squared term reflects the expected shape of the EKC. Note that the first equation has the dependent variable as per capita environmental change and the second equation has absolute environmental change. Differentiating either equation with respect to Y/POP gives

$$\left(\frac{Y}{POP}\right)^* = -\frac{b}{2c},$$

where $(Y/POP)^*$ is the turning-point of the inverted U, that is, the point at which environmental impact per capita or absolute environmental degradation declines with income per capita.[12]

Some authors provide other explanations of inverted U-shaped curves. Andreoni and Levinson (2001) show that the EKC can result from a simple model in which individual well-being is a positive function of consumption and a negative linear function of pollution, and in which pollution is a linear function of consumption and a negative function of abatement. The essence of the model is that the abatement function has increasing returns to scale. The authors suggest that this is typical of abatement expenditures and that their model embraces other models, including those that posit 'political economy' relationships involving various stakeholders in society, some demanding more abatement, some demanding less.

While the competing explanations for the shape of the EKC are interesting, implicit in the EKC is the notion that one of the factors producing the downturn in the curve, if the curve itself is identifiable, is the rise in the demand for environmental goods as income goes beyond the peak. This holds whether the explanatory model is a simple evolutionary model of how economies behave over time or a political economy model involving interest groups. This suggests that the demand for the environment is income-elastic. Due to data limitations—namely, the general absence of expenditure data for poorer countries—we cannot identify a 'full' EKC. But we can investigate the relationship between environmental expenditure and income for richer countries. More specifically, we can look at the elasticity of expenditure with respect to income. It is important to note that the conventional notion of an income elasticity of demand relates to private goods, while the relevant notion in the current context is that of a quantity-rationed public good. Essentially, public goods are exogenous to household and corporate decisions. Hence the relevant income elasticity is what has been called in the literature the 'price flexibility of income' (Randall and Stoll, 1980) or the 'income elasticity of virtual price' (Hanemann, 1991), the 'income elasticity of willingness to pay' (Flores and Carson, 1997), the 'income elasticity of environmental value' and the 'income elasticity of environmental improvement' (Kristrom and Riera, 1996). Appendix E sets out the basic relationships. The main point of relevance is that the elasticity of willingness to pay with respect to income is equal to the ratio of the conventional income elasticity of demand to the (negative) of the price elasticity of demand. In other words,

$$\varepsilon_W = \frac{\varepsilon_Y}{-\varepsilon_P},$$

where ε is elasticity and the subscripts denote willingness to pay with respect to income (W), quantity with respect to income (Y) and quantity with respect to price (P).

---

[12] There is a debate as to the functional form of the EKC. Some authors argue that cubic equations fit rich-country data better so that the declining section of the inverted U is followed by a further rising section, see, for example, Magnani (2000).

There are several views about the expected size of ε_W. Garrod and Willis (1999) argue that short-run price elasticities for environmental goods are less than one and income elasticities are positive and often greater than one. The latter finding is consistent with the intuition that 'the environment' is a luxury good (i.e. a normal good with conventional income elasticity greater than unity). Hence ε_W will be significantly greater than one in the short run and, arguably, smaller in the long run as price elasticities rise. Flores and Carson (1997) show that the size of ε_W cannot be determined from the size of ε_Y (as is clear from the equation above) and offer no empirical support for small or large values. Kristrom and Riera (1996) analyse contingent valuation studies of environmental change[13] and conclude that ε_W is *less* than one, that is, the 'consumption' of environmental goods accounts for a higher proportion of income of the poor than of the rich. If they are right, then 'environment' is a normal good but not a luxury good, contradicting the usual intuition about the demand for environmental quality.

We seek to offer some further evidence of relevance to this debate by estimating the income elasticity of environmental expenditure using the OECD database. To our knowledge, this is the first time that environmental expenditure data have been used for this purpose. Magnani (2000) purports to carry out such an exercise but has mistakenly used OECD data on environmental *research and development* (R&D) expenditures rather than the aggregate expenditure on environmental protection. Even if the data for R&D expenditures were reliable (what constitutes R&D expenditure is open to considerable interpretation), these expenditures add up to a few tens of millions of dollars in most OECD countries, and a few hundred millions in France, the UK, Japan and the USA. In the UK, for example, OECD-recorded R&D expenditures are around $180 million, compared with total environmental protection expenditures of over $12,000 million. In other words, Magnani's analysis relates to expenditures that constitute between 1 and 2 per cent of total pollution abatement expenditures (and even less if the total relates to environmental protection generally).

Table 6 summarises the available GDP and public environmental expenditure data. The data are derived from two OECD papers (OECD, 1996 and 1999). The earlier one contains data from 1972 to 1984, while the later one contains data from 1985 to 1997. To derive the 1972–84 absolute public expenditure figures, the absolute expenditure data from OECD (1996), given in 1980 prices, were multiplied by a GDP inflator[14] to obtain constant 1991 prices. GDP data in 1991 prices for this period were derived using public expenditure as a percentage of GDP (see Appendix A) and absolute public environmental expenditure in constant 1991 prices. For the period 1985–97, absolute public environmental expenditure was

---

[13] Contingent valuation studies elicit measures of willingness to pay directly via questionnaires, so that the resulting values can be related to socio-economic characteristics of respondents, such as income.

[14] The GDP inflator for each country was derived from a GDP index table given in OECD (1999, p. 321).

Table 6. *Data summary for environmental expenditure in OECD countries*

	Number of observations	Average GDP (US$ billion, constant 1991 prices)	Average public environmental expenditure (US$ billion, constant 1991 prices)	Average public environmental expenditure (% of GDP)
Australia	6	319.8	1.5	0.5
Austria	11	120.3	1.2	1.0
Belgium	3	187.6	0.9	0.5
Canada	22	454.1	3.5	0.8
Czech Republic	4	102.2	0.7	0.7
Denmark	18	90.5	0.6	0.7
Finland	5	81.4	0.4	0.5
France	17	920.7	7.0	0.8
Germany	5	1,395.4	12.6	0.9
West Germany	10	1,031.3	8.5	0.8
Greece	7	93.1	0.5	0.5
Hungary	5	76.5	0.3	0.4
Iceland	12	4.5	0.0	0.3
Ireland	3	26.3	0.3	1.0
Italy	3	337.6	1.9	0.6
Japan	15	822.3	8.1	1.0
Korea	6	461.2	3.9	0.8
Mexico	13	502.4	1.6	0.3
Netherlands	10	230.7	2.3	1.0
Norway	1	69.0	0.6	0.8
Poland	8	197.7	0.8	0.4
Portugal	7	101.2	0.6	0.6
Spain	7	474.8	2.5	0.5
Sweden	3	140.5	1.1	0.7
Switzerland	12	126.0	1.1	0.9
UK	4	766.4	5.1	0.7
USA	23	4,446.8	27.3	0.6

Sources: OECD, 1996 and 1999.

derived in the same way as described in Section III to get Figures 1a–1c, except that the percentage of GDP for *public* environmental expenditure was used only. GDP data for this period were also obtained from OECD (1999) using a GDP index. Thus data from two OECD papers were amalgamated, resulting in a cross-sectional time-series (or panel) dataset of 240 observations covering the period 1972–97, with all data in constant 1991 prices.

The USA spends by far the most in absolute terms, followed by Germany, France and Japan. As a percentage of GDP, the USA is behind a number of countries with regards to public environmental expenditure, with Japan, Austria, the Netherlands

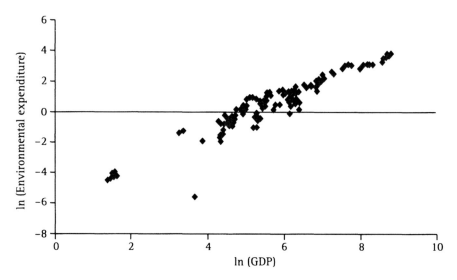

Figure 3. *Log of environmental expenditure (public only) against log of GDP:
all OECD countries, 1972–97*

Sources: OECD, 1996 and 1999.

and Ireland spending around 1 per cent of GDP on environmental goods. However, this dataset is limited by the large number of missing observations over the 1972–97 period, although the inclusion of even more limited private expenditure data would increase the number of missing observations. In addition, there were problems with amalgamating the two sets of OECD data, with some data anomalies occurring in the earlier paper as a result of its general unreliability.

Figure 3 displays the logs of public environmental expenditure against the logs of GDP of the panel dataset. As the graph shows, there appears to be a clear relationship between GDP and public environmental expenditure: as GDP increases, so does public environmental expenditure. However, this relationship does not control for any country-specific effects, that is, different countries having different levels of public environmental expenditure that are independent of time and GDP. Furthermore, the plot does not control for any time trend in that there may be growing environmental expenditure due to increasing pollution, population or environmental awareness over time that may be independent of country-specific effects or GDP.

Using the data from OECD (1996, 1999), a fixed-effects model,[15] which estimates a constant for each country and takes account of missing observations, was fitted to test the effects of a change in GDP on changes in absolute *public* environmental expenditure over the period 1972–97:

$$Y_{it} = \beta_0 + \beta_1 X_{it} + v_i + \varepsilon_{it}, \quad t = 0,1,2, \ldots , T\,(0 = 1972,\ 1 = 1973, \ldots),$$

$$i = 1,2,3, \ldots , N\,(1 = \text{Australia},\ 2 = \text{Austria}, \ldots),$$

---

[15] This is equivalent to an ordinary least squares (OLS) regression model with country-specific dummies.

Table 7. *Results from the regression analysis*

	Coefficient	Standard error	*t* statistic	$p > |t|$
ln GDP	1.194958	0.0655344	18.234	0.000
Time trend	−0.008117	0.0050999	−1.592	0.113
Constant	−6.048623	0.3343025	−18.093	0.000

Notes: Number of observations = 240.
R-squared = 0.6693.
Country-specific constants are available from the authors on request.

where $T = 26$ time periods covering 1972–97, $N = 27$ countries covered by the OECD data, Y_{it} denotes public environmental expenditure for country i in year t in 1991 prices (US\$ billion) and X_{it} denotes absolute GDP for country i in year t in 1991 prices (US\$ billion). In this model, $v_i + \varepsilon_{it}$ is the residual.

Next, a time-trend variable (t) is incorporated into the model to control for any increases in environmental expenditure that occur independently of country-specific effects and GDP, where an observation taken in 1972 is coded as 0, an observation in 1975 is coded as 3 and so on. In addition, the data were transformed. Natural logs were taken of both absolute public environmental expenditure and GDP since a log–log specification is the most readily interpretable, although the most general model would be to Box–Cox-transform[16] both variables.

This produces the final model:

$$\ln Y_{it} = \beta_0 + \beta_1 \ln X_{it} + \beta_2 t + v_i + \varepsilon_{it}, \quad t = 0, 1, 2, \ldots, T\,(0 = 1972, \ldots),$$

$$i = 1, 2, 3, \ldots, N\,(1 = \text{Australia}, \ldots).$$

The results in Table 7 show that the time-trend variable is not a significant determinant of public environmental expenditure, that is, β_2 is not significantly different from 0 ($p = 0.113 > 0.005$). Hence there is no evidence for growth in public environmental expenditure over time independent of growth in GDP. GDP[17] is a very significant determinant of public environmental expenditure, that is, β_1 is significantly different from both 0 and 1 ($p < 0.05$). The coefficient of GDP is greater than 1 and is also statistically significantly greater than 1. The results of this log–log model, where the coefficient can be interpreted as an elasticity, appear to show that the income elasticity of willingness to pay for the environment is just higher than unity, i.e. a 1 per cent increase in GDP leads to an average 1.2 per cent increase in public environmental expenditure. Finally, the *R*-squared from this

[16] Box–Cox transformations were attempted (results available from the authors on request) and showed that the log-log transformation was favoured to the linear model, semi-log model or reciprocal model.
[17] We recognise that GDP *per capita* is a better indicator of wealth than absolute GDP and ran a similar model, regressing GDP per capita on public environmental expenditure per capita. The results are almost the same (i.e. the coefficient of GDP per head is equal to 1.2, and significantly different from 0 and 1), which is due to OECD countries all being relatively similar to one another. The result would almost certainly differ if developing countries were included in the model as well.

model is relatively high, with around two-thirds of the variation in environmental expenditure being explained by the model.

VIII. WHAT DETERMINES ENVIRONMENTAL EXPENDITURE?

The links between environmental expenditure and GDP are clearly very strong. However, a more general theory of what explains environmental expenditures has, to date, been missing. The link to income could be interpreted in two ways. First, as incomes grow, the demand for environmental quality grows, as predicted in most versions of the EKC hypothesis. The evidence in the previous section can be interpreted as suggesting that the income elasticity of *willingness to pay* is just above unity.

Second, higher incomes are associated with a higher *ability to pay* and, once the EKC 'peak' has been achieved, countries begin to devote more of their resources to environmental protection in order to 'undo' past damage as the nation climbs up the upwards portion of the EKC. On this view, high expenditures reflect high (cumulative) damage. To some extent, the contrast between these two positions is artificial in that any decision to spend more resources on environmental protection must still reflect a shift in social preferences. Such preference shifts could come about because of greater awareness of environmental problems after the early stages of growth. In other words, preference shifts precisely because what were largely invisible problems become visible as the assimilative capacity of natural environments begins to be exhausted. Casual empiricism does not support this view, however, since environmental problems in poor countries are more than visible and there is a high potential demand for their solution, for example, safe water supply, sanitation and soil quality. Overall, then, we prefer to see the expenditure–income link as reflecting a more general change in social preferences as income rises. We therefore surmise that $\varepsilon_W < 1$ in poor countries.

If our hypothesis is correct, environmental expenditures reflect underlying social concerns about the environment, concerns that grow with income. As such, we would expect to see expenditures being correlated with some indicator or indicators of environmental concern. In turn, environmental concern may reflect other socio-economic influences such as education. Linking expenditures to some measures of social concern suggests analysing the issue in terms of a 'political economy' model of policy outcomes. Political economy models seek to explain policy outcomes in terms of the political forces that generate a political-economic equilibrium, that is, an equilibrium in which the amount of a public good is determined by governments facing differing demands from various stakeholders. The models are rooted in the early literature on public choice (e.g. Buchanan and Tullock, 1975) and bargaining solutions along the lines of the Coase theorem (Coase, 1960). While Aidt (1998) characterises the governmental implementation of policy as a Pigouvian feature of the models, in fact most environmental policy does not proceed along Pigouvian lines (essentially, environmental taxes) but through standard-setting.

In the current case, environmental expenditures would be the outcome of policy decisions made by government. Those decisions are, in turn, the outcome of some political compromise between the amount of environmental quality that households and corporations are willing to supply (through their taxes and for-gone income) and what lobby groups, including the government itself, demand. Several attempts have been made to explain environmental preferences and to develop political economy models of environmental policy (Black et al., 1997; Aidt, 1998; Marsiliani and Renström, 2000). One significant feature of some of these models is the inclusion of income distribution as an explanatory variable (Magnani, 2000; Marsiliani and Renström, 2000). The essential argument here is that poorer individuals will have a lower preference for environmental goods relative to private goods and that the poor's demand for redistribution of income will lower production due to production inefficiencies.[18] Evidence that the poor *care* less about the environment than the rich is, however, not strong—see, among others, Jones and Dunlap (1992). For the US, Elliott et al. (1997) find that public support for environmental spending varies positively with education, gender, the degree to which the individual is 'urbanised', 'liberalism' of the individual's view-point, and race (non-whites expressing more support). They also find that income is significant but less so than the previous factors. Age influences spending sup-port negatively, i.e. older people show less support for environmental spending.

Cross-country analysis obviously has to focus on fewer explanatory variables, since such things as age and gender will not vary substantially across countries. In what follows, we take the OECD data previously described and use environmental expenditure as a percentage of GDP as the dependent variable. The assumption here is that actual expenditures reflect the political-economic outcome of the various forces in the economy demanding different levels of environmental protection.[19] The independent variables are GDP per capita, an index of income inequality (the Gini index) and the strength of public opinion on environmental problems. These data are given in Table 8.

The data for this cross-country analysis are fully available for only 13 countries. Furthermore, while the index for income inequality for a particular country changes very little from one year to the next, changes in public concern for the environment are not so well known. Hence this analysis uses public opinion data collected between 1988 and 1990,[20] while some environmental expenditure data

---

[18] This second element of the argument is contentious, however, since lower production means lower throughput of materials and energy via the materials balance principle. This production effect appears to be ignored in the Marsiliani–Renström paper, for instance.

[19] Marsiliani and Renström (2000) adopt CO_2 per unit GDP as a proxy for the degree of environ-mental protection. However, environmental policy has only recently begun to address the issue of greenhouse gas emissions and, in most cases, only modestly. Carbon intensity is far more likely to reflect fossil-fuel endowments, energy prices and the state of technology and hence would appear to be a rather poor proxy for environmental protection.

[20] A more up-to-date survey of European public attitudes to the environment can be found in a report by the European Commission (1999), although it contains very little detailed data at a country level and instead focuses on European aggregates.

Table 8. *Determinants of environmental expenditure*

	Public environmental expenditure (% of GDP)	Year	Gini index[a]	Year	Public opinion (%)[b]	Year	GDP per capita (US$)[c]
Belgium	0.4	1995	25.0	1997	34	1988	18,359
Denmark	0.5	1988	24.7	1992	45	1988	20,421
Finland	0.6	1994	25.6	1991	39	1989	15,501
France	0.8	1988	32.7	1995	36	1988	17,207
Germany	0.8	1988	30.0	1994	45	1988	18,993
Greece	0.5	1990	32.7	1993	53	1988	9,941
Italy	0.6	1988	27.3	1995	62	1988	16,519
Japan	0.9	1990	24.9	1993	41	1990	18,497
Netherlands	0.9	1988	32.6	1994	54	1988	15,707
Portugal	0.4	1988	35.6	1994	41	1988	9,229
Spain	0.6	1988	32.5	1990	52	1988	12,669
UK	0.4	1990	36.1	1991	32	1988	16,184
US	0.6	1990	40.8	1997	58	1990	23,892

[a]The higher this is, the greater the income inequality between the poorest and richest within a single country.
[b]This is given as the average percentage of persons 'very concerned' with regards to national environmental problems: accidental damage to the marine environment, industrial waste disposal, water pollution and air pollution.
[c]GDP per capita and environmental expenditure are given for the same year.
Sources: OECD (1991, 1999) and World Bank (2001).

only become available in the mid-1990s, for example, for Belgium and Finland. Therefore, given the obvious data limitations where not all the data are collected for the same year, any conclusions drawn from this analysis should be treated with caution.

Consider the following model:

$$Y_i = \beta_0 + \beta_1 X_{1i} + \beta_2 X_{2i} + \beta_3 \ln X_{3i} + \varepsilon_i, \quad i = 1, 2, \ldots, N,$$

where $N = 13$ countries, Y_i denotes public environmental expenditure as a proportion of GDP, X_{1i} denotes income inequality for country i, X_{2i} denotes public opinion for country i and X_{3i} denotes GDP per capita (US$, 1991 prices) for country i. The results from this regression model are shown in Table 9.

For each independent variable, we test the null hypothesis that each variable has no effect on environmental expenditure and find that each coefficient is not significantly different from zero. Therefore the results from this limited regression analysis provide little evidence that income inequality, public concern for the environment or GDP per head has an effect on public environmental expenditure (as a proportion of GDP). Nonetheless, we acknowledge that the model has a very small sample and the results cannot be afforded firm credibility.

Table 9. *Results from the regression analysis*

	Coefficient	Standard error	*t* statistic	$p > |t|$
Income inequality	−0.005079	0.01169	−0.4345	0.6741
Public opinion	0.004844	0.007057	0.6865	0.5097
ln (GDP per capita)	0.1875	0.21148	0.8865	0.3984
Constant	−1.271	2.1151	−0.6008	0.5628

Notes: Number of observations = 13.
R-squared = 0.1548.

IX. CONCLUSIONS

Perhaps the overriding conclusion we would draw is that the data on environmental expenditure outside the USA, and probably Norway, are so poor that it is very much open to question whether econometric exercises are currently worthwhile. From a policy standpoint, this conclusion is somewhat startling. While there are several exercises in the USA whereby *some* idea can be obtained about the relative costs and benefits of environmental regulation generally (Freeman, 1982, 1990, 2000; Hahn, 1996; Portney, 1990, 2000), there are no such exercises outside the USA, nor do we see how they could take place. Ironically, while most of the controversy in cost–benefit procedures applied to the environment takes place in the context of the valuation of *benefits*, it turns out that we have little real idea of the *budgetary costs* of environmental protection, let alone the wide general equilibrium costs. In an era of renewed attention to efficiency in government, this finding is disturbing.

Despite the limitations of the data, we set out to see what the limited data could tell us about three questions:

- whether there has been a shift in the relative burdens of environmental expenditure borne by the state (national and local government) and the private sector (corporations and households);
- whether environmental expenditure acts as a 'drag' on economic growth; and
- how environmental expenditure might vary as economic development occurs and, a related issue, what determines environmental expenditure.

1. Inspecting the Data

Before addressing the three questions directly, we asked how reliable the data were. No tests of reliability have been carried out outside the USA, where the 'raw' data are far more detailed. Somewhat oddly, the assessments of reliability of US data provide contradictory results, several studies suggesting substantial understatements of true cost and one recent study suggesting significant overstatement of costs.

Inspection of the raw OECD data (Figures 2a–2c) suggests that, in per capita terms and for private and public expenditures combined, countries might be 'banded' as follows:

Per capita expenditure

Above $300	Austria, Netherlands, Switzerland, US
$200–299	Canada, Czech Republic, France, Germany, Japan, Norway, Sweden
$100–199	Australia, Belgium, Denmark, Finland, Italy, Korea, UK
<$100	Greece, Hungary, Mexico, Poland, Portugal, Spain

By and large, the banding is as one would expect but for the Czech Republic. Also, Korea appears to be highly placed. Inspection of the data shows that Korea significantly increased its expenditures in only six years, whilst the Czech Republic has more than doubled its per capita expenditure in the same period. The Netherlands, France and Sweden show substantial increases since the mid-1980s, and Poland has shown a big increase during the 1990s.

We turn now to the three questions.

2. The Public/Private Split in Environmental Expenditure

We hypothesised that we would expect to see a rise in the relative burden of expenditure being borne by the private sector because of (a) increased private spending due to regulation based on standard-setting, (b) growth of fiscal ideologies favouring the reduction in public spending generally and (c), related to (b), increased privatisation. Taking the OECD data at face value, Table 4 suggested that there has been no such rise in the share of expenditure borne by the private sector. The general trends are either fairly constant or slightly declining. There are no obvious reasons for these trends. Coverage of the data varies by country, but this should not affect time trends for single countries. It is possible that coverage of individual country data varies with time as data collection changes (we hesitate to say it improves), but the detail in the original sources is not sufficient to judge. At best, then, we can say that the available data do not show the expected shift towards an increasing private sector burden.

3. Environmental Drag

An important question concerns the role that increasing environmental expenditures have in economic growth. This has been addressed in a fairly large literature, although much of it is centred on the USA, historically arising because of the concern there to explain periods of low overall factor productivity growth. Cross-country generalisations may therefore be difficult. Various forms of the 'drag' hypothesis can be identified: the first concerns the export performance of environmentally heavily regulated industries relative to less regulated ones; the second concerns the notion that firms move out of national jurisdictions because of environmental regulation; the third suggests that inward investment will be less in heavily regulating countries; and the fourth concerns the impact of regulation on productivity. For all of the effects other than the impact on productivity, the literature finds little or no support for the drag hypothesis. This finding is consistent regardless of the methodologies used to identify impacts, ranging from case studies through to general equilibrium models. For those who espouse environmental concerns, this finding is important since the 'threat' that competitiveness and employment will suffer because of additional regulation is widely used by industry to lobby against regulations. Moreover, the regulations in question are dominated by traditional command-and-control measures. If environmental economists are right in arguing that market-based approaches are less costly, we would expect the drag hypothesis to be weakened even further.

The productivity literature is generally confined to the US and nearly all of the studies find a negative effect of regulation on productivity. At one extreme, however, one study raises the possibility of positive impacts and, at the other, the negative impacts are said to be significantly negative (Table 5). However, the extent to which this literature should be used to cast doubt on the wisdom of regulatory policies is open to question. First, for the periods in which the studies were carried out, the US was heavily reliant upon command-and-control measures. A market-based approach might not show the same productivity effects due to (a) initially lower compliance costs and (b) dynamic effects of inducing technological change. Second, the productivity literature adopts a highly partial view of the effects of environmental policies. By focusing on measured outputs, non-market effects are ignored entirely. This neglect has two effects. First, the beneficial effects of environmental policy on human well-being are not allowed to offset any of the negative output effects that are identified. The correct numeraire is not output but a welfare-adjusted measure of output such as output minus externalities. As the study by Repetto et al. (1996) shows, this can have a dramatic effect on the results. Second, it is unclear if the approaches account for any of the indirect but positive effects of environmental policy on output. One obvious link is from reduced pollution to improved human health and from health improvements to productivity impacts. Available but very limited evidence suggests that this indirect linkage could be important.

Overall, then, we doubt if the 'productivity' literature has significant implications for environmental policy, at least outside the US and, we suspect, within the US also. Nonetheless, it is important to keep such studies under review and to ensure that non-US experience is expanded by research in this area. A related issue concerns the potential contrast between the 'no effects' finding of the competitiveness literature and the 'negative effects' finding of most of the productivity literature since, a priori, one would expect these findings to be consistent.

We also investigated the view that, far from having negative impacts on economic growth, environmental policy might actually increase growth or, at least, increase competitiveness. This 'win–win' view is primarily associated with

Michael Porter. It has strong similarities with the corporate environmental litera-ture that argues that environmentally and socially responsible corporations are likely to fare better financially than those that neglect these social dimensions. But the Porter hypothesis has proved to be difficult to verify. Reassessments of the industries Porter claims do support the hypothesis have not been able to reproduce his results. We surmise that win–win arguments are likely to attract a degree of public and political attention out of proportion to the likelihood that they are correct. Win–win solutions avoid the necessity of facing up to real-world trade-offs. We do not reject the idea of win–win possibilities out of hand: few decision-makers are completely informed and few are completely economically rational. But for the Porter hypothesis to be right, bounded rationality and incomplete information must be pervasive, and we doubt if that is the case.

4. Environmental Expenditure and Economic Development

A large literature has developed that argues that the process of economic develop-ment will at first worsen environmental quality and then improve it. There is, it is argued, an inverted U-shaped curve linking environmental degradation to income per capita. How far these 'EKCs' actually prevail is open to question. Rather like the win–win hypothesis, the early literature was seized upon as supporting the notion that 'natural progress' will guarantee environmental sustainability. In practice, more and more empirical research is casting doubt on the robustness of the early findings. Nonetheless, if we take a crude indicator such as the ratio of primary energy use to GDP, it is well known that this exhibits a time trend of an inverted U-shaped curve. Energy per unit GDP rises at first and then declines. Structural economic change, changing energy mixes and technological change that improves energy efficiency all account for the change in the relationship. But it is also sug-gested that higher incomes induce a demand for environmental quality, a demand that should translate into increased environmental expenditure. To play a signifi-cant role, we would expect this linkage to show up in a high income elasticity of demand for the environment. As noted in the main text, what can actually be measured is the income elasticity of willingness to pay or expenditure, not income elasticities of demand in the conventional sense. Appendix E shows the relationship between the two elasticities. We therefore investigate the elasticity of expenditure with respect to income using the available OECD data. These suggest an elasticity of 1.2, which is perhaps less than we would have expected if the 'environmental demand effect' is to play a significant role in explaining the downward slope of the EKC.

Finally, we made an attempt to 'explain' environmental expenditure in terms of a political economy model. We regressed environmental expenditure as a percent-age share of GDP on a measure of inequality, GDP itself and public opinion. We found no statistically significant relationship but accept that the sample is probably too small to detect true relationships.

APPENDIX A. OECD ENVIRONMENTAL EXPENDITURES

Tables A.1 and A.2 set out the available OECD data for environmental expenditure in OECD countries, both private and public, as a percentage of each country's GDP. At best, the data are spotty, particularly those derived from OECD (1989). For each table, the data for 1972 up until 1984 originate from OECD (1989), while the data from 1985 to 1997 originate from OECD (1999). Data for public expenditures are better than those for total expenditures since private expenditures, that is, what corporations and households spend, are often not known.

Table A.1. OECD environmental expenditures for non-EU15 countries (per cent of GDP)

		Aus	Can	CzR	Hun	Ice	Jap	Kor	Mex	Nor	Pol	RuF	SR	Swi	US
1972	Public														0.55
	Private														0.67
	Pu + Pri														1.22
1973	Public														0.56
	Private														0.74
	Pu + Pri														1.31
1974	Public		1.07												0.62
	Private														0.82
	Pu + Pri														1.44
1975	Public		1.12				0.96							1.07	0.66
	Private														0.90
	Pu + Pri														1.55
1976	Public		1.16				1.17							1.08	0.66
	Private														0.90
	Pu + Pri														1.56
1977	Public		1.15				1.32							1.04	0.63
	Private														0.91
	Pu + Pri														1.53
1978	Public		1.12				1.50			0.80				0.97	0.66
	Private														0.89
	Pu + Pri														1.55
1979	Public		1.00				1.60							0.93	0.65
	Private														0.94
	Pu + Pri														1.59
1980	Public		1.05				1.59							0.89	0.63
	Private														0.96
	Pu + Pri														1.60

Year	Type								
1981	Public	0.96		1.55				0.85	0.56
	Private								0.95
	Pu + Pri								1.50
1982	Public	0.97		1.45				0.90	0.55
	Private								0.89
	Pu + Pri								1.44
1983	Public	0.93		1.33					0.55
	Private								0.88
	Pu + Pri								1.43
1984	Public	0.89		1.21					0.55
	Private								0.89
	Pu + Pri								1.44
1985	Public	0.5	0.3	0.9	0.4			0.7	0.5
	Private			0.1					0.9
	Pu + Pri			1.0					1.4
1986	Public	0.5	0.3	1.0	0.4				0.6
	Private			0.1					0.8
	Pu + Pri			1.1					1.4
1987	Public	0.5	0.3	1.0	0.2				0.6
	Private			0.1					0.8
	Pu + Pri			1.1					1.4
1988	Public	0.5	0.3	1.0	0.2			0.7	0.6
	Private			0.1					0.8
	Pu + Pri			1.1					1.4
1989	Public	0.6	0.3	1.0	0.3			0.8	0.6
	Private	0.3		0.1					0.8
	Pu + Pri	0.9		1.1					1.4
1990	Public	0.7	0.3	0.9	0.3	0.2	2.5		0.6
	Private			0.2		0.5			0.9
	Pu + Pri			1.1		0.7			1.5
		1.0			1.2				

Table A.1. (Contd.)

		Aus	Can	CzR	Hun	Ice	Jap	Kor	Mex	Nor	Pol	RuF	SR	Swi	US
1991	Public	0.4	0.7			0.3			0.3		0.2		2.4		0.7
	Private	0.2									0.8				0.8
	Pu + Pri	0.6		1.2	0.4						1.0				1.5
1992	Public	0.4	0.7		0.2	0.4		0.8	0.4		0.4		2.0	1.0	0.7
	Private	0.4			0.5			0.8			0.6				0.8
	Pu + Pri	0.8		1.9	0.7			1.6			1.0				1.5
1993	Public	0.5	0.6	0.5	0.3	0.3		0.8	0.4		0.4		1.8		0.6
	Private	0.4		1.4	0.2			0.7			0.6				0.9
	Pu + Pri	0.9		1.9	0.5			1.5			1.0	1.3			1.5
1994	Public	0.5	0.7	0.8	0.6	0.4		0.8	0.4		0.3		1.3	1.6	0.7
	Private	0.3	0.4	1.6	0.3			0.7			0.7				0.9
	Pu + Pri	0.8	1.1	2.4	0.9			1.5			1.0	1.7			1.6
1995	Public	0.5	0.6	0.8	0.4	0.3		0.8	0.3		0.3				
	Private	0.3	0.5	1.6	0.2			0.7	0.5		0.8				
	Pu + Pri	0.8	1.1	2.4	0.6			1.5	0.8		1.1	2.2			
1996	Public	0.5		0.8	0.3	0.3		0.8	0.3		0.6				
	Private	0.3		1.6	0.3			0.8			1.1				
	Pu + Pri	0.8		2.4	0.6			1.6			1.7	2.0			
1997	Public							1.0	0.2		0.6				
	Private							0.7			1.1				
	Pu + Pri				0.7			1.7			1.7	1.8			

Key: Aus–Australia, Can–Canada, CzR–Czech Republic, Hun–Hungary, Ice–Iceland, Jap–Japan, Kor–Korea, Mex–Mexico, Nor–Norway, Pol–Poland, RuF–Russian Federation, SR–Slovak Republic, Swi–Switzerland.
Sources: OECD (1989, 1999).

Table A.2. *OECD environmental expenditures for EU15 countries (per cent of GDP)*

		Au	Bel	Den	Fin	Fra	Ger[a]	Gre	Ire	Ita	Neth	Por	Spa	Swe	UK
1972	Public														
	Private	0.26													
	Pu + Pri														
1973	Public					1.43									
	Private	0.37													
	Pu + Pri														
1974	Public														
	Private	0.39												0.22	
	Pu + Pri														
1975	Public						0.81								
	Private	0.37					0.56								
	Pu + Pri						1.37								
1976	Public	0.76					0.82								
	Private	0.33					0.53								
	Pu + Pri	1.09					1.36								
1977	Public	0.72					0.78		0.98						0.82
	Private	0.44					0.52								0.84
	Pu + Pri	1.16					1.29								1.66
1978	Public	0.77		0.93			0.83	0.32	0.99		0.88			0.84	
	Private	0.33			0.57	0.48	0.50								
	Pu + Pri	1.10					1.33								
1979	Public	0.82		0.99			0.88								
	Private	0.30					0.49				0.34				
	Pu + Pri	1.13					1.37								
1980	Public			0.93			0.92		1.06		0.76				
	Private	0.39			0.46		0.53				0.34				
	Pu + Pri						1.45				1.10				

Table A.2. (Contd.)

		Au	Bel	Den	Fin	Fra	Ger[a]	Gre	Ire	Ita	Neth	Por	Spa	Swe	UK
1981	Public			0.92		0.67	0.88			0.00					0.81
	Private	0.36				0.39	0.58								0.76
	Pu + Pri					1.06	1.45								1.57
1982	Public			0.85		0.60	0.81			0.01	0.80				
	Private	0.47				0.33	0.63				0.34				
	Pu + Pri					0.93	1.45				1.13				
1983	Public			0.78	0.27	0.54	0.77			0.01					
	Private	0.50				0.30	0.64								
	Pu + Pri					0.85	1.41								
1984	Public			0.76		0.55	0.75			0.00					
	Private	0.47				0.29	0.62								
	Pu + Pri					0.84	1.37								
1985	Public	1.0		0.7		0.6	0.7				1.0				0.7
	Private					0.3	0.8				0.4				0.6
	Pu + Pri					0.9	1.5				1.4				1.3
1986	Public					0.6	0.8							0.2	
	Private					0.3	0.8							0.6	
	Pu + Pri					0.9	1.6								
1987	Public	1.0		0.8		0.6	0.8				0.9		0.5		
	Private	0.8				0.3	0.8				0.6				
	Pu + Pri	1.8				0.9	1.6				1.5				
1988	Public	1.0		0.5		0.8	0.8					0.4	0.5		
	Private	0.7				0.3	0.8					0.1			
	Pu + Pri	1.7				1.1	1.6					0.5			
1989	Public			0.6		0.8	0.8			0.6	0.9	0.4	0.6	0.4	
	Private					0.3	0.8			0.3	0.5	0.1			
	Pu + Pri					1.1	1.6			0.9	1.4	0.5			

Year	Type										
1990	Public	1.1	0.6	0.7	0.8	0.5	0.9	0.7	0.6		0.4
	Private	0.9		0.5	0.8		0.8	0.1	0.6		0.6
	Pu + Pri	2.0		1.2	1.6		1.7	0.8		0.8	1.0
1991	Public	1.2	0.6	0.8	0.9 (0.9)	0.5	1.1	0.6	0.6	0.6	
	Private	0.9		0.4	0.7 (0.7)		0.7	0.1		0.4	
	Pu + Pri	2.1		1.2	1.6 (1.6)		1.8	0.7	0.4	1.2	
1992	Public	1.1	0.6	0.8	1.0 (0.9)	0.6	1.2	0.7			
	Private			0.4	0.7 (0.7)		0.7				
	Pu + Pri			1.2	1.7 (1.6)		1.9				
1993	Public	1.2	0.7	0.9	0.9 (0.9)	0.6		0.7	0.5		
	Private			0.4	0.7 (0.6)				0.0		
	Pu + Pri			1.3	1.6 (1.5)				0.5		
1994	Public	1.0	0.6	0.9	0.9 (0.8)	0.5		0.6			
	Private	0.7	0.5	0.5	0.7 (0.7)			0.1			
	Pu + Pri	1.7	1.1	1.4	1.6 (1.5)			0.7			
1995	Public	0.4	0.6	1.0	0.8 (0.8)	0.5	1.3	0.7			0.3
	Private		0.6	0.4	0.7 (0.6)	0.3	0.5				

Table A.2. (Contd.)

		Au	Bel	Den	Fin	Fra	Ger[a]	Gre	Ire	Ita	Neth	Por	Spa	Swe	UK
	Pu + Pri				1.1	1.4	1.5 (1.4)	0.8			1.8				
1996	Public		0.5	0.6	0.6	1.0									
	Private		0.4	0.3	0.5	0.4									
	Pu + Pri		0.9	0.9	1.1	1.4									
1997	Public		0.5		0.6										
	Private				0.5										
	Pu + Pri				1.1										

Key: Au—Austria, Bel—Belgium, Den—Denmark, Fin—Finland, Fra—France, Ger—Germany, Gre—Greece, Ire—Republic of Ireland, Ita—Italy, Neth—Netherlands, Por—Portugal, Spa—Spain, Swe—Sweden.
[a]Data given in parentheses are the estimates for the former West Germany after reunification with East Germany in 1990.
Sources: OECD (1989, 1999).

APPENDIX B. EUROPEAN UNION ENVIRONMENTAL EXPENDITURES

European Union data on environmental expenditures are poor. This appendix assembles the available data.

Table B.1 shows early estimates of French expenditures. These are assumed to be a combination of government and industrial expenditures, and they also cover capital and operating costs.

Tables B.2 and B.3 report on early estimates of EU-wide expenditure.

Table B.1. *French environmental expenditures (Billion[a] ecus, 1983 prices)*

1967	1968	1969	1970	1971	1972	1973	1974	1975
5.9	6.4	6.9	6.8	7.0	7.8	7.9	8.1	8.7
1976	1977	1978	1979	1980	1981	1982	1983	
9.4	9.4	9.5	9.8	10.0	9.7	9.7	9.6	

[a]Billion = 10^9.

Source: French Ministry of the Environment, 1984.

Table B.2. *EU-wide expenditures: government and industry[a]*
(Million ecus, current prices)

	1978	1980	1988	1992
Austria	Not member	Not member	Not member	Not member
Belgium	290			1,200[b]
Denmark	435		1,000	1,200
Finland	Not member	Not member	Not member	Not member
France	2,970		8,300	12,900
Germany	7,854		16,500	20,500
Greece	107			300
Ireland	90		300	300
Italy			5,700	6,800
Luxemburg				See Belgium
Netherlands		1,412	2,700	3,500
Portugal	20		300	300
Spain	>175		1,800	3,900
Sweden	Not member	Not member	Not member	Not member
UK	3,608		2,000	12,400
EU total		45,300[c]	56,800[c]	63,300

[a]Assume it is both. 1992 = ERECO (1993) figures are definitely both; note that these estimates do not agree with the EUROSTAT (1999) figures, see below.
[b]Includes Luxemburg.
[c]1992 prices.

Sources: 1978 and 1980–SEMA-METRA (1986); 1988–European Commission (1992) based on ERECO (1993); 1992–ERECO (1993).

Table B.3. *EU total environmental expenditures: government and industry (Million ecus, 1992 prices)*

1980	1981	1982	1983	1984	1985	1986
45,314	45,240	45,340	45,641	45,948	49,105	52,285

1987	1988	1989	1990	1991	1992
54,458	56,831	59,150	61,618	62,544	63,340

Notes: Relates to EU before the accession of Austria, Finland and Sweden in January 1995. Unfortunately, the sources offer no country breakdown of the ERECO totals.

Source: ERECO (1993).

Table B.4. *EU total environmental expenditures: government and industry (Billion[a] Euros, current prices)*

	1992	1993	1994	1995
Austria			3.0	
Finland			0.8	
France		6.7	7.7	
Germany	13.5	15.6	19.4	18.7
Netherlands				5.0
Portugal			0.6	0.6
Spain		2.9		
EU total	53.2	56.2	64.6	65.5

[a]Billion = 10^9.

Source: EUROSTAT (1999).

Table B.4 gives data in current prices, based on EUROSTAT (1999). Note that the cell figures are the only independent figures, that is, based on country returns. The EU totals are artefacts based on EUROSTAT's assumption that expenditures vary directly with GNP.

Table B.5 repeats Table B.4 but in per capita terms. Again, note that the cell figures are the only independent figures and that the EU totals are artefacts, as in Table B.4.

Table B.6 provides estimates of government expenditure only. These are not summarised in EUROSTAT (1999) and have therefore been taken from the country tables.

Table B.7 shows EUROSTAT's estimates of industry expenditure, again taken from country tables.

Table B.5. *EU total environmental expenditures per capita: government and industry (euros, current prices)*

	1992	1993	1994	1995
Austria			373	
Finland			149	
France		116	133	
Germany	168	192	239	229
Netherlands				322
Portugal			58	63
Spain		73		
EU total	137	150	170	186

Source: EUROSTAT (1999).

Table B.6. *EU environmental expenditures: government only (million euros, current prices)*

	1988	1989	1990	1991	1992	1993	1994	1995	1996
Austria							1,745		
Denmark	282	248	279	339	372	393	432	507	509
Finland							420		
France			3,702	4,070	4,579	5,184	6,082	6,574	
Germany		4,518	4,413	4,788	5,441	6,694	8,457	8,938	9,672
Netherlands						2,642		3,215	
Portugal		94	171	159	189	213	255	264	
Spain	1,399	1,662	1,994	1,376	1,719	1,795			
Sweden				1,300					

Source: EUROSTAT (1999).

Table B.7. *EU environmental expenditures: industry only (million euros, current prices)*

	1992	1993	1994	1995
Austria		1,240		
Finland	506	457	396	
Netherlands			1,825	1,573
Portugal			109	109
Spain		1,210		
EU total		3,009		

Source: EUROSTAT (1999).

APPENDIX C. UK ENVIRONMENTAL EXPENDITURES

The earliest estimates of environmental expenditures for the UK relate to 1977. Table C.1 shows these estimates as recorded in ECOTEC (1989), together with conversion to 1991 prices. Once converted to a single base year, considerable fluctuations in total expenditure are observed and it seems likely that the very early estimates for 1977 are substantial exaggerations. The figures for 1977–85 are, in any event, only the broadest of guesses and were not supported by survey methods. The 1988 figures are the first to be supported by a more detailed survey of industrial costs.

More recent estimates are given in Table C.2.

Table C.3 shows the breakdown of industrial abatement costs for 1997, the year for which the most detailed study exists. The table shows that chemicals, metals, food and the energy and water utilities account for around 60 per cent of all pollution abatement costs in the industrial sector.

As noted in the text, pollution abatement costs are only part of total environmental expenditures. Only one attempt appears to have been made in the UK to estimate overall expenditures (UK Department of the Environment, 1992); the results are recorded in Table C.4. The estimate for pollution control expenditure in the corporate sector again reveals the formidable problems of attaching statistical significance to the estimates. Table C.4 suggests that corporate costs were some £5.9 billion in 1990–91 (at 1991 prices). This might be regarded as being broadly comparable to the £5.1 billion (at 1991 prices) for 1988 shown in Table C.1. But Table C.2 produces results that are significantly lower for 1990.

Table C.4 suggests that total pollution abatement costs from all sectors constitute about 60 per cent of all environmental expenditures. Conservation expenditures account for around 3 per cent of total environmental expenditures and include monies spent on conserving various protected areas and environmental improvements. R&D accounts for under 2 per cent of total expenditure, but the recorded sums do not include expenditure on 'clean technology' and hence R&D

Table C.1. *Environmental expenditures in the UK:*
pollution control only (£ million)

	1977 (1977 prices)	1978 (1984 prices)	1984 (1984 prices)	1985 (1985 prices)	1988 (1986 prices)
Public	1,193			2,380	1,511–1,940
Private	1,216			2,070	1,860–2,289
Total	2,410	3,300–3,800	3,000	4,450	3,371–4,229
Total, 1991 prices[a]	7,158	4,884–5,624	4,440	6,853	5,130

[a]1991/1977 price multiplier = 2.97; 1991/1984 price multiplier = 1.48; 1991/1985 price multiplier = 1.54; 1991/1986 price multiplier = 1.35. Price ratios from World Bank (annual).

Source: Adapted from ECOTEC (1989).

Table C.2. *Environmental expenditures in the UK*
(£ million, 1991 prices)

	1988, pollution control only	1990, pollution control only	1994	1997
Public	2,042–2,619		1,510	
Private	2,511–3,090[a]		2,766	3,592[a]
Households			2,539	
Total	4,553–5,709	4,190–4,793	6,815	

[a]'Private' includes households. Most sources remain silent on the treatment of households.

Sources: 1988–adapted from ECOTEC (1989) and converted to 1991 prices; 1990–broad judgement of ERL (1991); 1994–from ECOTEC (1996) with adjustments for arithmetic errors in the original (Brown (1998) also discusses the 1994 survey); 1997–from ECOTEC (1999).

Table C.3. *UK industrial abatement costs by industry, 1997*

Industry	Expenditure (£ million, 1997 prices)	Expenditure (% of total industrial)
Mining and quarrying	70	1.6
Food	560	13.1
Textiles and leather	130	3.0
Wood and wood products	110	2.6
Pulp and paper	350	8.2
Solid and nuclear fuels and oil refining	170	4.0
Chemicals	1,040	24.4
Rubber and plastics	140	3.3
Other non-metallic products	290	6.8
Metals	600	14.1
Machinery and equipment	100	2.3
Electrical equipment	100	2.3
Transport equipment	150	3.5
Other manufacturing	70	1.6
Energy and water supply	400	9.4
Total	4,270	100.0

Source: UK Department of the Environment, Transport and the Regions as recorded in Office for National Statistics, *United Kingdom National Accounts: The Blue Book, 1999 Edition*, The Stationery Office, London, Table 12.7.

expenditures are understated. Education and training relates mainly to expenditures on university courses in environmental sciences. Management of natural resources constitutes a significant portion of expenditure—around 25 per cent—and includes water company expenditures, flood defences and fisheries management; energy conservation is excluded. Finally, amenity improvement covers activities such as road cleaning and local park maintenance. Total expenditures of £14 billion in 1990 would have been some 2.5 per cent of UK GDP.

Table C.4. *Total environmental expenditures in the UK, 1990–91*
(£ million, 1991 prices)

Activity	Government	Firms	Households	Nature protection organisations	Total
Pollution abatement	2,200	5,900	680	–	8,780
Environmental conservation	290	–	–	160	450
R&D	250	–	–	–	250
Education and training	90	60	–	–	150
Sub-total	*2,830*	*5,960*	*680*	*160*	*9,630*
Management of natural resources	630	2,800	–	–	3,430
Amenity improvement	1,200	–	–	–	1,200
Total	4,660	8,760	680	160	14,260
Per cent	33	61	5	1	100

Source: Brown (1998).

APPENDIX D. ENVIRONMENTAL EXPENDITURES IN DEVELOPING COUNTRIES

Little is known about environmental expenditure in developing countries. The World Bank and the Asian Development Bank have sponsored studies of expenditure in Malaysia and Indonesia (personal communication with J. Vincent, 2001) but neither study appears to be publicly available. Hansen (1994) reports estimates produced by Phantumvanit and Panayotou (1990) for selected countries, as shown in Table D.1. Coverage of the data is unclear but the figures do suggest expenditures well below 1 per cent of GDP for poorer countries.

Table D.1. *Environmental expenditures in selected developing countries, 1987*

	As % of GDP	Per capita (US$)
Singapore	1.09	107
Republic of Korea	0.40	11
Thailand	0.24	2
China	0.70	2
Indonesia	0.38	1.7

Source: Authors' estimates.

APPENDIX E. THE 'INCOME ELASTICITY' OF DEMAND FOR ENVIRONMENTAL QUALITY

For a given demand function of the form

$$q = \alpha + \beta p + \gamma y,$$

where q=quantity, y=income and p=price, derive the inverse demand function

$$p = \frac{q - \alpha - \gamma y}{\beta}.$$

The 'conventional' income and price elasticities are then

$$E_q^y = \frac{\gamma y}{q}$$

and

$$E_q^p = \frac{\beta p}{q}.$$

From the inverse demand function, the elasticity of price with respect to income is

$$E_p^y = \frac{\gamma y}{\beta p}.$$

But $\gamma y = E_q^y q$ and $\beta p = E_q^p q$, so

$$E_p^y = \frac{E_q^y}{-E_q^p}.$$

REFERENCES

Aidt, T. (1998), 'Political internalization of economic externalities and environmental policy', *Journal of Public Economics*, vol. 69, pp. 1–16.

Albrecht, J. (1999), 'Environmental regulation, comparative advantage and the Porter hypothesis', University of Ghent, Faculty of Economics, mimeo.

Andreoni, J. and Levinson, A. (2001), 'The simple analytics of the environmental Kuznets curve', *Journal of Public Economics*, vol. 80, pp. 269–86.

Barbera, A. and McConnell, V. (1990), 'The impact of environmental regulations on industry productivity: direct and indirect effects', *Journal of Environmental Economics and Management*, vol. 18, pp. 50–65.

Black, D., Guppy, N. and Urmetzer, P. (1997), 'Canadian public opinion and environmental action: evidence from British Columbia', *Canadian Journal of Political Science*, vol. 30, pp. 451–71.

Brown, A. (1998), 'UK experience in collecting environmental expenditure information by industry', in P. Vaze (ed.), *UK Environmental Accounts 1998*, London: Office for National Statistics.

Bruvoll, A., Glomsrod, S. and Vennemo, H. (1995), 'The environmental drag on long-term economic performance: evidence from Norway', Statistics Norway, Discussion Paper no. 143.

Buchanan, J. and Tullock, G. (1975), 'Polluters' profit and political response: direct controls versus taxes', *American Economic Review*, vol. 65, pp. 139–47.

Coase, R. (1960), 'The problem of social cost', *Journal of Law and Economics*, vol. 3, pp. 1–44.

Conrad, K. and Morrison, C. (1989), 'The impact of pollution abatement investment on productivity change: an empirical comparison of the US, Germany and Canada', *Southern Economic Journal*, vol. 55, pp. 684–98.

ECOTEC (1989), *Industry Costs of Pollution Control*, Report to the UK Department of the Environment, London.

— (1996), *Environmental Protection Expenditure by Industry*, Report to the UK Department of the Environment, London.

— (1999), *Environmental Protection Expenditure by UK Industry: A Survey of 1997 Expenditure*, Report to the UK Department of the Environment, Transport and the Regions, London.

Elliott, E., Seldon, B. and Regens, L. (1997), 'Political and economic determinants of individuals' support for environmental spending', *Journal of Environmental Management*, vol. 51, pp. 15–27.

ERECO (1993), *Environmental Expenditure in the European Community*, Final Report to DG XI, Brussels: European Commission.

ERL (1991), *Pollution Abatement Cost Evaluation*, March, London: Environmental Resources Ltd.

Eskeland, G. and Harrison, A. (1997), 'Moving to greener pastures? Multinationals and the pollution haven hypothesis', World Bank, Policy Research Working Paper no. 1744.

European Commission (1992), *The State of the Environment in the European Community*, three volumes, COM(92) 23 Final, Brussels.

— (1999), *What Do Europeans Think about the Environment?*, the main results of the survey carried out in the context of Eurobarometer 51.1, DG XI Environment, Nuclear Safety and Civil Protection in conjunction with DG X Information, Communication, Culture and Audiovisual Media, Brussels.

EUROSTAT (1999), *Environmental Protection Expenditure in Member States: First Edition– 1988–1996*, Luxembourg: Eurostat. See also Eurostat web page: www.europa.eu.int/comm/ eurostat.

Flores, N. and Carson, R. (1997), 'The relationship between the income elasticities of demand and willingness to pay', *Journal of Environmental Economics and Management*, vol. 33, pp. 287–95.

Freeman, A. M. (1982), *Air and Water Pollution Control: A Benefit–Cost Assessment*, New York: Wiley.

— (1990), 'Water pollution policy', in P. Portney (ed.), *Public Policies for Environmental Protection*, Washington, DC: Resources for the Future.

— (2000), 'Water pollution policy', in P. Portney (ed.), *Public Policies for Environmental Protection*, Washington, DC: Resources for the Future.

French Ministry of the Environment (1984), *Données Economiques de l'Environnement*, Paris: Documentation Française.

Garrod, G. and Willis, K. (1999), *Economic Valuation of the Environment: Methods and Case Studies*, Cheltenham: Edward Elgar.

Gray, W. and Shadbegian, R. (1993), 'Environmental regulation and manufacturing productivity at the plant level', US Department of Commerce, Occasional Paper no. 93-6.

— and — (1995), 'Pollution abatement costs, regulation and plant-level productivity', National Bureau of Economic Research, Working Paper no. 4944.

Grossman, G. and Krueger, A. (1995), 'Economic growth and the environment', *Quarterly Journal of Economics*, May, vol. 110, pp. 353–77.

Hahn, R. (1996), 'Regulatory reform: what the government's numbers tell us', in R. Hahn (ed.), *Risks, Costs and Lives Saved: Getting Better Results from Regulation*, Oxford: Oxford University Press.

Hanemann, M. (1991), 'Willingness to pay and willingness to accept: how much can they differ?', *American Economic Review*, vol. 81, pp. 635–47.

Hansen, S. (1994), 'The market for environmental goods and services', in Asian Development Bank, *Financing Environmentally Sound Development*, Manila: Asian Development Bank.

Harbaugh, W., Levinson, A. and Wilson, D. (2000), 'Re-examining the empirical evidence for an environmental Kuznets curve', National Bureau of Economic Research, Working Paper no. 7711.

Heathfield, D. and Wibe, S. (1987), *Production Functions*, Houndmills: Macmillan.

Jaffe, A., Newell, R. and Stavins, R. (2000), 'Technological change and the environment', Washington DC, Resources for the Future, Discussion Paper no. 00-47.

—, Peterson, S., Portney, P. and Stavins, R. (1995), 'Environmental regulation and the competitiveness of US manufacturing: what does the evidence tell us?', *Journal of Economic Literature*, vol. 33, pp. 132–63.

Jones, R. and Dunlap, R. (1992), 'The social bases of environmental concern: have they changed over time?', *Rural Sociology*, vol. 57, pp. 28–47.

Jorgensen, D. and Wilcoxen, P. (1990), 'Environmental regulation and US economic growth', *RAND Journal of Economics*, vol. 21, pp. 314–40.

Joshi, J., Krishnan, R. and Lave, L. (2000), 'Estimating the hidden costs of environmental regulation', *The Accounting Review*, vol. 76, April.

Kristrom, B. and Riera, P. (1996), 'Is the income elasticity of environmental improvements less than one?', *Environmental and Resource Economics*, vol. 7, pp. 45–55.

Maddison, A. (1984), 'Origins and impacts of the Welfare State, 1883–1983', *Banca Nazionale del Lavoro Quarterly Review*, March.

— (1991), *Dynamic Forces in Capitalist Development*, Oxford: Oxford University Press.

— (1995), *Monitoring the World Economy 1820–1992*, Paris: Organisation for Economic Co-operation and Development.

Magnani, A. (2000), 'The environmental Kuznets curve, environmental protection policy and income distribution', *Ecological Economics*, vol. 32, pp. 431–43.

Marsiliani, L. and Renström, T. (2000), 'Inequality, environmental protection and growth', Milan, Fondazione Eni Enrico Mattei, Discussion Paper.

Morgenstern, R., Pizer, W. and Shih, J.-S. (1997), 'Are we overstating the real economic costs of environmental protection?', Washington DC, Resources for the Future, Discussion Paper no. 97-36REV.

—, — and — (2000), 'The cost of environmental protection', *Review of Economics and Statistics*, forthcoming. (Revised and shortened version of Morgenstern et al. (1997).)

Nestor, D. and Pasurka, C. (1994), *Productivity Measurement and Undesirable Outputs: A Distance Function Approach*, Washington, DC: Economic Analysis and Research Branch, US Environmental Protection Agency.

Ng, Y.-K. (2001), 'Is public spending good for you?', *World Economics*, vol. 2, no. 2, pp. 1–17.

Oates, W., Palmer, K. and Portney, P. (1994), 'Environmental regulation and international competitiveness: thinking about the Porter hypothesis', Washington DC, Resources for the Future, Discussion Paper no. 94-02.

OECD (1989), *Pollution Control Expenditure in OECD Countries: Statistical Compendium*, Paris: Organisation for Economic Co-operation and Development.

— (1990), *Pollution Abatement and Control Expenditure in OECD Countries*, Paris: Organisation for Economic Co-operation and Development.

— (1991), *OECD Environmental Data, Compendium 1991*, Paris: Organisation for Economic Co-operation and Development.

— (1993), *Pollution Abatement and Control Expenditure in OECD Countries*, Paris: Organisation for Economic Co-operation and Development.

— (1996), *Pollution Abatement and Control Expenditure in OECD Countries*, Paris: Organisation for Economic Co-operation and Development.

— (1999), *OECD Environmental Data, Compendium 1999*, Paris: Organisation for Economic Co-operation and Development.

Peacock, A. and Wiseman, J. (1961), *The Growth of Public Expenditure in the United Kingdom*, Oxford: Oxford University Press.

Pearce, D. W. (2000), 'The economics of technology-based environmental standards', in D. Helm (ed.), *Environmental Policy: Objectives, Instruments and Implementation*, Oxford: Oxford University Press.

Phantumvanit, D. and Panayotou, T. (1990), 'Industrialisation and environmental quality: paying the price', paper to Thailand Development Research Institute conference on industrialising Thailand and its impact on the environment, Chonburi, Thailand.

Porter, M. (1990a), 'The competitive advantage of nations', *Harvard Business Review*, March/April, pp. 73–95.

— (1990b), *The Competitive Advantage of Nations*, New York: Free Press.

— (1991), 'America's green strategy', *Scientific American*, April, p. 168.

— and van der Linde, C. (1995a), 'Toward a new conception of the environment–competitiveness relationship', *Journal of Economic Perspectives*, vol. 9, no. 4, pp. 119–32.

— and — (1995b), 'Green and competitive: ending the stalemate', *Harvard Business Review*, vol. 73, September/October, pp. 120–33.

Portney, P. (1990), 'Air pollution policy', in P. Portney (ed.), *Public Policies for Environmental Protection*, Washington DC: Resources for the Future.

— (2000), 'Air pollution policy', in P. Portney (ed.), *Public Policies for Environmental Protection*, Washington DC: Resources for the Future.

Randall, A. and Stoll, J. (1980), 'Consumer's surplus in commodity space', *American Economic Review*, vol. 70, pp. 949–1024.

Repetto, R., Rothman, D., Faeth, P. and Austin, D. (1996), *Has Environmental Protection Really Reduced Productivity Growth? We Need New Measures*, Washington, DC: World Resources Institute.

Robinson, J. (1995), 'The impact of environmental and occupational health regulation on productivity growth in US manufacturing', *Yale Journal of Regulation*, vol. 12, pp. 346–87.

Schaltegger, S. and Burritt, R. (2000), *Contemporary Environmental Accounting: Issues, Concepts and Practice*, Sheffield: Greenleaf Publishing.

SEMA-METRA (1986), 'Les flux économiques associés à la protection de l'environnement', paper to DG XI, European Commission, Brussels.

Sorsa, P. (1994), 'Competitiveness and environmental standards', World Bank, Policy Research Working Paper no. 1249.

Stewart, R. (1993), 'Environmental regulation and international competitiveness', *The Yale Law Journal*, vol. 102, pp. 2039–106.

Suri, V. and Chapman, D. (1998), 'Economic growth, trade and energy: implications for the environmental Kuznets curve', *Ecological Economics*, vol. 25, pp. 195–208.

Tanzi, V. and Schuknecht, L. (2000), *Public Spending in the Twentieth Century: A Global Perspective*, Cambridge: Cambridge University Press.

Tietenberg, T. (2000), *Environmental and Natural Resource Economics*, 5th edition, Reading, MA: Addison Wesley Longman.

UK Department of the Environment (1992), *The UK Environment*, London: HMSO.

World Bank (annual), *World Tables*, Washington, DC: World Bank.

— (1999), *Greening Industry: New Roles for Communities, Markets and Governments*, Washington, DC: World Bank.

— (2001), *World Development Report 2000–1*, Oxford: Oxford University Press.

9

Government Failure in US Urban Transportation

CLIFFORD WINSTON[1]

I. INTRODUCTION

Public provision of urban transportation is, in theory, socially desirable. Rail and bus operations exhibit economies of traffic density that could lead to destructive competition in an unregulated market. Highways are traditionally perceived as public goods that require enormous capital and maintenance investments that the private sector is unlikely to finance. Improving the urban mobility of elderly and low-income citizens is an important social goal that should be addressed by government. But in their official capacity as regulators, service providers and investors, public officials have generally instituted policies that have led to inefficient and inequitable urban transportation. A case for privatising urban transport is developing because these actual government failures most likely outweigh potential market failures.

Governmental involvement in the transportation systems of US cities illustrates the problem. Local governments, with state and federal financial support, are quasi-monopoly providers of urban bus and rail transit. Most US roads and bridges are owned and operated by federal, state or local governments. How has the public system performed? City roads are jammed at an ever expanding rush hour, causing infuriating delays. Bus service, never fast, has deteriorated over the years, while fares have risen. Pressures to expand rail service to outlying suburbs remain strong, even though current rail operations cannot attract enough riders to cover more than a small fraction of their total expenses including capital costs.

Popular opinion seems to be that the US can, and should, spend its way out of this mess by building more roads, running more buses and installing more track. Indeed, in the Transportation Equity Act for the 21st Century, T21 for short, Congress greatly increased federal support for transit and highways for 1998–2003. Many transportation analysts are sceptical and argue that, although more public spending

The author has received helpful comments from Kenneth Button, John Meyer, Steven Morrison, Don Pickrell, Chad Shirley, Kenneth Small and seminar participants at the Institute for Fiscal Studies. Alise Upitis provided valuable research assistance.

[1] Brookings Institution.

for urban transport may result in some improvements for travellers, its primary effects will be to swell transportation deficits and waste tax revenues. Instead, they suggest that government pursue more 'efficient' policies such as charging motorists for the congestion they cause and balancing costs and benefits when deciding transit frequencies, route coverage and vehicle sizes.

I have come to believe that it is futile to expect public officials to consider such changes because urban transportation policy is largely shaped by entrenched political forces. The forces that have led to inefficient prices and service, excessive labour costs, bloated bureaucracies and construction-cost overruns promise more of the same for the future. The only realistic way to improve the system is to shield it from those influences and expose it to market forces by privatising it. Preliminary evidence from the UK and elsewhere suggests that, although a private urban transportation sector should not be expected to perform flawlessly, it could eliminate most government failures and allow innovation and state-of-the-art technology to flourish free of government interference. The real uncertainty is what could spur policymakers to initiate change.

II. THE EVOLUTION OF THE US URBAN TRANSIT SYSTEM

The US government began subsidising urban transportation in the 1950s, funding urban extensions of the interstate highway system. Then, in response both to the deteriorating financial condition of private transit—an issue to which I will return—and to arguments by big-city mayors that subsidising transit would be more cost-effective than building highways, Congress passed legislation in the early 1960s that helped cities buy their transit companies. Federal operating subsidies followed in the 1970s. Today, most operating assistance comes from state and local governments, while Washington shoulders most capital investment.

Growing federal support of mass transit slowed the long-run decline in the use of buses and light-rail systems—trolleys and streetcars (Figure 1). By the late 1970s, federal subsidies had expanded bus and heavy-rail capacity.[2] Capacity has continued to increase in the past two decades, but other trends have revealed ominous weaknesses in service (Winston and Shirley, 1998). Many cities have cut bus frequency on their core routes to extend service to the suburbs. Many others, including New York, Chicago and San Francisco, have cut rail-service frequency and raised real fares. Indeed, since 1980, real transit fares per passenger-mile have increased 54 per cent.[3] Although federal support of public transit was intended to lure urban travellers from their cars, the share of commuters who use bus and rail

---

[2] It would be preferable to measure bus and rail capacity in terms of seat-miles instead of vehicle-miles. Information on seat-miles, however, is only available from the American Public Transit Association since 1980. Based on these data, bus and heavy-rail seating capacity has remained relatively constant, while light rail's seating capacity has increased somewhat. Thus using vehicle-miles instead of seat-miles understates the recent growth of light-rail capacity but does not have much impact on the growth of bus and heavy-rail capacity.

[3] American Public Transit Association, *Transit Fact Book*, various issues.

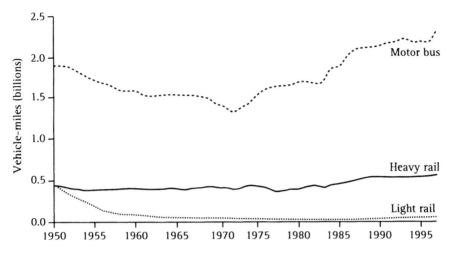

Figure 1. *Heavy- and light-rail and motor-bus vehicle-miles*[a]

[a]A number of smaller and rural systems are excluded before 1984.

Sources: American Public Transit Association–*1997 Transit Fact Book* (for 1984–95), *1991 Transit Fact Book* (for 1975–83), *1974–75 Transit Fact Book* (for 1960–73), *1981 Transit Fact Book* (for 1974) and *Transit Fact Book 1960* (for 1950–59).

has diminished since the 1960s. Rising incomes and suburban sprawl have rein-forced commuters' preferences for their automobiles, causing autos' share of work trips to climb to nearly 84 per cent by 1990 (Table 1).[4] Between 1960 and 1990, mass transit's share of *all* trips in large urban areas, where transit service should be most attractive, fell from more than 20 per cent to less than 10 per cent.[5] Transit's high share of empty seats attests to its inefficient operations. In the mid-1990s, rail filled roughly 18 per cent of its seats with paying customers, buses roughly 14 per cent (Winston and Shirley, 1998).

Public transit's long-run growth in capacity and decline in patronage have helped create deficits that are a serious drain on the public purse. By 1997, transit-operating expenses in the US were about $19 billion a year, almost twice the yearly $10.6 billion in operating revenues. Continuing capital investments are swelling this deficit (1998 capital subsidies amounted to $7.4 billion).[6] Government involve-ment portends better things for special interests than for travellers. According

---

[4] These mode shares are based on decennial censuses. Mode shares based on the 2000 census are not yet available.

[5] Passenger counts and mode shares for all types of trips are available from the US Federal Highway Administration, *Personal Transportation Survey*, Department of Transportation, 1990. Because the sample sizes are generally considered small, national estimates derived from these data should be regarded as preliminary. None the less, the data reveal trends and magnitudes that are consistent with those based on reliable samples of work trips.

[6] Operating subsidies are from the American Public Transit Association, *1998 Transit Fact Book*, Washington DC, and capital subsidies are from the National Transit Administration, *National Transit Database*, US Department of Transportation.

Table 1. *Journey-to-work passengers and mode shares in US urban areas with population greater than 1 million*

Mode	1960	1970	1980	1990
Millions of workers				
Privately owned vehicle	17.5	27.6	36.5	49.8
Bus	3.8	3.3	3.0	2.9
Subway/Rail	2.3	2.2	2.0	2.3
Walk	3.0	2.7	2.1	2.2
Other	5.2	1.2	1.7	2.4
Percentage of workers				
Privately owned vehicle	61.0	74.4	80.4	83.5
Bus	13.1	9.0	6.7	4.9
Subway/Rail	8.0	5.9	4.5	3.8
Walk	10.4	7.4	4.7	3.8
Other	7.5	3.3	3.7	4.0

Note: The 'other' category in 1960 and 1970 passenger trips includes walking, taxi, motorcycle, bicycle and respondents who work at home. The 'other' category in other years and in mode share includes these modes except walking. The mode share data for walking in 1960 and 1970 are based on US data rather than major urban area data. The set of major urban areas with population exceeding 1 million changes by decade.

Sources: Federal Highway Administration, *Journey-to-Work Trends in the United States and its Major Metropolitan Areas 1960–1990*, 1993, from census data; Federal Highway Administration, *Journey-to-Work Trends, based on 1960, 1970 and 1980 Decennial Censuses*, 1986; and author's calculations.

to Pickrell (1985) and Lee (1987), as much as 75 per cent of federal spending on mass transit ends up in the pockets of transit workers (as above-market wages) or goes to suppliers of transit capital equipment (as higher profits and interest). Just 25 per cent is used to improve transit and lower fares.

Although transit use has increased during the current US economic expansion, transit's market share has kept falling.[7] Moreover, according to data from the National Transit Database, transit use was lower in 1998 than in 1989. None the less, with growing government support for transit, cities will find it easier to build new (light-) rail systems or extend existing ones, ensuring that transit deficits will grow even larger.

A fundamental problem with rail construction projects is that ridership tends to be grossly overestimated at the planning stage, while capital and operating costs are underestimated. For example, after breaking ground in 1986, the new Los Angeles Red Line (light-rail system) finally opened in June 2000. The 17.4-mile system, costing more than $4.5 billion, now hopes to lure only 100,000 riders a day

---

[7] Wendell Cox, 'Report of public transit's "record" ridership questionable', June 2000 (available at www.heritage.org).

in a county with 10 million residents.[8] The system was originally intended to be much larger and carry more passengers, but after years of construction delays and cost overruns and faced with cost projections of some $75 billion over the next 20 years, Los Angeles voters decided in 1998 to block further use of local sales tax revenue for subway construction, effectively preventing expansion of the current Red Line.

Public transit authorities face growing financial pressures to maintain rail operations as these systems age. For example, the Washington, DC, Metro subway system, which began service only in 1976, is struggling with equipment break-downs, such as broken escalators and failed relays, and water seepage that is crippling power and communications systems and track infrastructure at an alarming rate. When faced with the likelihood that money would not be available over the next several years to make all necessary repairs and purchase additional equipment, regional planners concluded that far more people will have to drive cars than previously projected.[9]

In retrospect, the US public transportation experiment has been a major disappointment and done little to stem the growth of automobile travel. Policymakers are now confronted with the rising costs of this experiment.

III. US URBAN HIGHWAYS

The US has invested hundreds of billions of dollars—primarily from gas taxes (i.e. road fuel taxes)—in building and maintaining roads to accommodate auto and truck travel, but, like rail transit investments, the cost of some urban road projects has turned out to be much greater than anticipated. The most glaring example of cost overruns is the so-called Big Dig depression of Boston's central artery, considered to be the largest public works project in US history. Originally projected to cost $2.3 billion in 1984, it is now expected to cost $13.6 billion when finally completed in 2004, but even that figure could rise.[10] At a smaller scale, but indicative of the extent of the problem, transportation officials in the Washington, DC, region acknowledge that the cost of replacing a major highway interchange known as the 'Mixing Bowl' has ballooned from $350 million to $509 million and become the region's most expensive highway project. Officials fear costs could run higher and stall other transportation projects.[11]

The motoring public is less knowledgeable about construction cost overruns than about the increase in urban automobile congestion. Vehicle-miles travelled in urban areas increased 82 per cent from 1980 to 1997, while urban road mileage increased only 33 per cent.[12] The share of urban highways with peak-hour

---

[8] Todd S. Purdum, 'Los Angeles subway reaches end of the line', *New York Times*, 23 June 2000, p. 1.

[9] Alan Sipress, 'Transportation plan reveals funding gap', *Washington Post*, 13 July 2000, p. 1.

[10] Pamela Ferdinand, 'Boston's "Big Dig" buried in cost overruns', *Washington Post*, 12 April 2000, p. A3.

[11] Alan Sipress, 'Springfield interchange price tag rises 45%', *Washington Post*, 15 June 2000, p. B1.

[12] US Federal Highway Administration, *Highway Statistics*, various years.

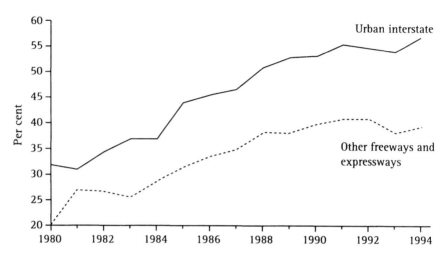

Figure 2. *Urban road miles at over 71 per cent capacity in peak periods*

Source: Table HM-61, Federal Highway Administration, *Highway Statistics*, Department of Transportation, various years.

traffic volume exceeding 71 per cent of design capacity–a common indicator of congestion–increased steadily during the 1980s to more than 50 per cent of urban interstate miles and 40 per cent of other freeway miles (Figure 2).[13] Although workplace and residential adjustments during the 1990s, such as working and living in outlying suburbs, have helped stabilise urban congestion, the current annual costs to travellers, mainly in the form of wasted time but also in the form of extra consumption of gasoline and vehicle wear and tear, have been estimated to run as high as $40 billion. The annual cost of congestion to shippers, in the form of higher inventories and more goods stuck *en route*, adds considerably to this figure.[14]

Even when roads are widened to keep up with demand, the expanded roads shortly fill to capacity. For example, the Montgomery County, Maryland, transportation director pressed the Maryland state government to widen its Interstate 270 six years ahead of schedule to accommodate growing traffic. Maryland responded with $200 million to widen more than a dozen miles of I-270, up to 12 lanes in some stretches. But less than eight years after the project was finished, county officials describe the highway as 'a rolling parking lot'.[15]

The US road system represents the nation's largest civilian public investment. None the less, congestion appears to have become an intractable problem because

[13] Measures of congestion after 1994 are based on a change in capacity calculation procedures, which makes it difficult to compare congestion in 1995 and years thereafter with that in previous years.

[14] Estimates of the costs of automobile congestion to travellers are produced by the Texas Transportation Institute at Texas A&M University.

[15] This is partly an outcome of Downs's (1962) law: on urban commuter expressways, peak-hour traffic congestion rises to meet maximum capacity because commuters shift from less preferred modes and times of day.

public expenditures to expand urban road capacity cannot keep up with growing automobile travel.

IV. ECONOMIC INEFFICIENCIES OF CURRENT URBAN TRANSPORT POLICY

The traditional theoretical justification for government management and operation of transit is that a private transit market would result in destructive competition.[16] Public transit agencies could maximise social net benefits by setting travellers' fares equal to the marginal cost of their trips and providing service, such as frequency and route coverage, where additional benefits to travellers equal the additional costs.[17] Government ownership and management of roads is justified on the grounds that roads are (for the most part) public goods that require enormous investments. Given congestion and road surface wear, the public highway authority could maximise social net benefits by charging users for the particular costs they incur and by making investments where marginal benefits equal marginal costs.

Large public transit deficits, low transit load factors and severe highway congestion, however, suggest that the US public sector is not setting urban transportation prices and service to maximise net benefits. Winston and Shirley (1998) explore this matter empirically by estimating the net benefits from two policies: replacing current transit prices and service frequency with marginal cost transit fares and optimal service frequency; and setting marginal cost automobile congestion tolls.[18] (The tolls, which can be assessed with current technology that does not disrupt motorists' journeys or invade their privacy, account for travellers' value of time and vary with the level of congestion throughout the day.) Policy simulations are based on an equilibrium model of urban transportation pricing and service where urban commuters choose among alternative modes (auto, bus, rail, taxi or car pool) and departure times. The effects of the pricing and service policies on consumer benefits and government balances are shown in Table 2.[19]

The net benefits from implementing only the pricing components of this policy total nearly $8 billion a year. Because optimal pricing means much higher fares

[16] Government intervention has also been justified on the grounds of 'Hotelling' bunching—competing transit companies would arrive at bus stops or rail stations at the same time. Bunching, however, occurs quite frequently in most public transit systems.

[17] If transit companies operate where there are increasing returns to scale, this first-best policy will require some subsidy because marginal costs are below average costs. If no subsidies are available (an unlikely situation in public transit), then Ramsey pricing represents the efficient second-best policy where the percentage mark-up of fares above marginal cost is inversely related to travellers' demand elasticities subject to a break-even constraint.

[18] Optimal service frequency is the level of bus and rail frequency that maximises net benefits, which are composed of the changes in travellers' benefits, congestion toll revenues, bus revenues and costs, and rail revenues and costs.

[19] Consumer benefits are measured by compensating variations that are based on the joint choice model of mode and departure time. Changes in government balances are based on changes in bus revenues and costs, rail revenues and costs, and toll revenues.

Table 2. *Effects of efficient urban transportation pricing and services in the US (Billions of 1998 dollars)*

Assumption and mode	Consumer benefits	Government balances	Net benefits
Efficient pricing only			
Auto, bus and rail total	−16.0	23.9	7.9
Auto toll	−8.2	12.0	3.8
Bus	−4.3	7.0	2.6
Rail	−2.4	2.8	0.4
Efficient pricing and optimal service frequency			
Auto, bus and rail total	−16.2	29.3	13.0
Bus	−4.3	11.7	7.3
Rail	−2.8	4.3	1.6

Source: Winston and Shirley, 1998.

and tolls, travellers themselves lose $16 billion.[20] But these private losses are more than offset by the reduced public transit deficits and accumulated toll revenues that bring the urban transportation budget into balance. It is, of course, questionable whether the average citizen will see benefits in policies that increase his or her costs, even as they lower public deficits. But voters are demonstrably inclined to support elected officials who reduce government spending (Peltzman, 1992; Winston and Crandall, 1994), so travellers wearing their hats as taxpayers would likely vote for their enlightened self-interest at the ballot box. In fact, the benefits noted in Table 2 are understated because they do not account for the cost of raising public funds (excess burden) to cover the transit deficit.

Some policymakers and analysts have tried to justify transit subsidies on second-best efficiency grounds because auto travel is implicitly subsidised, that is, travellers' costs of using their automobiles do not include the costs of congestion, pollution and the like. But the findings show that overall urban transportation efficiency would improve if *any* mode's prices were aligned with its marginal costs. Current transit fares are so out of line with costs that marginal cost pricing would reduce economic waste, even if the price of using auto travel remained unchanged. By the same token, raising the cost of driving to account for congestion without raising mass transit fares would also increase overall urban transportation efficiency.

Net benefits to society would climb to $13 billion a year if service frequency as well as prices were adjusted to maximise net benefits. Current transit frequency is excessive because of low ridership and oversized vehicles. Thus cutting frequency

---

[20] Congestion pricing provides benefits to peak-period auto travellers in the form of shorter travel time. The losses to travellers are net of these benefits.

generates benefits because public deficits are reduced by more than the value of service lost to urban travellers.

Government's failure to set efficient prices and service frequency for bus and rail transit and set optimal tolls for auto travel has generated large social costs, but these are only part of the allocative inefficiencies created by government involvement in urban transportation. Inefficiencies have also arisen because transit's service offerings are not optimised in other areas such as route coverage and because highway charges do not reflect the road damage caused by trucks.[21]

Public authorities have also failed to keep down the cost of urban transit service. The large share of empty bus and rail seats is one indication that costs are too high.[22] This excess capacity also prevents transit from realising its competitive advantage over auto. Transit's average operating costs per *seat*-mile are lower than auto's, but its empty seats drive its operating costs per *passenger*-mile above auto's (Winston and Shirley, 1998). Other indications of transit inefficiency include excessive wages (the typical Washington, DC, Metrobus driver, e.g. gets paid twice as much as drivers for the handful of private bus companies in the DC area) and declining productivity. Lave (1991) estimates that transit productivity has fallen 40 per cent since the public take-over in the mid-1960s.

Travel on urban thoroughfares is also not produced at minimum cost. Roth (1996) argues that highways make inefficient use of their capacity and actually run a substantial deficit when depreciation of highway capital is taken into account. Small et al. (1989) found that highway pavement is generally too thin, which raises maintenance costs. Public management of construction projects also raises costs because bureaucratic rules prevent the government from using the latest technologies, causing some investments to need upgrading shortly after completion. Project managers also specify detailed regulations that force contractors to adhere to the letter of the contract instead of seeking higher-quality, efficient alternatives. Finally, highway labour costs have been elevated by the Davis–Bacon Act, which requires that prevailing union wages must be paid on all federal construction contracts.

The legislative process also encourages waste. At the federal level, transportation bills are loaded with demonstration or 'pork barrel' projects to ensure passage (T21 is larded with some $9 billion of pork). A notorious example is the stretch of

---

[21] Road damage depends on a truck's weight per axle (the more axles a truck has for a given load, the less road damage) and should be covered by a user charge per mile based on axle weight. Small, Winston and Evans (1989) estimate that the efficiency improvements from replacing the gas tax, which is currently used to charge trucks for highway use, with an axle-weight tax amount to $8 billion (1996 dollars), using a GDP inflator. With respect to efficient pricing of other transport externalities, Winston and Shirley (1998) find there would be small net benefits from charging travellers for the cost of accidents and pollution.

[22] Transit's inherent operations—gradually increasing ridership in the primary commuting direction and consistently low ridership for the reverse commute—suggest that even an efficient transit system is unlikely to achieve average load factors that exceed 50 per cent. But public transit's average load factor is far below that figure and has been declining for some time. It was 22 per cent in 1975, 18 per cent in 1985 and 16 per cent in 1995.

I-99 connecting Wolfsburg and Bald Eagle, Pennsylvania. Dubbed the Bud Shuster highway after the influential local congressman, the road carries less traffic in a year than the Washington, DC, Capital Beltway carries in three days. None the less, Shuster supports extending it to the tune of $400 million.

For their part, state and city officials tend to prefer urban transportation projects that entail a large federal contribution over those that could yield greater social benefits. In addition, federal legislation in 1991 may have encouraged local officials to understate the potential costs of their projects by requiring that regions craft transportation programmes that included only those road and transit projects that had lined up funding. When the true, as opposed to wishful, costs of these projects have become apparent, officials have delayed other projects.

Until analysts better understand how both mass transit and auto can benefit travellers, it is premature to say whether a more efficient urban transportation system would shift travellers from mass transit to auto, or vice versa. Given the inescapable reality that the delivery of urban transportation by the public sector is creating substantial allocative and technical inefficiencies, researchers should consider how each mode's operations would improve in a privatised environment. Unfortunately, many analysts are preoccupied with how mode shares would change if policymakers followed their advice on how to design a 'better' public urban transportation system. What they fail to recognise is that current inefficiencies in the public sector are not simply an historical accident that can and will be easily corrected, but rather the predictable result of powerful political forces that are unlikely to change.

V. POLITICAL FORCES IN URBAN TRANSPORTATION

It is no secret that policymakers, appropriately, respond more to political forces than to market forces. Thus the subsidies that have become a fixture in urban transit largely accrue to powerful interests—higher wages to labour, including managers, operators and station agents, and higher profits to suppliers of transit capital. But a portion does go to keeping fares below cost and expanding service beyond what could be supported without subsidies. Winston and Shirley (1998) link much of transit's pricing and service inefficiencies with patrons' political influence: upper-middle-income rail riders benefit from more frequent service and route coverage, lower- and middle-income bus riders get more frequent service, and so on. Indeed, the recent debate about where to put the Red Line and new rapid bus lines in Los Angeles was more about the strength of homeowner groups and less about where the lines best integrate with the city.[23]

Transit inefficiencies might be more easily overlooked if they redistributed income from the well-to-do to the poor. But with the average annual household income of bus commuters approaching $40,000, with the average annual household income of rail commuters exceeding $50,000 and with train operators

---

[23] Glenn Gritzner and Katherine Perez, 'Something is missing in this Red Line picture', *Los Angeles Times*, 10 July 2000, p. 1 metro.

and station agents for the BART system in San Francisco, for example, being paid more than $40,000 a year, the poor are hardly transit's greatest beneficiaries.[24]

Highway spending also responds to strong interest groups, 'pork barrel' projects being an obvious example.[25] To maintain political support for a national highway system, the allocation of funds for highway repairs appears to be based on formulas that are biased in favour of (rural) states with relatively low highway use (Johnson and Libecap, 2000). In some cases, highway construction has been slowed because neighbourhoods (e.g. in Boston and San Francisco) resist demolitions for expressways that will mostly serve suburban commuting to downtown.

Efforts to implement congestion pricing on public highways have also been held hostage by politics. For example, a dispute between California public agencies and the state legislature over the redistribution of toll revenues prevented a congressionally authorised congestion toll experiment from being implemented on the San Francisco Bay Bridge (Shmanske, 1996). Given the wasteful spending of transportation funds, perhaps a silver lining in the nation's failure to introduce congestion pricing is that the 'pot of gold' represented by congestion toll revenues has not materialised in the public sector.

A fundamental question is how much travellers are willing to pay to save travel time by having road authorities set congestion tolls on highways. Calfee and Winston (1998) and Calfee et al. (forthcoming) suggest that automobile travellers' willingness to pay is much lower than once thought and that most travellers do not appear to value travel time savings enough to benefit substantially from optimal tolls. But it is clear in certain situations that auto travellers would be willing to pay considerable sums to travel faster. For example, a solo driver who was fined $50 for using a car-pool lane on a freeway in the Washington, DC, area viewed the fine as 'not a lot of money to pay to get to work an hour earlier'.[26]

Policymakers' preferred method of combating congestion has been to build more roads. Less politically expedient policies such as charging motorists efficiently for road use find less favour.[27] Car-pool lanes have been tried in some urban areas, but it is not clear whether these increase or decrease congestion. As funds for new roads are inevitably outstripped by demand and additions to existing roads fill up quickly with traffic, many urban officials are spending hundreds of thousands of dollars on commissions to 'study' ways to reduce congestion. But at least one commission concluded that political obstacles seem to put any strategy out of reach.[28]

---

[24] Winston and Shirley (1998) summarise evidence concluding that public transit programmes such as reverse commuting, which are designed to give low-income people greater access to suburban jobs, have not met with much success.

[25] Evans (1994) shows that the inclusion of highway demonstration projects is important to securing passage of legislation authorising the nation's highway and transit programmes.

[26] Alan Sipress and Josh White, 'Guilty, but feeling guilt-free', *Washington Post*, 16 July 2000, p. A1.

[27] Similarly, policymakers have only addressed road damage by repairing roads. They have not pursued efficient road wear taxes that would encourage truckers to shift to trucks that do less damage to the roads.

[28] Peter Behr, 'Area leaders hit traffic roadblock: political obstacles hamper solutions to driving woes', *Washington Post*, 28 September 1997, p. A1.

US policymakers at all levels of government have shaped an urban transportation system that benefits specific travellers and suppliers, but whose welfare costs are borne by all taxpayers. As long as transit is provided by the public sector, it is hard to see how the political forces that contribute to its current allocative and technical inefficiencies could be overcome. Efforts to improve the efficiency of public roads are also hamstrung by politics. Apparently, the federal government sees no reason to change matters because the T21 legislation indicates there will be no break with past transit or highway policy. Privatisation is therefore starting to be seen in a different light and is slowly attracting interest among transportation analysts as the only realistic hope for paring the huge inefficiencies that have developed in urban transportation under public management.

VI. BUILDING THE CASE FOR PRIVATISATION

Privatisation and deregulation could transform the US urban transportation system in the same way that deregulation has transformed US intercity transport. Starting in the mid-1970s, deregulation of the railroad, trucking and airline industries gave each the incentive and ability to become more efficient, innovative and responsive to customers, generating more than $50 billion in annual net benefits to consumers (Winston, 1998). Given deregulation's bipartisan political support, it is puzzling that privatisation conjures up ideological connotations among some policymakers instead of hope that it, combined with deregulation, can solve government failures. In fact, there is ample evidence that market forces in urban transit could accomplish a great deal of what public officials have been unable or unwilling to do. A conceptual case for privatising roads can be made, but it needs empirical analysis.

1. Urban Transit

It is true that the federal government got involved in urban transit during the 1960s because private transit failed. But Pashigian (1976) and Hilton (1985) provide evidence that private bus operations failed because they were weakened by government regulation. Meyer and Gomez-Ibanez (1981) point out that federal policy almost made it mandatory for cities to acquire their private transit companies instead of allowing them to raise fares to become more profitable. In response to those who claim that public transit's vehicle size and scale economies imply competition is unworkable in a private market, Walters (1982) argues that the extent of these economies indicates that public transit's operations are plagued by excess capacity. Such inefficiencies could be substantially eliminated in a private market where operators have the incentive and ability to improve their operations.

Just how would privatisation and deregulation reduce transit pricing and service inefficiencies? Winston and Shirley (1998) construct a model in which existing bus and rail companies are forced to compete with each other as well as automobiles and set prices and service frequency to maximise profits. They find that the effects of such competition are remarkably similar to the effects of marginal cost transit pricing and optimal service frequency. Society's gains from eliminating transit deficits—private carriers would earn profits—would substantially exceed travellers' losses from higher fares and reduced service.

These findings, however, greatly overstate the potential losses to travellers because they do not reflect the improvements in operations, marketing and service that could be achieved by private transit and the impact that new entrants would have on fares and service.

Deregulation of intercity transportation revealed that regulation had substantially raised carriers' costs and inhibited marketing and service innovations (Winston, 1998; Morrison and Winston, 1999). Given the freedom and incentive to use the latest technologies to improve routeing, scheduling and vehicle design, private transit companies could substantially raise load factors and improve productivity. Greater competition would put downward pressure on labour and capital costs. Such influences drove deregulated railroads', airlines' and truckers' real operating costs more than a third lower than they had been under regulation. It is likely that transit-operating costs would decline similarly if bus and rail companies were privatised.[29]

Under deregulation, airlines accelerated development of hub-and-spoke route structures to increase flight frequencies, railroads introduced double-stack trains and made greater use of intermodal (truck–rail) systems to improve service times, and truckers developed high-service megacarriers. Railroads and truckers also contracted with shippers for special services, such as expedited pick-up and delivery to facilitate just-in-time inventory policies. Similar service innovations by privatised bus and rail transit companies would also benefit travellers. Possibilities include new non-stop express van and bus services, specialised scheduled and non-scheduled van services, and door-to-door services.[30] Private bus and rail companies might also find it profitable to offer premium higher-fare service with seat and schedule guarantees. Transit service innovations could generate improvements in land use too, something rarely achieved by public transit (Pickrell, 1999).

These innovations go beyond what John R. Meyer characterises as 'transit's streetcar mentality'—scheduled stops by large buses or rail cars along a fixed route under all travel conditions. Transit operators, for example, might improve efficiency and service to travellers by providing looped express bus operations—turning some buses short instead of running all buses the full length of the route—and running minibus operations on the outer (lower-density) parts of the route (see Kerin, 1990). Indeed, as I discuss later, intensive minibus operations have been a beneficial outcome of British bus privatisation.

---

[29] Indianapolis is one of the few US cities that has privatised its transit system. Karlaftis and McCarthy (1999) estimate that, although the system is producing more vehicle- and passenger-miles, its operating costs have declined 2.5 per cent annually since privatisation. These savings are primarily efficiency gains, not transfers from transit labour.

[30] See, for example, Volpe National Transportation Systems Center (1998).

The deregulation experience has also shown that new market entrants, such as Southwest Airlines, often become the most efficient firms in a deregulated industry. In the transit industry, privatisation could lead to intense competition supplied by paratransit operations, such as jitneys, and other low-cost operations, such as minibuses. Competition among these new entrants and conventional bus, rail, taxi and auto modes would ensure that cost reductions would become fare reductions.[31]

Unlike airlines and trucks, railroads were deregulated because of their poor financial performance under regulation. It was expected that, in pursuit of greater profitability, the deregulated railroad industry would substantially reduce its operations, raise rates on much of its bulk freight and cede a lot of manufactured freight to truck. Railroads have indeed pruned their systems, but they have also become more efficient and responsive to customers—offering lower (contract) rates and better service. Thus instead of losing market share, deregulated railroads are actually carrying more freight, regaining market share and increasing their earnings. Depending on the behaviour of new entrants and what is done with the established transit authorities, there are numerous possibilities for how a privatised transit industry would supply peak and off-peak service.[32] None the less, the railroads' experience suggests that an efficient transformation of the transit industry's operations, technology, pricing and service could increase transit use and relieve taxpayers of subsidising transit's operations.

From a political perspective, deregulation succeeded because its benefits did not accrue to the rich at the expense of the poor. To be sure, some travellers and shippers benefited more than others, but the distribution of benefits generally had a rational economic basis. Public transit authorities have not aggressively pursued, let alone achieved, laudable social goals such as improving the urban mobility of the poor (Winston and Shirley, 1998). Thus a private system would not threaten to undermine any socially desirable income transfers. In fact, a private system may benefit low-income travellers because carriers would have the financial incentive and ability to develop a market for such customers. For example, Queens Van Plan, a private company, developed a highly valued and profitable service for low- to middle-income minority workers in New York's Queens and Nassau counties, who were largely neglected by public transit.[33]

---

[31] It would be desirable to deregulate taxis as part of a broader strategy to stimulate competition in urban transport. No longer enjoying a secure niche between the private car and the city bus or rail service, taxis would be forced, for example, to compete with vans that operate like taxis and offer links with rail and bus operations. The increased competition and co-ordination in the new urban transit system should lower taxi fares, improve service quality and enable taxi operations to impose some competitive pressure on transit.

[32] One strategy transit companies might pursue is to set capacity for off-peak periods and rely on part-time labour to develop peak capacity with extra scheduling and looping. Competition from private jitneys and other services with scheduled bus operations could be gradually introduced following the property rights approach developed by Klein et al. (1997).

[33] Hector Ricketts, 'Roadblocks made just for vans', *New York Times*, 22 November 1997, p. A15.

2. Roads

Public highways are characterised by pricing and design inefficiencies, inflated labour costs and expenditures on new construction and repair, and wasteful projects. Public authorities' delays in adopting technological innovations that could substantially improve the speed and safety of highway travel may also emerge as a large social cost.

At this point, the appeal of highway privatisation in US cities and intercity stretches is conceptual. Empirical evidence on its potential effects is not yet available. Thus I believe it is premature to recommend privatising US highways, but it is worth thinking about how market forces could reduce highway inefficiencies.

Let us begin with pricing. The conventional criticism of current road pricing is that it does not account for congestion. I have presented estimates of the benefits of congestion pricing in the US based on an average value of travellers' willingness to pay to save travel time. However, travellers differ, sometimes greatly, in how much they are willing to pay for transport capacity. For example, in airline travel, some business travellers are willing to pay the large costs that airlines incur for making seats available to them when they travel at the last moment. At the other extreme, some pleasure travellers make an effort to get low fares by planning their trips far in advance and being flexible about which day of the week they can travel. Other air travellers have preferences and constraints that fall between these extremes, and their fares are set accordingly. Thus by offering a range of fares and associated travel restrictions, the deregulated airline industry has greatly improved the use of its aircraft capacity and benefited travellers.

Some highway commuters are willing to pay a great deal to get to work much faster on a particular day, while others are not willing to pay much to speed up their trip. Highway capacity could be used more efficiently if motorists were offered a range of prices and service levels (e.g. travellers could choose among high-priced lanes with little congestion and lower-priced lanes with more congestion).

In fact, a few US highways have made a start in this direction by introducing value pricing. An example is the high-occupancy-toll (HOT) lanes on I-15 near San Diego, where solo drivers pay a toll to use less-congested car-pool lanes. By varying over the day, the toll more accurately reflects the value the road provides over alternate routes. But as pointed out by Small (2000), second-best pricing distortions may arise in highway travel because one or a few lanes are tolled but free alternate lanes and routes are close at hand. The efficient (first-best) policy would be to price all lanes (and alternate highways) in accordance with traffic conditions and travellers' willingness to pay to save travel time.

Could competition among highways develop and produce efficient tolls? New Zealand is considering a bold first step, called commercialisation, where the government turns its roads over to commercial road companies, which would be expected to charge for their use and earn a return on capital while being regulated as public utilities. Such a policy would be problematic in the US, where government regulation of public utilities is renowned for creating inefficiencies. Others have suggested that the US government franchise highways to private companies, although the devil would still be in the operating and financial constraints that the government placed on franchised companies and whether competition could evolve given these constraints.

Intercity deregulation offers a potentially useful analogy for solving this problem. Deregulated carriers have had to compete against each other, and in a certain sense against consumer 'organisations'. For example, railroads set most of their rates through contract negotiations with shippers. Among other factors, rates are affected by a shipper's traffic volume and competitive options. Shippers can improve their bargaining position by increasing their traffic volume as part of a group of firms that negotiates rates and by playing off one railroad against potential sources of competition. Such sources include other railroads in the market, other railroads reasonably close to the shipper, plants that compete with the shipper's plant in the product market, alternative origins from which the receiver could use alternative railroads to receive a product, alternative modes such as truck and barge, and so on. By enhancing their bargaining power, shippers can fully realise the benefits of rail-freight competition. Similarly, the benefits of airline competition are enhanced when travellers negotiate as a group to get lower fares or encourage a new entrant to provide service when they are dissatisfied with incumbent carriers.

Could highway users help road competition develop by organising as bargaining units that negotiate prices and service? Suppose the government distributes roads to commercial companies, as in commercialisation, but aims to allocate potentially competitive intercity stretches (e.g. California's Highway 101 and Interstate Route 5) and urban freeways and arterials to different companies. As in the railroad industry, a 'contract equilibrium' could develop where private companies negotiate prices (long-term contracts) with private organisations representing motorists, truckers, railroads, private transit companies and public sector transport. Public and private users *en masse* would therefore be able to bring competitive discipline on prices.

What would these prices look like? Customer groups would likely prefer a range of prices and levels of service. For example, Federal Express and other time-sensitive companies would want a lane (or even separate roads) to be available at a premium price, and time-sensitive automobile travellers would probably be willing to pay high tolls for travel on a less congested lane. It would take time for private road companies to explore various services that users were willing to pay for and for users' preferences to crystallise. But after that transition, the benefits could be large. Firms, and ultimately consumers, and households would gain from travel time savings. Out-of-pocket highway travel expenses would increase, especially for those who desire premium uncongested service, but price increases would be mitigated by, and taxpayers, in general, would benefit from, the lower cost of building, maintaining and operating highways.

Profit-seeking private road companies would have strong incentives to shed the inefficiencies developed over decades in the public sector. Cost-cutting measures would include using axle-weight truck taxes to charge for road damage, building stronger roads, placing much more control over construction and repair expenditures, reducing wages and managerial waste, and eliminating politically motivated projects.

Private road companies could improve the speed and safety of urban (and intercity) highway travel by implementing an intelligent transportation system (ITS). Such a system could include centrally controlled traffic signals, electronic toll collection, message signs about traffic conditions, and traffic control centres that, as needed, dispatch emergency vehicles, adjust signal timing and relay important road information to motorists. Under government management, the high-tech promises of this system could be compromised. One only has to think of the Federal Aviation Administration's management of air traffic control to understand how the US government would raise the cost and slow the implementation of ITS.[34]

The possibility of turning US roads over to private companies will seem less farfetched as the inefficiencies caused by the public sector increase and become more widely known. The best way to implement this experiment and estimates of its economic effects await further research.[35]

VII. THE BRITISH EXPERIENCE WITH URBAN TRANSPORT PRIVATISATION

Urban transport in the UK suffers from many of the same economic problems. Prices for all modes fall short of efficient prices (Peirson and Vickerman, 1998), urban bus and rail transit require large subsidies, road congestion is severe, and transit and highway infrastructure is in poor condition but funds are not available to finance required investments. Unlike the US, however, the UK has begun to address some of these problems by privatising and deregulating part of its urban transport system.

The Transport Acts of 1980 and 1985 largely privatised and deregulated the bus industry in the UK, with the exception of London and Northern Ireland. Although buses operating within London were not deregulated, individual routes were put out for competitive tender. Under the 1985 Act, public or private bus companies could offer virtually any bus service they deemed profitable by giving local authorities 42 days' (6 weeks') notice. The 70 subsidiaries of the National Bus Company, a nationalised entity, were sold and the other publicly managed bus companies that had dominated local bus service were reorganised as separate for-profit corporations. Many of these companies were subsequently sold to the

---

[34] Air traffic control has been criticised for decades for cost overruns and delays in introducing new technology that would make air travel safer and faster. Most recently, it has been under the gun for failing to introduce Global Positioning System (GPS) technology that could enable air carriers to choose speedier flight paths and to take off and land more quickly.

[35] Privatisation of roads could (and probably should) be introduced sequentially, beginning with bridges and bottleneck thoroughfares, and moving to entire highways.

private sector, while those that remained public could no longer receive direct government subsidies. Local authorities could supplement commercial routes by subsidising additional services that they felt were justified by social concerns, but these services had to be secured through competitive bidding.

The privatised UK bus industry has consolidated to a great extent and is currently dominated by large bus companies such as Stagecoach. None the less, the economic effects of the Transport Acts have been broadly consistent with the predictions of bus privatisation and deregulation in the US (Winston and Shirley, 1998). White (1997) found that improvements in labour productivity, lower wages and lower fuel and maintenance costs for minibuses—a major service innovation— reduced real bus operating costs. Kennedy (1995) found that competitive tendering for bus routes in London also lowered operating costs. As costs have fallen and fares have risen, the government has reduced bus subsidies from £237 million in 1985 to £117 million in 1998. Bus ridership has declined roughly a quarter, but in some areas of the country ridership has increased in response to intensive minibus operations.[36] Just three years after privatisation, minibuses providing local service outside of London have grown from a few hundred to nearly 7,000 (Gomez-Ibanez and Meyer, 1993). Minibuses operate at higher average speeds and offer greater frequencies than conventional buses, and their smaller sizes and manœuvrability allow some operators to offer 'hail-and-ride' service in which the minibus will stop at any point on the route to pick up and discharge passengers. White, Turner and Mbara (1992) estimate that travellers have benefited substantially from minibus services that have expanded into suburban areas.

The UK has not privatised inner-city rail operations, but in March 1998, Deputy Prime Minister John Prescott announced that the London Transport Group (now London Underground Limited) will award three private-sector contracts to maintain and modernise the London Underground. Successful bidders will be responsible for track, signals and stations, while trains will continue to operate within the public sector. The reform is expected to reduce rail infrastructure costs and the Underground's annual subsidy (now some £100 million). The economic effects of this policy will also depend on the rental charges that the public authority must pay the private companies to use the renewed facilities.

The UK has taken no steps to privatise roads, but in 1998 the government published *Breaking the Logjam,*[37] which proposed legislation to empower local authorities to 'charge drivers for using particular roads or roads in a specified area, and to levy a charge on workplace parking'. Although the object is to reduce congestion or traffic growth, Newbery and Santos (1999) point out that there has been little discussion of the principles that should guide these road charges. It appears that local authorities are primarily being encouraged to use them to help finance transport or land-use projects—a purpose that caused the California state legislature

---

[36] Bus ridership had been declining before privatisation. In light of this trend, one must be careful about attributing all of the recent decline in ridership to privatisation.

[37] Department of the Environment, Transport and the Regions, 1998.

to cancel one of the few congestion pricing demonstration projects ever proposed in the US.[38]

Budgetary pressures, rather than concern with allocative and technical inefficiencies created by the public sector, are motivating the UK's privatisation efforts in urban bus operations and rail infrastructure. From a US perspective, the UK experience is encouraging because it demonstrates that transit privatisation and deregulation can reduce costs and spur innovative services such as minibuses.[39] On the other hand, the US is not especially concerned with transit deficits, as indicated by the T21 legislation, which increases federal spending for transit (and highways). Thus it is not clear what will induce the US to pursue privatisation.

VIII. FINAL COMMENTS

Intercity deregulation in the US became politically attractive in the 1970s when the political benefits to policymakers from working in harness with carriers and labour were overwhelmed by the potential political gains from reducing inflation. When policymakers were ready to act, academic research was available to guide their understanding of the likely effects of deregulation.

Similarly, the probability of privatising urban transport in the US will increase if the prospect of major political gain becomes clear. Unfortunately, it won't in the near future because recent successes in eliminating budget deficits at all governmental levels have eased pressure to cut wasteful spending on urban transportation. None the less, researchers should continue to explore the effects of privatisation and provide guidance for how cities can conduct privatisation experiments. There is no escaping the evidence that the US government's activity in this area is marked by failure. Research should be available when the promise of political gains beckons policymakers to acknowledge this failure.

REFERENCES

Calfee, J. E. and Winston, C. (1998), 'The value of automobile travel time: implications for congestion policy', *Journal of Public Economics*, vol. 69, pp. 83–102.

—, — and Stempski, R. (forthcoming), 'Econometric issues in estimating consumer preferences from stated preference data: a case study of the value of automobile travel time', *Review of Economics and Statistics*, forthcoming.

Department of the Environment, Transport and the Regions (1998), *Breaking the Logjam: The Government's Consultation Paper on Fighting Traffic Congestion and Pollution through Road User and Workplace Parking Charges*, London.

[38] The newly elected Mayor of London, Ken Livingstone, has recently decided to charge motorists who wish to enter London's Inner Ring on weekdays between the hours of 7 a.m. and 7 p.m. A fee of £5 for cars is being seriously considered; fees would be higher for commercial vehicles. If this fee is charged, it is expected that traffic would fall 10 per cent and that the average speed would rise from 9 to 11 miles per hour.

[39] Gomez-Ibanez and Meyer (1993) support this conclusion based on the privatisation experience in several countries including the UK.

Downs, A. (1962), 'The law of peak-hour expressway congestion', *Traffic Quarterly*, vol. 16, p. 393.

Evans, D. (1994), 'Policy and pork: the use of pork barrel projects to build policy coalitions in the House of Representatives', *American Journal of Political Science*, vol. 38, pp. 894–917.

Gomez-Ibanez, J. A. and Meyer, J. R. (1993), *Going Private: The International Experience with Transport Privatization*, Washington, DC: Brookings Institution.

Hilton, G. W. (1985), 'The rise and fall of monopolized transit', in C. Lave (ed.), *Urban Transit: The Private Challenge in Public Transportation*, Cambridge, MA: Ballinger.

Johnson, R. N. and Libecap, G. D. (2000), 'Political processes and the common pool problem: the Federal Highway Trust Fund', University of Arizona, Department of Economics, Working Paper.

Karlaftis, M. and McCarthy, P. (1999), 'The effect of privatization on public transit costs', *Journal of Regulatory Economics*, vol. 16, pp. 27–43.

Kennedy, D. (1995), 'London bus tendering: the impact on costs', *International Review of Applied Economics*, vol. 9, pp. 305–17.

Kerin, P. D. (1990), 'Efficient transit management strategies and public policies: radial commuter arteries', Harvard University, Department of Economics, unpublished Ph.D. thesis.

Klein, D. B., Moore, A. T. and Reja, B. (1997), *Curb Rights: A Foundation for Free Enterprise in Urban Transit*, Washington, DC: Brookings Institution.

Lave, C. (1991), 'Measuring the decline in transit productivity in the US', *Transportation Planning and Technology*, vol. 15, pp. 115–24.

Lee, D. B. (1987), *Evaluation of Federal Transit Operating Subsidies*, Cambridge, MA: Transportation Systems Center, US Department of Transportation.

Meyer, J. R. and Gomez-Ibanez, J. A. (1981), *Autos, Transit, and Cities*, Cambridge, MA: Harvard University Press.

Morrison, S. A. and Winston, C. (1999), 'Regulatory reform of U.S. intercity transportation', in J. A. Gomez-Ibanez, W. B. Tye and C. Winston (eds), *Essays in Transportation Economics and Policy: A Handbook in Honor of John R. Meyer*, Washington, DC: Brookings Institution.

Newbery, D. M. and Santos, G. (1999), 'Road taxes, road user charges and earmarking', *Fiscal Studies*, vol. 20, pp. 103–32.

Pashigian, P. B. (1976), 'Consequences and causes of public ownership of urban transit facilities', *Journal of Political Economy*, vol. 84, pp. 1239–59.

Peirson, J. and Vickerman, R. (1998), 'The environment, efficient pricing, and investment in transport: a model and some results for the UK', in D. Banister (ed.), *Transport Policy and the Environment*, New York: E&FN Spon.

Peltzman, S. (1992), 'Voters as fiscal conservatives', *Quarterly Journal of Economics*, vol. 107, pp. 327–61.

Pickrell, D. H. (1985), 'Rising deficits and the uses of transit subsidies in the United States', *Journal of Transport Economics and Policy*, vol. 19, pp. 281–98.

— (1999), 'Transportation and land use', in J. A. Gomez-Ibanez, W. B. Tye and C. Winston (eds), *Essays in Transportation Economics and Policy: A Handbook in Honor of John R. Meyer*, Washington, DC: Brookings Institution.

Roth, G. (1996), *Roads in a Market Economy*, Aldershot: Avebury Technical.

Shmanske, S. (1996), 'The Bay Bridge blunder', *Regulation*, vol. 19, pp. 58–64.

Small, K. A. (2000), 'Pitfalls of road pricing demonstrations', UC Irvine, Department of Economics, Working Paper.

——, Winston, C. and Evans, C. A. (1989), *Road Work: A New Highway Pricing and Investment Policy*, Washington, DC: Brookings Institution.

Volpe National Transportation Systems Center (1998), *Autonomous Dial-a-Ride Transit*, Washington, DC: US Department of Transportation.

Walters, A. A. (1982), 'Externalities in urban buses', *Journal of Urban Economics*, vol. 11, pp. 60–72.

White, P. R. (1997), 'The experience of bus and coach deregulation in Britain and in other countries', *International Journal of Transport Economics*, vol. 24, pp. 35–52.

——, Turner, R. P. and Mbara, T. C. (1992), 'Cost benefit analysis of urban minibus operations', *Transportation*, vol. 19, pp. 59–74.

Winston, C. (1998), 'U.S. industry adjustment to economic deregulation', *Journal of Economic Perspectives*, vol. 12, pp. 89–110.

—— and Crandall, R. W. (1994), 'Explaining regulatory policy', *Brookings Papers on Economic Activity: Microeconomics*, pp. 1–49.

—— and Shirley, C. *Alternate Route: Toward Efficient Urban Transportation*, Washington, DC: Brookings Institution.

10

Public Financing of the Arts in England

ALAN PEACOCK[1]

I. INTRODUCTION

The justification for paying particular attention to public financing of the arts, including heritage and broadcasting, cannot be based on their relative significance in the public budget. This is soon apparent (cf. Section III) when it is realised that, by any acceptable definition, the arts represent less than 1.5 per cent of total government direct expenditure. Nevertheless, they have a high profile in public debates on the place of government in influencing the allocation of resources, which is also reflected in the amount of Parliamentary time devoted to them, particularly if the role of broadcasting in promoting cultural activities is included. Latterly, too, greater emphasis has been placed on the perceived economic benefits of the arts as a source of attraction to overseas tourists and of uncovenanted benefits to urban communities arising from development of cultural centres. This is demonstrated forcibly in the considerable percentage of Lottery money now devoted to capital spending on historical artefacts and refurbishment of theatres and cinemas and even to current expenditure on cultural goods. It is also recognised in our political structure by the promotion of the Minister responsible for the arts to Cabinet rank as from 1992.

It may be presumed that the framework for the study of this subject is similar to that found in the study of government subsidies to producers of goods and services. One would begin by identifying the relevant sector and the changing amount and composition of subsidy received from government, perhaps making comparison with other countries. The rationale of subsidy would then be discussed. The effects of subsidies would follow standard analysis duly incorporating recognition of the principal-agent problem that arises in government–industry relations. The analysis

[1] Sir Alan Peacock is the former Director (1985–91) of The David Hume Institute, Edinburgh and Honorary Professor of Public Finance at Heriot-Watt University. He owes a particular debt of gratitude to Stephen Creigh-Tyte for guidance through the maze of official reports on arts questions. He also wishes to thank Graham Berry, Paul Dwinfour, Andy Feist and Andrew Pinnock for helping to provide the data used in the statistical tables. Andrew Dilnot's perceptive comments as discussant have been taken into account. None of these persons bears any responsibility for the resultant text.

might then reveal policy issues, which would enable a judgment to be made on the suitability of the subsidy methods actually adopted.

That framework can be more or less adhered to, but the picture within it has to take account of a number of special features about the financing of the arts and of the economic analysis appropriate for the appraisal of cultural policies. Thus Section II devotes some space to identifying what is to be included in the arts and to unravelling the complicated skein of transactions between the central government and those bodies responsible for disbursing public funds. Such matters have an important bearing on the presentation of data on the amount and composition of funding and on attempted comparisons with funding in other countries (see Section III). Compared with, say, 20 years ago, public bodies are now called upon to produce reasoned arguments and not merely patrician effusions justifying their claims for funding, and economic analysis has begun to penetrate statements of their rationale. Welfare economics forms a convenient framework for presenting such statements and for summarising an important element in professional economics discussion of arts questions (see Section IV). With this descriptive and analytical background an attempt is made to appraise official attempts to achieve a satisfactory allocation of resources and efficiency in resource use, special attention being paid to the principal-agent problem in circumstances in which the agents are largely non-profit-making concerns (Sections V and VI). Three issues are selected for discussion of the future of public spending on the arts: the 'cost disease' and the performing arts; the controversy over heritage preservation; and public service broadcasting and the arts (Section VII). A final section (VIII) is an attempt to identify the major conclusions reached.

II. THE SCOPE OF EXPENDITURE ON THE ARTS

1. Definitional Problems

What is to be included in the arts? I avoid a direct answer to this question by presenting the 'stylised facts' of the recent history of the arts identified for subsidisation by government. At least since the Second World War, after the establishment of the Arts Council of Great Britain, well known as the brainchild of Keynes, it was accepted as the task of government to support cultural activities represented by the creative arts and their performance or presentation in the theatre, concert hall, opera house, museum or gallery and as heritage artefacts. Complementary to this support would be some investment in arts education, not only in order to continue the flow of creative artistic activity but also to encourage artistic appreciation. This approach embodied an important value judgment, namely that individuals would increase their welfare if they invested in knowledge which would 'improve their taste' and were encouraged to take seriously the professional views of *cognoscenti* in arriving at their purchasing decisions, for example, by reading reviews, attending lectures, by participation in amateur orchestras, play and painting groups, and as voluntary helpers in artistic ventures. The more idealistic supporters of this approach, Keynes included, envisaged that at some time in the future current funding could be gradually reduced as the change in individual tastes for the arts moved demand curves to the right.[2]

The aim of improving the quality of individual choices implied that the definition was too tightly drawn. There were soon complaints about the exclusion of popular art forms, not only because of their immediate appeal, but also as a point of entry for the appreciation of more demanding artistic presentations. The recent history of the evolution of government support could be written as the translation of 'the arts' into 'culture' with the latter term embracing a much wider range of 'products', of which the cinema, literature and crafts are the prime examples. The culmination of this process has been reached in the contemporary emphasis on 'social inclusion', that is to say the widening of the appeal of the arts not only through broadening the base of support to non-traditional art forms, including folk arts, action-type heritage displays, jazz and pop music, but by emphasis on active participation in art events.[3] In short, the definition of the arts is liable to frequent change and reflects the important role played by arts pressure groups attempting to influence the amount and composition of funding.

2. The Administrative Mechanism

The Department of Culture, Media and Sport (DCMS) is the principal source of central government funding of the Arts. It continues the tradition of 'arms length' organisation of support, by which funds are transferred to a range of disparate bodies with titles of differing degrees of grandeur from Commissions and Councils to mere Boards whose members are primarily those identified as arts *cognoscenti* who in turn are advised by experts in its various branches. The historical origins of these bodies resulted in a confusion of administrative command structure which involved several government departments as well as local authorities and private educational and cultural charities, but this has been simplified by bringing the major organisations responsible for the distribution of funds under the aegis of DCMS. The DCMS now makes Funding Agreements principally with Non-Departmental Public Bodies (NDPBS), in an endeavour to see that NDPBS plans conform with its general funding strategy and follow agreed methods of assessment of their efficiency and effectiveness. One interesting result is that the DCMS has control over something like 700 public appointments and makes what is probably the reasonable claim that selection is based mainly on merit and that the system is now more open and transparent. Whether that is an effective *modus operandi* is considered later (see Section V).

This system would appear to be simple enough if grants were made by DCMS to those directly concerned with producing arts services, but this is far from being the

---

[2] See Glasgow's (1975) fascinating account of working with Keynes on the foundation of the Arts Council.

[3] Particular emphasis is given to this aim by the then Secretary of State for the DCMS. See Chris Smith's Foreword to DCMS Annual Report, 1999.

Table 1. *Funding of arts and heritage*

Funding source	Funding body	Funding allocator	Principal clients
Treasury →	MoD →	MoD	Regimental Museums
→	DCMS →	DCMS →	National museums and galleries
Lottery (National Lottery Distribution Fund)		Arts Council →	Performing arts
		Crafts Council →	Decorative arts
		English Heritage →	Historic buildings and sites
		Film Institute →	Film production
		Museums and Galleries Commission	Non-state museums
		National Heritage Memorial Fund	Historic buildings and sites
Broadcasting Licence fee →	BBC →	BBC TV and Radio →	Drama and music (e.g. BBC orchestras)
Charges subscriptions →	National Trust →	National Trust →	Historic homes
Local taxation and charges →	Local governments →	Local government →	Local museums and galleries Local libraries

Notes: 1. Excludes central government grants to Local Authorities on which their cultural services may depend.
2. Excludes charges and subscriptions paid directly by the public to providers of arts and heritage services.

Source: Constructed from DCMS Annual Report, 1999.

case. National museums and galleries are directly funded, but bodies such as the Arts Council, the Museums and Galleries Commission and English Heritage themselves decide on the allocation of funds to arts clients. Some NPDBS receive considerable amounts of private funding whereas some private (normally non-profit-making) producers of arts services are highly dependent on public funding (Table 1). A schematic representation may give some idea of the complications of the administrative process. The inevitable result of these complications is that dissatisfied clients of NPDB who are disbursers of funds may adopt the practice of trying to subvert the authority of their funding supplier by various subterfuges, such as lobbying MPs, appealing directly to the Secretary of State of DCMS and public 'exposure' of what they regard as arbitrary action. They exploit their comparative advantage in articulate and persuasive rhetoric, and are often successful–the Covent Garden case comes to mind.[4]

[4] For illustrations, see my account of experiences as Chairman of the Scottish Arts Council and as a member of the Arts Council of Great Britain (1986–92)–Peacock (1993).

3. Finance

The DCMS is Exchequer-funded like other major government departments and the expenditure on the arts eventually emerges as direct current or capital grants and occasionally loans to (normally) artistic organisations usually registered as charitable corporations and therefore non-profit-making who employ artists, professional and administrative staff of all kinds. The precise legal form of such corporations differs but the fact that they are not normally profit-making has an important bearing on the motivation of those who control them and how their degree of discretion in using funds conforms or conflicts with the expressed desire of DCMS and other funding sources to achieve effectiveness and efficiency in their use. That is a matter for later discussion (see Section V).

The financing problem is complicated by the relative importance of government sources of finance other than that provided by DCMS. It is a moot point whether or not the BBC should be included in the enumerative definition of the arts, although clearly the DCMS regards it as 'a focal point for the identity and culture of the nation'.[5] The size of operation of the BBC crucially depends on the TV licence fee, a compulsory levy on TV sets, although latterly the BBC has generated a considerable amount of income from commercial activities. In 1997–98, the BBC's total income approached £2.5 billion with licence fee income representing just over £2 billion. Even if one maintained that only 15 per cent of this income represented support of artistic performances comparable with those included in our definition, at £375 million, this would add a large chunk to the total funding.

The National Lottery adds an even more complicated dimension. The funds available for distribution to 'good causes', including the arts, is a function of its popularity and certainly the current (2001) amount of about £4 million a day suggests that the lottery managers should shortly reach the agreed target. Sixteen per cent of the share of proceeds is earmarked for arts, sports, charities and national heritage. Originally funding was confined to capital projects on a co-funding basis but the present government extended the terms of reference to include current funding. The distributing bodies for the arts (including heritage) have been the Arts Councils and the Heritage Lottery Fund. The sums used or distributed by these bodies has become substantial.

Both of these methods of funding involve a direct financial link with the public, but that does not make these bodies any more responsive to the public's views on how the funds should be used as compared with representation to MPs or by direct lobbying. Whether a more direct link should be forged and how is another question worthy of further investigation.

One must also not forget the role of local authorities in promoting the arts. That this was perceived as important is demonstrated by post-war legislation which empowered local authorities to raise up to a 6d rate for the purpose of support of the arts, though this provision was abandoned in 1971. Although the Arts Council distributes funds to Regional Arts Boards, local authorities play a much more

---

[5] See DCMS (1999a, p. 172).

important role in a funding sense, provided that one is prepared to assign their library services to the category of expenditure on the arts. Many of them manage important art galleries and museums and library services are frequently one of the major items of expenditure. This may be observed in Table 2.

Finally, mention should be made of the alternative of tax relief as a government-supported method of helping the arts. Corporate sponsorship and donations can qualify for tax relief, though not applied to gifts in kind, and by the mid-90s represented about 10 per cent of arts sector income. A particular feature of this method was the Pairing scheme instituted in 1984 by which business support was matched by awards from Government. By 1994/95 the level of sponsorship raised by this means was £13.66 million of which 2/3rds came from business, but this total is a relatively low component of total business sponsorship, about 8 per cent. A naive view of recording support for the arts would entail adding proceedings from tax relief to the positive contributions by government, but this begs a number important questions about the impact of this tax relief and whether it would represent a net increase in arts funding corresponding to the recorded amount, not to speak of other effects that tax relief will entail if the lost revenue has to be made up by other tax adjustments or balanced by expenditure reductions elsewhere.[6]

4. Regulation

The influence of government on the arts is not confined to financial measures. Regulation offers an alternative way of making available historical artefacts for public enjoyment. The identification of buildings, monuments and sites of 'national importance' is carried out by the Royal Commission on Historical Monuments for England and Wales, covering both publicly and privately owned properties. By 1998 no fewer than 600,000 archaeological sites had been so identified with the aim, by 2003, of protecting 45,000 of them. Some half a million buildings are protected—buildings including anything from historic homes to walls and even early telephone boxes, though restrictions on their alteration or demolition, if rigorously enforced, cover something like 6 per cent of them. Moveable artefacts are covered by the Treasure Act 1996 which effectively nationalises discoveries of gold and silver relics leading to disputes over the compensation to be paid to discoverers. Exports of works of art require a licence from the DCMS as a means of checking whether efforts should be made to purchase them in the public interest before they disappear abroad.

The plethora of institutions and authorities concerned with arts provision by government is compounded by that very British institution, The National Trust for England and Wales. It is the largest British charity and largest English landowner, including in its patrimony 164 historic homes, 19 castles, making it a sizeable part of the heritage system. Although a private charitable corporation, the Trust made

---

[6] For a fuller discussion of these issues, see the report prepared for the Arts Council of England by London Economics (August 1997). See also Creigh-Tyte and Thomas (2001 ch. 15) and Selwood (2001).

a deal with government almost 100 years ago, with the passage of the National Trust Act of 1907, by which its properties became inalienable and therefore cannot be sold nor be acquired compulsorily by the State against the wishes of the Trust. In return the Trust holds its assets for the benefit of the Nation and not for its members. This arrangement has encouraged owners to donate properties in the expectation that they will be preserved and available for public enjoyment in perpetuity. It has also encouraged successive governments to give the Trust financial assistance or tax concessions over and above those normally available to charities.[7]

The final element in regulation of the arts is of growing importance—the government interest in the law of copyright which affects the returns of creative artists in respect of both the publication and performance of musical works and the sale of the products of artefacts. This is primarily the concern of the Department of Trade and Industry, but the DCMS has a particular interest in intellectual property of what it now describes as 'the creative industries'. It is closely involved in the discussions at national and international level with the determination of the scope of copyright material and how to protect it from the growth in piracy through CD and video recordings and the Internet. At the same time, these rights must be balanced against those who use copyright material, who can be at a disadvantage in bargaining with agencies collecting royalties.[8] An interesting illustration of the issues involved is to be found in the UK Government's dispute with some members of the EC who are pressing for a royalty right of resale which would entitle an artist and her heirs to a percentage of the price received when works are resold. It is claimed that artists would not benefit from this *droite de suite* because this right would be likely to reduce the price of original sale and that purchasers and art dealers would seek out markets in countries which do not recognise the right.[9] A compromise agreement seems likely to emerge.

III. PUBLIC FUNDING

The analysis of public funding of the arts in any meaningful way should start with the construction of a matrix in which the flow of funds between the suppliers, allocators, spenders and users of funds can be traced. This primary requirement cannot be met as the practical complications of data discovery, collection and interpretation are too great and recourse has to be made to more conventional presentations.[10] Worse still, while it is possible to illustrate trends in funding in a general way, using DCMS and Treasury data, this is barely possible in the case of other indicators of interest, such as international comparisons, so that one is left with point estimates.

---

[7] For an original and exhaustive discussion of the place of the Trust in heritage policy, see Sawers (1998).

[8] For further discussion, see MacQueen and Peacock (1995) and Towse (1997b).

[9] That this is a simplification of some very complicated issues is evident in the fascinating analysis of *droit de suite* in Solow (1998).

[10] Attempts by the author and Christine Godfrey to interest the then Central Statistical Office in presentation of cultural data only reached the stage of being allowed space in an early number of *Social Trends* (1973). I have tried to construct a matrix for the heritage sector, but the data are shaky (see Peacock, 1994). The compendious *The UK Cultural Sector* (Selwood, 2001) which appeared after this article was completed unfortunately does not tackle this problem.

Table 2. *Direct expenditure on the arts in England 1993/94 to 2001/02 (£ million)*

	1993/94	1995/96	1997/98	1999/00	2001/02
(1) Museums and galleries					
(a) Central government	221	219	205	220	246
(b) Local authorities	119	131	138	136	136
(2) Historic buildings	164	164	156	148	142
(3) Broadcasting and media	85	98	43	104	105
(4) Arts	235	200	196	230	253
(5) Libraries					
(a) National libraries	114	171	104	96	93
(b) Local govt. libraries	586	622	607	(658)	(658)
Total current expenditure	1524	1605	1449	1592	1633
(6) Capital expenditure					
(a) Arts Lottery Fund	–	–	73	(73)	(73)
(b) Local authorities					
(i) Museums & galleries	25	23	31	25	(25)
(ii) Libraries	29	25	30	24	(24)
(7) Total direct expenditure	1578	1653	1583	(1714)	(1753)
(8) 7 as % of direct expenditure of public authorities (DEPA)	1.02	1.07	1.11	–	–
(9) 7 as % of GDP (Eng)	0.48	0.47	0.49	–	–
(10) DEPA as % of GDP	38.9	36.9	34.0	–	–

Notes: (1) All figures are Cash Plans for relevant years.
(2) Broadcasting and Media: largely direct expenditure on Welsh Channel 4.
(3) Item 4. Arts is predominantly grant to the Arts Council of England and therefore for expenditure on performing Arts.
Source: DCMS Annual Reports (1999, 2000).
Public Expenditure Overview 1998/99.

Table 2 records the Cash Plans for the relevant NPDBs together with estimates of local government authorities' spending covering the period 1993/94 to 1998/99. It demonstrates the relative unimportance of expenditure on the arts within total government expenditure and as a percentage of England's GDP (cf. row 7 with rows 8 and 9). There is a small but perceptible rise in the relative position of the arts in later years, probably the result of lottery funding.[11] Expenditure in cash terms is

---

[11] It was feared that lottery funding would be used by the Government as a substitute for Exchequer funding—the so-called additionality issue. The matter was considered by the House of Commons Committee on Culture Media and Sport (1998) and the Treasury in evidence denied this. However, it is not known what the level of Exchequer Funding would otherwise have been in the absence of lottery funding so that the matter remains unresolved.

expected to rise in the immediate future, but this is not likely to represent a further relative increase. In any case, uncertainty attaches to the amount of lottery funding forthcoming and on the (as yet unknown) expenditure plans of local governments.

It is often alleged that arts spending per head in the UK is well below the standard expected in high-income countries. It is very difficult to offer precise evidence for this assertion. As Feist et al. (1998) show, in making international comparisons, definitional problems arise of the kind already referred to in Section II and point estimates only are possible. Table 3 shows that there are wide variations between countries both in respect of arts spending as a percentage of GDP and per head. This table can only be regarded as a useful point of departure for a full examination of funding methods which is beyond the scope of this paper, and contains the clear warning that public intervention cannot be measured in terms of expenditure data alone. Even confining attention to budgetary measures, the influence of tax relief measures, while having a tangible effect in the UK, is a major influence on art spending in the US.

One can measure the impact of public funding of the arts on those meant to benefit from them in a general way, but then only for recent years when NDPBS have been expected to develop sensible performance indicators (PIs). The problem of PIs is considered in detail in Section VI, but one can offer a general picture of the utilisation of arts expenditure through the use of data on audiences for performances and visitors to heritage sites.

Table 4 concentrates on the performing arts. The Arts Council of England imposes what is by international standards a rigorous test of financial targeting in expecting the performing arts organisations to raise about 50 per cent of their current income from sources other than grants from ACE and Local Authorities. In recent years, as Table 3 indicates, broadly speaking this target has been reached. In the case of Music and Drama companies in receipt of ACE grants, this target has been met by earned income (largely box-office receipts) alone, whereas dance companies have had to rely on generating a larger proportion from 'other receipts' such as donations and sponsorship in order to reach the target. Feist (1998) notes that in 1996/97, US and English orchestras raised about the same proportion of income from earned income (US: 59%; UK: 61%) but contributed income (donations, sponsorship, foundation income, etc.) represented 35% in the US and 9% in the UK, implying that public support in the US was negligible. In contrast, in the same year the German public theatres, which present a wide range of operas, plays, dance and concerts, derived only 13.8% of their income from earned income, practically nothing from central government funding and over 80% roughly equally divided between the *Länder* and *Gemeinden*. Another feature of Table 4 is the use of the crude general measure of audience numbers to illustrate utilisation of arts services. Along with virtually static direct state funding has appeared static and declining audience numbers, but the more striking feature is the relatively low ACE per capita grant for Drama and relatively high audience numbers which are over double those for Dance and Music. I have no supplementary data which would enable one to probe these differences in detail, but a reasonable guess is that the National

Table 3. *Direct expenditure on the arts and museums: selected countries*

	Australia	France	Germany	Ireland	Netherlands	Sweden	US	UK
Year	93/94	93	93	95	94	93/94	95	95/96
(1) Arts spending as % of Government final consumption spending	0.82	1.31	1.79	0.43	1.47	1.02	0.13	0.65 (0.74)
(2) Arts spending as % of GDP	0.14	0.26	0.36	0.07	0.21	0.29	0.02	0.14 (016)
(3) Arts spending per head (£)	16.4	37.8	56.5	5.6	30.3	37.5	3.8	16.0 (18.9)

Notes: (1) For detailed notes, see Feist et al. (1998).
(2) As it is difficult in individual countries to separate out capital spending, the data in brackets for the UK include capital spending.
(3) For problems in ensuring comparability, see text.

Source: Table 13.4, p. 166, *International data on public spending on the arts in eleven countries* by Andy Feist et al., Arts Council of England, Research Report No. 13, March 1998.

Table 4. *Public funding and utilisation of performing arts services (1994/95–1997/98)*

Art form	94/95	95/96	96/97	97/98
(1) Music				
Earned income	63.87 (48.8)	63.48 (49.2)	66.10 (50.3)	65.0 (47.0)
Government grants				
(a) ACE	44.88 (34.3)	45.57 (35.3)	46.13 (35.1)	54.0 (39.0)
(b) LG	6.50 (5.0)	6.38 (5.0)	7.10 (5.2)	6.6 (5.0)
Other income	15.53 (11.9)	13.55 (10.5)	12.27 (9.3)	11.7 (9.0)
Total	130.78 (100.0)	128.98 (100.0)	131.51 (100.0)	137.3 (100.0)
Audience nos. (Mns.)	2.53	2.59	2.63	2.81
ACE Grant p.c.	17.7	17.5	17.5	19.1
(II) Dance				
Earned income	21.09 (37.7)	19.91 (38.8)	19.02 (36.9)	21.5 (38.0)
Government grants				
(a) ACE	23.02 (43.5)	26.61 (47.7)	24.54 (47.6)	28.7 (51.0)
(b) LA	2.41 (4.5)	2.34 (4.5)	2.60 (5.1)	2.6 (5.0)
Other income	6.62 (11.5)	4.70 (9.7)	5.35 (10.4)	3.4 (6.0)
Total	53.14 (100.0)	51.56 (100.0)	51.52 (100.0)	57.2 (100.0)
Audience nos. (millions)	1.39	1.24	1.16	1.11
ACE grant p.c.	16.5	19.8	21.1	19.2
(III) Drama				
Earned income	77.60 (53.8)	71.83 (50.9)	72.16 (49.8)	66.7 (49.0)
Government grants				
(a) ACE	44.26 (30.7)	44.29 (31.4)	46.44 (32.0)	45.3 (34.0)
(b) LA	18.08 (12.6)	19.02 (13.50)	19.17 (13.2)	15.4 (11.0)
Other income	4.16 (2.9)	6.00 (4.2)	7.22 (5.0)	7.5 (6.0)
Total	144.10 (100.0)	141.14 (100.00)	144.99 (100.00)	134.9 (100.00)
Audience nos. (Mns.)	7.72	6.81	6.86	6.0
ACE grant p.c.	5.7	6.5	6.8	

Notes: (1) LA=Local authorities.
(2) Audience Numbers are for live performances only.

Source: Arts Council of Great Britain (until 1996/97) Annual Reports.
From 1997/98 Arts Council of England (ACE) Statistics Report No. 2.

Companies in receipt of 56% of ACE total funding in 1996/97 (see Table 6) are more heavily represented in Music and Dance than in Drama alongside non-national companies.

In Table 5, an attempt is made to provide similar data for English Heritage and a sample of the National Museums, Galleries and the British Library. Using the ratio of central government funding to total income as a PI, one notes that the ratio is higher than for the performing arts but that, with the exception of the British Library, the ratio falls through time. It has been deliberate policy to try to increase earned income, but future policy is complicated in the case of National Museums

Table 5. *Central government funding and utilisation of selected arts organisations
(1994/95–1999/00–1001/02: (estimates))*

	94/95	96/97	98/99	99/00	01/02
(I) British Museum					
(a) Grant-in-aid (£ million)	34.3	33.2	33.9	34.7	(34.9)
(b) as % of total income	73.3	72.2	73.4	75.6	(61.8)
(c) Visits (million)	6.44	6.5	5.50	5.00	(5.4)
(d) Grant per visitor (£s)	5.5	5.1	6.2	6.9	(6.5)
(II) Imperial War Museum					
(a) Grant-in-aid (£ million)	11.3	10.7	10.6	10.8	(11.3)
(b) as % of total income	55.6	44.5	40.6	35.0	(31.1)
(c) Visits (million)	1.27	1.30	1.4	1.35	(1.4)
(d) Grant per visitor (£s)	8.9	8.2	7.7	8.0	(8.1)
(III) Natural History Museum					
(a) Grant-in-aid (£ million)	27.6	27.5	27.0	29.6	(28.9)
(b) as % of total income	73.6	62.6	64.9	71.0	(72.1)
(c) Visits (million)	1.64	1.80	1.9	1.65	(1.65)
(d) Grant per visitor (£s)	16.8	15.2	14.5	17.9	(17.5)
(IV) Science Museum					
(a) Grant-in-aid (£ million)	21.9	20.6	20.3	24.6	(21.8)
(b) as % total income	77.9	65.6	42.8	49.9	(68.8)
(c) Visits (million)	2.51	2.54	2.20	2.70	(3.10)
(d) Grant per visitor (£s)	8.79	8.1	9.2	9.1	(7.0)
(V) British Library					
(a) Grant-in-aid (£ million)	80.4	84.3	81.5	80.8	(86.2)
(b) as % of total income	71.8	71.4	65.1	69.4	(71.0)
(c) Visits (million)	0.46	0.48	0.42	0.50	(0.54)
(d) Grant per visitor (£s)	174.0	177.5	193.6	161.6	(159.6)
(VI) English Heritage					
(a) Grant-in-aid (£ million)	104.5	107.6	102.4	114.1	(112.2)
(b) as % of total income	90.2	81.3	77.5	78.7	(78.3)
(c) Visits (million)	NA	9.8	11.0	11.2	(11.5)
(d) Grant per visitor (£s)	NA	11.0	9.3	10.3	(9.8)
(VII) National Gallery					
(a) Grant-in-aid (£ million)	18.2	18.7	18.7	19.2	(19.9)
(b) as % of total income	76.8	55.3	61.3	62.1	(69.6)
(c) Visits (Index)	100.0	114.0	109.0	110.0	(110.0)

Note: 1. Items in brackets are forward estimates.
2. National Gallery provides no estimates of annual number of visitors but only an index. An estimate of 'between 4 and 5 million visitors per annum is quoted' but estimate is not traceable in the Visits index. If 4 million is a reliable estimate for 1994/95, then the Grant per visitor could be estimated at £4.5 in that year.
Source: DCMS, Annual Reports, 1999–2000.

and Galleries by the abolition of admission charges. Again in recent years, using subsidy per visitor as a PI, individual institutions display remarkably little change even, in cash terms, but there are pronounced variations between them. While these data may be interesting in themselves, they must form the point of departure of wider penetration into the meaning and significance of PIs. To take one striking example, one can well imagine the Trustees of the British Library hitting its high roof at the very idea that its volume of output should be measured merely by reader visits unweighted by the number of documents consulted and without taking account of its obligations to act as a 'library of last resort' for all other libraries in the country.[12]

The issue of the distribution of the benefits of grant-in-aid is one of some political sensitivity because it is generally concluded from available data that there are pronounced inequities in the distribution of grant-in-aid according to social class and region.[13] Even if one accepts that placing subsidy per capita alongside distribution data is a very crude way of demonstrating the final incidence of subsidies and that possible 'spillover benefits' may be generated, calculations of the first impact of subsidies in this way show up differences which point towards the necessity for a careful analysis of the rationale of a subsidy policy which perpetuates them.

The Arts Council data provided on this issue reflects this sensitivity and only recently was it decided to publish data on its regional spending per capita. These data are displayed in Table 6. The data confirm the popular view that London benefits to a greater extent than any other region, even before account is taken of the location of the National Companies the expenditure on which is 'unallocated'. This makes the table a bit of a nonsense, given that their total grants represent 36 per cent of the total. At least the fiction of equality of benefits from such companies is not perpetuated by allocating their expenditure on an equal per capita basis per region.

More revealing would be a more comprehensive list of arts organisations covering the whole of the arts, as defined here, and which compared arts attendances by type of service with utilisation according to income group and social class. Table 7 is the best that can be done for a recent year, 1996/97.[14] It shows that the proportion of the adult population claiming to visit museums, galleries, and historic homes and to attend concerts, and stage performances which is compared with the expenditure per capita, so far as this can be identified. Historic homes turn out to be the most popular venue followed by museums, with opera and ballet at the other extreme. If the data on the utilisation by social class can still be accepted as a guide, then the least popular art forms, opera and ballet, not only receive much larger subsidies than others but are patronised largely by the AB social classes. Given the predilection of the present government to make the arts widely accessible, altering the balance of funding to reflect this, in the teeth of the understandable

---

[12] It has been claimed that the visitor numbers of museums and galleries which allow free admission cannot provide accurate checks. There is therefore a natural tendency to exaggerate them. [See Discussion following my Keynes Lecture to the British Academy (1994).] In the DCMS (1999), p. 106, no visitor numbers are given for individual years for The National Gallery, but only an index of growth is given. There is a mysterious bracketed observation that 'the number of visits is estimated to be between 4 and 5 million per annum'.

[13] For a thorough analysis of this issue and an examination of data which supports this conclusion for the early 1990s, see Towse (1994).

[14] See Feist (1998). The latest year for which there appears to be information on the proportion of social classes attending the various art forms is 1991, based on a survey commissioned by the Arts Council of Great Britain after some 'lobbying' by a few of its members, including the author—see Towse (1994).

Region	Total grants £ million	Total grants per capita			
		1998	1996/97	1995/96	1994/95
	(1)	(2)	(3)	(4)	(5)
Eastern	8.2	1.4	1.39	1.41	1.34
East Midlands	7.0	2.05	2.04	2.25	2.18
London	2.7	3.91	4.06	4.01	3.96
Northern	9.7	3.14	2.89	3.20	3.03
North West	16.4	2.53	2.49	2.42	2.49
Southern	10.9	2.30	2.19	2.26	2.05
South East	5.1	1.24	1.28	1.31	1.34
South West	8.7	2.24	2.31	2.37	2.29
West Midlands	10.5	1.97	1.90	1.95	1.88
Yorkshire &	12.8	2.54	2.54	2.70	2.17
Humberside	116.71	2.39	2.37	2.43	2.32
National companies	64.9	1.33	1.33	1.33	1.33
Totals	181.61	3.71	3.71	3.76	3.67

Notes: (1) Column (1) is the total direct spending in 1998 by the ACE in each region either directly or through the Regional Arts Boards.
(2) Columns (2)–(4) is the column (1) figure divided by the population in each region.
(3) The unallocated figure represents grants awarded in 1996/97 to the national companies (Royal Shakespeare Company, Royal Opera House, English National Opera, Royal National Theatre and the South Bank Board).
Source: Arts Council of England: Annual Reports.

Table 7. *Percentage of adult population claiming to attend arts events and museums and galleries (1996/97)*

	(i) %	(ii) Subsidy per capita (£s)
Historic Homes	33.0	9.8
Museums	32.0	8.1
Plays	24.1	6.8
Galleries	18.0	(8.2)
Classical Music	12.3	5.9
Opera	6.5	31.1
Ballet	6.5	21.13

Notes: 1. Historic Homes covers both public and private sector historical sites. The subsidy per capita only applies to English Heritage.
2. Galleries include national galleries and private galleries receiving subsidies, e.g. through the Museums and Galleries Commission. The subsidy per capita is bracketed as being an estimate based on data for national museums.
3. The subsidy p.c. is that provided only by central government.

Sources: Column (i) from Towse (1994), and ACE Annual Report (1998, p. 12). Column (ii) DCMS Annual Report 1999, ACE Statistical Report No. 2.

wishes of incumbent companies and institutions to defend their position, is bound to be difficult to achieve.

IV. THE RATIONALE FOR STATE SUPPORT OF THE ARTS[15]

The support that conventional welfare economics can offer for state funding of the arts turns out to be rather weak, but it does provide a familiar agenda for discussion. The main issue is whether instances of market failure can be identified that provide a rationale for the amount and form of public authorities' expenditure. The argument may be developed as follows.

(i) *Spillover benefits to other producers.* It is claimed that expenditure on performing arts benefits other producers through the creation of a cultural ambience attracting skilled factors of production and, as in the case of tourism, acts as a loss leader in attracting business from which other industries benefit (see DCMS, Annual Report 1998, p. 55–57). The claim assumes that such benefits cannot be captured other than by public subsidy. For the whole country such benefits must be largely pecuniary because any attempt to realise spillover effects by subsidy benefiting one area would require the reduction in incomes either by the extra taxation required or the reduction on other forms of government expenditure. Pushing the argument any further would require the introduction of interpersonal or interregional comparisons of utility. However, even if there were recognisable real benefits two further conditions would need to be fulfilled to justify state support. First of all, it would have to be demonstrated that extra inputs of cultural goods would be the most efficient way to produce the desired result; second, that beneficiaries would have no incentive to negotiate private agreements to support cultural loss leaders.

(ii) *Spillover benefits to consumers.* Here a distinction needs to be made between present generations and future generations. In the case of present generations, it is claimed that an option value attaches to the arts by which even those who never attend performances or visit museums and galleries derive satisfaction from the fact that others enjoy them, notably their friends and family, and from the prestige that the arts confer on their community or country (for a classic statement, see Robbins, 1963). This argument recurs with great frequency in official statements but amounts to special pleading for state subsidy. The resources to support the arts for this reason alone could be used to finance other activities that could produce the same result. The same argument could be used to support a whole range of options from space research to football teams. It will be noticed that interdependent utility functions have been introduced as a way of tracking spillover benefits to non-consumers of arts services. A more persuasive use of this familiar modification to welfare economics is found in the concern expressed for future generations who

---

[15] The argument in this section follows closely that developed in Peacock (1998). For a rather different approach concentrating on the measurement of market failure, see Creigh-Tyte and Stiven (2001) and Selwood (2001).

have no say in present decisions to preserve the arts (see, e.g. Baumol, 1987; Fullerton, 1991). I prefer an interpretation of this position which avers that present generations derive present utility from looking after the interests of their children and grandchildren. In other words, my welfare is affected by the expectation that future generations may disapprove of actions of mine which would deny them the enjoyment from preserved art forms. One should note, however, that the argument supposes that cultural resources which are destroyed cannot be re-created, but this only seems plausible in the case of historical artefacts. Even in this case, as with natural resources which are used up, new discoveries take place, and at present, as already observed, there are thousands of archaeological sites waiting examination. One has to adopt an extreme Ruskinian position to assert that all historical artefacts are unique and have an inalienable right to be preserved. Furthermore, there is no guarantee that future generations will approve of what we choose to preserve for them.

(iii) *Quality of choices.* Traditional welfare economics rests on the assumption that tastes and preferences are given. This neglects taking account of the fact that individuals derive utility from investing in knowledge of the goods and services available to them in order to improve their satisfaction, the arts being a prominent example of this process. That such investment should be encouraged must rest on a value judgment about the quality of choices. Libertarians might argue that taste formation should be regarded purely as a family responsibility in the case of minors leaving them in adult life to invest in self-education with a view to increasing their chances of individual enjoyment. However, those who claim that education provides spillover benefits to society will argue that cultural education is an integral part of the educational process and that inequality of access to education would imply that quality of choices would be impaired through under-investment. A more direct argument for cultural education is provided by Scitovsky (1983). The arts, he claims, can be presented in a form which rivals the excitement and danger associated with violent behaviour amongst the young. Teaching 'new consumption skills' which rely on artistic pursuits, might 'soothe the savage breast' and reduce the negative externalities by lowering the demand for the excitements associated with criminality. Certainly the sentiments expressed in such arguments frequently appear in official pronouncements. For example, recently the Davies Report in Annex 8 provides a lengthy examination of market failure in broadcasting in which is stated that '(t)elevision has the capacity either to restrict or expand knowledge, experience and imagination of individuals. If television is provided via the free market, there is a danger that consumers will under-invest in the development of their own tastes, experience and capacity to comprehend because it is only in retrospect that the benefits of such investment become apparent' (see DCMS, 1999c). As with the previous arguments, translating these arguments into a specific amount and form of public support is not usually attempted in their presentation and development.

(iv) *Trust the government rather than the market.* The maxim of freedom of choice must logically extend to choice over methods of choice themselves, and a variety of reasons may be given why individuals may prefer a political to a market solution in promotion of the arts. Individuals, while having different preferences scales may support community values which can only be given expression in some form of collective action, national heritage being quoted as an example (see particularly, Musgrave, 1987). Commercially operated theme parks may only partially fulfil any urge to derive utility from identification with the past. They are there to provide entertainment, often thereby creating a comfortable mythology, and have a very limited interest in preserving historical artefacts. Hence the proposition that government should support research designed to give a comprehensive account of our heritage and the public should assign to experts in art history, architecture and the like the task of selecting the artefacts that should be brought to their attention. The acceptance of this argument has wider implications which are examined below (see Section V) but the question of trust has been instanced as an important element in facilitating *voluntary* redistribution of cultural assets in order to make them more widely available to the public. Even the most ruthless captains of industry have been known to bequeath their historical artefacts to state museums and galleries and to the National Trust rather than to private institutions because it is considered that the former are more likely to abide by agreements to preserve and maintain them. (Of course the motive for bequests may lie in the utility derived from preserving the family's memory.) The Museums and Galleries Act 1992 does permit the National Gallery, the National Portrait Gallery and the Tate Gallery to overturn such agreements after 50 years, but this has caused bitter controversy (see, Goodison, 1997).

The merit goods position requires that choices are made by government appointees who presumably are expected to have superior knowledge of cultural benefits. These choices cannot be other than subjective, that is to say that at best they are well-informed value judgments.[16] The logic of consumer sovereignty therefore implies that consumers/taxpayers do not cease to be rational economic agents but will expect those who act on their behalf to be accountable to them through the political system. This is hardly a helpful conclusion for one is then forced to make a judgment as to whether the political system is sufficiently sensitive to operate in a way analogous to the competitive market. Rather than enter into an area embracing the more recondite areas of constitutional economics, it seems more sensible to take the political system as given and then to consider ways in which it might be modified to offer some prospect that consumer satisfaction is being taken as fully into account as possible.

While evidence has been presented here that those concerned with arts policy justify what they are doing with reference to welfare economics terminology, if only in incantatory form, forging a link between the public's preferences and the thrust of policy tends to be of a somewhat tenuous kind. The link tends to become stronger when arts organisations perceive that they are under threat because government

---

[16] For detailed consideration of this issue from the point of view of the art historian, see Gombrich (1979).

subsidies and/or direct receipts from the public are not considered sufficient to satisfy their aspirations. Indeed, whereas there is little demand for economists as devisers of optimal subsidy arrangements for the arts, there is a market for their services in a range of methods for measuring the degree of public support for existing programmes, a subject best treated below when methods of expenditure control are considered (see Section V).

A strong contrast can be observed between the forms of support suggested by welfare economics and those that actually exist. If reliance is placed on the doctrine of consumer sovereignty then this would appear to point towards the use of state financing, for example through a voucher system or tax relief, rather than state provision of arts ventures. Individuals would be encouraged to attend artistic events and to enjoy heritage services according to a pattern determined by themselves. This pattern will change according to their changing knowledge and appreciation of the arts. Bureaucratic interference in the production of arts services would be minimised, but companies would face more competition.[17] As already indicated, such a scenario has had little influence on methods of central and local government support. Heritage services, performing arts companies, state-funded museums and galleries provide services usually at well below cost and the difference is made up by direct production subsidies. The BBC receives a large part of its finance in the form of hypothecation of the licence fee.

The lack of correspondence between the prescriptions derived from welfare economics and the widespread intervention of governments in arts provision is the signal given to public choice economists, like the author, that attempts to rectify market failure may be frustrated by 'government failure'. It will at least be agreed that the amount and form of public expenditure on the arts in the UK will be characterised by discretionary behaviour on the part of government officials and the subsidised bodies. This fact is the basis of the argument that vested interests of producers are a dominant force in public management of the arts.

V. IMPLEMENTING POLICIES (1) THE ALLOCATION OF RESOURCES

Those wedded to a public choice approach to public expenditure on the arts in a normative sense would seek evidence for the degree of optimality in the allocation of resources in the extent of public participation in the decision-making process. It is for this reason that literature on cultural economics contains several major studies of methods for ensuring such participation, notably in countries where governments are obliged to respond to requests for referenda.[18]

Such pressures do not exist to anything like the same extent in our highly centralised democracy. The 'public interest' is decided by the elected government

---

[17] I have discussed this more fully with reference to the UK in Peacock (1993, ch. 3).
[18] Notably Switzerland where Frey and Pommerehne (1989) record that of 1,701 referenda conducted by Swiss municipalities between 1950 and 1983, no fewer than 108 concerned cultural matters.

whose degree of sensitivity to public opinion at any point in time depends on its perceived relationship between such opinion and its tenure of office. That relationship is a tenuous one in the case of arts expenditure both because of its relatively small size and the narrow range of classes that benefit directly from it. The exception is the BBC which, faced with growing competition, has increased considerably its efforts to detect a close connection between its programme making and consumer attitudes.

The present government is sensitive to the issue of public participation. In the case of DCMS, evidence of this is afforded by the large number of appointments to Quangoes which should take account of public attitudes. However, such persons are appointed to advise the Funded Bodies of the DCMS on the implementation of existing policies and not to formulate policies themselves. They are appointed and not elected by any constituency. They are not a cross-section of the public, nor is that claimed to be the case. The majority are recruited because of their knowledge of the art form in question, that is to say their interests are closely tied to those who receive public support. The strongest argument in favour of this approach derived from our previous discussion is that they can identify the appropriate 'merit goods' which the public should learn to enjoy, if they do not already.

Trustees of NDPBS are under no formal obligation to act as a sounding board for public opinion, which gives rise to the question how one might devise some forms of more direct public participation which does not depend on selection by DCMS. It would obviously be too complicated to devise constituencies of voters for so many different bodies as well as being very expensive to operate. However, several major arts organisations, notably The National Trust, English Heritage and large theatre, opera and orchestral companies, enlist subscribers as 'friends', but in few cases are they assigned seats on the Board of Management. Even with the National Trust, members have only limited powers in the election of the governing body. A case could therefore be made for insisting that publicly-funded (either by grants or by tax reliefs on covenanted income) institutions should give representation on the Board of Management to subscribers, the representatives being elected by the subscribers themselves. Of course, there could well be a tendency for subscribers to represent only a well-heeled minority, and that those willing to serve would be retired persons. However, this might be better than nothing at all, and at least compatible with other elements in a programme designed to combine public participation in and appreciation of artistic ventures. For example, those buying lottery tickets have no direct say in the allocation of National Lottery proceeds to 'good causes' and there is surely a case for polling punters so that preferences are taken much more fully into account.[19] It would be within the spirit of the lottery to allow punters to let their names go forward to serve for a fixed period on the Lottery Board and then to be chosen—by lot.

Of course, the general public do express their preferences for the arts through the box office in the performing arts and through charges made by museums, galleries

---

[19] How this might be done is briefly discussed in Peacock (1995).

and historical buildings and sites. As already observed, in the case of the performing arts alone, the grant-aided companies financed by the English Arts Council have in recent years raised just over 50 per cent of their current income form private sources (mainly box-office). The percentage for Museums and Galleries as Funded Bodies has been much lower and the dispersion in the percentage raised from admission fees and services much greater. The logic of subsidisation would suggest that the percentage of revenue provided in grant form should reflect the degree of market failure, but, apart from the formidable problems of calculation, neither the DCMS nor the Funded Bodies seem prepared to think in these terms. So far as the former is concerned, this can be explained by the emphasis in policy upon the expressed desire for 'the promotion of access for the many not just the few' (See DCMS, 1998, p.3), which adds an additional term to the 'social welfare function' alongside efficient allocation based on existing tastes and preferences. It is reflected in the recent scrapping of the entrance charges to publicly-funded museums and galleries. The NDPBS can readily accept financial arrangements which relieve the pressure on them to satisfy the general public by competing for their custom. This enables them more readily to achieve other objectives more congenial to their managers, such as the mounting of prestigious exhibitions, the pursuit of research interests which conform with the canons of their professional confrères and attendance at international conferences (see, Frey, 1994).

As an alternative approach to appraisal of the allocation of resources devoted to the arts is to judge the DCMS by identifying its 'utility function' and tracing its influence on the pattern of funding. There is little to add here to the exposition in Section III, except to say that the basic document describing aims and objects, *A New Cultural Framework*, was based on wide consultation to which the producer interests responded enthusiastically (see its appendix). Inevitably these aims and objects, as with many other major departments of government, are set out in very general terms with no clear idea of 'trade-offs' between 'the promotion of access for the many and not just the few', the pursuit of excellence and innovation' and 'the nurturing of educational opportunity'. This avoids the necessity of having to justify the precise pattern of funding and, indeed, although precise cash funding data are projected forward over a three-year planning period (subject to annual revision), it comes as no surprise to find that no attempt is made, nor the necessity recognised, to establish the nexus between objectives and the budget allocations to the various Funded Bodies.[20]

However, if the DCMS keeps its options open on funding allocations, and spends much of the space in the strategy document describing institutional changes rather than policy desiderata, it commendably emphasises the importance of improving the flow of information and the use of appraisal methods which are designed to guarantee that 'DCMS ties its expenditure to its objectives' and that 'public money is being used appropriately to meet public objectives'. These represent major and necessary changes in an area of public expenditure where there are particularly

---

[20] That this is a longstanding problem is evident in its first critical analysis by King and Blaug (1976).

difficult problems in achieving efficiency. These call for separate and extended treatment in the following section.

VI. IMPLEMENTING POLICIES (2) EFFICIENCY IN SPENDING

In common with other Government Departments, DCMS is subject to a series of expenditure controls which appear to be rigorous and effective. However, each department has its own particular difficulties in applying these controls and DCMS is no exception.

Consider first of all the standard controls:

- As the use of data and information already presented indicate, expenditure plans for the arts covered by the Funded Bodies of DCMS are set out in considerable detail within the framework of the annual Public Expenditure Reviews and are submitted in the normal way for Parliamentary approval. In the author's opinion the Annual Reports of the DCMS which convey this information and data to the public are very satisfactory.

- There has been a growing insistence on the presentation of Corporate Plans by both Executive Agencies such as English Heritage and national museums and galleries.[21] These have to include performance indicators. Evidence of this is to be found in the extraordinary case of the British Museum. The Edwards Report on the Museum (see Edwards, 1996), noted, alongside some trenchant criticism of its management, that until 1996 the British Museum published neither an annual report not a corporate plan. The bringing together of the Funded Bodies under the aegis of the DCMS has changed all that and now it must provide both. However, how such targets and indicators are chosen, who is to approve them and whether they are sensible in themselves is a separate, important matter and merits much further discussion (see below).

- The DCMS co-operates fully in the promotion of Treasury 'best practice' methods in economic appraisal of major investment projects and in minimising input costs through the use of competitive tendering. Cost benefit analysis (CBA) is extensively used, particularly in preservation and restoration work of historic buildings, but presents difficult problems in application, notably in the evaluation of benefits. Many heritage projects are justified in terms of intangible benefits, including those accruing to future generations, and where benefits to individuals are traceable, the price charged (in many cases zero) may not reflect these benefits. This accounts for the proliferation of evaluation procedures based on 'willingness-to-pay', notably the use of contingent valuation (CV). CV has been highlighted as of particular importance in the case of evaluating the contribution of historical artefacts to welfare because individuals in being asked to state the maximum that they are willing to pay to preserve some historical

---

[21] For comprehensive and highly detailed recommendations for managerial control, see DCMS (1999b).

object it seems possible to capture estimates of its so-called 'non-use value' (for further discussion, see Portney, 1994). Individuals can then express any benefits that they derive from option demand and bequest values (see Section III). The strong support for this method by architects and surveyors and by such bodies as English Heritage (see Allison et al., 1996) is in contrast to the criticisms of its methodology as highlighted in the example given later in this section. Nevertheless, the growing acceptance of sensible methods of appraisal is a notable development, although it is one thing to detect agreement amongst economic analysts on procedures and another to ensure their acceptance by those affected by the conclusions, upon whom access to information may depend.

• The accounts of the Funded Bodies are open to inspection to the National Audit Commission who may not only comment on their findings but also undertake *ad hoc* studies of the efficiency of their operations. These reports are meat and drink to the House of Commons Committee on Culture, Media and Sport which can summon the Chairs of such Bodies and their officials to explain and justify their actions. This Committee under the Chairmanship of Gerald Kaufman has been noticeably active, a striking example being their strong criticism of the financial administration of the Royal Opera at Covent Garden. In addition the Committee on Public Accounts has the specific task of reporting to Parliament on 'value for money' matters and has revealed that at present it has no access to the BBC in order to ascertain how it uses the licence fee. The Davies Committee has accepted this point and recommended that the National Audit Office should have access to the BBC's accounts, requiring an amendment to its Royal Charter.[22]

The above controls are clearly a necessary part of any planning and monitoring process designed to ensure that budgeting is properly carried out, but expenditure policy assumes that an attempt is being made to keep the costs of 'output' of arts services to a minimum. However, the opportunities for discretionary behaviour open to arts organisations present a major problem in fulfilling this condition.

This problem can be illustrated in a number of ways. A useful starting point is the analysis of the effects of an output subsidy on a single firm, which has been used to establish the proposition that a per unit of output subsidy will increase output in the case of both a profit-making firm and non-profit-making firm, with identical production functions, but, for a given amount of subsidy, more output will be achieved by the latter. This is because the profit-making firm will only increase output to the extent that it maximises profits. If the policy objective is to minimise the amount of subsidy to produce a given output, then subsidy should only be given to the non-profit-making firm. This has been used as an argument for discriminating in favour of arts organisations which are registered as charities (for further analysis, see Throsby and Withers, 1979; West, 1987; and comment by Peacock, 1998). Those who have advanced this argument are well aware that any approximation to reality involves further investigation of the relationship between the funding body and the

---

[22] The BBC has accepted the need for improved transparency and accountability but argues that this can be achieved without extending the remit of the NAO. See BBC (1999) response to the Davies Report.

firm. Unless that body can conduct some franchising arrangement which induces competitive tenders which reveal costs, a classic principal-agent situation arises with asymmetric information. That situation is no longer one of constrained maximisation by the firm but of bargaining. Well-established National arts institutions are clearly in this position, though it is conceivable that a bidding process of the kind applied in the case of operation of the National Lottery could be applied to the management of museums and galleries. Nevertheless, the DCMS would still have to rely on the 'firm' itself for information on its costs and close scrutiny of such costs is in itself a costly procedure. As West (1987) has put it, there is an 'implicit assumption of zero interdependence between the granting of the subsidy and reported costs'. There is therefore no guarantee that the response to a unit subsidy would be a movement along a minimum marginal cost curve, for the opportunity exists to accumulate rents by disguising them as costs. Of course, any such suggestion would be strongly denied by the subsidised firm. The case is usually associated with situations where there is a proposal to limit costs in which case it is invariably claimed that any reduction in subsidy will lower the quality of output. This is certainly the argument used by the BBC in questioning the tying of the licence fee to a consumer price index (see DCMS, 1999c passim).

The drawing up of a contract faces the further difficulty that in the case of NDPBS, they present themselves as multi-product firms whose 'outputs' are difficult to define. The convention has developed that PIs should be used to monitor their activities. Whereas in a profit-making enterprise, the assessment of the value of each product will be based on the relation between marginal cost and marginal revenue (subject to constraints reflecting objectives other than profit maximisation), the perceived importance of externalities in the case of the arts and the limited use of prices as indicators of consumer satisfaction means that trade-offs require the institution of some weighting system. Moreover, the implicit acceptance by the DCMS of the merit-goods argument means that performance indicators should reflect the preferences of the *cognoscenti* who advise it and not simply the satisfaction derived directly from NDPBS services enjoyed by the public. In short, the choice of performance indicators and their relative weighting reflects an interesting bargaining process between the DCMS and individual NDPBSs.[23] That considerable progress has been made in gaining acceptance of PIs is evident in the presentation of PIs for the directly funded NDPBSs in the most recent DCMS Annual Reports, which cover targets as well as reveal past trends (see e.g. Section II, DCMS Annual Report, 1999a).

It is beyond the scope of this chapter to offer a detailed critique of the PI system, but some brief conclusions can be drawn from the published data:

- The general method for measuring consumer demand is to index the number of visits by individuals or organised parties. It has been claimed that these data tend to

---

[23] Hence the considerable (and respectful) attention given to expert advice in the Deloitte and Touche Report (see footnote 21) on inventory management, storage and security of collections, though, significantly enough, without reference to budget constraints. The study arrives at conclusions about 'best practice' by what is described as 'iterative consultations' with National Museums and Galleries.

be exaggerated in the case of NDPBSs that do not charge for admittance (see footnote 11). It is noteworthy that those NDPBSs that charge for admission follow up with records of 'visitor satisfaction' which refine the crudity of the basic measure.

- Trade-offs are not recorded and there would be in any case some difficulty in knowing how to trade-off those PIs that, broadly speaking, refer to consumer satisfaction and those that record movements in inputs. The British Museum, for example, has adopted the conventional PI of number of visits per annum, actual and projected forward to 2001/02 along with a PI recording the number of 'objects loaned' and 'percentage of storage areas which are satisfactory'. Similarly the National Gallery offered 'No. of rooms refurbished since 1987' alongside an index of number of visits. In the case of the last-named PI, the number of visits could only be estimated (see footnote 11).
- PIs which purport to display movements in output are not by themselves measures of efficiency. As a minimum one requires data of inputs per unit of output, and a reasonable degree of homogeneity in the units of each measure. For example, the National Portrait Gallery entry in the DCMS Annual Reports tracks the Annual Grant-in-Aid per Visitor which is fairly constant through time (1993/94 to 2001/02(est.)), but this is an exception at this level of presentation of information. Several NDPBSs emphasise their attempts to improve the percentage of revenue raised from sources independent of government as a measure of efficiency.

It would be easy to conclude that the bargaining process regarding the choice of PIs makes it difficult to believe that the DCMS is able to minimise discretionary behaviour amongst NDPBSs. In particular, any attempt to measure *comparative* efficiency must be frustrated by the free-for-all manifested in the choice of PIs. Nevertheless, anyone who, like the author, can look back 30 years or so, is bound to admit that the information flow from arts organisations funded by government has improved beyond recognition.

VII. THE FUTURE OF PUBLIC SPENDING ON THE ARTS

1. The Performing Arts

One of the most influential propositions concerning the performing arts emanates from the identification of a 'cost disease' which is alleged to be endemic in the performing arts from which the conclusion has been drawn that their long-term survival depends on ever-growing amounts of public subsidy. The *locus classicus* of this proposition is the pioneer work of Baumol and Bowen (1966) which appeared in 1965.[24]

The 'disease' is 'caught' because personal services are an integral part of the provision of output and this limits the introduction of technology associated with changes in the input-mix which could improve the productivity of labour. No offsetting reduction in the relative cost of labour is possible because competition in

---

[24] For a full account of their work and Baumol's subsequent development of it, see Towse, 1997a.

labour markets offers alternative opportunities, in the longer run, for those with the capacity to become performing artists. It follows that as an economy grows and real wages increase, increases in costs in manufacturing output, where technological innovation can take place, are offset by increases in productivity per head through process innovation, whereas relative costs will rise in the 'unproductive' performing arts sector. Of course, if the income elasticity of demand for performing arts rises, the orchestras, theatre and opera companies may be able to survive, but even this assumption has been questioned by the introduction of the 'Linder effect' (see Linder, 1970). This requires that, as the economy grows and output per head rises, the price of time rises, implying that there is an offsetting reduction in demand for those goods and services where time is an important input, such as the performing arts. A favourite example of Baumol is the Purcell opera *Dido and Aeneas* which requires as many singers and orchestral performers to produce the same product today as in 1680 when it first appeared. One might add that the time input cannot be reduced by performing it at twice the speed, for that would destroy the product.

Baumol and his collaborators (see Towse, 1997a) have always been careful not to state a position on the question of public subsidy. Moreover, they have taken on themselves the responsibility of testing their propositions by detailed statistical enquiry and have offered a doughty defence against criticisms. Nevertheless, the identification of the 'Baumol Disease' has from time to time offered a heaven-sent opportunity for performing arts companies to demand progressive increases in subsidy, notably in the 1970s when the acceleration in the rate of inflation lead them to draw the inference that cost inflation was having an unfavourable differential effect on the performing arts (see Evidence before the House of Commons Education, Science and Arts Committee, 29 June 1981, HMSO, London). The Arts Council of Great Britain sought and expected detailed confirmation of this assertion in the report on *Inflation and the Performed Arts* which the author was asked to undertake together with Shoesmith and Milner (see Peacock et al., 1983). To their obvious disappointment, the report offered no evidence of a Baumol effect on the cost side. Unfortunately the Arts Council did not learn from this experience and conveyed the impression in later economic studies commissioned by them that they expected economists to act as hired guns (for further observations on this matter, cf. Peacock 1993). Nevertheless, this is not to dismiss the Baumol disease as a health scare, and there are aspects of the Baumol thesis that shed an important light on future relations between the performing arts and state funding authorities.

The question to be asked is why the large majority of the major performing arts companies have survived over the last four decades. Baumol's hypothesis emphasises the limited possibilities of substituting capital embodying new technologies for labour, but does not preclude reductions in the magnitude of *total inputs* without altering the relative factor proportions consistent with the attraction of the end-product. The commercial theatre has survived because new plays and shows are demanded by the public and this offers the opportunity of diminishing the size of casts down to the ultimate stage of the one-person show (for elaboration of this argument, see Peacock et al., 1983, pp. 43,44). The problem with orchestras and operas is the relative inflexibility in the repertoire caused by the preferences of audiences for 19th-century music, which requires large forces which cannot be reduced in size without a perceived fall in the quality of performance.

The Arts Councils have been placed in a dilemma by the perceived difficulties of factor substitution and the inflexibility of the repertoire. For many years they have sought to persuade the nine London and regional orchestras in receipt of grant to raise about half their income from box office and engagements. However, rising relative costs of labour illustrating the Baumol effect have resulted in periodic accumulation of large deficits reducing some regional orchestras to a position of near-bankruptcy, despite determined efforts by some of them to survive by 'down-market' concerts of popular music, including jazz and rock, and by seeking record-ings and broadcasting engagements in what has become a highly competitive market. While the Arts Councils tended in the past to adopt a Micawber-like strat-egy of waiting for funding to turn up as a result of public protests at orchestral 'under-funding', and then to bale out orchestras at the eleventh hour, the stark realities of projected funding have forced them to recognise that radical changes may be needed in orchestral management, and of the sort which the author advo-cated nearly 30 years ago (see, Arts Council of Great Britain, 1970 ('Peacock' Report)). It was announced in October 1999 that in return for wiping the deficit slate clean and providing a 'sound' financial footing for all orchestras, they would have to introduce much more flexible contracting arrangement with players which would increase the prospects of tackling a more extensive repertoire and to increase efforts at educational work (see Press Report, Arts Council of England, 13 October 1999). But, in keeping with a long tradition, the required changes will only be instituted by negotiation and agreement. It will be interesting to observe whether Baumol's disease can at least be controlled by these radical therapies, assuming that they are put into effect.

2. 'Sustainable' Heritage

A problem of growing concern in funding the arts must be having to square the growth in official inventories of heritage artefacts, whether moveable or immove-able, designed to identify what is worth preserving and restoring with the resources likely to be available to do so. These inventories are compiled largely on the advice of art historians and archaeologists (see Benhamou, 1998, comparing Britain and France) whose approach is nothing if not thorough. Their listings of everything from pebbles to palaces has a parallel with that adopted by environmentalists con-cerned about the possible demise of every species of beetle.

The practical purpose of these inventories must be to establish where the cut-off point is to be placed between what is to be preserved and restored and what is not, at least in respect of public funding. Co-operation to establish this point is under-standably difficult to obtain. First, there is bound to be professional disagreement about orders of priority as between buildings and moveable artefacts, between historical periods, and between art forms. This encourages a refusal to recognise the existence of an opportunity cost problem with respect to alternative ways of supporting the arts. The less resource constraints are brought into the argument, the less need to reveal these disagreements which undermine the authority of the arbiters of taste. Second, arbiters of taste are not only advisers to DCMS, as members of the various quangoes under its umbrella, but are frequently managers of the various outlets for public presentation of heritage. Not being answerable to the general public through having to 'sell' their product, they have a comparative advantage in making their case for moving the cut-off point as far down the list as possible, with the extreme position taken by those who appear to believe that all identifiable artefacts have an inalienable right to preservation. Third, the funding conventions make it much easier for managers-cum-experts to maximise a personal welfare function in which reputation with one's peer group is an important argument—as with university professors. This is because not only the additions to the heritage stock but also the stock itself fall within their control.

This is not to question the integrity of managers who may reasonably claim that reputation with their peer group ensures the standards of heritage preservation which promote the public interest and which they believe that the public, with their guidance, can learn to appreciate as merit wants. However, it leads to some questionable practices. The first is implicitly to reject the possibility that the public will ever move away from being passive adjusters to heritage services to becoming knowledgeable enough to demand a direct say in what is presented to them. The second is the refusal to accept that the non-material values that dominate their choice of artefacts to be acquired must be conditioned by the material base that supports them. Acquisitions must be allowed to accumulate indefinitely even if it means, as is commonly found, that the ratio of artefacts on display to the total stock reaches 1 : 4. (see Frey, 1994.) If this is rationalised by the proposition that this reflects the proper balance between what the public is to enjoy and what represents archival material for scholarly research, then an important issue of cultural policy is revealed. Third, these very research interests are not necessarily even closely related to the objective of preserving national heritage. A large part of our National Collections maintained at public expense consist of paintings, sculptures, etc. of a large variety of European Schools, and certainly have an educative value but it is a moot point whether heritage funds should be used to acquire them. Moreover, the major National Galleries are becoming vast storehouses of lesser-known paintings and other artefacts which no doubt cater for the more esoteric interests of scholars chasing new lines of artistic enquiry, but do not necessarily add to the enjoyment and understanding of those who have to provide the resources to maintain them.

A situation where the growth in the historical artefacts designed to reflect heritage policy will depend on such uncertainties as the artistic fashions, the state of the weather and the incidence of private sales of 'masterpieces' in dealers' catalogues cannot be sustained for much longer. There are already indications of this in the debate now centred on whether museums and galleries should be allowed to 'de-accession' artefacts with the proviso that the proceeds of sale should be used to alter the balance in the 'portfolio' of artefacts to reflect policy guidelines (for an account of this debate, see Elliot, 1998). The prediction may be hazarded that those guidelines will soon have to move towards the articulation of a 'sustainable heritage' offering an interesting parallel to attempts to devise a 'sustainable' natural environment (for further discussion see Getty Conservation Institute, 1998; Throsby, 1997; Peacock, 1997).

3. Broadcasting and the Arts

In the course of two decades, the standard arguments for vertical integration of broadcasting production, the restriction of access to broadcasting services, and the limitations on charging directly for such services have had to undergo drastic modification. Confining discussion to the influence of technological progress alone, spectrum scarcity has disappeared, modes of delivery of TV signals are no longer confined to terrestial transmission and charging systems such as subscription and pay-per-view even permit the exercise of active choice by viewers and listeners through two-way transmission, for example, in choosing between alternative programmes offered by one channel, and through the personal re-scheduling of programmes by the use of the VCR. If the purpose of broadcasting is to satisfy the tastes and preferences of viewers and listeners, then familiar economic analysis would offer workable competition as the appropriate policy model, and this seems achievable. However, this model would not preclude government intervention, where possible, to prevent anti-competitive practices, to exercise censorship to the degree sanctioned by public opinion, and to offer public funding for cultural and educational projects supported by 'market failure' arguments (for a rehearsal of these arguments, see Home Office, 1986 (Peacock Report) and DCMS, 1999c, (Davies Report) *passim*).

Changes in public policy over the last 15 years indicate the degree to which successive governments have had to accept the 'consumer sovereignty scenario'. The result has been that attention has now to be focused on defining the role of the government in influencing the content of programming which, in this context, means the use of broadcasting as a medium for improving access to the arts. A major part of the BBC's case for seeking a supplement to its licence fee for the development of digital services is based on its role 'to improve access to **British culture and creativity**, particularly for the many who can afford neither pay-per-view nor even ticket prices' (bold type in original).[25] Taking this assertion at its face value, one can certainly make a strong case for the BBC as having a leading role in encouraging private investment in cultural goods, not only through the stimulus of arts programmes as such but also in drawing attention to artistic events in general, including live productions in particular.[26] However, our general argument would

[25] See BBC's Response to the DCMS on the Davies Committee Report (1999).
[26] This ignores the interminable argument about whether TV productions are substitutes to or complements of live ones.

not support a case for assigning public funding to the exclusive use of the BBC. As it is, independent TV companies only receive their franchises on the assumption that they continue to produce public service programmes. The BBC may be right in assuming that the commercial sector will be forced 'downmarket' because of intense competition, but this does not make the case for conferring a cultural monopoly on the BBC buttressed by the licence fee. No such monopoly is assured in the case of the live arts, where competition between companies and between museums and galleries could be regarded as an important stimulus to creativity. A consistent policy in the field of broadcasting suggests that independent companies should be able to compete with the BBC for government funding for public service programming of this nature, and indeed for public service programming in general. If the licence fee were used for this purpose, this would entail the privatisation of the BBC, though not necessarily its transformation into a purely commercial concern.[27] The likelihood that logic will govern the future of provision for public service broadcasting can certainly not be taken for granted, and the BBC will remain a protected species at least until the review of its Charter in 2005.[28]

VIII. CONCLUSION

Government expenditure on the arts, including heritage and cultural programme in broadcasting, is 'peanuts' alongside the vast 'empires' of expenditure represented by defence, law and order, health, and education, but it may fairly be claimed that 'DCMS and its sponsored bodies have more to do with people's enjoyment of life than any other Government department' (DCMS, 1999 p. 4). It is therefore not altogether surprising to find that the DCMS in collaboration with other Government Departments and The Treasury influences the arts and heritage through instruments other than public funding, notably through tax concessions, regulation of conservation and disposal of historical artefacts, and copyright law (cf. Section II). The relative importance of this mix of measures will vary from time to time and from country to country, making international comparisons of government support for the arts very difficult indeed (cf. Section III).

A second feature of this study is the attention drawn to the analytics of cultural economics, which has only recently risen to the heights of separate classification (Z) in the bibliography of *The Journal of Economic Literature*. As a study of the provision of services, the economic analysis employed can be familiar, but there are two distinctive features in its use. The first is the emphasis placed on the dynamics of the preference structure which derives from investment in enjoyment of the arts and which implies that improving the quality of choices should be matters of public

---

[27] I admit that this is a 'plug' for the long-term recommendations of the Home Office *Report of the Committee on the Financing of the BBC* which was chaired by the author.

[28] For an enthusiastic defence of the BBC's traditional role as a public service broadcaster, see Thomson (2000) in the symposium *The Future of Broadcasting* (ed. Peacock, 2000). Other points of view are expressed in the same symposium by David Elstein and David Sawyers.

concern (see Section IV). This is not an issue that can be handled very readily in traditional welfare economics. The second is that cultural economics adds an interesting dimension to the development of principal-agent and bargaining models because it is concerned with the interface between the funding bodies and arts organisations which are typically non-profit-making (see particularly Section VI).

A final feature concerns the particular difficulties that a Department such as DCMS faces in developing techniques which are a substitute for market forces and which ensure proper and efficient use of public money. The fundamental problem is one of relating the aspiration of the DCMS to increase access to the grant-aided arts and heritage organisations to the latter's strong interest in promoting activities which satisfy the peer group assessment of its managers and advisers (see Sections VI and VII) as to what is in 'the public interest'. This aspiration, if it has anything to do with taxpayer/voter interest in the arts, could logically entail a major shifting of funds between art forms, such as preventing the 'top-slicing' of the arts budgets by entrenched 'national' companies, museums and galleries and encouraging art forms which more directly involve those who are supposed to benefit from them. A compromise is likely to be the result, with the DCMS placing conditions on the funding of powerful incumbents so that they demonstrate a concern for popularising their activities without reducing their standards. The DCMS has begun in the right place by instituting a formidable and welcome change in the flow of relevant information available to the public and in developing and applying methods of economic appraisal to expenditure proposals which must entail necessary adjustments in the perspective of arts managers. Economists who contend that funding bodies supporting activities as prestigious and elusive as the arts inevitably finish up as 'captives' may watch progress with considerable interest.

REFERENCES

Allison, G., Ball, S., Cheshire, P., Evans, A. and Stabler, M. (1996), *The Value of Conservation: A Literature Review of the Economic and Social Value of the Cultural Built Heritage*, London: Department of National Heritage, English Heritage and Royal Institution of Chartered Surveyors.

Arts Council of England (1999), *Annual Report*.

—— (1999), Press Report 13 October 1999.

Arts Council of Great Britain (1970), *A Report on Orchestral Resources in Great Britain*, Chairman: A. T. Peacock.

Baumol, W. J. (1987), 'Performing Arts' in J. Eatwell, M. Milgate, and P. Newman (eds), *The New Palgrave: A Dictionary of Economics*, vol. 3, London: Macmillan Press, pp. 841–3.

—— and Bowen, W. G. (1966), *Performing Arts: The Economic Dilemma*, New York: Twentieth Century Fund.

Benhamou, F. (1998), 'The evolution of heritage policies' in A. T. Peacock (ed.), *Does the Past Have a Future?* Readings 47, London: Institute of Economic Affairs, pp. 75–95.

British Broadcasting Corporation (1999), *The Future Funding of the BBC*, London: Press Report on Davies Committee, BBC.

Creigh-Tyte, A. and Thomas, B. (2001), 'Taxation' in S. Selwood (ed.), *The Cultural Sector*, London: Policy Studies Institute, ch. 15.

Creigh-Tyte, S. (1997), 'The development of British policy on built heritage preservation' in M. Hutter and I. Rizzo (eds), *Economic Perspectives on Cultural Heritage*, London: Macmillan, ch. 8.

— and Stiven, G. (2001), 'Why does government fund the cultural sector?', in S. Selwood (ed.), *The Cultural Sector*, London: Policy Studies Institute, ch. 15.

Department of Culture, Media and Sport (DCMS) (1998), *A New Cultural Framework*, London.

— (1999a), *Annual Report*, 1999, London.

— (1999b), *Efficiency and Effectiveness of Government-sponsored Museums and Galleries*, prepared by Deloitte and Touche, London.

— (1999c), *The Future Funding of the BBC*, Report of the Independent Review Panel, Chairman, Gavyn Davies, July, London.

Edwards, A. (1996), *The British Musuem, A Fundamental Review of the Museum's Operations*, British Museum, 8 October.

Elliot, G. (1998), 'Museums and galleries: storehouses of value?', in A. T. Peacock (ed.), *Does the Past Have a Future?* Readings 47, London: Institute of Economic Affairs, ch. 6.

Elstein, D. (2000), 'Competing with the public sector in broadcasting' in A. T. Peacock (ed.) *Does the Past Have a Future?* Readings 47, London: Institute of Economic Affairs.

Feist, A. (1998) 'Comparing the performing arts in Britain, the US and Germany: making the most of secondary data', *Cultural Trends*, no. 31, pp. 29–48.

—, Fisher, R., Gordon, C., Morgain C. with O'Brien, J. (1998), *International Data on Public Spending on the Arts*, Research Paper No. 13, London: Arts Council of England.

Frey, B. and Pommerehne, W. (1989), *Muses & Markets: Explorations in the Economics of the Arts*, Oxford: Basil Blackwell, ch. V.

— (1994), 'Cultural economics and museum behaviour', *Scottish Journal of Political Economy*, vol. 3, pp. 325–35.

Fullerton, D. (1991), 'On public justifications for public support of the arts', *Journal of Cultural Economics*, vol. 15, no. 2, pp. 67–82.

Glasgow, M. (1975), 'The concept of the arts council,' in M. Keynes (ed.), *Essays on John Maynard Keynes*, Cambridge: Cambridge University Press.

Getty Conservation Intitute (1999), *Economics and Heritage Conservation*, Los Angeles: Getty Institute.

Gombrich, E. (1979), 'Art history and the social sciences', in *Ideals and Idols*, London: Phaidon Press.

Goodison, N. (1997), 'Wishes that must be respected', *Quarterly*, London: National Arts Collection Fund.

Home Office (1986), *Report of the Committee on Financing the BBC*, Chairman: Alan Peacock, July, London: Her Majesty's Stationery Office.

King, K. and Blaug, M. (1976), 'Does the arts council know what it is doing?', in M. Blaug (ed.), *The Economics of the Arts*, London: Martin Robertson.

London Economics (1997), *New and Alternative Mechanisms for the Financing of the Arts*, Research Report No.12, London: Arts Council of England.

Linder, S. (1970), *The Harried Leisure Class*, New York: Columbia University Press.

MacQueen, H. and Peacock, A. T. (1995), 'Implementing performance rights', *Journal of Cultural Economics*, vol. 19, issue 2, pp. 157–75.

Musgrave, R. A. (1987), 'Merit goods' in J. Eatwell et al. (eds), *The New Palgrave: A Dictionary of Economics*, vol. 3, London: Macmillan Press, pp. 452–3.

Peacock, A. T. (1993), *Paying the Piper: Culture, Music and Money*, Edinburgh: Edinburgh University Press.

— (1994), 'A future for the past: the political economy of heritage', British Academy Keynes Lecture with Discussion, in *Proceedings of the British Academy*, vol. 87, Oxford: Oxford University Press, pp. 187–243.

— (1995), 'Roll up for a national lottery poll', *The Financial Times*, 10 July.

— (1996), 'The manifest destiny of the performing arts', *Journal of Cultural Economics*, vol. 20, no. 3, pp. 215–24.

— (1997), 'Towards a workable heritage policy' in M. Hutter and I. Rizzo (eds.), *Economic Perspectives on Heritage*, London: Macmillan, pp. 225–35.

— (1998), 'Subsidization and promotion of the arts', in H. Giersch (ed.), *Merits and Limits of Markets*, Berlin: Springer-Verlag, pp. 185–208.

— and Godfrey, C. (1973), 'Cultural accounting', *Social Trends* No. 4, London: HMSO.

—, Shoesmith, E. and Milner, G. (1983), *Inflation and the Performed Arts*, London: Arts Council of Great Britain.

— (ed.) (2000), 'The future of broadcasting', *Journal of Economic Affairs*, vol. 20. No. 4, December.

Portney, P. R. (1994), 'The contingent valuation debate: Why economists should care', *Journal of Economic Perspectives*, vol. 8, no. 4, pp. 3–17.

Robbins, L. C. (1963), 'Art and the state' in Lord Robbins (ed.), *Politics and Economics*, London: Macmillan, ch. 3.

Sawers, D. (1998), 'The national trust: the private provision of heritage services' in A. T. Peacock (ed.), *Does the Past Have a Future?* Readings 47, Institute of Economic Affairs, pp. 97–116.

— (2000), 'Public service broadcasting: a paradox of our time', *Journal of Economic Affairs*, vol. 20, No. 4, December.

Scitovsky, T. (1983), 'Subsidies for the arts: the economic argument', in Hendon, W. S. and Shanahan, J. L. (eds), *Economics of Cultural Decisions*, Cambridge, MA: Abt Books.

Selwood, S. (ed.) (2001), *The Cultural Sector*, London: Policy Studies Institute, ch. 10.

Solow, J. L. (1998), 'An economic analysis of *droit de suite*', *Journal of Cultural Economics*, vol. 22, no. 4, pp. 209–26.

Thomson, C. (2000), 'The public interest in converging communications', *Journal of Economic Affairs*, vol. 20, no. 4, December.

Throsby, C. D. (1997), 'Some questions in the economics of cultural heritage', in M. Hutter and I. Rizzo (eds), *Economic Perspectives on Cultural Heritage*, London: Macmillan, pp. 13–30.

— and Withers, G. A. (1979), *Economics of the Performing Arts*, London: Edward Arnold.

Towse, R. (1994), 'Achieving public policy objectives in the arts and heritage', in A. T. Peacock and I. Rizzo (eds), *Cultural Economics and Cultural Policies*, Dordrecht: Kluwer, pp. 143–65.

— (ed.) (1997a), *Baumol's Cost Disease: The Arts and other Victims*, Cheltenham: Edward Elgar.

— (1997b), 'Copyright as an economic incentive', in *Hume Papers on Public Policy*, vol. 5, no. 3, pp. 32–45.

West, E. G. (1987), 'Non-profit v. profit firms in the performing arts', *Journal of Cultural Economics*, vol. 11, no. 2, pp. 37–47.

11

Government Spending on Research and Development in the UK

PAUL STONEMAN[1]

I. INTRODUCTION

The UK government, in common with the governments of most developed economies, expends large amounts annually either directly upon, or in support of, scientific and technological activities. The aim of this paper is to review this expenditure. In the sections below, I will address several issues. I begin by looking at the extent of current government spending and place this in its recent historical context. I then move to consider what arms of government incur the relevant expenditures, the primary purposes of the expenditures undertaken and the extent to which the government performs as well as funds R&D. These patterns are then considered in the context of a comparison with other OECD economies.

Following this review of spending patterns, Section III addresses the political and institutional processes that determine the revealed patterns of expenditure in the UK, the rationales behind such spending and the aims and objectives of the main spending departments. A special discussion then follows in Section IV on how national patterns of such expenditure interact with EU expenditures on science and technology.

Section V of the chapter addresses the effectiveness of or pay-off to government support of this kind before the penultimate section addresses future spending plans. Some conclusions are provided in Section VII.

II. PATTERNS OF UK GOVERNMENT SUPPORT FOR SCIENCE AND TECHNOLOGY

1. Source and Definitions

In contrast to, for example, Germany or increasingly France, public support for science and technology in the UK is largely the preserve of central government

The author would like to thank participants in a Workshop at the Institute for Fiscal Studies in London on 6 July 1999, especially John Van Reenen for comments on an earlier draft. The views expressed here are a product of that time and to a degree matters may have moved on since then. The author would also like to thank Kim Kaivanto for permission to use his work on Launch Aid.

[1] Warwick Business School, University of Warwick.

Fiscal Studies (1999) vol. 20, no. 3, pp. 223–259. © Institute for Fiscal Studies, 1999

(defining central government to include the Scottish Office, the Welsh Office and the Northern Ireland Office). In Germany, on the other hand, the *Länder* are important providers of such support (for example, they are the main funders of universities), but the level of local authority spending on such activities is not important in the UK. Of course, this pattern may well change with devolution, especially if one redefines the Scottish Office and the Welsh Office as no longer part of central government.

The patterns of central government funding of science and technology have been well documented since the early 1980s in a series of publications. These included annual HMSO editions of the *Annual Review of Government Funded Research and Development*, which was followed by *Forward Look*, which in turn has been replaced by *Science, Engineering and Technology Statistics 1998* (SET98). Over the years, there have been refinements to the statistics and some redefinitions, but intertemporal comparisons are largely reasonable. SET98 is the source for all the data used here (except where otherwise stated) and covers realised outcomes in the accounting years 1986–87 to 1997–98 (the 1997–98 figures are estimated outcomes). The notes to the statistics in this publication detail the changes in methods of collection and calculation and thus any problems of intertemporal comparisons. Earlier data are taken from the other publications already mentioned except where specified.

In the period since the statistics were first published, there has been a changing emphasis in what is made available. The latest statistics emphasise science, engineering and technology (SET) activities in the UK, whereas earlier statistics emphasised research and development (R&D). SET is taken to include not only R&D but also technology transfer activities ('activities associated with research and development and contributing to the dissemination and application of scientific and technical knowledge'–SET98, p. 1) and scientific and technical postgraduate education and training.

In the statistics, science is defined as 'the systematic study of nature and behaviour of the material and physical universe' whereas technology is the 'practical application of this knowledge especially in industry and commerce'. This is not the only or even generally most useful means of distinction (see Dasgupta and David, 1987). Research and development concerns the 'gathering and use of new scientific and technological information, involving theoretical conjecture, observation, experiment, measurement and deduction' (SET98, p. 1). The OECD has for many years collected and published internationally comparative statistics on R&D on the basis of the definitions laid out in the (so-called) Frascati Manual. This makes international comparisons generally valid.

There is a mass of data available but I present data for only a limited number of years. I have chosen to concentrate upon 1997–98 as the latest year for which outturn data are available, the three years immediately prior to this as indicators of recent history, 1987–88 as an indicator of 10 years prior, and occasionally 1981–82 as an indicator of much more distant history, being the earliest date for which good data are available.

Table 1. *Total UK government spending on SET and R&D (£ million, 1996–97 prices)*

	1997–98	1996–97	1995–96	1994–95	1987–88	1981–82
Total GSET[a]	6,143	6,301.5	6,365.7	6,006.8	7,052.3	n.a.
NHS[a]	390	407.6	356.1	n.a.	n.a.	n.a.
Total GFR&D	5,625	5,759.3	5,798.5	5,491.5	6,643.9	6,704.3
EU contribution[b]	352	373.3	353.3	317.2	165.4	63.0
GFR&D/G%	3.0	2.9	2.9	2.8	4.0	n.a.
GFR&D/GERD%[c]	n.a.	31.8	33.2	33.2	38.8	n.a.
GFR&D/GDP%[c]	n.a.	0.6	0.7	0.7	0.9	n.a.

[a]NHS only included from 1995–96.
[b]An indicative measure of the UK contribution to the EU R&D budget and included in the R&D and SET totals.
[c]Sourced from OECD data.

Notes: GSET is total government expenditure on science, engineering and technology.
GFR&D is government expenditure on R&D.
G is total government expenditure.
GERD is gross national expenditure on R&D.
GDP is gross domestic product.

Sources: SET98, Table 7.1; Annual Review of Government Funded R&D (1991), Table 1.6.6.

2. Total UK Public Expenditure on SET and R&D

Table 1 provides data on a number of indicators of total UK government spending on SET and R&D. These data tell a very clear story. First, total government expenditure on SET and R&D has, over the last 10 years, been on a downward trend. Although an increase is recorded between 1994–95 and 1995–96, the increase is less than the NHS spend that is excluded from the 1994–95 statistics. In fact, government expenditure on R&D (excluding the NHS) peaked in 1985–86 at £6,955 million (in 1996–97 prices). This decline in government spend is obviously reflected in declines in such spends relative to GDP, total government spending and the total R&D spend in the economy. One may also note that the share of non-R&D activities in total SET (excluding the NHS) has been declining. This stood at 4.1 per cent in 1986–87 and had fallen to 2.2 per cent in 1997–98, although it did increase slightly between 1994–95 and 1995–96.

3. Departmental Spends

One means to explore the pattern of government R&D spending is to look at the spending by individual government departments. For this purpose, I split the data down by departments or ministries, with the Research Councils treated as if they were government departments. However, the Research Councils are really quite different organisations from government departments. Over the years, government departments have also been amalgamated and renamed, and thus presentation is

Table 2. *SET allocations by department (£ million, 1996–97 prices)*

Department[a]	1997–98	Department[a]	1987–88
OST	27	OST	n.a.
Research councils	1,276	Research councils	980.3
HE funding	1,042	HE funding	1,145.6
MAFF	142	MAFF	212.1
DFEE	83	DFE + ED	162.2
DETR	150	DOE + DOT	134.8
DH	57	DHSS	71.9
NHS	390	NHS	n.a.
DFID	82	ODA	49.0
DTI	341	DTI + DEn	864.9
Net Launch Aid	–107	Net Launch Aid	40.2
NI departments	35	NI departments	25.3
SO	73	SO	83.1
WO	3	WO	2.9
Other civil	76	Other civil	106.5
MOD	2,121	MOD	3,008.2
EU contribution	352	EU contribution	165.4
Total	6,143	Total	7,052.3

[a]A list of abbreviations appears at the end of this article.
Notes: Changes in the methods of calculation make comparisons of higher education research pre- and post-1993–94 problematic. New ways of collecting the NHS spend introduced in 1995–96 preclude the inclusion of a comparable figure prior to that date. The OST is entered as part of the science base although it is a (ring-fenced) part of the DTI.
Source: SET98 1998, Table 2.2.

a little messy. Table 2, however, presents some summary indications of spending patterns in 1997–98 and 1987–88.

Consider first the allocation of funding in 1997–98. We observe that the MOD share is 34.5 per cent, the total civil departments' share is 21.6 per cent, the science budget share (OST plus the Research Councils) is 21.2 per cent and the HE Funding Council share is 17 per cent. Compared with 1987–88, the MOD share has fallen from 42.7 per cent and the civil departments' share has fallen from 24.9 per cent whereas the science budget share has risen from 13.9 per cent and the higher education (HE) funding share has increased from 16.2 per cent. However, as these are shares in a reducing total, the actual changes in total expenditure are also worth noting. The MOD spend has fallen 29.5 per cent in real terms, the civil departments' spend has fallen by 24.4 per cent, the HE funding spend has decreased by 9 per cent and only the science budget has increased, that increase being 33 per cent.

Thus, although the MOD is still the largest public spender on R&D and spends more than all the civil departments put together, the MOD spend has been falling faster than that of the civil departments (both spends have been reducing).

The spend on HE funding has slightly increased its share, but within a falling total this means a reduced spend. The science budget has been increasing in real terms (although very recently, see below, the pattern is slightly different) and thus also increasing its share.

Within the civil departments, we observe a number of points worthy of comment. The major spenders in 1997–98 are, in order, the NHS, the DTI, the DETR, MAFF, the DFEE and the DFID. Compared with 1987–88, we have no figures for the NHS; for the DETR, the relative comparators are the DOE and the DOT whose total expenditure in 1987–88 was less, while MAFF spending has reduced considerably. This is at least partly attributable to a policy of progressive withdrawal from the provision of subsidised agricultural advice which was completed by March 1996.

The DTI is a slightly more complex case which will be discussed in some more detail in Section III. The current DTI incorporates the Office of Science and Technology (which is accounted for separately), has responsibility for aerospace and thus the Launch Aid scheme which is discussed in Section V, and also incorporates what used to be the Department of Energy. The DTI and the Department of Energy had a combined SET spend of £864.9 million in 1987–88. By 1997–98, the DTI spend (excluding Launch Aid and the OST) was only £341 million. Given that the DTI is the main department responsible for stimulating technological innovation in UK industry, the extent of this withdrawal of funding is dramatic.

One of the long-term trends in departmental civil spending on R&D has been the increasing importance of the DTI and the centralisation of responsibilities for civil R&D spending. Historically, support for civil technology development in UK industry (excluding agriculture and the NHS) was concentrated upon aerospace, nuclear energy, computers (or IT) and other general industry support programmes. At various times, these spending responsibilities have been allocated to the Department of Energy, an Aircraft Ministry and the Department of Industry, or their equivalents in name. In 1964, the new Labour government created the Ministry of Technology which was an attempt to centralise in one department nearly all government support for R&D spending directed at British industry. That department eventually disappeared. However, since then the DTI has become responsible for all these areas of policy. With the inclusion of the OST in the DTI (although ring-fenced), the concept of a Ministry of Technology has in fact been re-created under another name.

Finally, we may note that, in real terms, the EU contribution (which is discussed further in Section IV) has more than doubled between 1987–88 and 1997–98, indicating the growing involvement of the UK in EU technology programmes.

4. Military versus Civil R&D

The high level of government R&D funding attributed to the MOD exemplifies that UK government R&D spending has a strong defence bias. It is clear, however, that this bias is reducing over time. The MOD share in 1997–98 was 34.5 per cent but this compares with a 1987–88 share of 42.7 per cent. The Office for National Statistics (1999) illustrates that the 1997 government spend on military R&D represented 62 per cent of all military R&D spending in the UK, which is a slight increase on a figure of 60 per cent in 1992. Of the government spend, one-third was spent on government-performed R&D in 1997, compared with 30 per cent in 1992. Thus, although the military spend has reduced in real terms and as a share of the total government R&D spend, the government-funded share of military R&D and the government-performed share have remained approximately constant since 1992.

5. Primary Purposes

There are a number of ways of exploring the primary purposes or objectives of government expenditure on R&D. This section explores two. The first is a quite British classification that breaks down government spending according to the following categories (see SET98, p. 3):

(a) general support for research—all basic R&D that advances knowledge, including support for postgraduate studentships;
(b) government services—R&D relevant to any aspect of government service provision, including all of defence R&D;
(c) policy support—R&D to inform government policy;
(d) technology support—applied R&D that advances technology underpinning the UK economy, excluding defence;
(e) technology transfer;
(f) other, including postgraduate taught courses.

The relevant out-turn figures are included in Table 3. As can be seen, in 1997–98, government services is the largest funded primary purpose, taking almost half the funding. This includes all of defence R&D and thus the finding is not surprising. However, compared with 1989–90, the share of primary purpose (b) has reduced very little although the defence spend has reduced considerably. There has thus been a considerable shift from military spending directed at purpose (b)

Table 3. *Primary purposes (Per cent of government SET spend)*

Purpose	1997–98	1989–90
General support	38.7	27.2
Government services	48.0	49.8
Policy support	6.1	5.3
Technology support	4.3	13.5
Technology transfer	2.1	2.9
Other	0.8	1.1

Note: NHS included only in 1997–98 figures.

Source: SET98, Table 3.6.

towards civil spending directed at purpose (b). The second largest category in 1997–98 is general support, that is, all basic R&D that advances knowledge, including support for postgraduate studentships. Given that we have seen above that the science budget and HE spending are a large share of the total, this is again not surprising. However, this share has increased considerably since 1989–90 (largely at the expense of technology support). We thus observe a shift of resources from the support of applied R&D for support of technology in industry towards more support for the science and basic end of the spectrum. One must always hold in mind, however, that these changes in share are taking place in an environment where the total spend has been reducing.

A second way to look at primary purpose is through the socio-economic objectives of government funding. Here we constrain ourselves to just the R&D spend rather than the SET spend. The relevant data are presented in Table 4 (the latest data available are for 1996–97).

The first obvious point to make about these data is the overwhelming importance of defence and the advancement of knowledge in 1996–97. This reflects again the importance of military R&D in the UK government spend and also the spend on HE and the science budget. Of equal interest is the intertemporal comparison. Although the defence spend has reduced in importance somewhat, we also see (a) a large increase in the share going to the advancement of knowledge and (b) considerable reductions in the spend on energy and industrial development. This is as should be expected, given how we have seen departmental spends changing above.

Table 4. *Socio-economic objectives of UK government R&D spending (Per cent of total)*

Objective	1996–97	1986–87
Agriculture, forestry and fishing	4.5	4.7
Industrial development	2.5	10.5
Energy	0.7	4.4
Infrastructure	1.7	1.5
Environmental protection	2.2	1.1
Health	14.5	4.5
Social development and services	2.1	1.5
Earth and atmosphere	1.7	1.9
Advancement of knowledge	29.7	21.5
Civil space	2.8	2.9
Defence	37.2	45.1
nec[a]	0.4	0.3

[a]Not elsewhere classified.
Note: NHS included only in 1996–97 figures.

Source: SET98, Table 3.8.

Table 5. *Type of research activity (per cent of total government spend)*

Type	1996–97	1986–87
Total basic	32.1	19.6
Pure	23.0	
Orientated	9.1	
Total applied	40.6	37.5
Strategic	19.3	15.7
Specific	21.3	21.8
Experimental development	27.3	42.8

Note: NHS included only in 1996–97 figures.
Source: SET98, Table 3.5.

6. Basic R&D, Applied R&D and Experimental Development

Yet another way to explore the breakdown of government spending on R&D is to split it into basic and applied R&D and experimental development. These days, one may also separate basic R&D into pure and orientated and separate applied R&D into strategic and specific. The relevant data are presented in Table 5 (the 1996–97 data are the latest available). One should note that, by definition, the MOD is considered to undertake no basic R&D.

In 1996–97, applied research constitutes about 40 per cent of the total, basic 32 per cent and experimental development 27 per cent. It should be noted, however, that in defence, development is 67 per cent of the total and applied makes up the balance. In the civil departments, only 6 per cent is basic, 9 per cent is development and applied makes up 85 per cent of the total. In the Research Councils, not surprisingly, basic makes up 59 per cent, applied 40 per cent and experimental development only 0.7 per cent of the total.

One may note that the changes since 1986–87 are consistent with the patterns we have seen above. The total basic share has increased markedly, in line with the growing importance of the science spend in the total budget. The experimental development share has fallen considerably. This has occurred in both the defence and civil ministry spends. However, the reduction is more marked in the civil ministry spends and could be seen as a withdrawal by government from near market R&D, i.e. support for R&D aimed at technologies that are near to market launch. This will be discussed further below.

7. Government-Performed R&D

The UK government not only funds R&D. It also performs R&D. Table 6 details the share of economy-wide R&D performed by government and other relevant sectors (data for 1996 are the latest available; they are on an annual rather than financial-year basis). The total amount of R&D performed by government is approximately

Table 6. *UK R&D by performing sector (1996 prices)*

Sector	1996	1986
Total government	2,070	1,925
Government departments	1,495	
Research councils	575	
Higher education	2,792	2,045
Business enterprise	9,301	9,447
Private non-profit	177	273
Total	14,340	13,689

Source: SET98, Table 6.2.

14 per cent of total R&D performed in the UK. In 1986, it was also 14 per cent. This compares with the share of UK R&D funded by government of about 32 per cent in 1996. The government clearly funds more R&D than it performs. However, it is somewhat surprising that, with the process of 'privatisation' of government R&D facilities, there has not been a falling share of R&D performed by government. To some degree, this is because of accounting conventions. In the *Annual Review of Government Funded R&D* (1991), a timetable is presented (p. 59) of the dates at which formerly wholly government-controlled laboratories became or were to become executive agencies. However, it is also stated (p. 44) 'that staff engaged in and expenditure on R&D in agencies are included in the departmental total'. Where 'privatisation' meant the creation of executive agencies, therefore, the total department spends may not fully reflect the extent to which R&D performance was being privatised. However, with full privatisation of, for example, the Agricultural Development and Advisory Service (ADAS) from 1997, the Transport Research Laboratory (TRL) from 1996–97, British Rail Engineering (BRE) from 1997–98, Warren Springs from 1994, the Atomic Weapons Establishment (AWE) from 1993 and a number of other small agencies over the years, there may well be more reductions in government-performed R&D to be expected.

It is interesting to list for the main spending departments what proportion of their R&D was undertaken in-house (intramural) in 1997–98: MAFF, 57 per cent; MOD, 33 per cent; DFID, 3.6 per cent; DTI, 2.0 per cent; NI departments, 28 per cent; SO, 72.2 per cent; WO, 33 per cent. There are thus considerable differences across departments. The small figure for the DTI obviously reflects the true privatisation of its executive agencies. The extent to which MOD work is still in-house is an obvious contrast (although, as discussed below, this may well change in the future).

8. International Comparisons

Using OECD data, we may make a number of international comparisons. The usual countries considered in these comparisons are France (F), Germany (G), Italy (I),

Table 7. *UK R&D: international comparisons (per cent)*

Indicator	UK	F	G	I	J	US
(a) International comparisons (per cent)						
GERD/GDP 1996	1.94	2.31	2.28	1.13	2.77	2.52
GERD/GDP 1992	2.13	2.42	2.48	1.20	2.76	2.74
GFRD/GERD 1996	31.8	42.3	37.3	46.2	20.9	34.6
GFRD/GERD 1992	33.4	43.5	36.0	48.5	17.5	37.7
HERD/GDP 1996	0.38	0.39	0.43	0.25	0.40	0.38
HERD/GDP 1992	0.36	0.37	0.43	0.27	0.35	0.40
GPRD/GERD 1996	14.4	20.4	15.3	19.9	10.4	9.0
DEFENCE/GFRD 1996	37.2	28.9	9.8	4.7	5.8	54.7
DEFENCE/GFRD 1992	40.8	35.7	10.0	7.1	5.9	58.6
(b) Comparisons by Objectives, 1996 (per cent of government-funded R&D)						
Industrial development	2.5	4.8	13.3	8.8	3.4	0.6
Energy	0.7	4.7	3.4	3.1	23.3	3.6
Health	14.5	5.2	3.3	8.8	3.5	17.6
Advancement of knowledge	29.7	35.2	52.2	52.8	48.6	4.1
Civil space	2.8	10.9	5.0	8.7	6.6	11.4
Defence	37.2	28.9	9.8	4.7	5.8	54.7

Notes:
GERD is gross national expenditure on R&D.
GDP is gross domestic product.
GFRD is government-funded R&D.
HERD is higher education R&D.
GPRD is government-performed R&D.
DEFENCE is government-funded defence R&D.

Source: (a) SET98, Table 7.1; (b) SET98, Table 7.8.

Japan (J) and the US. The OECD data have a number of breaks in series between 1990, 1991 and 1992. We thus look at 1996 (the latest year) and 1992. The relevant data are presented in Table 7.

One may make a number of relevant observations upon these data.

- In terms of total gross expenditure on R&D (GERD) relative to GDP, only Italy is lower than the UK. The other four comparators all devote a greater share of their GDP to R&D. Moreover, except for Japan, all the comparators show declining shares of GDP devoted to R&D, and in this the UK is not out of line.
- The share of GERD financed by government is lower in the UK than in all the comparators except Japan. This share has also been falling in all the comparators except Germany (where reunification may have had a role to play) and Japan.
- The share of GDP devoted to higher education R&D differs little across countries (except for Italy where it is relatively low). The slight increase in this share shown in the UK between 1992 and 1996 is also present in France and Japan.

- The share of GERD performed by government, at 14.4 per cent, is low in the UK compared with France, Italy and Germany but high compared with Japan and the US. This reflects the greater prevalence of government-owned research establishments in the former countries and the greater share of R&D undertaken by private enterprise in the last two.
- The share of defence spending in total government-funded R&D is high in the UK, France and the US (mission-orientated countries according to the Ergas (1987) definition) and low in Germany, Italy and Japan (the more diffusion-orientated countries).

III. THE DETERMINATION OF UK GOVERNMENT R&D PRIORITIES AND SPENDING PATTERNS

1. The Process of Spending Determination

There is no centralised SET or R&D budget in UK government.[2] In this, the UK is similar to most other European economies (except perhaps France where one ministry has a centralised budget that it then distributes to other ministries). Instead, individual ministries determine their own R&D spends, given their own priorities and the limits of their annual total budgets agreed with the Treasury. The system is known as 'frame budgeting'.

Until recently, this system operated on an annual cycle, although since 1998 a three-year horizon has been employed. Given the limits upon the totality of government spending determined by the Chancellor of the Exchequer in Cabinet, rounds of bilateral meetings between the Treasury and individual ministries or departments take place. The main purpose of these meetings is to agree the total spending of each ministry or department. These discussions tend to be primarily concerned with the total spend rather than the detail of the spends of the individual departments. Thus, although discussion may take place relating to a department's spend on R&D, the discussion is unlikely to reduce to a discussion of individual projects (unless the projects are very large). Once the total budget has been agreed for any department, that department will then determine the allocation of the funding, including the allocation to R&D, according to its own priorities. The mechanism is slightly different for the science budget. The OST discusses the size of this budget directly with the Treasury. It is the case, however, that the Treasury will not, in general, discuss the detail of that budget but will be concerned more with the total size.

Such an arrangement may seem to be a very loose one, implying no overall technology or R&D strategy and with the potential to leave gaps or generate duplication in government spend on R&D. There are, however, a number of checks and balances in place to correct or prevent this. First, there are many interdepartmental committees and groups that address issues of departmental co-operation and interaction in the R&D process. Second, one of the functions of the OST is to oversee the totality of

---

[2] Much of this section is based upon Diederen et al. (1999).

government spend on R&D and to make recommendations to both departments and the Cabinet on duplication and omissions. Although these recommendations of the OST do not have executive authority, it is a brave minister who ignores them. Third, in the bilateral discussions with the Treasury, evaluations of past support activity may well be one of the factors discussed in the determination of future budgets and, if so, effectiveness in the R&D spend is a key to future budgets.

It is still, however, the case that this system does not necessarily generate a consistent unified technology strategy for the UK. The spending pattern is still very much the result of a number of different individuals and ministries making separate spending decisions. Partly as a reaction to such views, the last Conservative government instituted the Technology Foresight exercise. This exercise (which is currently being repeated) involved a process of widespread consultation upon those areas of science and technology in which the UK (as a whole) might best invest. The results of this exercise are being used to inform government R&D spending decisions (although it must be admitted that they appear to have had more influence on the Research Councils than on other spenders). The government, of course, has no control over the spending decisions of the private sector, and thus whether the recommendations have been influential in that area is another matter.

Technology Foresight exercises of this kind have also been undertaken in the Netherlands, Finland and Germany, for example. It is worth noting, however, that whereas in the UK the main objective was to spot technologies that might best contribute to improved competitiveness, in other countries (e.g. the Netherlands) there was also a matching concern with the quality of life. The UK Foresight exercise currently under way has to some degree redressed this imbalance.

Although individual government departments and ministries do have considerable freedom to determine their own R&D spending and priorities, the UK political system does tend to ensure that, at a general level at least, the different ministries and departments have common attitudes. Thus, for example, the various Conservative governments from 1979 to 1997 had a general belief in the efficacy of market forces. This led not only to privatisation but also to a general reconsideration of government R&D support programmes, especially in the DTI. The view that 'if it was worth doing, then the private sector would do it without government intervention' led to a wholesale withdrawal of the DTI from general technology support programmes and, in particular, withdrawal from support of near market R&D. Similarly, a belief in the importance of small and medium enterprises (SMEs) as a source of dynamism in the economy led to reorientation of support away from large firms towards smaller firms. In addition, desires to reduce government spending and to promote efficiency have led to growing demands for *ex post* evaluation of programmes.

This is not to say that individual government ministers did not or do not still have influence on individual departments' spends. One may observe many examples where, in individual ministries, a change of personality at the top has led to a change of policy. The point is that the prevailing political philosophy of the party in power tends to influence, at a general level, the size and nature of any public spending programmes in place. It also means that, as the party in power changes, so the underlying philosophy will tend to change. The election of a Labour government in 1997 has not seen a radical change in prevailing attitudes so far; however, we have already seen: (a) the introduction of an R&D tax credit for SMEs when such tax credits were always considered undesirable under the previous government; (b) announcements of future increased spending on science over and above the amount considered desirable by the previous government; and (c) an emphasis in the last Budget and in the latest Competitiveness White Paper on the importance of technology to the UK economy and in particular how the UK (especially the government) must invest to become a full member of the information economy.

The role of Parliament in the determination of government R&D spending is limited. There are effective House of Lords and House of Commons Select Committees on Science and Technology which over the years have issued critical reports on government R&D support activities. There is, however, little evidence that these reports have been particularly influential. In general, Parliament has not undertaken reviews of government SET support activities at a detailed level (except perhaps to investigate certain large defence projects that failed).

In addition to the general issues of the determination of the level of spending upon technology support and the areas to be supported, there is also an issue as to who should perform the technology activities being funded. From the late 1960s, there has been general acceptance in government of the 'contractor–customer' principle, whereby the same institution of government should not be both the funder and performer of research. This principle has two advantages in that the separation of customer and contractor (a) should promote efficiency in the research process and (b) should promote objectivity on the part of the contractor. This latter issue is one of the reasons for the separation of universities from government via the Research Councils.

In the 1991 *Annual Review*, the government argued that the spinning-off of previously in-house research establishments as executive agencies, many of which were then later more fully privatised, enabled an extension of the customer–contractor principle (as well as enabling such institutes to compete for privately funded research more effectively). This spinning-off may well have also been a further reflection of Conservative belief in the efficacy of the market. It is difficult to be precise as to the extent to which there is separation of customer and contractor in government R&D spending. We have seen above how the amount of government-funded R&D performed intramurally differs across ministries. There are, however, some data (Table 8) for 1996–97 that are more indicative of the current position. Although there are considerable difficulties in determining what is a competitive allocation mechanism and what is not (see, e.g. Cave et al., 1999), these figures suggest a considerable degree of competition in the allocation process.

2. Why Should Government Spend on SET?

The previous section has explored the process by which spending levels and patterns are determined. It does not answer the key question of why the government should

Table 8. *UK government expenditure on SET subject to competition, 1996–97*

	Science budget	Civil departments	MOD	Total
Total expenditure (£m)	1,302.5	1,444.7	2,143.7	4,890.9
Expenditure on contracts (£m)	705.9	1,193.2	1,800.7	3,699.8
Expenditure on competitive contracts (£m)	651.4	747.2	1,628.7	3,027.2
Percentage of total expenditure subject to competition	50.0	51.7	76.0	61.9

Source: SET98, Table 2.6.

spend on R&D and SET. In Table 3, some data were presented on the principal purposes of such spending, which to some degree help to answer why. In particular, we see that some spending is for policy support, that is, to inform government policy. This is quite appropriate. The government requires information in order to frame policy and also to negotiate with private sector contractors effectively. However, such spending is only about 6 per cent of the total. Another primary purpose is for government services, which is R&D relevant to any aspect of government service provision, including all of defence R&D. The principle here is that the government is the major provider of, for example, defence services, and, as such, should fund the R&D for such services. This element comprises almost 50 per cent of the government R&D spend. However, just because the government is the major customer, it does not necessarily mean that government should fund the R&D. The government, for example, instead of funding the development of a new torpedo, could promise to buy from a contractor a torpedo that the contractor had expended its own resources upon developing. In fact, over the last 10 years, there have been considerable changes in the relationships between the MOD and its suppliers whereby more of the responsibility for the funding of R&D is left with the contractor, as well as a move away from cost-plus to fixed-price contracts that have shifted the risk from government to the contractor. Having said this, however, such R&D is seen as somewhat different from the other R&D spends of government. It is, as its label implies, seen as a necessary part of delivering the services to the populace that the government considers to be part of its political remit.

The remaining 50 per cent of government R&D spending is for four other purposes: general support for research, technology support, technology transfer and others. Such spending is generally directed at stimulating the scientific and technological performance of the economy and, as such, has to be justified on other grounds. A prerequisite to such justification is a belief that innovation will yield improvements in competitiveness and economic welfare. Justification then tends to fall into two separate categories: (a) on the basis of international comparisons, i.e. UK economic performance is seen as not satisfactory and improvements in the scientific and technological performance of the economy would assist in overcoming this problem; and (b) the economy suffers from market failures in its SET perform-ance which means that the government should intervene. It should be noted that these are quite separate arguments. It may be that UK performance is not satisfac-tory in terms of international comparison, but this need not necessarily be due to market failures. All economies will suffer similar market failures and thus it is diffi-cult to argue that market failures cause differences in technological performance.

The international comparison argument as a justification for government support of R&D needs little further explanation. Policymakers will look at the performance of other economies and wish to replicate what the good performers are achieving. However, there is no strong evidence (see OECD, 1998) to suggest that policies can be simply transferred across national boundaries when there are extensive cultural and structural differences. Nor does there seem to be any acceptance in gov-ernment that a good rationale for any particular policy is that other countries are doing the same (note tax credits for R&D), although an academic literature on strategic trade policy might be used to support a contrary view. However, inferior relative performance can often be taken as a good general rationale for the need for policy. Of course, the desire to stimulate UK technological performance is not itself a justification for government spending on SET. There are many poli-cies open to government, of which direct spending is only one. The choice of actual policy is more a matter of consideration of what policies will be the most cost-effective.

The market failure argument—the argument most favoured by economists—merits greater discussion. Market failure is said to exist when the free market will not generate a welfare optimal outcome. All the literature (see, e.g. Stoneman, 1987) suggests that there is market failure in innovation. Reasons for market failure are various and encompass, *inter alia*: appropriability problems whereby the innovator is unable to appropriate (through, for example, externalities, copying or pricing) the whole social benefits of his or her innovative efforts; excessive risk aversion on the part of either innovators or capital markets in the presence of incomplete insur-ance markets; informational externalities; and indivisibilities. All of these will tend to lead to underinvestment in SET. On the other hand, common pool problems may lead to excessive repetition of R&D and/or excessive speed or overinvestment in the development and launching of new products and processes.

If market failure does lead to suboptimal investment, there is a rationale for gov-ernment intervention. The problem with this rationale, however, is that it is difficult to operationalise. Civil servants will often accept the potential for market failure but will query whether it is a practical tool for deciding where to direct intervention and the level of intervention required (see, e.g. Barber and White, 1987). It is also by no means obvious that government spending is the best means to correct market failure; it may be that tax breaks or information-spreading programmes will be more suitable.

The area where the market failure argument is used most frequently is basic R&D. It is commonly argued that, given that basic R&D has no particular applica-tion in view, there is little potential for the innovator to realise the benefits of his or her discoveries and thus, without intervention, there will be underinvestment in basic R&D. We have been informed that, in discussion about the size of the science budget in the annual spending rounds, the OST, which presents the case for the science budget, uses the market failure argument and the Treasury accepts the argument. However, little attempt is made to apply the argument on a project-by-project basis.

To a large extent, the market failure argument is thus used to justify government investment in science. Again, however, one might ask why direct government spending is employed. It would be possible to give tax breaks to private investors who fund science in universities instead.

Government investment in science raises a related issue. The basic justification for such investment is market failure. Thus the free market would not invest enough in science from a welfare point of view and, without government involvement, there would be insufficient knowledge and skills in the economy. However, the science budget is primarily allocated to universities. Although the Technology Foresight exercise has recently been put in place to inform the distribution of this budget to areas of greatest national technological advantage, it is still the case that the researchers in universities who are spending the budget are not primarily interested in the technological applications of the research that they undertake. They are generally producing information for the public domain that will raise their own estimation in the eyes of their peers. The actual process of allocating and spending the science budget may thus generate its own market failures (Dasgupta and David, 1987). This is not to suggest that there is no pay-off to the science budget (see below), nor is it to suggest that the potential pay-offs to basic research can be reliably predicted; it is more to suggest that current allocation mechanisms will not necessarily replicate the allocations that a free market might make in the absence of market failure.

Finally in this section, I might state the obvious. The existence of market failure or internationally comparative underinvestment in SET does not of itself merit government intervention. It must be the case that the intervention will be effective. I return to consider this point further below.

3. The Main Spending Departments

This section looks in some brief detail at the spends and policies of three main components of the government SET machine. It starts with the MOD, then considers the DTI, before finally considering the total OST, Research Councils and HE budget.

(a) The Ministry of Defence
Although the MOD spend on R&D has been declining recently, it is still the largest of all the government departments. The whole spend is considered to be non-basic. The MOD maintains that its prime responsibility is the defence of the UK and, as such, although civil spin-offs are to be welcomed, it has no particular responsibility towards wealth creation or competitiveness in the UK economy (although the MOD

involvement in arms exporting suggests that the MOD is concerned with the prosperity of the UK defence sector).

There are a number of issues that can be raised with respect to the MOD R&D spend:

- To what extent should the MOD commission new products and to what extent should it buy off-the-shelf equipment? Inclining towards the latter option would tend to reduce R&D spend.
- If the MOD wishes to commission new technology, to what extent should it finance the R&D? It is possible that new defence equipment can be commissioned, with the contractor funding the R&D. For example, in most supply chains, the final customer would not finance suppliers' R&D. One would expect the suppliers to fund the R&D and to recover that R&D through sales to the final ·customer. There are reasons why the final customer might fund the R&D (e.g. the supplier cannot raise the funding) but that seems unlikely in the case of the defence industry. Of course, if prototypes are being developed, there may be more of an argument for customer funding.
- If external contractors are to develop and produce new defence technologies, what are the optimal contractual arrangements? Some 20 years ago, nearly all contracts were of the cost-plus form. However, now there is a much greater emphasis upon fixed-price contracts. Such contracts not only provide a greater incentive for the contractor to be efficient but also shift the risk from the government to the contractor. However, such contract forms will require that the MOD spends more on R&D informing itself so that new contracts may be 'fair'.
- How efficient is defence R&D? There have been a number of high-profile failures of defence R&D projects (e.g. the UK AWACS aircraft and torpedo development). There is some evidence to suggest, however, that such failures are no more or less common in the defence sector than for similar complex projects in the civil sector (e.g. certain civil software development projects in the public sector).
- To what extent should MOD defence research be undertaken in-house? It has always been the case that much MOD research has been undertaken by private sector contractors. In addition, since 1991, the MOD has been trying to put greater distance between its research funding and research performance activities. Through the Defence Research Agency to 1994 and then the Defence Evaluation and Research Agency (DERA), the majority of the MOD's non-nuclear research performance activities have been amalgamated into a single organisation managed as a trading fund. This was undertaken in order to (a) impose a formal customer–supplier relationship, (b) encourage greater collaboration with the civil sector and (c) help ensure the exchange of technologies between the civil and military sectors.
- To what extent should defence technology be developed alone or as part of an international collaborative effort? Collaboration can, *inter alia*, share costs and spread risks as well as open up a wider market for products developed. Over the last 10 years, collaborative arrangements with Europe in particular have become more important.

- Are there externalities to defence R&D in terms of civil spin-offs? The MOD has for long attempted to encourage such spin-offs, and such externalities are often seen as a reason for supporting defence spending on R&D. However, the externalities cannot themselves justify the R&D. If civil usage is the objective, then surely it would be better to direct the spending into that area. In its list of prime contributions from its R&D spend, the MOD includes 'co-operating with industry and other government departments to ensure that scientific knowledge and technical innovation generated both within and outside the MOD is exploited both for defence purposes and by industry in support of wealth creation' (*Forward Look 1995*, vol. 2, p. 55).

Mechanisms considered to encourage civil spin-off include: (a) the use of private sector contractors to perform defence R&D who may spin off expertise into their civil activities; (b) the establishment of Dual Use Technology Centres to encourage collaboration between DERA, industry and academia; and (c) the granting of licences for technology developed by the MOD. One should note as well that, in 1995, the MOD was talking of the need for greater alignment between civil and defence sectors. This may also encourage spin-off. However, on the other hand, there may be spin-off from the civil sector to the defence sector that is at least as large as vice versa.

On an institutional level, the MOD maintains an overview of its SET activities through a Defence Research Committee chaired by the Department Chief Scientific Adviser. An independent view of its research programme is provided to the Minister by the Defence Scientific Research Council (DSRC) and its five supporting boards. These draw their members from academia and industry. In other work (Diederen et al., 1999), we have also been informed that the MOD has members sitting on a number of interdepartmental bodies that address issues of complementarity in departmental research programmes. This would be particularly relevant in cases such as aerospace where the DTI is responsible for civil aircraft and the MOD for military aircraft.

(b) The Department of Trade and Industry

Although, as explained above, the DTI has, over the last 15 years, taken on the responsibility for those areas of government industrial R&D policy that were the largest-spending (aircraft, IT, energy), its current R&D spend is only a shadow of the sums that once were being expended. In addition, as we have seen above, the DTI has 'privatised' nearly all of its in-house research institutes and thus the DTI now does very little in-house research.

In fact, the DTI now considers its main activities as regards innovation to be 'to give higher priority to supporting technology transfer, spreading best practice, and accessing and exploiting existing technology rather than to developing new technology. . . . DTI activities are now concentrating more on influencing the broad environment which allows innovative firms to flourish and less on the explicit development of technology' (*Forward Look 1995*, vol. 2, p. 112).

Of its 1997–98 estimated out-turn spend, £216 million (of a total SET spend of £341 million) was considered for technology support. Of this £216 million, £94 million went to the European Space Agency and £17 million to fusion research. Policy support received £55 million and technology transfer £79 million. One must not, of course, forget that, to some degree at least, responsibility for technology support has shifted to Brussels and away from Whitehall. This is discussed further below, but even so it is clear that the DTI has largely pulled back from not only the support of near market research but also the support of nearly all research.

There are many different programmes offered by the DTI in pursuit of its objectives. It would be tedious to list them all here. It is, however, worth stressing that its programmes emphasise help for SMEs, gaining access to overseas technology and also encouraging inward investment of R&D.

In early 1999, a new Competitiveness White Paper was issued by the DTI that laid out a conception of future policy. Although this does not contain any major change of strategic direction, it does have some new twists on existing policy. It is discussed below in the general discussion of the future. In addition, the March 1999 Budget introduced some future changes with respect to DTI innovation policy tied to the White Paper. Finally, the DTI is responsible for Launch Aid. This is one 'old-style' interventionist policy that the DTI has maintained and it is discussed separately below.

(c) The Science Budget

The whole science budget is made up of three parts—a small spend by the Office of Science and Technology, a much larger spend by the Research Councils and a large higher education budget.

The OST was originally created as part of the Cabinet Office but, with effect from 1996, was relocated as part of the DTI. Although many saw in this relocation a statement of the subservience of science and technology to the demands of wealth creation, civil servants argued that the shift had more to do with space in the Cabinet Office than any other issue. Within the DTI, the OST is headed by the government Chief Scientific Adviser (CSA). The CSA advises the Prime Minister, the Cabinet, the Secretary of State for Trade and Industry and the Minister for Science on SET matters. The Secretary of State for Trade and Industry has overall responsibility for the government's science policy and support for science and technology as a whole in his cross-departmental role as the Cabinet Minister for Science and Technology.

The OST has two main functions. The first is the overview function discussed above. The second is a responsibility for the science budget. Although the science budget is not spent by the OST but is instead allocated by the Research Councils, which are essentially intermediaries, it is the OST that negotiates with the Treasury on the size of the science budget. The Director General of the Research Councils is responsible for advising the Secretary of State for Trade and Industry and the Minster for Science on the allocation of the science budget and for securing the successful operation of the Research Councils, with support from the OST.

There also exists the Council for Science and Technology (COST) as an advisory body made up of independent members. The COST is advisory to the Prime Minister on all aspects of the government's science and technology activities and submits its reports to him through the Cabinet Minister for Science and Technology (the Secretary of State for Trade and Industry) who chairs the Council on behalf of the Prime Minister with the CSA as Deputy Chairman.

The higher education budget is the responsibility of the DFEE in England (but is spent by the HEFCE), of the Scottish Office in Scotland (but spent by the HEFCS), of the Welsh Office in Wales (but spent by the HEFCW) and of the Northern Ireland Office in Northern Ireland (with the NIHEC as the intermediary).

We have seen in Table 2 that Research Council spending has increased over the 10 years to 1997–98; the HE funding of R&D has, however, declined although the sum of the spends of the Research Councils and on HE funding has increased in real terms in the 10 years to 1997–98 within a declining total government R&D spend. To some degree, such comparisons are a little misleading. Although the comparison of Research Council spends is valid, more needs to be said of how the higher education R&D spends are calculated. There was a significant change of calculation methods and coverage in 1993–94; also in 1996 a new method was introduced to measure what proportion of HE expenditure could be considered as research. The new method basically uses grant income as a proxy for expenditure, with research, teaching and other grants separately identified. The block research grant is counted as research. One-third of the postgraduate element of the teaching grant is counted as research.

The 10-year comparison does not show, however, what has been happening more recently. The science budget (OST plus the Research Councils) peaked in 1995–96 at £1,331 million (1996–97 prices) and then fell to £1,303 million in 1997–98. HE funding peaked at £1,073.9 million in 1994–95 and then fell to 1996–97, recovering in 1997–98 to £1,042 million. Thus the 10-year comparison hides more recent reductions in the science budget.

The Research Council structure was changed in 1994 from a system with five such councils to a system with seven Research Councils. The Research Councils have extensive independence in the determination of the funds allocated to them by the Director General of the Research Councils. However, alignment with government objectives (such as Foresight) will tend to be rewarded by higher allocations. The main allocation mechanism used by the various councils is peer review. One might note, however, that the PPARC is a major funder of the European Space Agency and CERN on a long-term basis. The BBSRC, the MRC, NERC and the Council for the Central Laboratories of the Research Councils spent large proportions of their funding intramurally (most of the balance and the funding of the other Research Councils going to higher education institutions). This 'intramural' spend essentially funds research institutes 'owned' by the Research Councils.

One of the major changes that has affected the science spend over the last 10 years has been the growing demand for relevance. This can be interpreted in many ways but is essentially seen as a growing requirement that the science budget should support research that will be of relevance to wealth creation in the UK economy. There is considerable argument as to whether research that is basic can be so directed, and even whether it is possible to predict where basic research will be of value. I remember Paul David at a conference a few years ago stating that he saw the call for relevance in UK science as a sign that science had lost the trust of government. In the 1960s, all the scientists had to say was give us the money, trust us to spend it and society will benefit. However, an inability to show any material pay-off from such spending has since then led to greater and greater demands for accountability and relevance.

In higher education, the pressures have been more to do with quality and assessment. Teaching and Research Quality exercises across higher education institutions have been performed and are used to inform funding allocations across departments and institutions. It is not, however, clear that the criteria for the Research Assessment exercises well match the relevance criteria for Research Council funding allocations.

The potential pay-offs to the science budget are considered below. Here, a more fundamental question is addressed. Why should government fund the science budget? One could again consider international comparisons as one reason. The more interesting is market failure. The literature considers that there are many market failures in basic research, ranging from externalities (the supply of skilled manpower to UK industry) through to appropriability problems. As always, however, market failure arguments are an imprecise means of deciding the size of the budget (e.g. although the extent of market failure in basic research has probably not changed or has increased over the last 15 years, in the face of financial stringency UK universities have dramatically increased their income from non-government sources). One may also compare the funding of UK and US universities. In the US, private funding is more extensive. Questions that need to be answered are (a) should the government be responsible for the costs of education, especially postgraduate education, or should this be an individual responsibility? (b) to what extent should government fund basic research or should the private sector as the main potential user take more responsibility? and (c) to what extent do universities act as market institutions? (is it the case, e.g. that they are more interested in peer evaluation and international reputation than the market value of their products?). In many ways, perhaps the key issue that arises in the funding of science is whether there is an inherent incompatibility between institutions that largely consider their function to be the production of knowledge for the public domain and a government pushing for greater relevance of output to the needs of UK industry which will largely benefit from knowledge kept in the private domain.

IV. THE EUROPES SYSTEM

As can be seen from Table 1, the UK government contribution to the EU research budget has increased by 113 per cent in real terms over the 10 years to 1997–98.

Table 9. *Departmental attribution of*
EU contribution

Department	Percentage of EU contribution charged
DTI (excluding OST)	52.3
OST	18.7
DOE	8.5
MAFF	3.7
DOT	3.4
DFID	3.0
Others	<3.0[a]

[a]That is, no other was attributed more than 3 per cent.

Source: SET98, Table 2.9.

This reflects a growing involvement of the UK in EU-funded research support programmes.

The UK government treats contributions to EU programmes as part of departmental spending totals for the purposes of its public expenditure allocation process. Thus a contribution to an EU programme is considered as a charge against the spending total of the relevant government department. This is known as the EUROPES system. The percentage allocations of the 1996–97 £373.3 million are as in Table 9. Clearly, it is the DTI and the OST that carry most of this allocation of EU spending.

The implication of this EUROPES allocation is that, if the total departmental spend is controlled, then any EU programmes are completely non-additional to government spending. In principle, contributions to an EU programme are an alternative to a domestic spend and not an addition. The only other European country to have such a system of allocations is Germany. However, the German system seems to be largely non-binding (as we shall see, the UK system may well be).

The reasoning behind the EUROPES system was that, if government expenditure was to be controlled, then EUROPES was a way of controlling that part of such expenditure that was an R&D contribution to Europe. The EUROPES system will encourage ministries not to attempt to replicate EU programmes at home. The problem, however, is that, within the frame budgeting system, if the frame is not adjusted for the EUROPES contribution, then EU R&D will drive out domestic-funded R&D. If EU R&D is of a very different kind (e.g. involving more international collaboration or more technology support or more close to market) from the domestic R&D, then the plans of the department concerned may not be realised.

There are some doubts, however, as to how rigidly the government adheres to the EUROPES principles. In interviews (see Diederen et al., 1999), it was suggested to us that ministers may negotiate with the Treasury over a higher departmental budget if the EUROPES spending has much different objectives from those of the department.

One might also note that, to the extent that UK researchers are successful in gaining EU funds over and above the contribution of the government to EU R&D programmes, so there is an expansion of UK R&D spends. In 1996, the UK private sector received about £140 million from the EU Commission for R&D, with about £180 million going to universities. The total £320 million is about £50 million less than the EU contribution.

Of course, given the EUROPES system, ministries and departments have an incentive to argue for EU programmes that reflect their own objectives. The UK government plays a full role in the discussions over EU R&D budgets and spending, with the OST presenting the UK case.

V. THE EFFECTIVENESS OF THE SET SPEND

This section addresses issues relating to the effectiveness of UK government expenditure on science, engineering and technology through three separate discussions. The first concerns the general literature on the returns to government expenditure on R&D. The second concentrates upon government expenditure on basic research. This is relevant because, as we have seen above (and will see below), the science budget has (and will be) taking an increasing share of the total SET budget. Then we look at one particular policy, Launch Aid for civil aerospace. This is explored for two main reasons, first because of its peculiar position in the UK technology policy portfolio and second because it is an example of an old-style product support policy that has largely disappeared from the government (and especially DTI) portfolio.

When discussing effectiveness, a number of approaches can be taken. One is to ask whether the policy actually satisfies the objectives set for the policy itself. Many of the evaluation exercises undertaken within government (very few of which are available to me) are of this kind. Such an approach seems rather limited in scope and will not be explored here. A second approach is to consider the pay-offs to policy in terms of impact on economic welfare and then compare them with the cost of the policy. Although this leaves open the issue of how economic welfare is to be measured, it is the implicit approach taken here.

Of course, once effectiveness has been discussed, one can address the issue of whether current levels of expenditure are too high or too low. To answer such questions may require a degree of precision that is not available; however, they are relevant questions to ask.

1. The General Issue

Assessing the effectiveness of government R&D spending in welfare terms means the consideration of a number of different issues. First, the pattern of spending is heterogeneous. There is spending to inform government, to meet government objectives (e.g. defence), on training, on basic research, to create appropriate environments and (decreasingly) on particular new products or processes. What is sought from the different types of spending is different and the potential returns are different in character and probably value. Some returns will be particularly difficult to measure and value. Thus, for example, it would be particularly difficult to measure the social benefit of expenditure on defence R&D. One could, of course, explore whether the defence R&D met its objectives of developing the products targeted, but actually valuing the benefit of the resultant defence capability is much more problematic. Similarly, the social benefits of an informed government are difficult to value. In addition, the more that technology policy is directed towards the creation of appropriate innovation supportive environments, the more difficult it is to measure the return to such spending. There is, of course, a literature on the social returns to education that could be used to value training investments. It is fair to state, however, that generally the economic literature when considering the return or effectiveness of government spending on R&D has primarily concentrated upon those expenditures that are basically direct subsidies to commercial R&D. For example, a recent paper (the results of which are relied upon here to a large degree)–Klette et al. (1999)–surveys and adds to the general literature but constrains itself to the consideration of 'the impact on manufacturing performance of direct government support to commercial R&D projects and largely ignores . . . issues such as the impact of research in government labs, defence related R&D contracts, support to basic research in universities and tax breaks for R&D'.

Even taking a rather narrow approach to effectiveness does not make the measurement of social returns a simple exercise. There are many problems but the three most important conceptual problems are the following.

(a) If the effect of policy is to be measured, then some insight into the counterfactual (what would have happened in the absence of policy) is required. A necessary condition for a policy to have been effective is that it produced additionality, that is, socially desirable outcomes were generated by the policy that would not have arisen in its absence. At the most basic level, this might mean that the government support enabled a new product or process to be developed (or to be developed more quickly) that would not have been developed (or would have developed more slowly) in the absence of the policy.

(b) To measure the impact of policy in total, one also needs to obtain some insight into spillovers. Spillovers can be positive or negative but are essentially impacts that fall upon other than the direct recipients of support. Thus, for example, if government support enables a new product to be developed in one firm, then other firms might benefit from the knowledge generated and also develop new products. An evaluation of the returns to government support ought to take account of such advantages. However, spillovers need not always be positive. It may be the case that a firm receiving support develops a new product but this product drives (domestic) rivals from the market. The measure of the return to the intervention based solely upon the gains to the subsidised firm would then overstate the true returns, for, to some degree, the measurement will wrongly reflect redistribution.

(c) The final issue is the time dimension over which returns are to be measured. It may be the case that interventionist policy today not only yields benefits today but also provides a new base from which firm(s) may build for the future. Some benefits may thus be quite distant in time. The benefits may also be quite widely spread. Improvements in a firm's technological base may not only affect its profits but also lead to higher wages, greater profits for suppliers and also higher tax returns (thus perhaps enabling some reduction of the actual cost of any R&D support package) etc.

It is fair to say that, although the general literature addresses some of these issues, it has not managed to fully resolve them. Even so, the results of the literature are informative. Griliches (1995), in a survey of the literature to that date, argues that the returns to publicly funded R&D are less than those to privately funded R&D. He does, however, note estimates of the social returns to public R&D in agriculture in the range 20–80 per cent. Klette et al. (1999), in their more recent work, point out that there are a number of approaches in the literature addressing the effectiveness of R&D. They rule out discussion of case studies and I follow them in concentrating on econometric evaluation. I will not repeat their useful discussion of the methodological problems of this approach, but instead concentrate upon their conclusions. They first report upon four micro-level studies of government support for commercial R&D (in the US, Japan, Norway and Israel). Of the four examples reviewed, three show significant positive social benefits from government intervention. The Norwegian project is more problematic. Surveying the wider literature, Klette et al. quote a number of studies that show that the social return to R&D is much higher than the private return and that spillovers are significant in the evaluation of government support programmes. What is not supplied, however, is a single point estimate of the rate of return to government R&D spend of this kind. This is not surprising. Their conclusion is much more limited. They state that, if asked for a concise summary of the paper, the reply would be 'It is all very difficult'.

2. The Science Budget

Government expenditure on science could be considered a basic characteristic of a civilised society in a manner similar to expenditure on the arts. Knowledge is valuable for its own sake quite apart from any benefits to which it gives rise. The problem with this argument is that, if this is all that science yields, then there is little reason why the science spend should be more than the arts spend. It is therefore a dangerous argument upon which to rely for the justification of such spending. This is not to say that there is no such 'arts-like' benefit. It exists; however, it is very difficult to value.

Measures of the effectiveness of or the return to the science spend thus tend to rely upon the identification and measurement of more concrete returns. There is a growing literature in this field, neatly summarised by Martin and Salter (1996) in a report to HM Treasury, and thus to a large degree what I say below is based upon that report. The report argues that 'the traditional view of basic research as a source merely of useful codified information is too simple and misleading. It neglects the often larger benefits of trained researchers, improved instrumentation and methods, tacit knowledge and membership of national and international networks'.

Martin and Salter (hereafter M&S) quote estimates in the econometric literature of a rate of return to basic science of 28 per cent but they consider that the precision of this figure is open to doubt and that the methodology largely ignores the other benefits quoted immediately above. They do accept, however, that publicly funded basic research seems to have a substantial impact on national productivity and competitiveness, arguably through mastery over technology derived from better understanding of basic scientific processes underlying technology. Such understanding will be of increasing rather than lesser importance in the future. It is made clear that the relationship between basic research and technological advance differs across industries and products.

The less easily measurable benefits of basic research are more difficult to quantify. The ability to interconnect to international knowledge networks may be of increasing importance as knowledge becomes global. The supply of highly educated manpower is a key to understanding and utilising the world stock of knowledge. Improved instrumentation and methodology may well be crucial to maintaining or generating competitiveness in a number of industrial sectors.

Overall, the literature as reviewed by M&S indicates rates of return to basic research that are high. The quoted 28 per cent is imprecise and is only measuring part of the return. It would, however, suggest that greater levels of investment in basic research in the UK could be justified, the cost of capital being considerably less than 28 per cent.

However, the literature gives us no insight into, *inter alia*, whether the rate of return is being maximised. For example, are UK science resources being placed in the right technological areas and allocated to the most effective researchers and are the results being used to the greatest benefit of the UK economy? In fact, one might argue that, given the objectives of researchers (peer evaluation), there may well be means to improve the rate of return. However, as yet, no reliable means has been proposed that would enable reliable a priori evaluation of the potential returns to different basic science projects. Peer evaluation, i.e. the quality of the science, is still the main selection mechanism (even if within the framework of Technology Foresight guidelines). Although this may not maximise the return viewed in the traditional way, it may well be a reliable way of maximising the other returns (e.g. trained manpower, access to the world knowledge stock, instrumentation and methods).

Overall, therefore, one might consider UK expenditure upon basic research (the science budget) as generally effective. However, there is no guarantee that it is maximally effective. Nor have we any guidelines that would guarantee that the extra spending that the returns seem to suggest to be desirable is undertaken in the most desirable areas.

3. Launch Aid

Launch Aid is one of the longest lasting of all forms of technology policy in the UK.[3] First instituted in 1947 as a means to (re)generate a nascent civil aviation industry in the UK, it still survives, although in a modified form, today. It is the only form of technology policy that is embodied within an Act of Parliament (originally the 1948 and 1949 Civil Aviation Acts and subsequently the Civil Aviation Acts of 1968 and 1982). The principle of Launch Aid is that 'the government provides launch capital for non recurring development costs which is repaid from levies or royalties on the sale of aircraft or engines'. Launch Aid is administered by the Department of Trade and Industry and is now almost unique in the DTI portfolio in providing support for actual product and process development expenditures within large firms.

Launch Aid has generally been justified on the grounds that the risks involved in the launch of new civil aircraft and engines have been too large to expect the private firm (or its financiers) to bear. The principle behind it is thus to shift the risk to government. With Launch Aid being a sales-contingent contract, if the project fails then it is the government that bears the loss rather than the firm. Moreover, as the repayment terms are generally set such that the government only recoups its initial investment, if the project is a success then the firm will make at least the same net returns as if private funding had been used.

The actual terms of the Launch Aid contract have been changed over the years. The latest arrangements resulted from an EC–US argument over subsidies to national aircraft producers. The 1992 EC–US agreement entails

- restriction of Launch Aid to 33 per cent of total development costs, with 25 per cent to be repaid at the cost of government borrowing and the remaining 8 per cent to be repaid at that rate plus 1 percentage point;
- a maximum reimbursement period of 17 years, and 20 per cent of the repayment to be made over the first 40 per cent of aircraft deliveries (70 per cent over the first 85 per cent).

Launch Aid grants have always been discretionary: there is no standing or prior provisions for Launch Aid in the government budget and thus all applications are considered against other competing demand for government funds. There are no set criteria that guarantee success of an application, nor are there fixed rules for determining the government contribution.

It is worth noting that the national governments of most partners in the Airbus consortium have adopted Launch Aid schemes to assist these partners. It also worth noting that such risk-shifting policies exist in, e.g. the Netherlands and

---

[3] The commentry here is largely based upon Kaivanto (1995, 1996a,b). Kim Kaivanto is one of my doctoral students.

Finland for the support of project development in SMEs. However, in the UK, the aerospace industry is unique in having such assistance available to it.

As an 'old-style' product development policy, it is worth exploring the effectiveness of the policy. This may be done on a number of levels. First, one may ask whether the policy has managed to obtain returns equivalent to its internal targets, that is, a return equal to the investment made by government (plus the appropriate interest charge). If it has not, one might even consider the scheme as only a poorly veiled attempt to provide a general subsidy to the industry.

Gardner (1976), in an early review of Launch Aid experience, argued that of all the projects financed from 1948 through to the date of his review, only one—the Viscount—ever paid back receipts to government. Since 1970, only seven projects have actually been funded under Launch Aid: Concorde, RB211, Westland 30, V2500, A320, EH101 and the A330/340. These projects generated net disbursements (expenditure greater than receipts) on Launch Aid for each year between 1970–71 and 1991–92 (except for a small net receipt in 1977–78). However, by 1991–92, only the A330/340 and the EH101 were receiving Launch Aid whereas the RB211 and the A320 were generating government receipts. The last tranche of funding to the A330/340 was in 1992–93 so that, beyond that date, only the EH101 was still receiving Launch Aid. At the same time, receipts from the A320, the RB211 and the A330/340 started to build up. Since 1992–93, net Launch Aid expenditure has been negative in the range £40–60 million per year with estimated out-turns of −£110 million in 1997–98 and −£171 million in 1998–99. These net receipts may well be reversed if new applications currently sitting on the government's desk (e.g. the Airbus super jumbo) are approved.

Thus, post-Concorde, Launch Aid projects have been much more successful. Partly as a result of this and partly as a result of the unwinding of the scheme with few new projects being started when existing projects were in the pay-back phase, the scheme has been a net contributor to government for the last seven years. One cannot precisely calculate pay-backs and contributions project by project from publicly available data, but it looks as if Launch Aid has, of late at least, been close to meeting its own internal objectives of generating a pay-back of the loans made plus appropriate interest.

There is, however, a wider issue relating to Launch Aid. Is it effective in a more general sense? Representatives of the civil aircraft industry have argued that the industry is an important part of the UK economy with an impressive export record and that, to some degree at least, this is due to the continuing availability of Launch Aid. There are, however, a number of questions that must be answered before one could agree that the policy is effective:

(a) Does the policy produce additionality, that is, would the projects that have been undertaken not have been done without Launch Aid? The arguments here are, of course, complex. The rationale for Launch Aid is that the private sector would not fund the large risky projects involved. One must have some doubt with regard to this in the light of (i) the financing found for the Channel Tunnel

project and (ii) the extent to which, over the last 15 years, the aircraft manufacturers have been willing to take on large amounts of risk through a switch
of airlines policy from outright purchasing of civil aircraft to one of leasing,
often from manufacturers.

(b) What is the pay-off to the UK of having a civil aviation industry? There is a literature that argues that the existence of Airbus Industrie limits Boeing's monopoly
power and thus keeps down world aircraft prices to the benefit of the UK and
the world economy (Baldwin and Krugman, 1988). The UK share of this benefit
is, however, small. There are, of course, the high exports that the industry generates. However, one cannot but wonder whether the skills and knowledge used
in civil aircraft might be better employed elsewhere in the economy or whether
the use of Launch Aid to help SMEs in other industries to develop and launch
new products may have yielded a bigger pay-off.

(c) One might note, however, that, with the increasing internationalisation of the
civil aircraft industry and the involvement of the UK industry in international
projects where the partners are receiving Launch Aid from their national governments, it may be rather difficult to draw back from the policy.

VI. THE FUTURE

With the coming to power of the Labour government in May 1997, a major comprehensive spending review was initiated across all government departments and
all areas of spending including R&D. Published figures (in SET98) on spending
plans originating from prior to the conclusion of that review thus became obsolete
as new priorities and spending patterns were put in place. At the time of writing,
however, there are no publicly available data on the totality of the government's
future R&D spending plans (as of early July 1999, details of *Forward Look 1999*
and *Science, Engineering and Technology Statistics 1999* are just beginning to
appear on the DTI web page). This section thus considers just three areas, making
use of what data are available. The first area is science, where increased spending
plans have been announced. The second area is defence, where some material is
available. The third area is the DTI, where the Competitiveness White Paper gives
reasonable guidance as to the future.

1. The Science Budget 1999–00 to 2001–02

Information taken from the DTI/OST home page entitled 'Allocations of the science
budget 1999–00 to 2001–02' provides details of the outcome of the Comprehensive
Spending Review as it affects the science budget. The plan is to increase the science
budget by £700 million over three years in the context of additional support to the
science and engineering base (i.e. including the Higher Education Funding
Councils) of £1.4 billion. The planned spend and recent spends are as in Table 10.

The extra expenditure thus reverses recent (1996–97 to 1998–99) real declines
in the science budget and will probably reinforce the increasing share of the

Table 10. *The science budget, 1996–97 to 2001–02*

	Cash terms (£m)	Real annual growth (%)
Out-turn		
1996–97	1,312.4	−1.39
1997–98 (estimated)	1,338	−0.72
Plan		
1998–99	1,338	−2.76
1999–00	1,473	7.3
2000–01	1,587	12.7
2001–02	1,658	14.8

Source: 'Allocations of the science budget 1999–00 to 2001–02', from the DTI/OST web page.

government R&D budget going to the science and engineering base (SEB). The extra funding going to the SEB over and above the increase in the science budget is made up of three parts (over three years): an extra £300 million for the DFEE, £100 million to build a new synchroton radiation source at Daresbury (a project to which the Wellcome Trust will also contribute), plus another £300 million as half of a Joint Infrastructure Fund (joint with the Wellcome Trust) to address the infrastructure problem in universities. The direct collaboration with a research funding charity (the Wellcome Trust), especially on this scale, is a new initiative for the UK government.

The current government view of science funding can be transmitted through two relevant quotations from the source: 'The Science Base is the absolute bedrock of our economic performance' and 'A viable and internationally competitive research base is accepted as essential to the future industrial and commercial strength of the country, and hence also to the prosperity and well being of the UK population'. However, perhaps as a warning, this document also states

A key finding of the Comprehensive Spending Review was that, while much has been done in recent years to encourage exploitation of Science Base outcomes, still more is needed. In particular there is a need to increase the degree of interaction between UK firms and the Science Base, to ensure that UK firms maximise their opportunities to become fully competitive and to ensure that maximum value is realised from the public investment in the Science Base.

To facilitate such interaction, a University Challenge Fund (using £20 million from the science budget and £20 million from the Wellcome Foundation and the Gatsby Trust) has been initiated to encourage, through seed funding, the transformation of 'good research into good business'.

2. Defence R&D

Research Fortnight (28 April 1999) indicates that, in cash terms, the defence research budget planned for 1999–00 will be £453 million. This is seen as a fall of

15 per cent in cash terms since 1996–97 and of almost 50 per cent in real terms since 1985. The falling share of defence R&D in the total R&D spend will thus continue into the future. The source also suggests that the Defence Evaluation and Research Agency is poised for at least partial privatisation.

3. The Department of Trade and Industry

Although no hard data are available on future DTI R&D spends, it is clear from the Competitiveness White Paper (Department of Trade and Industry, 1998) that the department's current emphasis upon enabling innovation through creating an innovation-friendly environment will continue, as opposed to any return to explicit subsidies for particular product and process innovations. The White Paper also fully embraces the concept of the knowledge economy and expresses a desire and measures to ensure that the UK will be a full participant in the world knowledge economy. The environmental improvements encompass, *inter alia*, changes in regulations, reviews of tax regimes, encouraging private R&D spending, improving the functioning of capital markets, improving competitive pressures, improving the skills base and encouraging innovation and productivity in government.

4. The Future: An Overview

Although the future pattern of the government R&D spend is not entirely clear, the main characteristics appear to be an increased science spend, a reduced military spend and a technology policy that is more concerned with the innovative climate than with subsidising particular projects, processes or firms (except perhaps for Launch Aid). This is very much a reinforcement of recent trends. In terms of evaluation, it reflects the apparent effectiveness of basic research (although emphasises that full benefits will only be realised if the science base is fully exploited). The defence R&D reductions may also well reflect the current rather catholic view of the need for and pay-off from such spending. The continuing DTI emphasis on issues relating to the innovative environment is not fully consistent with the academic literature, which suggests that there may well be pay-offs to government support for particular products and processes. It may well, however, reflect some scepticism as to whether such spending has been effective in the UK in the past.

VII. CONCLUSIONS

Over the 10 years through to 1998, the UK government has reduced its expenditure on science, engineering and technology (SET) and research and development (R&D). The remaining spending has been reorientated towards science and the basic end of the spectrum, and away from both defence R&D and the support of technology and particularly the support of particular products and processes in large firms. Recent policy announcements of enhanced spending upon the science base will further emphasise the move towards the basic end of the spectrum.

There are a number of causes that lead governments to spend on R&D. The main primary purposes of government R&D in the UK are to support the provision of government services (largely defence) and general support (including the science spend). Technology support activity—that is, the stimulation of particular technologies in UK industry—is now relatively unimportant in the total spend. Different purposes are justified on different grounds. I have argued that market failure is endemic in technological change and market failure can and has been used to justify government spending both on science and on technology support. On the other hand, concern with the international competitiveness of the UK economy is also used as a justification.

This chapter has reviewed the SET activities of the two main spending departments—the MOD and the DTI—and the science budget. In doing so, it has raised more questions than answers. The effectiveness of general technology support policies, Launch Aid and the science spend has also been reviewed. My review of effectiveness is generally positive. This positive attitude indicates that further government R&D spending may be justified, and my quick look at the future suggests that, in science at least, higher spending is in prospect. For the MOD, the opposite appears to be the case. The DTI, on the other hand, appears to be continuing its emphasis upon the creation of an innovation-friendly environment rather than high levels of spending *per se*.

APPENDIX A: ABBREVIATIONS
(These abbreviations are not detailed elsewhere)

BBSRC   Biotechnology and Biological Sciences Research Council
DEn   Department of Energy
DETR   Department of the Environment, Transport and the Regions
DFE   Department for Education
DFEE   Department for Education and Employment
DFID   Department for International Development
DH   Department of Health
DHSS   Department of Health and Social Security
DOE   Department of the Environment
DOT   Department of Transport
DTI   Department of Trade and Industry
ED   Employment Department
HEFCE   Higher Education Funding Council (England)
HEFCS   Higher Education Funding Council (Scotland)
HEFCW   Higher Education Funding Council (Wales)
MAFF   Ministry of Agriculture, Fisheries and Food
MOD   Ministry of Defence
MRC   Medical Research Council
NERC   Natural Environment Research Council

NHS	National Health Service
NI	Northern Ireland
NIHEC	Northern Ireland Higher Education Council
ODA	Overseas Development Agency
OST	Office of Science and Technology
PPARC	Particle Physics and Astronomy Research Council
SO	Scottish Office
WO	Welsh Office

REFERENCES

Baldwin, R. and Krugman, P. (1988), 'Industrial policy and international competition in wide bodied jet aircraft', in R. Baldwin (ed.), *Trade Policy Issues and Empirical Analysis*, Chicago: University of Chicago Press.

Barber, J. and White, G. (1987), 'Current policy and problems from a UK perspective', in P. Dasgupta and P. Stoneman (eds), *Economic Policy and Technological Performance*, Cambridge: Centre for Economic Policy Research/Cambridge University Press.

Cabinet Office (various), *Annual Review of Government Funded Research and Development*, London: HMSO.

——/Office of Public Service and Science/Office of Science and Technology (1995), *Forward Look of Government Funded Science Engineering and Technology 1995*, London: HMSO.

Cave, J., Frinking, E., Malone, K., Van Rossum, W., Te Velde, R. and Stoneman, P. (1999), *Modalities of R&D Funding: An International Comparison*, report to the European Commission, March.

Dasgupta, P. and David, P. (1987), 'Information disclosure and the economics of science and technology', in G. Fiewal (ed.), *Arrow and the Ascent of Modern Economic Theory*, New York: New York University Press.

Department of Trade and Industry (1998), *Our Competitive Future: Building the Knowledge Driven Economy*, Competitiveness White Paper, London: HMSO.

—— /Office of Science and Technology (1998), *Science, Engineering and Technology Statistics 1998*, London: HMSO.

Diederen, P., Stoneman, P., Toivanen, O. and Wolters, A. (2000), *Innovation and Research Policies: An International Comparative Analysis*, Aldershot: Edward Elgar.

Ergas, H. (1987), 'The importance of technology policy', in P. Dasgupta and P. Stoneman (eds), *Economic Policy and Technological Performance*, Cambridge: Centre for Economic Policy Research/Cambridge University Press.

Gardner, N. K. (1976), 'The economics of Launch Aid', in A. Whiting (ed.), *The Economics of Industrial Subsidies*, London: HMSO.

Griliches, Z. (1995), 'R&D and productivity: econometric results and measurement issues', in P. Stoneman (ed.), *The Handbook of the Economics of Innovation and Technological Change*, Oxford: Blackwells.

Kaivanto, K. (1995), 'The structure and political economy of the UK civil aerospace industry', University of Warwick, December, mimeo.

—— (1996a), 'Post Concorde developments in the UK civil aerospace industry', Warwick Business School, Research Paper no. 206.

—— (1996b), 'Civil aerospace industrial policy: a wider perspective', University of Warwick, April, mimeo.

Klette, T., Moen, J. and Griliches, Z. (1999), *Do Subsidies to Commercial R&D Reduce Market Failures? Microeconomic Evaluation Studies*, National Bureau of Economic Research, Working Paper no. 6947.

Martin, B. and Salter, A. (1996), *The Relationship between Publicly Funded Basic Research and Economic Performance: A SPRU Review*, report prepared for HM Treasury, Sussex: Science Policy Research Unit.

OECD (1998), *Technology, Productivity and Job Creation: Best Policy Practices*, Paris: Organisation for Economic Co-operation and Development.

Office for National Statistics (1999), *Gross Domestic Expenditure on R&D 1997*, First Release, London, March.

Stoneman, P. (1987), *The Economic Analysis of Technology Policy*, Oxford: Oxford University Press.

Index

Lightning Source UK Ltd.
Milton Keynes UK
21 September 2009

144009UK00001B/101/P